Fodor's

W9-BFR-615

BELIZE

5th Edition

Where to Stay and Eat
for All Budgets

Must-See Sights
and Local Secrets

Ratings You Can Trust

Fodor's Travel Publications   New York, Toronto, London, Sydney, Auckland
www.fodors.com

FODOR'S BELIZE
Writer: Lan Sluder

Editor: Eric B. Wechter

Production Editor: Carrie Parker
Maps & Illustrations: David Lindroth, Inc.; Ed Jacobus, *cartographers;* Bob Blake,
Rebecca Baer, *map editors;* William Wu, *information graphics*
Design: Fabrizio La Rocca, *creative director;* Guido Caroti, *art director;*
Tina Malaney, Chie Ushio, Nora Rosansky, Jessica Walsh, *designers;*
Melanie Marin, *associate director of photography*
Cover Photo: Exactostock/SuperStock
Production Manager: Angela L. McLean

5th Edition

ISBN 978-0-307-92833-7

ISSN 1559-081X

SPECIAL SALES
This book is available at special discounts for bulk purchases for sales promotions or
premiums. Special editions, including personalized covers, excerpts of existing books,
and corporate imprints, can be created in large quantities for special needs. For more
information, write to Special Markets/Premium Sales, 1745 Broadway, MD 3-2, New
York, NY 10019, or e-mail specialmarkets@randomhouse.com.

AN IMPORTANT TIP & AN INVITATION
Although all prices, opening times, and other details in this book are based on information supplied to us at press time, changes occur all the time in the travel world, and
Fodor's cannot accept responsibility for facts that become outdated or for inadvertent
errors or omissions. So **always confirm information when it matters,** especially if you're
making a detour to visit a specific place. Your experiences—positive and negative—
matter to us. If we have missed or misstated something, **please write to us.** Share your
opinion instantly through our online feedback center at fodors.com/contact-us.

PRINTED IN THE UNITED STATES OF AMERICA

10 9 8 7 6 5 4 3 2 1

CONTENTS

CONTENTS

ABOUT THIS BOOK

Our Ratings

At Fodor's, we spend considerable time choosing the best places in a destination so you don't have to. By default, anything we recommend in this book is worth visiting. But some sights, properties, and experiences are so great that we've recognized them with additional accolades. Orange **Fodor's Choice** stars indicate our top recommendations; black stars highlight places we deem **Highly Recommended**; and **Best Bets** call attention to top properties in various categories. Disagree with any of our choices? Care to nominate a new place? Visit our feedback center at www.fodors.com/feedback.

> For expanded hotel reviews, visit **Fodors.com**

Hotels

Hotels have private bath, phone, TV, and air-conditioning, and do not offer meals unless we specify that in the review. We always list facilities but not whether you'll be charged an extra fee to use them.

Restaurants

Unless we state otherwise, restaurants are open for lunch and dinner daily. We mention dress only when there's a specific requirement and reservations only when they're essential or not accepted—it's always best to book ahead.

Credit Cards

We assume that restaurants and hotels accept credit cards. If not, we'll note it in the review.

Budget Well

Hotel and restaurant price categories from ¢ to $$$$ are defined in the opening pages of the respective chapters. For attractions, we always give standard adult admission fees; reductions are usually available for children, students, and senior citizens.

Listings
- ★ Fodor's Choice
- ★ Highly recommended
- ⊠ Physical address
- ✛ Directions or Map coordinates
- ⌖ Mailing address
- ☎ Telephone
- 🖷 Fax
- ⊕ On the Web
- ✎ E-mail
- ✒ Admission fee
- ☉ Open/closed times
- Ⓜ Metro stations
- ⊟ No credit cards

Hotels & Restaurants
- ⌨ Hotel
- ↩ Number of rooms
- ⌂ Facilities
- ⦿ Meal plans
- ✕ Restaurant
- ⊿ Reservations
- 🏛 Dress code
- ↘ Smoking

Outdoors
- 🏌 Golf
- ⚠ Camping

Other
- ♟ Family-friendly
- ⇨ See also
- ⊠ Branch address
- ☞ Take note

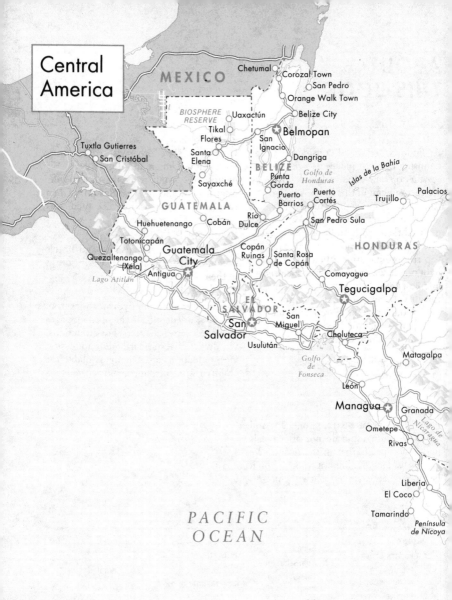

Central America

MEXICO

Chetumal

Corozal Town

San Pedro

Orange Walk Town

Belize City

Tuxtla Gutierres

San Cristóbal

BIOSPHERE
RESERVE

Uaxactún

Tikal

Flores

San
Ignacio

Belmopan

Santa
Elena

Dangriga

BELIZE

Sayaxché

Golfo de
Honduras

Islas de la Bahía

Punta
Gorda

GUATEMALA

Huehuetenango

Cobán

Río
Dulce

Puerto
Barrios

Puerto
Cortés

Trujillo

Palacios

San Pedro Sula

Totonicapán

Copán
Ruinas

Santa Rosa
de Copán

HONDURAS

Quezaltenango
(Xela)

Guatemala
City

Lago Atitlán

Antigua

Comayagua

Tegucigalpa

EL
SALVADOR

San
Miguel

San
Salvador

Choluteca

Matagalpa

Usulután

Golfo
de
Fonseca

León

Managua

Granada

Lago de Nicaragua

Ometepe

Rivas

PACIFIC
OCEAN

Liberia

El Coco

Tamarindo

Península
de Nicoya

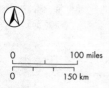

0   100 miles

0   150 km

JAMAICA

CARIBBEAN SEA

Puerto
Lempira
○ Mosquitia

La Rosita
○   ○ Puerto
                Cabezas

NICARAGUA

*Laguna de
Perkis*

Rama
○   Isla de
○ Bluefields   *San Andrés*
*Islas del
Maiz (Corn
Islands)*

*Bahía
Punta Gorda*

COSTA
RICA   ○ Tortuguero

Turrialba
San   ☆   ○ Puerto Limón
José   ○ Cartago
*Golfo
de   ○ Quepos   Bocas ·
Nicoya*   del Toro   *Panamá
                                    Canal*   El Porvenir   *San Blas
                                                   ○   Islands*
*Bahía de
Coronado*   ○ Boquete   *Golfo de los
                            Mosquitos*   Ciudad de
                                          ☆ Panama
La Palma ○   Puerto
Sirena ○ ○ David PANAMA   *Bahía de*   Obaldia
○ Matapalo   ○ Santiago   *Panamá*   ○
*Península
de Osa*   *Golfo de   *Isla del   ○ Yaviza
            Chiriquí*   ○ Chitré   *Rey*
                    ○ Las Tablas   *Golfo de
            Isla de   Panamá
             Coiba*

COLOMBIA

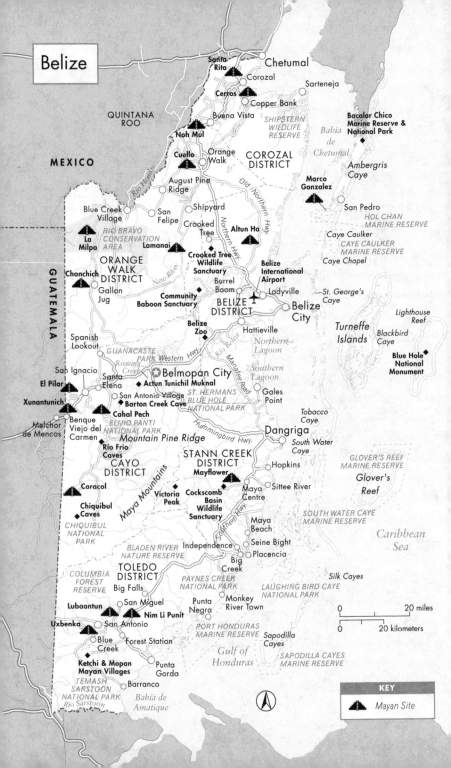

Belize

MEXICO

QUINTANA
ROO

GUATEMALA

Chetumal

Santa
Rita

Corozal

Cerros

Sarteneja

Copper Bank

Buena Vista

SHIPSTERN
WILDLIFE
RESERVE

Bahía
de
Chetumal

Bacalar Chico
Marine Reserve &
National Park

Noh Mul

COROZAL
DISTRICT

Ambergris
Caye

Cuello

Orange
Walk

August Pine
Ridge

Marco
Gonzalez

Blue Creek
Village

San
Felipe

Shipyard

Crooked
Tree

Altun Ha

San Pedro

HOL CHAN
MARINE RESERVE

La
Milpa

RIO BRAVO
CONSERVATION
AREA

Lamanai

Crooked Tree
Wildlife
Sanctuary

Belize
International
Airport

Caye Caulker
CAYE CAULKER
MARINE RESERVE

Caye Chapel

Chanchich

ORANGE
WALK
DISTRICT

New River

Gallon
Jug

Community
Baboon Sanctuary

Burrel
Boom

BELIZE
DISTRICT

Belize
Zoo

Ladyville

St. George's
Caye

Belize
City

Turneffe
Islands

Lighthouse
Reef

Blackbird
Caye

Blue Hole
National
Monument

Spanish
Lookout

GUANACASTE
PARK

Roaring
Creek

Western Hwy.

Rio Belize

Hattieville

Northern
Lagoon

Southern
Lagoon

Sán Ignacio

Santa
Elena

Belmopan City

Actun Tunichil Muknal

San Antonio Village

Barton Creek Cave

ST. HERMANS
BLUE HOLE
NATIONAL PARK

Manatee Road

Gales
Point

Tobacco
Caye

El Pilar

Xunantunich

Cahal Pech

Benque
Viejo del
Carmen

ELIJIO PANTI
NATIONAL PARK

Hummingbird Hwy.

Dangriga

South Water
Caye

GLOVER'S REEF
MARINE RESERVE

Glover's
Reef

Matchor
de Mencos

Río Frio
Caves

Mountain Pine Ridge

STANN CREEK
DISTRICT

Mayflower

Hopkins

Sittee River

Caracol

CAYO
DISTRICT

Maya Mountains

Victoria
Peak

Chiquibul
Caves

Cockscomb
Basin
Wildlife
Sanctuary

Maya
Centre

SOUTH WATER CAYE
MARINE RESERVE

Caribbean
Sea

CHIQUIBUL
NATIONAL
PARK

Maya
Beach

BLADEN RIVER
NATURE RESERVE

Independence

Seine Bight

Placencia

COLUMBIA
FOREST
RESERVE

TOLEDO
DISTRICT

Big Falls

Big
Creek

PAYNES CREEK
NATIONAL PARK

Silk Cayes

LAUGHING BIRD CAYE
NATIONAL PARK

Lubaantun

San Miguel

Nim Li Punit

Punta
Negra

Monkey
River Town

Uxbenka

San Antonio

PORT HONDURAS
MARINE RESERVE

Sapodilla
Cayes

SAPODILLA CAYES
MARINE RESERVE

Blue
Creek

Forest Station

Ketchi & Mopan
Mayan Villages

Punta
Gorda

Gulf of
Honduras

TEMASH
SARSTOON
NATIONAL PARK
Río Sarstoon

Barranco

Bahía de
Amatique

0   20 miles

0   20 kilometers

KEY

Mayan Site

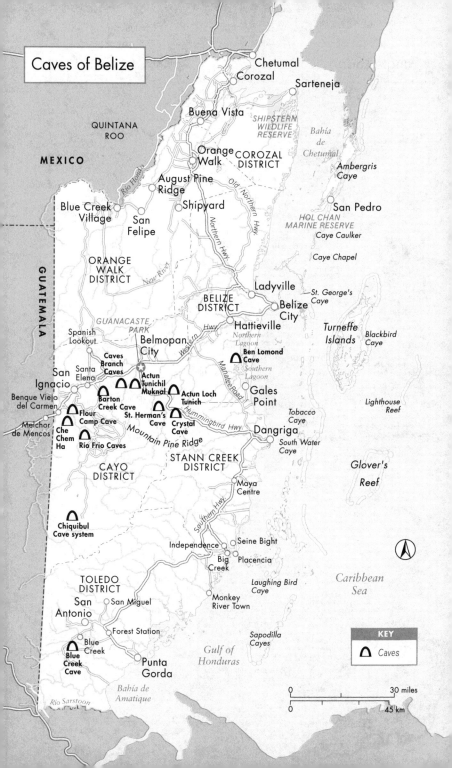

Caves of Belize

MEXICO

QUINTANA ROO

Chetumal
Corozal
Sarteneja

Buena Vista

SHIPSTERN WILDLIFE RESERVE

Bahía de Chetumal

Orange Walk
COROZAL DISTRICT

Ambergris Caye

August Pine Ridge

Shipyard

San Pedro

HOL CHAN MARINE RESERVE

Caye Caulker

Blue Creek Village

San Felipe

Río Hondo

Old Northern Hwy.

Northern Hwy.

ORANGE WALK DISTRICT

New River

Caye Chapel

GUATEMALA

Ladyville

St. George's Caye

BELIZE DISTRICT

Belize City

Guanacaste Park

Spanish Lookout

Hattieville

Northern Lagoon

Turneffe Islands

Blackbird Caye

Belmopan City

Caves Branch Caves

Santa Elena

San Ignacio

Benque Viejo del Carmen

Melchor de Mencos

Western Hwy.

Actun Tunichil Muknal

Ben Lomond Cave

Southern Lagoon

Gales Point

Barton Creek Cave

Actun Loch Tunich

St. Herman's Cave

Crystal Cave

Manatee Road

Lighthouse Reef

Flour Camp Cave

Che Chem Ha

Rio Frio Caves

Mountain Pine Ridge

Hummingbird Hwy.

Dangriga

Tobacco Caye

South Water Caye

CAYO DISTRICT

STANN CREEK DISTRICT

Glover's Reef

Maya Centre

Chiquibul Cave system

Southern Hwy.

Independence

Seine Bight

Big Creek

Placencia

Caribbean Sea

TOLEDO DISTRICT

San Antonio

San Miguel

Laughing Bird Caye

Monkey River Town

Sapodilla Cayes

Forest Station

Blue Creek

Blue Creek Cave

Punta Gorda

Gulf of Honduras

Bahía de Amatique

Río Sarstoon

| 0 | | 30 miles |
| 0 | | 45 km |

KEY

Caves

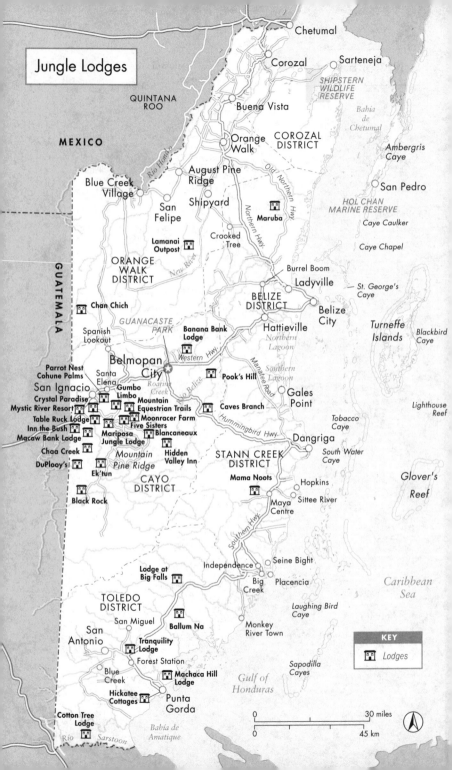

Jungle Lodges

Chetumal

Corozal
Sarteneja

SHIPSTERN
WILDLIFE
RESERVE

QUINTANA
ROO

Buena Vista

Bahía
de
Chetumal

CORZAL
DISTRICT

Orange
Walk

MEXICO

Ambergris
Caye

Blue Creek
Village

August Pine
Ridge

Shipyard

San
Felipe

Maruba

San Pedro

HOL CHAN
MARINE RESERVE

Crooked
Tree

Caye Caulker

Caye Chapel

Lamanai
Outpost

ORANGE
WALK
DISTRICT

New River

Burrel Boom

Ladyville

St. George's
Caye

Belize
City

Chan Chich

GUANACASTE
PARK

Spanish
Lookout

Banana Bank
Lodge

BELIZE
DISTRICT

Hattieville

Northern
Lagoon

Turneffe
Islands

Blackbird
Caye

GUATEMALA

Belmopan
City

Western Hwy.

Roaring
Creek

Pook's Hill

Southern
Lagoon

Gales
Point

Parrot Nest
Cohune Palms

Santa
Elena

Gumbo
Limbo

San Ignacio

Mountain
Equestrian Trails

Caves Branch

Lighthouse
Reef

Crystal Paradise

Mystic River Resort

Moonracer Farm

Belize River

Hummingbird Hwy.

Dangriga

Tobacco
Caye

Table Rock Lodge

Five Sisters

Inn the Bush

Mariposa

Blancaneaux

Macaw Bank Lodge

Jungle Lodge

STANN CREEK
DISTRICT

South Water
Caye

Chaa Creek

Mountain

Hidden
Valley Inn

DuPlooy's

Pine Ridge

Ek'tun

CAYO
DISTRICT

Mama Noots

Hopkins

Glover's
Reef

Black Rock

Sittee River

Maya
Centre

Southern Hwy.

Independence

Seine Bight

Lodge at
Big Falls

Big
Creek

Placencia

Caribbean
Sea

TOLEDO
DISTRICT

San Miguel

Ballum Na

Monkey
River Town

Laughing Bird
Caye

San
Antonio

Tranquility
Lodge

Forest Station

Blue
Creek

Machaca Hill
Lodge

Sapodilla
Cayes

Hickatee
Cottages

Punta
Gorda

Gulf of
Honduras

Cotton Tree
Lodge

Río
Sarstoon

Bahía de
Amatique

KEY	
🏠	*Lodges*

0   30 miles

0   45 km

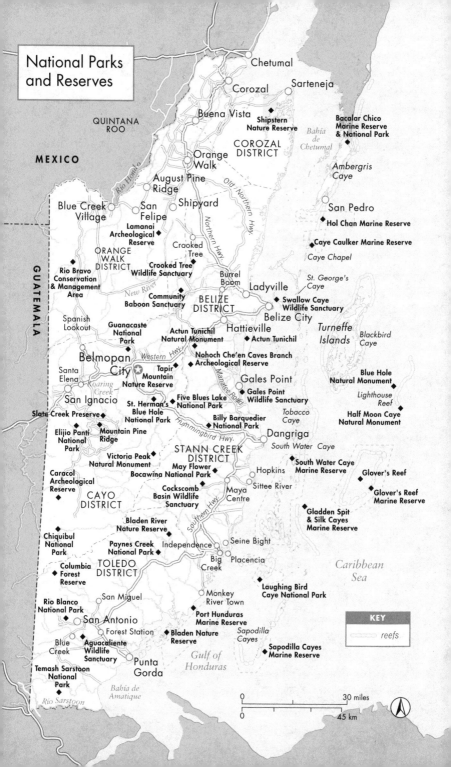

National Parks and Reserves

Chetumal

Corozal

Sarteneja

QUINTANA ROO

Buena Vista

Shipstern Nature Reserve

Bahía de Chetumal

Bacalar Chico Marine Reserve & National Park

MEXICO

COROZAL DISTRICT

Ambergris Caye

Orange Walk

August Pine Ridge

Shipyard

San Pedro

Blue Creek Village

San Felipe

Hol Chan Marine Reserve

Lamanai Archeological Reserve

Crooked Tree

Caye Caulker Marine Reserve

Caye Chapel

ORANGE WALK DISTRICT

Crooked Tree Wildlife Sanctuary

Burrel Boom

St. George's Caye

Rio Bravo Conservation & Management Area

New River

Community Baboon Sanctuary

BELIZE DISTRICT

Ladyville

Swallow Caye Wildlife Sanctuary

Belize City

Spanish Lookout

Guanacaste National Park

Actun Tunichil Natural Monument

Hattieville

Actun Tunichil

Turneffe Islands

Blackbird Caye

Belmopan City

Western Hwy.

Nohoch Che'en Caves Branch Archeological Reserve

Blue Hole Natural Monument

Santa Elena

Tapir Mountain Nature Reserve

Gales Point

Santa Elena

Roaring Creek

San Ignacio

St. Herman's Blue Hole National Park

Five Blues Lake National Park

Gales Point Wildlife Sanctuary

Manatee Road

Lighthouse Reef

Slate Creek Preserve

Billy Barquedier National Park

Tobacco Caye

Half Moon Caye Natural Monument

Elijio Panti National Park

Mountain Pine Ridge

Hummingbird Hwy.

Dangriga

South Water Caye

Victoria Peak Natural Monument

May Flower Bocawina National Park

STANN CREEK DISTRICT

South Water Caye Marine Reserve

Glover's Reef

Caracol Archeological Reserve

CAYO DISTRICT

Cockscomb Basin Wildlife Sanctuary

Hopkins

Maya Centre

Sittee River

Glover's Reef Marine Reserve

Chiquibul National Park

Bladen River Nature Reserve

Southern Hwy.

Gladden Spit & Silk Cayes Marine Reserve

Columbia Forest Reserve

Paynes Creek National Park

Independence

Seine Bight

Big Creek

Placencia

Caribbean Sea

TOLEDO DISTRICT

Rio Blanco National Park

San Miguel

Monkey River Town

Laughing Bird Caye National Park

San Antonio

Forest Station

Port Hunduras Marine Reserve

Sapodilla Cayes

Blue Creek

Aguacaliente Wildlife Sanctuary

Bladen Nature Reserve

Sapodilla Cayes Marine Reserve

Punta Gorda

Temash Sarstoon National Park

Gulf of Honduras

Rio Sarstoon

Bahía de Amatique

GUATEMALA

Old Northern Hwy.

Northern Hwy.

Rio Hondo

| 0 | | 30 miles |
| 0 | | 45 km |

KEY

reefs

Experience
Belize

WORD OF MOUTH

"Split your time [in Belize] between the coast and inland. [There are] lots of Mayan sites to choose from, many caving opportunities (don't miss ATM cave), awesome snorkeling/diving/fishing, plus zip-lining, canoeing, horseback riding, cultural visits, jungle hikes, zoos, and more. You certainly won't lack for things to do."

—rpowell

WHAT'S WHERE

The following numbers refer to chapters in the book.

2 Belize City. Depending on your perspective, Belize's commercial, transportation, and cultural hub is either a lively Caribbean port city of raffish charm or a crime-ridden, edgy backwater best seen through the rear-view mirror.

3 The Cayes and the Atolls. Hundreds of cayes (pronounced *keys*) dot the Caribbean Sea off Belize, both inside and outside the Barrier Reef. The largest are Ambergris, Belize's most popular visitor destination, and Caulker. Farther out are three South Pacific–style atolls.

4 Northern Belize. This is the land of sugarcane and sweet, off-the-beaten-path places to visit. Corozal Town, up against the Mexican border, has a lovely bayside setting, and Sarteneja is a fishing village just waiting to be discovered.

5 The Cayo. The rolling hills of Western Belize, anchored by San Ignacio, offer outdoor activities aplenty—caving, canoeing, hiking, horseback riding, and mountain biking. Several remarkable Mayan sites also await you, including Caracol and Actun Tunichil Muknal.

6 The Southern Coast. Want beaches? The best on the mainland are on the Placencia peninsula, especially in the Maya Beach area, and in Hopkins.

7 The Deep South. Rainy and lush, beautiful and remote, Punta Gorda in far southern Belize is the jumping-off point for the unspoiled Mayan villages of Toledo District and for onward travel to Guatemala and Honduras.

8 Side Trip to Guatemala. El Petén, Guatemala, is easily visited from the Cayo District of Belize. It's home to the most spectacular of all Mayan sites, Tikal, and the remains of many other ancient cities.

MEXICO

Carmelita

EL PETÉN

8 Tikal

Lake Petén Itzá

San José   El Remate

Flores

Santa Elena

Dolores

Poptún

San Luis

ALTA VERAPAZ   Río Santa Izabal

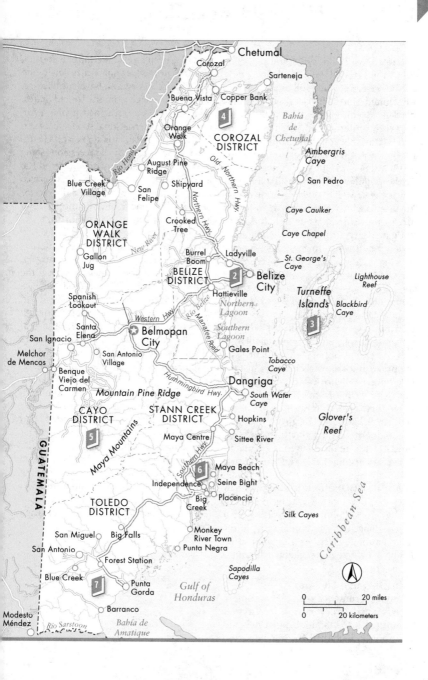

Chetumal

Corozal

Sarteneja

Buena Vista   Copper Bank

Bahía
de
Chetumal

4

Orange
Walk

**COROZAL
DISTRICT**

Ambergris
Caye

San Pedro

Rio Hondo

August Pine
Ridge

Blue Creek
Village

San
Felipe

Shipyard

Caye Caulker

Caye Chapel

Old Northern Hwy.

Northern Hwy.

**ORANGE
WALK
DISTRICT**

Crooked
Tree

New River

Gallon
Jug

Burrel
Boom

Ladyville

St. George's
Caye

Lighthouse
Reef

**BELIZE
DISTRICT**

2

**Belize
City**

Spanish
Lookout

Hattieville

Northern
Lagoon

Turneffe
Islands

Blackbird
Caye

Rio Belize

Western Hwy.

Santa
Elena

**Belmopan
City**

Southern
Lagoon

3

San Ignacio

San Antonio
Village

Manatee Road

Gales Point

Melchor
de Mencos

Benque
Viejo del
Carmen

Mountain Pine Ridge

Hummingbird Hwy.

Dangriga

Tobacco
Caye

South Water
Caye

Glover's
Reef

**CAYO
DISTRICT**

**STANN CREEK
DISTRICT**

Hopkins

5

Maya Centre

Sittee River

Maya Mountains

Southern Hwy.

Maya Beach

6

Independence

Seine Bight

Placencia

GUATEMALA

**TOLEDO
DISTRICT**

Big
Creek

Caribbean Sea

Silk Cayes

San Miguel   Big Falls

Monkey
River Town

Punta Negra

San Antonio

Forest Station

Sapodilla
Cayes

Blue Creek

7

Punta
Gorda

Gulf of
Honduras

Modesto
Méndez

Rio Sarstoon

Barranco

Bahía de
Amatique

0   20 miles

0   20 kilometers

WHAT'S NEW IN BELIZE

Belize's Own Politics of Change

Like the United States, Belize held national elections in 2008, and, also like the United States, Belize elected its first black leader in history. Dean Barrow, a lawyer by profession, educated in Jamaica and Miami, became prime minister. His party, the United Democratic Party (or UDP) swept into office with about 57% of the popular vote. In its first years in office, the new UDP generally took a low-key approach to governing. It followed a reform-oriented agenda in an effort to mitigate charges of high-level corruption levied against the former government. Seeking greater diversity in government, the UDP tapped Mayas and Mennonites for high office, in addition to the traditional core of Creole and Mestizo politicians. However, as the years since the election have passed, Belize's UDP government has faced growing challenges and increasing popular discontent. Rising prices and a slow economy (when the U.S. sneezes, Belize catches a bad cold) have cost Prime Minister Barrow some popularity, as has increasing crime, especially in Belize City. The government has become mired in messy efforts to renationalize the main telephone company, Belize Telemedia Ltd., and the electric company. There's been a popular backlash against UDP efforts to introduce new laws that many say would have reduced civil liberties. Political observers say that unless things change dramatically, in the next national elections the opposition People's United Party likely will gain a lot of ground.

Transportation Changes

Although a runway extension at Goldson International Airport near Belize City was completed in 2008, anticipated new airline service, including from Europe and Canada, hasn't yet materialized. Indeed, existing airlines serving Belize, including Delta and US Airways, have cut back on off-season service from the United States. One of Belize's airlines, Maya Island Air, started new international service between Belize and Mexico, Honduras, and Guatemala. However, with the recession, some of these routes didn't work out, and the long-awaited Cancún–Belize City service fizzled. Tropic Air has added daily service between Placencia and Belmopan and between San Pedro and Belmopan, making it easier to reach the centrally located capital. Construction on a new international airport near Placencia has slowed, and it's now unclear when or even if the airport will open. The national bus network, divided into northern, western, and southern zones, has been in a state of flux since the bankruptcy or closing of several large bus companies, but a large number of small regional bus lines have filled the gap, providing frequent and inexpensive, if not always comfortable, service on the main Northern, Western, and Southern highway routes and elsewhere. Belize's water-taxi network has expanded, and there are now three different companies providing service between Belize City and San Pedro and Caye Caulker. Also, two water-taxi companies are now running daily boats between Chetumal and San Pedro and Caye Caulker, making it easier for those flying into Cancún to reach Belize.

WHEN TO GO

Belize, like much of Central America and the Caribbean, has two basic seasons: the rainy season and the dry season. The rainy season is roughly June through October, extending in some areas through November or even December. The dry season usually runs from December through May. However, by "dry season" Belizeans usually mean specifically the months in late winter and spring, February through May, when temperatures inland may reach 100°F. April is usually the hottest month of the year.

If you want to escape crowds and high prices and don't mind getting a little wet, visit in the rainy—or green—season. Though some restaurants may close and hotels may offer limited facilities, especially in September and October, reservations are easy to get, even at top establishments, and you'll have the Mayan ruins and beaches to yourself. And the rains, which most often come at night, do make the entire country lush and green. The busiest time in Belize is the Christmas–New Year's period, followed by Easter, but most hotels count the high season as mid-November through April.

The dry season can be a less attractive time for inland trips, with dusty roads and wilting vegetation, but this is a good time to visit the coast and cayes, with their cooling winds from the sea.

Scuba enthusiasts can dive all year, but the water is clearest from March to June. Between November and February, cold fronts from North America can push southward, producing blustery winds known as "northers" that bring rain and rough weather and tend to churn up the sea, reducing visibility. Water temperatures, however, rarely stray far from 80°F, so many people dive without a wet suit.

Climate

Belize is a small country, but there's considerable variation in weather from north to south, and also from the cayes to the mainland. Rainfall, for example, varies dramatically depending on where you are: the Deep South gets as much as 160 to 200 inches of rain each year, but the rest of the country gets a lot less, as little as 50 inches in Corozal. The cayes generally get less rain than does the mainland. The rainy season doesn't mean monsoons, but, rather seasonal rains that green the countryside.

Belize's Caribbean coast often gets sweltering, humid weather, especially in summer, while the Mountain Pine Ridge, with elevations up to almost 3,700 feet, is cooler and less humid. Overall, Belize's subtropical temperatures generally hover between 70°F and 85°F (21°C and 29°C).

The western Caribbean's hurricane season is from June through November. September and October are the two prime months for tropical storms and hurricanes in Belize. Over the past century, about 85% of storms to hit Belize arrived in those two months; hurricanes, however, are relatively rare.

Forecasts

When you check weather forecasts for Belize, keep in mind the variations in weather around the country. It may be raining in Belize City but sunny in San Pedro, 36 mi (58 km) away. The Belize National Meteorological Service (⊕ *www. hydromet.gov.bz*) is a good source for weather information on Belize.

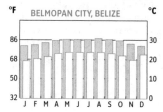

QUINTESSENTIAL BELIZE

The Jewel

Belizeans frequently talk about "the Jewel." They say, "Get yourself a piece of the Jewel." Or, "When are you coming back to the Jewel?" By Jewel, they simply mean Belize. And Belize is a jewel. It's a place of incredible natural beauty, of mint-green seas and emerald-green forests, of the longest Barrier Reef in the Western or Northern hemisphere, with more kinds of birds, butterflies, flowers, and trees than in all of the United States and Canada combined. Massive ceiba trees and graceful cohune palms stand guard in rain forests where jaguars still roam free and toucans and parrots fly overhead. Rivers, bays, and lagoons are rich with hundreds of different kinds of fish. And Belizeans themselves are jewels. The country is a gumbo of cultures—African, Hispanic, Mayan, Asian, European, and Caribbean. Belize? It's a Jewel.

Passing the Time

Nearly every country claims to be full of friendly, smiling, welcoming people, but in the case of Belize it's really true. The vast majority of Belizeans are open and gracious, and they're happy, even eager, to spend a few minutes chatting with you about nothing in particular—the weather, the beautiful morning, how you're enjoying the Jewel. In most cases they don't want anything from you, except to pass the time of day. So let your guard down, relax, smile, and share a few rewarding moments with the shopkeeper, the waitress, the fellow you meet in the bar, or the lady you sit next to on the bus.

If you want a sense of life in Belize, familiarize yourself with some of its simple pleasures. There are a few highlights that will send you home saying, "Ah mi gat wahn gud guf taim" ("I had a good time" in Creole).

Bird-Watching

Once you see toucans at Tikal or the hard-to-find motmot in the Cayo, you too might get caught up in the excitement of searching for some of Belize's 600 species of birds. Many Belizeans know all their local birds (although the names they have for them may differ from those in your birding guide) and where the best places are to find them. Crooked Tree, Chan Chich at Gallon Jug, the New River and New River Lagoon near Lamanai, and much of the Toledo District in the Deep South are wonderful areas for bird-watching; keep your eyes peeled to the treetops and don't forget your binoculars.

Archaeological Treasures

Though the ancient Mayan empire—which once occupied much of present-day Guatemala and extended into Belize, Mexico, Honduras, and El Salvador—began to collapse around AD 900, it still left one of the richest cultural and archaeological legacies in the world. Only a fraction of the thousands of Mayan ruins have been excavated from the jungle that over the centuries has swallowed the splendid temples and sprawling cities. Evidence of the Maya is everywhere in Belize, from the lagoon-side temples of Lamanai to the caves of Actun Tunichil Muknal. All together, Belize has more than 600 Mayan sites, most small and unexcavated, with likely hundreds or even thousands still to be discovered.

IF YOU LIKE

Luxury Resorts

Deluxe duvets. 1,200-thread-count sheets. Your own villa on a private island or a jungle hideaway with fine wines and gourmet dinners. You may be traipsing around Mayan ruins or diving the Blue Hole during the day, but at night you can look forward to pampering at Belize's luxury jungle lodges and beach resorts.

■ **Azul Resort, North Ambergris Caye.** It's all top-of-the-line at this hip and exclusive beach resort. Kick back with a frozen mojito at the Rojo Lounge and Market.

■ **Blancaneaux Lodge, Mountain Pine Ridge.** Francis Ford Coppola's riverside jungle lodge hints of Beverly Hills.

■ **Cayo Espanto, near Ambergris Caye.** Really want to splurge? A stay on this small, private island will cost you, but you'll have your own butler, chef, and gorgeous views of the sea.

■ **The Lodge at Chaa Creek, Cayo.** Soak up the carefully tended landscaping, deluxe garden suites, spa, Cuban cigars, and expensive cognac.

■ **Turtle Inn, Placencia.** Francis Ford Coppola hand-picked the Balinese furniture and art in these thatch cabañas, but that's not even the best part. Just wait until you see the garden showers.

■ **Victoria House, San Pedro.** Beautiful swimming pools, a fine beach, an excellent restaurant, and some of the best service in Belize await you at this stylishly barefoot resort south of town.

Fishing

Some of the world's most exciting sport-fishing lies off Belize's coast and cayes. Go for the "grand slam" of tarpon, bonefish, permit, and snook on the shallow flats between the mainland and the reef. Sailfish, wahoo, marlin, and barracuda abound farther out to sea. Several specialty resorts and fishing camps, such as Turneffe Flats and El Pescador, cater to the angler, but most hotels can help you organize excellent fishing trips. You'll need a fishing license for most sportfishing in Belize (except off piers and shores); your hotel or fishing guide can arrange it for you. In some marine reserves where fishing is allowed, such as Glovers Reef Marine Reserve, usage fees are also charged.

■ **Ambergris Caye.** There's surprisingly good saltwater fishing on the northern cayes—look for bonefish, permit, and tarpon.

■ **Glover's Atoll.** Shallow tidal flats around the atoll make for plenty of bonefish; there's also permit, jack, and barracuda.

■ **Placencia.** If you don't want to pay the big bucks that the resorts charge farther north, head here. Budget hotels start around BZ$50 a night. Permit's the number one catch inside the reef, or cast a line in the lagoon or the deep sea beyond the reef.

■ **Punta Gorda.** If you're serious about fishing, this is a great place to be. There's world-famous permit fishing.

■ **Turneffe Atoll.** Bonefish, tarpon, permit, snappers, jacks, barracuda, wahoo, dorado, and billfish all ply the waters.

Caving

One of the most exciting ways to tour Belize is to head underground—there are hundreds of caves all over the country. You can canoe down subterranean rivers in some, ducking under low-hanging stalactites while keeping your eyes trained for Mayan artifacts. The easiest caves to visit are in the Cayo; you don't need a guide to visit open caverns such as Rio Frio and St. Herman's. Before you head out to cave, make sure to find out whether it's open to the public, whether you need a guide, and, if the cave has a river, whether the water level is low enough for visitors.

■ **Actun Tunichil Muknal.** Go here for amazing limestone formations, many undisturbed Mayan artifacts, and calcified human remains. It's the top caving experience in Belize.

■ **Barton Creek Cave.** Canoe about a mile on an underground river through Barton Cave, which has some Mayan artifacts and skeletal remains.

■ **Caves Branch Caves.** The Caves Branch River cave system has become a popular place for cave tubing.

■ **Che Chem Ha.** This cave, once used by the Maya for grain storage and ceremonial rituals, is on private land about 25 minutes from San Ignacio in the Vaca Plateau.

■ **Hokeb Ha.** Blue Creek Cave (as it's known in English), near Blue Creek village, is Toledo's answer to Actun Tunichil Muknal, with vaulted limestone chambers and underground waterfalls.

■ **Rio Frio Cave.** Though it's more a natural tunnel than a cave, it's still worth a visit for its large entryway and path above the Cold River.

Scuba Diving and Snorkeling

Don your scuba or snorkeling gear and soak up the cast of aquatic characters offshore and around the Barrier Reef. One moment you may come upon an enormous spotted eagle ray; the next you may find the feisty little damselfish, a bolt of blue no bigger than your little finger. Bloated blowfish hover in their holes; barracuda patrol the depths; and queen angelfish shimmy through the water with puckered lips and haughty self-assurance. Graceful sea fans and great chunks of staghorn coral add to the exhilarating underwater experience.

■ **Blue Hole.** The underwater sinkhole, one of the most famous dives in Belize, forms a perfectly round, deep blue circle.

■ **Glover's Reef.** This is probably the least visited yet arguably most pristine dive and snorkel area in Belize. You can see nurse sharks and manta rays and go wreck diving.

■ **Hol Chan Marine Reserve.** Snorkel with nurse sharks and stingrays at Shark-Ray Alley and keep your eyes peeled for moray eels in the reserve.

■ **Sapodilla Cayes.** Fringe reefs and patch reefs in shallow water around the cayes support tropical fish like spadefish and parrot fish.

■ **South Water Caye.** If you want to shore snorkel, come here. The beach is sandy, and the island is one of Belize's most beautiful.

■ **Turneffe Islands.** Mangroves line a shallow lagoon, creating a rich nursery for sea life where snorkelers and divers alike can see reef sharks, dolphins, eagle rays, moray eels, and turtles.

GREAT ITINERARIES

RUINS, RAIN FORESTS, AND REEF

Day 1: Arrival

Fly into the international airport near **Belize City** and immediately head out to the **Cayo** in Western Belize, about two hours by road from the airport. Stay at one of the superb jungle lodges, such as the Lodge at Chaa Creek or duPlooy's, or, for less money, Black Rock, Table Rock, or Crystal Paradise.

Logistics: The best way to see the mainland is by rental car. Pick up a car at one of the car-rental agencies in kiosks just across the main parking lot at the international airport. If you'd rather not drive, you can arrange a shuttle van, take a bus, or ask your hotel in the Cayo to pick you up. Buses don't come to the international airport—if you're taking one, you have to take a taxi into town (BZ$50). There's currently no scheduled air service to San Ignacio, but Tropic Air has daily service from the international airport to Belmopan.

Day 2: Exploring the Cayo

On your first full day in Belize, get out and explore San Ignacio and the beautiful hill country around the Cayo. Among the top attractions are the small but interesting Mayan ruins at Xunantunich, Green Hills Butterfly Farm, the Rainforest Medicine Trail at Chaa Creek, and the Belize Botanical Gardens at duPlooy's. Save a little time for walking around and shopping in San Ignacio. After a full day of exploring, have cocktails and dinner at your lodge.

Logistics: You can do all four attractions and San Ignacio in one day if you have a rental car and if you don't dawdle. Sans car, you can hire a taxi for the day, or opt for your hotel's tours.

Day 3: Actun Tunichil Muknal (ATM)

Prepare to be wowed by the ultimate cave experience. Go into the mysterious and beautiful Mayan underworld and see untouched artifacts dating back thousands of years.

Logistics: You must have a guide for ATM, so book your trip the day before with an authorized tour guide. It's an all-day event, and you'll get wet—bring a change of clothes and wear walking shoes, not sandals. If you're badly out of shape or have mobility issues, this isn't a tour for you. You have to hike several miles, swim a little, and clamber through the dark.

Day 4: Tikal

Tikal, very simply, is the most awe-inspiring Mayan site in all of Central America, rivaling the pyramids of Egypt and the ruins of Angor Wat in Cambodia. It's well worth at least two days and nights, preferably staying in one of the three lodges at the park, but even on a day tour you'll get a sense of the majesty of this Classic-period city.

Logistics: Although you can go on your own, the easiest and most stress-free way to see Tikal is on a tour from San Ignacio—you'll leave around 6:30 am and return in the late afternoon; lunch is usually included. Note that in mid-2011 several warnings regarding travel to Tikal and the Petén were issued by the U.S. Embassy in Belize due to a series of drug-cartel-related murders. At press time most tours to Tikal had resumed operation.

Day 5: Caracol and the Mountain Pine Ridge

You can't pass up a trip to Caracol, the most important Mayan site in Belize. The trip there is part of the fun—you bump along winding roads through the Mountain Pine Ridge, past the Macal River,

and through broadleaf jungle. If you've seen enough Mayan ruins, skip Caracol and spend the day exploring the Mountain Pine Ridge—there's the Rio Frio cave and numerous waterfalls. A bonus: the higher elevation here means it's cooler and less humid than other parts of Belize. If you don't mind packing and unpacking again, for your last night in Cayo consider switching to one of the four lodges in the Pine Ridge. Our favorites are Blancaneaux and Hidden Valley Inn.

Logistics: From Blancaneaux or Hidden Valley it's around a two-hour drive to Caracol, and about an hour longer from most lodges around San Ignacio. The road can be near-impassable after heavy rains, and there have been some incidents with bandits from Guatemala, so check locally for the latest conditions and cautions.

Alternative: If you tire of rain forest and ruins, and long for the sea, head a day early to San Pedro.

Day 6: San Pedro

Return to Belize City by car, bus, or shuttle van. Then fly or take a water taxi to San Pedro (Ambergris Caye) for fabulous eating (our favorites include Rojo Lounge and Market at Azul Resort, Blue Water Grill, and Lazy Croc) and water activities (like snorkeling Shark-Ray Alley). Try to arrive early enough to take in a snorkel trip to Hol Chan and Shark-Ray Alley.

Alternative: San Pedro's a bustling town, so if you want a more laid-back experience on the coast, stay on Caye Caulker instead. You still have access to the same snorkel and dive sites.

Day 7: Blue Hole

Take a day trip to dive or snorkel the Blue Hole at Lighthouse Reef atoll. Dive boats also stop at Half Moon Caye for other dives (or snorkeling) besides the Blue Hole.

Logistics: A trip to the Blue Hole involves a full day on the water, so bring seasickness medicine, a hat, and plenty of sunscreen. Dive boats to Lighthouse leave early, usually before 7 am.

Day 8: Departure

Return to Belize City by plane or water taxi for your international flight.

Logistics: Plan on arriving at least two hours ahead of your international flight. There's often a long line at check-in.

FAQ'S

Is Belize a safe place to visit? The best answer is "Yes, but." Most visitors say they feel quite safe in Belize (except, they say, in some areas of Belize City). Tourist Police patrol areas of Belize City, Placencia, Ambergris Caye, and elsewhere, and many hotels and jungle lodges have security guards. Out of the hundreds of thousands of visitors, the number who are victims of any kind of crime, mostly petty theft, is perhaps a few hundred. So, while this is still a developing country, enjoy yourself and follow standard travel precautions: Don't wander into areas that don't feel safe; avoid deserted beaches and streets after dark; and don't flash expensive jewelry or cash. Be aware that there have been a few carjackings and robberies on remote roads or at little-visited parks and Mayan sites; travel in a group or with a guide to less popular places.

Where can we snorkel from shore? Belize has world-class snorkeling, but most of it requires a boat ride to the Barrier Reef. There are exceptions—the small islands that are on or near the reef, such as South Water, Ranguana, and Tobacco cayes, or the areas around the atolls, especially Glover's. Of course, you can go snorkeling off almost any beach, and see at least a few fish, even if there's no patch of coral nearby.

How much does it rain during the rainy season (June through October)? It depends on where you are in Belize and when you're there. Northern Belize gets about a third as much rain—around 50 inches—as the Deep South, which can get 150 inches or more. The seasonal rains begin in Toledo in early May, progress north over the next couple of months, and usually start in Corozal in late June. The cayes have different microclimates than the mainland and generally get less rain.

The rainy season typically peaks from June through September. By November, rainfall in nearly all areas of Belize averages 8 inches or less a month. The so-called rainy season is actually a good time to visit Belize, and that's not just a Tourism Board answer. Often the rains come overnight or in the early morning, and then the sun comes out. Many old Belize hands say they prefer traveling in summer or fall: prices are lower, hotel rooms are plentiful, and the landscape is lush after rains. It's also a little cooler than in the dry season months of April and May, and water visibility is usually very good.

Are the beaches in Belize nice? Although there are lovely stretches of beaches, many of them are not as good for swimming or sunbathing as the wide, sandy beaches of the main Caribbean or of Mexico's Yucatán. Belizean beaches are usually narrow ribbons of sand with clear but shallow water, sea grass, and an often-mucky sea floor. The best beaches on the mainland are on the Placencia peninsula and in the Hopkins area. Ambergris Caye has some beautiful beaches, though swimming isn't always good. South Water Caye and Belize's three atolls have excellent (nearly deserted) beaches as well. Beach resorts keep their beach areas clean, but elsewhere you may see garbage on the beach, brought in by the tides from other areas and from boats.

Does Belize have "real" jungles? "High bush" in Belize means undisturbed wilderness, and there's plenty of that. However, not all bush in Belize is the kind of canopied, broadleaf jungle that you may be thinking about. The Deep South, with its plentiful rainfall, has lush tropical and semitropical rain forest. The Cayo also has wide swaths of broadleaf bush. Northern Belize and parts of the Cayo have little classic jungle—it's primarily dry rain forest and agricultural lands.

Why are airfares to Belize so high, and how can we find cheaper flights? Belize is not a mass-market tourist destination. Air service is still limited, and service is mostly from a few hubs in the United States. Charter flights are rare, so fares tend to stay high. To find the most affordable flights, stay flexible on your dates, check the meta-fare comparison Web sites such as Kayak.com, avoid peak holiday travel (around Christmas and Easter), and sign up for Internet specials and email fare alerts on the airlines flying to Belize— currently Continental-United, American, US Airways, Delta, and TACA. Another option is to fly into Cancún, which usually has good air deals, bus to Chetumal at the Mexico-Belize border, and water taxi or bus from there.

Another option is the new ADO express overnight service from Cancún to Corozal Town, Orange Walk Town, and Belize City.

While traveling around the country, should we rent a car, take a bus, fly, or hire a taxi? Each has advantages and disadvantages. With a rental car you go when and where you want, including remote areas that don't have air or bus service or to sites that would otherwise require an expensive guided tour. However, auto rental costs are high, and gas is around BZ$11–$12 a gallon. Buses provide a true local experience, and fares are dirt cheap, but buses mainly run on the major roads and stop frequently to pick up and drop off passengers. Buses take up to twice as long as a private car. Flying is the fastest way to get

around the country; service is frequent on most routes, and the views from low altitudes are often dramatic. The downside? Fares—especially if you're traveling with a family—can add up, and not all destinations have service. In some cases, transfers by taxi can be an option, although taxis generally are quite expensive. For most long-distance trips there are no set fares, so the rate is a matter of negotiation and can vary considerably, depending on your bargaining skills. Drivers may also ask a little more if there are three or four going together, rather than just one or two. Expect to pay around BZ$3 a mile for longer taxi trips in Belize. Shuttles are another option, especially on popular routes such as between the international airport and San Ignacio, where shared shuttles operating on a fixed schedule are BZ$70 per person and private shuttles leaving anytime are around BZ$180 for up to three persons.

We want to spend time at the beach and also in the jungle. Where should we go? On a first and relatively brief visit to Belize, sample the best "surf and turf" by splitting your time between one of the popular beach areas—Ambergris Caye, Caye Caulker, Hopkins, or Placencia—and the rest in the Cayo, which has the largest concentration of popular mainland activities.

TOP EXPERIENCES

Explore the Belize Barrier Reef

The Belize Barrier Reef stretches along most of the coast of Belize, making it the longest Barrier Reef in the Western or Northern hemispheres. See it close up by snorkeling or diving. The reef is the sea's rain forest: More than 300 species of fish, 65 kinds of coral, plus sea turtles, manatees, and other sea life call Belize's reef home. Much of the reef is still in good condition, though it is threatened by climate change and development, and in 2009 it was put on UNESCO's watch list.

Get Festive

Lobsterfests, celebrating the all-too-delicious Caribbean spiny lobster and generally scheduled soon after the annual opening of lobster season June 15, are held in several areas in late June and early July including Caye Caulker, San Pedro, and Placencia. There are other fests, too: Cacao Fest, highlighting local chocolate, is held in Punta Gorda annually in May, and the Cashew Festival is observed in Crooked Tree Village, also usually in May. A Mango Festival is held in Hopkins in June.

Ride the Hummingbird

Belize's most scenic roadway begins at Belmopan with rolling hills, then cuts through the lush green Maya Mountains before gradually dipping to sea level as it approaches Dangriga (technically, the last few miles are the Stann Creek District Highway, but most people consider it all the Hummingbird.) The highway is paved and in good condition. You can drive it or go by bus.

Experience Belize the Way It Used to Be

Visitors flock to popular destinations like San Pedro, Placencia, and Cayo, and there are good reasons to spend time in those areas. But if you want to experience Belize the way it used to be, head to the edges—south to Toledo or northeast to Sarteneja. You'll find few tourists and a lot of beautiful scenery, friendly folks, and inexpensive lodging.

Put Your Money in ATM

Actun Tunichil Muknal (ATM) is more than a caving experience. It's a visit to the Xibalba, the Mayan underworld. You'll see ancient Mayan artifacts and human skeletons. While not cheap (a guided, full-day tour starts at BZ\$160–BZ\$180 per person) and requiring a little hiking and swimming, the ATM trip is one-of-a-kind. Many visitors consider it the highlight of their entire Central American experience. Due to the risk of damage to the cave and to the priceless Mayan artifacts there, we're not sure how much longer the Belize government is going to permit access to ATM. Go while you have the chance. You won't regret it.

Stay in the Jungle

While many visitors come to Belize for the diving, snorkeling, and other adventures on the Caribbean Sea, the Belize experience is only half complete without a stay in a jungle lodge. Just to hear the jungle at night—the rumble and roar of howler monkeys and the songs of tree frogs—is unforgettable. Jungle lodges come in all price ranges and in several parts of the country, including Cayo, Orange Walk, Stann Creek, and Toledo districts.

1

RETIRING IN BELIZE

So you fell in love with the Belize experience, outdoors and indoors, met some expats who bought their beachfront lot for a song, and want to do the same for your retirement years? Here's the scoop on what you can really expect if you decide to follow suit.

Belize can be enchanting for potential retirees. The climate is frost-free. Land and housing costs are still moderate, especially compared with already popular areas of the Caribbean. The official language is English, and the historical and legal background of the country is more comparable to that of the United States, Canada, and Great Britain than most other parts of Latin America and the Caribbean. Belize has a stable and democratic, if sometimes colorful, tradition. Recreational activities, on land and in the Caribbean, are almost limitless.

But there are some drawbacks: high costs for food, gas, and household items; high import duties; crime and drug problems; culture shock for those unaccustomed to the ways of a semitropical, developing country with a true multicultural society; growing resentment of foreigners; plenty of red tape; increasing taxes; a 5% transfer tax on real estate purchases by foreigners, payable by the buyer (buyers of new condos or houses pay 5% transfer tax plus 12.5% sales tax); and, most important for many retirees, medical care that in many cases isn't up to first-world snuff.

If retirement or relocation in Belize still sounds like a good option for you, there are three options to look into:

The Qualified Retired Persons Incentive Program. It's run by the Belize Tourism Board, and anyone at least 45 years old is eligible to participate in the program. It requires a pension or other reliable income of at least US$2,000 a month. Contact the tourism board for more information (⊕ *www.belizeretirement.org*).

Official Permanent Residency. Requirements and benefits are similar to those of the Retired Persons Incentive Act. With official residency, you can work in Belize. Before you can apply, you need to live in Belize for a year first, leaving for no more than two weeks. Permanent Residency applications are handled by the Belize immigration department and often take a long time for approval.

Regular Tourist Card. Many expats simply stay in Belize on a regular tourist card. Upon entry, you receive a free visitor permit, good for up to 30 days. This permit can be renewed for up to six months at BZ$50 a month. After that, renewals cost BZ$100 a month. After 12 months, it's usually necessary to leave the country briefly and start the process again. Renewals are never guaranteed, and the rules could change at any time.

The best advice for anyone contemplating retiring or relocating: Try before you buy. If possible, rent an apartment or house for a few months. Be cautious about buying property. Real-estate agents generally aren't licensed or regulated, and because the pool of qualified buyers in Belize is small, it's a lot harder to sell than to buy.

Easy Belize, by Lan Sluder (author of Fodor's Belize), is a handbook for those considering retiring or relocation in Belize. The author, with more than 20 years' experience in Belize, interviewed scores of expats and retirees in Belize to help provide readers with a realistic view of the pros and cons of living here.

FLAVORS OF BELIZE

The cuisine of Belize has three major influences: first, the spicy influence of its Latin neighbors and its own multicultural population; second, the influx of tourists with discerning palates who demanded, and eventually got, a higher standard of cooking at hotels and restaurants; and, third, the availability of fish, lobster, and conch fresh from the sea.

Rice and Beans

There is no single Belizean cuisine. Belize dining, like Belize itself, grew out of a gumbo of influences—Mexican, Guatemalan, African, Caribbean, Mayan, Garífuna, English, Chinese, and American. The most Belizean of all dishes is rice and beans. Although originally considered a Creole dish, today it's eaten daily by just about everyone. Recipes vary, but most use kidney beans, garlic, coconut milk, onion, and seasonings like black pepper, salt, and thyme. The kidney beans are boiled with seasonings and a little piece of meat—salt pork, pigtail, or pieces of bacon. Then the seasoned beans are cooked together with rice. A related but different dish is beans and rice, which is stewed beans served with white rice on the side, not cooked together as in its sister dish. In many restaurants you'll have a choice of rice and beans or beans and rice. Whatever and wherever you eat, you're likely to find a bottle of **Marie Sharp's** hot sauce on the table. This proud product of Belize—it's bottled near Dangriga—comes in a spectrum of heat, from Mild to Fiery Hot to No Wimps Allowed.

Regional Specialties

Among other Creole specialties are cowfoot soup (yes, made with real cows' feet), "boil up" (a stew of fish, potatoes, plantains, cassava and other vegetables, and eggs), and the ubiquitous "stew chicken."

Many Creole dishes are cooked in coconut milk and seasoned with red or black *recado*, a paste made from annatto seeds and other spices. You'll also find many Mestizo or Latin favorites such as Belizean *escabeche* (onion soup, with lime, vinegar, and chicken), *salbutes* (fried corn tortillas with chicken and a topping of tomatoes, onions, and peppers), and the similar *garnaches* (fried tortillas with refried beans, cabbage, and cheese). Many of these homey dishes are sold at street stands, and it's usually very safe to eat at these stands. In Dangriga and Punta Gorda or other Garífuna areas, try dishes such as *sere lasus* (fish soup with plantain balls) or cassava dumplings. The Chinese influence in Belize, unfortunately, focuses on the lowest culinary common denominator. Chinese restaurants abound, but they mostly serve dishes such as cheap chop suey, with ketchup on the side. The American influence is also less than haute cuisine, having been responsible for the widespread popularity of "fry chicken" and hamburgers (usually called beefburgers in Belize). Speaking of beef, it is generally not very good in Belize, as most local beef is grass-fed and can be tough. Fillets are generally the tenderest option. Belizean pork, however, is superb, and it's rare to get anything but a juicy, delicious pork chop in Belize. Chicken, the most popular meat in Belize, is also good. Most of Belize's chickens are provided by Mennonite farms in Spanish Lookout and elsewhere.

Seafood

On the coast and cayes, seafood is fresh, relatively inexpensive, and delicious. The Caribbean spiny lobster (*Panulirus argus*) is one of Belize's gourmet treats. Unlike its Maine cousin, it lacks claws, and most of the edible meat is in its tail.

It's perfect lightly grilled and served with drawn butter, but you can also enjoy it in fritters, soups, bisques, salads, and even burgers. Lobster season runs from June 15 to February 15. Conch, in season all year except for the months of July, August, and September, also is widely served in Belize, as conch steak, fritters, and soup. On restaurant menus you're most likely to find snapper and grouper, both tasty without being too fishy. Farm-raised tilapia is also widely available. Most shrimp, or "shrimps" as Belizeans say, are also farm-raised, from one of the large shrimp farms in Placencia or elsewhere.

Belizeans love their ceviche—raw seafood marinated in lime juice. You'll find a variety of ceviche dishes on menus everywhere—conch, shrimp, lobster, fish, and even octopus and squid. Usually the seafood is mixed with onion, hot peppers, salt, and herbs such as cilantro or *culantro* (culantro is similar to cilantro but stronger in flavor), and then "cooked" with lime or other citrus juices. It's all delicious!

Fruits and Vegetables

Belize offers a cornucopia of delicious fresh tropical fruits, although unfortunately not too much of the fruit makes its way to restaurant tables. You may have to stop at fruit stands and buy your own. In season, fruits in markets are remarkably inexpensive. For example, you can buy eight or 10 bananas or a huge pineapple for BZ$1. Papayas, mangoes, bananas, oranges, and watermelons are the most common fruits served usually on breakfast plates. But the markets have many other kinds of fruit: one is *craboo* or *nance*, a small yellow fruit the size of a cherry, which ripens in July and August. They're excellent mashed and served with

milk, or just eaten raw. Markets also have star fruit, soursop, breadfruit, dragon fruit, cashew fruit, and others. Among the best local markets in Belize are those in Corozal Town, Orange Walk Town, Belize City, Belmopan, San Ignacio, Dangriga, and Punta Gorda. Most operate daily, with Saturday using being the biggest day.

There are a few unusual vegetables to be found, too. *Cho cho*, a mild-flavored squash also known as *mirlton* or chayote, is commonly served raw in salads and also baked, fried, boiled, and stuffed. *Chaya* is a green leafy plant that is sometimes called Mayan spinach. It is rich in several vitamins and minerals. Chaya is often served as cooked greens or in scrambled eggs.

Beer, Wines, and Spirits

Nearly all restaurants serve beer—almost always the local brew, **Belikin**—and many bars offer terrific, tropical mixed drinks; a growing number offer wine. Imported liquor is expensive. Due to restrictive import laws, the beers of neighboring Mexico and Guatemala are rarely available, although due to Belize's membership in the Caribbean Community (CARICOM), Red Stripe and Heineken can be imported into Belize. Several Belize companies manufacture liquors, primarily rum, but also gin and vodka and variety of local fruit wines. **Traveller's "One Barrel" Rum**, with a slight vanilla-caramel flavor, is a favorite. Imported wines are available in supermarkets and better restaurants, at about twice the price of the same wines in the United States. There are wine stores in Belize City and San Pedro. Cashew, blackberry, and other local wines are available around the country. The legal drinking age in Belize is 18.

FLORA AND FAUNA

Belize is home to thousands of species of trees and flowers, hundreds of kinds of birds, butterflies, and moths. An amazing array of creatures makes its home in Belize. Many are not terribly difficult to see, thanks to their brilliant coloring. Others are likely to elude you completely. A rundown of some of the region's most attention-grabbing mammals, birds, reptiles, amphibians—even a few insects—is provided below. Also, we've listed a few of the more colorful or interesting plants and trees. Common names, in English and Spanish or Mayan, are given, so you can understand the local wild things lingo.

Anteater (*oso hormiguero*): Three species—giant, silky, and collared—are found in this region. Only the collared, or vested, anteater is commonly seen (and too often as a roadkill). This medium-size anteater (30 inches long with an 18-inch tail) has long sharp claws for ripping into insect nests. You may spot one lapping up ants and termites with its long, sticky tongue.

Bat (*murciélago*): There are more than 80 species of bats in Belize, making them by far the most common mammal found in the country. Belize has three species of vampire bats.

Black orchid (clamshell orchid, cockleshell orchid): The national flower of Belize is the black orchid, now *Prosthechea cochleata* and formerly *Encyclia cochleata*. The very dark purple flower is unusual among orchids, as the flower is effectively upside down. It is pollinated not by bees but by a small fly.

Bukut (stinking toe): Howler monkeys love the leaves of the bukut, which grows to almost 100 feet (30 meters) in open fields and pastures. You can see bukut trees at Community Baboon Sanctuary, along the Hummingbird Highway, and elsewhere in Belize. In April and May they are loaded with salmon-pink flowers. The long brown seedpods also are eaten by monkeys and birds, but they have an unpleasant smell, like sweaty socks. Hence the common name, stinking toe.

Cacao (wild cacao, kakaw): Most prevalent in Toledo District, the wild cacao is a small tree that grows to about 32 feet (10 meters). Its fruit pods, which are directly on the trunk, contain seeds that are the source of chocolate and cocoa powder. Cadbury's Green & Black's gets some of its organic cacao from Toledo, as do several small Belizean chocolate companies, including Goss Chocolate in Placencia, Cotton Tree Chocolate in Punta Gorda, Kakaw Belizean Chocolate in San Pedro, and Cyrila's Chocolate in San Felipe, Toledo. A Cacao Festival is held in Punta Gorda annually in May. The Toledo Cacao Growers' Association (TCGA) represents over 1,000 organic cacao growers in Southern Belize.

Caiman (*cocodrilo*): The spectacled caiman is a small crocodile that subsists mainly on fish. It's most active at night (its eyes glow red when illuminated by a flashlight), basking in the sun by day. It's distinguished from its American cousin by its sloping brow and smooth back scales.

Cashew (*marañon*): This tree, related to the mango, is about the size of a small apple tree, growing up to about 40 feet (12 meters), often in a serpentine fashion. In late spring and early summer it bears cashew apples, pear-shaped bright red or yellow pseudofruit. These can be eaten, though they have a somewhat unpleasant aftertaste, but a wonderful grape-like aroma. But the true fruit is the cashew nut, attached to the base of the cashew apple. The cashew nut shell contains a poisonous liquid. Before the nuts can be safely eaten they must be roasted twice. Crooked Tree village is the center of cashew cultivation in Belize, and cashew wine is also available here.

Ceiba (cotton tree, kapok, *yaaxche*): The national tree of Guatemala and the sacred tree of the ancient Maya, who cultivated it in their plazas, the ceiba (*say-ba*) is one of the giants of the bush, sometimes growing more than 230 feet (70 meters), rising out of the jungle canopy. It has a gray, cylindrical trunk supported by large buttresses at the ground and, high up, nearly horizontal branches. There is a fine specimen in the jaguar compound at the Belize Zoo and there are many at Tikal.

Cohune palm (*corozo* palm): The cohune is one of the most important trees for the Maya in Belize. Its leaves are used to thatch the roofs of buildings, its nuts are used for oil or soap and as fuel for fires, the sweet heart is eaten, traditionally in Belize during Easter week, and the heart sap can be used to make a wine. It is often a marker for ancient Mayan sites now hidden by jungle. Its distinctive fluted shape and tall height (up to 100 feet or more than 30 meters) make it easy to spot.

Cougar (puma): Growing to 5 feet in length, mountain lions are the largest unspotted cats in Central America. Rarely seen, they live in most habitats in the region and feed on vertebrates ranging from snakes to deer.

Crocodile (lagarto): Although often referred to by Belizeans as alligators, crocodiles reign supreme in this region. They are distinguished from the smaller caiman by their flat heads, narrow snouts, and spiky scales. Crocodiles seldom attack humans, preferring fish, birds, and the occasional small mammal. Both species are endangered and protected by international law.

Fer-de-lance (*barba amarilla*): One of the most dangerous of all pit vipers, the fer-de-lance has a host of names, such as tommygoff in Belize. This aggressive snake grows up to 8 feet in length and is distinguished by the bright yellow patches on its head.

Flamboyant (flame tree, royal Poinciana, *guacamayo*): This is perhaps the most visually striking tree in Belize, at least May–July when it is covered in blazing blossoms of flame-color orange. Originally from Madagascar, the flamboyant is easily identified, even when not in bloom, because of its umbrella shape, much wider than it is tall.

Frigate bird (*tijereta del mar*): These black birds with slender wings and forked tails are some of the most effortless and agile fliers of the avian world. When mating season approaches, males inflate a scarlet pouch beneath their beaks in an effort to attract females.

Frog (*rana*): More than 30 species of frogs can be found in Belize. Most are nocturnal in an effort to avoid being eaten, but the brightly colored poison dart frogs—whose brilliant red, blue, and green coloration warns predators that they don't make a good meal—can be spotted during the day. Red-eyed leaf frogs are among the showiest of nocturnal species. They firmly attach themselves to plants with neon-orange legs, scarlet eyes bulging out from a metallic green body splashed with white dots and blue patches. Large brown marine toads are also common at night.

Howler monkey (*mono congo*): These chunky-bodied monkeys travel in troops of up to 20. A bit on the lethargic side, they eat leaves, fruits, and flowers. The deep, resounding howls of the males serve as communication among and between troops. Erroneously termed "baboons" by Belizeans, these dark-faced monkeys travel only from tree to tree, limiting their presence to dense jungle canopy.

Iguana: The largest lizards in Central America, these scaly creatures can grow to 10 feet. They are good swimmers, and will often plop into a body of water when threatened by a predator. Only young green iguanas are brightly colored; adult females are grayish, while adult males are olive (with orangish heads during mating season). They are considered a delicacy among Belizeans, who call them "bamboo chicken."

Jaguar (*tigre*): The largest feline in the Western Hemisphere grows up to 6 feet long and can weigh up to 250 pounds. Exceedingly rare, this nocturnal predator is most often spotted near the Cockscomb Basin Wildlife Sanctuary in Belize.

Kinkajou (*martilla*): A nocturnal relative of the raccoon, kinkajous are known for their 20-inch-long prehensile tails. They actively and often noisily forage for fruit, insects, and the occasional sip of nectar. (If you're unsure that what you have spotted is a kinkajou, simply look at the picture on Belize's $20 note.)

Leaf-cutter ant (*zompopa*): Called wee wee ants in Creole, leaf-cutter ants are the region's most commonly noticed ants. They are found in all lowland habitats. Columns of these industrious little guys, all carrying clippings of leaves, sometimes extend for several hundred yards from plants to the underground nest. The leaves are used to cultivate the fungus that they eat.

Macaw (*lapas*): The beautiful scarlet macaw is the only species of this bird found in Belize. Huge, raucous birds with long tails, macaws use their immense bills to rip apart fruits to get to the seeds. Their nests are in hollow trees. They are endangered because of poachers and deforestation.

Mahogany (*caoba*): The national tree of Belize appears on the Belize flag, and the country's motto, *Sub Umbra Florero* (Under The Shade I Flourish), refers to the mahogany tree. Mahogany was the mainstay of the Belize (then British Honduras) economy for almost two centuries, from the mid-1700s until the 1950s. Most of the largest trees—the mahogany can soar to over 150 feet (45 meters) and reach trunk widths of over 6 feet (2 meters)—were cut down and exported to Europe where they were made into fine furniture and railway carriages. Some large specimens remain in the Programme for Belize lands in Orange Walk District.

Manatee: An immense and gentle mammal, the manatee is often called the sea cow. Living exclusively in the water, particularly in shallow and sheltered areas, manatees are said to be the basis of myths about mermaids. Fairly scarce today, these vegetarians have been hunted for thousands of years for their tasty flesh; their image frequently appears in ancient Mayan art.

Morpho (morfo): This spectacular butterfly doesn't fail to astound first-time viewers. Easy to overlook when resting, their color is only apparent when they take flight. One species has brilliant-blue wings, while another is distinguished by its intense violet color. Adults feed on fallen fruit, never flowers.

Ocelot (manigordo): These medium-size spotted cats have shorter tails than their cousins the margays. They are active night and day, feeding on rodents and other small animals. Their forepaws are rather large in relation to their bodies, hence the Creole name that translates as "fat hand."

Parrot (loro): A prerequisite of any tropical setting, there are five species of parrot in Central America. All are clad in green, which means they virtually disappear upon landing in the trees. Most have a splash of color or two on their head or wings.

Poisonwood (che chem, chechem negro): Avoid this low-growing small tree. Fairly common in Belize, it can be identified by the black, oily sap on the trunk. The bark, sap, and leaves of the poisonwood cause a reaction similar to poison ivy or poison oak. Fortunately, an antidote, the red gumbo limbo tree, usually grows next to or near the poisonwood. Rub a strip of gumbo limbo bark on the affected area, or boil the bark in water and apply with a sponge.

Red-footed booby: This bird received its unflattering name because it was unafraid of humans, which made it easy prey for hungry sailors landing at Belize's Half Moon Caye, where 4,000 now live in a protected nature reserve. Look for nests with fuzzy white chicks.

Scorpion (escorpión): Centruroides gracilis is the most common scorpion in Belize. It grows up to 6 inches in length. Its sting is poisonous, and painful—about like a wasp sting—but not serious or fatal except in the case of an allergic reaction. If you're stung, don't panic—wash the area with soap and water (the venom is water-soluble) and apply an icepack.

Sea turtle: Sea turtles on the coasts of Belize come in three varieties: green, hawksbill, and loggerhead. All have paddlelike flippers and have to surface to breathe.

Spider monkey (mono colorado, mono araña): These lanky, long-tailed monkeys hang out in groups of two to four. Their diet consists of ripe fruit, leaves, and flowers. Incredible aerialists, they can swing effortlessly through the trees using their long arms and legs and prehensile tails.

Tapir (danta): The national animal of Belize is also known as the mountain cow. Something like a small rhinoceros without the armor, it has a stout body, short legs, and small eyes. Completely vegetarian, it uses its prehensile snout for harvesting vegetation. The shy creature lives in forested areas near streams and lakes, where it can sometimes be spotted bathing.

Toucan (tucán, tucancillo): Recognizable to all who have ever seen a box of Fruit Loops, the toucan is common in Belize. The largest are the keel-billed and chestnut-mandibled toucans, growing to 22 inches long. The much smaller and stouter emerald toucanet and yellow-ear toucanet are among the most colorful. All eat fruit with their curved, multihued beaks.

Belize City

WORD OF MOUTH

"The zoo is totally worth it if you can swing it. It's tiny and very family-friendly and the schoolkids, every color of the rainbow, are so beautiful."
—SusanSDG

By Ian Sluder

Belize City is more of a town than a city—few of the ramshackle buildings here are taller than a palm tree, and the official population within the city limits is barely over 50,000. Not far beyond the city center, streets give way to two-lane country roads where animals outnumber people. Any dining room downtown could leave the impression that everybody knows everybody else in this town, and certainly among the elite who can afford to dine out, that's probably true.

Although on paper Belize City looks like an ideal base for exploring the central part of the country—it's two hours or less by car to San Ignacio, Corozal Town, Dangriga, and even less to Altun Ha, Belmopan, and the Belize Zoo—many old Belize hands will advise you to get out of Belize City as quickly as you can. They point to the high crime rate, similar to or higher than the rate in an inner-city area of a large U.S. city, and to drugs and gang activity. They also note the relative lack of attractions in Belize City. There are no good beaches in or near the city, except for one man-made beach at the Old Belize facility west of town, built to attract cruise-ship visitors. Although you can sometimes spot manatees and porpoises in the harbor, and birding around the city is surprisingly good, still this is not the wild rain forest visitors come to see.

All of that is true enough, and certainly any visitor to Belize City should take the usual precautions for travel in an impoverished urban area, which includes always taking a cab at night (and in rough parts of the city anytime), but Belize City does have an energy and excitement to it. There are good restaurants, including the best Chinese and Indian food in the country, a vibrant arts community, and, outside some of the rougher parts of town on the South Side, nice residential areas and a number of pleasant hotels and B&Bs. Belize City offers the most varied shopping in the country, and it's the only place to find sizeable supermarkets, department stores, and the Belizean version of big box stores. There is always some little treasure to be discovered in a shop with mostly junk. All in all, it's far more interesting than any modern mall.

Belize City also has an easygoing sociability. People meet on the street, talk, joke, laugh, and argue. Despite the Belize City streetscape's sometimes sketchy appearance, people in the shops and on the street tend to be friendly, polite, and helpful.

If you haven't spent time in Belize City, you simply won't understand Belize. Belize City is the commercial, social, sports, and cultural hub of the country. It's even the political hub, despite the fact that the capital, Belmopan, is an hour west. The current prime minister, Dean Barrow, a lawyer who came to power in February 2008, former prime ministers

TOP REASONS TO GO

Great Photo Ops. Belize City is highly photogenic, full of interesting faces, streets full of color, and charming old colonial houses. In short, Belize City has character.

Colonial Architecture. Belize City rewards the intrepid traveler with a surprising number of interesting sights and memorable places, among them the everyday colonial-era buildings in the Fort George and Southern Foreshore sections, where people still live and work. For the most part, buildings are wood, with tin or zinc roofs. Many are in need of a bit of repair, but they still ooze Caribbean port-of-call atmosphere.

Because You Have To. As a visitor to Belize, you'll almost certainly have to spend a little time in Belize City, whether you like it or not. The international airport is in Ladyville, at the northern edge of the city. Belize City is the transportation hub of the country, and most flights, buses, and car rentals originate here. If you're arriving late or leaving early, you'll have to overnight in or near the city. Make the best of it. Take care, but explore and enjoy the city.

including Said Musa, many of the other ministers, and nearly all of the country's movers and shakers live in or near Belize City.

One longtime Belize resident, a lodge owner who lives near San Ignacio, says that despite its problems she enjoys making day trips to the city and always encourages visitors to spend some time there: "Being a landlubber, I enjoy the boats, seabirds, and smell of the salt air, and of course the Swing Bridge, watching the fishermen on fishing boats sell their fish, and seeing what fish and sea creatures are for sale in the market. When I first came here I was amazed at the fish and meat stalls, at how they were out in the open, and weren't refrigerated like back home. I think it's good for tourists to see that there are other ways of living than what they are used to. Isn't that the point of traveling?"

Still—and we can't overemphasize this—you do have to be careful, as crime is not limited just to certain areas: When you're in Belize City, bring your street smarts and exercise caution at all times.

ORIENTATION AND PLANNING

GETTING ORIENTED

If you're prepared to go beyond a cursory excursion, Belize City will repay your curiosity. Belizeans are natural city dwellers, and there's an infectious sociability on streets like Albert and Queen, the main shopping strips. The finest British colonial houses—graceful white buildings with wraparound verandas, painted shutters, and fussy Victorian woodwork—are in the Fort George area, near the Radisson Fort George, the most pleasant part of the city for a stroll.

Fort George. The "colonial" section of Belize City is notable for its grand, if sometimes dilapidated, old 19th- and early-20th-century homes and buildings.

Marine Parade Harbor Front. Along the water near the Princess Hotel & Casino and BTL Park, there is more open, public space than there are buildings, making this a pleasant escape from the bustle of the city center.

The Commercial District. On the South Side, mainly on Albert and Regent streets, this is the commercial center of the city. Be advised, however, that it is also near some of the worst slums in Belize.

King's Park. Upscale residences line the streets near Princess Margaret Drive, about 2 mi (3 km) north of the city center.

The Northern Suburbs. Along the Northern Highway between the city center and the international airport, this is the fastest-growing part of the metropolitan area, with middle-class residential sections such as Buttonwood Bay and Belama, some of the city's stores and supermarkets, and several hotels and B&Bs.

The Western Suburbs. Several new tourist attractions have popped up here, such as the Old Belize complex. This multiuse commercial and residential area along the Western Highway, beginning at "Boot Hill" on Cemetery Road at the intersection of Central American Boulevard, is also on the way to the Belize Zoo, Belmopan, and Cayo.

> **TOURING TIP**
>
> If you're spending time in downtown Belize City, you're better off without a car. Parking is limited, and leaving a car on the street overnight, especially with any valuables in it, is just asking for trouble. Although most residents don't own a car and get around on bicycle or on foot, even a few cars on the narrow streets can cause a traffic backup. There are a few stoplights, but sometimes they're not working, and local drivers seem to know traffic rules that you don't know.

PLANNING

WHEN TO GO

As with the rest of Belize, the most pleasant time to visit Belize City is in the winter and early spring, December to March, when it's cooler and drier—similar to South Florida at that same time of year. The average high temperature in Belize City is 86.2°F, and the average low is 72.6°F. The coolest month is January, and the hottest is May. Hotel rates drop in the off-season, typically from just after Easter to U.S. Thanksgiving. September, a month marked by St. George's Caye Day (September 10) and Belize Independence Day (September 21) sees celebrations and parties; many expatriated Belizeans return home then for a visit to see family and friends. However, September is also peak time for tropical storms and hurricanes in the western Caribbean.

GETTING HERE AND AROUND

AIR TRAVEL

Philip S. W. Goldson International Airport (BZE) is near Ladyville, 9 mi (14 km) north of the city. The international airport is served from U.S. gateways by American, United, Continental, Delta, TACA, and US

Airways. Tropic Air has daily flights between the international airport and Flores, Guatemala, gateway to Tikal, and on to Guatemala City.

In addition to international flights, a domestic terminal at the international airport has flights on Maya Island Air and Tropic Air to Ambergris Caye and Caye Caulker and the coastal towns of Dangriga, Placencia, and Punta Gorda. Tropic Air also has a daily flight to the capital of Belmopan. A Maya Island flight goes to Savannah airstrip at Independence across the lagoon from Placencia. The Belize City municipal airport, on the seafront about 1 mi (2 km) north of the city center, has domestic flights only; Maya Island Air and Tropic Air serve most of the same domestic destinations from here as from the international airport. Fares from the municipal airport are about 10%–45% cheaper, depending on the destination, than similar flights departing from the international airport.

Contacts Maya Island Air ☎ 223/1140 ⊕ *www.mayaregional.com*. **Tropic Air** ☎ 226/2012, 800/422–3435 in U.S. or Canada ⊕ *www.tropicair.com*.

BUS TRAVEL

TO AND FROM BELIZE CITY

Belize City is the hub of the country's fairly extensive bus network, so there's service to most regions and to the Guatemalan and Mexican borders. The main bus terminal on West Collet Canal Street in Belize City—still locally referred to as Novelo's though the Novelo's bus company is no more—is used by most regional companies, including, on the Western Highway routes, Middleton's, Shaw's, Westline, Guerra's, and BBOC, a drivers' co-op; on the Northern Highway routes, Chell, Gilharry, Tillett's, BBOC, Venus, and others; and on the Hummingbird and Southern highways routes, James Bus Line, G-Line, and Usher. Take a cab to or from the bus terminal, as it is not in a safe area.

Bus service from Belize City on the main routes north, west, and south is frequent and inexpensive, although most of the buses, old Bluebird school buses from the United States, have cramped seating and lack air-conditioning. The fare from Belize City to San Ignacio is BZ$7, and to Corozal Town BZ$9; express buses, when available, are BZ$2 or $3 more.

For those going to Flores, Guatemala, or Chetumal, Mexico, two Guatemalan bus lines, Fuente del Norte and San Juan, have daily service from the Marine Terminal near the Swing Bridge. Fuente del Norte has the better equipment and service.

In late 2011 the Mexican bus line ADO began daily express service between Cancún and Belize City, with stops at Playa del Carmen, Tulum, Corozal Town, and Orange Walk Town. The overnight service, departing from both Cancún and Belize City in the evening and arriving about eight hours later in the early morning, is handy for those flying into or out of Cancún, an option that usually offers lower fares than flying to and from the international airport near Belize City. Service is on modern Mercedes buses with air-conditioning, reclining seats, bathrooms, and videos. ADO also added Mérida–Belize City service. In Belize City, ADO uses the Novelo's terminal on West Collet Canal.

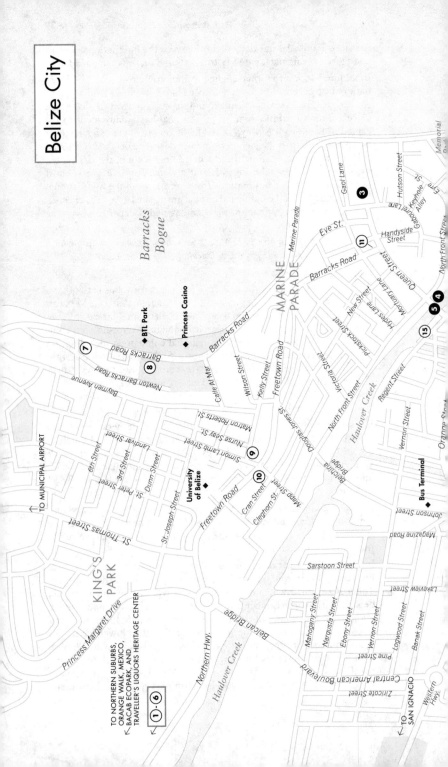

Belize City

Barracks Bogue

MARINE PARADE

KING'S PARK

◆ BTL Park
◆ Princess Casino

University of Belize ◆

◆ Bus Terminal

1 - 6

↑ TO MUNICIPAL AIRPORT

↙ TO NORTHERN SUBURBS, ORANGE WALK, MEXICO, BACAB ECOPARK, AND TRAVELLER'S LIQUORS HERITAGE CENTER

↙ TO SAN IGNACIO

3
11
4
5
15
7
8
9
10

Gaol Lane
Hutson Street
Eyre St.
Gabourel Lane
Keyhole Alley
North Front Street
Eve St.
Handyside Street
Marine Parade
Barracks Road
Queen Street
Mortuary Lane
New Street
Hydes Lane
Pickstock Street
Victoria Street
Barracks Road
Wilson Street
Kelly Street
Freetown Road
Calle Al Mar
Newton Barracks Road
Barracks Road
Baymen Avenue
6th Street
St. Peter Street
3rd Street
Landivar Street
Dunn Street
St. Joseph Street
St. Thomas Street
Matron Roberts St.
Nurse Seay St.
Simon Lamb Street
Douglas Jones St.
North Front Street
Hallover Creek
Regent Street
Vernon Street
Orange Street
Freetown Road
Cran Street
Mapp Street
Cleghorn St.
Belcan Bridge
Johnson Street
Magazine Road
Sarstoon Street
Lakeview Street
Mahogany Street
Narqusta Street
Ebony Street
Vernon Street
Logwood Street
Banak Street
Pine Street
Zirlcote Street
Central American Boulevard
Western Hwy.
Princess Margaret Drive
Northern Hwy.
Belcan Bridge
Hallover Creek
Memorial Park

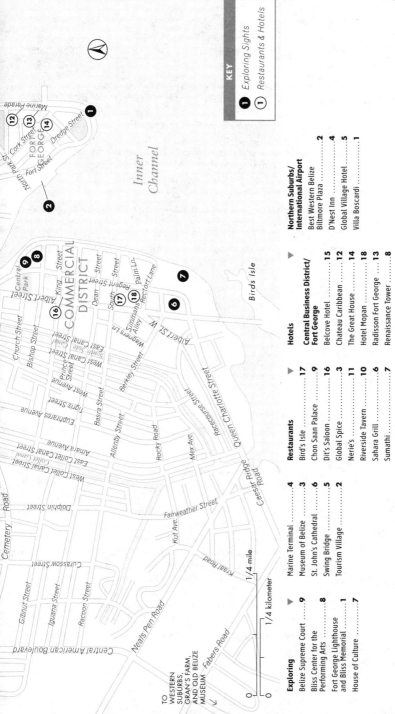

Inner Channel

FORT GEORGE

Marine Parade

Dredge Street

Fort Street

North Park St. Cork Street

COMMERCIAL DISTRICT

Central Park

Albert Street

King Street

Church Street

Bishop Street

West Avenue

Prince Street

Tigris Street

Euphrates Avenue

West Collet Canal Street

East Collet Canal Street

Amara Avenue

Allenby Street

Berkley Street

Basra Street

Dean Street

Regent Street

South Street

Magnus Ln.

Simmans Ln.

Palm Ln.

Rectort Lane

Albert St. W.

West Canal Canal

South Side Canal

East Side Canal

Racecourse Street

Queen Charlotte Street

Mex Ave.

Rocky Road

Caesar Ridge Road

Fairweather Street

Kut Ave.

Kraal Road

Dolphin Street

Curassow Street

Gibnut Street

Iguana Street

Racoon Street

Neals Pen Road

Fabers Road

Central American Boulevard

Cemetery Road

Birds Isle

TO
WESTERN
SUBURBS,
GRAN'S FARM,
AND OLD BELIZE
MUSEUM

0   1/4 mile
0   1/4 kilometer

Belize Bus Blog (⊕ *www.belizebus.wordpress.com*) is a good site for up-to-date information on bus travel in Belize.

Contacts Belize City Main Bus Terminal (locally called Novelo's) ⊠ *W. Collet Canal St.*

WITHIN BELIZE CITY
There is now limited bus service within Belize City on Lopez, Arrow Line, Haylock, and other independent lines. Fares are BZ$1 to BZ$2 depending on the route and the bus line. Ask locally about routes and times, as there are few if any published schedules. Also, local nonexpress buses will stop and drop off most anywhere on the standard route. For example, if you're going from West Collet Canal terminal downtown to Brodie's supermarket on the Northern Highway just north of downtown, you can be dropped off at or near Brodie's.

CAR TRAVEL

TO AND FROM BELIZE CITY
There are only two highways to Belize City: the Northern Highway, which stretches to the Mexican border, 102 mi (165 km) away, and the Western Highway, which runs 81 mi (131 km) to Guatemala. Both are paved and in good condition. Signs guide you to nearby destinations such as the Belize Zoo.

IN BELIZE WITH A CAR
Finding your way around the city itself can be confusing. With rare exceptions hotels in and near the city center offer mostly on-street parking, and you run the risk of a break-in if you leave the car overnight. Hotels in the suburbs north and west of the city usually have fenced or otherwise secured parking. Give your nerves a break and explore the city by taxi or on foot by day in safer sections like the Fort George area.

If you're driving between western and northern Belize, say from Belmopan to Orange Walk Town, you can take the Burrell Boom bypass around Belize City. The bypass runs between the roundabout on the Western Highway at Hattieville at Mile 15.5 and Mile 13 of the Northern Highway. The bypass, completely paved, is about 11.5 mi (18.5 km) in length; it saves you about 17 mi (28 km) and about a half hour of driving time.

TAXI TRAVEL

Cabs cost BZ$7–BZ$10 for one person between any two points in the city, plus BZ$1 for each additional person. Outside the city, and from downtown to the suburbs, you'll be charged by distance traveled. Traveling between the international airport and any point in the city (including the businesses and hotels along the Northern Highway) is BZ$50 (for the taxi, not per person). There are no meters, so be sure to agree on a price before you leave. Authorized taxis have green license plates. You can find taxis in the Market Square area near the Swing Bridge and at the Novelo's bus terminal, or hotels will call them for you (preferred, since the hotel people know the dependable drivers). Otherwise, for pickup, call Cinderella Plaza Taxi Stand if you are in the downtown area or Belcan Taxi Stand if you are on the north end of the city.

Contacts Belcan Taxi Stand ☎ *223/2916.* **Cinderella Plaza Taxi Stand** ☎ *223/0371.*

WATER TRAVEL

You can travel from Belize City on fast boats that hold up to 50 to 100 passengers to San Pedro (Ambergris Caye) and Caye Caulker. The boats also connect San Pedro and Caye Caulker. Caye Caulker Water Taxi boats (despite the name they go to San Pedro as well as Caye Caulker) depart from the Marine Terminal at 10 North Front Street near the Swing Bridge; San Pedro Belize Express boats (despite the name they also go to Caulker) leave from the nearby Brown Sugar dock at 111 North Front Street near the Tourism Village; Water Jets International boats, also confusingly known as San Pedro Water Jets Express, leave from the Marine Terminal at 10 North Front Street.

From Belize City it's a 45-minute ride to Caye Caulker and a 75-minute trip to San Pedro. Going between Caye Caulker and San Pedro takes about 30 minutes. Fares vary a little among these companies. One-way fares between Belize City and Caye Caulker are BZ$20 to BZ$24. Between Belize City and San Pedro, fares are BZ$30 to BZ$35.

Each service has boats departing every couple of hours during daylight hours. Current schedules and prices are on the operators' Web sites, but are subject to frequent change. There is no scheduled water-taxi service from Belize City to Placencia or other points south, nor to remote cayes.

Contacts Caye Caulker Water Taxi Association ⊠ *Marine Terminal, 10 N. Front St.* ☎ *223/5752* ⊕ *www.cayecaulkerwatertaxi.com.* **San Pedro Belize Express** ⊠ *Brown Sugar Terminal, 111 N. Front St., Belize City* ☎ *223/2225* ⊕ *www.belizewatertaxi.com.* **Water Jets International** ⊠ *Marine Terminal, 10 N. Front St.* ☎ *226/2194* ⊕ *www.sanpedrowatertaxi.com.*

EMERGENCIES

Karl Heusner Memorial, a public hospital, is the main medical center in the country. It offers competent and affordable care, though for serious injuries and illnesses many Belizeans who can afford it prefer to go to Miami or Houston or to Mexico or Guatemala. Belize Medical Associates and Belize Healthcare Partners are small private hospitals. Karl Heusner Memorial and Belize Medical Associates have 24-hour emergency rooms. Brodie's Pharmacy, at Market Square and on the Northern Highway, is open daily (hours vary). Belize Medical Associates Pharmacy has a pharmacist on call 24 hours.

In an emergency, dial 911. In Belize City only, for ambulance and fire, dial 90.

Hospitals Belize Healthcare Partners ⊠ *Corner Chancellor and Blue Marlin Aves., Belize City* ☎ *223/7870* ⊕ *www.belizehealthcare.com.* **Belize Medical Associates** ⊠ *5791 St. Thomas St., King's Park* ☎ *223/0303* ⊕ *www. belizemedical.com.* **Karl Heusner Memorial Hospital** ⊠ *Princess Margaret Dr.* ☎ *223/1548.*

Pharmacies Belize Medical Associates Pharmacy ⊠ *5791 St. Thomas St., King's Park* ☎ *223/0302.* **Brodie's Pharmacy** ⊠ *Regent St. at Market Sq.* ☎ *223/7070* ⊠ *Mile 2½, Northern Hwy.* ☎ *223/5587.*

THE BEST GALLERIES IN BELIZE

BELIZE CITY

Belizean Handicraft Market Place (formerly National Handicraft Center) ⊠ S. Park ☎ 223-3627

Image Factory ⊠ 1 N. Front St. ☎ 223-1149 ⊕ www. imagefactorybelize.com

BELMOPAN

Art Box ⊠ Mile 46, Western Hwy. ☎ 623-6129 ⊕ www.artboxbz.com

CAYE CAULKER

Caribbean Colors Art Gallery ⊠ Front St. ☎ 206-0206 ⊕ www. caribbean-colors.com

Cooper's Art Gallery ⊠ Front St. ☎ 226-0330 ⊕ www. debbiecooperart.com

COROZAL TOWN

Corozal Art Gallery ⊠ Reyes Plaza, 4th Ave. and 3rd St. N. ☎ 633-8679 ⊕ www.corozalartgallery.weebly.com

DANGRIGA

Garinagu Crafts and Art Gallery ⊠ 46 Oak St. at Tubroose St. ☎ 522-2596

PLACENCIA

Lola's Art ⊠ Seine Bight ☎ 601-1913 ⊕ www.jcasadart.com

Art 'n Soul ⊠ South end of the Sidewalk, Placencia village ☎ 503-3088

Spectarte ⊠ Maya Beach, opposite Green Parrot ☎ 523-8019

PUNTA GORDA

Fajina Craft Center ⊠ Front St.

Maya Bags ⊠ Workshop on Airport Rd. near Tropic Air office at PG airstrip ⊕ www.mayabags.com

SAN IGNACIO

Garcia Sisters Tanah Mayan Art Museum ⊠ Cristo Rey Rd., San Antonio ☎ 669-4023

Orange Gifts ⊠ Mile 60, Western Hwy. ☎ 824-2341 ⊕ www. orangegifts.com

Sak Tunich ⊠ Cristo Rey Rd., San Antonio ☎ 606-7806

SAN PEDRO, AMBERGRIS CAYE

Artesano ⊠ Buccaneer St. ☎ 226-2370 ⊕ www.artesanobelize.com

Belizean Arts ⊠ Barrier Reef Dr. at Fido's ☎ 226-3019 ⊕ www. belizeanarts.com

—Compiled by Lan Sluder

MONEY MATTERS

U.S. dollars are accepted everywhere in Belize, but if you need to exchange another currency, you can do so at one of the five banks in Belize City: Heritage Bank, Atlantic Bank, Belize Bank, First Caribbean International Bank, and ScotiaBank. All banks in Belize City have ATMs (Belize Bank has the largest number of ATMs), and, except for ATMs of Heritage Bank, all now accept cards issued outside Belize. If your ATM card has a Visa, MasterCard, PLUS, or CIRRUS symbol, it will work in at least some Belize ATMs, and you can generally withdraw up to BZ$500 a day. You get your cash in Belize dollars only. Note that other banks you may see in Belize City are international—that is, offshore—banks that do not offer local banking services.

Banks Heritage Bank. (Formerly Alliance Bank) ⊠ 106 Princess Margaret Dr. ☎ 223/6783. **Atlantic Bank** ⊠ Main Office, Corner Freetown Rd. and

Cleghorn St. ☎ 223/4123 ⊕ www.atlabank.com ✉ Mile 9, Northern Hwy. at Ladyville ✉ Cemetery Rd. ✉ Albert St. ✉ International Airport. **Belize Bank** ✉ Main Office, 60 Market Sq. ☎ 227/7132 ⊕ www.belizebank.com ✉ Coney Dr. ✉ International Airport. **First Caribbean International Bank** ✉ 21 Albert St. ☎ 227/7212 ⊕ www.firstcaribbeanbank.com. **ScotiaBank** ✉ 4 Albert St. ☎ 227/7027 ⊕ www.belizescotiabank.com ✉ Mile 2.5, Northern Hwy.

TOURS

From Belize City you can take day trips to Altun Ha, Crooked Tree Wildlife Sanctuary, and Lamanai. You can also do day trips to nearby islands, including Caulker and Ambergris cayes, either on your own or with a local tour operator. Your hotel can also arrange day trips.

Belize Trips' Katie Valk, a transplanted New Yorker, can organize a custom trip to almost any place in the country and also to Tikal in Guatemala. With her hotel connections she can even get you a room when everything seems booked. She's also a warden for the U.S. Embassy.

Several other Belize City–based tour companies are listed here. Keep in mind that most Belize City tour operators focus more on the booming cruise-ship market than on individual travelers. Some cruise-ship tour operators, while generally reputable, have no office and operate with a Web site and a cell phone, meeting customers at the Tourism Village.

Contacts Belize Trips ✉ Katie Valk, Belize Trips, P.O. Box 1108 ☎ 223/0376, 561/210–7015 U.S. number ✍ info@belize-trips.com ⊕ www.belize-trips.com.

Cave-Tubing in Belize ☎ 605/1575 ⊕ www.cave-tubing.com. **Discovery Expeditions** ✉ 5916 Manatee Dr., Buttonwood Bay ☎ 223/0748 ⊕ www.discoverybelize.com. **S&L Travel and Tours** ✉ 91 N. Front St. ☎ 227/7593 ⊕ www.sltravelbelize.com.

VISITOR INFORMATION

The Belize Tourism Board, downtown at 64 Regent St., is open Monday–Thursday 8–5, Friday 8–4.

Belize Tourism Board ✉ 64 Regent St. ☎ 227/2420 ⊕ www.travelbelize.org.

EXPLORING BELIZE CITY

Belize City is defined by the water around it. The main part of the city is at the end of a small peninsula, jutting out into the Caribbean Sea. Haulover Creek, an extension of the Belize River, running roughly west to east, divides the city into the North Side and the South Side. The North Side is, to generalize, more affluent than the South Side. The venerable Swing Bridge connects the two sides, although in modern times other bridges over Haulover Creek, especially the Belcan Bridge northwest of the city center, carry more traffic. At the mouth of the river, just beyond Swing Bridge, is the Belize Harbor (or Harbour, as it's written locally, in the English style).

Coming from the north, follow the Northern Highway through several roundabouts (traffic circles) to Freetown Road and Barracks Road to reach the center. Alternatively, you can swing west on Princess Margaret Drive to Barracks Road, along the seafront. From the west, the Western

Highway becomes Cemetery Road, which leads you to the center via the South Side and Orange Street. The city center itself is a confusing warren of narrow streets, many of them one-way.

If you're staying in either the northern or western sprawling suburbs, a car is handy, as there's limited municipal bus service. There are many taxis, however, with affordable rates starting at BZ$7. It's not customary to tip taxi drivers, unless they help you with luggage or perform other services. Most drivers are friendly and are happy to point out interesting sites to visitors. A few are licensed tour guides.

SAFETY AND PRECAUTIONS Belize City has a reputation for street crime. The government has made some progress in cleaning up the problem, despite gang activity and drugs. Crimes against tourists in Belize City are relatively rare. Still, the crime rate in Belize City is comparable to that of a distressed inner-city area in the United States, and the homicide rate is among the highest in the world. Take the same precautions you'd take in any city—don't wear expensive jewelry or watches, avoid handling money in public, and leave valuables in a safe. Ignore offers to buy drugs. On buses and in crowded areas hold purses and backpacks close to your body. Check with the staff at your hotel before venturing into any unfamiliar areas, particularly at night. After dark you should always take a taxi rather than walk even a few blocks. Avoid leaving your rental car on the street overnight. Generally the northern suburbs are safer than downtown.

FORT GEORGE

This is the most pleasant and appealing section of the city, much of it cooled by prevailing breezes from the sea. It has stately if sometimes run-down colonial buildings that escaped the hurricanes of 1931 and 1961, several embassies (though the U.S. embassy was transplanted to Belmopan in 2006), upmarket restaurants that attract the city's elite, and the city's better hotels, including the Radisson Fort George and the Great House, plus the Museum of Belize, Fort George lighthouse, and the Fort Street Tourism Village.

TOP ATTRACTIONS

★ **Museum of Belize.** This small but interesting museum was a Belize City jail from the 1850s to 1993. Displays on Belize history and culture include ancient Mayan artifacts, eclectic memorabilia, colorful Belize postage stamps, and an actual jail cell. Exhibitions change frequently. ⊠ *Gabourel La., Belize Central Bank Compound, Fort George* ☎ *223/4524* ⊕ *www.nichbelize.org* ⊠ *BZ$20* ☺ *Mon.–Thurs. 8–5; Fri. 8–4:30.*

Swing Bridge. As you might have guessed, the bridge spanning Haulover Creek actually swings, though not as regularly as it did in the past. When needed to allow a boat through or by special request of visiting dignitaries, four men hand-winch the bridge a quarter-revolution so waiting boats can continue upstream (when it was the only bridge in town, this snarled traffic for blocks). The bridge, made in England, opened in 1923; it was renovated and upgraded in 1999. It's the only one of its kind left. Before the Swing Bridge arrived, cattle were "hauled over" the creek in a barge. ⊠ *Haulover Creek where Queen and Albert Sts. meet, Fort George.*

HISTORY

The Maya had long had small fishing camps—but no large cities—near the present-day site of Belize City, but they abandoned the area in the 1600s. A few English adventurers and pirates then established camps at the mouth of the Belize River and on cayes just offshore. They began cutting logwood, which was valued in Europe as a source of black dyes. In the 1700s the Bay Settlement, as it was called, received influxes of new British settlers, termed Baymen, and African slaves from Jamaica.

Spain claimed Belize as a minor backwater of its New World domain, but Spain's influence dwindled after some of its navy ships were defeated by a ragtag group of Baymen in 1798 at the Battle of St. George's Caye, 9 mi (15 km) off Belize City. Belize Town, as it was then called, became the main export center for logwood, and, later, mahogany. Belize City became the capital of the British colony of British Honduras in 1892, and by 1904 its population had grown to about 10,000.

Belize was one of Pax Britannia's most neglected colonies. The British, who were usually generous in such matters, left little of either great beauty or interest in their former colony's capital. Belize City's rough reputation began after two devastating hurricanes caused authorities to move the capital to Belmopan.

Press accounts of street crime made Belize City sound like south-central Los Angeles. In 1995 a Tourism Police unit was created to help cut down on crime, and officers on foot or bicycle patrol are now a familiar sight. To make getting around the city easier, roads were resurfaced and traffic lights were installed. More and more colonial buildings were restored, making the Fort George area an increasingly pleasant place to stay. Casino gaming was legalized.

The city now gets more than 600,000 cruise-ship passengers annually. The cruise-ship terminal and shopping area called Fort Street Tourism Village was unveiled in 2001.

WORTH NOTING

★ **Fort George Lighthouse and Bliss Memorial.** Towering over the entrance to Belize Harbor, the lighthouse stands guard on the tip of Fort George Point. It was designed and funded by the country's greatest benefactor, Baron Bliss. The English nobleman never actually set foot on the Belizean mainland, but in his will he bequeathed most of his fortune to the people of Belize, and the date of his death, March 9, is celebrated as a national holiday. He is buried here, in a small, low mausoleum perched on the seawall, up a short run of limestone stairs. The lighthouse is for photo ops only—you can't enter it. ⊠ *Marine Parade, near Radisson Fort George Hotel, Fort George.*

Fort Street Tourism Village. In the former Customs House, the Tourism Village (sometimes also called the Tourist Village) is predominantly geared to cruise-ship passengers, being their official port of entry. In fact, Belizeans are discouraged from going into the Village, or may even be denied admittance. As a visitor, you may be required to show your passport and obtain a pass to enter. Inside and in the immediate vicinity of the

Tourism Village are several gift shops, restaurants, a car rental agency, tour companies, and taxi stands. On days when there are cruise ships in town, local vendors set up small stands selling crafts, food, and drink on the streets nearby. ⊠ *8 Fort St., Fort George* ☎ *223/7786* ⊕ *www. tourismvillage.com* ⊘ *Open when cruise ships are in port.*

SOUTH SIDE COMMERCIAL DISTRICT

This area, along Albert and Regent streets, two parallel streets running north–south from Haulover Creek, is the commercial heart of the city. It has many small stores, banks, and budget hotels, along with several places of interest, including the Supreme Court, St. John's Cathedral, and the House of Culture. A third parallel street, the Southern Foreshore, hugs the waterfront along the South Side.

WHAT TO SEE

★ **Belize Supreme Court.** Not the oldest building in the city but one of the most striking, the 1926 Belize Supreme Court building is patterned after its wooden predecessor, which had burned in 1918. An 1820 court building had also burned down. The current building, painted white, has filigreed iron stair and balcony rails, similar to what you might see in New Orleans (the construction company came from Louisiana), between two arms of the structure, and above the balcony a four-sided clock. This being Belize, the clock faces all seem to show different times. You can't enter the building, but it's worth admiring from the outside. ⊠ *Regent St., opposite Battlefield Park, Commercial District* ☎ *227/4387.*

Bliss Center for the Performing Arts. Overlooking the harbor from the Southern Foreshore near the Supreme Court, this building houses the Institute of Creative Arts and hosts cultural and arts events throughout the year. Renovated and expanded in 2004, the Bliss Center's 600-seat theater is headquarters for the Belize International Film Festival in February. A drama series, children's festivals, dance, art displays, and other cultural and musical performances take place at various times. It also houses a small art gallery with a George Gabb sculpture, Sleeping Giant, which appears as the watermark on Belize five-dollar bills. ⊠ *2 Southern Foreshore, between Church and Bishop Sts., Commercial District* ☎ *227/2110.*

★ **House of Culture.** Formerly called Government House, the city's finest colonial structure is said to have a design inspired by the illustrious British architect Sir Christopher Wren. Built in 1814, it was once the residence of the governor-general, the queen's representative in Belize. Following Hurricane Hattie in 1961, the governor and the rest of the government moved to Belmopan, and the house became a venue for social functions and a guesthouse for visiting VIPs. (Queen Elizabeth stayed here in 1985, Prince Philip in 1988.) Now it's open to the public. You can peruse its archival records, art, silver, glassware, and furniture collections, or mingle with the tropical birds that frequent the gardens. Although there's a gated parking area, this is not available for visitors—you'll need to park on Regent Street. ⊠ *Regent St. at Southern Fore-*

shore, opposite St. John's Cathedral, Commercial District ☎ 227/3050 🖼 *BZ$10* ⊙ *Weekdays 9–4.*

St. John's Cathedral. On Albert Street's south end is the oldest Anglican church in Central America and the only one outside England where kings were crowned. From 1815 to 1845, four kings of the Mosquito Coast (a British protectorate along the coast of Honduras and Nicaragua) were crowned here. The cathedral, built of brick brought to British Honduras as ballast on English ships, is thought to be the oldest building in Belize, other than Mayan structures. Its foundation stone was laid in 1812. Inside, it has whitewashed walls and mahogany pews. The roof is constructed of local sapodilla wood, with mahogany beams. ✉ *Albert St. at Regent St., Opposite the House of Culture, Commercial District* ☎ 227/3029 ⊙ *Daily 9–6, with Sunday services at 7 am, 9:30 am, and 6 pm.*

MARINE PARADE HARBOR FRONT

This rather nebulously defined area, which stretches from the Fort George section of Marine Parade to Barracks Road and then to the beginning of Princess Margaret Drive, could eventually be Belize City's equivalent of Havana's Malecón. Only a few years ago it was an unsightly conglomeration of old buildings and vacant lots. With cleaning up and some gentrification, the area now has several good restaurants, condominiums, a hotel-casino, and a park.

WHAT TO SEE

Princess Casino. Belize City's only casino is usually bustling with local residents out trying their luck. It also attracts some cruise-ship passengers. There are live blackjack and poker tables, roulette wheels, and about 400 slots. The gaming and hotel complex has two movie theaters and a dance club. ✉ *Newtown Barracks, King's Park, Commercial District* ☎ 223/2670 ⊕ *www.princessbelize.com.*

WESTERN SUBURBS

For visitors, this part of the metropolitan area mostly is just a place to pass through on the way to the Cayo. However, local entrepreneurs have opened several businesses targeted to cruise-ship passengers.

WHAT TO SEE

Old Belize. Many of the visitors here are tour groups from cruise ships, but you also can visit the museum at Old Belize on your own (it's a BZ$20 taxi ride each way from downtown Belize City). In a large warehouse-style building, exhibits are devoted to the rain forest and the Maya, Garífuna, and Creoles in Belize City, with displays on logging, chicle harvesting, and sugar production. Some of the artifacts formerly housed at the Maritime Museum at the Marine Terminal are now on display here. Also at the site of the museum are a marina; a restaurant, TGI Crazy Gringo, where you can get a decent hamburger (BZ$16) and other American-style dishes; a gift shop; and Cucumber Beach, a small man-made beach that's the only one near Belize City, a 600-foot zip line, and a waterslide. ✉ *Mile 5, Western Hwy., Western Suburbs*

⌨ 222/4129 ✉ *BZ$10 for museum; BZ$20 for beach and waterslide; BZ$40 for beach, waterslide and zip line* ⊙ *Daily 9 am–10 pm.*

NORTHERN SUBURBS

If you're arriving by air at the international airport, you'll pass through the Northern Suburbs on your way to the city, or (unless you take the Burrell Boom bypass) on your way to points south and west.

WHAT TO SEE

★ **Traveller's Liquors Heritage Center.** This museum celebrates Belize's love affair with rum and its oldest distillery, Traveller's. Although it's small, the museum is fascinating, with displays of old rum bottles and distillery equipment and the history of rum making in Belize. You can also look through a window and see rum and other potables being made and bottled at the little factory behind the museum. Best of all, you can get samples of the various rums made by Traveller's, along with samples of more exotic drinks such as cashew wine, Rumpope (rum with eggnog), Anise & Peppermint (called A&P, it may remind you of cough syrup and is usually mixed with milk), and Craboo Liquor. ✉ *Mile 2½, Northern Hwy., Northern Suburbs* ⌨ *223/2855* ⊕ *www.onebarrelrum. com* ✉ *BZ$2* ⊙ *Mon.–Fri. 10–6, Sat. 10–5.*

WHERE TO EAT

Though most restaurants here cater to locals, their number and quality rival those of tourist magnet San Pedro on Ambergris Caye. The city has inexpensive dives serving "dollah chicken" (fried chicken, a local favorite, though it no longer costs just a Belize dollar), Chinese joints of 1950s vintage specializing in chow mein, and lunch spots for downtown office workers seeking Creole dishes such as cow-foot soup and rice and beans. Belize City also has upmarket restaurants serving the city's affluent elite. Only a couple of these are "dressy" (by Belize standards, this means a nice collared shirt for men and perhaps a long tropical dress for women), and reservations are rarely necessary.

A few restaurants around the Tourism Village target cruise-ship passengers, typically for lunch and drinks, but the one thing you won't find here are chain restaurants.

WHAT IT COSTS IN BELIZE DOLLARS				
	¢	$	$$	$$$	$$$$
AT DINNER	under BZ$8	BZ$8–BZ$15	BZ$15–BZ$25	BZ$25–BZ$50	over BZ$50

Prices are per person for a main course at dinner, including tax and service.

$ ✕ **Bird's Isle.** This longtime local favorite is an open-air seafront bar and
SEAFOOD   restaurant on the little islet at the south end of Regent Street, also called Bird's Isle. The thatched-roof spot is a great place to sip tropical drinks and eat local seafood, away from the hustle of downtown. Hours are limited and seem to change frequently, so call before you go. ✉ *9 Albert*

Made in Belize

For such a little country, some of Belize's products pack a punch. Below is a list of possible souvenirs.

HOT SAUCE

Marie Sharp's. One of Belize's best-known products comes from a little plant near Dangriga. This spicy sauce was originally created by Marie Sharp in her kitchen in the early 1980s. It comes in a variety of heat levels, from the moderate Mild Habanero to the fiery No Wimps Allowed, and, finally, Beware. Marie Sharp's also makes less dangerous products, such as jams, jellies, and other spices and sauces. If you call ahead, you can tour the plant on Melinda Road near Dangriga. ✉ *Main Office, 3 Pier Rd., Dangriga* ☎ *522/2370* ⊕ *www.mariesharps-bz. com.*

RUM

Traveller's Liquors Ltd. A favorite of rum connoisseurs, One Barrel, from Traveller's Ltd., with a slight taste of vanilla and caramel, has won international tasting awards in the gold rum category. The company is run by the Perdomo family of Belize City. ✉ *P.O. Box 623* ☎ *223/2855* ⊕ *www. onebarrelrum.com.*

Cuellos. A good mixing white rum, and the one you'll see in most bars, is called Caribbean Rum. It is made by family-owned Cuellos distillery. ✉ *65 Main St., Orange Walk Town* ☎ *322/2141 refinery, 322/2183 Office.*

HARDWOOD FURNITURE

If the cost of shipping doesn't break your budget, the low-slung folding "clam chairs" are a favorite and made from the region's tropical hardwood.

New River Enterprises. New River Enterprises makes solid mahogany and other hardwood doors, some around BZ$2,400 plus shipping. It also makes patio furniture. ✉ *14 Westby St., Orange Walk Town* ☎ *322/2225* ⊕ *www.newriverenterprises.com.*

Hummingbird Furnishings. Hummingbird Furnishings uses bamboo, wicker, and rattan, sometimes mixed with mahogany, for indoor and outdoor furniture. ✉ *54 Hummingbird Hwy., Belmopan City* ☎ *822/3164* ⊕ *www.hummingbirdfurnishings. com* ✉ *20 Coconut Dr., San Pedro* ☎ *226/2960.*

COFFEE

Gallon Jug Estates in Orange Walk District is the only commercial coffee producer in Belize (and it is small, with only about 100 acres of coffee plantings). Made with only arabica beans, Gallon Jug coffees are shade-grown and don't use pesticides, herbicides, or fungicides. Whole-bean and ground coffee, packed in colorful gold and green, can be bought all over Belize.

BEER

Belize Brewing Co. Ltd. With a virtual nationwide monopoly on beer, Bowen & Bowen's Belize Brewing Co. Ltd. is one of the country's most profitable businesses. Perfect for sipping on the beach, there are four beers to choose from: Belikin lager, with 4% alcohol; Belikin Premium, also a lager, with 5% alcohol; Lighthouse, a pale lager, with 4.2% alcohol; and Belikin Stout, a dark beer with 6% alcohol. Some cruise-ship and Belize City tours include a stop at the Bowen brewery, with a half-hour tasting of the beers. ✉ *1 King St.* ☎ *227/7031* ⊕ *www. bowenbz.com.*

St., at south end of Regent St., across bridge on Bird's Isle, on South Side, Commercial District ☎ 207/6500.

$$
CHINESE
★
✗ **Chon Saan Palace.** Locally adored for more than 35 years, Chon Saan Palace is the best Chinese restaurant in Belize City, which is otherwise full of bad Chinese eateries. It has some 200 dishes on the menu, most Cantonese-style, such as sweet-and-sour pork. We like the Chinese-style crab legs. There's a live-seafood tank with lobster and the catch of the day, kept alive until you're ready to eat it. On Sunday, the restaurant switches gears a bit and makes sushi. ✉ 1 Kelly St., at Nurse Seay St., Commercial District ☎ 223/3008.

¢
LATIN AMERICAN
✗ **Dit's Saloon.** Probably the oldest restaurant in Belize City, Dit's is also one of the homiest, with simple, home-style Creole and Mestizo dishes. And it's cheap—it's hard to pay more than BZ$8 or $10 for stew chicken with rice and beans or a plate of garnaches or tamales. The baked goods are delicious—order a coconut cupcake to go. Bottom line: Dit's is unpretentious and authentic. ✉ 50 King St., off Albert St., Commercial District, Belize City ☎ 227/3330 ▭ No credit cards.

$
LATIN AMERICAN
✗ **Global Spice.** It's unusual to include an airport restaurant in any listing of restaurants, but Global Spice, a no-frills restaurant near the "waving gallery" on the second floor of the main terminal, will leave you with a nice taste of Belize. Chef Jason de Ocampo has been a winner in the annual "Taste of Belize" cooking contest, which focuses on Belizean national and regional cooking. It's not a gourmet restaurant: this is a good place to get that farewell plate of stew chicken with rice and beans and a cold Belikin. ✉ Philip S. W. Goldson International Airport, 2nd level of main terminal, Northern Suburbs ☎ 225/3339.

$
LATIN AMERICAN
✗ **Nerie's.** Always packed with locals, Nerie's is the vox populi of dining in Belize City. The many traditional dishes on the menu include fry jacks for breakfast and cow-foot soup for lunch. At dinner stew chicken with rice and beans and a soft drink will set you back only BZ$11. ✉ Queen and Daly Sts., Commercial District ☎ 223/4028 ▭ No credit cards ✉ Douglas Jones St., Commercial District ☎ 224/5199 ▭ No credit cards.

$$
AMERICAN
Fodor'sChoice
★
✗ **Riverside Tavern.** Owned and managed by the Bowen (Belikin beer) family, Riverside Tavern opened in 2006 and immediately became one of the city's most popular restaurants. The huge signature hamburgers are arguably the best in Belize. (The 6-ounce burger is BZ$16.) The Riverside has added new steak and prime rib dishes, from cattle from the Bowen farm at Gallon Jug. Sit inside in air-conditioned comfort, at tables set around a huge bar, or on the outside covered patio overlooking Haulover Creek. This is one of the few restaurants in Belize with a dress code—shorts aren't allowed at night. The fenced, guarded parking lot right in front of the restaurant makes it easy and safe to park for free. ✉ 2 Mapp St., off Freetown Rd., Commercial District ☎ 223/5640.

$
MEDITERRANEAN
✗ **Sahara Grill.** This new Mediterranean/Lebanese restaurant in the Northern Suburbs has kabobs, kofta, falafel, and hummus, with many vegetarian options. Hookahs also available. ✉ Vista Plaza, Mile 3½, Western Hwy., across from Belize Biltmore Plaza, Northern Suburbs, Belize City ☎ 203/3031.

CLOSE UP

Roots Belizean

If you spend time talking with Belizeans, sooner or later conversation will turn to "roots." It's not a vegetable, but a term referring to people born in Belize who share a certain set of values. Usually, but not always, it connotes ordinary folk, not wealthy Belizeans. These are Belizeans who ride the bus instead of driving a new Ford Explorer.

"Being roots Belizean is a way of life, a mindset, and a unique set of values," says Wendy Auxillou, a Belizean who spent much of her life on Caye Caulker. Roots Belizeans enjoy the simple pleasures of life: talking with friends they run into on the streets of Belize City; skipping work or school to swim in the sea, river, or lagoon; sitting on a veranda on a hot afternoon; fishing in an old wooden skiff; raising chickens in the backyard for Sunday dinner.

Roots is also about community involvement. Children are often looked after by aunts and grannies, as well as neighbors. Misbehaving children might find themselves answering to a slew of adults in addition to their parents.

It's going to the market and eating boiled corn, *dukunu* (boiled cornbread), *garnaches* (crispy tortillas topped with beans and rice), and Belizean-style hot dogs, which are wrapped in bacon and grilled with onions. It's buying bananas 10 for a Belizean dollar. It's enjoying the smell and taste of all the local fruits, like tambran, grocea, a dozen different kinds of mangoes, sapodilla, mamie, jicama, watermelon, pineapple, guava, and papaya. It's about going to restaurants with local flavor, like Caladium in Belmopan, Nerie's or Dit's in Belize City, and Clarissa Falls in Cayo.

"It's about eating johnnycakes or plucking chickens with your neighbor, just because," says one Belizean.

Some claim that the original and perhaps only roots Belizeans are Creoles, descendents of the rough-and-ready Baymen and freed African slaves. Others argue that anybody can be a roots Belizean, that there are roots Mestizos, roots Maya, even roots Mennonites.

—Lan Sluder

$$ ✕**Sumathi.** Sumathi serves tasty Northern Indian food, so don't let the
INDIAN   ugly concrete facade turn you away. The restaurant uses an authentic tandoori oven—a large clay oven with intense heat—that cooks meat and seafood quickly, leaving it crispy on the outside and juicy inside. Try the tandoori chicken, with cumin, ginger, and minty yogurt, served with naan (Indian flatbread). There are many vegetarian options, too. Service is attentive, and portions are generous. ✉ *190 Newtown Barracks, near Princess Hotel & Casino, Marine Parade Harbor Front* ☎ *223/1172* ☉ *Closed Mon.*

WHERE TO STAY

For expanded hotel reviews, visit Fodors.com.

Belize City has the country's largest hotels, though size is relative in Belize. The Radisson, Princess, and Biltmore Plaza each have 75 or more rooms and strive, not always successfully, for an international standard. The city also has its share of small inns and B&Bs with character, such as the Great House, D'Nest Inn, and Villa Boscardi. Although easy on the pocketbook, the city's budget hotels frequently have thin, inexpensive mattresses and scratchy sheets, and amenities such as room phones may be scarce. In Belize City safety is an issue, especially at the cheaper hotels, so be sure to check that doors and windows securely lock and that the entrance is well lighted. In the downtown areas, don't walk around after dark, even in groups; always take a taxi.

Several of the city's best hotels are in the Fort George area, but there are also good choices in the northern suburbs between downtown and the international airport. The Commercial District on the South Side (south of Swing Bridge) has a number of budget hotels.

WHAT IT COSTS IN BELIZE DOLLARS					
	¢	$	$$	$$$	$$$$
FOR TWO PEOPLE	under BZ$100	BZ$100–BZ$200	BZ$200–BZ$300	BZ$300–BZ$500	over BZ$500

Prices are for two people in a standard double room in high season, including tax.

¢   **Belcove Hotel.** Right in the middle of things, the Belcove is a popular budget hotel just south of Swing Bridge, literally at the edge of Haulover Creek. **Pros:** good value; friendly staff; central downtown location. **Cons:** slightly funky atmosphere; you need to be very careful downtown after dark. ⊠ *9 Regent St. West, just south of Swing Bridge, Commercial District* ☎ *227/3054* ⊕ *www.belcove.com* ⤢ *12 rooms, 4 with shared baths.*

$$ **Best Western Belize Biltmore Plaza.** This suburban motel gets guests who don't want to stay in the downtown area. **Pros:** comfortable, secure, motel-like suburban setting. **Cons:** not much atmosphere. ⊠ *Mile 3½, Northern Hwy., Northern Suburbs* ☎ *223/2302* ⊕ *www.belizebiltmore. com* ⤢ *75 rooms* ⚤ *In-room: safe, Wi-Fi. In-hotel: restaurant, bar, pool, gym, business center.*

$ **Chateau Caribbean.** The breezy Fort George seaside location of this hotel is its strongest point. **Pros:** waterfront location; colonial atmosphere in public areas. **Cons:** shabby rooms; you may see some bugs. ⊠ *6 Marine Parade, Fort George* ☎ *223/0800* ⊕ *www.chateaucaribbean. com* ⤢ *20 rooms* ⚤ *In-hotel: restaurant, bar.*

$ **D'Nest Inn.** In Belama Phase 2, a safe, middle-class suburb between the
Fodor's Choice   international airport and downtown, D'Nest Inn is run by a charming
★   couple, Gaby and Oty Ake. **Pros:** delightful B&B; charming and helpful hosts; delicious breakfasts included. **Cons:** only a few restaurant choices nearby. ⊠ *475 Cedar St., Northern Suburbs* ✛ *From Northern Hwy., turn west on Chetumal St., turn right at police station, go 1 short block and turn left, then turn right on Cedar St.* ☎ *223/5416* ⊕ *www.dnestinn. com* ⤢ *4 rooms* ⚤ *In-room: Wi-Fi* ⦿ *Breakfast.*

$ **Global Village Hotel.** This Chinese-owned hotel has little atmosphere, but it's sparkling clean, with modern furniture and fixtures, and a good value at BZ$100 plus tax for a double. **Pros:** clean, no-frills motel;

free airport pickup and drop-off; secure parking. **Cons:** no atmosphere; mainly for an overnight en route to other locations. ✉ *Mile 8½, Northern Hwy., just south of turnoff to international airport, Northern Suburbs* ☎ *225/2555* ⊕ *www.globalvillage-bz.com* ☞ *40 rooms* ⚷ *In-room: Wi-Fi. In-hotel: restaurant, bar, business center* ⊙*Breakfast.*

$$$ 🖭 **The Great House.** Among Fort
★ George's loveliest sights is the colonial facade of this large wooden house, across the street from the Radisson. **Pros:** lovely old inn; good location in the Fort George area. **Cons:** rooms are all upstairs on second and third floors, with no elevator. ✉ *13 Cork St., Fort George* ☎ *223/3400* ⊕ *www.greathousebelize.com* ☞ *16 rooms* ⚷ *In-room: safe, Wi-Fi. In-hotel: restaurant, bar.*

$ 🖭 **Hotel Mopan.** Established in 1973 by Jean Shaw, a pioneer in Belize tourism, the Hotel Mopan has been known for attracting interesting guests, including archaeologists, adventurers, and birders, though its best days are in the past. **Pros:** interesting clientele; Internet room; guest quarters are bright and clean; staff is helpful. **Cons:** not a safe area to walk in after dark; rooms are a bit pricey for what you get. ✉ *55 Regent St., at south end of Regent, on South Side, Commercial District* ☎ *227/7351* ⊕ *www.hotelmopan.com* ☞ *12 rooms* ⚷ *In-room: Wi-Fi. In-hotel: business center.*

$$$ 🖭 **Radisson Fort George.** This is the best international-style large hotel in
★ the city. **Pros:** Belize City's best international-style hotel choice; waterfront location in Fort George area. **Cons:** staff is sometimes distant; some rooms are small and could use updating. ✉ *2 Marine Parade, in Fort George area, Fort George* ☎ *223/3333, 800/395-7046 in U.S. and Canada* ⊕ *www.radissonbelize.com* ☞ *102 rooms* ⚷ *In-room: safe, Wi-Fi. In-hotel: restaurant, bar, pool, gym, business center.*

$$$ 🖭 **Renaissance Tower.** An alternative to staying in a hotel is this condominium tower, with some units available on a nightly basis; the new rates (BZ$318 including tax) make it even more attractive. **Pros:** spacious, 1,064-square-foot suites with kitchens at rates the same as or lower than the better hotels. **Cons:** lacks some hotel amenities such as restaurant and pool. ✉ *8 Newtown Barracks, Marine Parade Harbor Front* ☎ *223/2614* ⊕ *www.renaissancetower.bz* ☞ *27 2-bedroom suites* ⚷ *In-room: washer and dryer (for rentals only), kitchen, Wi-Fi. In-hotel: bar, business center.*

$ 🖭 **Villa Boscardi.** If you're edgy about downtown Belize City, this B&B
★ in the northern suburbs might be your cup of herbal tea. **Pros:** the Belgian-born owner is very helpful; cheerful B&B in safe area; attractive rooms. **Cons:** only a few restaurants nearby. ✉ *6043 Manatee Dr., Northern Suburbs* ✛ *Turn toward sea off Northern Hwy. at Golding Ave., then left on 2nd lane to 5th house on right* ☎ *223/1691* ⊕ *www. villaboscardi.com* ☞ *7 rooms* ⚷ *In-room: safe, Wi-Fi* ⊙ *Breakfast.*

NIGHTLIFE AND THE ARTS

Travelers who like to use their vacations to catch up on their nightlife rather than sleep will find Belize City's scene limited at best. Although locals love to party, safety concerns keep visitors away from most nightspots except hotel bars, such as the bar at the Radisson Fort George. After dark, take a taxi, or, if driving, park in a fenced and secured lot, such as at the Riverside Tavern.

Karaoke is a craze among many Belizeans. A hugely popular, locally produced karaoke television show, *Karaoke TV,* has been running on Tuesday nights on Channel 5 in Belize City since 2001. Most of the hotel bars have karaoke nights once or twice a week. Even in Belize you'll hear tried-and-true karaoke favorites such as "Crazy" by Patsy Kline and lots of Elvis and vintage Sonny and Cher, and you'll also hear songs like "Bidi Bidi Bam Bam" by Selena and "Greatest Love of All" by Whitney Houston. Singers may go from country to Motown and hip-hop to funk and R&B to reggae, ska, and Latin soca. Belizean taste in music is nothing if not eclectic. At live music shows and clubs in Belize City you can hear an equally diverse mix of music, although rap in all its variations is as popular in Belize City as in Los Angeles.

One uniquely Belizean style of music is punta rock. It's based on the traditional punta rhythms of the Garífuna, using drums, turtle shells, and rattles. In the late 1970s Pen Cayetano, a Garífuna artist in Dangriga, began writing punta songs, updating the music with an electric guitar, keyboard, and other electronic instruments. (Cayetano now lives in Germany, although he visits Belize regularly.) Punta rock, earthy and sexy, swept Belize and later became popular in other Central American countries, a result of the export of the music by the likes of Andy Palacio, "the ambassador of punta rock," who died unexpectedly at the peak of his career in early 2008.

BARS

The bars at the upmarket hotels, particularly those at the **Princess Hotel & Casino** and at the **Radisson Fort George,** are fairly popular—and safe—places to congregate for drinks. The Riverside Tavern is a popular place to have drinks, either indoors in air-conditioned comfort or on the outside patio next to the water.

Baymen's Tavern. This is the place to sip a rum and tonic, with live entertainment on weekends, usually a singer or a small band. Friday evenings often draw a local crowd. There's also a more casual section of the bar, on an open-air deck, with views of a garden and the sea. ⊠ *Radisson Fort George Hotel, 2 Marine Parade, Fort George* ☎ *223/3333.*

Club Next. At the Princess Hotel & Casino, Club Next is a venue for live music and dancing, especially on weekends. Admission to live concerts usually costs BZ$25 to BZ$50. ⊠ *In Princess Hotel & Casino, Marine Parade, Marine Parade Harbor Front* ☎ *223/7162.*

Riverside Tavern. At the Riverside Tavern you can have drinks before dinner on the covered patio overlooking Haulover Creek or inside at the bar. Park your car safely in a fenced, guarded lot next to the tavern and restaurant. ✉ *2 Mapp St., off Freetown Rd., Commercial District* ☎ *223/5640.*

Tinto and Blanco. Belize City's first and only wine bar is on the ground level of The Great House. Here you can sample wines and munch on tapas. ✉ *In The Great House, 13 Cork St., Fort George, Belize City* ☎ *223/4700.*

CASINOS

Princess Hotel & Casino. The only serious gambling in town is at the Princess Hotel & Casino, which has live tables for blackjack, roulette, and poker, along with about 400 slots. Dancers from Eastern Europe and Russia put on shows, and there are free drinks and a buffet for players. It's open 365 days a year. You'll have to show your passport and register (no charge) at the reception counter before you can go in. Gamble here if you like, but we don't recommend staying at the hotel. ✉ *Newton Barracks, King's Park, Marine Parade Harbor Front* ☎ *223/0638* ☉ *Noon–4 am.*

THEATERS

Bliss Center for the Performing Arts. The main venue for theater, dance, music, and the arts in Belize City is Bliss Center for the Performing Arts, which seats 600. It's rare to have more than one or two shows a week at the center, and most of these are local performances—a children's dance group or a young singer's debut concert. Concert organizers try to bring in performing talent from around the country, and on a Saturday night you could hear a Mayan singer from Toledo or a marimba band from Benque Viejo del Carmen. Most shows are in English, with Creole often mixed in. Ticket prices vary but typically range from BZ$10 to BZ$40. The Bliss Center is named after Baron Bliss, who died in 1926 while on his yacht off Belize City; he never set foot in Belize but donated his fortune to the country. ✉ *2 Southern Foreshore, between Church and Bishop Sts., Commercial District* ☎ *227/2110.*

SPORTS AND THE OUTDOORS

Belize City is a jumping-off spot for trips to the cayes and to inland and coastal areas, but the city itself offers little in the way of sports and outdoor activities. There are no golf courses, public tennis courts (there are courts at the private Pickwick Club), or other sports facilities of note around Belize City, other than a sports stadium named after the now-disgraced Olympic track star Marion Jones, a Belizean-American. Unless you're on a cruise ship or otherwise have only a short time in Belize, you'll be better off going elsewhere for your sporting activities— to the cayes and Southern Coast for snorkeling, diving, and fishing, and inland to the Cayo or Toledo for caving, cave tubing, hiking, horseback riding, canoeing, and other activities. Most of the dive, snorkel, and tour operators in Belize City do cater to the cruise-ship crowd, and prices usually are somewhat higher than you'd pay elsewhere. ⇨ *See chapters on The Cayo, Southern Coast, The Deep South, and The Cayes and Atolls, and also the Beyond Belize City section below.*

DIVING AND WATER SPORTS

Belize Dive Connection. This operation runs trips from the Radisson Fort George dock. Dive trips to the Belize Barrier Reef, about 30–45 minutes away, cost around BZ$180–BZ$230 per person. Those to Turneffe Atoll cost BZ$330–BZ$375 per person and involve an hour to 90 minutes of travel time one way. Snorkel trips are around BZ$120–BZ$200 per person. This dive shop also has locations in San Pedro and on Spanish Lookout Caye off Belize City. ⊠ *P.O. Box 1818* ☎ *220/4020 office, 223/5086 dive shop* ⊕ *www.belizediving.com.*

Sea Sports Belize. Sea Sports will take you to the Barrier Reef for snorkeling (BZ$190) or to Turneffe Atoll for diving (from BZ$286). Most of their business is with cruise ships, but they also work with visitors staying in Belize City. ⊠ *83 N. Front St.* ☎ *223/5505* ⊕ *www. seasportsbelize.com.*

FISHING

If you're a serious angler, you'll likely end up in Placencia, Punta Gorda, or even San Pedro, but you can arrange fishing charters from Belize City. Both the **Radisson Fort George** and the **Princess Hotel & Casino** have marinas, and there is also the Cucumber Marina at Old Belize, the city's best, and local fishing-guide services and lodges operate near the city. The oldest continuously operating fishing lodge, Belize River Lodge, is located near Belize City. Fishing licenses are now required for all but pier and shore fishing. Your fishing charter company can arrange them for you, at BZ$20 a day or BZ$50 a week.

Action Belize. Action Belize has 23-, 25-, and 27-foot boats that will take you out on the Belize River to try your luck with snook, cubera, and tarpon. Guided fishing packages including four nights of accommodations and three days of fishing are BZ$2,058 per person, double occupancy. Day fishing trips start at BZ$220-$300 per person. ⊠ *Mile 2, Northern Hwy.* ☎ *223/2987, 888/383–6319 in U.S.* ⊕ *www.actionbelize.com.*

Belize River Lodge. Owned by Mike Heusner and Marguerite Miles, Belize River Lodge is the oldest continuously operating fishing lodge in Belize. Three-night fishing trips with lodging, meals, guides, skiff, and transfers, start at BZ$2,800 per person, based on four people; six-night trips on a 52-foot Chris Craft are BZ$6,969 per person including meals, lodging, guide, and tax, based on four passengers. The Lodge now has an outpost at Long Caye (near Caye Chapel) for closer access to tarpon, permit, bonefish, jacks, and barracuda inside the reef. ⊠ *P.O. Box 459, Ladyville* ☎ *225/2002, 888/275–4843* ⊕ *www.belizeriverlodge.com.*

Sea Sports Belize. Choose from five- or six-hour barrier fishing trips from Belize City for BZ$1,350 for up to six people, including gear and lunch but not fishing license (BZ$20 per person). Flats and river fishing expeditions for up to three people cost BZ$900 for five hours of fishing. ⊠ *83 N. Front St.* ☎ *223/5505* ⊕ *www.seasportsbelize.com.*

GOLF

There are no golf courses in Belize City, but there's a 9-hole course at Roaring River, near Belmopan a little over an hour west by car—it's fun to play, and a bargain. The spectacular Caye Chapel course has closed.

Roaring River Golf Course. A little over an hour west of Belize City by car, Roaring River has a 9-hole executive-style "jungle course." Using the double tees, you can play 18 holes totaling 3,892 yards. All greens are elevated and bunkered, and the fairways are lined with native trees. Water traps are home to crocodiles. Play 9 holes for BZ$35 or 18 holes for BZ$50. ⊠ *Roaring River, Belmopan City ⊹ Turn south at Camelote Village, Mile 50¼, Western Hwy., and follow signs to golf course* ☎ *820/2031* ⊕ *www.belizegolf.net.*

HELICOPTER TOURS

Astrum Helicopters. This operation offers customized aerial tours of the Blue Hole, Mayan sites, the Belize Barrier Reef, and others, using five-seat Bell helicopters. It also provides helicopter transfers to upscale resorts and lodges on the cayes and inland. ⊠ *Cisco Base, Mile 3½, Western Hwy.* ☎ *223/5100, 888/278–7864 in U.S.* ⊕ *www. astrumhelicopters.com.*

SHOPPING

Belize City has the most varied shopping in the country. Rather than catering to leisure shoppers, most stores in Belize City cater to the local market and those from other parts of the country who need to stock up on supplies at lumberyards, home-building stores, appliance outlets, and supermarkets. Gift shops and handicraft shops are concentrated in the downtown area in and near the Tourism Village.

About a dozen cruise ships per week call on Belize City, and each time the Tourism Village shops open their doors. Wednesday is usually the biggest day of the week for cruise ships in Belize City, often with three to five in port, and Saturday is another popular day. Rarely is there a ship in port on Sunday.

Most stores in the downtown area are open Monday–Saturday from around 8 am to 6 pm. On Sunday, nearly all stores downtown are dark, although some stores in the suburbs are open Sunday afternoon.

The Queen's Square Market, with fruit, vegetable, and other food vendors, just south of the Novelo's bus terminal on West Collet Canal Street, has been renovated and also goes by the name of Michael Finnegan's Market, after a local politician.

SHOPPING CENTERS AND MALLS

Brodie's. To stock up on picnic supplies, head to the expanded, modern Brodie's, a mini-department store and pharmacy as well as a supermarket, in a safe area on the Northern Highway. Brodie's has been in Belize since 1887. ⊠ *Mile 2½, Northern Hwy.* ☎ *223/5587* ⊠ *16 Regent St.* ☎ *227/7070.*

Fort Street Tourism Village. Fort Street Tourism Village (also called Fort Point Tourism Village) is packed with day-trippers when cruise ships are in port and is nearly deserted, or closed, at other times. It has around 30 gift shops, clean restrooms, a cybercafé, a car rental kiosk, restaurants, and other services. On cruise ship days, vendors also set up booths on streets near the Tourism Village. ⊠ *Fort George cruise-ship docks, east of Swing Bridge, 8 Fort St.* ☎ *223/7789* ⊕ *www.tourismvillage.com* ⊙ *When cruise ships are in port.*

Mirab's. Mirab's is Belize's leading department store, worth a visit if you need to pick up something you forgot, like a flashlight or batteries. ⊠ *2 Fort St. at N. Front St., Belize City* ☎ *223/2933.*

Queen's Square Market. Queen's Square Market (also now known as Michael Finnegan Market, after a local politician) is a market primarily for local residents, with about 100 vendors, including meat stalls, fruit and vegetable vendors, and food stalls. Renovations on the market were completed in 2010. ⊠ *W. Collet Canal St., immediately south of Novelo's bus terminal.*

Save-U Supermarket. Save-U Supermarket is a good place for groceries, liquor, and sundries. ⊠ *San Cas Plaza, Northern Hwy. at Central American Blvd.* ☎ *223/1291.*

SPECIALTY SHOPS

Belizean Handicraft Market Place. Belizean Handicraft Market Place (formerly National Handicraft Center) has Belizean souvenir items, including hand-carved figurines, handmade furniture, pottery, and woven baskets. The prices are about as good as you'll find anywhere in Belize, and the sales clerks are friendly. It faces the small Memorial Park, which commemorates the Battle of St. George's Caye and is just a short stroll from the harbor front, the Tourism Village, and many of the hotels in the Fort George area, including the Radisson, Chateau Caribbean, and The Great House. ⊠ *2 S. Park St., in Fort George area across from Memorial Park* ☎ *223/3627.*

Image Factory. The leading edge of Belize City's art and hipster scene is at the Image Factory. Run by Yasser Musa, son of a former Belize prime minister, the Image Factory holds art shows and publishes books. Its shop on North Front Street sells books, artwork, and CDs. ⊠ *91 N. Front St., Belize City* ☎ *223/4093* ⊕ *www.imagefactorybelize.com* ⊙ *Open Mon.–Fri. 9–5.*

BEYOND BELIZE CITY

If you're like most visitors to Belize, you'll spend at most only a night or two, if that, in Belize City before moving on. If you're heading west to the Cayo, plan to make a stop at the wonderful Belize Zoo, about 30 mi (49 km) west of Belize City. Going north or west, you can visit the Community Baboon Sanctuary, as there is road access to Bermudian

Landing, where the sanctuary is located, via either the Northern Highway or the Western Highway. For other areas of interest, including Crooked Tree Wildlife Sanctuary and the Altun Ha Mayan site to the north, and Belmopan to the west, within an hour or so of Belize City, ⇨ *see the Northern Belize and Cayo chapters.*

BELIZE ZOO

Ⓒ **Belize Zoo.** Turn a sharp corner on the jungle trail, and suddenly you're
Fodor's Choice face-to-face with a jaguar, the largest cat in the Western Hemisphere.
★ The big cat growls a deep rumbling threat. You jump back, thankful that a strong but inconspicuous fence separates you and the jaguar.

One of the smallest, but arguably one of the best, zoos in the Americas, the Belize Zoo packs a lot into 29 acres. Containing more than 125 native species, the zoo has self-guided tours through several Belizean ecosystems—rain forest, lagoons, and riverine forest. Along with the spotted jaguar (the zoo's rare black jaguar died of natural causes in late 2008), you'll see the country's four other wild cats: the puma, margay, ocelot, and jaguarundi. Perhaps the zoo's most famous resident is April, a Baird's tapir that is more than a quarter-century old. This relative of the horse and rhino is known to locals as the mountain cow, and is also Belize's national animal. At the zoo you can also see jabiru storks, a harpy eagle, scarlet macaws, howler monkeys, crocodiles, and many snakes, including the fer-de-lance.

The zoo owes its existence to the dedication and drive of one gutsy woman, Sharon Matola. An American who came to Belize as part of a film crew, Matola stayed on to care for some of the semi-tame animals used in the production. She opened the zoo in 1983, and in 1991 it moved to its present location. She's also an active environmentalist. "The Zoo Lady" and her crusade against the Chalillo Dam is the subject of the 2008 book *The Last Flight of the Scarlet Macaw: One Woman's Fight To Save the World's Most Beautiful Bird* by *Outside* magazine writer Bruce Barcott.

■ TIP→ **If you're going to the zoo on a day when there are several cruise ships in port in Belize City, try to get to there early, when the zoo opens at 8. Crowds from cruise-ships tours don't arrive until about 9:30 or 10.** Besides touring the zoo, you can also hike or canoe through the nearby 84-acre Tropical Education Center, also called the Belize Zoo Jungle Lodge. Dormitory accommodations, with outdoor toilets, are available at the center for BZ$61 per person, and spiffier cabins go for BZ$132–BZ$143 double occupancy, all including breakfast, dinner, and taxes. Cameron Diaz and the late Steve Erwin have stayed here. Overnighters can take a nocturnal zoo tour for BZ$30 (minimum four persons). For Tropical Education Center accommodations, call in advance, and be aware that the lodging area is a long hike from the zoo. ✉ *Mile 29, Western Hwy., Belize City* ✉ *P.O. Box 1787, Belize City* ☎ *220/8004* ⊕ *www.belizezoo.org* ✉ *BZ$20 adults, BZ$10 children* ⊙ *Daily 8–5.*

COMMUNITY BABOON SANCTUARY

☺ **Community Baboon Sanctuary.** One of Belize's most fascinating wildlife conservation projects is the Community Baboon Sanctuary, which is actually a haven for black howler monkeys. Spanning a 20-mi (32-km) stretch of the Belize River, the reserve was established in 1985 by a group of local farmers. The howler monkey—an agile bundle of black fur with a disturbing roar—was then zealously hunted throughout Central America and was facing extinction. Today the sanctuary is home to nearly 1,000 black howler monkeys, as well as numerous species of birds and mammals. Thanks to ongoing conservation efforts, you can see the howler monkeys in a number of other areas, including at Lamanai in northern Belize, along the Macal, Mopan, and Belize rivers in western Belize, near Monkey River and around Punta Gorda in southern Belize. Exploring the Community Baboon Sanctuary is easy, thanks to about 3 mi (5 km) of trails that start near a small museum and visitor center. The admission fee includes a 45-minute guided nature tour during which you definitely will see howlers. ⊠ *Community Baboon Sanctuary, 31 mi (50 km) northwest of Belize City, Bermudian Village* ✢☎ *220/2181* ⊕ *www.howlermonkeys.org* ☒ *BZ$14 (includes monkey spotting tour)* ☉ *Daily 8–5.*

MONKEY BAY WILDLIFE SANCTUARY

☺ **Monkey Bay Wildlife Sanctuary.** Monkey Bay is a privately owned wildlife reserve on 1,070 acres near the Belize Zoo, established by Matt and Marga Miller in the 1980s. Here, you can canoe on the Sibun River, hike a 16-mi (31-km) nature trail along Indian Creek (only partly within Monkey Bay lands), or go bird-watching—some 250 bird species have been identified in the area. It has a natural history library with some 500 books and other reference materials, which visitors can use. The sanctuary also has educational and internship programs. Overnight accommodations are available, including tent camping (BZ$12 per person), a bunkhouse (BZ$22 a person), and rooms (BZ$35 per person) in the field research station, all with shared baths. Meals are also available at times, if an educational group is in residence. Otherwise you'll have to make your own meals. Homestays also can be arranged in nearby villages. Short-term volunteers (minimum stay one week) pay BZ$300 a week, which covers their lodging and meals while they volunteer about 30 hours of their time at Monkey Bay. Internships also are available January–August, with a minimum stay of one month. Most of the reserve's facilities demonstrate high ecological awareness. For example, the bathrooms collect methane gas for cooking. Most programs are geared for overnight or multinight visits, but you can come on a day visit. Call in advance to see what activities or facilities may be available when you want to come. ⊠ *31½ mi (51 km) northwest of Belize City, Mile 31, Western Hwy., Rural Belize District* ✍ *Monkey Bay Wildlife, P.O. Box 187, Belmopan City* ☎ *820/3032* ⊕ *www.monkeybaybelize.org.*

DIRECTIONS TO BABOON SANCTUARY

There are two routes to the sanctuary. If heading north on the Northern Highway, turn west at Mile 13.2 onto the Burrell Boom Road. Go 3 mi (5 km) and turn right just beyond the new bridge over the Belize River. Signs to Bermudian Landing mark the turn. Stay on this road approximately 12 mi (20 km) to Bermudian Landing. If going west on the Western Highway, turn north on the Burrell Boom Road at a roundabout at Mile 15½ of the Western Highway, and go 9 mi (15 km) to the new bridge over the Belize River. Just before the bridge, turn left. Signs to Bermudian Landing mark the turn.

Stay on this road approximately 12 mi (20 km) to Bermudian Landing. You can also use the Burrell Boom Road as a shortcut between the Northern and Western highways, avoiding Belize City. For this shortcut, stay on the Burrell Boom Road rather than turning toward Bermudian Landing. When on the Burrell Boom Road, you may want to stop at the Central Prison Gift Shop at the Central Prison, on the road to Burrell Boom about 3 mi (5 km) from the Western Highway. Prisoners at the "Hattieville Ramada" make small craft items and sell them at the gift shop.

WHERE TO STAY

For expanded hotel reviews, visit Fodors.com.

The most pleasant hotel near the Baboon Sanctuary is the Belizean-owned Black Orchid Resort on the Belize River. Orchid Garden Eco-Village, about halfway between Belize City and the Belize Zoo, is an option for those en route to the zoo. Or you could just stay at the Belize Zoo Jungle Lodge, part of the zoo's Tropical Education Center. Otherwise, for a broader choice of accommodations and dining, continue on to the Belmopan area.

$$ ⊞ **Black Orchid Resort.** This resort in a pleasant and safe rural setting
RESORT northwest of Belize City perches at the edge of the Belize River, and you
★ can launch a canoe or kayak from the hotel's dock, or just laze about the riverside swimming pool and thatch palapa. **Pros:** most upscale lodging near Baboon Sanctuary; lovely riverside setting; good food. **Cons:** not directly in the Baboon Sanctuary. ⊠ *12 mi (20 km) from Baboon Sanctuary, 2 Dawson La., Northern Suburbs, Burrell Boom Village* ☎ *225/9158, 866/437–1301* ⊕ *www.blackorchidresort.com* ⤢ *16 rooms, 1 3-bedroom villa, 2 2-bedroom cabins* ♿ *In-room: kitchen. In-hotel: restaurant, bar, pool, water sports.*

$$$ ⊞ **Orchid Garden Eco-Village.** A friendly, hardworking, and promotion-minded couple from Taiwan runs this little hotel and budding eco-complex on the Western Highway. **Pros:** centrally located; clean rooms; tasty meals. **Cons:** not in a particularly scenic part of Belize; a little pricey. ⊠ *Mile 14½, Western Hwy., Belize City* ☎ *225/6991* ⊕ *www.trybelize.com* ⤢ *18 rooms* ♿ *In-room: no TV. In-hotel: restaurant, bar* ⭐ *Some meals.*

The Cayes and Atolls

WORD OF MOUTH

"We loved the snorkeling at Hol Chan. [We] saw sea turtles, nurse sharks, huge rays, and lots of colorful tropical fish. There's sea grass along a lot of the shore, so for the best snorkeling, you'll most likely want to take a tour. Belize is beautiful."

—volcanogirl

By Lan Sluder

Imagine heading back to shore after a day of snorkeling, the white prow of your boat pointing up toward the billowing clouds, the sky's base darkening to deep lilac, spray from the green water pouring over you like warm rain. To the left, San Pedro's pastel buildings huddle among the palm trees like a detail from a Paul Klee canvas. To the right, the surf breaks in a white seam along the reef.

You can experience such adventures off the coast of Belize, where more than 400 cayes dot the Caribbean Sea like punctuation marks in a long, liquid sentence. A caye, sometimes spelled "cay" but in either case pronounced "key," is simply an island. It can be a small spit of sand, a tangled watery web of mangroves, or, as in the case of Ambergris Caye, a 25-mi-long (41-km-long) island about half the size of Barbados. (Ambergris is locally pronounced Am-BUR-griss.)

Besides being Belize's largest island, Ambergris Caye is also Belize's top visitor destination. Around half of all visitors to Belize make at least a stop at Ambergris, and many visit only this island. There are several reasons why Ambergris Caye is so popular. First, it's easy to get to from Belize City and the international airport, by water taxi or a quick commuter flight. It has the largest concentration of hotels, from budget spots to the ultradeluxe, and the most (and some of the best) restaurants in Belize. While the island's beaches may not compare to classically beautiful beaches of the Yucatán or main Caribbean, Ambergris has miles and miles of beachfront on the east or Caribbean side, and the amazing Belize Barrier Reef is just a few hundred yards offshore. Finally, against all odds given the growth in tourism on this island, Sanpedranos remain authentically friendly and welcoming to visitors.

Though it's developing fast, San Pedro, the only real town on Ambergris Caye, still remains mostly laid-back and low-rise. Some of the main streets have been paved with concrete cobblestones, but the side streets are still sand. Golf carts are still the main form of transportation, although the number of cars on the island continues to rise, and in some areas of downtown the traffic on the narrow streets is really bad.

Caye Caulker is Ambergris Caye's "little sister" island—smaller, less developed, and a cheaper date. Caulker, whose name derives from the Spanish word for coco plum, *hicaco*, has the kind of laid-back, sandy-street, tropical-color, low-key Caribbean charm that some travelers pay thousands to experience. Here they can have it almost for peanuts. Less than 10 mi (16 km)—about 30 minutes by boat—from San Pedro, Caye Caulker is definitely worth a day visit, and some people may decide they like Caulker as much, or better, than San Pedro.

Most of Belize's cayes lie inside the Barrier Reef, which allowed them to develop undisturbed by tides and winds that would otherwise have swept them away. The vast majority of them are uninhabited but for

TOP REASONS TO GO

Scuba Diving. Dive destinations are often divided into reefs and atolls. Most reef diving is done on Belize's northern section, particularly off Ambergris Caye, but head to the atolls for some of the world's greatest diving opportunities.

No Shoes, No Shirt, No Problem. Unlike some parts of the mainland, the cayes are all about relaxing. "Go Slow" street signs dot the sandy roads, and you spend a lot of time lazing in hammocks or sipping beer in a beachside palapa alongside vacationing Belizeans.

Snorkeling. You don't have to don scuba gear to enjoy the colorful fish and psychedelic vistas under the surface of the sea. Some of the best

snorkeling in the Caribbean is off the coast of Belize. Jump in a boat for a short ride out to the reef or to patch coral.

Good Eats. Because they attract so many free-spending tourists, Ambergris Caye and Caye Caulker have more restaurants than anywhere else in Belize, and some of the best, too.

Beaches. While not your typical wide, sandy spreads, they're still classic postcard material, with wind-swept coco palms facing expanses of turquoise, green, and purple waters. You'll usually have a front-row seat, because most hotels in all price ranges are actually right on the beach.

3

pelicans, brown- and red-footed boobies, and some creatures curiously named wish-willies (a kind of iguana). Island names are evocative and often humorous: Wee Caye, Laughing Bird Caye, and—why ask why?—Bread and Butter Caye. Names can suggest the company you should expect: Mosquito Caye, Sandfly Caye, and Crawl Caye, which is supposedly infested with boa constrictors. Several, like Cockney Range or Baker's Rendezvous, simply express the whimsy or nostalgia of early British settlers.

Farther out to sea, between 30 mi and 45 mi (48 km and 74 km) off the coast, are Belize's atolls, Glovers (or Glover's), Lighthouse, and Turneffe, impossibly beautiful when viewed from the air. There are only four true Pacific-style atolls in the Americas, and Belize has three of them (the fourth is Chinchorro, off Mexico). At their center the water is mint green: the white sandy bottom reflects the light upward and is flecked with patches of mangrove and rust-color sediment. Around the atoll's fringe the surf breaks in a white circle before the color changes abruptly to ultramarine as the water plunges to 3,000 feet.

ORIENTATION AND PLANNING

GETTING ORIENTED

Belize's two most important cayes, Ambergris and Caulker, are both off the northern end of the country, easily reached from Belize City. Ambergris was actually once connected to Mexico's Yucatán Peninsula. Other, smaller cayes dot the Caribbean Sea off the coast all the way south to

Punta Gorda. The Belize Barrier Reef, a part of the MesoAmerican Barrier Reef system that begins in Mexico and ends in Honduras, runs all along most of the coast of Belize. You're closest to the reef when you're on a beach on Ambergris Caye. As you go south, the reef is farther from shore, 20 mi (12 km) or more off the Southern Coast. The three atolls are outside the reef, as much as 45 mi (74 km) offshore.

The Cayes. Ranging from tiny stretches of sand, mangrove, and palms to large islands like Ambergris and Caulker, Belize's cayes have excellent swimming, diving, fishing, and snorkeling.

The Atolls. Ovals of coral, majestic and remote, Belize's three atolls offer some of the best diving and snorkeling in the Western Hemisphere. The catch? They're difficult and time-consuming to get to, typically requiring a two-hour boat ride on open seas.

PLANNING

WHEN TO GO

Island weather tends to be a little different from that on the mainland. The cayes are generally drier. Storm squalls come up suddenly, but just as quickly they're gone, leaving sunny skies behind. Keep in mind that if you see rain in the forecast for Belize City, this doesn't necessarily mean it'll be wet in San Pedro. Late summer and early fall are prime tropical-storm season, a time when island residents keep a worried eye out for hurricanes; more than eight out of 10 hurricanes that hit Belize arrive in either September or October. If a hurricane does threaten, the cayes are evacuated, and islanders try to get inland. The Christmas to Easter period, when the northern climes are cold and blustery, is the most popular time to visit the islands, even though in winter "northers" occasionally blow down from Canada, creating rough seas and chilly weather (by subtropical standards, anyway). While winter is a delightful time to enjoy the cayes, we also like the late spring and early summer, when the risk of storms is low, hotel prices drop, and the sea is like bathwater.

GETTING HERE AND AROUND

Island hopping in the northern cayes is simple, though getting to other cayes and the atolls can be more complicated. Water taxis connect Belize City, Ambergris Caye, and Caye Caulker. There is also frequent air service between Belize City and San Pedro and Caye Caulker. For the other cayes, you're generally stuck with whatever boat transport your hotel provides.

Once on the islands, you'll get around by golf cart, bike, or on foot. Ambergris Caye is the only island where you'll see many cars and trucks, but even here you can only rent a golf cart, scooter, or bike. Ambergris Caye is also the only caye with ferry service up and down the island.

AIR TRAVEL

Maya Island Airways and Tropic Air operate flights to Ambergris Caye and Caye Caulker from both the municipal and international airports in Belize City. Each has roughly hourly service every day to Ambergris Caye between about 7:30 am and 5:30 pm. Flights stop at

Caye Caulker on request. In high season additional flights are added to accommodate demand. Tickets can be booked online using the airlines' Web sites. In mid-2009 Tropic Air opened a beautiful new terminal in San Pedro, complete with a small aquarium. Round-trip fares on both Tropic and Maya Island to either San Pedro or Caye Caulker for the 15- to 20-minute flight are about BZ$144 (municipal) and BZ$250 (international). In addition, there is also a BZ$5 ticket fee each way, and a BZ$1.50 security fee if leaving from the international airport, but sometimes this is included in quoted fares. Note that you save over BZ$105 round-trip by flying from the municipal airport in Belize City rather than the international airport north of the city. The catch is that on international flights you have to transfer by cab between the two airports—about a 25-minute ride—and a cab is BZ$50 (for the taxi, up to four persons, not per-person) each way. Calculate your savings including the taxi fares. Usually, factoring in the extra time and hassle, using the municipal airport only makes sense if you're traveling in a group of at least three. Three people would save a total of BZ$218 round-trip by using the municipal airport. ■ TIP → **Both airlines usually offer a 10% discount if you pay cash rather than use a credit card, and sometimes more. But you'll have to ask for the discount, which only applies in person, not online, and usually not on Saturdays.**

Leaving San Pedro, there are roughly hourly flights to Belize City on Tropic Air and Maya Island Air, both to the international and municipal airports. Flights stop to drop off or pick up passengers on Caye Caulker on demand. In addition, from San Pedro Tropic Air flies twice daily to Belmopan and to Corozal Town six times a day, with stops on demand in Sarteneja on three of those Corozal flights. Maya Island has four flights daily from San Pedro to Corozal Town. Tropic Air has twice-daily service from San Pedro to Flores, Guatemala (gateway to Tikal), with continuing serving to Guatemala City, but flights require a change of planes at the international airport in Belize City.

Contacts Maya Island Airways ⊠ *Municipal Airport, Building 1, Belize City* ☎ *223/1140, 223/0734* ⊕ *www.mayaregional.com.* **Tropic Air** ⊠ *Box 20, San Pedro* ☎ *226/2012, 800/422–3435 in U.S.* ⊕ *www.tropicair.com.*

BOAT, FERRY, AND WATER-TAXI TRAVEL
There are no scheduled water-taxi services up and down the coast of Belize, so for example you can't hop a boat in Belize City and go down the coast to Hopkins or Placencia or to one of the southern cayes. Likewise, except from Belize City, and between busy Ambergris Caye and Caye Caulker, there is no scheduled boat service to Belize's cayes. (There is also limited water-taxi service to these northern cayes from Corozal and from Chetumal, Mexico.)

Several private boats do make the run from Dangriga to Tobacco Caye for around BZ$35 per person one-way. They leave Dangriga around 9:30 am and return from Tobacco Caye midmorning. Check at the Riverside Café in Dangriga or ask your hotel on Tobacco Caye.

Other than that, you're generally left to your own devices for private boat transportation to the cayes. You can charter a small boat with driver—typically BZ$500 and up a day—or negotiate a one-way or round-trip price, up to BZ$800 or more one-way to the atolls. (Gas is near BZ$12 a gallon, and boats capable of handling the open water to the atolls have big dual or triple outboards.) You'll have little luck renting a powerboat on your own, as boat owners are reluctant to risk their crafts, and new laws require that you need a captain's license before you can operate a boat in Belize waters (sailing charters are excepted).

> ### SAN PEDRO TAXI
>
> There is now limited vehicular taxi service between San Pedro Town and North Ambergris Caye, along with water-taxi service. Taxis, along with local vehicles, are permitted on the golf-cart path from 7 am to 9 pm as far north as Las Terrazas Resort, about 4 mi (6.6 km) from the center of San Pedro, road conditions permitting. Las Terrazas is a BZ$50 fare, including the BZ$12 vehicle fee to cross the bridge. Fares to closer hotels are less.

BELIZE CITY TO SAN PEDRO There are three main water-taxi companies with fast boats that hold 50 to 100 passengers, connecting Belize City with San Pedro (Ambergris Caye) and Caye Caulker. They also connect San Pedro and Caye Caulker. From Belize City it's a 45-minute ride to Caulker and 75 minutes to San Pedro. Going between Caulker and San Pedro takes about 30 minutes.

Note: At this writing, the water-taxi business is still in a state of flux, and at the very least schedules and rates are very likely to change.

Caye Caulker Water Taxi Association. Caye Caulker Water Taxi boats (despite the name they go to San Pedro as well as Caye Caulker) depart from the Marine Terminal at 10 North Front Street near the Swing Bridge. They arrive at the Main Public Pier on Front Street on Caye Caulker, and on San Pedro they arrive at the Texaco Marina. ✉ *Marine Terminal, 10 N. Front St., near Swing Bridge, Belize City* ☎ *223/5752 in Belize City, 226/0992 in Caye Caulker* ⊕ *www.cayecaulkerwatertaxi. com* 🖃 *BZ$20 between Belize City and Caye Caulker; BZ$30 one-way between Belize City and San Pedro.*

San Pedro Belize Express Water Taxi. On Caye Caulker, San Pedro Belize Express boats arrive at the pier near the basketball court on Front Street, and in San Pedro they arrive at the pier at on Black Coral Street on the east (sea) side of the island, next to Wahoo's Bar & Grill. They also provide daily service between the Muelle Fiscal or municipal pier in Chetumal, Mexico and San Pedro and Caye Caulker. ✉ *111 N. Front St., San Pedro* ☎ *223/0225, 983/119–1431 in Mexico* ⊕ *www. belizewatertaxi.com* 🖃 *BZ$20 one-way between Belize City and Caye Caulker; BZ$30 one-way between Belize City and San Pedro.*

Water Jets International. Water Jets International boats, also confusingly known as San Pedro Water Jets Express, leave from the Marine Terminal at 10 North Front Street. On both Caye Caulker and Ambergris Caye the Water Jets International terminals are on the back (lagoon) side of the islands. They also provide daily service between the Muelle Fiscal or municipal pier in Chetumal, Mexico, and San Pedro and Caye Caulker. ✉ *Black Coral St., Dock next to soccer field on back side of island, San Pedro* ☎ *226/2194* ⊕ *www.sanpedrowatertaxi.com*

🚢 *BZ$24, one-way between Belize City and Caye Caulker; BZ$35 one-way between Belize City and San Pedro.*

COROZAL **Thunderbolt.** Thunderbolt has daily service between Corozal Town and San Pedro. The trip takes 90 minutes to two hours, depending on weather conditions and whether there is a stop in Sarteneja. In Corozal, the Thunderbolt leaves from the Reunion Pier in the center of town; it arrives in San Pedro at the dock on Black Coral Street on the back side of the island near the soccer field. ⊠ *Dock on back side of island near soccer field, San Pedro* ☎ *610/4475* 🚢 *BZ$45 one-way.*

UP AND DOWN **Coastal Xpress.** Coastal Xpress provides scheduled ferry service up and
AMBERGRIS down the island. It offers about a dozen daily trips between the Ami-
CAYE gos del Mar pier in town and Pelican Reef hotel in the south, and the same number between Amigos del Mar and Blue Reef Island Resort in the north, with stops and pickups on demand at all private docks and hotels and restaurants. At this writing, service starts at 5:30 am and ends around 2:15 am. Coastal Xpress also offers charter boat service to many cayes and coastal locations. ⊠ *Amigos del Mar Pier, Beachfront, San Pedro* ☎ *226/2007* ⊕ *www.coastalxpress.com* 🚢 *From BZ$8 to BZ$40; weekly pass also available.*

GOLF CART TRAVEL

On Ambergris Caye and Caye Caulker there are no car rentals, but you can rent a golf cart. Most carts are gas-powered. Golf-cart rentals cost about as much as a car rental in the United States—around BZ$120 a day, or BZ$500 a week, plus 12.5% tax. Golf-cart-rental companies spring up like weeds, and many hotels have a few carts to rent. Compare prices and ask for discounts.

Contacts Castle Cars ⊠ *1 Barrier Reef Dr., San Pedro* ☎ *226/2421* ⊕ *www. castlecarsbelize.com.* **Cholo's** ⊠ *San Pedro* ☎ *226/2406* ⊕ *www.choloscarts. com.* **Moncho's** ⊠ *11 Coconut Dr., near airstrip, San Pedro* ☎ *226/3262* ⊕ *www. sanpedrogolfcartrental.com.* **Island Golf Carts** ⊠ *Coconut Dr., near airstrip, San Pedro* ☎ *226/4343* ⊕ *www.islandgolfcarts.com.*

TAXI TRAVEL

Regular taxicabs are available in San Pedro and in the developed area south of town on Ambergris Caye. Most trips in and close to town are BZ$10 for up to four persons. For trips north of the bridge over Boca del Rio, cabs charge BZ$25 to $50, including the BZ$12 vehicle bridge fee. Currently, taxis go only as far as Las Terrazas, Have your hotel arrange for a cab, or hail one of the cabs cruising the downtown area. On Caulker there are golf-cart taxis, which charge BZ$5 per person for most trips.

HEALTH AND SAFETY

In San Pedro Town and nearby, the water comes from a municipal water system and is safe to drink, although most people including local residents prefer to drink bottled water. On North Ambergris, water may come from cisterns or wells. On Caye Caulker the water, usually from brackish shallow wells, often smells of sulfur. A new village reverse osmosis system began operation in early 2011, but not everyone is on it. To be safe, drink bottled water. On other remote cayes, the water usually comes from cisterns. Stick to the bottled stuff, unless you're assured that the water is potable. To be green, you can buy water in large one- or five-gallon bottles and refill your carry-around bottle rather than throwing away liter bottles after use; you'll save a little money, too.

In terms of crime risk, the cayes are among the safest areas of Belize. However, petty thefts—and sometimes worse—do happen. With some 20,000 people on Ambergris Caye, if you count tourists and itinerant construction workers, the island has the same crime problems, including rapes and murders, as any area of similar population. There are drugs, including crack cocaine, on both Caye Caulker and Ambergris Caye. Ignore any offers to buy drugs.

EMERGENCIES

The San Pedro Lions Polyclinic on Ambergris Caye has services just short of a full-scale hospital and is open weekdays from 8 to 8 and Saturday from 8 to noon. A doctor and nurse are on 24-hour call. Two other clinics, at least five doctors, four pharmacies, a chiropractic clinic, four dentists, and a hyperbaric chamber (with affiliation with about 40 Belize dive shops) are also on the island. For serious medical emergencies, patients are usually transferred to Karl Heusner Memorial Hospital, the nation's main public referral hospital, in Belize City, or to one of the private hospitals in Belize City, Belize Medical Associates or Belize Healthcare Partners. Belize Medical Associates is affiliated with Baptist Health Systems of South Florida.

On Caye Caulker the Caye Caulker Health Center, usually staffed by a doctor, is open weekdays 8–11:30 and 1–4:30. For dental care or serious ailments you need to go to Belize City. There are no medical facilities on any of the other cayes, but if you have an emergency, call your embassy or contact Karl Heusner Memorial Hospital, Belize Medical Associates, or Belize Healthcare Partners.

Astrum Helicopters provides emergency airlift services.

For police emergencies, call 911. On marine radios, channel 16 is the international distress channel.

Clinics Caye Caulker Health Center ✉ *Front St., about 2 blocks south of main pier, Caye Caulker* ☎ *226/0166.* **Subaquatics of Belize** ✉ *Near airstrip, San Pedro* ☎ *226/2851.* **San Pedro Lions Polyclinic** ✉ *Near airstrip, San Pedro* ☎ *226/4052, 600/9071 for emergencies.*

Other Emergency Contacts Astrum Helicopters ✉ *Cisco Base, Mile 3½, Northern Hwy., Belize City* ☎ *222/5100, 888/278–7864 from U.S.* ⊕ *www.astrumhelicopters.com.* **Belize Healthcare Partners** ✉ *Corner Chancellor and Blue Marlin Aves., West Landivar, Belize City* ☎ *223/7870* ⊕ *www.belizehealthcare.com.* **Belize Medical Associates** ✉ *5791 St. Thomas St., Kings Park, Belize City* ☎ *223/0303* ⊕ *www.belizemedical.com.* **Karl Heusner Memorial Hospital** ✉ *Princess Margaret Dr., Belize City* ☎ *223/1548.* **United States Embassy in Belize** ✉ *Floral Park Rd., Belmopan City* ☎ *822/4011* ⊕ *belize.usembassy.gov.*

MONEY MATTERS

Five banks operate on Ambergris Caye: Atlantic Bank, Belize Bank, First Caribbean International Bank, Heritage Bank, and ScotiaBank. Most are open weekdays from 8 until midafternoon, with longer hours on Friday afternoon. All the local banks except Heritage Bank accept ATM cards issued outside Belize, giving cash in Belize dollars. Cash advances on your Visa or MasterCard are also available from these banks.

On Caye Caulker there's just one bank with an ATM machine that accepts foreign-issued ATM cards, Atlantic Bank. There are no banks on any other islands.

3

Contacts **Heritage Bank.** ✉ 33 Barrier Reef Dr., San Pedro ☎ 226/2136 ⊕ www.heritageibt.com. **Atlantic Bank** ✉ Pescador Dr., Office is on Pescador Dr., but ATM is on Barrier Reef Dr., San Pedro ☎ 226/2195 ⊕ www.atlabank. com ✉ Avenida Langosta, Caye Caulker ☎ 226/0207 ⊕ www.atlabank.com. **Belize Bank** ✉ 49 Barrier Reef Dr., San Pedro ☎ 226/2482 ⊕ www.belizebank. com. **First Caribbean International Bank** ✉ 45 Barrier Reef Dr., San Pedro ☎ 226/3834 ⊕ www.firstcaribbeanbank.com. **ScotiaBank** ✉ 12 Coconut Dr., San Pedro ☎ 226/3730 ⊕ www.belize.scotiabank.com.

ABOUT THE RESTAURANTS

Ambergris Caye has the biggest selection of restaurants of any destination in Belize, and among them are some of the country's best. They range from simple beach barbecue joints to upscale, sophisticated eateries, where, especially if you eat lobster, you can easily spend BZ$100 a person or more, including a drink or two or wine. You have a wide choice of kinds of food on Ambergris: seafood, of course, but also steak, pizza, sushi, tapas, Chinese, Italian, Thai, Mexican, and French.

Caye Caulker has a number of small bistros where fish arrives at your table fresh from the ocean, and sometimes you find yourself eating with your feet in the sand. On other islands you're usually limited to eating at your dive lodge or resort.

On both Caye Caulker and Ambergris Caye street vendors set up barbecue grills and cook chicken, fish, shrimp, and lobster. Use your own judgment, but we've found in almost all cases the food from these vendors is safe, tasty, and inexpensive.

ABOUT THE HOTELS

The more budget-oriented cayes, such as Tobacco and Caulker, have mostly small hotels and simple cabins, often built of wood and typically without any amenities beyond a fan or two, though this is changing on Caulker, which now has a number of somewhat upscale hotels. At the other end, notably on Ambergris Caye, are deluxe "condotels" (condo developments where individual owners rent their units on a daily basis through a management company) and an increasing number of vacation villas, usually rented by the week. Nearly all accommodations on Ambergris Caye have air-conditioning, and most also have swimming pools. Regardless of which caye you're staying on, lodgings have several things in common: they're small (usually fewer than 30 rooms), low-rise, and almost always on the water.

Off-season (typically just after Easter to around Thanksgiving), most island hotels, except some budget hotels, reduce rates by around 20% to 40%.

ABOUT THE WATER ACTIVITIES

The cayes are all about diving, snorkeling, fishing, sea kayaking, windsurfing, sailing, and even parasailing. Diving and snorkeling are excellent on the Barrier Reef and world-class around the atolls. There's great fishing, whether for bonefish, tarpon, or permit on the flats, or snapper, grouper, or barracuda near the reef, or sailfish, marlin, tuna, and other big fish in the blue water outside the reef. Caye Caulker is known for its excellent windsurfing, especially in spring, and the Belize cayes are famous for kayaking. Boating and sailing are good in the protected waters inside the reef. Beach swimming, however, is only fair in many areas because of the shallow waters, mucky bottoms, and large amounts of sea grass near shore. Still, most resorts have a swimming area off a pier or on a part of a sandy beach where they've cleared the sea grass. The Caribbean here is usually crystal clear and around 80°F. Swimming pools are now common except at budget hotels.

WHAT IT COSTS IN BELIZE DOLLARS					
	¢	$	$$	$$$	$$$$
RESTAURANTS	under BZ$8	BZ$8–BZ$15	BZ$15–BZ$25	BZ$25–BZ$50	over BZ$50
HOTELS	under BZ$100	BZ$100–BZ$200	BZ$200–BZ$300	BZ$300–BZ$500	over BZ$500

Restaurant prices are per person for a main course at dinner. Hotel prices are for two people in a standard double room, including tax and service.

TOURS

From Ambergris and Caulker, and from smaller cayes with advance planning, you can do day trips to the mainland to see Mayan ruins, try cave tubing, visit the Belize Zoo, and do other activities. However, because you have to get from the islands to the mainland and then to your destination, the cost will be higher than if you did the tour from a closer point. *(⇨ Caye Caulker and Ambergris Caye sections.)*

VISITOR INFORMATION

The best source of information on the islands is online. Operated by Marty Casado, AmbergrisCaye.com (⊕ *www.ambergriscaye.com*) has thousands of pages of information on San Pedro, and to a lesser extent on Caye Caulker. The Taco Girl blog (⊕ *www.tacogirl.com*) has up-to-date information on happenings on the island, though some of it is a little commercial. Caye Caulker's official Belize Tourist Industry Association (BTIA) Web site is ⊕ *www.gocayecaulker.com*. Belize Explorer (⊕ *www.belizeexplorer.com*), formerly Toucan Trail, focuses on low-cost accommodations on the islands and elsewhere. The *San Pedro Sun* (⊕ *www.sanpedrosun.com*) newspaper publishes a free weekly tabloid-size visitor newspaper, the *San Pedro Sun Visitor Guide*. *Ambergris Today* (⊕ *www.ambergristoday.com*) is an online weekly newspaper for San Pedro.

THE CAYES

ST. GEORGE'S CAYE AND OTHER CAYES NEAR BELIZE CITY

9 mi (15 km) northeast of Belize City.

Just a stone's throw from Belize City, St George's Caye is steeped in history. The country of Belize had its origins here, as St. George's Caye held the original British settlement's first capital. In 1798 the island was the site of a decisive battle with the Spanish. Islanders had only one sloop, while the Spanish had 31 ships. Their knowledge of the sea, however, helped them to defeat the invaders in two hours. Some affluent Belize City residents weekend in their private cottages here. Although St. George's Caye has great places to dive, many serious scuba enthusiasts choose to head out to the more pristine atolls. Swimming from shore here is not very good.

Another option about 9 mi (15 km) from Belize City is Royal Palm Island Resort on Little Frenchman Caye. This caye is indeed little, but it offers modern air-conditioned accommodations in two-bedroom cottages.

St. George's Caye Aquarium. While at St. George's Caye, don't miss the little aquarium, run by the son of the owners of St. George's Caye Resort, Karly Ricky Bishof, a primary school student, who says he wants to be a marine biologist when he grows up. Karly speaks four languages. The aquarium, in a boathouse at the southeast end of the caye, has about 100 kinds of tropical fish. Admission is BZ$6. ✦ *From St. George's Caye Resort, walk south on the beach and look for the aquarium sign.*

GETTING HERE AND AROUND

St. George's Caye Resort and Royal Palm Island Resort will meet you at the international airport and handle your 20-minute boat transfer to the islands.

WHERE TO STAY

For expanded hotel reviews, visit Fodors.com.

$$$$ 🏨 **Royal Palm Island Resort.** A newer option for an island vacation near Belize City is Royal Palm Island, a resort just 20 minutes by boat from the mainland on Little Frenchman Caye—and it is in fact French-owned. **Pros:** relaxing getaway near Belize City; friendly service. **Cons:** not directly on reef; tiny island; expensive. ✉ *Little Frenchman Caye, 9 mi (15 km) east of Belize City* ☎ *621/6762, 888/969–7829* ⊕ *www.royalpalmisland.com* ➥ *5 cottages* ✦ *In-hotel: restaurant, bar, spa, beach, water sports* ⊙ *All meals.*

$$$$ 🏨 **St. George's Caye Resort.** In colonial days this long-established resort was a British favorite because of its proximity to Belize City, about 20 minutes away by boat; today visitors favor the Canadian-owned resort for its casual style and good diving program. **Pros:** comfortable, historical setting; good diving. **Cons:** drinks are expensive. ☎ *800/813–8498, 220/4444* ⊕ *www.gooddiving.com* ➥ *12 cabañas, 8 rooms* ✦ *In-room: no TV. In-hotel: restaurant, bar, pool, spa, beach, water sports, business center* ⊙ *All meals.*

GREAT ITINERARIES

It's difficult to recommend itineraries on the cayes, because what you do and where you go depends greatly on the island where you're staying. If you're on a remote caye or atoll, your activities and itineraries are defined partly by your interests (whether it's diving, fishing, or just lazing in a hammock), and by the lodge's daily schedule (or lack of one). Your basic itinerary might go a little like this: dive, eat, sleep, and dive.

On the other hand, if you're on Ambergris Caye or Caye Caulker, you can set your itinerary around a wide choice of daily island activities, day trips to the mainland, snorkeling or diving on the Barrier Reef, and day trips to the atolls.

IF YOU HAVE 5 DAYS ON AMBERGRIS CAYE OR CAYE CAULKER

Spend your first full day getting to know the island. On Ambergris Caye, rent a golf cart or bike and explore the north and south ends of the caye. Have a beach picnic or enjoy one of the many good restaurants. If you're on Caulker, which is much smaller, you can explore on foot, or, if you prefer, on a bike or in a golf cart. On your second day on either caye, take a boat trip to Hol Chan Marine Reserve and Shark-Ray Alley for snorkeling, and spend the rest of the day on the beach or just hanging out in San Pedro town or Caulker village. On your third day, take a full-day dive or snorkel trip to Lighthouse Reef, with stops at the Blue Hole and Half Moon Caye. On your fourth day, if you're not planning to spend a few days on the mainland this trip, take a tour to the Lamanai Mayan ruins, which includes an exciting boat ride up the New River; or, for some pampering, take one of the combined day trips to Maruba Spa and the Altun Ha Mayan site. If you do plan a mainland stay, then use Day 4 to try windsurfing on Caye Caulker, parasailing on Ambergris Caye, bonefishing in the flats, or sea or lagoon kayaking. On your final day, take a relaxing daylong catamaran snorkeling trip with a beach barbecue.

IF YOU HAVE 5 DAYS ON A REMOTE CAYE OR ATOLL

On arrival, take off your shoes, take a deep breath, grab a cold drink, and relax. This is what the islands are all about, with the cooling trade winds in your hair and no decisions to make except whether you want the grilled fish or the lobster for dinner. If you're on a dive package, you typically do two to three dives a day, weather permitting. On a fishing package you'll be out on the flats or the reef all day every day. If you're not tied to a package, get up early and watch the sunrise on your first full day. Then spend the day exploring the island: go swimming, spend some time beachcombing, or snorkel off the shore. On your second day, take a dive or snorkel trip to the nearest atoll. On the third day, hire a guide and try your hand at fishing for bonefish or permit on the flats. On your fourth day, take a catamaran sail along the Barrier Reef, with stops for snorkeling and a barbecue on a deserted beach. On your final day, go kayaking around the island and relax on the beach.

The Cayes, Atolls, and Barrier Reef

COROZAL DISTRICT

Bay of Chetumal

BACALAR CHICO MARINE NATIONAL PARK & RESERVE

Barrier Reef

Deer Caye

Ambergris Caye

Cayo Espanto

Marco Gonzales

HOL CHAN MARINE RESERVE

San Pedro see detail map

Cangrejo Caye

Caribbean Sea

Santana

Altun Ha

Hick's Cayes

CAYE CAULKER MARINE RESERVE

Caye Caulker see detail map

Caye Chapel

Montego Caye

Crawl Caye

Three Corner Caye

Belize City

St. George's Caye

BELIZE

Ladyville

Western Hwy.

Drowned Cayes

Northern Caye

Belize Harbour

Douglas Caye

Blackbird Caye

Lighthouse Reef Atoll

Northern Lagoon

Water Caye

Belmopan City

Middle Long Caye

Inner or Main Channel

Turneffe Atoll

Calabash Caye

Blue Hole

Southern Lagoon

Alligator Caye

Colson Cayes

Long Caye

HALF MOON CAYE NATIONAL MONUMENT

Gales Point

Southern Long Caye

Deadman's Cayes

Mullins River

Mosquito Caye

Big Caye Bokel

Sandfly Cayes

Silk Cayes

Fly Range

Dangriga

Columbus Caye

Silk Grass

Coco Plum Caye

Cross Caye

STANN CREEK DISTRICT

Hopkins

Man-of-War Caye

Tobacco Reef

GLOVER'S REEF MARINE RESERVE

Twin Cayes

Sittee Point

Tobacco Caye

All Pines

Bread & Butter Caye

South Water Caye

Glover's Reef Atoll

Northeast Caye

Wee Wee Caye

Southwest Caye

Norval Caye

SOUTH WATER CAYE MARINE RESERVE

Maya Beach

Seine Bight

Placencia

Lark Caye

Big Creek

LAUGHING BIRD CAYE MARINE RESERVE

Gladden Split

TOLEDO DISTRICT

Laughing Bird Caye

PORT HONDURAS MARINE RESERVE

Gulf of Honduras

Sapodilla Cayes

SAPODILLA CAYES MARINE RESERVE

Old Northern Highway

Northern Highway

Hummingbird Highway

Southern Hwy.

KEY	
◩	Dive Site

0   10 miles

0   10 kilometers

AMBERGRIS CAYE AND SAN PEDRO

35 mi (56 km) northeast of Belize City.

At 25 mi (40 km) long and 4½ mi (7 km) wide, Ambergris (in Belize pronounced Am-BUR-griss) is the queen of the cayes. On early maps it was often referred to as Costa de Ambar, or the Amber Coast, a name supposedly derived from the blackish substance secreted by sperm whales—ambergris—that washes up on the beaches. Having never seen any ambergris in Belize, or a sperm whale, we're not sure we buy this explanation.

Here the reef is just a few hundred yards from shore, making access to dive sites extremely easy: the journey by boat takes as little as 10 minutes. Because Ambergris Caye was the first to cater to those hoping to witness Belize's undersea world, it's generally superior in the number of dive shops, experience of dive masters, and range of equipment and facilities it offers. San Pedro even has Belize's only hyperbaric chamber and an on-site doctor to tend to divers with the bends. Many dive shops are attached to hotels, where the quality of dive masters, equipment, and facilities can vary considerably.

But there's more than diving to Ambergris Caye. Today the majority of visitors to the island don't dive at all. They snorkel, fish, splash in the sea, go parasailing or sailboarding, or just laze around the hotel pool until it's time to sample one of the dozens of restaurants on the island. With an island population of around 20,000, according to many local observers who point to the many mainlanders who have come to the island to find work, or 11,510, according to the 2010 Belize Census, Ambergris and its only real town, San Pedro, remain friendly and prosperous. The caye has one of the country's highest literacy rates and an admirable level of awareness about the reef's fragility.

GETTING HERE AND AROUND
Hard-packed sand streets are giving way to the concrete cobblestones of Barrier Reef Drive, Pescador Street, and Coconut Drive and other island streets, and everyone complains about the worsening car traffic in town, but the most common forms of transportation remain golf cart, bike, and foot.

TIMING
Belize's most popular destination merits a significant chunk of your vacation time. Indeed, some visitors to Belize only experience Ambergris Caye. With its many restaurants, bars, and shops, plus myriad opportunities for water sports, you can easily spend a week or more on the island without beginning to run out of things to do.

SAFETY
With rapid growth and an influx of workers from other parts of Belize and Central America, Ambergris Caye has seen an increase in all types of crime. However, nearly all visitors to Ambergris Caye say they feel perfectly safe. Use common sense and avoid walking on dark streets and deserted beaches after nightfall. Most of the larger hotels have full-time security.

HISTORY

Because of their strategic locations on trade routes between the Yucatán in the north and Honduras in the south, the northern cayes, especially Ambergris Caye and Caye Caulker, were long occupied by the Maya. Then, as now, the reef and its abundance of fish provided a valuable source of seafood.

The origin of Belize's atolls remains a mystery, but evidence suggests they grew from the bottom up, as vast pagodas of coral accumulated over millions of years. The Maya were perhaps the first humans to discover the atolls, but by the time the first Spanish explorers arrived in 1508, the Mayan civilization had already mysteriously collapsed and few remained on the islands.

In the 17th century, English pirates used the cayes and atolls as a hideout, plotting their attacks on unwary ships. The most famous battle in Belize history happened on September 10, 1798, when a ragtag band of buccaneers defeated a Spanish armada at the Battle of St. George's Caye.

The economy on the islands has ebbed and flowed, as pirates were replaced by wealthy plantation owners, who were eventually usurped by lobster fisherman. The atolls' first hotel opened in 1965 and soon began attracting divers from around the world. Today tourism is by far the top industry.

WATER ACTIVITIES
CHARTERS
El Gato. A 30-foot catamaran, *El Gato* does day cruises to Caye Caulker, with two stops for snorkeling, for BZ$130 per person (minimum three persons). Also, half-day sails to Mexico Rocks or Hol Chan, BZ$100 per person (minimum three). ⊠ *San Pedro* ☎226/2264 ⊕*www.ambergriscaye.com/elgato.*

Winnie Estelle. This vessel is a 66-foot Chesapeake Bay trawler built in 1920 and restored during the 1980s. *Winnie Estelle* is large, able to carry up to 40 passengers, making charter day trips to Caye Caulker and to snorkeling areas (BZ$1,320 for up to 12 people, additional persons BZ$110 per person). Noncharter trips are available several times a week, at BZ$110 per person. Longer trips also are available. ⊠ *San Pedro* ☎226/2427 ⊕*www.ambergriscaye.com/winnieestelle.*

FISHING
Although southern Belize, especially Placencia, is the main sportfishing center in Belize, Ambergris Caye also has good opportunities for flats, reef, and deep-sea fishing. Expect to pay about BZ$500–BZ$600 for one or two people for a day of flats fishing for bonefish, permit, or tarpon, including a guide and a boat. May to September is the best time for catching tarpon off Ambergris Caye; April to October is the best time for bonefish; and March through May is best for permit. Reef fishing for snapper, grouper, barracuda, and other reef fish runs BZ$600 or more, including a guide and a powerboat. Deep-sea fishing outside the reef for billfish, sailfish, wahoo, and tuna costs around BZ$1,200–BZ$1,500 a day, depending on the number in your party and the size of the boat.

Although there's still a lot of confusion about it, a sportfishing license is now required to fish in Belize waters (except for fishing off piers or from shore). Licenses are BZ$20 a day or BZ$50 a week. You can buy a license online from the Belize Coastal Zone Management Authority and Institute (⊕ *www.coastalzonebelize.org*) or your fishing guide may be able to help you get it.

El Pescador. This is an upscale fishing lodge on North Ambergris, one of the top fishing centers in the region. It offers bonefish, permit, and tarpon fishing packages including room, meals, boat, and guide, starting at around BZ$3,300 per person, double occupancy, for three nights (two days of fishing). ☎ *226/2398, 800/242–2017* ⊕ *www.elpescador.com.*

For fishing that's easier on the pocketbook, you can fish for snapper, barracuda, and other fish from piers and docks on the island. No license is required. Bring your own gear or buy tackle at local hardware stores and ask local anglers about bait. Horse conch and small sardines work well. For fly-fishing aficionados, there's a fly-fishing shop at El Pescador (see above) and at Go Fish Belize. You can also wade out in the flats near shore on North Ambergris, north of the river channel on the back (west) side, and try your luck with bonefish. Keep an eye out for the occasional crocodile. You'll catch more with a guide and boat, but fishing on your own is inexpensive fun.

FISHING
GUIDES
George Bradley. Local guide George Bradley specializes in fly-fishing for bonefish. ⊠ *Pescador Dr., San Pedro* ☎ *226/2179.*

Fishing San Pedro. A fishing service run by Steve DeMaio, Fishing San Pedro works with about a half-dozen guides on the island. You call Steve, tell him what kind of fishing you want to do, and he will arrange a guide and boat for you and your party. ⊠ *San Pedro* ☎ *607/9967* ⊕ *www.fishingsanpedro.com.*

Pete Graniel. Local guide Pedro "Pete" Graniel does both deep sea and reef trips and has a boat that's good for trolling. ⊠ *Almond St., San Pedro* ☎ *226/2584.*

Go Fish Belize. Local fishing guide Abbie Marin arranges fly-, reef, and deep-sea fishing charters, and Go Fish Belize also has a fly-fishing shop. ⊠ *7 Boca Del Rio Dr., San Pedro* ☎ *226/3121.*

JET SKIS
Extreme Adventures. Extreme Adventures, formerly Fido's Fun Sports, has parasailing setups for one, two, or three persons. ⊠ *Beachfront at Fido's, Barrier Reef Dr., San Pedro* ☎ *226/3513.*

San Pedro Water Sports. Based at the dock of the SunBreeze Hotel at the south end of San Pedro, with a branch at Coco Beach Resort on North Ambergris, San Pedro Water Sports has around 10 Jet Skis for rent and also does Jet Ski tours. ⊠ *SunBreeze Hotel, San Pedro* ☎ *226/2888* ⊕ *www.sanpedrowatersports.com* 🖃 *Rental rates, BZ$130 for 30 min; BZ$220 for an hr.*

SAILING
Belize will probably never rival the British Virgin Islands for sailing. The shallow water kicks up a lot of chop, and hidden coral heads and tidal currents are dangerous for even those familiar with the area. When

you charter a boat you have to stay inside the Barrier Reef, but there's a lot of beautiful territory to explore.

TMM Belize. These operators have about a half-dozen catamarans (38 feet–46 feet), with weeklong bareboat (sailing experience required) and captained charters out of San Pedro. Rates vary, depending on boat type and time of year, but range from around BZ$6,000 to more than BZ$16,000 a week, not including provisions (available through TMM for BZ$60 per person per day), cruising fee (BZ$20 per person), and incidentals. Skippers are an additional BZ$300 per day, plus food and gratuity; cooks are BZ$220 a day, also plus food and gratuity. Bareboat charters must stay inside the reef. Split among three to eight people, sailing charter prices are competitive with hotel rates. ⊠ *Coconut Dr., San Pedro* ☎ *226/3026, 800/633–0155* ⊕ *www.sailtmm.com.*

SCUBA DIVING AND SNORKELING

Dives off Ambergris are usually single tank at depths of 50 to 80 feet, allowing about 35 minutes of bottom time. Diving trips run around BZ$90 for a single-tank dive, BZ$150 for a two-tank dive, BZ$90–BZ$110 for a one-tank night dive, and BZ$470–BZ$650 for day trips with three dives to Turneffe Atoll or Lighthouse Reef. Dive gear rental is usually extra—a full package of gear including wet suit, buoyancy compensator, regulator, mask, and fins is around BZ$60–BZ$80. Snorkeling by boat around Ambergris generally costs BZ$70–BZ$100 per person for two or three hours or BZ$140–BZ$200 for a day trip, including lunch. If you go to Hol Chan Marine Reserve there's a BZ$20 park fee, but this fee is often included in the quoted rate. A snorkel trip to the Blue Hole is around BZ$470, including the BZ$80 Marine Reserve fee. In most cases, gear rental is additional. In some cases, these prices do not include 12.5% tax. (Businesses are supposed to include the 12.5% GST in their quoted prices, but not all do.) Most dive shops will pick you up at your hotel or at the nearest pier.

⚠ Be careful when snorkeling off docks and piers on Ambergris Caye. There's heavy boat traffic between the reef and shore, and boat captains may not be able to see snorkelers in the water.

★ **Bacalar Chico National Park and Marine Reserve.** Development on Ambergris continues relentlessly, but most of the far north of the island remains pristine, or close to it. At the top of the caye, butting up against Mexico, Bacalar Chico National Park and Marine Reserve spans 41 square mi (105 square km) of land, reef, and sea. Here, on 11 mi (18 km) of trails you may cross paths with whitetail deer, ocelots, saltwater crocodiles, and, according to some reports, pumas and jaguars. There are excellent diving, snorkeling, and fishing opportunities, especially off Rocky Point, and a small visitor center will get you oriented. You'll need a boat and a guide to take you here. An all-day snorkel trip to Bacalar Chico from San Pedro costs around BZ$170–BZ$200. Trips from Sarteneja also are offered for about the same cost. ⊠ *North end of Ambergris Caye* 🎫 *BZ$10 or BZ$30 for weekly pass.*

Belize Barrier Reef. The longest barrier reef in either the Western or Northern hemispheres, the Belize Barrier Reef is off the eastern shore of Ambergris Caye. From the island, you see the coral reef as an almost unbroken chain of white surf. Inside the reef, the water is clear and shallow, and the reef itself is a beautiful living wall formed by billions of small coral polyps. Just outside the reef, the seabed drops sharply, and from a distance the water looks dark blue or purple. ⊠ *½ mi (1 km) east of Ambergris Caye (it's closer to shore the farther north you go on the island).*

Fodor's Choice
★ **Hol Chan Marine Reserve.** The reef's focal point for diving and snorkeling near Ambergris Caye is the Hol Chan Marine Reserve (Maya for "little channel"), 4 mi (6 km) southeast of San Pedro at the southern tip of Ambergris. It's a 20-minute boat ride from San Pedro. Hol Chan is a break in the reef about 100 feet wide and 20 feet–35 feet deep, through which tremendous volumes of water pass with the tides.

The 3-square-mi (8-square-km) park has a miniature Blue Hole, a 12-foot-deep cave whose entrance often attracts the fairy basslet, an iridescent purple-and-yellow fish frequently seen here. The reserve is also home to a large moray eel population.

Varying in depth from 50 feet to 100 feet, Hol Chan's canyons lie between buttresses of coral running perpendicular to the reef, separated by white, sandy channels. You may find tunnel-like passageways from one canyon to the next, and not knowing what's in the next "valley" as you come over the hill can be pretty exciting.

Because fishing is off-limits here, divers can see abundant marine life, including spotted eagle rays. There are throngs of squirrelfish, butterfly fish, parrotfish, and queen angelfish, as well as Nassau groupers, barracuda, and large shoals of yellowtail snappers. Altogether, more than 160 species of fish have been identified in the marine reserve, along with 40 species of coral, and five kinds of sponges. Hawksbill, loggerhead, and green turtles have also been found here, along with spotted and common dolphins, several species of sharks, and West Indian manatees. ⊠ *Off southern tip of Ambergris Caye* ☎ *526/2247 Hol Chan office in San Pedro* ⊕ *www.holchanbelize.org.*

★ **Shark-Ray Alley.** Shark-Ray Alley is a sandbar within Hol Chan where you can snorkel alongside nurse sharks and stingrays (which gather here to be fed) and even larger numbers of day-trippers from San Pedro and from cruise ships. Sliding into the water is a small feat of personal bravery—the sight of sharks and rays brushing past is spectacular yet daunting. Although they shouldn't, guides touch and hold sharks and rays, and sometimes encourage visitors to pet these sea creatures (which you shouldn't do, either). ■TIP→ **A night dive at Shark-Ray Alley is a special treat: bioluminescence causes the water to light up, and many nocturnal animals emerge, such as octopus and spider crab. Because of the strong current you'll need above-average swimming skills, especially at night.** ⊠ *Southern tip of Ambergris Caye in Hol Chan Marine Reserve* ☎ *226/2247 Hol Chan office* ⊕ *www.holchanbelize.org* 🗀 *BZ$20 marine reserve fee included as a part of Hol Chan fee.*

LESSONS AND
EQUIPMENT
Amigos del Mar. Amigos del Mar, established in 1991, is perhaps the island's most consistently recommended dive operation. The PADI facility offers a range of local dives as well as trips to Turneffe Atoll and Lighthouse Reef in a fast 48-foot dive boat. Amigos charges BZ$150 per

person for a local two-tank dive, not including equipment rental, and BZ$500 for a 12-hour trip to the Blue Hole, including park fee and lunch but not equipment rental. ✉ *On water off Barrier Reef Dr., near Mayan Princess Hotel* ☎ *226/2706* ⊕ *www.amigosdive. com.*

Ecologic Divers. Fairly new to the dive scene on the island, this PADI shop has won a good reputation for safety, service, and ecologically sound practices. Local two-tank dives are BZ$150 per person, not including equipment rental or 12.5% tax. Full-day Turneffe trips are BZ$400 including equipment, breakfast and lunch, but not 12.5% tax. ✉ *Beachfront, on pier at north end of San Pedro* ☎ *226/4118.*

3

SUBMERSE YOURSELF

Those who want to see the underwater world but don't dive or snorkel may want to try the *Nautilus IV,* (☎ 541/782–8687 ⊕ *www.belizesubmarinetour*) a semisubmersible submarine. The 45-minute tours leave from San Pedro and also, on alternate days, from the Tourist Village in Belize City. As of this writing, the exact schedule has not been set. The air-conditioned sub with large glass windows cruises about 6 feet below the surface. Cost is BZ$158 for a regular tour, or BZ$198 for a 90-minute sunset cruise.

Lil' Alphonse Tours. Offering snorkeling only, Lil' Alphonse himself usually captains the tours, doing a fabulous job making snorkelers feel comfortable in the water. ✉ *Coconut Dr., across street from Changes in Latitudes B&B, San Pedro* ☎ *226/3136* ⊕ *www.ambergriscaye.com/ alfonso.*

Patojo's Scuba Center. Operated by Elmer "Patojo" Paz, who has nearly 20 years of diving experience, Patojo's Scuba Center at The Tides Hotel is a small dive shop with a good reputation. ✉ *At Tides Hotel, at north end of San Pedro* ☎ *226/2283* ⊕ *www.ambergriscaye.com/tides/dive. html.*

SEAduced by Belize. This well-run snorkeling, sailing, and tour company does full-day snorkeling trips to Bacalar Chico and to Mexico Rocks and Robles Point. Trips include a lovely beach barbecue. ✉ *Vilma Linda Plaza, Tarpon St., San Pedro* ☎ *226/2254* ⊕ *www.seaducedbybelize. com.*

SEArious Adventures. This long-established snorkeling and sailing shop does day snorkel trips to Caye Caulker (BZ$100 plus park fees and equipment rental), along with a variety of other snorkel and sail trips. ✉ *Beachfront, on dock, between Tarpon and Black Coral St., San Pedro* ☎ *226/4202.*

White Sands Dive Shop. This operation isn't at White Sands Resort but at Las Terrazas. Never mind, this PADI dive center is run by Elbert Greer, a noted diver and birder who has taught scuba in San Pedro for more than 20 years, getting more than 2,400 divers certified. ✉ *Las Terrazas, North Ambergris Caye* ☎ *226/2405* ⊕ *www.whitesandsdiveshop.com.*

Many dive shops and resorts have diving courses. A half-day basic familiarization course or "resort course" costs around BZ$300–BZ$350. A four-day PADI open-water certification course costs

HOW TO CHOOSE A DIVE MASTER

Many dive masters in Belize are former anglers who began diving on the side and ended up doing it full-time. The best have an intimate knowledge of the reef and a superb eye for coral and marine life.

When choosing a dive master or dive shop, first check the Web. Participants on forums and newsgroups such as ⊕ www.ambergriscaye.com field many questions on diving and dive shops in Belize. On islands where there are multiple dive shops, spend some time talking to dive masters to see which ones make you feel most comfortable. Find out about their backgrounds and experience, as well as the actual crew that would be going out with you. Are they dive masters, instructors, or just crew? Get a sense of how the dive master feels about reef and sea life conservation.

Besides questions about costs and equipment, ask:

■ How many people, maximum, go out on your dive trips?

■ Is there a minimum number of divers before you'll make the trip?

■ What dive sites are your favorites, and why?

■ What kind of boat do you have, and how long does it take to get where we're going?

■ Who is actually in the water with the divers?

■ What kind of safety and communications equipment is on the boat?

■ What's the procedure for cancellation in case of bad weather?

■ How do you decide if you're going out or not?

■ If you're not comfortable with the answers, or if the dive shop just doesn't pass your sniff test, move on.

BZ$800–BZ$1,000. One popular variant is a referral course, where the academic and pool training is done at home, but not the required dives. The cost for two days is about BZ$550 to BZ$600. Prices for dive courses vary a little from island to island, generally being a little less expensive on Caye Caulker. However, even prices on Ambergris Caye, which tends to have higher costs for most activities, are a little lower than on the mainland.

If you're staying on Ambergris Caye, Glover's Reef is out of the question for a day trip by boat. Even with perfect weather—which it often isn't in winter—a trip to Lighthouse Reef takes between two and three hours. Most trips to Lighthouse and the Blue Hole depart at 6 am and return at 5:30 or 6 pm, making for a long day in the sun and water. Turneffe is more accessible, though it's still a long and costly day trip, and you're unlikely to reach the atoll's southern tip, which has the best diving.

DIVE BOATS   If you want to hit the best dive spots in Belize and dive a lot—five or six dives a day—live-aboard dive boats may be your best bet. Live-aboards concentrate on dives around Belize's three atolls—Lighthouse, Turneffe, and Glover's—with most dives at Lighthouse and Turneffe. The boats depart from Belize City.

Expect to pay about US$2,000 to US$3,000 per person double occupancy for six days of diving. The Belize Aggressor III is at the high end of that range, and the Dancer Fleet's Sun Dancer II is at the lower end. The price includes all dives, meals, airport transfers, and stateroom accommodations on the dive boat. It doesn't include airfare to Belize, overnight stays at a hotel before or after the dive trip if necessary, tips, U.S. port fees (US$95), some alcoholic beverages, equipment rentals, Nitrox, marine park fees, port charges, and incidentals.

Belize Aggressor III. The itinerary of the *Belize Aggressor III* has passengers embarking in Belize City, at the Radisson Fort George, on a Saturday and spending time until the following Friday at Turneffe and Lighthouse atolls, with as many as five or six dives each day. This orderly operation is run by a crew of five, mostly Belizeans, along with the captain and dive master. The *Aggressor III* can accommodate up to 18 passengers. It uses a 110-foot luxury cruiser, refitted in 2009, powered by twin 500-horsepower engines and equipped with ultramodern communication systems. There's a hot tub and sundeck. Staterooms are spacious double-berth cabins brightened with blue fabrics, light wood trim, and multiple windows instead of small portholes. All have private baths, TVs, and DVDs, plus individual climate controls. Rates for 2012 are US$2,695 to US$2,895 per person, plus US$95 for U.S. port fees. ☎ *706/993–2531 U.S. office, 800/348–2628 in the U.S., 223/0748 shore office in Belize ⊕ www.aggressor.com.*

Dancer Fleet. Dancer Fleet (formerly Peter Hughes Diving) runs trips on the 138-foot *Sun Dancer II,* which can hold up to 20 passengers in 10 staterooms. It has a white-uniformed crew of nine, mostly from Central America and the Caribbean. The *Sun Dancer II* departs from the Radisson Fort George Hotel dock in Belize City on Saturday afternoon and moors at either Turneffe or Lighthouse Atoll. For the next 5½ days, divers explore these two atolls, diving as many as five times a day. The ship moves two or three times a day. Rates for 2012 are US$1,995 to US$2,195, plus US$95 port fees. Rates include stateroom, dives, Belize international airport transfers, and local beers and well-brand alcohol. ✉ *15291 NW 60th Ave., Suite 201, Miami Lakes, Florida, USA ☎ 305/669–9391 office in U.S., 800/932–6237 in the U.S., 610/5173 agent in Belize ⊕ www.dancerfleet.com.*

WINDSURFING AND KITESURFING

Caye Caulker is better known as a windsurfing destination, perhaps because it attracts a younger crowd than Ambergris Caye, but the winds are equally good and consistent off Ambergris Caye. February through July sees the windiest conditions, with winds 12 to 20 knots most days. Kitesurfing, combining a windsurfing-type board pulled by a large kite, is also available on Ambergris Caye.

Aquatic Sports Belize. Aquatic Sports rents all kinds of water sports equipment, including windsurfers, paddleboats, kayaks, water bikes, snorkel gear, paddleboards, and catamarans. Windsurfing boards are BZ$50 per hour for the first hour, then BZ$30 per hour. ✉ *Barrier Reef Dr. and Black Coral St., in purple building near La Playa bar, San Pedro ☎ 226/4601 ⊕ www.aquaticsportsbelize.com.*

Sailsports Belize. Sailsports Belize at Caribbean Villas offers private windsurfing instruction at BZ$98 an hour, with equipment rental at BZ$44–BZ$54 an hour, or from BZ$98 a day. Five hours of intensive kitesurfing instruction costs BZ$660, and your initial kite-board rental, with an instructor on hand to assist, is BZ$132 for two hours. After that, kitesurfing equipment (kite and board) rentals are BZ$164 for a full day. All rates plus 12.5% tax. Sailsports Belize also rents catamarans. ⊠ *Beachfront, Caribbean Villas, San Pedro* ☎ *226/4488* ⊕ *www.sailsportsbelize.com.*

MAINLAND TOURS

You can do tours of mainland sights including Mayan ruins, the Belize Zoo, and cave tubing from San Pedro, though the cost will be higher than from the mainland. From Ambergris Caye a full-day cave-tubing trip, combined with lunch and a visit to the zoo, runs BZ$250–BZ$270. A visit to Altun Ha is BZ$150–BZ$200. Considered by many as the best San Pedro tour operator for mainland trips, Tanisha specializes in full-day Lamanai trips (BZ$220 per person, plus 12.5% tax). The full-day Lamanai trip includes a boat ride up the New River and also includes a light breakfast, lunch, beer, rum punch, and soft drinks. Tanisha also offers cave tubing (BZ$240 to BZ$340, plus tax), trips to Altun Ha (BZ$180 including tax), and other tours. SEAduced by Belize is unrivaled for its nature and kayak tours. SEAduced and SEArious Adventures both do a variety of trips, including manatee spotting, visits to Altun Ha, and others. If tour prices from San Pedro seem too high, you can take a water taxi to Belize City and rent a car or take a cab for your own DIY tour, though the hassle factor may be higher.

Contacts SEAduced by Belize ⊠ *Vilma Linda Plaza, Tarpon St., San Pedro* ☎ *226/2254* ⊕ *www.seaducedbybelize.com.* **SEArious Adventures** ⊠ *Beachfront, between Tarpon and Black Coral sts., San Pedro* ☎ *226/4202* ⊕ *www.seariousadventures.com.* **Tanisha Tours** ⊠ *Middle St., San Pedro* ☎ *226/2314* ⊕ *www.tanishatours.com.*

WHERE TO EAT

Ambergris Caye has the largest and most diverse selection of restaurants in the country. Here you can buy cheap tacos or grilled chicken from a street vendor, eat barbecued fish on the beach, or, at the other end, dine on lobster, crab claws, and steak at upscale eateries. Even the most upmarket spots have a casual atmosphere, some with sand floors and screenless windows open to catch the breezes from the sea.

The largest concentration of restaurants is in town, but many, including some of the best on the island, are opening on the South End and on North Ambergris.

SAN PEDRO TOWN

¢ ✕ **The Baker.** Come to the Baker for Artisan breads based on Belizean, Swiss, French, Russian, Mexican, Italian, and German recipes, from BAKERY BZ$2 to BZ$8, along with pastries and coffee. Try their cakes and other desserts, too. The Baker's breads are featured at many of San Pedro's better restaurants. Bakery is open daily from 7 to 7. ⊠ *Barrier Reef Dr., between Buccaneer and Black Coral Sts. across from Town Council, San Pedro* ☎ *206/2036* ⊕ *www.thebaker.bz* ⊟ *No credit cards.*

$$$
SEAFOOD
★

× **Blue Water Grill.** Close to the beach and perpetually busy, this restaurant's seats are on a raised, covered deck with views of the Barrier Reef a few hundred yards away. The emphasis here is on seafood (grilled grouper or snapper with sides run BZ$42–$44), but there are wood-fired pizzas (around BZ$28) and pastas, too. The owners run a tight ship, and by island standards the service is top-notch. The crispy coconut shrimp appetizer (BZ$22) is our favorite. Open daily for breakfast, lunch, and dinner. ⊠ *Beachfront at SunBreeze Beach Hotel, Coconut Dr.* ☎ *226/3347* ⊕ *www.bluewatergrillbelize.com.*

$$
CARIBBEAN

× **Caliente.** Come here for a seat where you can catch sea breezes, and dig into spicy Mexican dishes with a Caribbean twist, such as margarita shrimp or *caracol al mojo de ajo* (grilled conch with garlic sauce). If you like tacos, don't miss Taco Fridays, when you can choose from steak, conch and lobster (in-season), fish and shrimp, or Hawaiian with chicken and pineapple tacos, along with half-price margaritas. ⊠ *Barrier Reef Dr., in Spindrift Hotel* ☎ *226/2170* ⊘ *Closed Mon.*

$$$
MEXICAN

× **Cocina Caramba.** You'll quickly sense the frenetic energy of this noisy and often packed restaurant operated by Rene Reyes, who worked in restaurants in Miami and San Pedro before opening his own spot. There's nothing very fancy on the menu here—just basics like grilled snapper (BZ$30), fried shrimp, pork chops, and Mexican fajitas and burritos—but everything is well prepared, prices are moderate (though they've increased in recent years), and the service is snappy and enthusiastic. ⊠ *Pescador Dr.* ☎ *226/4321* ⊕ *www.carambasbelize.com* ⊘ *Closed Wed.*

¢
CAFÉ
★

× **DandE's Frozen Custard & Sorbet.** Dan and Eileen (DandE, get it?) Jamison, who used to run the local weekly paper, the *San Pedro Sun,* opened shop in 2005, serving creamy custards and cooling sorbets. For something with an island flavor, try the mango sorbet or the soursop frozen custard. The rum raisin custard is our favorite. ⊠ *Pescador Dr., next to Cocina Caramba* ☎ *608/9100* ⊕ *www.dande.bz/* ▭ *No credit cards* ⊘ *Closed Wed.*

$
LATIN AMERICAN

× **El Fogon.** Open only for lunch, El Fogon serves down-home Belizean cooking like *chaya* tamales and stew chicken in a thatch building with dirt floor. Food is prepared in cast iron pots in a traditional *fogon*, a wood-burning stove. Though it's in town just two blocks from the airstrip, it's a little hard to find. ⊠ *2 Trigger Fish St., near airport, between Esmeralda and Tarpon Sts., San Pedro* ☎ *206/2121* ▭ *No credit cards* ⊘ *No dinner.*

$$$
SEAFOOD

× **Elvi's Kitchen.** In the old days, in 1974, Elvi Staines sold burgers from the window of her house. Soon she added a few tables on the sand under a flamboyant tree. Today the sandy floor is still here, and the tree remains (though now lifeless and cut back to fit inside the roof), but everything else is changed. Enter through massive mahogany doors and you'll be tended to by a staff of a couple of dozen. The burgers are still good, but for dinner Elvi's now specializes in upmarket dishes such as shrimp in watermelon sauce (BZ$37) or crab claws with garlic butter (BZ$75). There's a "Mayan Feast" on Friday nights, when you can dine on traditional Mayan dishes. For dessert, don't pass on the coconut pie.

It's all a bit touristy, but we always enjoy Elvi's. ✉ *Pescador Dr., near Ambergris St.* ☎ *226/2176* ✆ *Closed Sun.*

$$
AMERICAN

✕ **Estel's Dine by the Sea.** This is San Pedro's absolute best place for a hearty American-style breakfast of eggs, bacon, fried potatoes, fry jacks, and freshly squeezed juice. Estel's even has grits! Later in the day you can order burgers, Mexican meals, and good seafood dishes. The little white-and-aqua building is on the beach, as you might infer from the sandy floor and porthole-shaped windows. Best seats for breakfast are on the terrace outside where you can sit and watch pelicans. There's a beachside barbecue on weekends. ✉ *Beachfront, Barrier Reef Dr.* ☎ *226/2019* ⊟ *No credit cards.*

$$
AMERICAN

✕ **Fido's Courtyard.** Sooner or later you're sure to end up at Fido's (pronounced Fee-dough's), sipping something cold and contemplating the sea views, under what the owners claim is the largest thatch palapa in Belize. If not the largest in Belize, it may at least be the largest on Ambergris Caye. This casual joint serves mediocre burgers, fish-and-chips, tacos, and other bar food but it's a great place to get a cold beer and enjoy the live music most nights. ✉ *Barrier Reef Dr., Beachfront, just north of Catholic church* ☎ *226/3176.*

$$$
SEAFOOD
★

✕ **Red Ginger.** With its stylishly minimalist decor and ice-cold air-conditioning, this restaurant could be in L.A., but it's actually at The Phoenix condos at the north end of San Pedro. No sea views here—you gaze at deep red and mocha cream walls, with brown earth-toned accents, and tropical wild ginger plants in glass vases. After a ginger or basil mojito, start with ceviche, your choice of grouper, conch, or shrimp. In-season, spring for the grilled lobster tails or enjoy the pan-seared snapper with coconut milk–curry sauce and ginger rice. On Wednesdays and Sundays there's also a tapas menu, each item for BZ$12. The service is a couple of notches above most other places in San Pedro. ✉ *Barrier Reef Dr., in The Phoenix* ☎ *226/4623* ⊕ *www. redgingerbelize.com* ✆ *Closed Tues.*

$$$
SEAFOOD

✕ **Sunset Grill.** At this casual restaurant, under new management in 2011, you can behold gorgeous sunset views on the lagoon side of the island and enjoy a juicy grilled snapper. While you're comfortably ensconced in the thatch-roof dining room set partly over the water, tarpon, stingrays, and eagle rays swim up to the restaurant and wait to hear a bell, telling them food is on the way. ✉ *10 Black Coral St., on lagoon side* ☎ *226/2600.*

$$$
LATIN AMERICAN
★

✕ **Wild Mango's.** Noted local chef Amy Knox made Wild Mango's one of the most interesting dining choices on the island. Many of the dishes have a Mexican base but with Knox's sophisticated twist. She calls her cooking "New Wave Latin"—Caribbean food infused with spicy Latin flavors from Cuba, Argentina, and Mexico. It's good enough to have earned her Belize Chef of the Year honors twice. Start with the Tres Amigos, three kinds of ceviche with shrimp and fish (Knox does not use conch or lobster, because she believes it is not sustainable.) Try the Budin Azteca, a Mexican version of lasagna, or the huge fish burritos (enough for two). Seating is beach casual, with stools at tables on a covered, open-air veranda. ✉ *Beachfront, 42 Barrier Reef Dr., near south end of town* ☎ *226/2859.*

NORTH OF SAN PEDRO

Unless you are staying near one of the North Ambergris restaurants listed below, you may want to take a water taxi—the Coastal Xpress—to these restaurants, especially after dark. Cabs from town now go as far north on the golf-cart path as Las Terrazas Resort, though the cost is steep (BZ$30 to BZ$50 for most destinations, including the BZ$12 vehicle bridge fee). In a golf cart, the cart path is bumpy and buggy and sometimes impassable after heavy rains.

$$$ ✕ **Aji Tapa Bar and Restaurant.** Relax in a shady seaside patio, with views
SEAFOOD   of the beach and barrier reef in the distance, and snack on delicious
★   small plates of barbecue shrimp, bacon-wrapped dates, fried *calamares a la andaluza,* and a heavenly artichoke dip. For a special treat, try the seafood paella, the best in Belize. Great iced tea, too. If there's a downside, it's inconsistency, with the food suffering on nights Chef Hugo is off. If you decide you want to stay longer, follow the winding path through tropical gardens and cross a small bridge over a lagoon and you'll find four cute one-bedroom rental cottages. Come by golf cart, cab (BZ$35 from San Pedro), or water taxi—get off at Grand Caribe. ✉ *Beachfront, Buena Vista Point, North Ambergris Caye, 2½ mi (4 km) north of town* ☎ *226/4047.*

$$$$ ✕ **Capricorn.** Capricorn is consistently excellent and one of the more pop-
SEAFOOD   ular upscale restaurants on the island. If there's a weakness, it's that the
★   chef stays with proven winners, such as filet mignon, stone crab claws, and grilled lobster (each BZ$70, plus tax and service) and rarely opts for innovation. The seaside setting is romantic. Although the focus here has always been on the restaurant, there are three cute little cabañas. You can get here by golf cart, cab, or water taxi. ✉ *3 mi (5 km) north of San Pedro* ☎ *226/2809* ⊕ *www.capricornresort.net* ⚓ *Reservations essential.*

$$ ✕ **Lazy Croc BBQ.** You'll smell the smoky aroma of barbecue well before
BARBECUE   you enter this popular spot about 1½ mi (2½ km) north of the bridge.
★   As befits a barbecue joint, the menu is short and sweet—pulled pork, barbecue chicken, ribs, Buffalo wings, chili, and a few other items, with sides of coleslaw, french fries, barbecue beans, fried okra, and baked macaroni and cheese. Barbecue platters with garlic toast and two sides are BZ$15 to BZ$30. Lazy Croc has very limited hours: it is only open Friday–Sunday 11 am–6 pm. And, yes, there are real crocs in the lagoon near (and even under) the restaurant, but don't give them leftovers—feeding wild crocodiles is illegal. Go by golf cart, cab (BZ$35 one-way from town), or Coastal Xpress water taxi (get off at Grand Caribe). ✉ *Beachfront, Buena Vista Point, 15 Buena Vista, North Ambergris Caye* ⚓ *2½ mi (4 km) north of center of town and 100 yards north of Grand Caribe* ☎ *226/4015* ▭ *No credit cards* ☉ *Closed Mon.–Thurs.; closes at 6 pm other days; closes in mid-July for off-season.*

$ ✕ **Legends Burger House.** You can get a big, thick American-style burger
BURGER   here, at this slightly funky hamburger joint (formerly Sweet Basil) in a two-story clapboard building by the side of the golf cart path on North Ambergris. Try the Wyatt Earp burger, piled high with onions, bacon, and cheese, or the "old school" Jerry Garcia, with Swiss cheese and grilled mushrooms. Don't let them overcook your burger. Fries are excellent, and the beer is cold. ✉ *¼ mi (½ km) north of the*

bridge, Ambergris Caye ☎ 226/2113 ⊕ www.legendsburgerhouse.com ☉ Closed Mon.

$$$ ✕ **Rendezvous Restaurant & Winery.** Belize's only Thai-French-Belizean

THAI restaurant combines local seafood with Thai spices and French and

★ Asian presentation. The menu changes frequently, with daily specials. Our favorites include pad thai and spider crabs served with a spicy Singapore sauce (BZ$65). The owners, Glen and Colleen Schwenginger, who have lived and worked in Thailand and Singapore, also produce and bottle their own wines using imported grape concentrate. It's not bad. There's a casual beach bar underneath the restaurant. ⊠ 4 mi (6½ km) north of San Pedro ☎☎ 226/3426.

$$$$ ✕ **Rojo Lounge.** Chef Jeff Spiegel, who was formerly a punk-rock record

SEAFOOD producer, heads the hippest restaurant and bar on the cayes. Rojo

Fodor's Choice Lounge, in a sultry open-air palapa on a beautiful beach, is definitely

★ red-hot. If you feel like cooling off, there a swimming pool just for restaurant guests. Lunch offers a selection of sophisticated snacks like chili-dusted cold shrimp, lobster salad, and conch sausage pizza. Dinner is romantic and delicious, with surprising combinations such as chorizo, shiitake, and lobster wontons with mango–star fruit ponzu, sinfully sticky-sweet guava-glazed ribs, and Belikin-glazed pork *baos* with pickled cucumbers. Believe us: Rojo's succulent version of lobster tails is unsurpassed. The bar serves killer frozen mojitos and all kinds of fascinating, boozy concoctions. Rojo Market has groceries and prepared foods for takeout. ⊠ Beachfront, North Ambergris, 5 mi (8 km) north of town ☎ 226/4012 ⊕ www.azulbelize.com/rojo.html ⚑ Reservations essential ☉ Closed Mon.

SOUTH OF SAN PEDRO

$ ✕ **Ali Baba.** This is the spot for takeout roast chicken, falafel, hummus,

MIDDLE EASTERN and other Middle Eastern dishes, at modest prices. ⊠ Coconut Dr., across from Tropic Air terminal, San Pedro ☎ 226/4042 ▭ No credit cards.

$$$ ✕ **Hidden Treasure.** Hidden away on a back street in a residential neigh-

SEAFOOD borhood south of town, Hidden Treasure opened in 2008 and was quickly discovered by visitors and locals. At dinner, you dine romantically by candlelight, in the sultry tropical air under a pitched roof set off by bamboo, mahogany, and cabbage-bark wood. The signature barbecue ribs are seasoned with traditional Garífuna spices and glazed with pineapple or papaya sauce. Mojarro a la Lamanai (BZ$39) is snapper seasoned with Mayan spices and cooked in a banana leaf. ⊠ Escalante Residential Area, San Pedro ⊹ About 1½ mi (2½ km) south of town; go south on Coconut Dr. past Royal Palm Villas and watch for signs ☎ 226/4111 ⊕ www.ambergriscaye.com/hiddentreasure/index.html ☉ No lunch Tues.

$$$$ ✕ **La Palmilla.** La Palmilla at Victoria House is classy without being

ECLECTIC stuffy and romantic without being precious. The setting, near one of

★ the Victoria House pools with views of the sea, in manicured grounds, is among the most attractive in San Pedro. Chef Jose Luis Ortega does a fine job with local seafood, especially grilled lobster. Although there's a lovely indoor dining room, in good weather you might prefer dining on the patio in the open air, with views and a nice breeze from the water. ⊠ Coconut Dr., at Victoria House, San Pedro ☎ 226/2067.

Where to Eat and Stay South of San Pedro

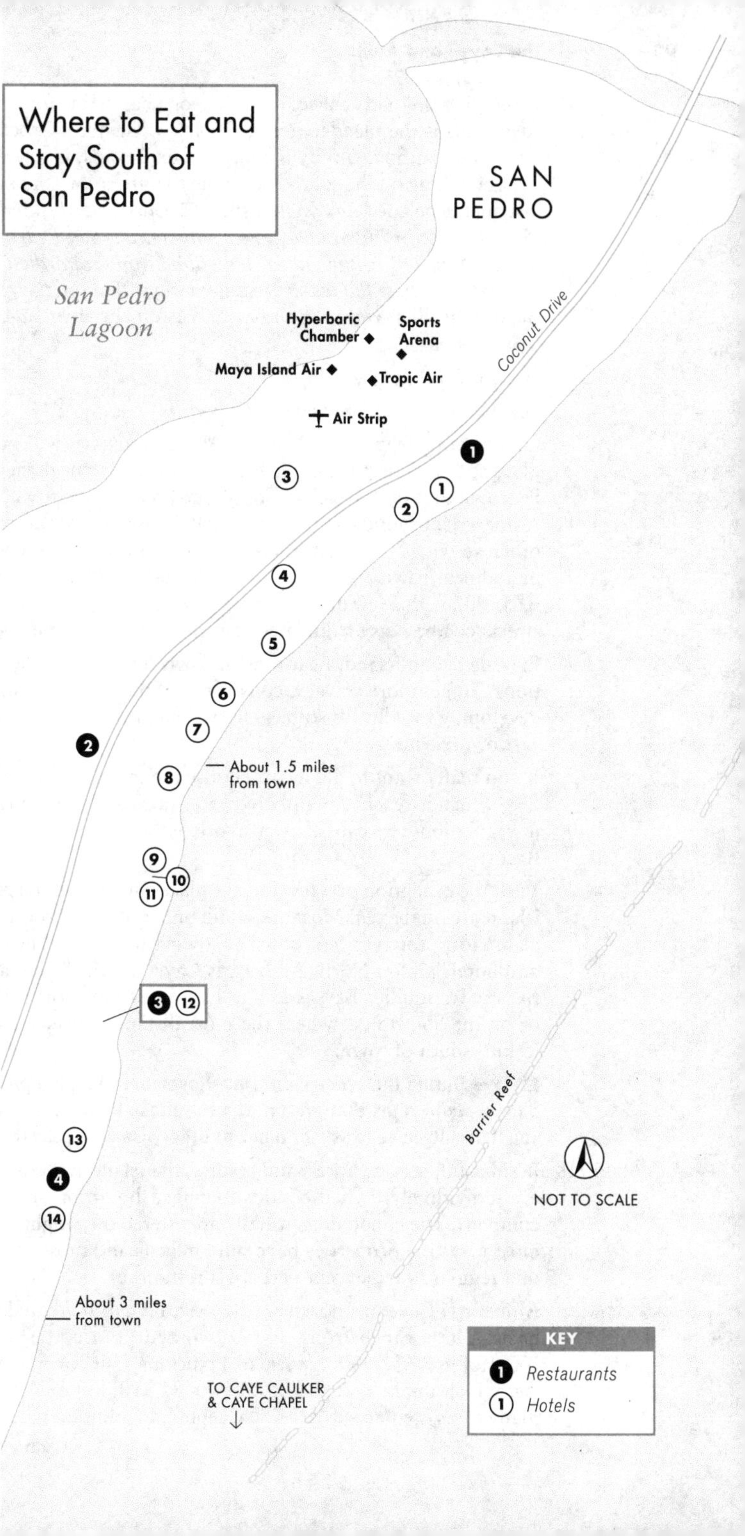

SAN PEDRO

San Pedro Lagoon

Hyperbaric Chamber ◆

Sports Arena ◆

Maya Island Air ◆

◆ Tropic Air

✈ Air Strip

Coconut Drive

①

③

② ①

④

⑤

⑥

⑦

❷

⑧ — About 1.5 miles from town

⑨

⑩

⑪

③ ⑫

Barrier Reef

⑬

❹

⑭

About 3 miles from town

NOT TO SCALE

TO CAYE CAULKER & CAYE CHAPEL ↓

KEY	
❶	*Restaurants*
①	*Hotels*

$$ ✕ **Lone Star Grill and Cantina.** If you've got a hankering for a chicken-fried
SOUTHERN steak, this is the place to get it. Formerly Mr. Joe's Grocery, Lonestar
Grill and Cantina, run by a couple of ex-Texans, is a new outpost of
Texas cooking on the south end of the island. Enjoy cold beer, margaritas, and some good Tex-Mex dishes. ✉ *South end of island, about 3 mi
(5 km) south of town, near police sub-station, San Pedro* ✛ *Go south
on Coconut Dr. to the end of the cobblestones and then continue on
the dirt road past the water treatment plant. Follow the road to police
substation. Bear right, and Lone Star is on the right side of the road.*
☎ *No phone.*

WHERE TO STAY
For expanded hotel reviews, visit Fodors.com.

One of your biggest decisions in Ambergris Caye will be choosing a
place to stay. There are three basic options: in or near the town of San
Pedro, in the South Beach or South End area beyond town, or on North
Ambergris, beyond the river channel. Access to restaurants, bars, and
other activities is easiest in and around San Pedro. Accommodations
in and near town are generally simple and reasonably priced (BZ$50–
BZ$300), with a few notable upscale exceptions, but rooms on the main
streets can be noisy from late-night revelers and traffic.

For silence and sand, head out of town for resort-style accommodations. To get more privacy, consider the South End. Though it, too, is
developing rapidly, it's still less hectic than in town, and it's only a golf
cart or taxi ride away.

If you really want to get away, choose the more remote North Ambergris, which is reached mainly by water taxis and, with a recent change
in regulations, by cabs that currently go as far north as Las Terrazas
Resort.

With the exception of a few budget places, nearly all the resorts on the
island are on the sea. Most are small, under 30 or 40 rooms, and nearly
all are four stories or less. Some are owner-managed. The newer resorts
and hotels are on North Ambergris Caye, of which the farthest-north
resort, Tranquility Bay, is about 12 mi (20 km) north of San Pedro,
or on the South End, where the most distant resorts are around 3 mi
(5 km) south of town.

■ TIP→ During the off-season (May–November), lodging properties often
have walk-in rates that are up to a third less than advertised rates. But
you'll usually have to ask for them, as otherwise you'll pay the regular rate.

CONDOTELS Besides full-service hotels and resorts, the island has condotels, which
are individually owned condos managed by an on-site management
company. The condo units usually are offered on a nightly basis, and in
most cases the properties have full kitchens and most of the amenities
of a regular hotel, except perhaps a restaurant.

VACATION Ambergris Caye has dozens of homes that can be rented on a weekly
HOMES basis. These range from simple two-bedroom cottages that go for
BZ$1,000–BZ$2,000 a week to luxurious four- or five-bedroom villas, which might rent for BZ$5,000–BZ$10,000 or more weekly. In
many cases credit cards are not accepted. In addition to the local rental

management companies listed here, also check online for Vacation Rentals By Owner (⊕ *www.vrbo.com*). VRBO lists well over 100 vacation rentals, more than any local management company.

$$$$ 🏠 **Caye Management.** This is the island's oldest rental management company. ☎ 226/3077 ⊕ *www.cayemanagement.com* ⏎ *Around 20 vacation rental houses and suites* ▭ *No credit cards.*

$$$ 🏠 **M & M Rentals.** M & M Rentals manages around 8–10 vacation rentals and condos. ☎ 949/258 *in the U.S.* ⊕ *www.ambergriscaye.com/m-m/ index.html* ⏎ *10 vacation rental houses and condo suites.*

Also on the island are clusters of upscale homes or villas that are offered for weekly, and sometimes nightly, rental. These luxury homes, often with 4,000–5,000 square feet of space or more, typically have a shared pool and other resort-like amenities. Although they usually have no restaurant, they may offer food service prepared by a chef and delivered to guests in the homes.

TIME-SHARES Time-shares have been on the island for years. Captain Morgan's is one of them. It opened a small casino at its property in mid-2011. Reef Village, on North Ambergris just beyond the bridge, was known for its aggressive time-share touts, but in 2011 it ran into financial and management problems with its time-shares, and the future of this development is up in the air. Fairly new to the island are upscale "fractional ownership" or "residential club" resorts, which sell longer-term memberships and rights to use the property, typically for two, four, or six months a year. One of these, Sueño del Mar, opened on North Ambergris in 2006 but shut down in 2010, leaving more than 100 owners at least temporarily out in the cold, before reopening in 2011. The moral? Think twice before putting any money in a time-share or fractional ownership scheme.

SAN PEDRO TOWN

$$ ⚑ **Caye Casa.** Longtime Belize resident Julie Babcock built these three beachfront condo villas, which opened in 2007, to go with her two small casitas, at the north end of town. **Pros:** pleasant, well-designed small condo colony; quiet; beachfront spot. **Cons:** older casitas are fairly basic. ✉ *Boca del Rio Dr., beachfront, at north end of town* ☎ *226/2880, 800/936–3433 in U.S.* ⊕ *www.cayecasa.com* ⌕ *3 villas, 2 casitas, 2 rooms* ⌂ *In-room: kitchen, Wi-Fi. In-hotel: pool, beach, laundry facilities.*

$$$ ⚑ **Mayan Princess.** Sitting pretty and pink in the middle of town, this seafront three-story condo hotel has rattan furniture covered with pastel-color fabrics, lacking only a pool to make it a perfect mid-level choice. **Pros:** central in-town location; pleasant one-bedroom efficiencies with sea views; near good dive shop. **Cons:** no swimming pool on-site; beach area has heavy boat and pedestrian traffic. ✉ *Beachfront, Barrier Reef Dr., in center of town* ☎ *226/2778, 800/850–4101* ⊕ *www.mayanprincesshotel.com* ⌕ *23 1-bedroom suites* ⌂ *In-room: kitchen. In-hotel: beach, business center.*

$$$$
Fodor's Choice
★
⚑ **The Phoenix.** Bold geometric forms mark this luxury beachfront condominium resort; spacious units are outfitted with beautiful hardwoods, stainless steel, original art, and even washer/dryers. **Pros:** deluxe, beautifully designed condo suites; in-town's most luxurious hotel. **Cons:** for some it lacks a get-away-from-it-all feel. ✉ *Barrier Reef Dr., beachfront, at north end of town* ☎ *226/2083, 877/822–5512 in U.S.* ⊕ *www.thephoenixbelize.com* ⌕ *30 apartments (not all in rental pool)* ⌂ *In-room: kitchen, Wi-Fi. In-hotel: restaurant, bar, pool, gym, spa, beach.*

¢ ⚑ **Ruby's.** No wonder budget-minded travelers flock to this clean, simple hotel on the beach: air-conditioned rooms with private baths and balconies facing the ocean go for around BZ$100, while the original rooms with fans and private bath, facing the street, are BZ$70 for a double plus tax. **Pros:** best budget accommodations in town. **Cons:** bring earplugs as rooms on the street side can be noisy. ✉ *Beachfront, south end of town, Barrier Reef Dr.* ☎ *226/2063* ⊕ *www.ambergriscaye.com/rubys* ⌕ *23 rooms, 21 with bath* ⌂ *In-room: no TV. In-hotel: restaurant, beach.*

$$ ⚑ **San Pedro Holiday Hotel.** Trimmed in cheery pink-and-white colors, this spic-and-span quartet of colonial-style houses on the water is near the center of San Pedro. **Pros:** central location; affordable, clean rooms. **Cons:** no pool; in-town beach isn't very good for swimming. ⊠ *Beachfront, Barrier Reef Dr.* ☎ *226/2014, 713/893–3825 in U.S.* ⊕ *www.sanpedroholiday.com* ☞ *16 rooms, 1 apartment* ⚐ *In-room: no TV, Wi-Fi. In-hotel: restaurant, bar, beach, water sports.*

$$$ 🛏 **SunBreeze Hotel.** A midsize resort across from the airstrip at the town's busy southern edge (though there's no issue with aircraft noise), the waterfront SunBreeze has large rooms that surround a U-shaped, plant-filled courtyard. **Pros:** comfortable, motel-like lodging; handicap-accessible; excellent restaurant on-site. **Cons:** not much of a beach; rates have crept up. ⊠ *Coconut Dr., across from Tropic Air terminal and airstrip* ☎ *226/2191, 800/688–0191 in U.S. and Canada* ⊕ *www.sunbreeze.net* ☞ *43 rooms* ⚐ *In-room: Wi-Fi. In-hotel: restaurant, bar, pool, beach, water sports.*

$$ 🛏 **The Tides Beach Resort.** If diving is your reason for being, and you
★ don't want to spend a ton of money, you couldn't do better than this beachfront hotel, owned by Patojo Paz, one of the island's most experienced dive masters, and his wife. **Pros:** locally owned beachfront hotel; respected dive shop on-site; good value. **Cons:** rooms aren't overly large; beds and furnishings in some rooms need upgrading. ⊠ *Boca del Rio Dr., Beachfront, north end of town* ☎ *226/2283* ⊕ *www.ambergriscaye.com/tides* ☞ *12 rooms, 3 suites* ⚐ *In-room: kitchen, no TV. In-hotel: bar, pool, beach, water sports* ❘◎❘ *Breakfast.*

NORTH OF SAN PEDRO

$$$ 🛏 **Ak'bol Yoga Retreat & Eco-Resort.** This hip little beach resort has seven simple thatch cabanas, some with sea views, around a natural stone swimming pool. **Pros:** cool, small, laid-back resort; rooms and restaurant are good values. **Cons:** you may feel like an outcast if you can't do the downward dog. ⊠ *North Ambergris, 1¾ mi (3 km) north of center of town* ☎ *226/2073* ⊕ *www.akbol.com* ☞ *7 cabañas, 30 rooms with shares baths* ⚐ *In-room: no a/c, no TV. In-hotel: restaurant, bar, pool, beach, water sports.*

$$$$ 🛏 **Azul Resort.** This resort has only two beach villas, but what beach
Fodor's Choice houses they are! The two-level, 3,000-square-foot, two-bedroom vil-
★ las on 10 private acres of beachfront have an open floor plan, 20-foot ceilings, and beams of mylady wood. **Pros:** amazing private beachfront villas with every luxury; fabulous food; five-star service. **Cons:** not for those on a budget. ⊠ *North Ambergris, 5 mi (8 km) north of San Pedro* ☎ *226/4012* ⊕ *www.azulbelize.com* ☞ *2 beach houses* ⚐ *In-room: kitchen, Wi-Fi. In-hotel: restaurant, bar, pool, beach* ❘◎❘ *All-inclusive.*

$$$ 🛏 **Belizean Shores.** If you're looking for a peaceful setting and well-maintained rooms at competitive prices, this beachfront condotel with one-bedroom units is a good choice. **Pros:** comfortable condos; great pool; lots of on-site sports activities. **Cons:** poor beach swimming; getting into town requires a boat ride. ⊠ *5 mi (8 km) north of San Pedro* ☎ *226/4478, 800/319–9026* ⊕ *www.belizeanshores.com* ☞ *48 suites* ⚐ *In-room: kitchen, Wi-Fi. In-hotel: restaurant, bar, pool, tennis court, spa, beach, water sports.*

$$$$ 🛏 **Blue Reef Island Resort.** Luxury in a remote setting is what you get at this resort about 8 mi (13 km) north of town. **Pros:** beautiful rooms;

quiet, far north location. **Cons:** remote setting means it's not for those who want to try a different restaurant every night. ⊠ *North Ambergris, 8 mi (13 km) north of San Pedro* ☎ *866/825–8500* ⊕ *www.bluereefresort. com* 🏬 *23 units* 🛇 *In-room: kitchen, Wi-Fi. In-hotel: restaurant, bar, pool, gym, beach, water sports, laundry facilities, business center.*

$$$$ 🏨 **Coco Beach Resort.** Coco Beach Resort is one of the top-end condotels
★ on the island, with spacious one- and two-bedroom suites and large rooms on an attractive stretch of beach, though it lacks some amenities like an on-site restaurant and in-room Wi-Fi. **Pros:** big, beautiful suites; gorgeous swimming pools; nice beach. **Cons:** no restaurant (not even for breakfast); getting to town requires a boat ride; bar drinks are pricey; no Wi-Fi in rooms. ⊠ *Beachfront, 4 mi (7 km) north of San Pedro, Ambergris Caye* ☎ *226/4840* 🏬 *45 1- and 2-bedroom condo suites, 17 rooms* 🛇 *In-room: kitchen. In-hotel: bar, pool, beach, water sports, business center.*

$$ 🏨 **Cocotal Inn & Cabanas.** If you're looking for small, homey spot on the beach, Cocotal could be it. **Pros:** friendly, small resort on the beach; affordable rates. **Cons:** no restaurant on-site. ⊠ *North Ambergris, 2½ mi (4 km) north of the center of town, San Pedro* ☎ *226/2097* ⊕ *www.cocotalbelize.com* 🏬 *1 casita, 2 cabañas, 1 1-bedroom suite, 1 2-bedroom suite* 🛇 *In-room: kitchen, Wi-Fi. In-hotel: bar, pool, beach, water sports.*

$$$$ 🏨 **El Pescador.** Nearly every hotel on Ambergris Caye claims that it offers fishing trips, but this resort has the best angling resources. **Pros:** this is the place for saltwater anglers. **Cons:** rooms in original lodge are not as spacious as they could be. ⊠ *2½ mi (4 km) north of San Pedro* ☎ *226/2398* ⊕ *www.elpescador.com* 🏬 *13 rooms, 8 villas* 🛇 *In-room: kitchen, no TV, Wi-Fi. In-hotel: restaurant, bar, pool, gym, beach, water sports* 🍴 *All-inclusive.*

$$$$ 🏨 **Grand Caribe Resort and Condominiums.** Set in an arc on a 5-acre beach-
Fodor'sChoice front site, Grand Caribe's 72 super-luxury condos, in eight four-story,
★ red-tiled-roof clusters, face the sea and a 500-foot stretch of sandy beach. **Pros:** super-luxury condos, all with views of the sea; short bike, golf cart ride, or taxi ride to restaurants and to town. **Cons:** pricey but worth it if you want the best; taxi to town is BZ$35. ⊠ *Tres Cocos area of North Ambergris, 1¼ mi (2 km) north of bridge* ☎ *226/4726* ⊕ *www. grandcaribe.com* 🏬 *72 condominium suites* 🛇 *In-room: kitchen, Wi-Fi. In-hotel: restaurant, bar, pool, beach, water sports, laundry facilities.*

$$$$ 🏨 **La Perla del Caribe.** Twelve deluxe villas (eight for rental) command the beachfront about 6 mi (10 km) north of town. **Pros:** very upscale villas with every amenity; lovely beach. **Cons:** expensive; somewhat remote; no on-site restaurant. ⊠ *North Ambergris, 6 mi (10 km) north of San Pedro* ☎ *226/5888, 866/290–6341 in U.S. and Canada* ⊕ *www. laperladelcaribe.com* 🏬 *8 rental villas* 🛇 *In-room: kitchen, Wi-Fi. In-hotel: pool, beach, water sports, laundry facilities.*

$$$$ 🏨 **Las Terrazas.** Developed by the owners of the nearby Journey's End Resort, Las Terrazas is a luxury condominium project with one-, two-, and three-bedroom suites available on a nightly basis. **Pros:** luxury condos on over 500 feet of beachfront. **Cons:** prices higher than at other comparable resorts on the island; part of resort complex

remains unfinished. ⊠ *North Ambergris, 4 mi (6.5 km) north of town* ☎ *226/4249, 713/780–1233 in U.S., 800/447–1553 in U.S. and Canada* ⊕ *www.lasterrazaresort.com* ⊅ *39 condo suites (39 additional units planned)* ⚭ *In-room: kitchen, Wi-Fi. In-hotel: restaurant, bar, pool, gym, beach, water sports.*

$$$$ ▥ **Matachica Resort & Spa.** Thatch casitas in shades of mango, banana, ★ and blueberry offset by brilliant white sand give this deluxe beachfront resort a Gauguin-like quality. **Pros:** charming collection of casitas on the beach; friendly staff and good management; postcard-pretty beach. **Cons:** restaurant and bar prices are steep. ⊠ *5 mi (8 km) north of San Pedro* ☎ *226/5010, 223/0002* ⊕ *www.matachica.com* ⊅ *21 casitas, 2 2-bedroom villas, 1 3-bedroom house* ⚭ *In-room: no TV, Wi-Fi. In-hotel: restaurant, bar, pool, spa, beach, water sports, business center, some age restrictions.*

$$$$ ▥ **Portofino.** Even if you're not a newlywed, you'll enjoy the honeymoon ★ suite at this tranquil North Ambergris resort, operated by a Belgian couple. **Pros:** attractive small beachfront resort; gorgeous pool; good management. **Cons:** somewhat remote. ⊠ *6 mi (10 km) north of San Pedro* ☎ *678/5096, 888/240–1923 in U.S.* ⊕ *www.portofinobelize.com* ⊅ *8 beach cabañas; 3 suites; 1 honeymoon suite; 4 garden cabañas* ⚭ *In-room: kitchen, no TV, Wi-Fi. In-hotel: restaurant, bar, pool, beach, water sports* ⎨⎬ *Some meals.*

$$$$ ▥ **Seascape Villas.** Six posh homes spread across 4 beachfront acres are ★ among the island's most exclusive properties. **Pros:** deluxe private villas. **Cons:** no restaurant on-site. ⊠ *North Ambergris, 4 mi (6 km) north of San Pedro* ☎ *226/2119, 888/753–5164* ⊕ *www.ambergriscaye.com/ seascape/index.html* ⊅ *6 beach houses* ⚭ *In-room: kitchen, Wi-Fi. In-hotel: pool, tennis court, beach, water sports.*

SOUTH OF SAN PEDRO

$$ ▥ **Banana Beach Resort.** Thanks to its affordable rates and friendly staff's ★ accommodating attitude, this mid-level beachfront resort has one of the island's higher guest-occupancy rates. **Pros:** good value; friendly staff. **Cons:** some furnishings are a little dated; beach has a seawall. ⊠ *Coconut Dr., 1½ mi (2½ km) south of San Pedro, San Pedro* ☎ *226/3890, 877/288–1011 in U.S. and Canada* ⊕ *www.bananabeach.com* ⊅ *28 rooms, 43 suites* ⚭ *In-room: kitchen, Wi-Fi. In-hotel: restaurant, bar, pool, beach* ⎨⎬ *Breakfast.*

$$ ▥ **Caribbean Villas.** It may not be as flashy as some of the newer resorts ★ on the island, but Caribbean Villas, with its 2½ acres of gardens, a bird sanctuary, and lovely quiet beachfront, is a pleasant, affordable, and low-key alternative to the glitzier developments. **Pros:** haven of quiet in developed area; good value: good beach. **Cons:** no full-service restaurant; some units could use updating. ⊠ *Seagrape Dr., 1 mi (1½ km) south of town, San Pedro* ☎☎ *226/2715, 866/290–6341 in U.S. and Canada* ⊕ *www.caribbeanvillashotel.com* ⊅ *5 rooms, 9 suites* ⚭ *In-room: kitchen. In-hotel: bar, pool, beach, water sports, business center.*

$$ ▥ **Changes In Latitudes.** Friendly, helpful owners Renita and Cindy have done good things with the only true B&B on the island. **Pros:** helpful owners; good value; cheerful B&B atmosphere. **Cons:** smallish rooms; not on water; close to busy street. ⊠ *36 Coconut Dr., ¼ mi (½ km)*

NAVIGATING AMBERGRIS CAYE

Since places around here lack proper addresses, here's a list of hotels and restaurants in this area from north to south.

- Tranquility Bay Resort
- Blue Reef Island Resort
- Costa Maya Reef Resort
- Portofino
- La Perla del Caribe
- Matachica and Mambo
- Azul Resort and Rojo Lounge
- Rendezvous

- Las Terrazas
- Seascape Villas
- Belizean Shores
- Coco Beach
- Capricorn
- El Pescador
- Aji
- Lazy Croc
- Grand Caribe
- Ak'bol
- Cocotal

south of San Pedro ☎ *226/2986, 800/631–9834 in U.S. in Canada* ☎ *317/536–5160 U.S. number* ⊕ *www.ambergriscaye.com/latitudes* ⊟ *6 rooms, 1 suite* ⚒ *In-room: kitchen, no TV* ⊺⊙⊺ *Breakfast.*

$$ ⊞ **Corona del Mar Apartments and Hotel.** One of the best values on the island, Corona del Mar has rooms from BZ$202 (double in-season, including 19% tax and service); the apartment suites for BZ$309 including tax and service can sleep six. **Pros:** top value; pleasant seafront rooms; friendly staff. **Cons:** no pool. ⊠ *Coconut Dr., 1 mi (1½ km) south of town* ☎ *226/2055* ⊕ *www.ambergriscaye.com/coronadelmar/* ⊟ *12 rooms, 4 suites* ⚒ *In-room: kitchen. In-hotel: beach* ⊺⊙⊺ *Breakfast.*

$$$$ ⊞ **Grand Colony Villas.** These are some of the most upscale condos on the island: two- and three-bedroom, two-bath apartments, ranging from 1,100 to more than 1,900 square feet, with tall ceilings, marble or hardwood floors, mahogany doors and cabinets, and luxurious furnishings. **Pros:** deluxe condo villas; beautifully finished and furnished; on a lovely beach. **Cons:** spendy; no restaurant on-site. ⊠ *Coconut Dr., 1½ mi (3 km) south of town, San Pedro* ☎ *226/3739, 866/620–9521 in U.S. and Canada* ⊕ *www.grandcolonyvillas.com* ⊟ *21 condo apartments* ⚒ *In-room: kitchen, Wi-Fi. In-hotel: pool, beach, laundry facilities.*

$$$ ⊞ **Mata Rocks Resort.** Squeaky-clean rooms at this intimate, midlevel hotel right on the beach, about a 25-minute walk from town, have perfect sea views and breezes. **Pros:** small beachside resort; good value. **Cons:** no restaurant on-site. ⊠ *Coconut Dr., 1½ mi (2½ km) south of town, San Pedro* ☎ *226/2336, 888/628–2757 in U.S. and Canada* ⊕ *www.matarocks.com* ⊟ *17 rooms* ⚒ *In-room: kitchen. In-hotel: bar, pool, business center* ⊺⊙⊺ *Breakfast.*

$$$$ ⊞ **The Palms Oceanfront Suites.** Stay here for the sea views from the oceanfront units and the convenient location. **Pros:** comfortable beachfront apartments; convenient location near town; next to best in-town beach. **Cons:** small, shaded pool; not as upscale as some of the island's new condo developments; rates have crept up; there's a BZ$50 charge per stay for Wi-Fi. ✉ *Coconut Dr., at south edge of town, San Pedro* ☎ *226/3322* ⊕ *www.belizepalms. com* ⇆ *8 2-bedroom apartments, 5 1-bedroom apartments* ♿ *In-room: kitchen, Wi-Fi. In-hotel: pool, beach, water sports* ⦿ *No meals.*

$ ⚏ **Pedro's Hotel.** Gregarious (and sometimes quarrelsome) British expat Peter Lawrence opened the island's only backpacker-style accommodations in 2003, and now he has opened a budget hotel across the street, along with a sports bar and pizza joint, which has become a local expat hangout. **Pros:** good value; handy to the bar; the inimitable owner. **Cons:** not on water; a bit of a hike to town. ✉ *Seagrape Dr., south of town, San Pedro* ☎ *226/3825, 212/796–4897 U.S. phone* ⊕ *www.pedroshotel.*

com ⇆ *32 hotel rooms and 14 hostel rooms* ♿ *In-room: no a/c, Wi-Fi. In-hotel: restaurant, bar, pool.*

$$$$ ⚏ **Pelican Reef Villas.** While listening to the pool's trickling turquoise
★   waterfall, it's easy to believe you've stumbled upon a hidden tropical treasure; however, the faux cave is a swim-up bar, and Pelican Reef is only a little south (2½ mi or 4 km) of San Pedro's bustle. **Pros:** well-run condo colony in quiet south-end location; luxurious accommodations; friendly staff; good beach area. **Cons:** no full-service restaurant on-site; at the far south end of current development on the island. ✉ *Coconut Dr., 2½ mi (4 km) south of town, San Pedro* ☎ *226/2352, 281/394– 3739 in U.S.* ⊕ *www.pelicanreefvillas.com* ⇆ *24 condo apartments* ♿ *In-room: kitchen, Wi-Fi. In-hotel: bar, pool, beach, water sports, laundry facilities.*

$$$ ⚏ **Ramon's Village Resort.** One of the first resorts on the cayes, Ramon's has grown into one of the largest, but it still retains its appealing thatch-and-sand atmosphere. **Pros:** good in-town beach; has island atmosphere many are looking for. **Cons:** busy location across from the airstrip, in an area that's increasingly congested. ✉ *Coconut Dr., across from airstrip just south of town* ☎ *226/2071, 800/624–4215 in U.S. and Canada, 601/649–1990 U.S. reservations office* ⊕ *www.ramons.com* ⇆ *61 rooms, 8 cottages* ♿ *In-room: kitchen, no TV. In-hotel: restaurant, bar, pool, beach, water sports, business center.*

$$$ ⚏ **Victoria House.** With its bougainvillea-filled gardens, this property
Fodor'sChoice   about 2 mi (3 km) south of San Pedro has the style and seclusion of
★   a diplomatic residence, if the diplomat lived on a stunning beach and liked to run around barefoot. **Pros:** quiet and lovely grounds away from bustle of town; variety of gorgeous beachside accommodations; idyllic spot for breakfast outside overlooking the pool and beach.

Cons: not a budget spot. ⊠ *Coconut Dr., 2 mi (3 km) south of town* ☎ *226/2067, 800/247–5159 in U.S. and Canada, 713/344–2340 U.S. number* ⊕ *www.victoria-house.com* ⇆ *14 rooms, 4 casitas, 3 suites, 8 villas* ⚖ *In-room: safe, kitchen, Wi-Fi. In-hotel: restaurant, bar, pool, beach, water sports.*

$$$$ ▦ **Villas at Banyan Bay.** If you enjoy little luxuries like a whirlpool bath in your room, this red tile–roofed complex about 1½ mi (2½ km) south of town will suit you splendidly. **Pros:** well-maintained two- and three-bedroom condos, ideal for families or two couples; one of island's best beaches. **Cons:** restaurant is expensive. ⊠ *Coconut Dr., 1½ mi (2½ km) south of town, San Pedro* ☎ *226/3739, 866/352–1163 in U.S.* ⊕ *www. banyanbay.com* ⇆ *42 suites* ⚖ *In-room: kitchen. In-hotel: restaurant, bar, pool, beach, business center.*

$$$ ▦ **Xanadu Island Resort.** It's billed as the "world's first monolithic dome
★   resort," a description that might appeal only to engineers, but happily these look much nicer than they sound, with thatch roofs over the domes, and the result is a beach resort that can withstand winds up to 300 mph. **Pros:** friendly management; attractive suites; tropically perfect pool; convenient location. **Cons:** seawall at beach; no restaurant or bar on-site. ⊠ *Coconut Dr., 1 mi (1½ km) south of town, San Pedro* ☎ *226/2814* ⊕ *www.xanaduresort-belize.com* ⇆ *19 suites* ⚖ *In-room: safe, kitchen, Wi-Fi. In-hotel: pool, beach, water sports.*

CAYO ESPANTO

$$$$ ▦ **Cayo Espanto.** This super-luxury resort with seven villas, all there is on
Fodor's Choice   the small island, has a staff-to-guest ratio of two to one. **Pros:** over-the-
★   top luxury and service. **Cons:** island is on the back side of Ambergris Caye, not on the main Caribbean Sea. ⊠ *3 mi (5 km) west of Ambergris Caye, Cayo Espanto* ⊡ *P.O. Box 90, Cayo Espanto, Cayo Espanto* ☎🏠 *221/3001* ☎ *888/666–4282 in U.S.* ⊕ *www.aprivateisland.com* ⇆ *7 villas* ⚖ *In-room: Wi-Fi. In-hotel: pool, spa, beach, water sports* ℴℓ *All-inclusive.*

NIGHTLIFE

San Pedro has the most active nightlife scene in Belize, but, still, don't expect Miami's South Beach. A few in-town spots such as Fido's have live music. At Big Daddy's and Jaguar's Temple nightclubs, the action starts after 10 or 11 and often goes until almost daybreak. (Be careful going back to your hotel in the middle of the night after sampling rums—take a taxi if possible.) There are plenty of spots just to have a cold one, including some classic beach bars like BC's, Tackle Box, and Palapa Bar, or tonier spots like Rojo Lounge. New in mid-2011 is a small casino at Captain Morgan's on North Ambergris. Karaoke is big in Belize, and some bars and clubs in San Pedro have karaoke nights, which are more for locals than visitors. In late January and early February, singer Jerry Jeff Walker holds "Camp Belize," two weeklong events in San Pedro during when Walker puts on shows for his loyal fans.

BARS AND CLUBS

BC's Beach Bar. BC's Beach Bar is a popular seafront bar at the south edge of town that hosts all-you-can-eat barbecues on Sunday afternoon. ⊠ *Beachfront, just south of SunBreeze Hotel, San Pedro* ☎ *226/3289.*

PARADISE THEATER

Ambergris Caye now has a movie theater. The Paradise Theater, just across the bridge on North Ambergris, is part of the troubled Reef Village condo and time-share development, though it is now under new management. Here you can watch first-run movies in air-conditioned comfort and with Dolby 5.1 sound for as little as BZ$5. The theater is also used for live shows. If you're thirsty, there's a bar. ■TIP→ If you don't want to pay the BZ$10 fee to take your golf cart across the bridge, you can park it on the south side of the bridge and walk over (no toll for pedestrians), as the theater is a just a few hundred feet from the bridge. ✉ *Golf cart path, North Ambergris, just across the bridge in the Reef Village development, San Pedro* ☎ *610/0574.*

Big Daddy's. This spot is the scene of much of the action in downtown San Pedro. It's right on the water, and there's a beachside barbecue some nights. The music and real boozing don't get started until 10 or 11. The bar closes at 2, but the nightclub continues on until the wee hours, especially on weekends. ✉ *Barrier Reef Dr., North side of Central Park, San Pedro* ☎ *604/1425.*

Fido's. Under a giant thatch palapa, Fido's is always jumping and has live music some nights. ✉ *Barrier Reef Dr., San Pedro* ☎ *226/3176.*

Jaguar's Temple. Across the street from Big Daddy's is Jaguar's Temple, San Pedro's largest dance club. You can party here on weekends until 4 am. ✉ *Barrier Reef Dr. and Pelican St., San Pedro* ☎ *226/4077* ☉ *Open Thurs.–Sat.*

La Playa Lounge. This open-air beachfront bar has breakfast all day and karaoke a couple of nights a week. ✉ *Beachfront, Black Coral St. and Barrier Reef Dr., San Pedro* ☎ *206/2101.*

Palapa Bar and Grill. The setting and festive atmosphere at this thatch-roof bar are what draw the crowds here, not the food. The breezy two-story palapa at the end of a pier, about ½ mi (1 km) north of the bridge, has stunning views of the sea and reef by day; by night, the colorful bar lighting lends a festive air. Bring a bathing suit and jump in the sea beside the pier (there are handy inner tubes). ✉ *Beachfront, North Ambergris, about 1½ mi (2½ km) north of the bridge, San Pedro* ☎ *206/2101* ⊕ *www.palapabarandgrill.com.*

Pedro's Sports Bar. If all you want is to enjoy a cold drink and watch sports on TV, and maybe have a pizza, Pedro's Sports Bar is your spot. It attracts some island expats, and there are poker games a few nights a week. ✉ *Seagrape Dr., south of town, San Pedro* ☎ *226/3825, 206/2198.*

Rojo Lounge. You can act like a sophisticate at this stunning beachfront bar and restaurant on North Ambergris, sipping a Shark Bite (light rum, coconut rum, Meyer's rum, mango juice and pineapple juice) or slurping a frozen mojito. ⊠ *Beachfront, North Ambergris, Ambergris Caye* ☎ *226/4012.*

Tackle Box. The motto of this burgers-and-beer waterfront spot is "Lunch all day—party all night." ⊠ *On Caye Caulker Water Taxi pier, San Pedro* ☎ *226/4313* ☉ *Closed Mon.*

Wahoo's Lounge. On the odd side of the nightlife spectrum is the Chicken Drop, held on Thursday night's at Wahoo's (formerly Pier Lounge) at the spendthrift hotel. Bet on a numbered square, and if the chicken poops on your square, you win the pot of BZ$1,000. ⊠ *At Spindrift Hotel, Barrier Reef Dr., San Pedro* ☎ *226/2002.*

Wet Willy's. Wet Willy's is a wood-paneled, thatch-roof bar at the end of 340-foot pier. There's indoor and outdoor seating, a grill that serves bar food like burgers, and live music some nights. ⊠ *At Wet Willy's pier, Beachfront, San Pedro* ☎ *226/4136.*

CASINOS

Captain Morgan's Retreat Casino. Opened mid-2011, the small casino at Captain Morgan's is billed as "Las Vegas–style" with slot machines, live table games, and a full bar. ⊠ *3 mi (5 km) north of the bridge, North Ambergris Caye, Ambergris Caye* ☎ *226/2207, 888/653 in U.S. and Canada.*

SHOPPING

Barrier Reef Drive, formerly sandy Front Street, but sadly paved with concrete cobblestones in 2007, is San Pedro's Street of Shopping Dreams—it's lined with souvenir shops complemented by restaurants, small hotels, banks, and other anchors of tourist life on the island. Stores with more local appeal are on Pescador Drive (Middle Street) and Angel Coral Street (Back Street), especially at the north end of town. Barrier Reef Drive is closed to golf carts and vehicles on weekends, starting around 6 pm Friday, and local vendors set up shop selling locally made jewelry and wood carvings (they're also out during the week in high season). Except for these items, few are made on the island. Most of the souvenir shops sell crafts from Guatemala and Mexico, along with carved wood and slate from the mainland.

Belizean hot sauces, such as Marie Sharp's and Gallon Jug's Lissette Sauce, along with local rums, make good souvenirs; they're cheaper in grocery stores (try Pescador Drive and Angel Coral Street) than in gift shops. To avoid worsening the plight of endangered sea life, avoid buying souvenirs made from black coral or turtle shell.

Vendors on the beach occasionally try to sell you carvings, jewelry, Guatemalan fabrics, and sometimes drugs, but they're not pushy.

BEST SHOPS

Ambar. Ambar offers locally made jewelry of amber, jade, and silver. Jeweler Elisabeth Ouvrard creates original designs. ⊠ *Fido's Courtyard, Barrier Reef Dr., San Pedro* ☎ *226/2824.*

Belizean Arts. The first art gallery in Belize, established more than 20 years ago by Londoner Lyndsey Hackston, Belizean Arts today has the largest selection of art by Belizeans and Belize residents of any gallery in the country, with paintings by Walter Castillo, Pen Cayetano,

Nelson Young, Leo Vasquez, Piva, Eduardo García, Curvin Mitc, Jorge Landero, and others. The gallery also carries art by Cuban ar: other Caribbean artists, along with ceramics, jewelry, and other crafts. ⊠ *Fido's Courtyard, Barrier Reef Dr., San Pedro* ☎ 226/3019 ⊕ *www. belizeanarts.com.*

Graniel's Dreamland. Graniel's Dreamland, the showroom for Armando Graniel's beautiful carpentry, has high-quality wood chairs, tables, and other furniture and furnishings, made from Belizean tropical hardwoods, some of which the shop will break down and package for carrying back on the airplane or for shipping. ⊠ *Pescador Dr., San Pedro* ☎ 226/2938 ⊕ *www.granielsdreamlandbelize.com.*

Habaneros S.A. This may be the only place on the island to get authentic Cuban cigars. Many other shops claim to offer Cuban cigars, but more than 90% of cigars advertised as Cuban are fake. Expect to pay BZ$40–$50 or more for the real deal. ⊠ *Barrier Reef Dr., just south of intersection with Black Coral St., San Pedro* ☎ *No phone.*

Island Supermarket. Island Supermarket has the largest selection of groceries, liquor, and beer, along with hot sauces and other Belizean-produced items, though it's not the cheapest place in San Pedro. Grocery prices in San Pedro generally are 20% to 75% higher than in supermarkets in the United States, except for a few items, such as rum, produced in Belize, and Island Supermarket's prices are high even by San Pedro standards. ⊠ *Coconut Dr., south of town, across from Bowen & Bowen Belikin distributors, San Pedro* ☎ 226/2972.

Lagniappe Provisioning. For those chartering a sailboat or staying in a condo, Lagniappe Provisioning will deliver groceries and other provisions to your boat or condotel for a bit more than you'd pay in a grocery. ☎ 610/3326 ⊕ *www.lagniappe-belize.com.*

Marina's Store. Marina's Store has good prices for groceries but a small selection. ⊠ *Coconut Dr., about 1 mi (1½ km) south of town, San Pedro* ☎ 226/3647.

Mata Grande Grocery. This little grocery serves residents and condo guests on North Ambergris. You can order and pay online, and Mata Grande will deliver groceries to your vacation home rental or condo north of the Boca del Rio bridge. ⊠ *4½ mi (7½ km) north of the bridge, North Ambergris, Ambergris Caye* ☎ 629/7411 ⊕ *www.matagrandegrocery. com.*

Orange Gifts. Orange Gifts, a branch of the Cayo store of the same name, is a higher-end gift shop, with crafts, local furniture, original art, and better souvenirs. ⊠ *Coconut Dr., south of the air strip, San Pedro* ☎ 226/4066.

San Pedro Supermarket. One of the less expensive places to buy groceries is San Pedro Supermarket. ⊠ *Lagoon St., at traffic circle at north end of town off Pescador Dr., San Pedro* ☎ 226/3446.

Super Buy. Many local residents buy their groceries at Super Buy. ⊠ *Angel Coral St., San Pedro* ☎ 206/2039.

Toucan Gift Shops. For gaudy geegaws and unabashedly touristy souvenirs, the Toucan Gift Shops, including Toucan Too and Di Bush Toucan, sporting the bright green, yellow, and red Toucan logo, are hard to ss. ⊠ *Barrier Reef Dr., San Pedro* 📞 *226/2431.*

ne De Vine. Wine De Vine has a good selection of wines, many from ile and Argentina, and imported cheeses, at prices (due to import es) roughly double the cost in the United States. ⊠ *Coconut Dr., next to Island Supermarket, San Pedro* 📞 *226/3430* ⊕ *www.winedevine.com.*

SPORTS AND THE OUTDOORS

TENNIS

The San Pedro Family Fitness Club. The San Pedro Family Fitness Club has two hard-surfaced outdoor tennis courts, along with a large swimming pool and a fully equipped air-conditioned gym open to the public. Day, weekly, and monthly passes available. ⊠ *½ mi (1 km) south of town, San Pedro* ✛ *From town, go south on Coconut Dr. until you reach Crazy Canucks and Road Kill bars, at corner of Coconut and Hurricane Sts. Turn west toward lagoon. Go 3 blocks to Fitness Club.* 📞 *226/4749* ⊕ *www.sanpedrofitness.com.*

CAYE CAULKER

5 mi (8 km) south of Ambergris Caye, 18 mi (29 km) northeast of Belize City.

A half-hour away from San Pedro by water taxi and sharing essentially the same reef and sea ecosystems, Caye Caulker is very different from its big sister island, Ambergris Caye. It's smaller (with a population of around 1,300), less developed, way more relaxed, and less expensive.

Caye Caulker has long been a stop on the Central America backpacker trail, and it remains Belize's most popular budget destination, although more upscale lodgings are opening and the island now has several condo developments. Still, flowers outnumber cars ten to one (golf carts, bicycles, and bare feet are the preferred means of transportation).

As you might guess from all the "no shirt, no shoes, no problem" signs at the bars, the living is relatively easy here. This is the kind of place where most of the listings in the telephone directory give addresses like "near football field." However, Caye Corker, as it's sometimes called in Belize (or Cayo Hicaco in Spanish, a reference to the coco plums on the island), isn't immune to change. Many hotels have added air-conditioning, and the island now has cybercafés and several upmarket restaurants. Still, Caye Caulker remains the epitome of laid-back, and as development continues at a fevered pace on neighboring Ambergris Caye, Caulker's simpler charms exercise considerable appeal to those who seek an affordable and relaxing island experience.

For those used to researching and booking everything online, here's a caution about Caye Caulker: As is common with budget destinations, some of the tour operators and cheaper lodging choices on Caulker don't have Web sites. In fact, some tour operators work from a spot on the beach and have only a cell phone, if that. Those that are online often have Web sites that are done on the cheap, with poor graphics and servers that are down intermittently. Consider it part of the charm of Caye Caulker.

WORD OF MOUTH

"While it looked like many operators [on Caye Caulker] are willing to take you to the manatees, Chocolate seems to be the most famous. Other popular dive areas include the local reef five minutes from Caye Caulker and the Hol Chan Reserve between Caye Caulker and Ambergris Caye. I would recommend the Hol Chan trip, even though it will be crowded. We had some great lobster at Rose's, but I think the best food we had was at Fran's. She has a little yellow food hut right near the water and is only open for dinner. She pulls out her grill right by the street and cooks lobster, snapper, and other meals. It's more street food than a more proper sit-down meal—you get your food in a Styrofoam container and sit at the nearby picnic tables to eat it—but the food is great. "

—Gritty

3

GETTING HERE AND AROUND

Other than a few emergency vehicles and several private cars, there are few cars on Caye Caulker. Most locals and visitors get around the island's sand streets on foot, although you can rent a golf cart or bike. (Golf-cart taxis charge around BZ$5–BZ$10 per person to most destinations in the village.)

Like Ambergris Caye, Caye Caulker can be used as a base for exploring part of the mainland. It's only about 45 minutes by water taxi, or 15 minutes by air, to Belize City. Two water-taxi companies now offer daily service between Caye Caulker and Chetumal, Mexico. Tours run from Caulker to the Mayan ruins at Lamanai and Altun Ha, and other tours go to the Belize Zoo and to the Caves Branch River for cave tubing.

Caye Caulker is a fairly small island, only 5 mi (8 km) long and a little over 1 mi (2 km) wide at the widest point—most of the island is only a few hundred feet wide. The island itself is divided by "the Split," a small channel of water separating the north area and the south area. The area north of the Split is mostly mangroves and lagoons, accessible only by boat, while the only village occupies most of the area south of the Split. From the Split to the airstrip, which is at the south end of the island, is about a mile (2 km). Directions in the village usually use the main public pier or dock, where you come in on the Caye Caulker Water Taxi boat, as the reference point. (To confuse things, other water taxis come into a different pier just north of the original public pier.) Things are either north of the main pier or south of it. The village has only three main streets: Front, Middle, and Back running north and south; Back Street just runs on the south side of the village. The main east-west street between the public pier and the lagoon-side dock is called Center Street or Dock Street. All the streets on the island are hard-packed sand. On the east side you can also walk along the beachfront. Officially, the streets are named, from front to back, Avenida Hicaco, Avenida Langosta, and Avenida Mangle, but rarely does anyone use these names.

Generally, the north end of the village bustles more than the south end, which is primarily residential.

TIMING

Caye Caulker's low-key charms take a while to fully appreciate. Stay here a day, and you'll complain that there's nothing to do. Stay a week, and you'll probably tell everyone how much you hate overdeveloped islands like Ambergris.

SAFETY

Several high-profile muggings, rapes, and stabbing of visitors, along with the murder of the local Tropic Air station manager in 2009 brought Caulker unwanted attention. Despite these crimes, and the general disreputable vibe of some Rasta-phonians who hang out at bars or call out to passing tourists, Caye Caulker remains one of the safest places in Belize. Just don't bring the barfly back to your room or wander around dark alleys at night. Also, keep your camera, wallet, and other possessions close to you, especially in cheaper hotels.

WATER ACTIVITIES AND TOURS

When you see the waves breaking on the Barrier Reef just a few hundred yards from the shore, boats full of eager snorkelers and divers, and the colorful sails of windsurfers dashing back and forth in front of the island, you know you've come to a good place for water sports and activities. You can dive, snorkel, and fish the same areas of the sea and reef as you can from San Pedro, but usually for a little less dough. One area where Caulker suffers by comparison with its neighboring island is in the quality of its beaches. Caulker's beaches, though periodically nourished by dredging to replenish the sand, are modest at best, mostly narrow ribbons of sand with shallow water near the shore and, in places, a mucky sea bottom and lots of sea grass. You can, however, have an enjoyable swim at "the Split," a channel cut through the island by Hurricane Hattie in 1961, at the north end of the village, or from the end of piers.

FISHING

Caye Caulker was a fishing village before it was a visitor destination. From Caulker you can fly-fish for bonefish or permit in the grass flats behind the island, troll for barracuda or grouper inside the reef, or charter a boat to take you to blue water outside the reef for deep-sea fishing. Ambergris Caye offers more options for chartering boats for deep-sea fishing than Caye Caulker. For a guide and boat for flats and reef fishing, you'll pay around BZ$600 a day for one or two people. If you're a do-it-yourself type, you can fish off the piers or in the flats. Anglers Abroad has a small fly-fishing and tackle shop where you can rent fishing gear, if you didn't bring your own. Blue marlin weighing more than 400 pounds have been caught beyond the reef off Caye Caulker, along with big sailfish, pompano, and kingfish. If you can find a charter on Caulker for blue-water deep-sea fishing, you'll pay BZ$1,000–$1,200 and up for a full day's fishing for up to four people.

CHARTERS, LESSONS, AND EQUIPMENT **Anglers Abroad.** Haywood Curry, a transplanted Texan, and his crew run all types of fishing trips, starting with half-day trips at BZ$440 for two persons up to three-day camping and fishing expeditions, at around

BZ$1,200 per person. He also has a fly-fishing and tackle shop on Front St. ⊠ *At Seadreams Hotel near the Split, Hattie St., Caye Caulker* ☎ *226/0303, 866/863–5374.*

Porfelio "Piggy" Guzman. Porfelio "Piggy" Guzman is one of the the best-known fishing guides on the island, and he may charge a little more than others. ⊠ *Calle Almendro* ☎ *226/0152.*

Tsunami Adventures. Tsunami Adventures offers reef and flats fishing trips starting at BZ$400 for a half day for two persons, including boat and guide. ⊠ *Front St.* ☎ *226/0462* ⊕ *www.tsunamiadventures.com.*

MANATEE SPOTTING
Several operators do boat trips to see West Indian manatees. The 9,000-acre Swallow Caye Wildlife Sanctuary, established in 2002 in great part due to the efforts of Chocolate Heredia and his wife Annie Seashore, is home to many of these endangered mammals. It's just 10 minutes by boat from Caye Caulker. It's illegal in Belize to get into the water with the gentle sea cows, but a few tour operators unfortunately do permit it. Half-day tours typically cost around BZ$75–BZ$100 per person, including the BZ$10 sanctuary admission fee. Some stop at Goff's Caye, which has excellent snorkeling.

CHARTERS, LESSONS, AND EQUIPMENT

Carlos Tours. Carlos Tours, one of the most recommended tour operators on Caye Caulker, runs snorkeling trips with stops at some of the best snorkel spots near Caye Caulker, and also at Hol Chan Marine Reserve and other places, along with manatee-spotting tours. ⊠ *Front St., at Calle del Sol* ☎ *226/0058* ✎ *carlosayala10@hotmail.com.*

Chocolate. Lionel "Chocolate" Heredia, who was instrumental in establishing Swallow Caye Wildlife Sanctuary as a safe home for the manatees and who has pioneered responsible manatee tours, now only occasionally does tours. But if one is available (around BZ$100 including Sanctuary fee), jump at the chance. ⊠ *Front St.* ☎ *226/0151* ✎ *chocolateseashore@gmail.com.*

Red Mangrove Eco Adventures. Red Mangrove Eco Adventures offers "ecologically sensitive" manatee-watching tours—no swimming with the manatees. ⊠ *Front St.* ☎ *607/1440* ⊕ *www.mangrovebelize.com.*

SAILING
A few small sailboats offer sailing and snorkeling trips to nearby areas. One company, Raggamuffin Tours, also offers multiday combination sailing, snorkeling, and camping trips to Placencia.

CHARTERS, LESSONS, AND EQUIPMENT

Raggamuffin Tours. Raggamuffin Tours has day sails and sunset and moonlight sails for BZ$60–BZ$100. A full-day trip by motorboat to Turneffe with snorkeling is BZ$150. Two-night/three-day camping and sailing trips to Placencia, with nights at Tobacco Caye and Ranguana Caye, are BZ$700 per person one-way. These normally depart Caye Caulker twice a week, on Tuesdays and Fridays, weather permitting. ⊠ *Front St.* ☎ *226/0348* ⊕ *www.raggamuffintours.com.*

Seahawk Sailing. Seahawk Sailing offers snorkeling, overnight camping, and charter trips on a 30-foot sailboat. ⊠ *Front St., next to De Real Macaw* ☎ *607/0323* ⊕ *www.nickmela.com/seahawk.*

Stuart Trent. If you want to learn to sail, Stuart Trent gives sailing lessons and also rents small sailboats, providing sailing lessons with the rentals if needed. Hobie Cats go for BZ$150 for a half-day. ⊠ *Front St., near Sandbox restaurant, Caye Caulker* ☎ *631/9134.*

SCUBA DIVING AND SNORKELING

Hol Chan Marine Reserve at the southern tip of Ambergris Caye *(⇨ see Ambergris Caye section, above)* is a popular destination for snorkel and dive trips from Caye Caulker. At Hol Chan you can swim with nurse sharks and stingrays and see hundreds of tropical fish, some quite large due to the no-fishing restrictions in the reserve. On the way, your boat may be followed by a pod of frolicking dolphins, and you may spot sea turtles or even a manatee. Boats from Caulker also go to Lighthouse and Turneffe atolls.

The Caye Caulker Marine Reserve north and east of Caye Caulker, with its coral canyons, is a favorite of divers, especially for night dives. Caulker has its own mini version of San Pedro's Shark-Ray Alley, called Shark-Ray Village.

CHARTERS, LESSONS, AND EQUIPMENT
A plethora of dive and snorkel operators offer reef tours (some of them are "cowboys"—unaffiliated and unreliable—so make sure you use a reputable company). Plan on spending about BZ$40–BZ$60 for a snorkel trip around the island or BZ$70–BZ$100 for a six-hour snorkel trip to Hol Chan Marine Reserve.

Local two-tank reef dives typically run about BZ$150, and those to Hol Chan or other nearby areas cost about BZ$160–BZ$180. Day trips to Lighthouse or Turneffe atoll, with three dives, cost around BZ$250–BZ$300. If you stop at Half Moon Caye, there's an additional BZ$80 park fee. At Hol Chan, the park fee is BZ$20, and at Caye Caulker Marine Reserve, BZ$10. These park fees, which apply for divers and snorkelers, are sometimes not included in the quoted prices for dive and snorkel trips. The 12.5% Goods and Services Tax (GST) may—or may not—be included in the price you're quoted. Ask, to be sure.

Anwar Tours. Anwar Tours runs snorkel trips to see manatees at Swallow Caye, with a visit at St. Georges Caye, and stops at three other good snorkel sites. Rate for this full-day trip is BZ$130. A night snorkel trip is BZ$90. Anwar, like other tour operators, provides various snorkel and other tour options, depending on demand. Stops and length of trips vary depending on weather and sea conditions. ⊠ *Front St.* ☎ *226/0327.*

Belize Diving Services. Established in 1978, Belize Diving Services has been around long enough to know all the best spots. They train around 500 divers every year, with a full open water course running around BZ$700. A two-tank local reef dive is BZ$130, not including gear rental, 12.5% tax and BZ$10 reserve admission fee. A two-tank Turneffe trip is BZ$180 plus tax and gear rental. ⊠ *Chapoose St., near soccer field and Iguana Reef Inn* ☎ *226/0143* ⊕ *www.belizedivingservices.net.*

Carlos Tours. Carlos Tours runs snorkel trips to Hol Chan Marine Reserve and elsewhere, manatee-spotting trips to Swallow Caye, and full-day snorkel and sightseeing trips with several stops on the Barrier Reef, at San Pedro, and at small cayes. Prices vary according to the destination but range from around BZ$70 to BZ$160 per person. ✉ *Front St.* ☎ *226/0058.*

Frenchie's Diving Services. If you're looking for someone to take you out to the reef for diving, or to the Blue Hole, Frenchie's Diving Services is a respected local operator. Frenchie's leaves early for the Blue Hole, to try to be the first boat there. The three-dive, full-day trip, including gear, breakfast, lunch, BZ$80 park fee, and tax is BZ$393 per person. ✉ *Front St., on dock north of main pier* ☎ *226/0234* ⊕ *www.frenchiesdivingbelize.com.*

Raggamuffin Tours. Go out for a snorkel on a sailboat with Raggamuffin Tours, which goes to Hol Chan for BZ$100, including the park entrance fee, lunch, and cocktails. ✉ *Front St.* ☎ *226/0348* ⊕ *www.raggamuffintours.com.*

Red Mangrove Eco Adventures. Red Mangrove Eco Adventures offers "ecologically sensitive" snorkel and mainland trips—no touching or hugging the sharks on their tours. ✉ *Front St.* ☎ *607/1440* ⊕ *www.mangrovebelize.com.*

Tsunami Adventures. Tsunami Adventures runs full-day snorkeling trips to Hol Chan for BZ$90 including the park entrance fee and lunch. A three-hour local reef snorkel trip is BZ$50. This company also offers a number of other snorkel trips, including a trip to Turneffe Atoll (BZ$150) and another to the Blue Hole (BZ$280 including breakfast and lunch and BZ$80 park fees). ✉ *Front St.* ☎☎ *226/0462* ⊕ *www.tsunamiadventures.com.*

WINDSURFING AND KITESURFING

With brisk easterly winds most of the year, Caye Caulker is one of Belize's premier centers for windsurfing. The island gets winds over 12 knots most days from November to July. The best windsurfing is in the morning and afternoon, with lulls around midday. In the late winter and spring, winds frequently hit 20 knots or more.

CHARTERS, **KiteXplorer.** KiteXplorer offers beginning and advanced kitesurfing les-
LESSONS, AND sons. An intensive nine-hour training program over three or four days
EQUIPMENT costs around BZ$740. Private lessons are BZ$130 an hour. KiteXplorer also sells and rents equipment. ✉ *Beachfront* ☎ *635/4967* ⊕ *www.kitexplorer.com.*

WHERE TO EAT

Once your dining choice on Caulker was fish, fish, or fish, but now you can also enjoy Italian, Mexican, and Chinese, as well as wonderful fresh conch and lobster and, of course, fish. Several restaurants serve wholesome natural foods and vegetarian dishes. Prices for meals here are generally lower than on other islands, and even a lobster dinner is usually less than BZ$45. The cheapest way to eat on the island is to buy grilled fish, chicken, lobster, and other items from the folks with barbecue grills who set up along Front Street and elsewhere. Though you should use good judgment, the food is almost always well prepared and safe to eat. Locals also sell meat pies, tacos, tamales, cakes, and other homemade items at very low prices. Do what local people do and buy your snacks and some of your meals from these street vendors.

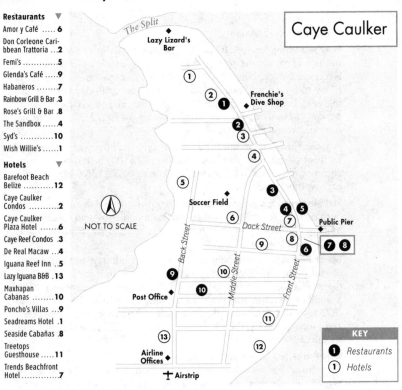

Caye Caulker

NOT TO SCALE

KEY

1 *Restaurants*

① *Hotels*

$ ✕ **Amor y Café.** This is the best spot on Caye Caulker for love, coffee
CAFÉ (including espresso and lattes), and breakfast. Sit on the front porch, do some people-watching on Front Street, and try the fruit with granola and homemade yogurt, or the yummy fresh-baked breads. ✉ *15 Front St., 1 block south of main pier* ☎ *632/4141* ⊕ *www.aguallos.com/ amorycafe* 🖃 *No credit cards.*

$$$ ✕ **Don Corleone Caribbean Trattoria.** If you're tired of fried seafood and
ITALIAN beans and rice, the Italian food at Don Corleone, under new management, is an offer you can't refuse. Try the pasta carbonara, cooked al dente as it should be, or the seafood linguine. The snapper, cooked simply in olive oil with capers (BZ$30) is excellent. We have heard some recent grumblings about the service and the pizza here, and we hope any problems get quickly ironed out. ✉ *Front St., halfway between main public pier and the Split, on west side of street* ☎ *226/0025* 🕐 *Closed Sun.*

$ ✕ **Femi's.** Popular with younger travelers, Femi's is on the beach, with
SEAFOOD no walls to spoil the view. Try the Mexican dishes at lunch, the snapper at dinner, or the smoothies any time. In the evening, Femi's is more of a bar. ✉ *Beachfront, south of the public pier, Front St.* ☎ *622/3469.*

¢ ✕ **Glenda's Café.** The menu here is on a chalkboard, short and sweet, and
CAFÉ you place your order at the window. At breakfast, when this café is most popular, you can get a hearty breakfast of eggs, bacon, beans, homemade

cinnamon roll or johnnycakes and fresh orange juice for a pittance. It opens at 7 am. ⊠ *Back St., north of post office* ☎ *226/0148* ▭ *No credit cards* ⊙ *Closed Sun. No dinner.*

$$$
ECLECTIC
★
✕ **Habaneros.** The most expensive dining spot on Caye Caulker, Haberneros is also a place that tends to generate mixed reactions: One diner goes ga-ga over the coconut encrusted snapper with mixed fruits and loves the dramatic light-

ing, while another guest sniffs at the combination of pork topped with crab and thinks the restaurant is too dark. Chef-owner Darren Casson hits for the fences with some of his dishes, and he doesn't always connect, with too many competing flavors and over-the-top presentations, but for a splurge on Caye Caulker this is your most interesting choice. Just be aware that with drinks, tip, and taxes (Haberneros doesn't include the 12.5% GST in the menu price), you'll face a hefty check. ⊠ *Front St., due west from main public pier* ☎ *226/0487* ⊙ *Dinner only; closed Thurs.*

$$
SEAFOOD
✕ **Rainbow Grill & Bar.** To catch the sea breezes, the Rainbow is built out over the water. Seafood of course is the thing here—our favorites are the grilled or fried fish dishes. There are burgers and fajitas, too, along with several vegetarian dishes. Prices are moderate. This place is always buzzing. ⊠ *Front St., on beachfront midway between public pier and the Split* ☎ *226/0281* ⊙ *Closed Sun.–Mon.*

$$$
SEAFOOD
★
✕ **Rose's Grill & Bar.** This little restaurant has some of the best word of mouth on the island, and the tables on the porch and inside are often packed. The specialty is seafood, and it's all fresh. As you arrive you pick out your snapper, grouper, barracuda, lobster or other seafood from the fresh selection displayed, and then it's grilled in front of the restaurant. On a recent visit, there was a mix-up on our order and a long wait, but the final product was perfectly prepared. Open daily for lunch and dinner. ⊠ *Calle del Sol (Center St.) at Front St., behind Habaneros* ☎ *206/0407.*

$
SEAFOOD
✕ **The Sandbox.** Whether outside under the palms or indoors under the lazily turning ceiling fans, you'll always have your feet in the sand here. The Sandbox, located right in the center of town near the public pier, has a large menu, with tasty items such as lobster omelet with fry jacks for breakfast, lobster or conch fritters and barbecue chicken for lunch, and red snapper for dinner. Prices are reasonable, and portions are large. ⊠ *Front St. at Dock St., near the main public pier* ☎ *226/0200.*

$
MEXICAN
✕ **Syd's.** If you ask a local resident for a restaurant recommendation, chances are you'll get a vote for Syd's. It serves Belizean and Mexican favorites like beans and rice, stew chicken (BZ$12), *garnaches,* and tostadas, along with (in-season) lobster and conch at prices lower than you'll pay at most other eateries. The fried chicken (BZ$9) is the best on the island. Especially popular for lunch. ⊠ *Middle St. at Aventurera St.* ☎ *226/0294* ⊙ *Closed Sun.*

Permanent Vacations in Belize

That well-tanned lady relaxing under a palm tree on the beach may not be a tourist after all. She could be an expatriate who decided to chuck it all and move to Belize. Thousands of Americans, Canadians, Europeans, and Asians have already done so or have bought property and plan to move later, perhaps after retirement.

Attracted by low real-estate prices, a frost-free climate, and an awesome spectrum of activities, many expats are drawn to Belize, especially to Ambergris Caye, Corozal, Placencia, and the Cayo. Ambergris Caye has an idyllic Caribbean island atmosphere. Corozal Town and its environs have Belize's lowest living costs, and Mexico is right next door. The Cayo appeals to those who want land for growing fruit trees or keeping a few horses. Placencia has some of the best beaches in Belize.

With nice houses renting for as little as BZ$600 a month (though some in San Pedro go for 10 times that amount), and land selling at prices last seen in the United States in the 1970s, retirement dollars can stretch far here. Beachfront building lots go for as little as BZ$150,000—still pricey, but cheap in comparison to ocean-front lots in Florida or California. There are no restrictions against foreigners owning land in Belize. Moreover, with English as an official language and English Common Law forming the basis of Belize's legal system, Belize is very accommodating to expats.

In late 2001 the government unveiled a program called the Qualified Retired Persons Incentive Program to attract retirees to Belize. In exchange for depositing US$2,000 a month in a Belize bank for living expenses, and proving that you have the pension or other resources to do so, anyone aged 45 and older can get official residency, along with the right to import household goods, a car, boat, and even an airplane tax-free. The application costs about BZ$2,900 and is relatively painless. After getting Qualified Retired Persons status, you have many of the rights of Belizeans except you can't vote or work for pay. The Belize Tourist Board (BTB) administers the program, and details are available on its Web site, ⊕ www.travelbelize.org.

Hundreds of QRP applications have been approved to date. It's a wonder that more people haven't applied: 75 million baby boomers in the United States alone are expected to retire over the next 20 years. Many of them will be looking for alternatives to cold winters and high prices up north.

For those not quite ready to retire, it's still possible to move to Belize, although work permits are difficult to obtain and salaries are a fraction of those in the United States, Canada, or Western Europe. The best option may be to invest in or start a business in Belize that employs Belizean workers, thus paving the way for a self-employment work permit and residency.

Of course, Belize isn't for everyone. And Belize, as seen from the perspective of a full-time resident, isn't the same as the Belize that's experienced by vacationers. Expats anywhere face culture shock, and Belize presents some special situations, including lack of high-tech medical care and a higher risk of theft and burglary than back home.

$$
SEAFOOD
★

✕Wish Willie's. You eat in the sandy backyard of the owner, Maurice Moore, and he will tell you what's on the menu for the day. It may be fresh fish, lobster, or chicken. In most cases, the prices are very low, and the rum drinks cost less than almost anywhere else on the island. You may have to share a table with other guests, and the service is sometimes slow, but keep in mind the money you're saving and the good time you're having! ⊠ *Park St., off Front St. due west of Frenchies* ☎ *660/7194* ▭ *No credit cards* ☉ *Usually closed Sept.–Oct.*

WHERE TO STAY

For expanded hotel reviews, visit Fodors.com.

Caye Caulker has more than 40 hotels, mostly small places with just a few rooms. The older budget hotels are mostly clapboard, with fans but no air-conditioning, and usually without TV or room phones. If they're not on the water where they can catch the prevailing sea breezes, they are often burning hot during the day. Hotels built in the last decade or so are generally constructed of concrete, and most newer properties have air-conditioning. There are only a handful of swimming pools on the island.

$

Barefoot Beach Belize. This little seafront hotel (formerly the Seaview Guest House) has three basic rooms and a suite set in a pastel blue, concrete building with pink and yellow trim, along with three cottages. **Pros:** choice of accommodations; pier is nice spot to enjoy the water. **Cons:** short walk from main restaurant area; some units need upgrading. ⊠ *Beachfront, south of main public pier* ☎ *226/0205* ⊕ *www.barefootbeachbelize.com* ⇆ *3 rooms, 1 suite, 3 cottages* ⚒ *In-room: kitchen, Wi-Fi. In-hotel: beach, water sports.*

$$

Caye Caulker Condos. If you want a full kitchen to prepare some of your own meals, these condos are a good choice. **Pros:** small apartments with kitchens; good location near water and most restaurants. **Cons:** units are not particularly large. ⊠ *Front St., Corner of Calle Almendro, near Split* ☎ *226/0072* ⊕ *www.cayecaulkercondos.com* ⇆ *8 apartments* ⚒ *In-room: safe, kitchen, Wi-Fi. In-hotel: pool.*

$

Caye Caulker Plaza Hotel. This 32-room, three-story hotel, built by Alan Chan, is an attractive new option for modern and modest-cost accommodations in the center of the island. **Pros:** new, modern hotel in the center of the village. **Cons:** not on beach; no pool. ⊠ *Middle St. at Calle del Sol, Caye Caulker* ☎ *226/0780* ⇆ *32 rooms.*

$$$
★

Caye Reef Condos. Caye Reef Condos are among the most upmarket and spacious digs on the island. **Pros:** upscale condo apartments; lots and lots of space; pool; convenient location. **Cons:** some furnishings are already looking a little worn. ⊠ *Front St. at Park St., near Split* ☎ *226/0381, 610/0240* ⊕ *www.cayereef.com* ⇆ *6 2-bedroom condo apartments* ⚒ *In-room: safe, kitchen, Wi-Fi. In-hotel: pool.*

$

De Real Macaw. De Real Macaw was a pioneer in the "new Caulker" trend in guesthouses: better service, bigger rooms, more amenities like air-conditioning and cable TV—all at a good value. **Pros:** clean and well-run; good location near water and most restaurants. **Cons:** not many frills. ⊠ *Front St., corner of Crocodile St., north of main* *public pier* ☎ *226/0459* ⊕ *www.derealmacaw.biz* ⤴ *6 rooms, 2 suites, 1 2-bedroom condo, 1 house* ⚿ *In-room: no a/c, kitchen, Wi-Fi. In-hotel: laundry facilities.*

$$ ▦ **Iguana Reef Inn.** One of Caye Caulker's most upscale lodgings, Iguana
★ Reef has just about everything but a concierge. **Pros:** attractive, well-designed lodging, with pool. **Cons:** on back side of island. ⊠ *Near north end of Middle St., next to soccer field* ☎ *226/0213* ⊕ *www. iguanareefinn.com* ⤴ *12 1-bedroom suites and 1 2-bedroom penthouse suite* ⚿ *In-room: safe, no TV, Wi-Fi. In-hotel: bar, pool, water sports, some age restrictions* ℟ *Breakfast.*

$$ ▦ **Lazy Iguana B&B.** This B&B is one of the tallest structures on the island; the sunset views from the fourth-floor terrace are spectacular. **Pros:** laid-back, nicely furnished B&B; big homemade breakfast included. **Cons:** not on sea; back-of-island location is 10-minute walk to main restaurant area. ⊠ *Alamina Dr., On back side of island north of airstrip* ☎ *226/0350* ⊕ *www.lazyiguana.net* ⤴ *4 rooms* ⚿ *In-room: no TV, Wi-Fi. In-hotel: some age restrictions* ℟ *Breakfast.*

$ ▦ **Maxhapan Cabañas.** This little spot is in the center of the village and not on the water, but it makes up for it by being neat and clean and a fine value, and set in a small, shady, sandy garden. **Pros:** inexpensive, clean rooms. **Cons:** not on the water. ⊠ *55 Av. Pueblo Nuevo, in center of village south of the main public pier* ☎ *226/0118* ⤴ *3 rooms.*

$ ▦ **Pancho's Villas.** Cutesy name aside, Pancho's Villas offers six attractive, modern one-bedroom suites in a lemon-yellow three-story building. **Pros:** pleasant one-bedroom suites. **Cons:** not on beach. ⊠ *Pasero St., between Front and Middle Sts. south of main pier* ☎ *226/0304* ⊕ *www.panchosvillasbelize.com* ⤴ *6 suites* ⚿ *In-room: Wi-Fi.*

$ ▦ **Seadreams Hotel.** Seadreams is ideal for those who like to fish or enjoy taking in beautiful sunsets from a private pier on the lagoon. **Pros:** Convenient location near Split; ideal for anglers; private pier on lagoon. **Cons:** Not on beach. ⊠ *Off Front St., near the Split, Caye Caulker* ☎ *226/0602* ⤴ *5 rooms, 3 apartments* ⚿ *In-room: Wi-Fi. In-hotel: water sports* ℟ *No meals.*

$$ ▦ **Seaside Cabañas.** If your Belizean dreams include lounging pool-
★ side, Belikin in hand, get thee to Seaside, a delightful beachfront inn with one of the few swimming pools on the island. **Pros:** a top choice on the island; pool; convenient location. **Cons:** beach swimming in front of hotel is not good. ⊠ *Front and Dock Sts., at main public pier* ☎ *226/0498* ⊕ *www.seasidecabanas.com* ⤴ *16 rooms, 1 suite* ⚿ *In-room: Wi-Fi. In-hotel: bar, pool, beach, water sports.*

$ ▦ **Treetops Guesthouse.** Austrian-born owner Doris Creasey brings inter-
★ national flair and Teutonic cleanliness to this seaside guesthouse, which is so well run and such a good value (rooms start at around BZ$112 double year-round) that it's almost always full. **Pros:** meticulously clean and well run; quiet location near the water; excellent value. **Cons:** some guests complain about rules. ⊠ *Playa Asunción, south of main public pier* ☎ *226/0240* ⊕ *www.treetopsbelize.com* ⤴ *4 rooms, 2 with shared bath, 2 suites* ⚿ *In-room: Wi-Fi. In-hotel: beach, some age restrictions.*

¢ 🏠**Trends Beachfront Hotel.** One of the first things you see when you arrive at the island's pier is this little hotel, painted tropical turquoise. **Pros:** central location; comfortable no-frills rooms. **Cons:** busy area can occasionally be noisy. ✉ *Dock St. near Front St., at main public pier* ☎ *226/0094* ⊕ *www.trendsbze.com* ⤵ *6 rooms, 1 cabaña* ♨ *In-room: no a/c, no TV. In-hotel: beach.*

VACATION HOME RENTALS

A handful of privately owned homes are available for rent on the island, either daily or by the week. Expect to pay around BZ$100–BZ$200 a night or BZ$800–BZ$2,000 a week. In most cases, credit cards are not accepted.

$ 🏠**Caye Caulker Rentals.** The largest rental source on the island, Caye Caulker Rentals has houses from BZ$100 to BZ$1,000 a night, plus 9% tax. ✉ *Front St., north of the main public pier* ☎ *226/0029* ⊕ *www. cayecaulkerrentals.com* ⤵ *25 rental houses.*

NIGHTLIFE

You don't come to Caye Caulker for the hot nightlife, but the island does have its share of laid-back bars.

I&I Reggae Bar. Knock back a Belikin or two to the beat of reggae music at I&I Reggae Bar. Swings hang from the ceiling, replacing bar stools, on the first floor, and the top floor has hammocks and a thatch roof. The second floor is for dancing. There's really nothing else like this three-story bar in Belize. ✉ *South of public pier—go south on Front St. to dead end, then turn right, Middle St. at Luciano Reyes St.* ☎ *No phone.*

Lazy Lizard. "Sunny place for shady people" is the slogan of the Lazy Lizard. During the day you can swim at the Split and then cool off with some Belikins on the barstools at the Lizard, which sits right at the edge of the water at the northernmost tip of the village. Sunsets are amazing here. After dark there's a spotlight pointed into the water, so you can see fish, small sharks, and occasionally even a crocodile swimming around. Lazy Lizard is usually open very late. ✉ *At the Split* ☎ *623/1454.*

Oceanside. For live music, your best bet is Oceanside on weekends. Other nights, you can enjoy karaoke and dance music. ✉ *Front St. at Pasero St.* ☎ *226/0233.*

SHOPPING

You won't find nearly as many shops here as in San Pedro, but there are a few standout stores to poke around in for some interesting souvenirs. Every day vendors set up on a section of Front Street north of the main public pier, selling crafts and souvenirs. A few vendors can be aggressive.

Caribbean Colors. Caribbean Colors has colorful watercolors and silk screenings by the owner, Lee Vanderwalker-Kroll, along with handmade jewelry, scarves, and art by other artists. ✉ *Front St., just south of main public pier* ☎ *226/0206, 877/809–1659* ⊕ *www.cafepress.com/ caribbeancolors.*

Chan's. Chan's is the largest grocery in the village. Pick up your basic groceries and Marie Sharp's here. ✉ *Middle St. at Calle del Sol* ☎ *226/0165.*

National Symbols of Belize

National Tree: **Mahogany** (*Swietenia macrophilla*)

This prized tree has been heavily logged in Belize, and large specimens are found in only a few areas. The "big leaf" mahogany tree can grow more than 150 feet high and takes 80 years to reach maturity. The wood has a coppery red sheen, a tight, knot-free grain, and a single mature tree can be worth US$100,000 or more.

National Flower: **Black Orchid** (*Prosthechea cochleata*)

The name is deceiving. Only the lip of the flower is black, and the long, slender sepals and petals are yellow-green. These fragrant little flowers bloom year-round and can be found growing on trees in damp areas.

National Bird: **Keel-Billed Toucan** (*Ramphastos solfurantus*)

The toucan, with its huge canoe-shape beak and bright yellow cheeks, can be found in open areas all over the country and loves to eat fruit.

National Animal: **Baird's Tapir** (*Tapirello bairdii*)

Called the mountain cow by most Belizeans, the tapir is actually related to the primitive horse and rhinoceros. A beefy vegetarian, it can weigh up to 600 pounds and is often found in heavy bush, near rivers and streams.

National Motto: *Sub Umbra Florero*

"Under the Shade I Flourish" refers to the shade of the mahogany tree, which is on Belize's coat of arms and flag.

National Drink: **Orange Fanta** and **Belikin Beer** (unofficially, of course).

Chocolate Gift Shop. Established three decades ago, this is the oldest gift shop on the island, run by Annie Seashore and husband Chocolate Heredia. It has textiles from Guatemala along with some from Indonesia. ⊠ *Front St., opposite Frenchie's pier, Caye Caulker* ☎ *226/0151.*

Cooper's Art Gallery. Cooper's Art Gallery has paintings and prints by Walter Castillo, Nelson Young, and other Central American artists, along with pieces by owner Debbie Cooper. ⊠ *Front St., north of main public pier* ☎ *226/0330* ⊕ *www.debbiecooper.artspan.com.*

Friendship Grocery. This convenience store on Front Street has rum, beer, and other necessaries. ⊠ *Front St., between Calle del Sol and Aventurera St., north of main public pier, Caye Caulker* ☎ *226/0378.*

SOUTHERN CAYES

GETTING HERE AND AROUND

The southern cayes are specks of land spread out over hundreds of square miles of sea. There is no scheduled air or boat service to any of these islands. In the case of Tobacco Caye, private boats leave Dangriga daily around 9 to 9:30 am. To other cayes and atolls you'll have to arrange transportation with the lodges or resorts on the islands, or charter your own boat at high cost.

TIMING

Because of the difficulty and expense of getting to the islands, most resorts have minimum-stay requirements, sometimes as little as three days but often a week. Bring several beach novels, and be prepared to enjoy a quiet vacation filled with salty adventures on and under the sea.

TOBACCO CAYE

11 mi (18 km) southeast of Dangriga.

Tobacco Caye is at the northern tip of the South Water Caye Marine Reserve, a 62-square-mi (160-square-km) reserve that's popular for diving and fishing and has some of the most beautiful islands in Belize. Visitors to the South Water Caye Marine Reserve pay BZ$10 a day for up to three days, or BZ$30 a week, park fee. Rangers come around and collect it from guests at the Tobacco Caye hotels.

The island has no shops or restaurants, except those at the hotels, and just a couple of bars, but there is one small dive shop. Boats leave from the Riverside Café in Dangriga for the 40-minute, BZ$35 trip to Tobacco Caye. Get to the Riverside by 9 am; most boats leave around 9:30 (though at busy times such as Easter they come and go all day long). You can get information on the boats, as well as breakfast, at the Riverside Café. ⇨ *See Southern Coast chapter.*

If you don't want to pay a lot for your place in the sun, Tobacco Caye may be for you. It's a tiny island—barely 4 acres, and a walk around the entire caye takes 10 minutes—but it's right on the reef, so you can wade in and snorkel all you want. Though the snorkeling off the caye is not as good as in some other areas of Belize (some of the coral is dead and most of the fish are small), you can see spotted eagle rays, moray eels, octopuses, and other sea life.

WHERE TO STAY

All the accommodations are budget places, basically simple wood cabins, some not much larger than sheds. Since a half-dozen hotels vie for space, the islet seems even smaller than it is. Periodically the hotels get blown away by storms but are rebuilt, usually a little better than they were before. Unfortunately, garbage tends to pile up on the island, and the hotels don't always use the most ecologically sound methods for disposing of it.

Though some places are increasing rates, most prices remain affordably low, around BZ$80–BZ$145 a day per person, including meals.

⚠ **Hotels can be casual about reservations. After making reservations months in advance, you may arrive to find that your reservation has been lost and the hotel is fully occupied.** Fortunately, it's usually easy to find a room in another hotel. Lana's on the Reef, Gaviota Coral Reef Resort, and Tobacco Caye Paradise are the cheapest hotels, with rates starting around BZ$70 per person, including meals, but with tiny rooms and shared baths.

$ ▦ **Tobacco Caye Lodge.** This cluster of pastel blue cabins is a few feet from the turquoise sea. **Pros:** most "upscale" of Tobacco Caye hotels; solar-powered lights. **Cons:** still pretty basic. ☎ *520/5033* ⊕*www. tclodgebelize.com* ⊷ *6 cabins* ⎮ *In-room: no a/c, no TV. In-hotel: restaurant, bar, beach, water sports* ⦿ *No meals.*

$ ⊞ **Tobacco Caye Paradise.** Whether it's paradise or not depends on your expectations, but if what you're seeking is a little hut built partly over the water, backed by cocopalms, with snorkeling and swimming right out your door, and all for BZ$80 a person including meals, this could be it. **Pros:** huts on the beach with meals at low prices; snorkeling is 15 ft. away. **Cons:** very basic; bring a mosquito net, as rooms aren't screened. ⊠ *Tobacco Caye* ☎ *520/5101* ⇥ *6 cabins* ▭ *No credit cards* ⎁*All meals.*

THATCH CAYE
WHERE TO STAY

$$$$ ⊞ **Thatch Caye.** In a process that took years of hard, mostly hand
★ labor, the owners of Thatch Caye put up bamboo seawalls and raised boardwalks around the island, built 11 guest cottages, and the rest of the infrastructure of this "hand-built" island. **Pros:** beautiful private island with congenial hosts; plenty of marine activities; attractive cabañas directly on the water. **Cons:** limited snorkeling off beach; not on reef. ⊠ *Part of the Coco Plum Caye, 9 mi (15 km) or about 25 minutes by boat from Dangriga, Thatch Caye* ⊠ *P.O. Box 143, Dangriga* ☎ *603/2414, 800/435–3145* ⊕ *www.thatchcayebelize.com* ⇥ *11 cabañas* ⎔ *In-room: no a/c, no TV, Wi-Fi. In-hotel: restaurant, bar, beach, water sports* ⎁*All meals.*

COCO PLUM CAYE
WHERE TO STAY

$$$$ ⊞ **Coco Plum Island Resort.** It all comes down to this: Relax in a hammock
★ on the veranda of your cottage, sip a cold drink, and gaze at the Caribbean at this all-inclusive private island resort. **Pros:** air-conditioned cabins on tranquil island; very friendly staff. **Cons:** only fair snorkeling off beach; not on reef; sand flies can be a real nuisance, though spraying has helped control them. ⊠ *Coco Plum Caye, 8 mi (13 km) from Dangriga, Coco Plum* ⊠ *P.O. Box 239, Coco Plum* ☎ *522/2200, 512/786–7309 U.S. reservations number* ⊕ *www.cocoplumcay.com* ⇥ *10 cottages* ⎔ *In-room: no TV, Wi-Fi. In-hotel: restaurant, bar, beach, water sports* ⎁*All-inclusive.*

SOUTH WATER CAYE
Fodor's Choice *14 mi (23 km) southeast of Dangriga.*
★

This is one of our favorite underrated spots in Belize. The 15-acre South Water Caye has good off-the-beaten-reef diving and snorkeling in a stunning tropical setting, and the beach at the southern end of the island is one of Belize's sandy beauties. The reef is only a short swim from shore. The downside of the small caye? The sand flies here can be a nuisance, and there aren't any facilities other than those at the island's two resorts and the International Zoological Expeditions' student dorm.

Smithsonian Institution's Marine Research Laboratory. The Smithsonian Institution's Marine Research Laboratory, conducting a long-term Caribbean Coral Reef Ecosystems Program study, accepts visitors and study groups who come to Carrie Bow Caye for periods of one to three weeks. Reservations usually are made months in advance. For information contact the Smithsonian Marine Station in Fort Pierce, Florida. It also sometimes accepts shorter-term visitors by appointment; contact the Blue Marlin Lodge on South Water Caye for more information. ⊠ *Carrie Bow Caye in South Water Caye Marine Reserve* ☎ 772/462–6220 *Smithsonian Marine Station in Fort Pierce, Florida.*

WHERE TO STAY

$$$$ 🔅 **Blue Marlin Lodge.** A good, though pricey, base for fishing, snorkeling, and diving trips, this Belizean-owned resort at the north end of the island is only 50 yards from the reef. **Pros:** Belizean-owned; great snorkeling and diving nearby; friendly staff. **Cons:** some rooms need upgrades. ⊠ *South Water Caye* ☎ 522/2243, 800/798–1558 in U.S. ⊕ *www.bluemarlinlodge.com* ➹ *9 rooms, 8 cottages* ᐃ *In-room: no TV. In-hotel: restaurant, bar, beach, water sports.*

$$$$
★ 🔅 **Pelican Beach Resort/Pelican's Pouch South Water Caye.** Steps from one of Belize's best beaches, where you can swim, snorkel, and dive from shore, and fish to your heart's content, is this former convent turned peaceful island retreat on 3½ seaside acres. **Pros:** on great little beach, with snorkeling from shore; tasty Belizean food; comfortable no-frills accommodations. **Cons:** you have to make your own entertainment. ⊠ *South Water Caye* ⊠ *P. O. Box 2, Dangriga* ☎ 522/2044 ⊕ *www. pelicanbeachbelize.com* ➹ *5 rooms, 4 cottages with 7 rooms, 1 student dorm* ᐃ *In-room: no a/c, no TV. In-hotel: restaurant, beach, water sports* ⦿ *All-inclusive.*

SOUTHERN CAYES OFF PLACENCIA AND SOUTHERN COAST

8–18 mi (13–30 km) east of Placencia.

A few miles off the coast of southern Stann Creek District are several small islands with equally small tourism operations. If Placencia and Hopkins aren't far enough away from civilization for you, consider an overnight or longer visit to one of these quiet little paradises surrounded by fish. French Louie Caye is one of them, a private two-acre island with a nice coral sand beach. You can do a day trip here from Placencia, or stay overnight in basic cabins.

WHERE TO STAY

$$$ 🔅 **French Louie Caye.** Rent your own private island with a lovely coral sand beach and a reef for snorkeling and fishing, and enjoy lobster and fish freshly prepared by your own cook, all at an affordable rate. *rench Louie Caye, 8 mi (13 km) east of Placencia* ☎ 523/3636, 800/886–4265 in U.S. ⊕ *www.frenchlouiecaye.com* ➹ *1 cabin* ᐃ *In-room: no a/c, no TV. In-hotel: restaurant, beach, water sports, drinking water, showers, electricity, swimming* ⦿ *All meals.*

$$$$ 🔅 **Whipray Caye Lodge.** Whipray Caye (also called Whippari Caye) lures anglers with some of the best permit and bonefish fishing in Central America, and owner Julian Cabral (who claims he is descended from a pirate who stopped off in Belize in the 17th century) is a top-flight fishing guide and fly fisherman. **Pros:** good choice for hard-core anglers. **Cons:** basic accommodations; expensive. ⊠ *9 mi (15 km) from Placencia village, Whipray Caye* ⊠ *General Delivery, Placencia Village* ☎ 610/1068 ⊕ *www.whipraycayelodge.com* ➹ *4 rooms in 2 cottages* ᐃ *In-room: no a/c, no TV. In-hotel: restaurant, beach, water sports* ⦿ *All-inclusive.*

THE ATOLLS

There are only four atolls in the Western Hemisphere, and three of them are off Belize (the fourth is Chinchorro Reef, off Mexico's Yucatán). Belize's atolls—Turneffe, Lighthouse, and Glover's—are oval-shape masses of coral. A few small islands, some sandy and others mostly mangrove, rise up along the atolls' encircling coral arms. Within the coral walls are central lagoons, with shallow water 10 to 30 feet deep. Outside the walls, the ocean falls off sharply to 1,000 feet or more, deeper than any diver can go.

Unlike the more common Pacific atolls, which were formed from underwater volcanoes, the Caribbean atolls began forming millions of years ago, atop giant tectonic faults. As giant limestone blocks slowly settled, they provided platforms for coral growth.

Because of their remoteness (they're 25 mi [40 km] to 50 mi [80 km] from the mainland) and because most of the islands at the atolls are small, the atolls have remained nearly pristine. Only a few small dive and fishing resorts are here, and the serious divers and anglers who favor the area know that they have some of the best diving and fishing in the Caribbean, if not the world. The atolls are also wonderful for beachcombing, relaxing, and snorkeling—just bring plenty of books, as there are no shops or restaurants other than at the hotels. Of course, paradise has its price: most of the atoll resorts are expensive and have minimum-stay requirements.

GETTING HERE AND AROUND

Getting to the atolls usually requires a long boat ride, sometimes rough enough to bring on *mal de mer*. You'll need to take one of the scheduled boats provided by your lodge or ride out on a dive or snorkel boat with a group; otherwise, you'll likely pay BZ$600 to BZ$1,600 or more to charter a boat one-way. Remember, there are no commercial services at the atolls, except those associated with an island dive or fishing lodge. To charter a boat, check with a lodge on the atoll where you wish to go, or ask locally at docks in Belize City, San Pedro, Dangriga, Hopkins, or Placencia.

Glover's Reef Resort has two boats, including a 68-foot catamaran, which can be chartered to Glover's. Rates for up to six people are BZ$700 from Dangriga or Hopkins/Sittee River, BZ$800 from Placencia, and BZ$1,600 from Belize City, one-way. For up to 12 people, the rates jump to BZ$1,400 from Dangriga or Hopkins/Sittee River, BZ$1,600 from Placencia, and BZ$3,200 from Belize City, one-way. Dive shops and sailing charters in San Pedro, Caye Caulker, Placencia, and Hopkins also make regular trips to the atolls, and may take additional passengers, for a fee, if space is available. ⇨ *See Dive sections of the pertinent destination chapter for contact information on dive shops.*

TIMING

Because of the difficulty and expense of getting to the atolls, most resorts have minimum-stay requirements, sometimes as little as three days but more often a week. There's nothing to do on the atolls except dive, snorkel, fish, eat, sleep, and drink.

TURNEFFE ATOLL

25 mi (40 km) east of Belize City.

The largest of the three atolls, Turneffe, is the closest to Belize City. It's one of the best spots for diving, thanks to several steep drop-offs. Only an hour from Lighthouse Reef and 45 minutes from the northern edge of Glover's Reef, Turneffe is a good base for exploring all the atolls.

The best-known attraction, and probably Belize's most exciting wall dive, is the **Elbow**, at Turneffe's southernmost tip. You may encounter eagle rays swimming nearby. As many as 50 might flutter together, forming a rippling herd. Elbow is generally considered an advanced dive because of the strong currents, which sweep you toward the deep water beyond the reef.

Though it's most famous for its spectacular wall dives, the atoll has dives for every level. The leeward side, where the reef is wide and gently sloping, is good for shallower dives and snorkeling; you'll see large concentrations of tube sponges, soft corals such as forked sea feathers and sea fans, and plenty of fish. Also on the atoll's western side is the wreck of the *Sayonara*. No doubloons to scoop up here—it was a small passenger and cargo boat that sank in 1985—but it's good for wreck dive practice.

Fishing here, as at all of the atolls, is world-class. You can fly-fish for bonefish and permit in the grassy flats, or go after migratory tarpon from May to September in the channels and lagoons of the atoll. Jack, barracuda, and snappers lurk in the mangrove-lined bays and shorelines. Billfish, sailfish, and other big creatures are in the blue water around the atoll.

WHERE TO STAY

For expanded hotel reviews, visit Fodors.com.

$$$$ ⬚ **Turneffe Flats.** The sound of the surf is the only thing you'll hear at these smart blue-and-white, red-roofed beachfront air-conditioned cabins. **Pros:** focus here is on fishing. **Cons:** focus here is on fishing. ✉ *Turneffe Atoll, Turneffe Atoll* ☎ *220/4046, 888/512–8812* ⊕ *www.tflats.com* ➭ *8 cottages* ☒ *In-room: no TV. In-hotel: restaurant, bar, beach, water sports, business center, some age restrictions* ¶◎¶ *All-inclusive.*

$$$$ ⬚ **Turneffe Island Resort.** White dive tanks serving as fence posts and ★ a rusty anchor from an 18th-century British warship set the tone at this remote upscale resort offering fishing, diving, beachcombing, and more, including a spa. **Pros:** beautiful atoll setting near great diving and snorkeling; delicious and varied meals. **Cons:** very expensive. ✉ *Coco Tree Caye, Turneffe Atoll* ☎ *713/236-7739, 800/874–0118* ⊕ *www. turneffelodge.com* ➭ *12 rooms, 8 cabañas* ☒ *In-room: no TV. In-hotel: restaurant, bar, spa, beach, water sports, business center* ☉ *Closed Sept. and Oct.* ¶◎¶ *All-inclusive.*

LIGHTHOUSE REEF ATOLL, THE BLUE HOLE, AND HALF MOON CAYE

50 mi (80 km) east of Belize City.

If Robinson Crusoe had been a man of means, he would have repaired here for a break from his desert island.

Lighthouse Reef is about 18 mi (29 km) long and less than 1 mi (2 km) wide and is surrounded by a seemingly endless stretch of coral. Here you'll find two of the country's best dives.

At this writing, visiting Lighthouse Reef is best done as a side trip from Ambergris Caye, Caye Caulker, or another location in northern Belize.

Blue Hole. From the air, the Blue Hole, a breathtaking vertical chute that drops several hundred feet through the reef, looks like a dark blue eye in the center of the shallow lagoon. The Blue Hole was first dived by Jacques Cousteau in 1970 and has since become a diver's pilgrimage site. Just over 1,000 feet wide at the surface and dropping almost vertically to a depth of 412 feet, the Blue Hole is like swimming down a mineshaft, but a mineshaft with hammerhead sharks. This excitement is reflected in the thousands of stickers reading, "I Dived the Blue Hole."

Half Moon Caye. The best diving on Lighthouse Reef is at this classic wall dive. Half Moon Caye begins at 35 feet and drops almost vertically to blue infinity. Floating out over the edge is a bit like free-fall parachuting. Magnificent spurs of coral jut out to the seaward side, looking like small tunnels; they're fascinating to explore and invariably full of fish. An exceptionally varied marine life hovers around this caye. On the gently sloping sand flats behind the coral spurs, a vast colony of garden eels stirs, their heads protruding from the sandlike periscopes. Spotted eagle rays, sea turtles, and other underwater wonders frequent the drop-off.

Half Moon Caye National Monument. Belize's easternmost island offers one of Belize's greatest wildlife encounters, although it's difficult to reach and lacks accommodations other than camping. Part of the Lighthouse Reef system, Half Moon Caye owes its protected status to the presence of the red-footed booby. The bird is here in such numbers that it's hard to believe it has only one other nesting ground in the entire Caribbean (on Tobago Island, off the coast of Venezuela). Some 4,000 of these birds hang their hats on Half Moon Caye, along with iguanas, lizards, and loggerhead turtles. The entire 40-acre island is a nature reserve, so you can explore the beaches or head into the bush on the narrow nature trail. Above the trees at the island's center is a small viewing platform—at the top you're suddenly in a sea of birds that will doubtless remind you of a certain Alfred Hitchcock movie. Several dive operators and resorts arrange day trips and overnight camping trips to Half Moon Caye. Managed by the Belize Audubon Society, the park fee here is a steep BZ$80 per person.

GLOVER'S REEF ATOLL

Fodor's Choice *70 mi (113 km) southeast of Belize City.*

★ Named after the pirate John Glover, this coral necklace strung around an 80-square-mi (208-square-km) lagoon is the southernmost of Belize's three atolls. There are five islands at the atoll. Visitors to Glover's Reef are charged a BZ$20 park fee (BZ$25 for fly-fishing).

Emerald Forest Reef. Although most of the best dive sites are along the atoll's southeastern side, this is the exception. It's named for its masses of huge green elkhorn coral. Because the reef's most exciting part is only 25 feet down, it's excellent for novice divers.

Long Caye Wall. This is an exciting wall with a dramatic drop-off hundreds of feet down. It's a good place to spot turtles, rays, and barracuda.

Southwest Caye Wall. Southwest Caye Wall is an underwater cliff that falls quickly to 130 feet. It's briefly interrupted by a narrow shelf, then continues its near-vertical descent to 350 feet. This dive gives you the exhilaration of flying in blue space, so it's easy to lose track of how deep you are going. Both ascent and descent require careful monitoring.

Kayaking is another popular sport here; you can paddle out to the atoll's many patch reefs for snorkeling. Most hotels rent kayaks.

WHERE TO STAY

For expanded hotel reviews, visit Fodors.com.

¢ **Glover's Atoll Resort.** If you want to experience the stunning Glover's Atoll setting on the cheap, this is your best bet. **Pros:** beautiful setting; great snorkeling, fishing, and diving. **Cons:** extremely basic accommodations; food and supplies on island are expensive; limited service. ⊠ *Northeast Caye* ⊠ *Box 2215, Belize City* ☎ *520/5016* ⊕ *www. glovers.com.bz* ⇆ *12 cabins with shared bath, 1 dorm, campground* ⚲ *In-room: no TV. In-hotel: beach, water sports* ☒ *Closed Sept. and Oct. most years* ⍿ *No meals.*

HOTEL

$$$$ **Isla Marisol.** At Isla Marisol, after a good night's sleep in an air-conditioned cabaña, and a breakfast of mango and johnnycake, you can dive "The Pinnacles," where coral heads rise 40 feet from the ocean floor. **Pros:** beautiful setting; great diving; you can see whale sharks in the late spring. **Cons:** prices aren't a bargain; sand flies sometimes are bad. ⊠ *Southwest Caye* ☎ *520/2056, 866/990–9904 in U.S. and Canada* ⊕ *www.islamarisolresort.com* ⇆ *10 cabins, 1 2-bedroom house* ⚲ *In-room: no TV. In-hotel: restaurant, bar, beach, water sports* ⍿ *Some meals.*

$$$$ **Off the Wall Dive Center & Resort.** Though this lodge on Glover's Atoll focuses on diving, there's excellent snorkeling and fishing as well. **Pros:** competitive price (for an atoll lodge); easy access to great diving; knowledgeable dive staff. **Cons:** bugs can be a nuisance. ⊠ *Long Caye, Glover's Reef Atoll* ⊠ *P. O. Box 195, Dangriga* ☎ *614/6348* ⊕ *www. offthewallbelize.com* ⇆ *4 cabañas* ⚲ *In-room: no a/c, no TV. In-hotel: restaurant, bar, beach, water sports* ⍿ *All meals.*

Northern Belize

WORD OF MOUTH

"I have been to Chan Chich twice and LOVED both trips. It is definitely geared more towards nature/wildlife lovers since there aren't really other types of tours. . . . The food, staff, and lodging at CC is second to none in our travels and worth the cost. Plus, there is no better place in Central America to spot a wild cat. We have seen three ocelots in our two trips as well as fresh puma and jaguar tracks."

—atdahl

By Lan Sluder

Razzmatazz and bling are in short supply in northern Belize. Here you'll find more orange groves than beach bars, more sugarcane than sugary sand, and more farms than restaurants. Yet if you're willing to give in to the area's easygoing terms and slow down to explore back roads and poke around small towns and villages, this northern country will win a place in your traveler's heart. You'll discover some of Belize's most interesting Mayan sites, several outstanding jungle lodges, and a sprinkling of small, inexpensive inns with big personalities.

Northern Belize includes the northern part of Belize District and all of Orange Walk and Corozal districts. Altogether, this area covers about 2,800 square mi (7,250 square km) and has a population of nearly 90,000. The landscape is mostly flat, with mangrove swamps on the coast giving way to savannah inland. Scrub bush is much more common than broadleaf jungle, although to the northwest near the Guatemala border are large, wild tracts of land with some of the world's few remaining old-growth mahogany trees. The region has many cattle ranches, citrus groves, sugarcane fields, and, in a few areas, marijuana fields.

The only sizable towns in the region are Orange Walk, about 53 mi (87 km) north of Belize City, with about 14,000 residents, and the slightly smaller Corozal, with a population of around 10,000, 85 mi (139 km) north of Belize City. Both are on the Northern Highway, a paved two-lane road that runs 95 mi (156 km) from Belize City up the center of the region, ending at the Mexican border.

Northern Belize gets less rain than anywhere else in the country (roughly 50 inches annually in Corozal), a fact that's reflected in the sunny disposition of the local population, mostly Maya and Mestizos. Both Orange Walk and Corozal towns have a Mexican ambience, with central plazas serving as the focus of the downtown areas. Most locals speak Spanish as a first language, though many also know English. Offering little in the way of tourism facilities itself, Orange Walk Town is a jumping-off point for trips to Lamanai and other Mayan ruins, to Mennonite farmlands, and to several well-regarded jungle lodges in wild, remote areas. Corozal Town, next door to Chetumal, Mexico, is a place to slow down, relax, and enjoy the laid-back atmosphere of a charming small town on the beautiful Corozal Bay (or, as Mexico calls it, Chetumal Bay).

If you tire of small-town pleasures, the Belize side of the Mexican border has three casinos, including one called Las Vegas that claims to be the largest casino in Central America, and a duty-free zone (though the shopping here is mostly for cheap clothing and appliances, with little of interest to international visitors). Corozal has begun to draw foreign

TOP REASONS TO GO

Mayan Sites: Several of the most interesting Mayan sites in the region are in northern Belize. These include Altun Ha, Lamanai, and Cerros. Altun Ha gets the most visitors of any Mayan site in Belize, and Lamanai, on the New River Lagoon, and Cerros, on Corozal Bay, are notable because of their beautiful locations.

Wild, Open Spaces: This part of Belize has some of the country's wildest tracts of land. The quarter-million acres of Rio Bravo Conservation and Management Area host only a few thousand visitors each year. Although people are scarce, Rio Bravo teems with wildlife. Other

large tracts of land include the Gallon Jug lands, 130,000 privately owned acres around Chan Chich Lodge. The Shipstern Reserve is a 22,000-acre expanse of swamps, lagoons, and forests on the Sarteneja peninsula. Huge numbers of birds nest at the Crooked Tree Wildlife Sanctuary.

Jungle Lodges: Northern Belize is home to several first-rate lodges, including Chan Chich Lodge, a paradise for birders and the place where you're most likely to spot the jaguar in the wild. Lamanai Outpost, on the New River Lagoon, is a center for crocodile research.

4

expats looking for inexpensive real estate and proximity to Chetumal, the Quintana Roo Mexican state capital, whose metropolitan population is nearly as large as that of the entire country of Belize. Chetumal offers urban conveniences that Belize doesn't, including a modern shopping mall, fast food, a multiplex cinema, and big-box stores including Walmart and Sam's Club. Sarteneja Village, in the far northeastern part of Corozal District, about 35 mi (57 km) from Corozal Town, is a still undiscovered fishing village at the edge of the sea, near the Shipstern Wildlife Reserve. On the way are several pristine lagoons, including the lovely Progresso Lagoon.

ORIENTATION AND PLANNING

GETTING ORIENTED

The Northern Highway, a paved two-lane road, is the transportation spine of the region, running about 95 mi (156 km) from Belize City to the Mexican border at Chetumal, passing the two main towns in northern Belize, Orange Walk and Corozal. A bypass around Orange Walk provides a way to avoid the congested downtown.

Branching off the Northern Highway are a number of tertiary roads, mostly unpaved, including the road to Crooked Tree Wildlife Sanctuary; the Old Northern Highway that leads to the Altun Ha ruins and Maruba Spa; a road to Shipyard, a Mennonite settlement, which also connects with roads to the Lamanai ruins and to La Milpa ruins and Chan Chich Lodge at Gallon Jug; the San Estevan Road that is a route to Progresso, Copper Bank, and the Cerros Mayan ruins, or, via a different branch, to Sarteneja. About 16 mi (27 km) of the San Estevan

Road from Orange Walk to Progresso are scheduled to be paved in 2012. Another route, unpaved, to Sarteneja runs from Corozal Town and requires crossing the New River and the mouth of Laguna Seca on hand-pulled auto ferries.

Crooked Tree Wildlife Sanctuary. A paradise for birders and animal lovers, this wildlife sanctuary is an "inland island" surrounded by a chain of lagoons, in total covering about 3,000 acres. Traveling by canoe among countless birds, you're likely to see iguanas, crocodiles, coatis, and turtles.

Altun Ha. Easy to get to from the Northern Cayes or Belize City, Altun Ha is the most visited Maya site in Belize. After the ruins, treat yourself to a cold drink or mud bath at nearby Maruba Resort Jungle Spa.

Northwest Orange Walk District. A fascinating combination of Mennonite farm country, wild jungle, and Mayan sites including Lamanai, La Milpa, and Chan Chich, this remote part of Belize is anchored by two remarkable jungle lodges, Chan Chich Lodge and Lamanai Outpost.

Corozal Bay. It's so low-key you may doze off occasionally, but for relaxation at modest cost you can't find a better spot than the shores of Corozal Bay. Copper Bank and Sarteneja are especially laid-back. Corozal Town is an expat magnet.

PLANNING

WHEN TO GO

Corozal Town and the rest of northern Belize get about the same amount of rain as Atlanta, Georgia, so even the "rainy season"—generally June to November—here is not to be feared. It's hot and humid for much of the year, except in waterfront areas where prevailing breezes mitigate the heat. December to April is usually the most pleasant time, with weather similar to that of south Florida. In winter, cold fronts from the north occasionally bring rain and chilly weather, and when the temperature drops to the low 60s, locals sleep under extra blankets.

GETTING HERE AND AROUND

AIR TRAVEL

Corozal Town has flights only to and from San Pedro (Ambergris Caye), and some of these flights stop at Sarteneja. Tropic Air and Maya Island Air each fly four to six times daily between Ambergris Caye and the airstrip at Corozal, about 2 mi (3 km) south of town off the Northern Highway. The journey takes 20 minutes and costs around BZ$100 one way. There's no direct service to Belize City or other destinations in Belize. Charter service is available to Chan Chich Lodge and the Indian Church/Lamanai area. From San Pedro to Corozal, two Tropic Air flights daily stop at Sarteneja. The one-way fare is BZ$100. There is no scheduled air service to Orange Walk Town.

Contacts Tropic Air ☎ 226/2012, 800/422–3435 in U.S. ⊕ www.tropicair.com. **Maya Island Air** ☎ 422/2333, 223/1140 ⊕ www.mayaregional.com.

BOAT AND WATER-TAXI TRAVEL

Ferry from Corozal. An old, hand-pulled sugar barge ferries passengers and cars across the New River from just south of Corozal Town to the road to Copper Bank, Cerros, and the Shipstern peninsula. The ferry is free from 6 am to 9 pm daily. ⊹ *To get to the ferry from Corozal, take the Northern Highway south toward Orange Walk Town and look for the ferry sign. Turn left and follow the unpaved road to the ferry landing.*

Ferry between Copper Bank and Sarteneja. A second, hand-pulled auto ferry has been added between Copper Bank and Sarteneja, at the mouth of Laguna Seca. ⊹ *From Copper Bank, follow the ferry signs. Near Chunox, at a T-intersection, turn left and follow the unpaved road 20 mi (32 km) to Sarteneja.*

Water Taxi between Corozal Town and Ambergis Caye. A daily water taxi operates between Corozal Town and Ambergris Caye, with a stop on demand at Sarteneja. The *Thunderbolt* departs from Corozal at the pier near Reunion Park behind Corozal Cultural Center at 7 am and also goes from a pier on the back side of San Pedro near the soccer field to Corozal at 3 pm. Fare is BZ$45 one-way. The trip usually takes nearly two hours but may be longer if there's a stop at Sarteneja, or if the weather is bad.

Chetumal to San Pedro and Caye Caulker. Two Belize-based water-taxi companies now provide service direct from Chetumal to San Pedro and Caye Caulker.

San Pedro Belize Express. The San Pedro Belize Express departs from the Muelle Fiscal in Chetumal at 3:30 pm, returning from Caye Caulker (the pier on Front St. near the basketball court) at 7 am and from San Pedro (pier at Black Coral St.treet, on the front side, near Wahoo's Bar & Grill) at 7:30 am. The advertised rate is are US$30 (BZ$60) between Chetumal and San Pedro, and US$37.50 (BZ$65) between Chetumal and Caye Caulker. The water taxi takes about 90 minutes between Chetumal and San Pedro and 2 hours between Chetumal and Caye Caulker. If you are buying your ticket in Chetumal—the ticket office is near the entrance to the pier—you may be able to negotiate a lower price than the advertised rate, sometimes as little as US$20 (BZ$40). ⊠ *Pier at Black Coral St., San Pedro Town* ☎ *226/3535* ⊕ *www.belizewatertaxi. com.*

San Pedro Water Jets Xpress. The San Pedro Water Jets Xpress boat departs leaves Chetumal from the Muelle Fiscal (Municipal Pier) daily at 3 pm, arriving at the pier on the back side of San Pedro near the soccer field. The boat continues on to Caye Caulker. From Caye Caulker to Chetumal, the boat departs daily at 7:30 am; from San Pedro to Chetumal, the boat departs daily at 8 am. The advertised rate is US$35 (BZ$70) between San Pedro and Chetumal, and US$40 (BZ$80) to or from Caye Caulker. Higher rates may be in effect on holidays and some weekends. This water taxi takes about 90 minutes between Chetumal and San Pedro and two hours between Chetumal and Caye Caulker. If you are buying your ticket in Chetumal—ticket offices are near the entrance to the pier—you may be able to negotiate a lower price than the advertised rate, sometimes as little as US$20 (BZ$40) ✉ *San Pedro Town* ☎ *226/2194.*

Tour boats run from near Orange Walk on the New River to Lamanai. Boats from San Pedro and Caye Caulker bring visitors from those islands to Altun Ha and environs via Bomba, a small coastal village.

BUS TRAVEL

Buses between Belize City and Corozal run about every half hour during daylight hours in both directions, and some of these continue on to Chetumal, Mexico.

Several small bus lines, including Belize Bus Owners Cooperative (BBOC), Chell, Gilharry, Russell, Tillett, T-Line, Venus, and others, make the 3- to 3½-hour journey between Belize City and Corozal Town, with service by one line or another approximately every half hour during the day.

Northbound buses from Belize City. Northbound buses depart beginning at 5:30 am, with the last departure around 7:30 pm.

Southbound buses from Corozal. Southbound buses begin at 3:45 am, with the last departure at 7:30 pm.

Some buses continue on to the Nuevo Mercado (New Market) bus terminal in Chetumal, Mexico. As of this writing, none of the Belize buses arrives at or departs from the main bus station in Chetumal, the ADO terminal. Any non-express bus will stop and pick up almost anywhere along the highway.

The cost between Belize City and Corozal is about BZ$9 or $10, or BZ$12 for express service; the cost between Belize City and Orange Walk Town is around BZ$5. ■ TIP→ Bus service to the villages and other sites off the Northern Highway is limited, so to reach them you're best off with a rental car or a guided tour. There's some bus service on the Old Northern Highway and from Orange Walk to Sarteneja. Bus franchises and routes in Belize, which are controlled by the government, are in a state of flux. Ask locally for updates on bus lines, routes, and fares.

To Guatemala. In addition to regular buses, a Guatemalan tourism bus operator, San Juan Travel Services, operates a daily bus from the main Chetumal ADO bus terminal, currently leaving at 5 am and going all the way to Flores, Guatemala, near Tikal, with a stop at the Marine Terminal in Belize City. The three-hour trip to Belize City costs BZ$20; it's a total of about eight hours and BZ$70 from Chetumal to Flores.

CAR TRAVEL

Corozal is the last stop on the Northern Highway before you hit Mexico. The 95-mi (153-km) journey from Belize City will probably take about two hours, unless you're slowed by sugarcane trucks. The Northern Highway is a two-lane paved road in fairly good condition. Other roads, including the Old Northern Highway, roads to Lamanai, Río Bravo, and Gallon Jug, and the road to Sarteneja are mostly unpaved. Because tour and long-distance taxi prices are high, especially if you're traveling with family or in a group, you likely will save money by renting a car.

Car-rental agencies in Belize City will usually deliver vehicles to Corozal and Orange Walk, but there will be a drop fee, starting at around BZ$150. Two small local car-rental agencies, Corozal Cars and Belize VIP Service, have a few cars to rent, at rates starting around BZ$140 a day.

Contacts Belize VIP Service ⊠ *South End, Corozal* ☎ *422/2725.* **Corozal Cars** ⊠ *Mile 85, Northern Hwy., Corozal* ☎ *422/3339* ⊕ *www.corozalcars.com.*

TAXI TRAVEL

To get around Corozal, call the Taxi Association or ask your hotel to arrange for transportation. Fares to most destinations in town are low, at BZ$10 or less, but rates to points outside town can be expensive; agree on a price beforehand. Likewise, in Orange Walk call the Taxi Association or ask your hotel to arrange a taxi.

Contacts Taxi Association in Corozal ⊠ *1st St. S, Corozal* ☎ *422/2035.* **Taxi Association in Orange Walk** ⊠ *Queen Victoria Ave., Orange Walk* ☎ *322/2560.*

EMERGENCIES

For dental and medical care, many of Corozal's residents go to Chetumal, Mexico. In Corozal, call Bethesda Medical Centre if you need medical care. The Corozal Hospital, with only limited facilities, is on the Northern Highway. In Orange Walk, the Northern Regional Hospital doesn't look very appealing, but it provides emergency and other services. Consider going to Belize City or Chetumal for medical and dental care, if possible.

Emergency Contacts Bethesda Medical Centre ⊠ *Mile 85½, Northern Hwy., Corozal* ☎ *422/3000.* **Corozal Hospital** ⊠ *Northern Hwy., Corozal* ☎ *422/2076.* **Northern Regional Hospital** ⊠ *Northern Hwy., Orange Walk* ☎ *322/2752.*

MONEY MATTERS

Although American dollars are accepted everywhere in Corozal and Orange Walk, money changers at the Mexico border and in Corozal Town exchange Belize dollars for U.S. and Mexican currency, usually at better rates than in banks. The three banks in Corozal—Atlantic Bank, Belize Bank, and ScotiaBank—have ATMs, and all three accept ATM cards issued outside Belize. Orange Walk Town also has branches of Atlantic Bank and ScotiaBank with ATMs that accept foreign ATM cards. There are no banks in Sarteneja or the Copper Bank area, or around Altun Ha or near the jungle lodges in remote areas of Orange Walk District.

Contacts Atlantic Bank ⊠ *4th Ave. and 3rd St. N., Corozal* ☎ *422/3473.* **Atlantic Bank Orange Walk** ⊠ *Main St., Orange Walk Town* ☎ *322/1575.* **Belize Bank** ⊠ *5th Ave. at 1st St. S, Corozal* ☎ *422/2087* ⊠ *Main and Park Sts., Orange Walk* ☎ *322/2019.* **ScotiaBank** ⊠ *4th Ave., Corozal* ☎ *422/2046* ⊠ *Main and Park Sts., Orange Walk* ☎ *322/2194.*

TOURS

Your hotel in Orange Walk Town or Corozal Town can usually arrange tours to Lamanai, Cerros, and other sites, starting at around BZ$80 per person. In Orange Walk, Jungle River Tours, Beyond Touring, and J. Avila & Sons run boat trips (BZ$80 per person, plus BZ$10 admission fee) up the New River to Lamanai and can help arrange other tours and trips. In Corozal Town, local tour operator Vitalino Reyes can arrange tours to Shipstern (BZ$160) and Cerros (BZ$180), although most of his business is in cave-tubing tours for the cruise ships in Belize City. From Sarteneja, Sarteneja Adventure Tours can take you to Bacalar Chico Marine Reserve and National Park off North Ambergris Caye. Rates are BZ$170 per person for a full-day snorkel tour, including guide, park admission, snorkeling gear, and lunch.

Two shuttle services based in Corozal Town, Belize VIP Transfers and George and Esther Moralez Travel, provide inexpensive and handy transportation across the border between Corozal and Chetumal. These services, which cost BZ$60 to $70 one way for up to three or four people, make crossing the border easy and hassle free.

The transfer services also provide shuttles to and from Cancún and other destinations in the Yucatán and in Belize. To or from Cancún, you'll pay around BZ$800 for up to four persons.

Contacts J. Avila & Sons River Tours ⊠ *42 Riverside St., Orange Walk* ☎ *322/0419.* **Belize VIP Transfers (Henry Menzies)** ⊠ *Caribbean Village, South End, Corozal* ☎ *422/2725* ⊕ *www.belizetransfers.com.* **Beyond Touring** ⊠ *Indian Church Village* ☎ *954/415–2897 in the U.S.* ⊕ *www.beyondtouring. com.* **George & Esther Moralez Travel Service** ⊠ *3 Blue Bird St., Corozal* ☎ *422/2485* ⊕ *www.gettransfers.com.* **Jungle River Tours** ⊠ *20 Lovers La., Orange Walk* ☎ *302/2293.* **Sarteneja Adventure Tours** ⊠ *N. Front St.* ☎ *633/0067* ⊕ *www.sartenejatours.com.* **Vitalino Reyes** ⊠ *Corozal* ☎ *602/8975.*

ABOUT THE RESTAURANTS

With the exception of dining rooms at upscale jungle lodges, where four-course dinners can run BZ$70 or more, restaurants are almost invariably small, inexpensive, family-run places, serving simple meals such as stew chicken with rice and beans. Here, you'll rarely pay more than BZ$25 for dinner, and frequently much less. If there's a predominant culinary influence, it's Mexican, and many restaurants serve tacos, tamales, *garnaches* (small, fried corn tortillas with beans, cabbage, and cheese piled on them), and soups such as *escabeche* (onion soup with chicken). A few places, mostly in Corozal Town, cater to tourists and expats with burgers and steaks. For a quick snack, restaurants on the second floor of the Corozal market, including H&L Diner, sell inexpensive breakfast and lunch items (usually closed Sunday). You can also buy delicious local fruits and vegetables at the market—a huge papaya, two lovely mangoes, and a bunch of bananas cost as little as BZ$2.50 or $3.

ABOUT THE HOTELS

As with restaurants, most hotels in northern Belize are small, family-run spots. In Corozal and Orange Walk towns, hotels are modest affairs with room rates generally under BZ$150 for a double, a fraction of the cost of hotels in San Pedro or other more popular parts of Belize. Generally, the hotels are clean, well maintained, and offer a homey atmosphere. They have private baths and plenty of hot and cold water, and most also have air-conditioning. Hotels and lodges in Crooked Tree, Sarteneja, and Copper Bank are also small and inexpensive; few have air-conditioning. The jungle lodges near Lamanai, Gallon Jug, and Altun Ha, however, are a different story. Several of these, including Chan Chich Lodge, Maruba Jungle Lodge and Spa, and Lamanai Outpost Lodge, are upscale accommodations, with gorgeous settings in the jungle or on a lagoon and prices to match, typically BZ$500 or more for a double in-season; meals and tours are extra.

WHAT IT COSTS IN BELIZE DOLLARS					
	¢	$	$$	$$$	$$$$
RESTAURANTS	under BZ$8	BZ$8–BZ$15	BZ$15–BZ$30	BZ$30–BZ$50	over BZ$50
HOTELS	under BZ$100	BZ$100–BZ$200	BZ$200–BZ$300	BZ$300–BZ$500	over BZ$500

Restaurant prices are per person for a main course at dinner. Hotel prices are for two people in a standard double room, including tax and service, in high season.

SAFETY

Corozal is one of Belize's safer areas, but petty theft and burglaries aren't uncommon, so use common sense when traveling through the area. Both Corozal Town and Orange Walk Town have some crack cocaine users. Often, they stand on the street with a pigtail bucket (a 5-gallon bucket) of water and try to earn money by washing car windshields—ignore them if you can.

VISITOR INFORMATION

Excellent sources of general information on northern Belize are the Web sites Northern Belize, ⊕ *www.northernbelize.com*, and Belize North, ⊕ *www.belizenorth.com*. For information about Corozal, check ⊕ *www.corozal.com*. Local information on Orange Walk managed by the Orange Walk Town Council is at ⊕ *www.owtowncouncil.com*.

CROOKED TREE WILDLIFE SANCTUARY

33 mi (54 km) northwest of Belize City.

GETTING HERE AND AROUND

An easy 25-minute drive north from the international airport takes you to the entrance road to Crooked Tree Wildlife Sanctuary at Mile 30.8 of the Northern Highway. From there it's another 2 mi (3 km) on an unpaved causeway to the sanctuary visitor center and Crooked Tree village. If you don't have a rental car, any of the frequent nonexpress buses going north to Orange Walk or Corozal will drop you at the entrance road, but you'll have to hike across the causeway to the village (or arrange a pickup by your Crooked Tree hotel). Jex buses leave from the corner of Regent Street West and West Canal Street in Belize City and go directly to the village, currently three times daily except Sunday (BZ$4).

GREAT ITINERARIES

IF YOU HAVE 3 TO 5 DAYS IN NORTHERN BELIZE

If you are starting in Belize City, rent a car and drive to Crooked Tree Wildlife Sanctuary, which has great birding and offers the chance to see the jabiru stork, the largest flying bird in the Americas. Spend a few hours here, canoeing on the lagoon and hiking trails. If you have an interest in birding, you'll want to overnight here at one of the simple lagoon-side lodges, such as Bird's Eye View Lodge or Crooked Tree Lodge. Otherwise, you could drive on to Maruba, an upscale jungle lodge and spa. The drive from Crooked Tree takes about 45 minutes. While you're at Maruba, visit the Altun Ha Mayan site, which you can see in a couple of hours. On the second day, drive to Corozal Town, about 1½ hours from Maruba or Crooked Tree. Base here in Corozal Town for two days, at one of the small hotels on Corozal Bay such as Corozal Bay Resort, Tony's, or Sea Breeze Hotel, making day trips by boat to Lamanai and Cerros ruins (or you can drive). If you have additional days in the north, you can add a visit to Sarteneja or cross the border into Chetumal, Mexico. Alternatively, after the first night in Crooked Tree or at Maruba,

drive to the Lamanai Mayan site and spend the night there at one of the lodges on the New River Lagoon, or, for a different experience, proceed to Blue Creek Village, a Mennonite area, and spend the night at Hillside B&B. Then, continue on through Programme for Belize lands to Chan Chich Lodge and spend the rest of your time in northern Belize at this amazing jungle lodge. If money isn't much of an object and you want one of the best jungle lodge experiences in Central America, then ditch the car and fly from Belize City to Chan Chich, where you can spend all your time looking for jaguars and listening to the howler monkeys.

IF YOU HAVE 1 DAY IN NORTHERN BELIZE

With only one day, head to Lamanai, which with Caracol in the Cayo District is the most interesting of Belize's Mayan sites. Although you can drive, the most enjoyable way to get to Lamanai is by a 1½-hour boat trip up the New River. Tour boats (BZ$80 per person) leave around 9 am from docks near the Tower Hill bridge over the New River just south of Orange Walk Town. If you're staying overnight at Lamanai, your hotel can arrange boat transportation.

TIMING

One full day is enough to do a canoe trip on the lagoon, hike local trails, and see the small Creole village. But if you're a birder, you'll want at least another day.

Bus Info Jex and Sons Bus Service ⊠ *Crooked Tree Village* ☎ *225/7017.*

EXPLORING

★ **Crooked Tree Wildlife Sanctuary.** Crooked Tree Wildlife Sanctuary is one of Belize's top birding spots. The 16,400-acre sanctuary includes more than 3,000 acres of lagoons, swamp, and marsh, surrounding what is essentially an inland island. Traveling by canoe, you're likely to see

LOCAL FOOD FESTIVALS

Belizeans love to party, and festivals celebrating lobster, chocolate, cashews, and other local foods give them—and you—the chance to join in the fun. Here are some of the food festivals in Belize. Note that dates can change from year to year.

Cashew Festival, Crooked Tree in early May. Crooked Tree village is named for the cashew tree that often grows in a serpentine fashion, curling and growing sideways as well as up. The yellow cashew fruit, which tastes a little like mango and smells like grapes, ripens in late spring, and the Crooked Tree Festival celebrates the cashew in all its forms: fruit, nut, juice, jam, and wine.

Cacao Festival, Toledo in late May. Toledo's increasingly popular Cacao Fest celebrates the home of chocolate in Belize, with tours of small chocolate factories in Punta Gorda and nearby, visits to organic cacao farms, and local music and dances.

Hopkins Mango Festival and Cultural Jam in early June. New in 2011, the Hopkins Mango Festival is devoted to the sweet, juicy mango, spiced by local Garifuna culture. Events include a Garifuna drumming competition, along with bicycle and canoe races.

Placencia LobsterFest in late June. Belize's biggest and best salute to the spiny lobster is held in Placencia village, usually on the last weekend in June. Booths sell local lobster grilled, fried, curried, and in fritters, and there's music, dancing, and lots of Belikin. LobsterFests also are held, typically in late June or early July, in San Pedro and Caye Caulker.

iguanas, crocodiles, coatis, and turtles. The sanctuary's most prestigious visitors, however, are the jabiru storks, which usually visit between November and May. With a wingspan up to 12 feet, the jabiru is the largest flying bird in the Americas. For birders the best time to come is in the dry season, roughly from February to late May, when lowered water levels cause birds to group together to find water and food, making them easy to spot. Birding is good year-round, however, and the area is more scenic when the lagoons are full. Snowy egrets, snail kites, ospreys, and black-collared hawks, as well as two types of duck—Muscovy and black-bellied whistling—and all five species of kingfishers native to Belize can be spotted. Even on a short, one- to three-hour tour, you're likely to see 20 to 40 species of birds. South of Crooked Tree, on Sapodilla Lagoon and accessible by boat, is a small Mayan site, Chau Hiix.

At the Crooked Tree **visitor center,** open 8–4, at the end of the causeway where you pay your BZ$8 sanctuary admission fee, you can arrange a guided tour of the sanctuary or rent a canoe (around BZ$10 per person per hour) for a do-it-yourself trip. The sanctuary is managed by the Belize Audubon Society. You can also walk through the village and hike birding trails around the area. If you'd prefer to go by horseback, you'll pay around BZ$30 an hour. The visitor center has a free village and trail map. If you're staying overnight, your hotel can arrange canoe or bike rentals and set up tours and trips. A typical tour takes about three hours and costs around BZ$160–BZ$200 for up to four persons. It starts at

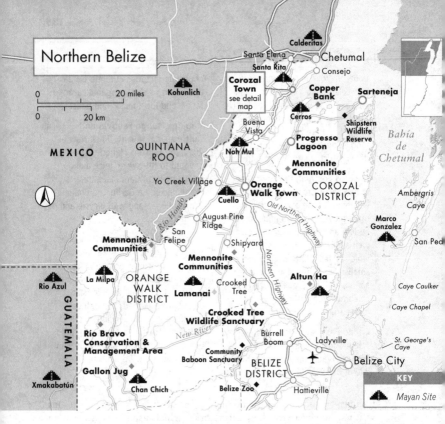

Northern Belize

| 0 | | 20 miles |
| 0 | | 20 km |

MEXICO

QUINTANA ROO

Kohunlich

Calderitas

Santa Elena
Chetumal

Santa Rita
Consejo

Corozal Town
see detail map

Copper Bank
Sarteneja

Buena Vista

Cerros

Shipstern Wildlife Reserve

Progresso Lagoon

Bahía de Chetumal

Noh Mul

Yo Creek Village

Orange Walk Town

Mennonite Communities

COROZAL DISTRICT

Cuello

Old Northern Highway

Ambergris Caye

August Pine Ridge

San Felipe

Marco Gonzalez

San Ped

Mennonite Communities

Shipyard

ORANGE WALK DISTRICT

Mennonite Communities

Northern Highway

Caye Caulker

La Milpa

Rio Azul

Lamanai

Crooked Tree

Altun Ha

Caye Chapel

GUATEMALA

Crooked Tree Wildlife Sanctuary

St. George's Caye

Xmakabatún

Río Bravo Conservation & Management Area

New River

Burrell Boom

Ladyville

Belize City

Gallon Jug

Community Baboon Sanctuary

BELIZE DISTRICT

Chan Chich

Belize Zoo

Hattieville

KEY

🔺 Mayan Site

your hotel or the visitor center with a boat ride on the lagoon, then up Spanish Creek, where you are met by a car and returned to your hotel or visitor center. Although tours can run at any time, the best time is early in the morning, when birds are most active.

One of Belize's oldest inland villages, established some 300 years ago, **Crooked Tree** is at the reserve's center. With a population of about 900, most of Creole origin, the community has a church, school, and one of the surest signs of a former British territory: a cricket pitch. There are many large cashew trees around the village, the serpentine growth pattern of which gave the village its name. The cashews are highly fragrant when in bloom in January and February, and when the cashew fruit ripen to a golden yellow color in May and June, they taste something like mango and smell like sweet grapes. The cashew nuts require roasting to make them edible. Villagers make and sell cashew wine. A Cashew Festival is held annually in early May. ⊠ *Turn west off Northern Hwy. at Mile 30.8, then drive 2 mi (3 km)* ☎ *223/4987 for Belize Audubon Society* ⊕ *www.belizeaudubon.org/parks/ctws.htm* 🖂 *BZ$8.*

WHERE TO STAY

For expanded hotel reviews, visit Fodors.com.

$ **Bird's Eye View Lodge.** This modern concrete hotel, with a two-story main building and a new annex next door, covered with bougainvillea and other flowers, occupies a prime location at lagoon's edge, and you'll find that the friendly and welcoming service is consistent with Belize's down-home reputation. **Pros:** on shores of Crooked Tree Lagoon; delicious meals made with local ingredients; breezy second-floor patio with great lagoon views. **Cons:** undistinguished, blocky buildings; no-frills guest rooms. ⊠ *Crooked Tree* ⊠ *P.O. Box 1976, Belize City* ☎ *203/2040* ⊕ *www.birdseyeviewbelize.com* ⤳ *20 rooms* ⚘ *In-room: no TV. In-hotel: restaurant, water sports.*

$ **Crooked Tree Lodge.** Owned by a British-Belizean couple on the site
★ of the old Paradise Lodge, this lodge has six comfy hardwood cottages on a gorgeous 11½-acre site on the shores of the Crooked Tree Lagoon. **Pros:** wonderful lagoon-side location; friendly hosts; good food. **Cons:** no air-conditioning. ⊠ *Crooked Tree* ☎ *626/3820* ⊕ *www.crookedtreelodgebelize.com* ⤳ *5 cabañas and 1 2-bedroom cottage* ⚘ *In-room: no TV. In-hotel: restaurant, bar, water sports.*

> **GOOD GUIDE**
>
> **Crooked Tree Visitor Center.** For an introduction to the sanctuary, and for a guide, visit the Crooked Tree Visitor Center at the end of the causeway. Although the visitor center itself does not provide guides, it can put you in touch with all the best local guides. Expect to pay about BZ$20–BZ$30 an hour for guide services. Admission to the sanctuary is BZ$8 per person. ⊠ *Crooked Tree Village* ☎ *223/5004* ⤳ *BZ$8* ⊙ *8–4.*

ALTUN HA

28 mi (45 km) north of Belize City.

GETTING HERE AND AROUND

Altun Ha is easily visited on your own—if you have a car. From Belize City, drive north on the Northern Highway to Mile 18.9; turn right on the *Old* Northern Highway and go 10½ mi (17 km). The Old Northern Highway is a mix of gravel areas, broken pavement, and paved sections. The turnoff from the Old Northern Highway to Altun Ha, on the left, is well marked. If coming from Corozal or Orange Walk, you can also enter the Old Northern Highway at Mile 49 of the Northern Highway. There's limited bus service from Belize City to Maskall Village near Altun Ha.

TIMING

You can see Altun Ha in a couple of hours. If you add lunch and a spa treatment at the nearby Maruba Resort Jungle Spa, you'll spend most of the day in the area.

SAFETY AND PRECAUTIONS

Marijuana is illegally grown in remote areas off the Old Northern Highway. Avoid hiking off trail, where you might accidentally stumble on someone's weed plantation.

EXPLORING

Altun Ha. If you've never experienced an ancient Mayan city, make a trip to Altun Ha, which is a modern translation in Mayan of the name "Rockstone Pond," a nearby village. It's not Belize's most dramatic site—Caracol and Lamanai vie for that award—but it's one of the most accessible and most thoroughly excavated. The first inhabitants settled before 300 BC, and their descendants finally abandoned the site after AD 1000. At its height during the Classic period the city was home to 10,000 people.

A team from the Royal Ontario Museum first excavated the site in the mid-1960s and found 250 structures spread over more than 1,000 square yards. At Plaza B, in the Temple of the Masonry Altars, archaeologists unearthed the grandest and most valuable piece of Mayan art ever discovered—the head of the sun god Kinich Ahau. Weighing nearly 10 pounds, it was carved from a solid block of green jade. The head is kept in a solid steel vault in the Central Bank of Belize, though it is occasionally displayed at the Museum of Belize. The jade head appears on all denominations of Belize currency. If the Masonry Altars temple looks familiar to you, it's because an illustration of the Masonry Altars structure appears on Belikin beer bottles. Because the Altun Ha site is small, it's not necessary to have a tour guide, but licensed guides may offer their services when you arrive.

Tours from Belize City, Orange Walk, and Crooked Tree also are options. Altun Ha is a regular stop on cruise ship excursions, and on days when several ships are in port in Belize City, typically midweek, Altun Ha may be overrun with cruise passengers. Several tour operators in San Pedro and Caye Caulker also offer day trips to Altun Ha, often combined with lunch at the nearby Maruba Resort Jungle Spa. Most of these tours are by boat, landing at Bomba Village. From here, a van makes the short ride to Altun Ha. If traveling independently, you also can stop at Maruba for a drink, lunch, or a spa treatment. *(See ⇨ Maruba.)* ✛ *From Belize City, take Northern Hwy. north to Mile 18.9. Turn right (east) on Old Northern Hwy., which is only partly paved, and go 10½ mi (17 km) to signed entrance road to Altun Ha on left. Follow this paved road 2 mi (3 km) to visitor center* ☎ 822/2106 *Belize Institute of Archeology* 🖾 *BZ$20* ⊗ *Daily 9–5.*

WHERE TO STAY

For expanded hotel reviews, visit Fodors.com.

$$$ **Maruba Resort Jungle Spa.** "Neo-primitive tribal chic" is how Maruba ★ describes its style, and the resort definitely delivers an exotic experience in a jungle setting, complete with 24-hour electricity, air-conditioned

HISTORY

The Maya settled this area thousands of years before the time of Christ. Cuello, near Orange Walk Town, dates from 2500 BC, making it one of the earliest known Mayan sites in all of Mesoamerica (the region between central Mexico and northwest Costa Rica). In the Pre-Classic period (2500 BC–AD 300) the Maya expanded across northern Belize, establishing important communities and trading posts at Santa Rita, Cerros, Lamanai, and elsewhere.

During the Classic period (AD 300–AD 900), Santa Rita, Lamanai, Altun Ha, and other cities flourished. To feed large populations perhaps totaling several hundred thousand, the Maya developed sophisticated agricultural systems, with raised, irrigated fields along the New River and other river bottoms. After the mysterious collapse of the Mayan civilization by the 10th century AD, the region's cities went into decline, but the Maya continued to live in smaller communities and rural areas around the many lagoons in northern Belize, trading with other settlements in Belize and in Mexico. Lamanai, perched at the edge of the New River Lagoon, was continuously occupied for almost three millennia, until late in the 17th century.

The Spanish first set foot in these parts in the early 1500s, and Spanish missionaries made their way up the New River to establish churches in Mayan settlements in the 16th and 17th centuries. You can see the remains of a Spanish church at the entrance of Lamanai near Indian Church Village. About this same time, small groups of shipwrecked British sailors established settlements in Belize but the Battle of St. George's Caye in 1789 effectively put an end to Spanish control in Belize.

In the second half of the 19th century, the so-called Caste Wars (1847–1904), pitting Maya insurgents against Mestizo and European settlers in Mexico's Yucatán, had an important impact on northern Belize. Refugees from the bloody wars moved south from Mexico, settling in Corozal Town, Orange Walk Town, Sarteneja, and also on Ambergris Caye and Caye Caulker.

Today more than 40,000 acres of sugarcane are harvested by 4,000 farmers in northern Belize. Mennonites, who came to the Blue Creek, Shipyard, and Little Belize areas in the late 1950s, have contributed greatly to agriculture in the region, producing rice, corn, chickens, milk, cheese, and beans. And tourism, foreign retirement communities, and casino gaming are becoming important, especially in northern Corozal District.

cabañas, fresh flowers in the rooms, high-thread-count sheets, and, in some suites, hot tubs. **Pros:** wild, sexy, hip. **Cons:** some find it outlandish; can be buggy; not in a particularly scenic area. ⊠ *Mile 40½ Old Northern Hwy., Maskall Village* ☎ *225/5555, 800/627–8227 in U.S.* ⊕ *www.maruba-spa.com* ➷ *8 rooms, 10 suites* ⟁ *In-hotel: restaurant, bar, pool, gym, spa.*

NORTHWEST ORANGE WALK DISTRICT

This district borders both Mexico and Guatemala, and holds four areas well worth the time it takes to visit them: Lamanai Archeological Reserve, at the edge of the New River Lagoon; the Mennonite communities of Blue Creek and Shipyard; the 260,000-plus acres of the Río Bravo Conservation Area; and Gallon Jug lands, 130,000 acres in which the remarkable Chan Chich Lodge nestles.

These areas, especially Río Bravo and Gallon Jug, are best visited on an overnight or multinight stay. You can visit Lamanai on a day trip by boat or road from Orange Walk Town (and guided day tours are also available from Belize City, San Pedro, and Caye Caulker), though it's well worth at least an overnight stay. If you're staying in Blue Creek, you can go to Río Bravo, Lamanai, and even Gallon Jug and Chan Chich on a day trip, but the poor roads will slow you down, and you'll have little time to explore. Both the Gallon Jug and Programme for Belize (Río Bravo) lands are private, with gated entrances, so you'll need advance permission to visit.

ORANGE WALK TOWN

52 mi (85 km) north of Belize City.

Orange Walk Town is barely on the radar of visitors, except as a jumping-off point for boat trips to Lamanai, road trips to Gallon Jug and Río Bravo, or as a place to gas up en route from Corozal to Belize City. Though its population of around 14,000, mostly Mestizos, makes it the third-largest urban center in Belize (after Belize City and San Ignacio), it's more like a "county seat" in an agricultural area than a city. In this case, it's county seat of Belize's sugarcane region, and you'll see big tractors and trucks hauling sugarcane to the Tower Hill refinery. Happily, the new bypass around Orange Walk Town has reduced through traffic.

The town's atmosphere will remind you a little of Mexico, with signs in Spanish, a central plaza, and sun-baked stores set close to the streets. The plaza, near the Orange Walk Town Hall, has a small market (daily except Sunday and holidays) with fruits, vegetables, and inexpensive local foods for sale. This was once the site of Fort Cairns, which dates to the Caste Wars of the 19th century.

GETTING HERE AND AROUND

Orange Walk Town is about midway between Belize City and Corozal Town, a drive of an hour or so from either one. Most buses on the busy Northern Highway route will drop you in Orange Walk Town. There is no scheduled air service.

TIMING

The only reason most visitors stop at Orange Walk Town is to take a day trip to Lamanai, up the New River. An excellent restaurant, Nahil Mayab, makes a stopover in Orange Walk more pleasant.

SAFETY AND PRECAUTIONS

While generally safe, Orange Walk Town does have its share of crack problems, and the cheap bars can get rough on weekend nights.

CLOSE UP

What's in a Name?

The name *Belize* is a conundrum. According to *Encyclopaedia Britannica,* it derives from *belix,* an ancient Mayan word meaning "muddy water." Anyone who's seen the Belize River swollen by heavy rains can vouch for this description. Others trace the name's origin to the French word *balise* (beacon), but no one can explain why a French word would have caught on in a region once dominated by the English (Belize was known as British Honduras). Perhaps nothing more than a drinker's tale, another theory connects Belize to the Mayan word *belikin* (road to the east), which also happens to be the name of the national beer. A few even think the name may have come from Angola in West Africa, where some of the slaves who were brought to the West Indies and then to Belize originated, and where today there is a town called Belize. Some say Belize is a corruption of Wallace, the name of a Scottish buccaneer who founded a colony in 1620; still others say the pirate wasn't Wallace but Willis, that he wasn't Scottish but English, and that he founded a colony not in 1620, but in 1638.

There was indeed a pirate named Wallace, a onetime lieutenant of Sir Walter Raleigh's who later served as Tortuga's governor. Perhaps it was liquor or lucre that turned him into a pirate, but at some point in the early to mid-1600s he and 80 fellow renegades washed up near St. George's Caye. They settled in and lived for years off the illicit booty of cloak-and-dagger raids on passing ships. In 1798 a fleet of 31 Spanish ships came to exterminate what had now blossomed into an upstart little colony. Residents had a total of one sloop, some fishing boats, and seven rafts, but their maritime knowledge enabled them to defeat the invaders in two hours. That was the last Spanish attempt to forcibly dislodge the settlement, though bitter wrangles over British Honduras's right to exist continued for nearly a century.

We may never know whether Wallace and Willis were one and the same, but what's in a name, anyway? Grab a Belikin and come up with a few theories of your own.

WHAT TO SEE

Las Banquitas House of Culture. Las Banquitas House of Culture is worth an hour of your time. This small museum—the name refers to the little benches in a nearby riverside park—presents changing exhibitions on Orange Walk District history and culture. Among the permanent displays are artifacts from Lamanai and Cuello. An outdoor auditorium is used for occasional events. ⊠ *Main and Bautista Sts.* ☎ *322/0517* 🖃 *Free, some exhibits have small fees* ☉ *Mon.–Fri. 8:30–4:30.*

WHERE TO EAT AND STAY

For expanded hotel reviews, visit Fodors.com.

$ ✕ **El Establo Bar & Grill.** This friendly, family-run eatery is at the edge of
LATIN AMERICAN town near the northern end of the Orange Walk bypass. The dining room has a rustic charm, with displays of antiques and old photographs. It's a great place to stop for lunch or dinner (open daily) on a trip between Belize City and Corozal Town. Enjoy local dishes such as

cow-foot soup, *escabeche, relleno negro,* and, of course, rice and beans. A house speciality is shrimp with garlic and spices. ⊠ *Northern Hwy. Bypass* ☎ *322/0094.*

$$
LATIN AMERICAN
★
✗ **Nahil Mayab.** Orange Walk Town may be the last place you'd expect to find an upscale restaurant like this, with its Maya-inspired decor and well-prepared food. Nonetheless, it opened here, on a corner behind the Shell station, in December 2008 to rave reviews and has enjoyed steady business since. Sit in the tropical gardens in the back, or in air-conditioned comfort in the main dining room, and enjoy a cold drink and a delicious shrimp or conch ceviche appetizer (the small is only BZ$6, enough for two). For a main course try the smoky-flavor pork fajitas (BZ$18) or one of the Yucatán-inspired dishes such as Hor'och, corn balls cooked in back beans and served with stew chicken. ⊠ *Corner of Santa Ana and Guadeloupe sts., 2 blocks behind Shell Station* ☎ *322/0831* ⊕ *www.nahilmayab.com* ☉ *Closed Sun.*

¢
★
🖽 **Hotel de la Fuente.** Orlando de la Fuente's place is a step up from the other hotels in Orange Walk Town, and the low room rates, starting at BZ$70 with air-conditioning (plus 9% tax), complimentary Wi-Fi, fridge, and cable TV, put it among the best values in northern Belize. **Pros:** excellent value; attractive and modern rooms; central location. **Cons:** no pool. ⊠ *14 Main St.* ☎ *322/2290* ⊕ *www.hoteldelafuente.com* ➥ *18 rooms, 2 suites* ♿ *In-room: kitchen, Internet, Wi-Fi.*

$
🖽 **Lamanai Riverside Retreat.** It's many miles from the Lamanai ruins (though on a street called Lamanai Alley), but this hotel with just three cabins is pleasantly set right beside the New River, the water route to the famous Mayan ruins. **Pros:** Relaxing riverside setting; friendly owners; open-air riverside dining. **Cons:** It's a short hike into town; pesky mosquitoes at times. ⊠ *Lamanai Alley* ☎ *302/3955* ✉ *lamanairiverside@ hotmail.com* ➥ *3 cabañas* ♿ *In-room: Wi-Fi. In-hotel: restaurant, bar.*

¢
🖽 **St. Christopher's Hotel.** On a quiet street near the Banquitos House of Culture and backing up on the New River, this family-run hotel has simple but clean rooms, with tile floors and brightly colored bedspreads, at reasonable rates. **Pros:** unpretentious, family-run hotel; central location near market and the river; a good value. **Cons:** no-frills rooms. ⊠ *10 Main St.* ☎ *302/1064* ⊕ *www.stchristophershotelbze.com* ➥ *25 rooms* ♿ *In-room: a/c, Wi-Fi.*

LAMANAI

About 2½ hrs northwest of Belize City, or 24 mi (39 km) south of Orange Walk Town.

GETTING HERE AND AROUND

There are several ways to get here. One option is to drive on the mostly unpaved road from Orange Walk Town. Turn west at the Orange Walk fire station. From here go to Yo Creek, then southwest to San Felipe Village, a total of 24 mi (39 km). In San Felipe, go straight for another 12 mi (19 km) to reach the ruins. Another route by road is via Shipyard—the unpaved road to Shipyard is just south of Orange Walk. The best way to approach the ruins, however, is by boat, which takes about an hour and a half from Orange Walk. Boats leave around

9 am from the Tower Hill bridge over the New River on the Northern Highway, about 6 mi (10 km) south of Orange Walk. The cost is BZ$80 per person. If you are staying at Lamanai Outpost, the lodge has its own boats to take you up the river, departing from a dock just south of the dock where the other boats depart. Some hotels in Orange Walk Town arrange Lamanai tours, with pickup and drop-off at the hotel, also for around BZ$80 per person. You can also take a 15-minute charter plane trip from Belize City, around BZ$400 for up to four persons.

A SPECIAL PLACE

What makes Lamanai so appealing is its setting on the west bank of a beautiful 28-mi-long (45-km-long) lagoon, one of only two waterside Mayan sites in Belize (the other is Cerros, near Corozal Town). Nearly 400 species of birds have been spotted in the area and a troop of howler monkeys visits the archaeological site regularly. Lamanai Outpost Lodge offers guided tours of the ruins, but you can also explore the site on your own.

TIMING

Most people visit Lamanai as a day trip, but to see the ruins and explore the New River Lagoon, you'll want to overnight at least, and preferably stay two to three nights.

Contacts Jungle River Tours ✉ *20 Lovers La., Orange Walk Town* ☎ *615/1712.* **Reyes and Sons** ✉ *Tower Hill Bridge, Northern Hwy., Orange Walk Town* ☎ *322/3327.*

EXPLORING

Lamanai. Lamanai ("submerged crocodile" in Yucatec Maya) is Belize's longest-occupied Mayan site, inhabited until well after Christopher Columbus discovered the New World in 1492. In fact archaeologists have found signs of continuous occupation from 1500 BC until AD 1700.

Lamanai's residents carried on a lifestyle that was passed down for millennia, until the Spanish missionaries arrived. You can still see the ruins of the missionaries' church near the village of Indian Church. The same village also has an abandoned 19th-century sugar mill. With its immense drive wheel and steam engine—on which you can still read the name of the manufacturer, Leeds Foundry of New Orleans—swathed in strangler vines and creepers, it's a haunting sight.

In all, 50 to 60 Mayan structures are spread over this 950-acre archaeological reserve. The most impressive is the largest Pre-Classic structure in Belize—a massive, stepped temple built into the hillside overlooking the New River Lagoon. Many structures at Lamanai have only been superficially excavated. Trees and vines grow from the tops of temples, and the sides of one pyramid are covered with vegetation. On the grounds you'll find a visitor center with educational displays on the site, and pottery, carvings, and small statues, some dating back 2,500 years. Local villagers from the Indian Church Village Artisans Center set up small stands on the grounds to sell handmade carvings, jewelry, and other crafts, along with T-shirts and snacks. ✉ *Near Indian Church Village, Orange Walk District* ⌂ *BZ$20* ⊙ *Daily 8–5.*

WHERE TO STAY

For expanded hotel reviews, visit Fodors.com.

$$$ ⬛ **Lamanai Outpost Lodge.** Perched on a low hillside on the New River
★ Lagoon, this eco-lodge's well-designed thatch cabañas sit amid lovely
gardens and have porches with lagoon views. **Pros:** gorgeous setting
on the New River Lagoon; easy access to Lamanai ruins; good tours.
Cons: high rates; not easy to get to. ⊠ *Indian Church* ☎ *220/9444,
954/636–1107 in U.S., 888/733–7864 U.S. reservation office* ⊕ *www.
lamanai.com* ⬅ *20 cabañas* ⚷ *In-room: no a/c, no TV. In-hotel: restau-
rant, bar, business center* ⦿| *Multiple meal plans.*

MENNONITE COMMUNITIES

2½ hrs northwest of Belize City.

GETTING HERE AND AROUND

The progressive Blue Creek Mennonite community is about midway
between Orange Walk Town and Chan Chich Lodge—it's 33 mi (54
km) from Orange Walk Town via Yo Creek, August Pine Ridge, and
San Felipe, and 36 mi (59 km) from Chan Chich. About 6 mi (10 km)
beyond Blue Creek, you'll enter the Río Bravo reserve managed by Pro-
gramme for Belize. Shipyard is accessed via an unpaved road that turns
west off the Northern Highway just south of Orange Walk Town. Little
Belize is visited by driving northeast from Orange Walk Town via San
Estevan. Keep in mind that these are conservative communities; they
shun the use of cars and motorized farm equipment.

TIMING

Unless you have a particular interest in Mennonite culture or farming
methods, you'll probably just drive through the Mennonite communi-
ties in Northern Belize, as there are no specific tourist sites or activities.
With rare exceptions, Mennonites shun tourism development.

EXPLORING

The Mennonite religion emerged in Holland during the Protestant
Reformation in the 16th century. These Anabaptists (so called for the
practice of baptizing adults) first moved to Germanic lands—many in
Belize still speak Low German, which combines elements of German
and Dutch—and then to Prussia, the United States (mainly Pennsyl-
vania), and Manitoba, Canada. In the 1950s some 3,000 Mennonites
emigrated to Belize, where they established communities in the Orange
Walk and Cayo districts. Today there are an estimated 12,000 Men-
nonites in Belize.

The Blue Creek Mennonite community is predominantly progressive,
which means the Mennonites accept modern conveniences such as auto-
mobiles and electricity. Near the Linda Vista shopping center is a small
bed-and-breakfast where you can stay and learn a little about Men-
nonite life in Belize.

Both Little Belize and Shipyard are primarily farming areas, and have
no hotels or tourist facilities, but the unexpected sight, on dusty rural
roads, of pale-skin folks in old-fashioned dress—the women in long plaid

dresses and the men with suspenders and straw hats—in horse-pulled buggies will remind you of how diverse Belizean culture really is.

WHERE TO STAY

For expanded hotel reviews, visit Fodors.com.

$ ⬚ **Hillside Bed and Breakfast.** After Mennonites John and Judy Klassen finished raising their 10 children, they opened this small B&B in Blue Creek village. **Pros:** beautiful vistas over Blue Creek; nice way to get to know a little of the Mennonite community. **Cons:** basic, motel-like rooms; cabañas require a steep climb; B&B accessible only if you have your own transport. ⊠ *Main Rd., Blue Creek Village* ☎ *323/0155* ✍ *bchillsideb_b@yahoo.com* ⬚ *5 rooms, 2 cabañas* ⬚ *In-room: a/c, kitchen, no TV* ⊟ *No credit cards.*

RÍO BRAVO CONSERVATION AND MANAGEMENT AREA

2½ hrs west of Belize City.

GETTING HERE AND AROUND

By car from Belize City or Corozal Town, drive to Orange Walk Town, going into town rather than taking the bypass. Turn west at the crossroads near the Orange Walk fire station toward Yo Creek. Continue on through Yo Creek, following the road that turns sharply south and goes through San Lazaro, Trinidad, and August Pine Ridge villages. At San Felipe, 24 mi (40 km) from Orange Walk Town, the road turns sharply to the west (right) at a soccer field. Follow this road for about 7 mi (12 km) to the Río Bravo bridge and into Programme for Belize lands. If you don't have your own car, contact Programme for Belize and ask if they can arrange transportation for you from Orange Walk Town, Belize City, or elsewhere.

Contact Programme for Belize ☎ *277/5616* ⊕ *www.pfbelize.org.*

TIMING

If you decide to visit this remote part of Belize, you'll want to spend a minimum of two days, and preferably longer, so you can explore the jungle, La Milpa, and nearby Mestizo villages.

SAFETY AND PRECAUTIONS

Once away from the Field Station grounds, you're in the bush. Keep a wary eye out for poisonous snakes, scorpions, stinging insects, and other denizens of the wild.

EXPLORING

Río Bravo Conservation & Management Area. Created with the help of distinguished British naturalist Gerald Durrell, the Río Bravo Conservation & Management Area spans 260,000 acres near where Belize, Guatemala, and Mexico meet. The four-hour drive from Belize City takes you through wildlands where you may encounter a troupe of spider monkeys, wildcats, flocks of ocellated turkeys, a dense shower of butterflies—anything but another vehicle.

Managed by Belize City–based Programme for Belize, a not-for-profit organization whose mission is the wise use and conservation of Belize's natural resources, the Río Bravo Conservation Area contains some 400 species of birds, 70 species of mammals, and 200 types of trees. About half of Río Bravo is managed as a nature reserve, and the rest is managed to generate income, from forestry and other activities, including tourism. Programme for Belize is actively involved in research and conservation programs to protect endangered species including the Yellow Headed Parrot.

Within the reserve's borders are more than 60 Mayan sites; many have yet to be explored. The most important is **La Milpa,** Belize's largest site beside Caracol and Lamanai. At its height between AD 400 and 830, La Milpa was home to almost 50,000 people. The suburbs of this city spread out some 3 mi (5 km) from the city center, and the entire city encompassed some 30 square mi (78 square km) in area. So far, archaeologists have discovered 20 large courtyards and 19 stelae.

Visiting Río Bravo, like the other areas of northwestern Orange Walk, is best done in a four-wheel-drive vehicle. You must make arrangements to visit in advance with **Programme for Belize** (☎ 227/5616 *in Belize City* ⊕ *www.pfbelize.org*), as the entire Río Bravo conservation area is managed by this private, nonprofit organization, and the main road through its lands is gated. You also need advance reservations to stay at La Milpa Field Station *(see below)*. Staying overnight or longer at this field station is the best way to see Río Bravo, but you can visit it briefly on a day trip. Another field station, at Hill Bank, primarily serves as a research base for sustainable forest management but visitors with an interest in forest research can be accommodated in two cabañas and a dorm that sleeps six. Contact Programme for Belize *(see above)* for information.

Guides and information are available at La Milpa Field Station. Chan Chich Lodge, Lamanai Outpost Lodge, and other hotels also can arrange visits with guides to La Milpa and the Río Bravo Conservation & Management Area.

WHERE TO STAY

For expanded hotel reviews, visit Fodors.com.

$$ ☒ **La Milpa Field Station.** About 3 mi (5 km) from La Milpa Mayan site, this field station is a combination of hotel and summer camp. **Pros:** You'll feel like an archaeologist here; quiet and remote setting surrounded only by nature; dining room serves filling Belizean dishes. **Cons:** Not for the party crowd; not easy to get to. ⊠ *Programme for Belize, 1 Eyre St., Belize City* ☎ *227/5616* ⊕ *www.pfbelize.org* ⤴ *8 rooms in 4 cabins, 1 dormitory (30 beds)* ⚅ *In-room: no a/c, no TV. In-hotel: restaurant* ⦿ *Multiple meal plans.*

GALLON JUG

3½ hrs west of Belize City.

GETTING HERE AND AROUND

The easiest and fastest way to get here is by charter airplane (about BZ$500, depending on the number of people, to Gallon Jug Estates' own 3,000-foot airstrip). Javier Flying Service in Belize City has three- and five-passenger Cessna airplanes, and charter flights are also available through Maya Island Air and Tropic Air. Chan Chich will arrange the flights for you. With advance permission, you can also drive to Chan Chich, about 3½ hours from Belize City. Follow the route to Río Bravo *(see above)* and continue on through Programme for Belize lands to the Cedar Crossing gatehouse and into Gallon Jug lands. It's a long but beautiful drive, and you're almost certain to see a considerable amount of wildlife along the dirt road.

Contacts Javier Flying Service ✉ *Municipal Airport, Belize City* ☎ *824/0460* ⊕ *www.javiersflyingservice.com.*

TIMING

You'll want to spend at least two to three days at Chan Chich, longer if you have a keen interest in birding or wildlife spotting.

SAFETY AND PRECAUTIONS

Despite its remote location, Chan Chich is one of the safest places in Belize.

EXPLORING

Gallon Jug. The 130,000 acres of Gallon Jug Estates, owned by the family of the late Sir Barry Bowen, is home to old-growth mahogany trees and many other tropical hardwoods along with more than 350 species of birds and many mammals and reptiles. Jaguar sightings are fairly common around the Chan Chich Lodge, averaging around one a week. You're likely to see toucans, many different hummingbirds, and flocks of parrots.

This is a working farm that produces coffee and raises cattle, cacao, and corn. It's the only truly commercial coffee operation in Belize—elevations in Belize are too low to grow high-quality Arabica coffees that thrive at over 4,000 feet—producing Gallon Jug Estates coffee from coffee trees on more than 100 acres. Gallon Jug Estates also produces hot sauces and delicious mango jams, which are for sale in Belize and elsewhere. Tours of the coffee plantings and the production facility, along with other farm tours, can be arranged through Chan Chich Lodge.

Chan Chich is one of the best jungle lodges in Central America, if not the world. This is the only place to stay in the area. It's possible to visit on a day trip from La Milpa Field Station, Blue Creek Village, or even Lamanai or Orange Walk Town, but you need your own transportation and advance permission to come on the gated Gallon Jug lands.

WHERE TO STAY

For expanded hotel reviews, visit Fodors.com.

$$$$ ⊡ **Chan Chich Lodge.** Coca-Cola, Belikin, and shrimp farming "Belizeanaire" Sir Barry Bowen, who died in a crash of his private plane in 2010, built this remote jungle lodge, arguably the best lodge in Belize and one of the top lodges in Central America. **Pros:** The best birding and wildlife spotting in Belize; so safe you don't lock your cabaña's door; magnificent setting within Mayan site; understated but eminently comfortable accommodations. **Cons:** somewhat difficult to get to; definitely splurge prices. ✉ *Chan Chich Lodge, P.O. Box 37, Belize City* ☎ *223/4419, 800/343–8009 in U.S.* ⊕ *www.chanchich.com* ⟿ *12 cabañas, 1 2-bedroom villa* ⚅ *In-room: a/c, no TV, Wi-Fi. In-hotel: restaurant, bar, pool, business center* ⦿ *Multiple meal plans.*

Fodor's Choice
★

COROZAL BAY

Corozal Bay, or Chetumal Bay as it's called on most maps, has tropically green and turquoise waters. It provides a beautiful waterside setting for Corozal Town and a number of villages along the north side of Corozal District. Tarpon, bonefish, permit, and other game fish are not hard to find. The drawback is that there are few natural beaches in Corozal District, although some hotels have trucked in sand to build human-assisted beach areas. Also, there's no good snorkeling or diving locally, and the Belize Barrier Reef is several long hours away by boat. However, the Mexican border and the outskirts of the city of Chetumal are only 9 mi (14½ km) away. Chetumal, capital of Quintana Roo state, with a modern mall, big-box stores such as Walmart and Sam's Warehouse, and air-conditioned multiplex movie theaters, provides a bustling counterpoint to easygoing Corozal.

At the border, the Commercial Free Zone (usually called the Corozal Free Zone, though that's not its official name) promises duty-free goods and cheap gas. The reality is a little less appealing. Most of the duty-free items are cheap trinkets from China and Taiwan, and the gasoline, while one-third cheaper than in Belize, is more expensive than in Mexico. Plus, to sample the questionable enticements of the Free Zone, visitors have to formally exit Belize, paying exit taxes and fees totaling BZ$37.50 per person.

Casinos have sprung up on the Belize side of the border, at the edge of the Commercial Free Zone. There are three casinos: the **Princess Casino**, the larger **Royal Princess Casino** (both associated with the Princess Hotel & Casino in Belize City), and the largest of the three, the **Las Vegas Casino**. The Las Vegas casino has 54,000 square feet of gaming area, making it, according to management, the largest in Central America. In addition to more than 300 slot machines, plus blackjack, roulette, and poker, the casino has gaming areas designed to appeal to visitors from Asia, with Pai Gow, mah-jongg, and other games. There's also a private club area for high rollers from Mexico and elsewhere. The casinos are busy on weekends, but the crowds thin out during the week.

COROZAL TOWN

95 mi (153 km) north of Belize City.

Settled by refugees from the Yucatán during the 19th-century Caste Wars, Corozal is the last town before Río Hondo, the river separating Belize from Mexico. Though thoroughly ignored by today's travelers, this friendly town is great for a few days of easy living. It's hard not to fall into the laid-back lifestyle here—a sign at the entrance of a local grocery used to advertise "Strong rum, 55 Belize dollars a gallon."

English is the official language in Corozal, but Spanish is just as common here. The town was largely rebuilt after Hurricane Janet nearly destroyed it in 1955, so it's neat and modern. Many houses are clapboard, built on wooden piles, and other houses are simple concrete-block structures, though the growing clan of expats is putting up new houses that wouldn't look out of place in Florida. One of the few remaining colonial-era buildings is a portion of the old fort in the center of town.

GETTING HERE AND AROUND

Corozal Town is the last stop on the Northern Highway before the Mexico border. There's frequent bus service from early morning to early evening on the Northern Highway from Belize City. Maya Island Air and Tropic Air have a total of 10 daily flights to San Pedro, Ambergris Caye (some flights also stop in Sarteneja), but no other scheduled air service. A daily water taxi operated by San Pedro-Belize Express Water Taxi runs between Corozal Town and San Pedro with a stop on demand at Sarteneja.

Contacts Maya Island Air ☎ 223/1140 ⊕ www.mayaregional.com. **San Pedro Belize Express** ✉ Ambergris Caye, San Pedro ☎ 226/2194 ⊕ www.sanpedrowatertaxi.com. **Tropic Air** ✉ San Pedro, Ambergris Caye ☎ 226/2012 ⊕ www.tropicair.com.

HOT PROPERTY

Corozal District has become a hot spot for expats seeking property for retirement and snowbirds looking for a vacation home. Several hundred foreign expats live in Corozal District, and the numbers are growing. They're attracted by the home prices—a two-bedroom, modern home in a nice area near the water can go for less than US$150,000, though you can always pay more. An expat "friendship luncheon" is held the second Tuesday of every month at 1:30 pm at the Purple Toucan Restaurant and Bar, 7th Avenue South in Corozal Town. Newcomers and wannabes welcome.

TIMING

Although from your base in Corozal Town you can make day trips to the ruins at Cerros and Lamanai, the main activity for visitors in Corozal is simply relaxing and hanging out.

SAFETY AND PRECAUTIONS

Corozal Town and the rural parts of the district are among the safer places in Belize, but crack cocaine has made its ugly appearance here (police seem oddly unable to find and close down the crack houses), which makes petty thefts an issue.

Contacts ADO Bus Line ✉ ADO Terminal, Av. Insurgentes and Av. Belice, Chetumal, Quintana Roo, Mexico ☎ 51/33–24–24, 01/800–009–9090 ⊕ www.ado.com.mx.

EXPLORING

Corozal Art Gallery. Opened in mid-2011, the Corozal Art Gallery offers the work of many Belizean artists, often at lower prices than at galleries in San Pedro and elsewhere, along with art by owner Anne de Strijcker who signs her paintings "Iver." ✉ Reyes Plaza, 4th Ave. & 3rd St. N, Corozal Town ☎ 633/8679 ⊕ www.corozalartgallery.weebly.com ⊘ Closed Sun.

Corozal Town Hall. The history of Corozal, including a graphic portrayal of the brutality of colonial rule on the indigenous people, is depicted in a strikingly beautiful mural by Manuel Villamar Reyes on the wall of the Corozal Town Hall. ⊠ *1st St. S.* ☎ *422/2072* 🎟 *Free* ⊙ *Mon.–Sat. 9–noon and 1–5.*

Corozal Cultural Center. A landmark 1886 former lighthouse houses the Corozal Cultural Center, along with a museum and the Belize Tourist Industry Association information center. As of this writing the Center is closed, but efforts are underway to get it open again. If it reopens, you can see the spiral staircase and parts of the original beacon. Also on display are handblown rum bottles and a traditional Mayan thatch hut. ⊠ *Off 1st Ave. at edge of Corozal Bay* ☎ *422/3176.*

Gabrielle Hoare Market. This market on 6th Avenue has stalls selling a good selection of local fruits and vegetables. ⊠ *6th Ave., Corozal Town* ☎ *No phone* ⊙ *Mon.–Sat 6:30–5:30; Sun. 6:30–3.*

Santa Rita. Not far from Corozal are several Mayan sites. The closest, Santa Rita, is a short walk from the town's center. It's on a low hill across from the Coca-Cola plant. Only a few of its structures have been excavated, and there's currently no visitor center open, so it takes some imagination to picture this settlement, founded in 1500 BC, as one of the district's major trading centers. You can walk around the site without paying an admission fee. 🎟 *Free.*

WHERE TO EAT

¢ ✕ **Cactus Plaza.** For a great bargain, grab a seat at this popular nightspot
MEXICAN and order a plateful of tacos, tostadas, *salbutes* (stuffed tortillas), and other Mexican finger foods. You won't be stuck with a big check: most entrées are less than BZ$8. Everything is freshly made and tasty. ⊠ *6 6th St. S, 2 blocks west of bay* ☎ *442/0394* ▭ *No credit cards* ⊙ *Closed Mon.–Wed.; no lunch.*

$ ✕ **Patty's Bistro.** Relocated to a new, slightly larger location, Patty's Bistro
LATIN AMERICAN (sometimes spelled Patti's) still serves the best food in town, the service
★ is sprightly and friendly, and prices are low. For a local treat, try the conch ceviche or conch soup. A delicious fried-chicken dinner with salad and mashed potatoes is only BZ$9. Stew chicken with rice and beans is BZ$8. ⊠ *2nd St. N* ☎ *402/0174* ⊙ *Closed Sun.*

$ ✕ **Venky's.** For takeout curries and other Indian food at modest prices,
INDIAN Venky's is the spot. It's run by an Indian who formerly was a chef at Las Vegas Casino in the Free Zone and at a leading Belize City Indian restaurant. As for atmosphere, Venky's has absolutely none, and you're likely to find laundry hanging near the takeout counter, but the delicious curries, mostly BZ$12 to BZ$18, come in servings big enough for two, with rice and tortillas on the side. Also try the chicken tikka masala. ⊠ *5th Ave., across from immigration office* ☎ *402/0536* ▭ *No credit cards.*

WHERE TO STAY

For expanded hotel reviews, visit Fodors.com.

$ 🏨 **Almond Tree Hotel Resort.** Directly on the bay just south of town,
★ Almond Tree Hotel Resort raises the bar on Corozal Town lodging. **Pros:** Newest and nicest accommodations in town; attractive rooms; swimming pool; bayside setting with views. **Cons:** On the South End, a bit away from the main part of town; restaurant is hit-or-miss. ⊠ *425*

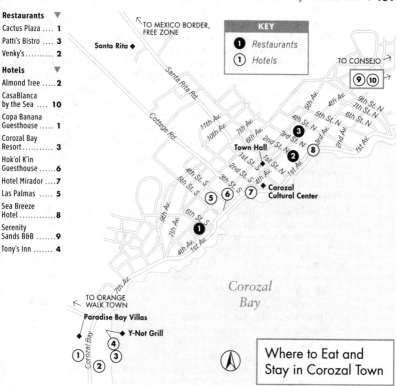

KEY

❶ *Restaurants*

① *Hotels*

TO MEXICO BORDER,
FREE ZONE

Santa Rita ◆

TO CONSEJO →

Corozal
Cultural Center

Town Hall

*Corozal
Bay*

TO ORANGE
WALK TOWN

Paradise Bay Villas

◆ Y-Not Grill

Where to Eat and
Stay in Corozal Town

Bayshore Dr., South End ☎ *628/9224* ⊕ *www.almondtreeresort.com* ⤶ *6 rooms, 3 suites* ⟳ *In-room: kitchen, Wi-Fi. In-hotel: restaurant, bar, pool* ⧆ *No meals.*

$ ⊞ **CasaBlanca by the Sea.** In a quiet village, with views of Chetumal across Corozal Bay, this is a fine place to get away, but be aware that the location is off the beaten path, and there's not much to do around the hotel. **Pros:** Charming bayside setting; great place to get away; well-maintained. **Cons:** Taxi or your own transportation required to visit town; no pool or real beach; bay swimming is only so-so. ⊠ *8 mi (13 km) northeast of Corozal Town, Consejo* ⟴ *From Corozal Town, take 4th Ave. north, which becomes unpaved Consejo Rd. Stay on Consejo Rd. 7 mi (10 km), through Consejo village. CasaBlanca is at end of road on bay* ☎ *423/1018* ⊕ *www.casablancabelize.com* ⤶ *7 rooms, 3 suites* ⟳ *In-hotel: restaurant, bar.*

$ ⊞ **Copa Banana Guesthouse.** This homelike hotel, painted bright yellow, has five sunny suites with air-conditioning and cable TV carved out of two houses across the street from Corozal Bay, at BZ$110 plus 9% hotel tax. **Pros:** handy to have kitchen privileges; tastefully decorated; close to bay. **Cons:** bike ride or long walk to heart of town. ⊠ *409 Bay Shore Dr.* ☎ *422/0284* ⊕ *www.copabanana.bz* ⤶ *5 rooms, 1 apartment* ⟳ *In-room: kitchen, Wi-Fi. In-hotel: pool.*

$ ⊡ **Corozal Bay Resort.** This casual bayside resort has nicely done, moderately priced thatch cabañas in pastel colors and a restaurant and bar beside the pool. **Pros:** nice tropical feel to thatch cabañas; breezy bayside setting. **Cons:** beach has seawall. ⊠ *Almond Dr., Off Northern Hwy. at south end of Corozal Town* ☎ *422/2691* ⊕ *www.corozalbayinn.com* ↩ *10 cabañas* ⚐ *In-room: Wi-Fi. In-hotel: restaurant, bar, pool, beach.*

$ ⊡ **Hok'ol K'in Guest House.** Yucatec Maya for "coming of the rising sun," Hok'ol K'in, founded by an American Peace Corps veteran and now operated by Belizeans, is a friendly small budget hotel on the Corozal bayfront. **Pros:** breezy bayfront location within walking distance of most shops and restaurants; friendly management; some handicap-accessible rooms. **Cons:** no-frills rooms. ⊠ *89 4th Ave., Corozal Town* ☎ *422/3329* ⊕ *www.corozal.net* ↩ *10 rooms and 1 2-bedroom apartment* ⚐ *In-room: no a/c. In-hotel: restaurant, bar.*

¢ ⊡ **Hotel Mirador.** Breathless as you may be when climbing to the fifth-level terrace of this budget hotel—the highest point in Corozal Town—it's worth it for the breathtaking views of Corozal Bay and town. **Pros:** beautiful views from top-floor patio; good value in the heart of town. **Cons:** layout of stairs precludes bay views from many rooms; mediocre food at Chinese restaurant; not for those who have trouble with a lot of stairs. ⊠ *4th Ave. and 2nd St. S* ☎ *422/0189* ⊕ *www.mirador.bz* ↩ *24 rooms* ⚐ *In-room: Wi-Fi. In-hotel: restaurant, bar.*

¢ ⊡ **Las Palmas.** Totally renovated and rebuilt, this whole property is upmarket but still a good value with doubles starting at BZ$90 plus 9% tax. **Pros:** handy central location in town; good value. **Cons:** not on the water; limited secure parking. ⊠ *123 5th Ave.* ☎ *422/0196* ⊕ *www.laspalmashotelbelize.com* ↩ *20 rooms* ⚐ *In-room: Wi-Fi.*

¢ ⊡ **Sea Breeze Hotel.** Run by a Welshman who lived for years in Antigua, Guatemala, the Sea Breeze is your best budget choice in Corozal, with rooms starting at BZ$35 plus tax. **Pros:** good value in a budget hotel; convivial owner; cheapest breakfasts in town. **Cons:** rooms are simple; those without A/C can be hot. ⊠ *23 1st Ave.* ☎ *422/3051* ⊕ *www.theseabreezehotel.com* ↩ *7 rooms* ⚐ *In-room: a/c (some), Wi-Fi. In-hotel: restaurant, bar.*

$$ ⊡ **Serenity Sands B&B.** This upscale, eco-oriented B&B is hidden away
★ off the Consejo Road north of Corozal Town, with four tastefully decorated rooms on the second floor with private balconies overlooking the gardens, Belizean art, and locally made hardwood furniture. **Pros:** beautiful rooms; family-friendly; eco-oriented management. **Cons:** in an out-of-the-way location, best visited with a rental car; not directly on the water. ⊠ *Mile 3, Consejo Rd.* ✛ *From Corozal Town, take 4th Ave. north, which becomes unpaved Consejo Rd. Stay on Consejo Rd. 3 mi (5 km). Turn right at Serenity Sands sign. Follow this road .75 mi (1.2 km); turn at first right and follow this road turning left, then right until you reach Serenity Sands* ☎ *669/2394* ⊕ *www.serenitysands.com* ↩ *4 rooms and 1 2-bedroom house* ⚐ *In-room: no TV* ⦿ *Breakfast.*

$ ⊡ **Tony's Inn.** One of the oldest hotels and restaurants in Corozal, Tony's
★ Inn is still going strong, with spacious rooms with ice-cold A/C and a popular bayside restaurant and bar. **Pros:** breezy bayside setting; excellent open-air restaurant on-site; safe guarded parking. **Cons:** rooms

have been here a long time and while updated could still use some work. ⊠ *South End* ☎ *422/2055* ⊕ *www.tonysinn.com* ⇆ *24 rooms* ⌂ *In-room: a/c, Wi-Fi. In-hotel: restaurant, bar.*

COPPER BANK

12 mi (20 km) southeast of Corozal Town.

Copper Bank is a tidy and small (population around 500) Mestizo fishing village on Corozal Bay. The village is something of a footnote to the nearby Mayan site, Cerros.

Cerros. Like the Tulum site in Mexico, Cerros Maya is unusual in that it's directly on the water. With a beautiful setting on Corozal Bay, at the mouth of the New River, the late Pre-Classic center dates to 2000 BC and includes a ball court, several tombs, and a large temple. Altogether, there are some 170 structures, many just mounds of stone and earth, on 52 acres. Bring plenty of bug spray—mosquitoes can be fierce here. ⊠ *2½ mi (4 km) north of Copper Bank* ⊹ *The easiest way to get to Cerros is to charter a boat in Corozal Town, for a 15-minute ride across the bay. By car, follow signs from the south end of Corozal Town and cross the New River on the Pueblo Nuevo hand-cranked ferry. At the T-intersection, go left to Copper Bank Village and follow signs west to Cerros* ☎ *No phone* ☜ *BZ$20* ⊙ *Daily 8–5.*

GETTING HERE AND AROUND

One way to get here is by boat from Corozal, which costs around BZ$80–BZ$160 for up to four people. You can also drive from Corozal Town, crossing the New River on the hand-pulled ferry. To get to the ferry from Corozal, take the Northern Highway south toward Orange Walk Town (watch for ferry sign). Turn left and follow this unpaved road for 2½ mi (4 km) to the ferry landing. After crossing the river, drive on to a T-intersection and turn left for Copper Bank. The trip to Copper Bank takes about a half hour, but longer after heavy rains, as the dirt road can become very bad. As you enter Copper Bank, watch for signs directing you to "Cerros Maya."

TIMING

Most visitors do only a day trip to see the Cerros ruins, although if you want a quiet, off-the-main-path place to finish writing that novel, you won't find a better place than Cerros Beach Resort.

WHERE TO STAY

For expanded hotel reviews, visit Fodors.com.

$ ▦ **Cerros Beach Resort.** Cerros Beach Resort is an off-the-grid option for good food and simple lodging on Corozal Bay, near the Cerros ruins. **Pros:** low-key, crowd-free small resort on the bay; tasty food; good value. **Cons:** mosquitoes sometimes can be pesky. ⊹ *Near Cerros Maya site on north side of Cerros peninsula; entering Copper Bank village, watch for signs to Cerros Beach Resort. The resort will arrange for a pickup by boat from Consejo or Corozal Town for parties of 5 or more* ☎ *623/9763* ⊕ *www.cerrosbeachresort.com* ⇆ *4 cabañas* ⌂ *In-room: no TV, Wi-Fi. In-hotel: restaurant, bar, beach, water sports* ⊙ *Restaurant closed Mon.*

¢ ⊡ **Copper Bank Inn.** If you want to get away from it all: Copper Bank Inn, your only lodging option in the village of Copper Bank, is a white, two-story, 10,000-square-foot house, with a small bar and restaurant, serving tasty local food at modest prices. **Pros:** you may be the only guest at the hotel; pool. **Cons:** you'll likely be the only guest. ⊠ *Copper Bank Village* ☎ *665/7907, 619/278–9823 in U.S.* ⊕ *www.copperbankinn. com* ⊅ *10 rooms* ⚬ *In-room: a/c, Wi-Fi. In-hotel: restaurant, bar, pool.*

SARTENEJA

40 mi (67 km) from Corozal Town.

This small Mestizo and Creole community, the largest fishing village in Belize, enjoys a bay setting that makes it one of the most relaxed and appealing in all of Belize. You can swim in the bay here, though in many places the bottom is gunky.

Lobster fishing and pineapple farming are the town's two main industries, and Sarteneja is also a center for building wooden boats. Most residents speak Spanish as a first language, but many also speak English.

Visitors and real-estate buyers are beginning to discover Sarteneja, and while tourism services are still minimalist, several small guesthouses are now open, and there are a few places to get a simple, inexpensive bite to eat.

GETTING HERE AND AROUND

Driving to Sarteneja from Corozal Town takes about 1½ hours via the New River ferry and a second, bay-side ferry across Laguna Seca. The road is unpaved and can be very muddy after heavy rains. You also can drive to Sarteneja from Orange Walk Town, a trip of about 40 mi (67 km) and 1½ hours. There are several Sarteneja Bus Line buses a day, except Sunday, from Belize City via Orange Walk Town. The trip from Belize City takes 3½ to 4 hours and costs BZ$10.

The daily water taxi between Corozal Town and San Pedro will drop you at Sarteneja on request. You also can hire a private boat in Corozal to take you and your party to Sarteneja.

Sarteneja has an airstrip, with two flights daily on Tropic Air from San Pedro (BZ$191 round trip).

Contacts Tropic Air ⊠ *Ambergris Caye, San Pedro* ☎ *226/2012* ⊕ *www. tropicair.com.*

TIMING

Once you visit Shipstern and take a splash in the sea, you've just about exhausted all there is to do in Sarteneja. So bring several good books and enjoy the slow-paced village life.

EXPLORING

Shipstern Wildlife Reserve. About 3½ mi (6 km) west of Sarteneja on the road to Orange Walk or Corozal is the Shipstern Wildlife Reserve. You pass the entrance and visitor center as you come into Sarteneja. The 31 square mi (81 square km) of tropical forest forming the reserve are, like the Crooked Tree Wildlife Sanctuary, a paradise for bird-watchers. Currently, Shipstern is owned and operated by a Swiss conservationist nongovernmental organization, but it is slated to become a Belize national park managed by the Belize Audubon Society. More than 300 species of birds have been identified here. Look for egrets (there are 13 species), American coots, keel-billed toucans, flycatchers, warblers, and several species of parrots. Mammals are in healthy supply as well, including pumas, jaguars, and raccoons. The butterfly farm next to the visitor center is now a small education area, and butterflies are being repopulated.

Nearby, the museum at Mahogany Park focuses on the history and uses of this beautiful tropical hardwood. There is a botanical trail leading from the visitor center, with the names of many plants and trees identified on small signs. Admission, a visit to the butterfly farm, and a one-hour guided tour of the botanical trail is BZ$10 per person. You can add a tour of the Mahogany Park for BZ$5. Other tours are available, including a full-day lagoon tour for BZ$150 for a group of up to six. Bring plenty of bug juice. ☎ 223/4533 ⊕ *www.belizeaudubon.org* 🎫 *BZ$10* ⊙ *8–5.*

WHERE TO EAT

¢ ✕**Liz Fast Food.** Some of the tastiest and certainly the cheapest food in Sarteneja is at this little restaurant, hardly more than a glorified street stall. Liz Perez and her sister prepare and serve delicious, inexpensive tacos, salbutes, and garnaches for breakfast, lunch, and dinner. At lunch, locals stop by for spicy Buffalo chicken wings. It's hard to spend more than BZ$5 here for a filling meal. ⊠ *Primitivo Aragon St., opposite the old church* ☎ *No phone* ▭ *No credit cards.*

MEXICAN

$ ✕**Ritchie's Place.** This no-frills, family-run restaurant serves the freshest seafood in Sarteneja, from a whole fried snapper (BZ$15) to fish empanadas to conch and lobster in season. Owner Ritchie Cruz lives next door to his restaurant, which is just a few tables on a screened porch. Even a hungry family of four will find it difficult to spend more than BZ$50 for dinner unless you buy specials such as lobster. ⊠ *Front St., near public pier* ☎ *423/2031* ▭ *No credit cards.*

SEAFOOD

WHERE TO STAY

For expanded hotel reviews, visit Fodors.com.

$ 🏠**Candelie's Seaside Cabañas.** Our picks for the best, and best-value, lodging in Sarteneja are two seaside cottages at Candelie's. **Pros:** Spacious private cottages; lovely waterside location; good value; friendly manager. **Cons:** Mattresses are a little thin. ⊠ *On waterfront at west end of village, N. Front St.* ⊠ *P.O. Box 77, Orange Walk Town* ☎ *423/2005* ✉ *candeliescabanas@yahoo.com* ⇆ *2 cottages* ▭ *No credit cards* ✱ *No meals.*

¢ 🏠**Fernando's Seaside Guesthouse.** Lounge on the second-floor veranda of this small waterfront guesthouse and watch the fishing boats anchored just a few hundred feet away. **Pros:** seaside location; water views from the comfy second-floor porch. **Cons:** rooms at back lack a sea view and can be hot. ⊠ *North Front St.* ☎ *423/2085* ⊕ *www.cybercayecaulker. com/sarteneja.html* ⇆ *4 rooms* ♿ *In-room: a/c.*

4

The Cayo

WORD OF MOUTH

"Don't miss out on the ATM [Actun Tunichil Muknal] cave—it's is one of the coolest and most interesting things we've ever done! Our guide Ben was awesome. This was way more adventurous than they describe—maybe it's so the fun isn't spoiled or maybe it's just because the safety regulations are different in Central America (I really can't believe we didn't have to sign a waiver for this). Regardless, we are avid swimmers and hikers so we loved it."

—sessa

By Lan Sluder

When the first jungle lodges opened in the early 1980s in the Cayo, few thought this wild area would become a tourist magnet. The mountainous region was too remote. Roads were bad. Restaurants were few. What would visitors do, besides visit cattle ranches and orange groves? After three decades of thoughtful development, and remarkable growth in lodging, restaurants, and other infrastructure, more than half of those touring Belize visit the Cayo during their trip, making this the country's second most popular destination after Ambergris Caye.

You'll be lured by the rugged beauty of the region, with its jagged limestone hills, low green mountains where tapirs, peccaries, and jaguars still roam free, and its boulder-strewn rivers and creeks. You'll also appreciate its diversity, in a compact and accessible package. Even on a short stay, you can canoe or kayak rivers, hike remote mountain trails, visit a Mayan ruin, explore underground cave systems, go birding or wildlife-spotting, shop at a busy local market, chill out at a sidewalk café, and dine in style at a good restaurant or by lamplight at a jungle lodge.

You'll know when you've entered the Cayo a few miles east of Belmopan. Running along the Belize River for miles (though it's usually not visible from the road), the Western Highway then winds out of the valley and heads into a series of sharp bends. In a few minutes you'll see cattle grazing on steep hillsides and horses flicking their tails. The Creole people who live along the coast give way to Maya and Mestizos; English is replaced by Spanish as the predominant language (though English is also widely spoken). The lost world of the Maya comes alive through majestic, haunting ruins. And the Indiana Jones in you can hike through the jungle, ride horseback, canoe down the Macal or Mopan River, and explore incredible caves such as Actun Tunichil Muknal, which some call the highlight of their entire Central American experience.

The best of Cayo is mostly found in its scenic outdoors—nearly two-thirds of the district is in national parks and forest reserves. But you should also take time to appreciate its towns and villages. Belmopan, once just a sleepy village, is in the middle of a boom, with new government and residential construction fueled by real-estate speculation. These days, it's officially known as Belmopan City, one of only two such official government destinations, the other of course being Belize City. San Ignacio is a thriving little town, its downtown area usually busy with locals come to buy supplies and backpackers looking to book tours or grab a bite and a Belikin at one of San Ignacio's many inexpensive eateries. The village of San Antonio is predominantly Mayan. Benque

Viejo del Carmen, just 2 mi (3 km) from the border, feels more Guatemalan than Belizean, and Spanish Lookout, the Mennonite center, with its well-kept farms and no-nonsense farm-supply and general stores, could as well be in the U.S. Midwest.

El Cayo is Spanish for "the caye" or key. Local residents still call San Ignacio Town "El Cayo," or just "Cayo," which can potentially create some confusion for outsiders. The name is thought to have originally referred to the small island formed where the Macal and Mopan rivers meet at San Ignacio.

ORIENTATION AND PLANNING

GETTING ORIENTED

The Cayo's main connection to the coast is the Western Highway, a paved two-lane road running 78 mi (128 km) between Belize City and the Guatemala border. The highway is in generally good condition, but shoulders are narrow, and parts of the highway can be slick after rains. Secondary roads, mostly unpaved and sometimes difficult to drive on, branch off the Western Highway, leading to small villages and to the Mountain Pine Ridge, the Spanish Lookout Mennonite area, and various jungle lodges. The Mountain Pine Ridge is crisscrossed by an extensive network of gravel and dirt roads, some formerly logging trails.

At Belmopan the paved Hummingbird Highway is Belize's most scenic road, cutting 54 mi (90 km) southeast through the Maya Mountains to Dangriga, passing Five Blues Lake and Blue Hole national parks. Mile markers on the Hummingbird start in Dangriga.

Belmopan City. While hardly a tourism hot spot, Belmopan is Belize's newest city (in Belize the government designates urban areas as cities, towns, or villages) with a growing number of restaurants and hotels. The U.S. Embassy has a US$50 million compound here, and around Belmopan are several excellent jungle lodges.

San Ignacio. The hub of western Belize, San Ignacio is a bustling little town. Here you can arrange tours (often at lower prices than from jungle lodges), shop at the local market, and get a good meal, whether you're hungry for Indian, Italian, French, Chinese, Belizean, or even Sri Lankan.

Benque Viejo. The last town in Belize before you reach Guatamala, Benque Viejo has modest art and cultural attractions worth checking out, as well as a Mayan burial cave.

Mountain Pine Ridge. The largest forest reserve in Belize, the Mountain Pine Ridge covers almost 300 square mi (777 square km). Crisscrossed by old logging roads and small rivers, and dotted with waterfalls, the Mountain Pine Ridge—at elevations up to 3,000 feet and higher, and noticeably cooler than other parts of Cayo—is the gateway to the Chiquibul wilderness and to Caracol.

TOP REASONS TO GO

National Parks and Reserves. About 60% of the Cayo District is national parks and reserves. Good news if you like hiking, birding, wildlife-spotting, canoeing, or engaging in other outdoor activities.

Caves. Although there are caves in Toledo and elsewhere in Belize, the Cayo has the biggest and most exciting ones. Actun Tunichil Muknal is the top caving experience in Belize.

Mayan Sites. The Cayo is home to the largest and most important Mayan site in Belize; Caracol has more than 35,000 buildings, though so far only a handful have been excavated. Cayo also has the most easily accessible Mayan sites in the country, Cahal Pech and

Xunantunich, along with dozens of smaller ones.

Jungle Lodges. With more than 30 jungle lodges, the Cayo has far more than all the other districts of Belize combined. There's a lodge for every budget, from bare-bones cabins along the Mopan River to ultradeluxe villas on the Macal River and in the Mountain Pine Ridge.

Mountains. The Mountain Pine Ridge's 2,000–3,500 foot mountains, with their waterfalls, caves, and rivers, provide a welcome respite from the heat and humidity of lowland Belize, though most of it is not broad-leaf jungle but piney woods not too different from the Southern Appalachians in Alabama or Georgia.

Caracol. The largest and most important Mayan site in Belize, Caracol rivals Tikal in Guatemala in historical importance and archaeological interest.

PLANNING

WHEN TO GO

The best time to visit the Cayo is late fall and winter, when temperatures generally are moderate. During the peak of the dry season, March to May or early June, at the lower elevations around San Ignacio and Belmopan daytime temperatures can reach 100°F, though it does cool off at night. Seasonal rains usually reach the Cayo in June. In summer, after the rains begin, temperatures moderate a little, but humidity increases. Year-round the Mountain Pine Ridge is noticeably cooler and less humid than anywhere else in Belize, and at times in winter it can be downright chilly.

GETTING HERE AND AROUND

AIR TRAVEL

Most people bound for the Cayo fly into Belize City. Tropic Air has flights from Belize City, San Pedro, and Placencia to Belmopan, but there are no scheduled flights to San Ignacio. For charter flights, there is an airstrip near San Ignacio at Central Farm. Blancaneaux Lodge and Hidden Valley Inn in the Mountain Pine Ridge have their own private airstrips and helipads.

BUS TRAVEL

A number of bus lines provide frequent service—about once every half hour during daylight and early evening hours—between Belize City and Cayo, with a stop in Belmopan. Among small bus companies authorized to operate on the Western Highway are BBOC, Westline, Shaw's, Guerra's, and Middleton. James Line runs from Belize City to Belmopan, and then down the Hummingbird and Southern highways to Dangriga and Punta Gorda. The cost between Belize City and San Ignacio is BZ$7 on a local, and BZ$9 on an express if you can find one. From Belize City it is about BZ$5 to Belmopan and BZ$8 to Benque Viejo. Buses are typically old U.S. school buses and are not air-conditioned. Most buses from Belize City leave from what is still called the Novelo's terminal on West Collet Canal Street, even though the Novelo's bus line is defunct. Look for any bus with "Cayo" or "Benque" on the front. There is a bus station in Belmopan, while buses stop at an unmarked stand in Memorial Park in the center of San Ignacio. A new visitor center, under construction in San Ignacio, is expected to include a bus terminal. If in doubt, ask locally where to catch buses, or simply flag down the next bus you see. The Belize Bus Blog (⊕ *www.belizebus.wordpress.com*) has helpful information on bus travel.

CAR TRAVEL

Other than the well-maintained two-lane Western Highway, most roads in the Cayo are unpaved and dusty in the dry season, muddy in the rainy season. To get to the Cayo, simply follow the Western Highway from Belize City. Watch out for "sleeping policemen" (speed bumps) near villages along the route. If you didn't rent a car in Belize City, you can rent one in San Ignacio. Of the handful of car-rental companies in San Ignacio, Cayo Auto Rentals is the cheapest, with vehicles from around BZ$90 a day plus tax.

Information Cayo Auto Rentals ⊠ *81 Benque Rd., San Ignacio* ☎ *824/2222* ⊕ *www.cayoautorentals.com.* **Flames Auto Rental** ⊠ *Joseph Andrews Dr., San Ignacio* ☎ *824/3198* ⊕ *www.flamesautorentals.com.* **Matus Car Rental** ⊠ *18 Benque Rd., San Ignacio* ☎ *824/2005* ⊕ *www.matuscarrental.com.*

TAXI TRAVEL AND SHUTTLES

Taxis are plentiful in and around San Ignacio, but they're expensive if you're going to a remote lodge. For example, a taxi from San Ignacio to one of the Mountain Pine Ridge lodges is likely to be BZ$100 or more, and to one of the lodges west of San Ignacio on the Macal River, about BZ$50–$60 (rates are negotiable). Taxis within San Ignacio shouldn't be more than BZ$6 to most points and around BZ$15 to Bullet Tree. Collective taxis (they pick up as many passengers as possible) run to the Guatemala border for BZ$5 or less. Colectivos to Bullet Tree are BZ$2. You can find taxis at Market Square in the middle of town, near Burns Avenue, or call **Cayo Taxi Association** (☎ *824/2196*) or **Savannah Taxi** Association (☎ *824/2155*), or have your hotel call one.

Many Cayo hotels and lodges provide van transportation from the international airport and other points in Belize City for about BZ$250–BZ$300 for up to four people one way. Several operators run shuttle vans between Belize City and San Ignacio for around BZ$70–BZ$100 per person. Among those currently offering shuttles are William's Shuttle, Belize Shuttles and Transfers, and Aguada Hotel. Of these, we highly recommend William's Shuttle. Dutch expat William Hofman is reliable, friendly, and knowledgeable; he charges around BZ$90 per person for two between Belize City and San Ignacio, or BZ$70 per person for three or more. Belize Shuttles and Transfers has both on-demand and fixed-time shuttle trips, the fixed-time shuttles costing BZ$70 per person. Cahal Pech Village Resort does transfers from Cancún, Mexico, to San Ignacio, an eight- or nine-hour trip, for BZ$800 for up to three persons.

A taxi from the international airport near Belize City to San Ignacio will cost around BZ$180–BZ$250 (for the cab, not per person), depending on your bargaining ability.

Shuttle Vans Aguada Hotel ⊠ *On street opposite La Loma Luz hospital, Santa Elena* ☎ *804/3609* ⊕ *www.aguadahotel.com.* **Belize Shuttles and Transfers** ⊠ *Philip Goldson International Airport, Ladyville* ☎ *631/1749, 757/383–8024 U.S. number* ⊕ *www.belizeshuttlesandtransfers.com.* **Cahal Pech Village Resort** ⊠ *Cahel Pech Hill, San Ignacio* ☎ *824/3740* ⊕ *www.cahalpech.com.* **William's Shuttle** ☎ *620/3055* ⊕ *www.parrot-nest.com/belize-shuttle.html.*

EMERGENCIES

In case of emergency, there's the private Seventh Day Adventist hospital La Loma Luz, in Santa Elena, east of San Ignacio, as well as the public hospital, San Ignacio Hospital, in a new facility west of town on Bullet Tree Road. Belmopan is home to the Western Regional Hospital, and there is a clinic in Benque Viejo.

For police and fire, dial 911.

Hospitals La Loma Luz Hospital ⊠ *Western Hwy., Santa Elena* ☎ *824/2087.* **San Ignacio Hospital** ⊠ *Bullet Tree Rd., San Ignacio* ☎ *824/2066.* **Police.** San Ignacio ☎ *911, 824/2022.***Western Regional Hospital** ⊠ *North Ring Rd., Belmopan* ☎ *822/2263.*

MONEY MATTERS

Although U.S. dollars are accepted everywhere, you can exchange money at the border crossing near Benque Viejo. Money changers at the border often give slightly better rates. Banks in San Ignacio include Atlantic Bank, Belize Bank, and ScotiaBank. They are all downtown on Burns Avenue. Belmopan has branches of all five of Belize's retail banks—Atlantic Bank, Belize Bank, First Caribbean International Bank, Heritage Bank, and ScotiaBank. ScotiaBank also has an office in Spanish Lookout. All these bank offices have ATMs, and all but Heritage Bank accept ATM cards issued outside Belize.

Banks Atlantic Bank ⊠ *17 Burns Ave., San Ignacio* ☎ *824/2347* ⊠ *Garden City Plaza, Belmopan* ☎ *822/0693.* **Belize Bank** ⊠ *Constitution Dr., Belmopan* ☎ *822/2303.* ⊠ *16 Burns Ave., San Ignacio* ☎ *824/2031.* **First Caribbean International Bank** ⊠ *Market Square, Belmopan* ☎ *822/2382.* **Scotia-Bank** ⊠ *Burns Ave. at Riverside St., San Ignacio* ☎ *824/4191.* ⊠ *Center Rd.* ☎ *823/0328* ⊠ *1915 Constitution Dr., Belmopan* ☎ *822/1412.*

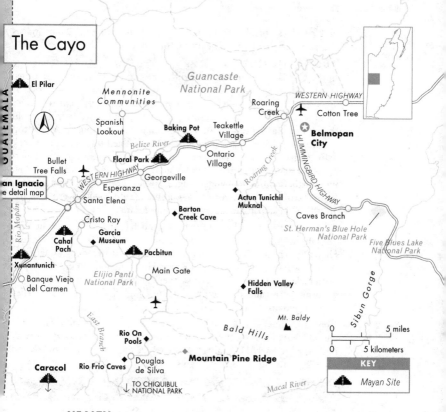

The Cayo

HEALTH

While the Cayo normally has relatively few mosquitoes, thanks to the porous limestone terrain that doesn't allow water to stand in puddles, there are occasional outbreaks of dengue fever. Dengue, which causes flu-like symptoms, and, in more serious cases, death from internal bleeding, is transmitted by the bite of *Aedes aegypti* and *Aedes albopictus* mosquitoes. These species are most active in the early morning and late afternoon. Travelers, especially during the rainy season, should consider using insect repellent with DEET. There is no preventative medicine for dengue.

Health standards in the Cayo are high. The water in San Ignacio and Santa Elena comes from a treated municipal system, so it's safe to drink, though many people prefer the taste of bottled water. Resorts in the region have their own safe water systems.

ABOUT THE RESTAURANTS

San Ignacio is the culinary center of the Cayo, with some two dozen restaurants. Most are small spots with only a few tables. Restaurants offer Indian, French, German, and even Sri Lankan fare as well as burritos and beans. Prices, designed to appeal to the budget and mid-level travelers who stay in town, rarely rise above the moderate level. At the jungle lodges outside San Ignacio prices are much higher. Some lodges charge BZ$65 or BZ$70, or more, for dinner.

ABOUT THE HOTELS

In the Cayo you have two very different choices in accommodations: jungle lodges and regular hotels. Jungle lodges, regardless of price or amenities, offer a close-to-nature experience, typically next to a river or in a remote mountain setting. Most lodges house their guests in thatch cabañas patterned after traditional Mayan houses. At the top end, lodges such as Blancaneaux Lodge and The Lodge at Chaa Creek deliver a truly deluxe experience, with designer toiletries, imported mattresses, and decor that wouldn't be out of place in *Architectural Digest*. At the other end, some budget lodges have outdoor bathrooms and thin foam mattresses. In between are a number of mid-level lodges providing an off-the-beaten-path experience at moderate prices.

Whereas the district's lodges are back-a-bush (a Belizean expression for "out in the jungle"), the Cayo's hotels are in towns or along the Western Highway. The area's least expensive hotels are clustered in San Ignacio, one of the backpacker centers of Belize. Hotels in and around Belmopan are a little more expensive because they cater to people in the capital on government business. Whether hotel or jungle lodge, most properties in the Cayo are small, typically run by the owner.

Generally, inexpensive hotels and lodges maintain the same rate year-round, though some may discount a little in the off-season (generally mid-April to early December). More expensive places have off-season rates 20% to 40% less than high season.

WHAT IT COSTS IN BELIZE DOLLARS					
	¢	$	$$	$$$	$$$$
RESTAURANTS	under BZ$8	BZ$8–BZ$15	BZ$15–BZ$25	BZ$25–BZ$50	over BZ$50
HOTELS	under BZ$100	BZ$100–BZ$200	BZ$200–BZ$300	BZ$300–BZ$500	over BZ$500

Restaurant prices are per person for a main course at dinner. Hotel prices are for two people in a standard double room, including tax and service.

VISITOR INFORMATION

There's currently no official tourism information office in the Cayo. However, a new BZ$3 million welcome center in the heart of San Ignacio is under construction, with completion scheduled for late 2012. The welcome center is expected to have a visitor information center, along with several shops and kiosks and a bus terminal. The Belize Tourism Board Web site, ⊕ *www.travelbelize.org*, has some information on visiting the Cayo. Eva's restaurant, when run by Englishman Bob Jones and his wife, was known as the place to get the latest news and gossip about Cayo. It is now under new management and is a ghost of its former self.

The Cayo Star, a weekly tabloid newspaper published by veteran journalist Alberto August and edited by his wife Nyani Azueta-August, has news about the Cayo and particularly about San Ignacio. It's available online at ⊕ *www.belizenews.com* and elsewhere. San Ignacio Town (⊕ *www.sanignaciotown.com*), though a commercial site, has considerable information on the Cayo. Best of Cayo (⊕ *www.bestofcayo.com*) offers opinionated recommendations of the best places to stay, eat, shop, and drink in San Ignacio. For an idiosyncratic local perspective, visit Santa Elena resident Ray Auxillou's blog, Western Belize Happenings (⊕ *westernbelizehappenings.blogspot.com*). Belmopan City Online (⊕ *www.belmopancityonline.com*) has tourism information on the Belmopan area, along with local news of the capital city. For information on how Belize is governed, visit the National Assembly of Belize Web site (⊕ *www.nationalassembly.gov.bz*)—the site also explains how you can request a visit to the legislative assembly.

BELMOPAN CITY

50 mi (80 km) southwest of Belize City.

It used to be said that the best way to see Belize's capital was through the rearview mirror as you head toward San Ignacio or south down the Hummingbird. It's a dreary cluster of concrete office buildings plunked in the middle of nowhere, surrounded by residential areas that may remind you of a central Florida town, proving that cities can't be created overnight. However, with the opening of the main campus of the University of Belize in Belmopan in 2002, the relocation of several embassies (including the U.S. embassy) from Belize City to Belmopan, and new commercial activity around the capital, Belmopan—finally—is showing signs of life. The population has grown to more than 18,000. Commercial and retail activities are booming, and there's a minor real-estate gold rush going on. Despite all this, however, except for a brief ride around the city to see the government buildings and perhaps a stop for lunch or to shop the local market, we recommend that you spend your time at nearby sites rather than in the city itself.

GETTING HERE AND AROUND

Belmopan is about 48 mi (79 km) on the Western Highway from Belize City. By car, it takes about an hour. As you approach the turnoff to Belmopan from the east, Guanacaste National Park is on your right. Turn south at Mile 47.4 on the Hummingbird Highway. In about 1¼ mi (2 km) you'll come to the main entrance road to Belmopan City. Turn left and soon you come to the Ring Road, a two-lane road that circles the city and provides access to the streets inside the ring. The jungle lodges near Belmopan are located either off the Western or Hummingbird highways.

TIMING

The highlights of Belmopan City itself can easily be seen in a couple of hours. If you're staying at a jungle lodge nearby, you can easily spend two to three days exploring the wider area, or longer, if you want to see the San Ignacio area while basing here.

GREAT ITINERARIES

IF YOU HAVE 3 DAYS IN THE CAYO

Upon arrival at the international airport, immediately head to the Cayo by rental car, bus, or shuttle van. If you have time, stop en route at the Belize Zoo. Stay at one of the jungle lodges around San Ignacio if it's within your budget. On your first full day in the Cayo, explore the area around San Ignacio, visiting the Xunantunich Mayan ruins, the Belize Botanic Gardens on the grounds of duPlooy's Lodge, and Green Hills Butterfly Farm. Assuming you have the energy, walk the Rainforest Medicine Trail and spend a few minutes at the Natural History Center, both at the Lodge at Chaa Creek. On the second day, if you're not planning to move on to Tikal in Guatemala after your stay in the Cayo, at least take a day tour there. Guided tours from San Ignacio usually include van transportation to the Tikal park, a local guide at the site, and lunch. Alternatively, if you're heading to Tikal later, take a day trip to Caracol in the Mountain Pine Ridge. Bring a picnic lunch and make stops at Río

On pools, the Río Frio cave, and a waterfall, such as Five Sisters. On your final day, take a full-day guided tour of Actun Tunichil Muknal. Have dinner at a restaurant in San Ignacio.

IF YOU HAVE 5 DAYS IN THE CAYO

Rent a car at the international airport and drive to a jungle lodge near Belmopan. If you have time, stop en route at the Belize Zoo and do a quick driving tour of the capital. On your first full day, go cave tubing and take a zip-line canopy tour at Jaguar Paw. Alternatively, for a more strenuous day, take a trip with Caves Branch Adventure Camp, or do its cave-tubing trip. End your day with dinner at your lodge and a night wildlife-spotting tour. On your second day, drive down the Hummingbird Highway and take a dip in the inland Blue Hole. Also, visit St. Herman's Cave or go horseback riding at Banana Bank Lodge. On the third day, move on to a jungle lodge near San Ignacio or in the Mountain Pine Ridge and follow the three-day itinerary.

EXPLORING THE BELMOPAN CITY AREA

At the edge of Belmopan City is **Guanacaste**, Belize's smallest national park. The **Belize Zoo** (⇨ *See Chapter 2*), one of the country's top sights, is only a half hour east of Belmopan via the Western Highway. **Actun Tunichil Muknal**, the cave that many view as one of the top sights and experiences in the region, is not far from Belmopan, off Mile 52.5 of the Western Highway. Neither is the **Nohoch Che'en Caves Branch** archeological park, accessible on a paved road off the Western Highway at Mile 37, with its exhilarating cave tubing. Belmopan is also the gateway to the **Hummingbird Highway**, Belize's most scenic roadway and home to the inland **Blue Hole** and **Five Blues Lake**. If you have an interest in Belizean history and politics, the **George Price Centre for Peace and Development** is a museum, library, and cultural center focused on Belize's Founding Father and first prime minister.

George Price Centre for Peace and Development. A permanent exhibit at this cultural center, library, and museum follows the life story of the Right

BUTTERFLY MIGRATIONS

Belize is on the flyway for Sulphur and other butterfly migrations from the U.S. and Canada to and through Central America. The summer migration usually starts in June and can last for several weeks. Among the species of butterflies migrating at this time are Cloudless Sulfur (*Phoebis sennae*), Orange Banded Sulfur (*Phoebis philea*), Ruddy Daggerwing (*Phoebis philea*), Great Southern White (*Ascia monuste*), and Giant Swallowtail (*Heraclides cresphontes*), among many others. Monarchs (*Danaus plexippus*) usually migrate south to and through Belize in the late fall, and northward in the early spring. (Monarchs are believed to be the only species that migrate both north and south.) Butterfly and moth expert Jan Meerman at Green Hills Butterfly Farm estimates that as many as two million butterflies and moths migrate through Belize in a single day during migration season.

Honorable George Price as he led the British colony to independence. Born in 1919 in Belize City, George Price was Belize's first and longest-serving prime minister. The "George Washington of Belize" is widely respected for his incorruptible dedication to the welfare of Belize and Belizeans. There's a sizeable library of books on human rights, peace, and national development, and the center hosts art shows, concerts, and film screenings. George Price passed away September 19, 2011, at age 92, just two days short of the 30th anniversary of Belize's independence. ⊠ *Price Centre Rd., Belmopan* ☎ *822/1054* ⊕ *www.gpcbelize. com* 🎫 *Free* ☉ *Mon.–Thurs. 9–6; Fri. 9–5; Sun. 9–11:30; closed Sat.*

Guanacaste National Park. Worth a quick visit on the way in or out of Belmopan is Belize's smallest nature reserve, Guanacaste National Park, named for the huge guanacaste trees that grow here. Also called monkey's ear trees because of their oddly shaped seedpods, the trees tower more than 100 feet. (Unfortunately, the park's tallest guanacaste tree had to be cut down in 2006, due to safety concerns that it might fall.) The 50-acre park, managed by the Belize Audubon Society, has a rich population of tropical birds, including smoky brown woodpeckers, black-headed trogons, red-lored parrots, and white-breasted wood wrens. You can take one of the eight daily hourly tours, or you can wander around on your own. After, cool off with a refreshing plunge in the Belize River; there's also a small picnic area. ⊠ *Mile 47.7, Western Hwy.* ☎ *223/5004 Belize Audubon Society in Belize City* 🎫 *BZ$5* ☉ *Daily 8:30–4:30; tours every hr 8:30–3:30.*

Hummingbird Highway. Hands down, Hummingbird Highway is the most scenic roadway in Belize. The Hummingbird, a paved two-lane road, runs 54½ miles (91 km) from the junction of the Western Highway at Belmopan to Dangriga. Technically, only the first 32 mi (53 km) is the Hummingbird—the rest is the Stann Creek District Highway, but most people ignore that distinction. As measured from Belmopan at the junction of the Western Highway—the road has a few mileposts running from Dangriga north, but we'll ignore them—the Hummingbird first winds through limestone hill country, passing St. Herman's Cave (Mile 12.2) and the inland Blue Hole (13.1). It then starts rising steeply, with the Maya Mountains on the west or right side, past Five Blue Lake (23). The views, of green mountains studded with cohune palms and tropical hardwoods, are incredible. At the Hummingbird Gap (Mile 26, elevation near 1,000 feet, with mountains nearby over 3,000 feet), you're at the crest of the highway and now begin to drop down toward the Caribbean Sea. At Middlesex village (32), technically the road becomes the Stann Creek District Highway. Now you're in citrus country, with groves of grapefruit and Valencia oranges. At Mile 48.7 you pass the turn-off to the Southern Highway and at Mile 54.5 you enter Dangriga, with the sea just ahead. ⊠ *Belmopan to Dangriga, Hummingbird Hwy., Belmopan* ☎ *No phone.*

⟳ **St. Herman's Blue Hole National Park.** Less than a half hour south of Belmopan, the 575-acre St. Herman's Blue Hole National Park has a natural turquoise pool surrounded by mosses and lush vegetation, wonderful for a cool dip. The "inland Blue Hole" is actually part of an underground river system. On the other side of the hill is St. Herman's Cave, once inhabited by the Maya. There's a separate entrance to St. Herman's. A path leads up from the highway, but it's quite steep and difficult to climb unless the ground is dry. To explore St. Herman's cave beyond the first 300 yards or so, you must be accompanied by a guide (available at the park), and no more than five people can enter the cave at one time. With a guide, you also can explore part of another cave system here, the Crystal Cave (sometimes called the Crystalline Cave), which stretches for miles; the additional cost is BZ$20 per person for a two-hour guided tour. The main park visitor center is 12½ mi (20½ km) from Belmopan. St. Herman's Blue Hole National Park is managed by the Belize Audubon Society. ⊠ *Mile 42.5, Hummingbird Hwy.* ☎ *223/5004 Belize Audubon Society* 🌐 *BZ$10* ⊙ *Daily 8–4:30.*

A WACKY TALE

Five Blues Lake National Park. At Five Blues Lake National Park, until 2006 you were able to hike 3 mi (5 km) of trails, explore several caves, and canoe and swim in this lake with five shades of blue. The lake was a cenote, a collapsed cave in the limestone. In July 2006, despite heavy rains, the water level in the lake began to recede. On July 20, 2006, local residents heard a strange noise "as if the lake were moaning." A giant whirlpool formed, and most of the water in the lake was sucked into the ground. Many of the fish died, and the lake looked like a dry pit. Researchers believe that a sediment "plug" dissolved and the lake drained, like water from a bathtub, into underground sinkholes and caves. As of this writing, the lake has refilled with water, but the park isn't what it was before 2006. The park entrance is about 3½ mi (5¾ km) from the Hummingbird Highway, via a narrow and very rough dirt road. Bikes can be rented in St. Margaret's village, from which village volunteers manage the park, and homestays and overnight camping in the village also can be arranged. ⊠ *At end of Lagoon Rd., off Mile 32, Hummingbird Hwy., St. Margaret's Village.*

CAYO HISTORY

The Maya began settling the Belize River Valley of the Cayo some 4,000 years ago. At the height of the Maya civilization, AD 300 to 900, Caracol, El Pilar, Xunantunich, Cahal Pech, and other cities and ceremonial centers in what is now the Cayo were likely home to several hundred thousand people, several times the population of the district today.

Spanish missionaries first arrived in the area in the early 17th century, but they had a difficult time converting the independent-minded Maya, some of whom were forcibly removed to the Petén in Guatemala.

The first significant Spanish and British settlements were logwood and mahogany logging camps. The town of San Ignacio and its adjoining sister town, Santa Elena, were established later in the 1860s. Though only about 70 mi (115 km) from Belize City, San Ignacio remained fairly isolated until recent times, because getting to the coast by horseback through the bush could take three days or longer. The Western Highway was paved in the 1980s, making it easier to get here. The first jungle lodges began operation, and tourism now vies with agriculture as the main industry.

WHERE TO EAT

In addition to the restaurants listed here, the food and produce stalls at the Belmopan market (**Market Square,** open Monday–Saturday, off Bliss Parade next to the bus terminal on Constitution Drive) are good places to buy tasty Belizean food, snacks, and fruit at inexpensive prices—for example, you can get 10 bananas for BZ$1. On the way to Belmopan, near the Belize Zoo, is a well-known roadside eatery where you can grab a burger and a beer, **Cheers** (⊠ *Mile 31, Western Hwy.* ☎ *822–8014*).

$$ ✕**Barn and Grill.** That's no typo—it is Barn and Grill, and the specialties

BARBECUE here, served in a rough and rustic open-air shed, are beef burgers and steak. The flank steak (BZ$20) is excellent. We've never tried it, but if you're with a group or just have a gigantic appetite, try the Rodeo Big Plate with three flank steaks, two sirloin steaks, two rib eye steaks, and four pork chops, served with mashed potatoes, salad, cole slaw, and tortillas. Serves six, BZ$225 with tax, and you need to give them 24-hours notice. ⊠ *Mile 53, Western Hwy., Belmopan* ☎ *667/5684* ⊙ *Closed Mon.*

$ ✕**Caladium.** In business since 1984, the Caladium is one of the old-

LATIN AMERICAN est businesses in this young capital. Most Belizeans know it, since it's next to the bus station at Market Square. Here you'll find many of the country's favorites on the menu, including fried chicken, tender barbecued pork ribs, traditional rice and beans with chicken, beef, or pork, and cow-foot soup. It's authentic, clean, well-run, and air-conditioned. ⊠ *Market Sq.* ☎ *822/2754* ⊙ *Closed Sun.*

$$ ✕**Chon Saan Palace.** A branch of the well-known Belize City Chinese

CHINESE restaurant has been successfully transplanted to Belmopan, with food that rivals the original. Try local favorites like the shrimp fried rice or curried Singapore noodles from the lengthy Cantonese and Szchuan menu. ⊠ *7069 George Price Blvd., Belmopan* ☎ *822/3388*.

$$ ✕ Corker's. This new dining option, run by the husband-and-wife team
ECLECTIC of Geoff Hatto-Hembling and Sam Buxton from the U.K., has a second-
★ floor space between two banks, Belize Bank and First Caribbean, and
it's next door to the Hibiscus Hotel. To catch any breezes, sit in the cov-
ered, open-air patio, or you can dine inside in the cozy air-conditioned
dining room. The menu is eclectic, ranging from classic English fish and
chips (BZ$18) to a grilled American cheeseburger with fries (BZ$16)
to Indian curries, pasta, steak, pork ribs, and a nice variety of salads.
Drink prices are reasonable—imported Jack Daniels is BZ$6. Open for
lunch and dinner. ⊠ *Hibiscus Plaza, Belmopan* ☎ *822/0400* ⊕ *www.
corkersbelize.com* ☉ *Closed Wed.*

WHERE TO STAY

For expanded hotel reviews, visit Fodors.com.

$$ ⌂ Banana Bank Lodge. Set on the banks of the Belize River, this jungle
★ lodge is one of the best spots for families. **Pros:** good choice for families
and horse lovers; lodge has a swimming pool; guests and owners mingle
at meals. **Cons:** pesky mosquitoes; some object to the lodge's caged birds
and animals. ⊹ *There are two ways to reach Banana Bank. To go by
boat across the Belize River, turn north at Mile 47 of the Western Hwy.
Continue to a split in the road and keep right. At the next sharp turn,
keep right and continue ½ mi (1 km) to the end of the road, park, and
bang the gong to summon a boat from Banana Bank. To go by road:
From the Western Hwy., turn north at Mile 46.9 and cross bridge over
Belize River. Follow gravel/dirt road 3 mi (5 km) to Banana Bank sign.
Turn right and follow dirt road for 2 mi (3 km) to lodge* ☎ *832/2020*
⊕ *www.bananabank.com* ➘ 7 rooms, 7 cabañas, 2 suites △ In-room:
no TV, Wi-Fi. In-hotel: restaurant, bar, pool ⦿ Breakfast.

$$ ⌂ Belize Jungle Dome. This well-appointed small inn near the Belize River
★ has four attractively furnished suites, with tile floors, lots of windows,
and an uncluttered look. **Pros:** intimate upscale accommodations in a
lovely setting; large selection of tours; access to hiking trails, horse-
back riding, and other facilities at nearby Banana Bank Lodge. **Cons:**
stairs to some rooms and the café may be a problem for guests with
mobility limitations. ⊹ *From Western Hwy. turn north at Mile 46.9
and cross bridge over Belize River. Follow gravel/dirt road 3 mi (5 km)
until you see Banana Bank sign. Turn right and follow dirt road 2 mi
(3 km). Belize Jungle Lodge is on the right just before Banana Bank
Lodge* ☎ *822/2124* ⊕ *www.belizejungledome.com* ➘ 1 room, 4 suites,
1 3-bedroom house △ In-room: kitchen, Wi-Fi. In-hotel: restaurant,
bar, pool.

$ ⌂ Bull Frog Inn. More of a mom 'n' pop motel than an inn, with retro-
style furnishings reminiscent of the 1960s, the Bull Frog caters mainly
to government workers and Belizeans on business in Belmopan. **Pros:**
cheerful service; pleasant restaurant. **Cons:** furnishings are a bit run-
down; rooms a bit more expensive than they should be. ⊠ *25 Half
Moon Ave.* ☎ *822/2111* ⊕ *www.bullfroginn.com* ➘ 25 rooms △ In-
hotel: restaurant, bar, business center.

$$ ★ **Caves Branch Adventure Co. & Jungle Camp.** As part of general upgrading, this former no-frills adventure lodge has added hillside "treehouse suites" 20 feet above the ground (from BZ$660 single or double), a multilevel swimming pool with Jacuzzi, and a botanical garden featuring orchids and bromeliads. **Pros:** some of the best adventure tours in Belize; lush jungle setting; swimming pool and botanical gar-

den. **Cons:** in dry weather the river often goes completely dry; not a cheap date. ⊠ *12 mi (19½ km) south of Belmopan, Mile 42½, Hummingbird Hwy.* ☎ *822/2800* ⊕ *www.cavesbranch.com* ⊅ *8 suites, 3 bungalows, 10 cabañas with shared bath, 8 beds in bunkhouse* ☐ *In-room: no a/c, no TV. In-hotel: restaurant, bar, pool, water sports, business center.*

$ **Hibiscus Hotel.** If you want to sleep well and also do some good, try the Hibiscus Hotel, where one-half of the profit from your stay goes to the bird rescue and rehab program at Belize Bird Rescue near Belmopan. **Pros:** central location; good value; some of profits go to a good cause. **Cons:** no pool; basic rooms. ⊠ *Hibiscus Plaza, Melhado Parade, Belmopan* ☎ *822/0400* ⊕ *www.hibiscusbelize.com* ⊅ *6 rooms* ☐ *In-room: a/c, Wi-Fi.*

$$$ ★ **Pook's Hill.** When the lamps are lighted each night on the polished rosewood veranda, this low-key jungle lodge is one of the most pleasant places in the Cayo. **Pros:** well-managed jungle lodge in true jungle setting; on doorstep of Actun Tunichil Muknal; bar and dining room are conducive to guest interaction. **Cons:** insects can be a nuisance. ✛ *At Mile 52 of Western Hwy., head south on unpaved track for 5 mi (8 km)* ☎ *820/2017* ⊕ *www.pookshillbelize.com* ⊅ *11 cabañas* ☐ *In-room: no a/c, no TV. In-hotel: restaurant, bar, business center.*

$ **Yim Saan.** The 25 rooms of this Chinese-owned hotel and restaurant near the entrance to Belmopan's Ring Road may make you think you're in an interstate motel in Alabama rather than in Belize's capital, but they're sparkling clean, with tile baths, air-conditioning, cable TV, Wi-Fi, and in-room phones. **Pros:** clean rooms. **Cons:** not very atmospheric. ⊠ *4253 Hummingbird Hwy.* ☎ *822/1356* ⊅ *25 rooms* ☐ *In-room: Wi-Fi. In-hotel: restaurant, bar.*

THE OUTDOORS

Belmopan and San Ignacio offer a similar lineup of outdoor activities, and since they're only about 20 mi (33 km) apart, even if you are staying in San Ignacio you can enjoy the activities near Belmopan.

BIRDING

Pook's Hill. Although there's good birding in many areas around Belmopan, Pook's Hill lodge (⇨ *see review*), 5½ mi (9 km) off the Western Highway at Mile 52½ is in a league of its own. The birding list from

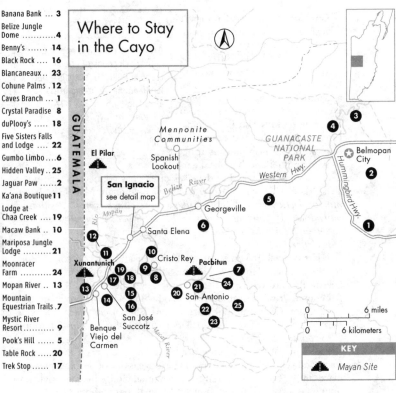

Where to Stay in the Cayo

Pook's Hill includes the Mealy Parrot, Spectacled Owl, Aztec Parakeet, and Keel-billed Toucan. ☎ *820/2017.*

CANOEING AND KAYAKING

The Belize River, wide and mostly gentle (Class I–II) offers good canoeing and kayaking. It was once used by loggers to transport mahogany to Belize City and hosts the annual La Ruta Maya Mountains to the Sea Canoe Race. The multiday race is held in March during the Baron Bliss holiday. You can also canoe or kayak portions of the Caves Branch River (also Class I–II). Many hotels and lodges arrange canoe or kayak trips, including **Caves Branch Adventure Co. & Jungle Lodge** (☎ *822/2800*), off the Hummingbird Highway. Full-day canoe or kayak trips start at around BZ$120 per person.

CANOPY TOURS

You may feel a little like Tarzan as you dangle 80 feet above the jungle floor, suspended by a harness, moving from one suspended platform to another.

Jaguar Paw/Chukka Caribbean. Jaguar Paw, formerly a jungle lodge and now a tour operation and part of the Chukka Caribbean tours empire, off Mile 37 of the Western Highway, has eight zip-line platforms set 100 to 250 feet apart. At the last platform you have to rappel to the ground. There's a 240-pound weight limit. Zip-line tours often are combined

TO AI OR NOT AI

Quite a few lodges and resorts in Belize offer a tweaked version of the sort of all-inclusive you often find in Mexico or Jamaica: optional packages that include nearly everything, such as all meals, guided tours, and sports (fishing, diving, or snorkeling). So when is it worth your money to choose one of these over selecting room, meals, and activities à la carte?

The answer is: It depends. If you're going to a remote caye resort or jungle lodge, you may not have a choice. When you're two hours away from the nearest restaurant, you're pretty much stuck eating at your hotel. On the other hand, at a destination such as Ambergris Caye, Caye Caulker, Placencia, or even San Ignacio, there are many excellent restaurants to choose from. It would be a shame to lock yourself into a single dining experience. A few resorts on Ambergris Caye, mainly those located on the far north end of the island (a long boat ride away from San Pedro), do offer all-inclusive or near all-inclusive packages; however,

for most people, one of the main reasons for coming to Ambergris Caye is the opportunity to sample the variety of restaurants.

The main advantage of an all-inclusive or mostly inclusive package is that you don't have to worry about the details of travel planning. Once you've paid your fixed price, all you have to do is show up at the airport with your bags packed. The resort or lodge picks you up at the Belize International Airport, takes you on guided tours, provides your meals, and practically holds your hand. It's almost like being on a cruise, with few decisions to make. If you're the type of person who likes an organized travel experience, an AI package is probably a great bet for you.

Before you book, be sure to total up the value of what you expect to get at the all-inclusive, and compare that with what you probably would pay on an à la carte basis. If some of the included activities don't appeal to you, it might actually be more expensive to go with an AI.

with cave tubing in the Caves Branch River. The cost is around BZ$120–BZ$180, depending on the tour and whether lunch and transportation are included. ☎ 223/4438 ⊕ *www.chukkacaribbean.com.*

CAVING

The area around Belmopan, with its karst limestone topography, is a paradise for cavers.

Fodor'sChoice ★ **Actun Tunichil Muknal.** The Actun Tunichil Muknal (ATM) cave system runs some 3 mi (5 km) through the limestone of Cayo, just a few miles from Belmopan. ATM is the resting place of the Crystal Maiden, a Maya girl who was sacrificed here, along with at least 13 others, including seven children, hundreds of years ago. If you visit Actun Tunichil Muknal ("Cave of the Stone Sepulcher" in the Mayan language), you will experience what many say are the most awesome sights in all of Central America. You'll see amazing limestone formations, thousand-year-old human calcified skulls and skeletons, and many Mayan artifacts including well-preserved pottery. As long as you are in adequate physical condition—you have to hike almost an hour, swim in neck-deep water, and clamber through dark, claustrophobic underground chambers—this is sure to be the most memorable tour you'll take in Belize. ■ TIP➜ **Although you can drive on your own to the staging area for ATM, you *must* have a licensed and specially trained guide to visit it, as you'll be up close and personal with priceless Maya artifacts.** It's easiest to do an all-day tour from San Ignacio or Belmopan. These tours run around BZ$160–$200, including lunch and the BZ$50 admission fee. ✉ *Mile 52.5, Western Hwy., Belmopan* ☎ *822/3302 National Institute of Culture & History (NICH)* ✇ *BZ$50, plus required guide fee* ☉ *Daily 8–4:30.*

PACZ Tours. The best ATM tour operator, PACZ is operated by Emilo Awe and Jamal Crawford, with help by Bob Jones, formerly of Eva's. The tour costs around BZ$180—including lunch, if you book directly with PACZ. Your hotel or lodge can arrange an ATM or other caving trip but may add an additional fee. ✉ *30 Burns Ave., San Ignacio* ☎ *824/0536* ⊕ *www.pacztours.net.*

St. Herman's Blue Hole National Park. At St. Herman's Blue Hole National Park (⇨ *see review*), at Mile 42 of the Hummingbird Highway, there are two large caves, St. Herman's and the Crystal Cave. Both require a guide to explore (guides are available at the national park visitor center), though you can go without a guide into the first 300 yards of St. Herman's.

CAVE TUBING

♻ The most popular outdoor activity around Belmopan is cave tubing. You float down the Caves Branch River in an inner tube, at points going through dark limestone caves in the subterranean sections of the river.

Caves Branch River has two main entry points: near the former **Jaguar Paw Lodge** (✉ *Off Mile 37 of Western Hwy.*) at **Nohoch Che'en Caves Branch Archeological Reserve** and near **Caves Branch Adventure Co. & Jungle Lodge** (✉ *Off Hummingbird Hwy.* ☎ *822/2800*). The Jaguar Paw access attracts more people, and when several cruise ships are in port at Belize City the river here can be jammed. There's a parking area about ½ mi (1 km) from Jaguar Paw, and here you'll find a number of independent tour guides for cave-tubing tours, which vary in length, generally costing from BZ$50 to BZ$70. Cave-tubing tours from Belize City, Belmopan, and San Ignacio, including transportation and perhaps lunch, cost more, generally BZ$120–$180. ⇨ *See tour operators in Belize City Essentials and the San Ignacio section of this chapter.* Cave-tubing trips from Caves Branch Lodge are longer, require more hiking, and cost more. For example, the "River of Caves" trip, through 7 mi (12 km) of underground caves, takes much of a day and costs BZ$190 per person.

Cave tubing is subject to changes in the river levels. In the dry season (February–May or June), the river levels are often too low for cave tubing. Also, after heavy rains, the water level in the river may be too high to safely float through caves, so in the rainy season (June–November) cave-tubing trips may occasionally be canceled. Always call ahead to check if tours are operating.

Nohoch Che'en Caves Branch Archeological Reserve. Nohoch Che'en Caves Branch is the most-visited archeological site in Belize, mainly because of the number of cruise-ship day-trippers who come here. However, that doesn't diminish the grandeur—and just plain fun—you'll experience when you float on inner tubes in the Caves Branch River through caves that the ancient Maya held sacred. Many Belize City, Belmopan, and San Ignacio tour companies offer cave tubing tours that include transportation, equipment, and a guide, typically for a charge of BZ$100 to BZ$130 per person, although you can drive to the park and do cave tubing on your own with a guide for lower cost. The site, now fairly commercial with a large paved parking lot, changing rooms, concession stands, bar, and shops, is at the end of a paved road off Mile 37 of the Western Highway, near Jaguar Paw (which is no longer operating as a hotel). Tour operators at the site including Caves Branch Outpost (☎ *671/0987* ⊕ *www.cavesbranchoutpost.com*) provide guides and equipment, and independent guides wait to offer tours. With an independent guide you'll pay around BZ$50 to BZ$70, depending on how many caves you want to go float through. Tours start with a 30-minute hike to the cave entrance, and then you float back to a point near the parking lot. There is also a zip line at this site, operated by Jaguar Paw/ Chukka Caribbean. ⊠ *Nohoch Che'en Caves Branch, off Mile 37, Western Hwy., Frank's Eddy Village* ✛ *From Belize City, follow the Western Hwy. to Mile 37. Turn south (left) on a paved road and follow about 6 mi (10 km) to Nohoch Che'en Caves Branch Archeological Reserve parking lot* ☎ *226/2882* 🎟 *BZ$20.*

GOLF

Roaring River Golf Course. The only public golf course on the mainland is Roaring River Golf Course. This 9-hole, 1,933-yard, par-32 jungle course (watch out for the crocs in the water traps) with double tees that let you play 3,892 yards at par 64, was the pet project of an expat South African, Paul Martin, who found himself with some extra time and a lot of heavy earth-moving equipment on his hands. Before long, he'd carved out the greens and bunkered fairways. It's not Pebble Beach, but it's fun, and affordable, too, as fees are only BZ$35 for 9 holes or BZ$50 for 18 holes. After a round of golf, you can sip a Belikin at the clubhouse. Roaring River Golf Course also has air-conditioned cottages for rent, and a restaurant, The Meating Place, for guests and groups. ⊠ *Off Mile 50 1/4, Western Hwy., near Camalote village* ✛ *Turn south at Camalote village at Mile 50¼ of Western Hwy. and follow signs* ☎ *820/2031* ⊕ *www.belizegolf.net.*

HORSEBACK RIDING

Banana Bank Lodge. The best equestrian operator in this part of Belize is Banana Bank Lodge, off the Western Highway near Belmopan. Run by John Carr, a former Montana cowboy and rodeo rider, Banana Bank has more than 100 horses, mostly quarter horses, a large round-pen riding arena, stables, and miles of jungle trails on a 4,000-acre ranch. A two- to three-hour ride costs BZ$120. Night rides are available also, as are horseback riding vacation packages (four-day riding packages from BZ$1,330). ☎ *832/2020* ⊕ *www.bananabank.com.*

5

SAN IGNACIO

23 mi (37 km) southwest of Belmopan.

When you see the Hawksworth Bridge, the only public suspension bridge in Belize, you'll know you've arrived at San Ignacio, the hub of the Cayo district. San Ignacio, with its twin town Santa Elena just to the east, is an excellent base for exploring western Belize. Nearby are three Mayan ruins, as well as national parks and a cluster of butterfly farms.

With its well-preserved wooden structures, San Ignacio is a Belizean town where you might want to linger. Evenings are comfortable and usually mosquito-free, and the colonial-era streets are lined with funky bars and restaurants. It's worth coming at sunset to listen to the eerily beautiful sounds of the grackles, the iridescent black birds that seem to like the town.

GETTING HERE AND AROUND

San Ignacio is less than two hours by car on the Western Highway from Belize City. Coming into San Ignacio is a little confusing. As you go through the "twin town" of Santa Elena and head into San Ignacio, you'll see the Hawksworth Bridge straight ahead. The bridge is one way coming from the west but this is not well marked; those coming from the east and unfamiliar with the area often try to drive across the bridge the wrong way. A sign noting a detour has been erected, directing vehicles to another bridge.

To keep from running afoul of traffic rules, turn right before the Hawksworth Bridge, following the detour to what is called the "lower bridge" or "low lying bridge." Cross this and follow Savannah Road around the sports stadium and, if you're lucky, you'll soon end up back on Western Highway just to the west of San Ignacio. Alternatively, after you cross the river, you can turn left and go through to Burns Avenue, the main street in town.

From San Ignacio, the Western Highway continues on about 9 mi (15 km) to the Guatemala border. This stretch is locally known as the Benque Road.

TIMING

San Ignacio and the jungle lodges around it are used by many visitors to explore western Belize, which easily takes a week or more if you want to see it all.

SAFETY AND PRECAUTIONS

On several occasions in the past decade, armed bandits from nearby Guatemala robbed tourists around San Ignacio. At this writing, the U.S. Embassy had issued a warning about highway banditry on unpaved roads near the Guatemala border, and trips to Caracol may be made only in convoys accompanied by Belize Defence Forces soldiers. Ask locally about any recent incidents before starting road trips to remote areas. However, most visitors say they feel quite safe. As a visitor, you're unlikely to encounter any problems.

EXPLORING SAN IGNACIO AND ENVIRONS

TOP ATTRACTIONS

Fodor's Choice ★ Most tours to **Actun Tunichil Muknal** leave from San Ignacio, although this amazing cave is actually near Belmopan. (⇨ *See Belmopan section above for information.*)

★ **Belize Botanical Gardens.** The life's work of Ken duPlooy, an ornithologist who died in 2001, the personable Judy duPlooy, and their family, is the 45-acre Belize Botanical Gardens, a collection of hundreds of trees, plants, and flowers from all over Central America. Enlightening tours of the gardens, set on a bank of the Macal River at duPlooy's Jungle Lodge, are given by local guides who can tell you the names of the plants in Maya, Spanish, and English as well as explain their varied medicinal uses. An orchid house holds the duPlooys' collection of more than 100 orchid species, and there also is a palm exhibit. The gardens and duPlooy's Lodge in general offer great birding. On some days duPlooy's runs shuttles from San Ignacio. The BZ$38 per person fee includes the round-trip shuttle and self-guided tour. Call for information and schedule. A taxi will likely cost at least BZ$50 one-way. ⊠ *Chial Rd.* ✛ *From San Ignacio, head 4¾ mi (7½ km) west on Benque Rd., turn left on the unpaved Chial Rd. and go about 5 mi (8 km) to duPlooy's Jungle Lodge* ☎ *824/3101* ⊕ *www.belizebotanic.org* ✎ *BZ$10 self-guided tour, BZ$15 guided tour* ☉ *Daily 7–5.*

WORTH NOTING

Cahal Pech. Just at the western edge of San Ignacio is a third major Mayan area ruin, the unfortunately named Cahal Pech ("Place of the Ticks"). It was occupied from around 900 BC to AD 1100. At its peak, in AD 600, Cahal Pech was a medium-size settlement of perhaps 10,000 people with some three dozen structures huddled around seven plazas. It's thought that it functioned as a guard post, watching over the nearby confluence of the Mopan and Macal rivers. It may be somewhat less compelling than the area's other ruins, but it's no less mysterious, given that these structures mark the presence of a civilization we know so little about. Look for answers at the small visitor center and museum. ⊠ *On hill at western edge of San Ignacio* ☎ *822/2016* ✎ *BZ$20* ☉ *Daily 6–6.*

Chaa Creek Natural History Centre. The Chaa Creek Natural History Centre has a small library and lots of displays on everything from butterflies to snakes (pickled in jars). Outside is a screened-in Blue Morpho butterfly-breeding center. If you haven't encountered Blue Morphos in the wild, you can see them up close here and even peer at their slumbering pupae, which resemble jade earrings. Once you're inside the double doors, the electric blue beauties, which look boringly brown when their wings are closed, flit about or remain perfectly still, sometimes on your shoulder or head, and open and close their wings to a rhythm akin to inhaling and exhaling. Tours are led by a team of naturalists. You can combine a visit here with one to the Rainforest Medicine Trail. ⊠ *The Lodge at Chaa Creek, Chial Rd.* ☎ *824/2037* ⊕ *www.chaacreek.com* ✎ *BZ$20 combined with Rainforest Medicine Trail; free to Chaa Creek guests* ☉ *Daily 9–4.*

El Pilar. El Pilar is still being excavated under the direction of Anabel Ford, a professor at the University of California at Santa Barbara. El Pilar is three times larger than Xunantunich, but due to its location—at the end of a 7-mi (12 km) rough dirt road—it gets only a few hundred visitors a year. Excavations of Mayan ruins have traditionally concentrated on public buildings, but at El Pilar the emphasis has been on reconstructing domestic architecture—everything from houses to gardens with crops used by the Maya. El Pilar, occupied from 800 BC to 1000 AD, at its peak may have had a population of 20,000. Several well-marked trails take you around the site. Because the structures haven't been stripped of vegetation, you may feel like you're walking through a series of shady orchards. ■ TIP➔ **Don't forget binoculars: In the 5,000-acre nature reserve there's terrific bird-watching.** Behind the main plaza, a lookout grants a spectacular view across the jungle to El Pilar's sister city, Pilar Poniente, on the Guatemalan border. There is a visitor center, the Be Pukte Cultural Center of Amigos de El Pilar, in Bullet Tree Falls (open daily 9–5), where you can get information on the site and pay the BZ$20 admission fee. Note that several incidents of robbery have occurred at or near El Pilar. You may want visit this site on a tour, available from several tour operators in San Ignacio including duPlooy's and Crystal Paradise/Birding in Paradise. ⊠ *7 mi (12 km) northwest of Bullet Tree Falls, off Bullet Tree Rd., Bullet Tree Falls* ⊹ *Take the Bullet Tree Road in San Ignacio to Bullet Tree Falls. In Bullet Tree Falls, just before the bridge over the Mopan River on the left you will see the Be Pukte Cultural Center of the Amigos de El Pilar. To go on to El Pilar, cross the Mopan River Bridge and you will see signs to the El Pilar Road* ☎ *822/2106 NICH Institute of Archeology in Belmopan, 824/3612 Dr. Anabel Ford in Belize* ⊠ *BZ$20* ⊙ *Daily 8–5.*

☾ **Rainforest Medicine Trail.** The Rainforest Medicine Trail, originally developed by natural medicine guru Rosita Arvigo, gives you a quick introduction to traditional Mayan medicine. The trail takes you on a short, self-guided walk through the rain forest, giving you a chance to study the symbiotic nature of its plant life. Learn about the healing properties of such indigenous plants as red gumbo-limbo and see some endangered medicinal plants. The shop here sells Mayan medicinal products like Belly Be Good and Flu Away. ⊠ *Next to Lodge at Chaa Creek, Chial Rd.* ☎ *824/2037* ⊕ *www.chaacreek.com* ⊠ *BZ$10 for Rainforest Medicine Trail, BZ$20 including Natural History Centre and Blue Morpho Breeding Center; free to Chaa Creek guests* ⊙ *Daily 9–5.*

San Ignacio Market. On Saturday mornings, San Ignacio Market, in a field across from the soccer stadium, comes alive with farmers selling local fruits and vegetables. Vendors also hawk crafts, clothing, and household goods. Some vendors show up on other days as well, but Saturday has by far the largest market. A smaller vegetable and fruit market is open weekdays near Burns Avenue, closer to town. ⊙ *Sat. 7–noon, though some vendors stay later.*

Spanish Lookout. The hilltop community of Spanish Lookout, population 2,500, about 5 mi (8 km) north of the Western Highway, is one of the centers of Belize's 11,000-strong Mennonite community, of which nearly 3,000 are in Cayo District. The easiest access to Spanish Lookout is via the paved Route 30 at Mile 57½ of the Western Highway. The village's blond-haired, blue-eyed residents may seem out of place in this tropical country, but they're responsible for much of the construction, manufacturing, and agriculture in Belize. They built many of Belize's resorts, and most of the chickens, eggs, cheese, and milk you'll consume during your stay come from their farms. Many of the small wooden houses that you see all over Belize are Mennonite pre-fabs built in Spanish Lookout. In conservative communities, women dress in cotton frocks and head scarves, and the men don straw hats, suspenders, and dark trousers. Some still travel in horse-drawn buggies, though most Mennonites around Spanish Lookout have embraced pickup trucks and modern farming equipment. The cafés and small shopping centers in Spanish Lookout offer a unique opportunity to mingle with these sometimes world-wary people, but they don't appreciate being gawked at or photographed any more than you do. Stores in Spanish Lookout are modern and well-stocked, the farms wouldn't look out of place in the U.S. Midwest, and many of the roads are paved (the Mennonites do their own road paving). Oil in commercial quantities was discovered in Spanish Lookout in 2005, and several wells now pump about 5,000 barrels of black gold daily.

Tropical Wings. Besides thoughtful displays on the Cayo flora and fauna, Tropical Wings, a little nature center, raises 20 species of butterfly including the Blue Morpho, Owl, Giant Swallowtail, and Monarch varieties. The facility, at The Trek Stop *(⇨ see below)*, also has a small restaurant and gift shop, along with cabins. ⊠ *6 mi (10 km) west of San Ignacio, Mile 71.5, Western Hwy. (aka Benque Rd.), San José Succotz* 📞 *823/2265* 🌐 *www.thetrekstop.com/tropwings.htm* 💰 *BZ$6 adults, BZ$3 children 12 and under* 🕐 *Daily 9–5.*

WHERE TO EAT

SAN IGNACIO

Besides the restaurants listed here, most of the jungle lodges in the Cayo have their own restaurants. Those at Table Rock Lodge, Mystic River Lodge, The Lodge at Chaa Creek, and duPlooy's Lodge are especially good. Nearer town, the restaurants at Ka'ana Boutique Resort and San Ignacio Resort Hotel also are noteworthy. On the other end of the price scale, street vendors set up barbecue grills and food stalls on the Western Highway just east of the Hawksworth Bridge in Santa Elena, and you can get big plates of food for little money.

$ ✕ **Erva's.** Nothing fancy here, just down-home Belizean dishes at modest
LATIN AMERICAN prices. Go for the traditional beans and rice dishes or *escabeche (onion soup with chicken);* the ceviche is quite good, too. The waiters are extra-friendly. It's a couple of blocks off the main drag, so it's quieter and more relaxing here, whether you dine on the veranda or inside in the homey dining room. Open for breakfast, lunch, and dinner except Sunday. ⊠ *2 Far West St., San Ignacio* 📞 *824/2821* 🕐 *Closed Sun.*

$ ✕ **Hode's Place Bar & Grill.** With a large shaded patio next to a citrus
AMERICAN grove and swings, slides, and an ice-cream bar (cones BZ$2) for the
★ kids in the back, Hode's is even bigger than it looks from the outside.

It's popular for cold beers, karaoke, and billiards and is often the busiest place in town. There's even a mini-casino. Hode's has good food in large portions at moderate prices. The escabeche (BZ$12) is terrific, and the fried chicken with french fries (BZ$10) is the best in Cayo. Entrée prices range from BZ$5 for a beef burger and BZ$6 for a chicken burrito or small plate of stew chicken with rice and beans to BZ$26 for a sirloin steak. ⊠ *Savannah St., across from sports field* ☎ *804/2522.*

$　✕ **Ko-Ox Han-Nah.** Formerly called Hannah's (the new name in the
ECLECTIC　Mayan language means, roughly, "Let's go eat"), by whatever name
★　this is one of San Ignacio's most popular restaurants, and deservedly so. It's far from fancy—you eat on simple tables in what is essentially a large shed on busy Burns Avenue—but service is cheerful, and the food is inexpensive and well-prepared. Dinner entrées range from BZ$6 to BZ$25. Much of the food is raised on the farm of the Zimbabwean-born owner. In addition to the usual Belizean beans-and-rice dishes, Ko-Ox Han-Nah serves fusion food influenced by Mexican, Southeast Asian, and North and South Indian cooking, with salads, sandwiches, burritos, Burmese dishes, Cambodian and Korean chicken dishes, and Indian lamb curries. Across the street the owner has opened a butcher shop that also has sandwiches. ⊠ *5 Burns Ave.* ☎ *824/3014.*

$　✕ **Mr. Greedy's Pizzeria.** Located in the heart of downtown on Burns
AMERICAN　Avenue, with open-air seating on a covered street-side deck, this is the best place in Cayo for pizza by the slice or whole. Buffalo wings and subs are also good. In the afternoons, a cheap happy hour (BZ$2 rum and cokes) draws a crowd. There's free Wi-Fi, too. ⊠ *34 Burns Ave., across from Venus Hotel* ☎ *804/4688.*

¢　✕ **The Old French Bakery.** All the tasty French temptations that you can't
BAKERY　get elsewhere in Cayo are available at this little bakery. Pick up a crusty baguette and an authentic croissant for only a couple of Belize dollars. This shop is associated with The Baker in San Pedro. ⊠ *Manzanero Complex, Whyatt St.* ☎ *604/4657* ⊟ *No credit cards* ⊘ *Closed Sun.*

$$　✕ **Sanny's Grill.** With a hot grill and sizzling spices, this restaurant trans-
LATIN AMERICAN　forms Belizean basics like chicken or pork chops beyond standard fare. Try the pork chops in brandy-mustard sauce, coconut chicken, or grilled fish with coriander. Eat in the casual dining room or out on the covered deck. In a residential area off Benque Road, the place can be hard to find after dark. Consider taking a taxi. ⊠ *18th St., heading west of San Ignacio, look for sign just beyond Texaco station* ☎ *824/2988* ⊘ *No lunch.*

$$　✕ **Serendib.** What's a Sri Lankan restaurant doing here? The original
AMERICAN　Ceylonese owner and his wife came to Belize with the British Army, and like many other squaddies (enlisted men), decided to stay on and open a business. Over the years, the menu here has migrated more to Belizean, Chinese, and American dishes than Sri Lankan, but you can still get authentic Sri Lankan curries (you choose the heat level) and a nice choice of teas. Save room for the Wattalappan dessert, a Ceylonese coconut custard with cardamom. The restaurant is a comfortable, cool escape from the crowds on busy Burns Avenue outside. ⊠ *27 Burns Ave.* ☎ *824/2302* ⊘ *Closed Sun.*

WHERE TO STAY

SAN IGNACIO

For expanded hotel reviews, visit Fodors.com.

Hotels in downtown San Ignacio are all budget to moderate spots. As you near the western edge of town, with hotels such as the San Ignacio Resort Hotel, lodgings become more upscale. The lodges along the Mopan River, a dark jade–color river that winds into Belize from Guatemala, tend to be in the budget to moderate range. Most lodges on the Macal River, such as The Lodge at Chaa Creek and duPlooy's Lodge, are upmarket, though there are some exceptions. A number of new lodges, including Mystic River, Inn the Bush, Table Rock, and Mariposa have opened on the Cristo Rey Road en route to the Mountain Pine Ridge, most with access to the Macal River.

¢ **Aguada Hotel & Restaurant.** Penny-pinching travelers jump at the opportunity to stay in this tidy, attractive, and inexpensive hotel with air-conditioned rooms and a swimming pool in Santa Elena, the low-key town adjoining San Ignacio. **Pros:** clean, inexpensive rooms with air-conditioning; one of the few budget hotels with a pool. **Cons:** location is a bus or BZ$7 taxi ride away from downtown San Ignacio. ⌧ *Off Western Hwy. across from La Loma Luz hospital, Santa Elena* ☎ *804/3609* ⊕ *www.aguadahotel.com* ⤶ *25 rooms* ⌂ *In-room: no TV, Wi-Fi. In-hotel: restaurant, bar, pool.*

$ **Cahal Pech Village Resort.** Once you make it up the steep hill, you'll ★ enjoy the best views in the Cayo at this hotel set on a high hill at the western edge of San Ignacio, near the Cahal Pech Mayan site. **Pros:** great views; enticing pool; good value. **Cons:** some rooms are a bit dowdy and need upgrading; limestone dirt road up to hotel is very steep, especially if you're walking. ⌧ *1 mi (2 km) west of town, off Western Hwy., Cahal Pech Rd.* ☎ *824/3740* ⊕ *www.cahalpech.com* ⤶ *16 rooms, 6 suites, 25 cabañas* ⌂ *In-hotel: restaurant, bar, pool, business center.*

¢ **Casa Blanca Guest House.** Though it's in the center of San Ignacio, on ★ bustling Burns Avenue, this small hotel is an oasis of peace and one of Belize's top budget choices. **Pros:** central downtown location; extremely clean, appealing rooms; good value. **Cons:** limited parking nearby. ⌧ *10 Burns Ave.* ☎ *824/2080* ⊕ *www.casablancaguesthouse.com* ⤶ *9 rooms.*

¢ **Hotel El Pilar.** Hotel El Pilar near Bullet Tree Falls is a new, no-frills lodging choice for those who are looking to save money while enjoying some amenities like cable TV and air-conditioning. **Pros:** clean, modern motel with cable TV and a/c. **Cons:** no restaurant or bar; not near the action. ⌧ *Bullet Tree Rd., Bullet Tree Falls* ☎ *824/3059, 665/6125* ⤶ *19 rooms.*

$$ **La Casa del Caballo Blanco.** Caballo Blanco is named after a resident white horse that whinnies affably on the ecolodge's sloping lawn with a panorama of hills in the distance. **Pros:** beautiful hilltop views; comfortable accommodations; part of a bird rehab center. **Cons:** owners aren't in residence full-time. ⌧ *Bullet Tree Rd., next to San Ignacio Hospital* ☎ *707/974–4942 U.S. reservations number, 824/2098* ⊕ *www. casacaballoblanco.com* ⤶ *6 rooms* ⌂ *In-room: no a/c, no TV. In-hotel: restaurant, business center.*

5

$ 🏠 **Martha's Guesthouse and Restaurant.** With clean rooms, a popular restaurant, handy laundry, and convenient tours, Martha's provides just about everything you need in an affordable package right in the heart of downtown San Ignacio. **Pros:** handy downtown location. **Cons:** can be noisy; rates are a little higher than most other downtown hotels. ✉ *10 West St.* ☎ *804/3647* ⊕ *www.marthasbelize.com* ➫ *16 rooms, 7 with shared baths, 1 suite* ⚒ *In-room: no a/c, kitchen, Wi-Fi. In-hotel: restaurant, bar, laundry facilities, business center.*

$ 🏠 **Maya Mountain Lodge.** Designed with the nature lover in mind, this hilltop lodge aspires toward comfort rather than luxury. **Pros:** comfortable; unpretentious; good food. **Cons:** roadside location. ✉ *1 mi (2 km) south of San Ignacio, Cristo Rey Rd.* ☎ *824/2164* ⊕ *www.mayamountain.com* ➫ *8 cottages, 6 rooms* ⚒ *In-room: no TV, Wi-Fi. In-hotel: restaurant, pool, business center* ❑ *Some meals.*

$$$ 🏠 **San Ignacio Resort Hotel.** Queen Elizabeth II stayed here once, and while you may not feel like royalty, you'll appreciate the comfortable rooms with verandas facing a hillside. **Pros:** safe, comfortable choice at the edge of town. **Cons:** expensive for what you get. ✉ *Buena Vista Rd.* ☎ *824/2034* ⊕ *www.sanignaciobelize.com* ➫ *24 rooms, 2 suites* ⚒ *In-room: Wi-Fi. In-hotel: restaurant, bar, pool, tennis court, spa.*

$$$ 🏠 **Windy Hill Resort.** The cabañas at this lodge all have private verandas and are perched on a low hill across the landscaped grounds. **Pros:** handy roadside location; offers many tours; pleasant cabins on hillside. **Cons:** not a jungle lodge. ✉ *1 mi (1½ km) west of San Ignacio, Western Hwy. (aka Benque Rd.)* ☎ *824/2017, 800/946–3995* ⊕ *www.windyhillresort.com* ➫ *25 cabañas* ⚒ *In-room: no a/c. In-hotel: restaurant, bar, pool, gym, business center* ❑ *Multiple meal plans.*

ALONG THE MOPAN RIVER

$ 🏠 **Clarissa Falls Resort.** The low gurgle of nearby Mopan River rapids ⚙ is the first and last sound of the day at this small colony of thatch cabañas. **Pros:** quiet, pastoral riverside setting; good food; you'll want to hug the owner. **Cons:** resort is on a ranch and not in a true jungle setting. ✉ *5½ mi (9 km) west of San Ignacio, Mile 70, Western Hwy. (aka Benque Hwy.), San Ignacio* ☎☎ *824/3916* ⊕ *www.clarissafalls.com* ➫ *11 cabañas, 1 bunkhouse with 10 beds* ⚒ *In-room: no a/c, no TV. In-hotel: restaurant, bar, water sports.*

$$ 🏠 **Cohune Palms River Cabañas.** This charming spot in Bullet Tree has five thatched cabañas set among palms on a small peninsula on the Mopan River. **Pros:** excellent moderately priced lodge; good food. **Cons:** you need to take a taxi or *colectivo* (group taxi) into San Ignacio. ✉ *Bullet Tree Falls* ☎ *824/0166* ⊕ *www.cohunepalms.com* ➫ *5 cabañas* ⚒ *In-room: no a/c, no TV, Wi-Fi. In-hotel: restaurant, bar.*

$$$$ 🏠 **Ka'ana Boutique Resort and Spa.** Ka'ana brings a welcome level of ★ luxury to San Ignacio with tranquil gardens, a wine cellar, spacious rooms outfitted with iPod docks, espresso machines, high-end toiletries, and flat-screen TVs. **Pros:** terrifically comfortable beds; convivial staff; nice selection of amenities; good bar and restaurant. **Cons:** not a jungle lodge; pricey. ✉ *Mile 69 1/4, Western Hwy. (aka Benque Rd.), San Ignacio* ☎ *824/3350, 877/522–6221 in U.S.* ⊕ *www.kaanabelize.com* ➫ *15 rooms* ⚒ *In-room: safe, Wi-Fi. In-hotel: restaurant, bar, pool, spa.*

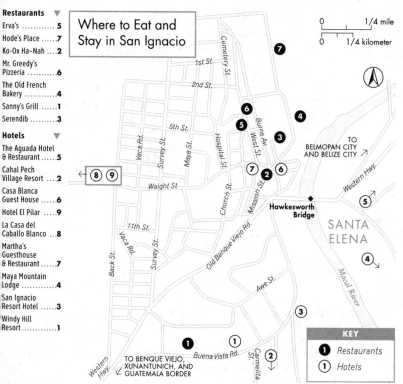

Where to Eat and Stay in San Ignacio

$$\$\$\$ \quad \text{⊡ Mahogany Hall Boutique Resort.}$$ An upmarket alternative to fancy jungle lodges is this new resort in, of all places, Bullet Tree Falls, on the banks of the Mopan River. **Pros:** gorgeous suites; lovely views of the Mopan River; super comfortable beds. **Cons:** somewhat unusual location—neither a jungle lodge or in-town hotel. ⊠ *Paslow Falls Rd., Bullet Tree Falls* ☎ *664/7747* ⊕ *www.mahoganyhallbelize.com* ➟ *8 rooms* ⌂ *In-room: Wi-Fi. In-hotel: restaurant, bar, pool.*

$$\$ \quad \text{⊡ Parrot Nest.}$$ If ever since you were a kid you've wanted to sleep in a tree house by a river, this is your chance. **Pros:** rustic but cute cabañas and tree houses; good value; helpful, friendly owners. **Cons:** you're not really in the jungle here; cabañas are small. ⊠ *Off Bullet Tree Rd., On Mopan River, Bullet Tree Falls* ☎ *820/4058* ✉ *parrotnestlodge@yahoo. com* ⊕ *www.parrot-nest.com* ➟ *2 tree houses, 4 cabañas, all with share baths* ⌂ *In-room: no a/c, no TV.*

ALONG THE MACAL RIVER

$$\$\$ \quad \text{⊡ Black Rock River Lodge.}$$ Some 800 feet above limestone cliffs and the Macal River gorge, Black Rock has one of the most beautiful settings of any lodge in the country. **Pros:** remote, beautiful setting; eco-conscious management. **Cons:** you're stuck here for somewhat pricey meals and tours unless you have a car. ⊠ *On Macal River, 13 mi (22 km) upriver from San Ignacio, San Ignacio* ☎ *820/4049* ⊕ *www.blackrocklodge.com*

🛏 *13 cabins* ⚕ *In-room: no a/c, no TV. In-hotel: business center.*

$$$ 🏨 **duPlooy's Lodge.** High above a ☾ bend in the Macal River called Big ★ Eddy is this remarkable, relaxing lodge whose grounds include the 45-acre Belize Botanic Gardens. **Pros:** variety of lodging choices; excellent food; botanic gardens on-site; first-rate birding; eco-conscious management. **Cons:** costs for meals, transfers, and tours add up. ⊹ *Head 4¾ mi (7½ km) west on Western Hwy. (also called Benque Rd.), turn left on Chial Rd., and go about 5 mi (8 km) to duPlooy's* ☎ *824/3101, 425/254–3481 U.S. number* ⊕ *www.duplooys. com* 🛏 *1 house, 4 cabañas, 3 suites, 15 rooms* ⚕ *In-room: no a/c, no TV. In-hotel: spa, business center* ¶◎¶ *Breakfast.*

$$$$ 🏨 **The Lodge at Chaa Creek.** This was the first true jungle lodge in the **Fodor's Choice** Cayo, and the gracefully landscaped grounds, surrounded by 365 acres ★ on the Macal River are magnificent, as are the whitewashed stone cottages. **Pros:** stunningly beautiful grounds; excellent staff and service; lovely cabañas and suites; gorgeous pool. **Cons:** lodging and meal prices have jumped in recent years. ⊠ *Chial Rd., San Ignacio* ⊠ *The Lodge at Chaa Creek, P.O. Box 53, Cayo District, San Ignacio* ⊹ *From San Ignacio go 4¾ mi (7½ km) on Benque Rd., aka Western Hwy., turn left on Chial Rd. and go about 4½ mi (7 km). Follow signs to Chaa Creek* ☎ *824/2037 local reservations, 877/709–8708, 834/4010 front desk* ⊕ *www.chaacreek.com* 🛏 *14 rooms in duplex cottages, 6 suites, 4 villas, 10 casitas, 1 2-bedroom suite* ⚕ *In-room: no a/c, no TV. In-hotel: restaurant, bar, pool, spa, business center* ¶◎¶ *Breakfast.*

THE OUTDOORS

San Ignacio is the center for touring in western Belize. Just walk along busy Burns Avenue and you'll see signs for all kinds of tours and find the offices of several tour operators. Individual tour guides, who by law must be Belizean citizens and be licensed by the government, may work for tour operators, for a lodge or hotel, or they may freelance on their own. Some hang out at restaurants in town, especially those on busy Burns Avenue, and post notices at bulletin boards in downtown hotels and restaurants. PACZ Tours and others have offices downtown. You can compare prices and sign up for the next day's tours. Obviously, the more layers of costs involved, the higher the price for you, but on the other hand larger operators and hotel tour companies have more resources, and they have their long-term reputations to protect, so they may be more reliable. Tours from lodges usually are more costly than if booked with an independent tour operator. Also, some lodges try to sell packages of tours rather than individual ones.

Most jungle lodges offer a full range of day trips, using either their own guides or working with independent guides and tour companies. The largest lodge-affiliated tour operations are Chaa Creek Expeditions and Windy Hill Tour Company, but Crystal Paradise, duPlooy's, Maya Mountain, Cahal Pech Village, San Ignacio Resort Hotel, Moon Racer Farm, and other hotels and lodges also do many tours and trips.

If you have a rental car, you can visit all of the Mayan sites in the Cayo on your own, along with other attractions such as the butterfly farms, the Belize Botanic Gardens, Rainforest Medicine Trail, and many of the attractions in the Mountain Pine Ridge. However, for most caving tours, notably Actun Tunichil Muknal, you'll need a guide, and for canoe and kayak trips, you'll need drop-off and pickup. Local guides also are critical for nature hikes and birding trips, as many of these guides have remarkable local knowledge and ability to spot things you probably wouldn't see otherwise.

BIRDING

The area around San Ignacio is good for birding because it contains such a variety of habitats—river valleys, foothills, lagoons, agricultural areas, and broadleaf jungle—each of which attracts different types of birds. For example, Aguacate Lagoon near Spanish Lookout attracts waterbirds such as night herons, neotropic cormorants, and whistling ducks. Open land and pastures are good for spotting laughing falcons, vermillion flycatchers, eastern meadowlarks, and white-tailed kites.

There's good birding on the grounds of most of the lodges along the Mopan and Macal rivers, including **Chaa Creek, duPlooy's, Crystal Paradise,** and **Clarissa Falls.** In addition, local guides and tour companies run birding trips.

Paradise Expeditions. Associated with Crystal Paradise Lodge, Paradise Expeditions leads first-rate birding trips. ☎ 670/2473 ✍ info@birdinginbelize.com.

CANOEING AND KAYAKING

The Cayo's rivers, especially the Mopan and Macal, make it an excellent place for canoeing and kayaking. Most of the larger resorts, like **Chaa Creek** and **duPlooy's,** have canoes or inflatable kayaks. Generally you put in the Macal and paddle and float down to the Hawksworth Bridge at San Ignacio, a trip that takes two or three hours depending on your starting point. You'll pay about BZ$50 per person for canoe rental and pickup. You'll see iguanas and birdlife on the banks, and if you dip in for a swim, don't be surprised if tiny (toothless) fish school around you to figure out whether you're food.

Do exercise caution. You won't believe how fast the rivers, especially the Macal, can rise after a heavy rain. Following rains in the Mountain Pine Ridge, it can reach a dangerous flood stage in just a few minutes. Also, in the past there have been a few rare incidents of visitors in canoes being stopped and robbed on the Macal. Watch weather forecasts, and ask locally about safety on the rivers.

BUDGETING YOUR TRIP

Here are a range of rates you can expect to pay for selected trips. These charges are per person and usually include transportation, lunch (on full-day trips), and, in the case of river trips, drop-off and pickup. Admission to Mayan sites (usually BZ$20 to BZ$30, except about US$20 at Tikal), border fees (BZ$37.50 to go from Belize to Guatemala), may or may not be included—you should ask. Gratuities for guides are almost always extra. On some trips, such as to Tikal or Caracol, there's often a flat fee for one to three or four persons, so the more going together, the cheaper. Keep in mind that, especially off-season, rates for some of these tours may be negotiable.

■ Guided nature walk, at lodge: BZ$20–BZ$60

■ Morning birding walk, at lodge: BZ$10–BZ$30 (sometimes free)

■ Day tour to Tikal: BZ$200–BZ$400 (cheaper for larger parties)

■ Overnight trip to Tikal: BZ$400–BZ$750

■ Day trip to Caracol: BZ$150–BZ$250 (cheaper for larger parties)

■ Half-day tour of Xunantunich: BZ$40–BZ$100

■ Mountain Pine Ridge tour: BZ$100–BZ$250

■ Actun Tunichil Muknal: BZ$180–BZ$240

■ Barton Creek Cave with canoe: BZ$75–BZ$160

■ Self-guided canoe or kayak trip on Macal or Mopan rivers: BZ$50–BZ$70

■ Half-day horseback riding: BZ$60–BZ$140

■ Mountain bike rental: BZ$25–BZ$70 a day (complimentary at some lodges)

■ Overnight camping trip, with guide: BZ$300 per night for up to three persons, plus supplies

River Rat. River Rat arranges canoeing and kayaking trips, both for beginners and experienced river runners, as well as tours to Caracol, ATM, El Pilar, and elsewhere. ☎ *628/6033* ⊕ *www.riverratbelize.com.*

CAVING

Fodor's Choice ★ Over the millennia, as dozens of swift-flowing rivers bored through the soft limestone, the Maya Mountains became pitted with miles of caves. The Maya used them as burial sites, and, according to one theory, as subterranean waterways that linked the Cayo with communities as far north as the Yucatán. Previously, the caves fell into a 1,000-year slumber, disturbed only by the nightly flutter of bats. In recent years, the caves have been rediscovered by spelunkers.

Caves Branch Adventure Co. & Jungle Camp. First on the scene was Ian Anderson, owner of Caves Branch Adventure Co. & Jungle Camp. He and his friendly staff of trained guides run exhilarating adventure-theme caving, tubing, and hiking trips from a tiki-torchlighted jungle camp just south of Belmopan. (⇨ *See Belmopan lodging.*) ⊠ *12 mi (19½ km) south of Belmopan, Mile 42½, Hummingbird Hwy., Belmopan* 📞📞 *673/3454* ☎ *866/357–2698* ⊕ *www.cavesbranch.com.*

DON'T MISS

Arts & Crafts of Central America. In town, Arts & Crafts of Central America has a small selection of crafts, at competitive prices. ⊠ *24 Burns Ave.* ☏ *824/2253.*

Celina's Superstore. The friendliest little grocery in Belize is Celina's Superstore, which has almost anything you'll need, including picnic supplies, toiletries, snacks, booze, and more. ⊠ *43 Burns Ave.* ☏ *824/2247.*

Orange Gifts. Orange Gifts (formerly Caesar's Place) has one of the best selections of Belizean and Guatemalan crafts in Belize. It has an especially good selection of wood items from tropical hardwoods, including bowls, small pieces of furniture, and carvings. If you're hungry after shopping, the restaurant here is surprisingly good. ⊠ *Mile 60, Western Hwy., east of San Ignacio* ☏ *824/2341* ⊕ *www.orangegifts.com.*

PACZ Tours. PACZ specializes in tours to the spooky, wonderful Actun Tunichil Muknal near Belmopan. ⊠ *30 Burns Ave., San Ignacio* ☏ *824/0536* ⊕ *www.pacztours.net.*

HIKING

Most of the lodges have hiking trails. **Black Rock River Lodge, Chaa Creek, Maya Mountain, Crystal Paradise,** and **duPlooy's** all have especially good areas for hiking. If you want even more wide-open spaces, head to the Mountain Pine Ridge, which offers hundreds of miles of hiking trails, mostly old logging roads. (⇨ *See Mountain Pine Ridge, below.*) For more adventurous hikes and overnight treks, you'll want to go with a guide. (⇨ *See also Caves Branch Adventure Co. & Jungle Camp listing above for another great guide.*)

Marcus Cucul, Maya Guide Adventures. Marcus Cucul is a Kekchi Mayan who is trained in cave and wilderness rescue. He can guide you to Victoria Peak (BZ$1,000) on a three-night/four-day hike or teach you about jungle survival with just a machete and a medical kit on a four-day trip (BZ$700, minimum two persons.) ⊠ *P. O. Box 485, Belmopan* ☏ *670/3116* ⊕ *www.mayaguide.bz.*

HORSEBACK RIDING

The Lodge at Chaa Creek. The Lodge at Chaa Creek has a stable of riding horses. Two- to three-hour guided horseback trips cost BZ$90 per person. A horseback tour to Chaa Creek's Maya organic farm is BZ$90. ⊠ *Chial Rd.* ☏ *824/2037* ⊕ *www.chaacreek.com.*

Moonracer Farm. Moonracer Farm has half-day (BZ$100) and full-day (BZ$130) horseback rides with a local Maya guide. ⊠ *Mountain Pine Ridge Rd., just outside Mountain Pine Ridge, San Antonio* ☏ *585/200–5748 Skype number* ⊕ *www.moonracerfarm.com.*

Mountain Equestrian Trails. When it comes to horseback-riding adventures, whether on the old logging roads of the Mountain Pine Ridge or on trails in the Slate Creek Preserve, the local experts are found at Mountain Equestrian Trails. Full-day rides range from BZ$166 to BZ$180.

Five-night riding packages including accommodations but not meals are BZ$4,880 double in-season. ✉ *Mile 8, Mountain Pine Ridge Rd.* ☎ *669/1124, 800/838–3918* ⊕ *www.metbelize.com.*

BENQUE VIEJO

7 mi (11 km) southwest of San Ignacio

Old Bank, or Benque Viejo in Spanish, is the last town in Belize before you reach Guatemala. Modest in size and population (about 9,000), Benque is low-key in other ways, too, but the little House of Culture is worth a stop, and neighboring San José Succotz village is home to the Xunantunich Mayan site. The Poustinia Land Art Park is perhaps the most unusual element of Belize's art scene.

EXPLORING

Actun Chechem Ha. On private land, Actun Chechem Ha, which means "Cave of the Poisonwood Water," is a Mayan burial cave with artifacts that date back three millennia. There are many pots and a stela used for ceremonial purposes. To examine some of the pottery, you'll have to climb ladders, and getting to the cave requires a 35-minute walk, mostly uphill. The cave is on private property, and the landowner gives tours. Tour companies, with registered guides, also visit here from San Ignacio and Belmopan, charging from BZ$130 per person. ✉ *10 mi (17 km) south of Benque Viejo* ☎ *820/4063 to arrange a visit* 💲 *BZ$50 for guided tour for up to 3 people, if arranged with owner; tours including transportation from San Ignacio or your lodge and often including lunch and swimming at Vaca Falls are around BZ$130 per person and up* ⊙ *By appointment.*

Benque House of Culture. The mission of Benque House of Culture, one of four government-sponsored houses of culture in Belize (others are in Belize City, Orange Walk Town, and San Ignacio/Santa Elena), is "promoting beauty and goodness." Who could argue with that? Housed in the former Benque police station, this little museum has displays on the history of Benque Viejo, which celebrated its centennial in 2004, and also offers classes for local schoolchildren and their teachers. ✉ *64 Joseph St., 7 mi (11½ km) west of San Ignacio, Benque Viejo del Carmen* ☎ *823/2697* 💲 *By donation* ⊙ *Weekdays 8–5.*

Poustinia Land Art Park. One of the most unusual attractions in Belize, Poustinia Land Art Park is a collection of about 30 original works by artists from a dozen countries, including Belize, Norway, Guayana, Brazil, Guatemala, and England, scattered about some 60 acres of a former cattle ranch. It's owned by an architect, who calls Poustinia an "environmental project." *Poustinia* is Russian for "desert of the soul." Among the works of outdoor art, which some would call funky and others fascinating, are "Downtown," by Venezuelan artist Manuel Piney, and "Returned Parquet," a reference to Belize's colonial history in mahogany parquet flooring by Tim Davies, a British artist. Getting around the park, which is open by appointment only, requires sometimes strenuous hiking. Bring insect repellent. Make arrangements to visit the park and for a tour guide at the Benque House of Culture in Benque Viejo. Two simple cabins at the site are available for rent "to artists and short-term visitors" for around BZ$80 per night. For information, contact the owner Luis Alberto Ruiz at 822–3532. ✉ *2½ mi (5 km) south of Benque Viejo, 8 mi (13 km) southwest of San Ignacio, Hydro Rd., Benque Viejo del Carmen* ☎ *823/2697 Benque House of Culture* ✑ *BZ$20; guided tours BZ$50* ☾ *By appointment.*

○ ★ **Xunantunich.** Pronounced *shoo-nan-too-nitch*, Xunantunich is one of the most accessible Mayan sites in Belize, located on a hilltop site above the Mopan River. You can ask to work the crank yourself as you ride a hand-pulled ferry across the river, near the village of San José Succotz. As you hike through the profusion of maidenhair ferns to the ruins, you may encounter numerous butterflies flitting through the air. A magnificent avenue of cohune palms announces your arrival at an important ceremonial center from the Maya Classic Period. Xunantunich means "stone maiden." The structures here, in six plazas with more than two dozen buildings, date from 200 to 900 A.D. El Castillo, the massive 120-foot-high main pyramid, still the second-tallest structure in Belize after Caana at Caracol, was built on a leveled hilltop. The pyramid has a spectacular 360-degree panorama of the Mopan River valley into Guatemala. On the eastern wall is a reproduction of one of the finest Mayan sculptures in Belize, a frieze decorated with jaguar heads, human faces, and abstract geometric patterns telling the story of the Moon's affair with Morning Light. Drinks and snacks are available at a visitor center that provides the history of the site. ✉ *Near San José Succotz Village, 6½ mi (11 km) southwest of San Ignacio, Benque Rd., San José Succotz* ☎ *822/3302 National Institute of Culture and History (NICH) Belmopan* ✑ *BZ$20* ☾ *Daily 8–4.*

WHERE TO EAT AND STAY

For expanded hotel reviews, visit Fodors.com.

¢ ✕ **Benny's Kitchen.** This little open-air restaurant near Xunantunich has
LATIN AMERICAN won many fans who come for hearty Mayan and Creole dishes at rock-bottom prices. Most items on the menu are BZ$10 or less, including *chilimole* (chicken with mole sauce), cow-foot soup, escabeche, and stew pork with rice, beans and plantains. The classic Mayan *pibil* (pork cooked in an underground oven), when available, is BZ$12. The banana *licuados* (milk shakes) are delicious. ✉ *Across Benque Rd., (Western Hwy.) from ferry to Xunantunich, San José Succotz* ✛ *Turn south just west of ferry and follow signs about 3 blocks* ☎ *823/2541* ▭ *No credit cards.*

$$$$ ▥ **Mopan River Resort.** Belize's first truly all-inclusive resort is still one of
★ the best values in the Cayo, although rates have increased significantly—once you've taken the short, private ferry trip across the Mopan River to the resort's manicured, palm-studded, 90-acre grounds, you're in your own private bit of paradise, and everything except border fees and site admission charges is included in the price, from meals and drinks to trips to Tikal and Barton Cave, transfers from Belize City, and even taxes and tips. **Pros:** excellent value in a true all-inclusive; beautiful

grounds. **Cons:** not a true jungle lodge, with a location near Benque Viejo town. ⊠ *Riverside North, Benque Viejo del Carmen* ☎ *823/2047* ⊕ *www.mopanriverresort.com* ⊅ *12 cabañas* ⚴ *In-room: safe, kitchen. In-hotel: restaurant, bar, pool, business center* ⦿ *All-inclusive*.

¢ ⛺ **The Trek Stop.** After a day spent out and about, a cold Belikin and ★ filling Mexican and Belizean dishes await you at this cluster of neat-as-a-pin cabins at affordable prices. **Pros:** top value for the money; friendly management. **Cons:** just a couple steps up from camping; location means you'll have to take a bus or taxi to most sights, except Xunantunich. ⊠ *6 mi (9 km) west of San Ignacio, Western Hwy. (aka Benque Rd.), near Xunantunich, San José Succotz* ☎ *823/2265* ⊕ *www. thetrekstop.com* ⊅ *9 cabins, 7 with shared bath* ⚴ *In-room: no a/c, no TV, Wi-Fi. In-hotel: restaurant, bar.*

MOUNTAIN PINE RIDGE

17 mi (27 km) south of San Ignacio.

★ **Mountain Pine Ridge Forest Reserve.** This reserve is a highlight of any journey to Belize and an adventure to reach and explore. The Mountain Pine Ridge Forest Reserve is in the high country of Belize—low mountains and rolling hills are covered in part by vast pine forests and crisscrossed with old logging roads. The higher elevations provide cooler temperatures and outstanding views. The best way to see this area, which covers more than 106,000 acres, is on a mountain bike, a horse, or your own feet, not bouncing around in an SUV. Aside from pines, 80% of which were damaged by the Southern Pine Beetle but are now recovering, you'll see lilac-color mimosa, Saint-John's-wort, and occasionally a garish red flower appropriately known as hotlips. Look out for the craboo, a wild tree whose berries are used in a brandylike liqueur believed to have aphrodisiacal properties. Birds love this fruit, so any craboo is a good place to spot orioles and woodpeckers. You may not see them, but the Pine Ridge is home to many of Belize's large mammals, including tapirs, cougars, jaguars, and ocelots. In the streams are a few Morelet's crocodiles. ▦ *Free, but check in at the entrance gate.*

GETTING HERE AND AROUND

From the Western Highway, there are two routes into the Mountain Pine Ridge, both just east of San Ignacio: the Mountain Pine Ridge Road (also sometimes called the Chiquibul Road or the Georgeville Road), at Georgeville at Mile 61.6 of the Western Highway; and the Cristo Rey Road, with the turnoff at Mile 66.5 of the Western Highway. From the Western Highway, the entrance to the Mountain Pine Ridge is 10.2 mi (17 km) via the Mountain Pine Ridge Road and 14.8 mi (25 km) via the Cristo Rey Road. Both roads cut through limestone and are rough, but currently the Georgeville Road is rougher.

Heading southeast from San Ignacio on the Cristo Rey Road, a little beyond San Antonio, the Cristo Rey Road meets the Mountain Pine Ridge Road coming from Georgeville. Turn right to go into the Mountain Pine Ridge. After 2½ mi (4 km) a guard at a gatehouse will record your name, destination, and license-plate number. The main road through the Mountain Pine Ridge is a dirt road that can become almost impassable after heavy rains.

There is no public bus transportation into the Mountain Pine Ridge. Charter flights from Belize City can fly into private airstrips at Blancaneaux Lodge and Hidden Valley Inn. Tropic Air offers service to Hidden Valley Inn on demand.

TIMING

You could spend a week or longer exploring the streams, waterfalls, and distant trails of the Mountain Pine Ridge.

SAFETY AND PRECAUTIONS

The Mountain Pine Ridge is a remote and lightly populated area. Occasionally, bandits have taken advantage of this to stop and rob visitors, and some Guatemalan squatters have tried to move across the border in search of free land, prompting run-ins with Belize authorities. Currently, Belize Defence Forces soldiers will accompany vehicles to Caracol. However, the main danger to most visitors is not bandits but getting lost on a hiking trail or old logging road, or being stung by a scorpion.

Contacts Javier Flying Service ☎ 824/0460 ⊕ www.javiersflyingservice.com. **Tropic Air** ☎ 226/2012, 800/442–3435 in U.S. and Canada ⊕ www.tropicair. com.

EXPLORING

Barton Creek Cave. This wet cave in a remote area off the Mountain Pine Ridge Road offers a canoeing adventure in Xibalba (the Mayan underworld.) You'll float through a long underground chamber and see Mayan ceramics along with the ancient calcified skeletal remains and skulls of several individuals. You can go on a tour from San Ignacio—PACZ Tours offers a six-hour tour, including lunch and the BZ$20 admission to the cave, for BZ$130 plus tax. You can also do it yourself by driving to the cave and renting a boat and gear and getting a guide from Mike's Place near the cave. Getting to the cave is also an adventure, requiring a long drive on rough roads. Part of the road and the cave itself may be inaccessible after hard rains. Be careful in the cave— one visitor drowned in a boating accident here in 2011. ✛ *Turn at Mile 62 of the Western Hwy. onto Mountain Pine Ridge Rd. Go about 3 mi (5 km) and, at Cool Shade, turn left. Go 4 mi (6½ km) on a very rough unpaved road through Lower Barton Creek Mennonite community to Upper Barton Creek and the cave. Watch for signs for Barton Creek Outpost, Mike's Place, and the cave* 🎫 *BZ$20.*

Elijio Panti National Park. Named after the famed Guatemala-born herbal healer who died in 1996 at the age of 106, Elijio Panti National Park, also known as Noj Kaax Panti National Park, is the latest addition to Belize's already extensive national parks system. It spans about 16,000 acres around the villages of San Antonio, Cristo Rey, and El Progreso and into the Mountain Pine Ridge. The boundaries of the park roughly follow the Macal River on the west, Barton Creek on the north, Rio Frio Caves on the south, and the Mountain Pine Ridge reserve on the east. The hope is that with no hunting in this park, more wildlife will return to western Belize. Inside the park are Sapodilla Falls and a Mayan ceremonial cave, Offering Cave. At this writing, a visitor center near the village of San Antonio is under construction, with a natural healing medicine trail, which is also a work in progress. Entry to the park including a visit to Sapodilla Falls and Offering Cave currently requires that you be accompanied by a licensed tour guide. For information on the park and how to visit it, check with tour guides in San Ignacio or ask at the Garcia Sister's gift shop at the Tanah Art Museum in San Antonio village. ⊠ *Off Cristo Rey Rd., San Antonio* ☎ *820/4023* ⊕ *www.epnp.org* 🖃 *BZ$10.*

Green Hills Butterfly Ranch and Botanical Collections. This is the largest and best of Belize's butterfly farms open to the public. For a closer look at the creatures, the facility, located outside the Mountain Pine Ridge reserve, at any one time has about 30 species in a huge flight area. (Some 90 species have been raised at the farm.) Jan Meerman, who's published a book on Belize's butterflies, runs the place with Dutch partner Tineke Boomsma. On the grounds also are many flowers, including passion flowers, bromeliads, heliconias, and orchids. Birding is good here as well. ⊠ *Mile 8, Mountain Pine Ridge Rd., San Antonio* ☎ *820/4017* ⊕ *green-hills.net/protected_area.htm* 🖃 *Guided tour BZ$12.50 adults, BZ$7.50 children under 10* ☯ *Daily 8–4, last tour 3:30.*

Hidden Valley Falls. Inside the Mountain Pine Ridge Forest Reserve, Hidden Valley Falls, also known as the Thousand Foot Falls, actually drops nearly 1,600 feet. A thin plume of spray plummets over the edge of a rock face into an ostensibly bottomless gorge below. The catch is that the viewing area, where there is a shelter with some benches and a public restroom, is some distance from the falls. Many visitors find the narrow falls unimpressive from this vantage point. To climb closer requires a major commitment: a steep climb down and up the side of the mountain is several hours. ⊹ *From the Mountain Pine Ridge gate, go 2 mi (3.2 km) and turn left toward Hidden Valley Inn. Go 4 mi (6½ km) to the falls observation area. It is well-signed.* 🖃 *BZ$4* ☯ *Daily 7–5.*

Ka'ax Tun Rock Shelters. Local people are trying to develop Ka'ax Tun, Mayan for "Big Rock," into a tourist destination. (Don't confuse this with the other Big Rock, another site on the Privassion Creek.) Ka'ax Tun is a labyrinth of caves and rocks sculpted by water. At one time, it may have been used by the Maya for religious ceremonies. You can walk the trails at this 20-acre site near the village of El Progresso. Moonracer Farm organizes tours to this evolving site. ⊹ *From the Western Hwy., at about Mile 62, take the Mountain Pine Ridge Rd. to Mile 7 and turn left to the village of El Progreso* 🖃 *BZ$8; guided tour BZ$30 for one or two persons.*

Río Frio Caves. Río Frio Caves are only a few miles by car down a steep track, but ecologically speaking, these caves are in a different world. In the course of a few hundred yards, you drop from pine savanna to tropical forest. Nothing in Belize illustrates its extraordinary geological diversity as clearly as this startling transition. A river runs right through the center of the main cave—actually it's more of a tunnel, open at both ends—and, over the centuries, has carved the rock into fantastic shapes. Swallows fill the place, and at night ocelots and margays pad silently across the cold floor in search of slumbering prey. Seen from the dark interior, the light-filled world outside seems more intense and beautiful than ever. About a mile away (2 km) are the Cuevas Gemelas (Twin Caves), best seen with a guide. Due to occasional bandit activity in the area, at times a Belize Defence Forces escort is required to visit to the Rio Frio Caves—if driving on your own, ask at your hotel or at the Douglas de Silva forestry station. ✛ *From the entrance gate of the Mountain Pine Ridge, go 14 mi (23 km). Turn right Douglas de Silva forestry station at Rio Frio sign and drive 5 mi (8 km) to the caves.* 🎬 *Free.*

Río On. At the Río On, just north of the Rio Frio Caves, you can sunbathe on flat granite boulders or dunk yourself into crystal clear pools and waterfalls. 🎬 *Free.*

WHERE TO STAY

NEAR MOUNTAIN PINE RIDGE
For expanded hotel reviews, visit Fodors.com.

In addition to the lodges in the Mountain Pine Ridge itself, which include the top-end Blancaneaux Lodge and Hidden Valley Inn, along with the moderate Five Sisters Lodge, several jungle lodges, some recently opened and all in the moderate price category, are on the two roads leading to the Mountain Pine Ridge—the Chiquibul Road from Georgeville (also called the Mountain Pine Ridge Road or the Georgeville Road) and the Cristo Rey Road from Santa Elena. Of the lodges en route to the Mountain Pine Ridge, Table Rock Lodge, Mystic River Lodge, Macaw Bank Lodge, Inn the Bush, and Crystal Paradise Resort are on the Macal River, while Mariposa Jungle Lodge, Gumbo Limbo Village Resort, Moonracer Farm, and Mountain Equestrian Trails are not.

$$ 🎬 **Crystal Paradise Resort.** There's a range of accommodations here—from two simple rooms to a collection of thatch cabañas with views of the Macal River—run by the Tut (pronounced *Toot*) family—Mom and Dad Tut and 10, yes, 10, children. **Pros:** Belizean-owned; good guided tours. **Cons:** no-frills rooms and cabañas. ⊠ *Cristo Rey Rd., Cristo Rey Village* ☎ *820/4014* ⊕ *www.crystalparadise.com* ↩ *13 cabañas, 1 cottage, 2 rooms* ⚠ *In-room: no TV. In-hotel: business center.*

$$$ 🎬 **Gumbo Limbo Village Resort.** Well-priced, with a lovely hilltop setting, and amenities such as a pool, this lodge is an attractive option just 2 mi (3 km) from the Western Highway at Georgeville. **Pros:** attractive cottage accommodations; lovely views from hilltop setting; swimming pool. **Cons:** steep hill on dirt access road is a doozy. ⊠ *Mile 2, Mountain Pine Ridge Rd. (also called Chiquibul Rd. or Georgeville Rd.), Georgeville* ☎ *650/3112* ⊕ *www.gumbolimboresort.com* ↩ *4 cottages* ⚠ *In-room: no TV, Wi-Fi. In-hotel: restaurant, bar, pool.*

$$ 🎬 **Inn the Bush.** Even if you wince at the punning name of this new ecolodge, you'll probably enjoy a stay here. **Pros:** small eco-lodge with personal service; reasonable rates; swimming pool; peace and quiet. **Cons:** not a party place. ⊠ *Mile 6, Cristo Rey Rd., Macaw Bank, off Cristo*

Rey Rd., Cristo Rey Village ☎ 670/6364 ⊕ *www.innthebushbelize.com* ↪ *2 cabañas* ⚘ *In-room: no a/c, no TV. In-hotel: restaurant, bar, pool.*

$$ ▦ **Macaw Bank Lodge.** This small, laid-back eco-lodge on 50 acres adjoining the Macal River is for travelers seeking a frill-free spot where you can hear the jungle hum outside your doorstep and where the air bristles with the promise of bird and animal sightings. **Pros:** laid-back eco-lodge with moderate rates. **Cons:** a bit of a hike to the river for swimming; no cell phone access. ⊠ *Cristo Rey Rd.* ⊠ *P.O. Box 248, San Ignacio* ☎ 603/4825 ⊕ *www.macawbankjunglelodge.com* ↪ *5 cottages* ⚘ *In-room: no a/c, no TV, Wi-Fi* ⅋ *No meals.*

$$$ ▦ **Mariposa Jungle Lodge.** Two American lawyers, Jim and Sharyn Brinker, opened these six well-designed cabañas set in the shade, with pimento walls, thatch roofs, a nd handmade furniture. **Pros:** personalized service; attractive cabañas; new pool. **Cons:** bumpy 30-minute drive from San Ignacio. ⊠ *Cristo Rey Rd., near junction with Mountain Pine Ridge Rd., San Antonio Village* ☎ 670/2113, 304/244–2136 *in U.S.* ⊕ *www.mariposajunglelodge.com* ↪ *6 cabañas* ⚘ *In-room: no a/c, no TV. In-hotel: restaurant, bar, pool.*

$ ▦ **Moonracer Farm.** This small lodge combines down-home friendliness, a comfortably rustic setting, and lots of outdoor activities, all at a modest price. **Pros:** comfortable, moderately priced, small lodge; helpful owners; tasty meals. **Cons:** rustic setting; leave your hair dryer at home. ⊠ *Mountain Pine Ridge Rd., 600 feet (190 meters) south of junction with Cristo Rey Rd., San Antonio* ☎ 667/5748, 585/200–5748 *in U.S.* ⊕ *www.moonracerfarm.com* ↪ *4 rooms* ⚘ *In-room: no a/c, no TV, Wi-Fi. In-hotel: restaurant, bar.*

$ ▦ **Mountain Equestrian Trails.** If horses are your thing, this is your place. **Pros:** equestrian charm abounds; other activities include caving and birding; affordable room prices. **Cons:** rustic facilities; the focus is on horseback riding. ⊠ *Mike 8, Mountain Pine Ridge Rd. (aka Chiquibul Rd. or Georgeville Rd.), San Antonio* ☎ 669/1124, 800/838–3918 *U.S. reservations* ⊕ *www.metbelize.com* ↪ *10 cabañas,* ⚘ *In-room: no TV* ⅋ *Some meals.*

$$$$ ▦ **Mystic River Resort.** Operated by a French-American couple formerly ★ of Ambergris Caye, this jungle resort on the Macal River is a step up in luxury, service, and dining from run-of-the-mill lodges. **Pros:** stylishly decorated cottages all with river views and fireplaces; excellent food; friendly owners and staff. **Cons:** a little pricey. ⊠ *Mile 6, Cristo Rey Rd., San Antonio Village* ☎ 834/4100 ⊕ *www.mysticriverbelize. com* ↪ *6 cottages* ⚘ *In-room: no a/c, no TV. In-hotel: restaurant, bar.*

$$$ ▦ **Table Rock Lodge.** Though but a fledging lodge, this intimate jungle Fodor's Choice spot offers the seamless service and mature landscaping of a veteran ★ resort that has long since mastered the art of accommodation, and the delicious meals are yet another reason to stay here. **Pros:** low-key, relaxing, off-the-beaten-path ecolodge; good value; wonderful food. **Cons:** it's a bumpy 20-minute ride to San Ignacio. ⊠ *Cristo Rey Rd., San Antonio Village* ☎ 834/4040 ⊕ *www.tablerockbelize.com* ↪ *3 cabañas* ⚘ *In-room: no a/c, no TV. In-hotel: restaurant, bar.*

MOUNTAIN PINE RIDGE

$$$$ ⊡ **Blancaneaux Lodge.** Owned by Francis Ford Coppola, this special
Fodor's Choice lodge is comprised of stunning villas with Japanese-style baths, plunge
★ pools, and screened porches. **Pros:** fabulous grounds; deluxe cabañas
and villas; wonderful food and service. **Cons:** many steep steps may pose
problems for the infirm or elderly; very expensive. ✛ *Turn right at Blancaneaux sign 4½ mi (7½ km) from Mountain Pine Ridge entrance gate*
☎ *824/4912, 800/746–3743 in U.S.* ⊕ *www.blancaneaux.com* ⇨ *10
cabañas, 7 villas, 1 house* ⬧ *In-room: no a/c, safe, kitchen, no TV,
Wi-Fi. In-hotel: restaurant, bar, pool, spa, business center* ¦◎¦ *Breakfast.*

$$ ⊡ **Five Sisters Falls & Lodge.** With a laid-back and romantic style, this
Belizean-owned lodge is perched on a steep hill above the five small
waterfalls that give the place its name. **Pros:** appealing combination
of value and comfort in the Mountain Pine Ridge; no need for a gym
if you walk the steps up from the river. **Cons:** some standard cabañas
lack a view. ✛ *Turn right at Blancaneaux and Five Sisters signs 4½ mi
(7½ km) from Mountain Pine Ridge entrance gate. Continue past air-
strip about 1 mi (1½ km)* ☎ *820/4005, 800/447–2931 in U.S.* ⊕ *www.
fivesisterslodge.com* ⇨ *14 cabañas, 4 suites, 1 2-bedroom villa* ⬧ *In-
room: no a/c, no TV. In-hotel: restaurant, bar, business center.*

$$$ ⊡ **Hidden Valley Inn.** Owned by a prominent Belize City family, Hidden
★ Valley Inn sits on 7,200 acres and has more than a dozen waterfalls,
at least two private caves, and 90 mi (150 km) of hiking and mountain biking trails. **Pros:** charming lodge atmosphere; wonderful waterfalls; excellent birding. **Cons:** meals are pricey; loss of many mature
pines due to the pine beetle means it can be hot and dry on the trails.
✛ *Turn left at Hidden Valley Inn sign 3¾ mi (6¼ km) from Mountain
Pine Ridge entrance gate* ☎ *822/3320, 866/443–3364 in U.S.* ⊕ *www.
hiddenvalleyinn.com* ⇨ *12 cottages* ⬧ *In-room: no a/c, no TV. In-hotel:
restaurant, bar, pool, business center.*

HE OUTDOORS

BIRDING

Birding is great in the Mountain Pine Ridge, and, surprisingly, it's even
better now that many of the pines were felled by the southern pine
beetle. Without the tall pines, it's much easier to spot orange-breasted
falcons, blue crown motmots, white king vultures, stygian owls, and
other rare birds. Some of the best birding is at **Hidden Valley Inn,** a destination for numerous birding tours, and open only to guests.

CAVING

Easily accessible in the Cayo is the Río Frío Cave *(⇨ see above).* You
can also do trips to Barton Creek Cave, about 8 mi (13 km) northwest
of Mountain Pine Ridge entrance gate, off Mountain Pine Ridge Road,
and to Actun Tunichil Muknal from Mountain Pine Ridge. Hidden Valley Inn has two caves open only to guests of the inn.

HIKING

With its karst limestone terrain, extensive network of old logging trails
and roads, and cooler temperatures, the Mountain Pine Ridge is ideal
for hiking. All of the lodges here have miles of marked trails. You can

CLOSE UP

A Crime of Flowers

A rather plain-looking palm leaf has become a big-money target for poachers in Belize—and a huge problem for the Forestry Department. The leaves in question, Xate (pronounced Sha-tay), are widely used in the floral industry because they stay fresh-looking for 45 to 60 days after harvest. They come from three *Chamaedorea* palm species: *C. elegans,* known as parlor palm; *C. oblongata,* called Xate macho; and *C. ernesti-augustii,* or fishtail. The latter is the most sought-after, fetching up to US$1 at its final destination, though poachers get only a fraction of that.

Xate grows wild in Belize, and also in parts of Guatemala and Mexico. Guatemalan Xate collectors, called *xateros,* have stripped much of their own El Petén jungles and have now moved on to Belize, crossing the border into the Chiquibul and other remote areas. Xateros earn more collecting Xate than working at regular jobs, if they can even find work in the economically depressed rural areas of El Petén. Not surprisingly, Belizeans are increasingly joining the ranks of Xate poachers. The harvesters sweep through the jungle, removing the palm leaves with a pocketknife or machete. Each palm plant produces two to five usable leaves.

Unfortunately, the poachers do more than just collect Xate. They sometimes stumble across Mayan sites and loot them for priceless artifacts. Some trap toucans, parrots, and the endangered scarlet macaw for sale on the black market, and they hunt wild animals, including protected tapirs, for food. The Belize Forestry Department has reported significant depletion of native wildlife in areas with large numbers of Xate collectors. In a few cases, xateros have been implicated in robberies or in attacks on researchers and on Belize Defence Forces soldiers. With little chance of getting caught and only modest fines if they are, Xate poachers are working at minimal risk.

What can you do to reduce the damage done by illegal Xate collectors? First, avoid buying flower arrangements that contain Xate, unless you're sure that the Xate was harvested legally. You can also support an effort by the Natural History Museum in London, in cooperation with the Belize Ministry of Natural Resources and the Belize Botanic Gardens at duPlooy's Lodge near San Ignacio, to encourage sustainable, organic growing of Xate by Belizean farmers.

—Lan Sluder

also hike along the roads (mostly gravel or dirt), as there are very few cars in the Pine Ridge. Most people find this more pleasant than trying to fight their way through the bush. The mountain area around Baldy Beacon is especially beautiful; it may remind you of part of the Highlands of Scotland.

All of the Mountain Pine Ridge and Chichibul Wilderness is lightly populated, and some of the residents, such as unemployed squatters who have moved into this remote area, may not always have your best interests at heart. Cell phones don't usually work here, although there has been talk of installing some cell-phone towers as a security measure.

Lodges such as Hidden Valley Inn provide radio phones to guests who are hiking. Always leave word with a responsible party about your hiking plans and time of expected return. Carry plenty of water, food, a compass, and basic medical supplies, especially on long hikes to remote areas. You may want to hire a guide.

HORSEBACK RIDING

In this remote area with virtually no vehicular traffic and many old logging roads, horseback riding is excellent. **Blancaneaux Lodge** and **Hidden Valley Inn** offer horseback riding, and Mountain Equestrian Trails runs horseback tours into the Pine Ridge.

Mountain Equestrian Trails. "MET" runs riding trips into the Pine Ridge. A full-day trip costs around BZ$166. ⊠ *Mile 8, Mountain Pine Ridge Rd.* ☎ *820/4041* ⊕ *www.metbelize.com.*

MOUNTAIN BIKING

Mountain Pine Ridge has the best mountain biking in Belize on hundreds of miles of remote logging roads. Blancaneaux and Hidden Valley Inn provide complimentary mountain bikes to guests.

ZIP-LINING

Calico Jack's Jungle Canopy & Zip Line. This zip line is more than a half mile (1 km) long. The "Ultimo Explorer" zip line tour has nine runs on 15 platforms over 2,700 feet (825 meters). Calico Jack's Village also has cabañas moved from its original location on the Placencia peninsula. ⊠ *Off Mile 7, Mountain Pine Ridge Rd.* ☎ *301/792–2233 U.S. number, 820/4078* ⊕ *www.calicojacksvillage.com.*

HOPPING

Tanah Art Museum. The village of San Antonio, on the way to the Mountain Pine Ridge reserve, is home to the Garcia sisters' Tanah Art Museum, run by four sisters with clever hands and great business acumen. Look for their eye-catching slate carvings. Maria Garcia, who is usually at the shop, has been a driving force behind the Elijio Panti National Park. ⊠ *Cristo Rey Rd., San Antonio* ☎ *669/4023.*

Magaña Zaac-tunich Art Gallery. At one end of San Antonio village is the Magaña family's arts-and-crafts shop, Magaña Zaac-tunich (sometimes spelled Sac-Tunich) Art Gallery, which specializes in wood and limestone carvings. ⊠ *Cristo Rey Rd., San Antonio* ☎ *606/7806.*

ARACOL

55 mi (98 km) south of San Ignacio

GETTING HERE AND AROUND

Caracol is about 55 mi (92 km) from San Ignacio, and about 35 mi to 40 mi (57 km to 66 km) from the major lodges in the Mountain Pine Ridge. Because roads are mostly unpaved and often in poor condition, cars or tour vans take 1½ to 2 hours from the Pine Ridge lodges and about 2½ to 3 hours from San Ignacio, sometimes longer after heavy rains.

TIMING

You can't overnight at Caracol, except on a very expensive overnight tour by Ka'ana Boutique Resort in San Ignacio, so you have to visit on a day trip. You can see the excavated area of Caracol in a few hours.

SAFETY AND PRECAUTIONS

Occasional holdups of tourists by armed gangs believed to be from Guatemala occurred here over the past several years. For caution's sake, trips to Caracol are now in a group convoy, protected by Belize Defence Forces troops. As off-putting as that may seem, Caracol is well worth seeing. The robbery incidents have occurred only rarely, and not a single one has taken place with the Belize Defence Forces on hand. The tour operators to Caracol know the ropes, and will work to make sure your trip to Caracol is rewarding and safe.

Fodor's Choice ★

Caracol. Caracol (Spanish for "snail") is the most spectacular Mayan site in Belize, as well as one of the most impressive in Central America. It was once home to as many as 200,000 people (two-thirds the population of modern-day Belize). It was a metropolis with five plazas and 32 large structures covering almost a square mile. In AD 650, the urban area of Caracol had a radius of approximately 6 mi (10 km) around the site's center. It covered an area larger than present-day Belize City. Altogether it is believed there are some 35,000 buildings at the site, though only a handful of them have been excavated. Excavations at Caracol are being carried on by Diane and Arlen Chase of the University of Central Florida. The latest excavations are in the Northeast Acropolis area east of Caana. Once Caracol has been fully excavated it may dwarf even the great city of Tikal, which is a few dozen miles away (as the toucan flies) in Guatemala. The evidence suggests that Caracol won a crushing victory over Tikal in the mid-6th century, a theory that Guatemalan scholars haven't quite accepted. Until a group of *chicleros* (collectors of gum base) stumbled on the site in 1936, Caracol was buried under the jungle of the remote Vaca Plateau. It's hard to believe it could have been lost for centuries, as the great pyramid of Caana, at nearly 140 feet, is still Belize's tallest structure. ✣ *From Mountain Pine Forest Ridge reserve entrance, head south 14 mi (23 km) to village of Douglas DiSilva, turn left and go 36 mi (58 km)* ⊕ *www.caracol.org* 🎫 *BZ$30* ☉ *Daily 8–5.*

THE RUINS

The main excavated sections are in four groups, denoted on archaeological maps as A, B, C, and D groups. The most impressive structures are the B Group at the northeast end of the excavated plaza. This includes Caana (sometimes spelled Ca'ana), or "Sky Palace," listed as Structure B19-2nd, along with a ball court, water reservoir, and several large courtyards. Caana remains the tallest structure in Belize. The A Group, on the west side of the plaza, contains a temple, ball court, and a residential area for the elite. The Temple of the Wooden Lintel (Structure A6) is one of the oldest and longest-used buildings at Caracol, dating back to 300 BC. It was still in use in AD 1100. To the northwest of the A Group is the Northwest Acropolis, primarily a residential area. The third major plaza forming the core of the site is at the point where a causeway enters the "downtown" part of Caracol. The D Group is a group of structures at the South Acropolis.

Near the entrance to Caracol is a small but interesting visitor center. A guide usually can be hired at the site, but you can also walk around on your own. Seeing all of the excavated area involves several hours of hiking around the site. Be sure to wear comfortable shoes and bring insect repellent, as mosquitoes and other bugs can be a nuisance. Also, watch for anthill mounds and, rarely, snakes. This part of the Chiquibul Forest Reserve is a good place for birding and wildlife spotting. Around the ruins are troops of howler monkeys and flocks of oscellated turkeys, and you may also see deer, coatimundis, foxes, and other wildlife at the site or on the way.

TIPS

Advance permission to visit Caracol is no longer required. Although only about a 10-mi (17-km) section of the road to Caracol from San Ignacio is paved, once into the Mountain Pine Ridge the road is generally in good shape. The Belize government has plans to eventually pave the entire road to Caracol. Belize Defence Forces soldiers accompany vehicles going to Caracol. The convoys leave from Augustine/Douglas DiSilva village. Check with your hotel for current departure times of the convoys. You can drive your own rental vehicle in the convoy or go in a tour van.

TOURS

Most visitors to Caracol come as part of a tour group from San Ignacio, or from one of the lodges in the Mountain Pine Ridge. Full-day tours from San Ignacio, which often include a picnic lunch and stops at Río Frio Cave, Río On, and other sights in the Mountain Pine Ridge, cost from about BZ$140 to BZ$220 per person, including the BZ$30 admission fee to Caracol, depending on what is included and the number of people going. Tours from independent operators generally cost less than those from lodges. Lodges in the Mountain Pine Ridge charge around BZ$200–$250 per person for tours to Caracol, including tax.

Because of its remote location, Caracol gets only about 12,000 visitors a year. That's about one-tenth the number who visit Altun Ha, one-fifth the number who visit Xunantunich, and a smaller fraction of the number who see Tikal. Thus, you're in an exclusive company, and on some slow days you may be one of only a handful of people at the site. Excavations by a team from the University of Central Florida usually are carried out in the winter, typically January through March.

The Southern Coast

WORD OF MOUTH

"Although there's not much to do in Hopkins other than enjoy the beaches and water, great hiking is within reach in the Cockscomb Reserve and at the Mayflower site. You could also access adventures like cave tubing and zip-lining from there. The reef is quite a ways out from there (unlike from Ambergris and Caye Caulker). So you'd have some time on a boat to access snorkeling and diving. If you go, don't miss the drumming at the Lebeha Center."
—hopefulist

By Lan Sluder

As always in Belize, the transition from one landscape to another is swift and startling. As you approach the Hummingbird Highway's end in coastal Dangriga, the lush, mountainous terrain of the north gives way to flat plains bristling with orange trees. Farther south, the Stann Creek Valley is where bananas, the nation's first bumper crop, and most other fruits are grown. Equally noticeable is the cultural segue: whereas San Ignacio has a Spanish air, the Southern Coast is strongly Afro-Caribbean.

The Southern Coast isn't so much a melting pot as a tropical stew full of different flavors. A seaside Garífuna village recalls Senegal, while just down the road a Creole village evokes the Caribbean. Inland, Maya live much as they have for thousands of years next door to Mestizos from Guatemala and Honduras who've come to work the banana plantations or citrus groves. Sprinkled in are expats from the northern climes, looking for a retirement home or trying to make a buck in tourism.

Tourist dollars, the staple of contemporary Belize, have largely bypassed Dangriga to land in Hopkins, and, even more tellingly, in Placencia, the region's most striking destination. Several years ago there were only three small resorts on the peninsula north of Placencia Village. Now there are more than 20, stretching up to the village of Seine Bight, Maya Beach, and beyond. Despite the global recession, plans are in the works for new condos and hotels, although some of these developments have been stalled by a shortage of financing and a scarcity of buyers. A few have shut down, victims of the real-estate bust, or are rotting away in the tropical humidity. Still, owners of small beach resorts and inns are cashing in, selling out to developers, who are in turn combining several small tracts into one, hoping to put together larger residential or resort projects.

With the paving of the Placencia road now completed, with the on-again, off-again construction of a new international airport going on just north of the peninsula, and with talk of a new cruise-ship port in Placencia village, many believe that the tipping point for the Placencia peninsula has been reached and that the new wave of resorts and residential developments will be larger, more upscale, and more multinational. Local residents appear divided about the dramatic changes coming to the peninsula. Some embrace the development in hopes of a better economic future; others bitterly oppose it, citing the impact on the narrow peninsula's fragile ecosystems. With the exception of a few shop owners and some guides, most Placencia residents appear to oppose the coming of mass cruise-ship tourism to the fragile peninsula.

The surfacing of the Southern Highway from Dangriga all the way to Punta Gorda has made the region much more accessible. Off the main

TOP REASONS TO GO

Beaches. The mainland's best beaches are on the Placencia peninsula and around Hopkins. Although they're narrow ribbons of khaki rather than wide swaths of talcum-powder sand, they're ideal for lazing in a hammock under a coco palm. And you don't have to fight the crowds for a spot—at least not yet.

Jaguars. The world's first and only jaguar preserve is the Cockscomb Basin Wildlife Sanctuary. Chances are you won't actually see one of these big, beautiful cats in the wild, as they roam the high bush mainly at night, but you may see tracks or hear a low growl in the darkness.

Water Sports. Anglers won't be disappointed by the bonefish, tarpon, and other sportfishing. The Barrier Reef here is generally 15 mi (25 km) or more off the coast, so it's a long trip out, even with the fast boats the dive shops use, but there are patch reefs around closer islands, with excellent snorkeling. Serious divers will find two of Belize's three atolls, Turneffe and Glover's, within reach. In a charter sailboat you can island-hop in the protected waters inside the reef.

highway, however, most roads consist of red dirt and potholes. The road that once was the worst in the region, the dirt track from the Southern Highway to Placencia Village, has been transformed, thanks to a loan from the Caribbean Development Bank, into a smooth, paved, two-lane thoroughfare.

Real-estate sales are a driving force in Placencia, Hopkins, and elsewhere along the coast. The lure is the beaches. The Southern Coast has the best beaches on the mainland, although as elsewhere inside the protecting Barrier Reef, the low wave action means the beaches are narrow and there's usually sea grass in the water close to shore. (Sea grass—not seaweed, which is an algae—may be a nuisance for swimmers, but it's a vital part of the coastal ecosystem, acting as a nursery for sea life.) Much of the seafront land has been divided into lots awaiting development; if things continue at this pace, the area will one day rival Ambergris Caye as Belize's top beach destination.

ORIENTATION AND PLANNING

GETTING ORIENTED

From the north, two roads lead to the Southern Coast: the Hummingbird Highway from Belmopan, and the Coastal Road from La Democracia. The Hummingbird is paved, and the most scenic drive in all of Belize. The Coastal Road is unpaved, dusty, or muddy, depending on the amount of rain. Despite the name, it does not hug the coast; in fact you never glimpse the sea from it. The loose gravel roadway is an accident waiting to happen. In short, if you're driving, take the Hummingbird.

Off the spine of the Southern Highway, various shorter roads lead to villages on the coast and inland: from the highway it's about 4 mi (7 km) on a partly paved road to Hopkins; 25 mi (42 km) to Placencia Village, nicely paved all the way, and 5 mi (8 km) to Big Creek/Independence on a paved road.

Gales Point and Dangriga. Gales Point is a small Creole village, with a beautiful waterside setting, known for the manatees in nearby lagoons. Dangriga is the largest Garífuna settlement in Belize, and a jumping-off spot for several offshore cayes. However, neither Gales Point nor Dangriga is a tourism center.

Hopkins. The most accessible and friendliest Garífuna village in Belize, Hopkins has good beaches and a growing tourism industry. It's similar to what Placencia was like 15 years ago.

Placencia Peninsula. This peninsula has the best beaches on the mainland. With the paving of the Placencia road, real-estate development and tourism are taking off, bringing more high-quality accommodations and dining, along with problems associated with development.

PLANNING

WHEN TO GO

The weather on the Southern Coast is similar to that in central and northern Belize, only a little wetter. On average, for example, the Cayo District has rain, or at least a shower, on 125 days a year, while in Stann Creek District there's some rain on 183 days—usually thanks to late fall and winter cold fronts or summer tropical fronts passing through. These showers are generally followed by sunshine. Summer daytime temperatures along the coast reach the high 80s, occasionally the 90s. Humidity is high most of the year, typically 80% or more.

GETTING HERE AND AROUND

AIR TRAVEL

You'll arrive fresher if you fly. From Belize City (both international and municipal airports) there are frequent flights to Dangriga and Placencia on Maya Island Air and Tropic Air. There are more than 20 flights daily between Belize City and Placencia, and more than a dozen to Dangriga. You'll generally fly in small turbine or prop aircraft, such as the 13-passenger Cessna Caravan C208. Fares to Placencia are BZ$159–$169 one way from the Belize City municipal airport, BZ$194–$199 from the international airport; to Dangriga, fares are BZ$83–$93 from the municipal airport, BZ$131–$136 from the international airport. If not included in the ticket price, as they usually are on Maya Island Air, fares are plus a BZ$5 Airport Authority ticket fee for each ticket. There's also a BZ$1.50 security fee from the international airport. New in 2011 is the opportunity to fly between Belmopan and Placencia, with at least one flight daily each way on Tropic Air (BZ$115).

Contacts Maya Island Air ⊠ *Placencia airstrip, Placencia* ☎ *523/3475 in Placencia, 223/1140 in Belize City* ⊕ *www.mayaregional.com.* **Tropic Air** ⊠ *Placencia airstrip, Placencia* ☎ *523/3410 in Placencia, 226/2012 in Belize City, 800/422–3435 in the U.S.* ⊕ *www.tropicair.com.*

CLOSE UP

Missing Bridge

Tropical Storm Arthur, which formed off the coast of Belize on May 31, 2008, and quickly moved ashore, in a few hours dumped up to 15 inches of rain on the country. The flooding was the worst in three decades, and seven Belizeans drowned. Belize's tourism industry managed to escape mostly unscathed. However, one lingering impact for visitors is the loss of the Kendal Bridge over the Sittee River, at Mile 13.7 of the Southern Highway. This major bridge, between Maya Centre and Hopkins, was washed away. Only a temporary and low-lying bridge is in place over the Sittee River, and during the rainy season (June–December in the south), the bridge is sometimes flooded, cutting off the only road between the Hopkins and the far south. No one seems to know for sure when a permanent replacement bridge will be in place. In the rainy season, check locally before driving or busing south of the Hopkins area. Air service to all airstrips in the south continues normally, so if necessary you can fly to Placencia, Independence, or Punta Gorda.

6

BOAT AND FERRY TRAVEL

There are no scheduled boat or ferry services from Belize City to points along the Southern Coast, nor are there any scheduled water taxis or ferries between those points or to offshore cayes. However, there's a scheduled water taxi, a small boat named the *Hokey Pokey,* between Placencia Village and Mango Creek/Independence, two adjacent villages on the west side of Placencia Lagoon. Fare is BZ$10 one-way. Currently there are seven trips each way daily, with reduced service on Sunday.

From Placencia, a weekly boat, the *D'Express,* runs to Puerto Cortes, Honduras, on Friday, with a stop in Big Creek across the lagoon to clear immigration and customs. It returns from Puerto Cortes on Monday. Get information from the Placencia Tourism Center in Placencia village. From Dangriga, another boat, *Nesymein Nedy*, also goes weekly to Puerto Cortes on Friday and returns from Puerto Barrios on Monday. Fares to Honduras are BZ$110 one-way.

Also from Dangriga, boats go out daily to Tobacco Caye. There are no fixed schedules, but the boats generally leave around 9 to 9:30 am, and the fare is BZ$35–$40 per person one-way. Ask at the Riverside Café.

Contacts D' Express ✉ *Placencia* ☎ *523/4045 in Placencia, 2665–0726 in Honduras* ⊕ *www.belizeferry.com.* **Hokey Pokey** ✉ *Placencia MnM Dock, Placencia* ☎ *523/2376.* **Nesymein Nedy Charter Boats** ✉ *North Riverside, Dangriga* ☎ *522/0062, 604/4738.*

BUS TRAVEL

In the south, James Bus Line runs from Belize City via Belmopan to Dangriga and Independence and then Punta Gorda. Schedules are subject to change, but James Bus Line has about 10 buses daily. Ritchie's Bus Line also has three to four buses daily each way between Dangriga to Placencia, with reduced service on Sunday. Fares from Belize City are around BZ$15 to Dangriga and BZ$20 to Placencia (BZ$10 between Dangriga and Placencia).

With connections, the trip from Belize City to Dangriga and Hopkins is three to four hours; Placencia is around five to six hours or more, depending on the number of stops. Buses are usually old U.S. school buses or ancient Greyhound buses, are often crowded, and don't have air-conditioning or restrooms. The James Bus Line buses generally are in the best condition.

Contacts James Bus Line ⊠ *7 King St., Punta Gorda* ☎ *702/2049*. **Ritchie's Bus Line** ⊠ *Placencia* ☎ *523/3806*.

CAR TRAVEL

To get to Placencia, head southeast from Belmopan on the Hummingbird Highway. The highway is one of Belize's better roads, as well as its most scenic. On your right rise the jungle-covered Maya Mountains, largely free of signs of human habitation except for the occasional field of corn or beans. As you approach Dangriga you'll see large citrus groves.

Three small local outfits, Barefoot Services, Car Rental of Placencia, and Jagz Auto Rental, rent cars in Placencia. Some, including Car Rental of Placencia, also rent golf carts, which can be driven on the roads. Jagz (sometimes written Jag) is an agent of Hertz in Belize City. Also, Budget, based in Belize City, has a branch in Placencia. Rates in Placencia start at around BZ$160 per day, plus tax.

Contacts Budget ⊠ *Placencia* ☎ *223/2435 in Belize City* ✉ *reservations@ budget-belize.com* ⊕ *www.budget-belize.com*. **Car Rental of Placencia** ⊠ *Placencia Rd., 1 mi (1⅔ km) north of the airstrip, Placencia* ☎ *625/9573* ⊕ *www. carrentalofplacencia.com*. **Jagz Auto Rental** ⊠ *Placencia Airstrip, Placencia* ☎ *604/7471* ⊕ *www.genietravelbelize.com/auto_rental_placencia.htm*. **Barefoot Services** ⊠ *Caribbean Travel and Tours Office, Main St., Placencia* ☎ *607/5133, 629/9602* ✉ *info@barefootservicesbelize.com* ⊕ *www.barefootservicesbelize. com* ⊗ *Closed Sat. and Sun.*

TAXI TRAVEL

If you need a ride to the airport in Dangriga, have your hotel call a taxi. The fare from downtown Dangriga to the airstrip at the town's north end is about BZ$6–BZ$8. From Dangriga to Hopkins the fare is around BZ$100–BZ$120. Taxis are expensive in Placencia, given the relatively short distances involved and the fact that the road is now paved. Fares within Placencia village are BZ$6 for one or two persons and BZ$6 each for three or more. From the village to the airstrip the fare is BZ$12 for one or two persons, and BZ$6 each for three or more. It's BZ$22 for one or two persons between Placencia village and Seine Bight, and BZ$8 each for three or more. Between Placencia village and the north end of the peninsula, where The Placencia condotel is, it's BZ$50 one-way for one to three persons and BZ$15 per person for four or more, and BZ$40 one-way between Placencia village and Maya Beach for one to three persons and BZ$15 per person for four or more. Your hotel can arrange a taxi for you, or call Radiance Ritchie or Gilly Garbutt.

Contacts Gilly Garbutt ⊠ *Placencia* ☎ *620/9387*. **Radiance Ritchie** ⊠ *Placencia* ☎ *622/3197*.

EMERGENCIES

Placencia has a small medical clinic with a physician and nurse. Seine Bight, Hopkins, and Independence also have medical clinics. For more serious medical attention you should go to the Southern Regional Hospital in Dangriga or one of the hospitals in Belize City. The Belize Emergency Response Team, based in Belize City, provides ambulance and air transport all over the country. A pharmacy with limited supplies is Placencia Pharmacy, and Wallen's Market also has a small pharmacy. Dial 911 in case of emergency.

Hospitals **Belize Emergency Response Team** ✉ *1675 Sunrise Ave., Belize City* ☎ *223/3292.* **Independence Medical Center** ✉ *Independence* ☎ *523/2167.* **Placencia Medical Clinic** ✉ *In center of village, near primary school, Placencia* ☎ *523/3326.* **Placencia Pharmacy** ✉ *Main Rd., Independence* ☎ *523/3346.* **Southern Regional Hospital** ✉ *Stann Creek District Hwy., Dangriga* ☎ *522/2078.* **Wallen's Market and Pharmacy** ✉ *Main Rd., Independence* ☎ *523/3128.*

MONEY MATTERS

There are three banks in Placencia. Atlantic Bank has an office on the road just north of Placencia Village, as well as a second ATM in Placencia Village, and ScotiaBank is also in the village. Belize Bank has an office at Placencia Point. All three banks have ATMs that accept foreign-issued cards.

Belize Bank in Dangriga accepts foreign-issued ATM cards. First Caribbean International Bank in Dangriga has an ATM that accepts foreign cards. There are no banks in Hopkins.

Banks **Atlantic Bank** ✉ *Placencia Rd., Placencia* ☎ *523/3386.* **Belize Bank** ✉ *24 St. Vincent St., Dangriga* ☎ *522/2903* ✉ *Placencia Point, Placencia* ☎ *523/3144.* **First Caribbean International Bank** ✉ *Commerce St., Dangriga* ☎ *522/2015.* **ScotiaBank** ✉ *Main Rd., Placencia* ☎ *523/3277.*

ABOUT THE RESTAURANTS

Broiled, grilled, fried, sautéed, cooked in lime juice as ceviche, or barbecued on the beach: any way you eat it, seafood is the life-stuff on the Southern Coast. Restaurants serve fish, lobster, conch, and shrimp, often fresh from the boat, or, in the case of shrimp, straight from the shrimp farms near Placencia.

Expect mostly small, locally owned restaurants; some breezy beachside joints with sand floors, others wood shacks. Placencia has by far the largest number of eateries, with Hopkins a distant second. Some of the upscale restaurants are in resorts, such as Inn at Robert's Grove and Turtle Inn. The Bistro at Maya Beach Hotel is one of the country's best. And it's worth making a trip to Placencia just to sample the incredible gelato at Tutti-Frutti.

Off-season, especially in late summer and early fall, restaurants in Placencia and Hopkins may close for a few weeks, and on any day the owners may decide to close early if there are no customers, so call ahead. It's also a good idea to make reservations so the cooks will have enough food on hand.

ABOUT THE HOTELS

There are two kinds of lodging to choose from on the Southern Coast: small, basic hotels, often Belizean-owned, and upscale beach resorts, usually owned and operated by Americans or Canadians. The small hotels are clustered in Placencia Village, Hopkins village, and in Dangriga town. The beach resorts are on the Placencia peninsula north of Placencia Village and also near Hopkins. Several of these resorts, including Francis Ford Coppola's Turtle Inn and Hamanasi in Hopkins, are among the best hotels in Belize. There also are a small number of vacation rental houses near Hopkins and on the Placencia peninsula.

At least a dozen condo developments have opened, are under construction, or are in the planning stages on Placencia peninsula and near Hopkins. Only time will tell whether all these plans will fully materialize (one large condo development, Bella Maya, on the Placencia peninsula, has closed, leaving some owners in the lurch) or whether supply will outstrip demand, but it's clear that this area has reached the point where, sooner or later, development by large international companies is inevitable.

WHAT IT COSTS IN BELIZE DOLLARS				
	¢	$	$$	$$$	$$$$
RESTAURANTS	under BZ$8	BZ$8–BZ$15	BZ$15–BZ$25	BZ$25–BZ$50	over BZ$50
HOTELS	under BZ$100	BZ$100–BZ$200	BZ$200–BZ$300	BZ$300–BZ$500	over BZ$500

Restaurant prices are per person for a main course at dinner. Hotel prices are for two people in a standard double room, including tax and service.

TOURS

Altogether, Placencia has about 80 licensed tour guides. Most of the guides, except the fishing guides, work on a contract basis for resorts or tour operators. These tour guides and operators offer dive and snorkel trips to Laughing Bird or other cayes and to the Barrier Reef, wildlife tours to Monkey River, birding tours to Red Bank, hiking trips to Cockscomb Basin Wildlife Sanctuary, and excursions to Mayan ruins such as Mayflower, Nim Li Punit, or Lubaantun.

The larger resorts on the peninsula, including Inn at Robert's Grove, Turtle Inn, and others, offer a variety of tours and trips, using tour guides they have come to trust. ⇨ *See Where to Eat and Stay sections for contact information.*

Mary Toy's Destinations Belize is a full-service tour and travel operation, offering fishing, boating, sailing, and other trips with some of the best guides in the region, along with hotel reservations. Other tour operators include Caribbean Tours and Joy Tours.

For first-time visitors, taking a couple of sea and land tours is a good way to become familiar with what the area offers. If you have a rental car, you can do some of the trips, such as to Cockscomb, Mayflower, and the ruins near Punta Gorda, on your own. To book tours and trips, check with your hotel or walk along the Sidewalk in Placencia

GREAT ITINERARIES

IF YOU HAVE 3 DAYS ON THE SOUTHERN COAST

Base yourself in Placencia. On your first full day, walk the Sidewalk in Placencia Village, hear the latest gossip, and get to know a little of village life. Hang out on the beach at your hotel and get on Belize time, then have drinks and dinner in the village, perhaps at Rumfish y Vino, Wendy's, or La Dolce Vita. If you still have energy, have some Belikins at the Barefoot or Tipsy Tuna. On your second day, take a snorkel trip to Laughing Gull Caye or another snorkel area, or, if you dive, do a full-day dive trip to Turneffe or Glover's atoll. On your final day, drive or take a guided tour to Cockscomb Basin Wildlife Sanctuary. Be sure to stop at the Maya Centre craft cooperative for gift shopping. If there's time, also visit the Mayflower Mayan site and waterfall. End the day with dinner at the Bistro at Maya Beach Hotel.

IF YOU HAVE 5 DAYS ON THE SOUTHERN COAST

Drive or fly to Dangriga (the closest airport to Hopkins). While in Dangriga, stop by the Garífuna museum, then proceed by taxi or rental car to Hopkins to stay at one of its beach resorts. On your first full day, take a walk on the beach in the morning, then tour Cockscomb Basin Wildlife Sanctuary and hike the jungle trails. Be sure to stop at the Maya Centre craft cooperative. Have dinner at one of the local restaurants in Hopkins Village or at Chef Rob's. On your second full day, visit the Mayflower Mayan site and waterfalls in the morning, and spend the rest of the day on the beach. On your third day, rise early and drive (or go by taxi) to Placencia. If the weather's good, take a snorkel trip. Have dinner in Placencia Village. On your fourth day, if you dive, do a day dive trip to Turneffe or Glover's atoll, or go fishing for permit or tarpon. If you catch anything edible, have one of the local restaurants prepare it for you for dinner. Or simply spend a lazy day in a hammock at the beach and around the pool. On your final day, if you're interested in Mayan sites, do a day trip to Lubaantun and Nim Li Punit near Punta Gorda, or else go on a tour of Monkey River.

6

Village, where several of the tour operators have small shops. You can also check with the Belize Tourism Industry Association (BTIA) visitor information office, which publishes a monthly tabloid and online newspaper, Placencia Breeze. You'll probably pay a little less by booking in the village instead of at your hotel, but the savings may not be worth the effort.

Day trips to Nim Li Punit and Lubaantun Mayan sites near Punta Gorda cost around BZ$160–BZ$190 per person, while day trips to the Mayflower ruins and waterfalls run about BZ$120. Half-day snorkeling trips inside the reef, to Laughing Bird Caye and other snorkel spots, are around BZ$100, while a full-day snorkel trip might run BZ$140. Boat trips to Monkey River are around BZ$120, while a boat excursion on the Placencia Lagoon to look for manatees is around BZ$80–$100. Cockscomb day trips run about BZ$160. Most full-day trips include a picnic lunch. If you're going to an area with an admission fee, such as Cockscomb, the fee is additional.

HISTORY

As elsewhere in Belize, the Maya were here first. They had settlements in what is now Stann Creek District at least from the Early Classic period (around AD 300) until the Post-Classic period (about AD 1200). However, this part of Belize did not have the large Mayan cities that existed elsewhere. Few of the known Mayan sites in the area have been extensively excavated, but they appear to have been small ceremonial centers.

In the 1600s, small numbers of English, some of whom were pirates, settled on the Placencia peninsula, though most eventually left the area. Creoles from Jamaica came to Stann Creek in the 1700s, mainly to work in logging, and, later, in fishing. In the next century English traders and farmers arrived in what is now Dangriga. They called their coastal trading posts "stands," which was corrupted to "stann." Hence the name Stann Creek. On November 19, 1823, a group of Garinagu from the Bay Islands of Honduras, former African slaves who had intermarried with Carib Indians in the southern Caribbean, arrived at the mouth of the Stann Creek River, at what was then called Stann Creek Town. This date is still celebrated in Belize as Garífuna Settlement Day. Later, the name of Stann Creek Town (but not the district) was changed to Dangriga, which means "sweet water" in the Garífuna language.

In the late 1800s several families, originally from Scotland, Portugal, Honduras, and elsewhere, arrived in Placencia. The names of these families—Garbutt, Leslie, Westby, and Cabral—are still common on the peninsula. In the 19th and early 20th century the fertile soils of the coastal plain were found to be ideal for growing bananas and citrus, and soon agriculture became the most important industry in the region. The first railroad in Belize, the Stann Creek Railway, built by the United Fruit Company to transport bananas, started operation around World War I. The railroad closed in the 1950s.

The first small tourist resorts were developed on the Placencia peninsula in the 1960s and '70s, but the bad roads and lack of infrastructure meant that few visitors got this far south. The first fishing cooperative was established in Placencia in 1962. Although fishing is still a way of life for a few people on the coast, the big money now is real-estate development and tourism. Shrimp farming, once an up-and-coming industry around Placencia, has run into problems due to competition from Asia, and several Belize shrimp farms have closed. At one point in 2011 there was even a shortage of shrimp in Belize due to lack of supply from local shrimp farms.

Hurricane Iris in October 2001 devastated much of the Southern Coast south of Maya Beach, Tropical Storm Arthur in late May 2008 caused extensive flooding, and an earthquake in May 2009 damaged some homes in Placencia and Monkey River, but the area has bounced back stronger than ever, and you will see few signs of the natural disasters.

Dave Vernon's Toadal Adventure is a leading operator of adventure kayaking, hiking, and biking tours in Southern Belize. Seakunga offers kayak and camping trips on the cayes off Placencia, as well as an array of kayak, Windsurfer, and small catamaran rentals for independent adventuring.

Contacts **Caribbean Travel and Tours** ⊠ *Skip Jeck St., Placencia* ☎ *523/3481* ⊕ *www.ctbelize.com.* **Destinations Belize** ⊠ *Placencia* ☎ *253/4018, 610/4718* ⊕ *www.destinationsbelize.com.* **Joy Tours** ⊠ *Placencia* ☎ *253/3325* ⊕ *www. belizewithjoy.com.* **Seakunga** ⊠ *Placencia Rd., 1 mi (1½ km) north of airstrip, Placencia* ☎ *800/781, 523/3644.* **Toadal Adventures Belize** ⊠ *Point Placencia, Placencia* ☎ *523/3207* ✆ *info@toadaladventure.com* ⊕ *www.toadaladventure. com.*

VISITOR INFORMATION

The Placencia office of the Belize Tourism Industry Association is on the main road near Tutti-Frutti and Rumfish y Vino. The BTIA publishes the *Placencia Breeze*, an informative monthly newspaper, and has a very helpful Web site listing all accommodations, restaurants, and bars, ⊕ *www.placencia.com.* Another helpful site on Placencia is put together by local resident Mary Toy, ⊕ *www.destinationsbelize.com.* Hopkins has several interesting Web sites put together by local residents, including ⊕ *www.hopkinsbelize.com* and ⊕ *www.cometohopkins.com.*

Information **Belize Tourism Industry Association** ⊠ *In village, behind Tutti-Frutti, Main Rd., Placencia* ☎ *523/4045* ⊕ *www.placencia.com.*

FROM GALES POINT TO PLACENCIA

Thanks to its good beaches, the Southern Coast—the area from Gales Point to Placencia—is the up-and-coming part of Belize, with a growing number of resorts and restaurants, especially in Hopkins and Placencia.

DANGRIGA

99 mi (160 km) southeast of Belmopan.

With a population of around 9,000, Dangriga is the largest town in the south and the home of the Garífuna or Black Caribs, as they're also known (though some view the latter term as a remnant of colonialism). Strictly speaking the plural is Garinagu, but Garifunas also is used. There's not much to keep you in Dangriga. Though the town is on the coast, there are no good beaches, no truly first-class hotels, few restaurants, and, except for a small museum on Garífuna culture in the outskirts of town, not much to see. Rickety clapboard houses on stilts and small shops line the downtown streets, and the town has a kind of end-of-the-road feel. Dangriga isn't really dangerous, and in fact it's friendlier than it first seems, though it has a rough vibe, a little like Belize City, that's off-putting for many visitors.

Each year, on November 19 and the days around it, the town cuts loose with a week of Carnival-style celebrations. Garífuna drumming, costumed Jonkunu dancers, punta music, and a good bit of drinking make

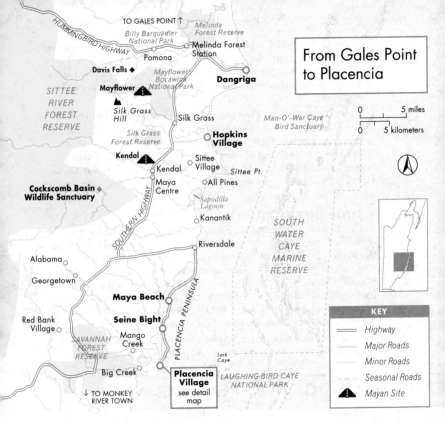

up the festivities of Garífuna Settlement Day, when these proud people celebrate their arrival in Belize and remember their roots.

GETTING HERE AND AROUND

You can arrive in Dangriga by car, bus, or airplane. The Hummingbird, Belize's most scenic road, runs 54 mi (89 km) from Belmopan to Dangriga. As it approaches Dangriga, it technically becomes the Stann Creek District Highway, but most people simply refer to the entire road as the Hummingbird Highway. James Line and other bus lines have frequent service during the day from Belize City via Belmopan to Dangriga. The bus station in Dangriga is seven blocks south of town on the main road, near the Texaco and Shell stations. By air, Maya Island and Tropic together have around a dozen flights daily from the international and municipal airports in Belize City.

Contacts James Bus Line ✉ 7 King St., Punta Gorda ☎ 664/2185.

TIMING

Candidly, Dangriga isn't exactly a mecca for tourists. (Some hotels have Dangriga mailing addresses, even though they're physically located in Hopkins or elsewhere.) Unless you have a special interest in Garífuna culture, need to overnight there on your way to Tobacco Caye, Southwater Caye, or another offshore caye, or simply have a yen to visit quirky, Graham Greene-ish spots, you'll probably spend only a few hours in Dangriga, if that. We do note that the best french fries we've ever had in Belize are at the Pelican Beach Hotel in Dangriga, the best hotel in town.

SAFETY AND PRECAUTIONS

Visitors may get hassled a little on the streets of Dangriga, and care should be exercised if walking around town after dark.

EXPLORING

Billy Barquedier National Park. Billy Barquedier National Park is a 1,500-acre park along the Hummingbird Highway in Stann Creek District. Established in 2001, the park is still in its infancy. While it offers no spectacular sights, it does have primitive hiking trails and the Barquedier Waterfall (locally sometimes called Bac-a-Der Waterfall). It's part of a community co-management program for parks and reserves, in this case with the Steadfast Tourist and Conservation group of Steadfast village, along with the Belize Forestry Department. It's best to enter the park via the northern entrance at Mile 16½ of the Hummingbird Highway. Entrance fee is to the park BZ$8, and a three-hour guided tour to the falls by Holistic Eco Tours is BZ$120 for up to four persons. Camping is available in the park for BZ$20 per person, plus the park entrance fee. ⊠ *Main entrance at Mile 16½, Hummingbird Hwy., and a second entrance is at Mile 17½* ☎ *603/0863 for park caretaker and Holistic Eco Tours guide* ⊕ *billybarquediernp.webs.com* ☑ *BZ$8* ☉ *Daily 9–4:30.*

Davis Falls. Getting to Davis Falls requires a four-wheel-drive vehicle or tractor and wagon and an arduous 2-mi (3 -km) hike, but the falls here are about 500 feet high and are the second highest in the country (after 1,000-Foot Falls in the Mountain Pine Ridge), and the natural pool at the base of the falls is 75 feet deep. The swimming is wonderful, and the undisturbed forest around the falls is great for a picnic or enjoying nature. Before going to Davis Falls, stop at the Citrus Products of Belize plant (Mile 42) or at Awe & Sons store in Alta Vista village (Mile 40), for information and to pay your admission fee. Tours of Davis Falls are offered by several tour guides including IBTM Tours near Punta Gorda and by Holistic Eco Tours at Steadfast village. ⊠ *Off Mile 42, Hummingbird Hwy.* ☎ *722/0112 for IBTM Tours, 603/2339 for Holistic Eco Tours* ☑ *BZ$10* ☉ *Daily 9–4:30.*

Gales Point. The small Creole village of Gales Point, population about 500, set beside the lagoon, is home to several drum makers, including Boombay Andrewin, who gives Creole-style drumming lessons (about BZ$16 an hour) at the Maroon Creole Drum School. Emmeth Young, a founder of the drum school and a long-time Gales Point drummer and drum maker, has moved to San Pedro Columbia, Toledo.**Sugar Shack.** Artist Jill Burgess runs this crafts, snack, and gift shop next to the Maroon Creole Drum School. Handmade drums of coconut wood, cashew wood, or mahogany cost BZ$100–BZ$800. ⊠ *Gales Point Village* ☎ *603/6051* ☉ *Hrs vary but generally Mon.–Sat. 9–5* ✢ *To Gales Point: From Dangriga, go northwest on Hummingbird Hwy. 8½ mi (14 km) to village of Melinda; turn right on Manatee Hwy. (Coastal Rd) and follow 13 mi (21 km) to turnoff, a sharp right turn. This dirt road to Gales Point Village runs about 2½ mi (4 km) until it ends at lagoon* *and Manatee Lodge ☎ 209/8031 community phone for Gales Point, 603/6051 Maroon Creole Drum School.*

🕐 **Gulisi Garífuna Museum.** Named after a Garífuna heroine who came to Belize with her 13 children and founded the village of Punta Negra in Toledo District, this museum has a number of displays on Garífuna history and life. Exhibits cover the Garífuna migration from Africa to St. Vincent, then to Roatan and Belize. Another exhibit is on Thomas Vincent Ramos, a visionary Garífuna leader who, in 1941, established the first Garífuna Settlement Day. Other displays are on Garífuna food, clothing, medicinal plants, and music and dance. The museum also displays paintings by Garífuna artists including Benjamin Nicholas. ✉ *Chuluhadiwa Park, Stann Creek Valley Rd., about 2 mi (3 km) from Dangriga* ☎ *605/1272, 699/0639* 💵 *BZ$10* ⊙ *Weekdays 10–5, Sat. 8–noon.*

Marie Sharp's Factory. You can visit the source of one of Belize's few well-known exports, Marie Sharp's Hot Sauce. The small factory, with about 20 workers, established and still run by Marie Sharp and family, is open to interested visitors weekdays, but for a factory tour it's best to call ahead at least a day in advance. Marie Sharp's main office is in Dangriga (✉ *3 Pier Rd.* ☎ *522–2370*), where there is a small shop. Her products also are sold in nearly every grocery in Belize. ✉ *1 Melinda Rd., 8 mi (13 km) south of Dangriga, Stann Creek Valley* ☎ *520/2087* ⊕ *www.mariesharps-bz.com.*

Mayflower Bocawina National Park. Declared a national park in 2001, Mayflower Bocawina National Park has three minor Mayan ceremonial sites: Mayflower, T'au Witz, and Maintzunum, near Silk Grass Creek. Nearby are the three waterfalls Bocawina Falls, Three Sisters Falls, and Antelope Falls. Access to Mayflower is easiest from Hopkins, about 20 minutes by car. However, tours are offered from Placencia and Dangriga as well as from Hopkins. The entrance to the park is about 4½ mi (7½ km) off the Southern Highway. From the visitor center, to get to Bocawina and Three Sisters Falls, which are close together, it's an easy hike of about 1¼ mi (2 km) on the marked Bocawina Falls trail. The trail to Antelope Falls, about 1¾ mi (3 km), is somewhat more difficult due to some steep sections that can be slick after rains. Maps of the trails are available at the small visitor center. So far, little excavation has been conducted at the Mayan sites, but the parklike setting at the base of the Maya Mountains is beautiful. A nearby jungle lodge, Mama Nootsis an option for food and drinks, or overnight stays. ✉ *Off Mile 6* ✛ *From Mile 6 on Southern Hwy, go west 4½ mi (7½ km) west on dirt road to park visitor center* 💵 *BZ$10* ⊙ *Daily 8–4.*

Southern Lagoon. One of the most beautiful lagoons in Belize, Southern Lagoon, is about 25 mi (41 km) north of Dangriga—a 45-minute car ride. This lagoon is home to many West Indian manatees, and on beaches nearby, hawksbill turtles nest May to October. The Northern and Western lagoons also are in this area. ✛ *From Dangriga, drive west on the Stann Creek Hwy./Hummingbird Hwy. to Melinda; turn right on the unpaved Coastal Hwy. and go about 12 mi (20 km) to the turnoff for Gales Point and follow 2½ mi (4 km) to the lagoon and Gales Point village.*

WHERE TO EAT

$ ✕**King Burger.** Formerly called Burger King, but a far cry from the chain
LATIN AMERICAN of the same name, this is one of the best places in Dangriga to get an
honest plate of stew chicken and rice and beans. The fresh fish is good,
and, yes, so are the hamburgers. Everything's affordable, too. Open for
breakfast, lunch, and dinner daily except Sunday. ✉ *135 Commerce St.*
☎ *522/2476* ▭ *No credit cards* ✆ *Closed Sun.*

$ ✕**Riverside Café.** Information, rather than the food or atmosphere, is
LATIN AMERICAN what you usually come here for, although the Creole and Garífuna
dishes are hearty and tasty, too, and the restaurant is usually busy.
Fishermen and the guys who run boats out to Tobacco Caye and other
offshore cayes hang out here, and if you're going to the islands you can
arrange transportation while you're sipping a beer or having a plate
of rice and beans. Open daily for breakfast, lunch, and dinner. ✉ *S.
Riverside Dr., on south side of North Stann Creek river* ☎ *523/3499*
▭ *No credit cards.*

WHERE TO STAY

For expanded hotel reviews, visit Fodors.com.

DANGRIGA

$ ⊞ **Bonefish Hotel.** If you're overnighting in Dangriga before heading out
to Tobacco Caye or another offshore caye, this little hotel, painted
aquamarine and white, is an acceptable option. **Pros:** handy location;
clean rooms. **Cons:** won't win any interior-design awards; staff not as
friendly as they could be. ✉ *15 Mahogany St.* ☎ *522/2243* ⊕ *www.
bluemarlinlodge.com* ⌑ *7 rooms* ⚓ *In-hotel: restaurant.*

$$ ⊞ **Pelican Beach Resort.** This waterfront hotel on the north end of Dan-
griga, near the airstrip, is the best the town has to offer. **Pros:** charming
colonial-era main building; breezy seaside location; the best lodging in
Dangriga. **Cons:** not the beach of your dreams. ✉ *Scotchman Town,
North End* ✉ *P.O. Box 2* ☎ *522/2044* ⊕ *www.pelicanbeachbelize.com*
⌑ *20 rooms* ⚓ *In-room: no a/c, no TV, Wi-Fi. In-hotel: restaurant, bar,
beach, water sports.*

NEAR DANGRIGA

$$ ⊞ **Manatee Lodge.** This colonial-era lodge, just feet from the Southern
Lagoon and surrounded by flowers, has a stunning setting, though ser-
vice and facilities do not always live up to its location. **Pros:** beautiful
waterside setting; interesting colonial atmosphere. **Cons:** off-the-beaten-
path location; à la carte tours fairly expensive; lodge would benefit from
upgrades. ✉ *Gales Point Village* ☎ *220/8040* ⊕ *www.manateelodge.
com* ⌑ *8 rooms* ⚓ *In-room: no a/c, no TV, Wi-Fi. In-hotel: restaurant,
bar, water sports.*

SHOPPING

Dangriga has some interesting, offbeat shopping, notably for Garífuna
arts and crafts. Collectors may want to spend a day looking for items
that are rarely available outside Belize and in some cases may not be
available elsewhere in Belize. Austin Rodriquez sells his handmade
drums here. Noted Garífuna artist Pen Cayetano has a studio and

gallery. Garífuna cultural expert Frank Swaso has a gallery selling local drums, dolls, masks, and wood carvings.

Austin Rodriquez. Come to this seafront store for locally made drums. ✉ *Seafront at North Stann Creek River, Dangriga* ☎ *502/3752.*

Garinagu Crafts Gallery. This small gallery sells Garífuna drums, masks, wood carvings and other locally made items. In the gallery is a small museum on Garífuna life. ✉ *46 Oak St. at Tubroose St., Dangriga* ☎ *522/2596.*

Pen Cayetano Studio Gallery. Punta rocker and internationally known artist Pen Cayetano displays his bold, colorful paintings at his gallery. Work by his wife, Ingrid Cayetano, and daughter, Mali, are also displayed. ✉ *3 Aranda Crescent, Dangriga* ☎ *501/3156* ✍ *BZ$5.*

HOPKINS VILLAGE

10 mi (17 km) south of Dangriga on the Southern Hwy., then 2 mi (3 km) east on a partially paved road.

Hopkins is an intriguing Garífuna coastal village of about 1,400 people, halfway between Dangriga and Placencia. Garífuna culture is more accessible here than in Dangriga. Hopkins has the same toast-color beaches as those in Placencia, and a number of new resorts have opened to take advantage of them. Americans, Canadians, and Europeans are snapping up beachfront land here at prices a bit lower than in Placencia or on Ambergris Caye, but so far only a few vacation homes and condos have been built. If there's a downside to the area, it's the biting sand flies, which can be vicious at times.

GETTING HERE AND AROUND
The turnoff to Hopkins from the Southern Highway is 10 mi (16 km) south of the junction of the Hummingbird and Southern highways. The Hopkins road, partly paved, is rutted and potholed. A longer, but less potholed, route to Hopkins is via the Sittee River Road, 2½ mi (4 km) farther south on the Southern Highway. Buses on the Southern Highway will drop you at the entrance road to Hopkins, and a few stop in Hopkins itself. Hopkins has no air service. You can fly to Dangriga and take a taxi to Hopkins (about BZ$100–BZ$120), if your hotel doesn't provide a shuttle.

Contacts James Bus Line ✉ *7 King St., Punta Gorda* ☎ *722/2049, 664/2185.*

TIMING
The highlights of Hopkins can be seen in much less than a day, but if this is your beach destination, you can profitably spend several days, or longer, here enjoying activities on the water.

WHAT TO SEE
Lebeha Drumming Center. In the center of town you can watch local Garífuna boys hone their drumming skills at the Lebeha Drumming Center. *Lebeha* means "the end" in the Garífuna language, a reference to the school's location at a small guesthouse (rooms from BZ$35) and bar near the north end of the village. Visitors are welcome. The drums, mostly made by a noted drum maker in Dangriga, Austin Rodriquez,

CLOSE UP

The Garífuna Struggle

Perhaps the most unusual of the ethnic groups calling Belize home, the Garífuna have a story that is both bizarre and moving, an odyssey of exile and dispossession in the wake of the confusion wrought in the New World by the Old. The Garífuna are descended from a group of Nigerian slaves who were shipwrecked on the island of St. Vincent in 1635. The Caribs, St. Vincent's indigenous population, fiercely resisted the outsiders at first, but they eventually overcame their distrust.

In the eyes of the British colonial authorities, the new ethnic group that developed after years of intermarriage was an illegitimate and troublesome presence. Worse still, the Garífuna sided with, and were succored by, the French. After nearly two centuries of guerrilla warfare, the British decided that the best way to solve the problem was to deport them en masse.

After a circuitous and tragic journey across the Caribbean, during which thousands perished of disease and hunger, the exiles arrived in Belize.

That the Garífuna have preserved their cultural identity testifies to Belize's extraordinary ability to encourage diversity. They have their own religion, a potent mix of ancestor worship and Catholicism; their own language, which, like Carib, has separate male and female dialects; their own music, a percussion-oriented sound known as punta rock; and their own social structure, which dissuades young people from marrying outside their community. In writer Marcella Lewis, universally known as Auntie Madé, the Garífuna also had their own poet laureate. In 2002 the United Nations designated the Garífuna as a World Heritage culture.

6

are of mahogany or mayflower wood, with deerskin on the drumhead. Other instruments include *shakas,* or shakers, calabash gourds filled with fruit seeds and turtle shells. The drumming goes on nightly, though the most activity is on weekends. Donations are accepted, and you can purchase a CD of Lebeha drumming. Drumming lessons are around BZ$30. ☎ 666/6658 ⊕ *www.lebeha.com.*

WHERE TO EAT

$$$ ✕ **Barracuda Bar & Grill.** Owners Tony and Angela Marsico traded run-
ECLECTIC ning a restaurant in Alaska for operating a beachside bistro in Belize.
★ They've turned this restaurant, part of Beaches and Dreams Seafront Inn, into one of the best eateries on the Southern Coast, with delicious dishes like fresh grilled snapper, pork shank osso bucco, and baked fish with shrimp in a tamarind sauce. Also try the blackened barracuda bits. Catch the sea breezes on the covered, open-air deck while you munch a handmade pizza or enjoy a burger. The restaurant usually closes for a few weeks off-season. ⊠ *Sittee Point* ☎ *523/7259.*

$$$ ✕ **Chef Rob's Gourmet Cafe.** You'll recognize this restaurant by the big sign
ECLECTIC out front made from one side of a red 1964 Peugeot 404, but inside the
★ charming clapboard building Chef Rob Pronk's Caribbean-style food is surprisingly contemporary. And delicious. A four-course (soup, salad,

entrée, and dessert) prix fixe menu is BZ$50–$70; the menu changes daily, but the entrée might be lobster, rib-eye steak, fresh fish, or ribs, all presented creatively and with interesting sauces. If ordering à la carte, try the lobster sautéed with garlic and rum or the signature bouillabaisse. In-season, you'll definitely need reservations. As of this writing, Chef Rob planned to open a second location in Hopkins at Parrot Cove resort. ⊠ *Front St., opposite All Seasons Guest House, Hopkins* ☎ *670/0445* ⌫ *Reservations essential* ☯ *Closed Mon.*

$$
PIZZA
✕ **Driftwood Beach Bar and Pizza Shack.** Driftwood arguably has the best pizza in Southern Belize, and some would say in all of Belize, served up in a friendly, casual atmosphere in a beachfront thatch palapa by outgoing British-American owners. Try the Driftwood veggie pizza, with white sauce, eggplant, zucchini, spinach, and sun-dried tomatoes (in three sizes, BZ$25 to $45) or the classic with pepperoni, black olives, and mushrooms (BZ$20 to $36). If pizza isn't your thing, go for the catch of the day or one of the pasta dishes. Plenty of cold beer at BZ$3.50 a bottle. ⊠ *North end of Hopkins, Hopkins* ☎ *667/4072* ▭ *No credit cards* ☯ *Closed Wed.*

$
LATIN AMERICAN
✕ **Innies Restaurant.** At Innies, as at most of the other local restaurants in Hopkins, you're eating in a spot that was once somebody's house or back porch. In this pink dining room with linoleum floor, you dine on picnic tables with oilcloths, and the inexpensive food is well prepared. Fried chicken with rice and beans or french fries is around BZ$10, burritos BZ$4, and fish dinners are a little more. Traditional Garífuna dishes such as *hudut* (fish cooked in coconut milk and served with mashed plantains) are also available. ⊠ *South end of village* ☎ *523/7026* ▭ *No credit cards.*

$
SEAFOOD
✕ **King Cassava Cultural Restaurant and Bar.** Some call this bar and restaurant the soul of Hopkins. Located at the entrance to the village on the road from the Southern Highway, with its sand floors it doesn't look like much, but when the rum and beer start flowing, the drums start drumming, and the action at the pool table in the back room gets hot, this is the place to be in Hopkins. The food here is now just so-so, but the beer is cold and patrons are friendly. ⊠ *Main T-intersection entering village* ☎ *503/7305* ▭ *No credit cards* ☯ *Closed Mon.*

$
CAFÉ
✕ **Thongs.** This European-run coffee shop and bistro has good coffee, well-prepared breakfast omelettes, and satisfying smoothies. For lunch, try the salads. It's open for dinner on weekends only. Thongs is small but stylish, with Belizean wood carvings and paintings on the walls. Free Wi-Fi and helpful, friendly owners. ⊠ *South of main T-intersection, Front St.* ☎ *622/0110* ☯ *Closed Mon.–Tues.*

$
LATIN AMERICAN
✕ **Yugadah Café.** The Nuñez sisters, all good cooks, run this café at the Yugadah Inn on the sea (*Yugadah* means "coastal village" in the Garífuna language). They prepare food in a traditional, freestanding kitchen. Garífuna dishes not readily available in most restaurants, such as hudut (fish with coconut water and plantains) and cassava bread, are often available here, along with traditional beans and rice and other Belizean dishes. ⊠ *Front St., about ½ mi (1 km) south of the Hopkins Rd.* ☎ *503/7089* ▭ *No credit cards* ☯ *Closed Wed.*

CLOSE UP

Development, Belize-Style

"People are building $500,000 houses on $5,000 roads!" This is the sentiment of many who watch in amazement as huge condos and luxury houses sprout up along narrow, muddy golf-cart trails. In some areas huge 4,000- to 6,000-square-foot homes are being built where there is no municipal water or sewage system, and in more remote parts of the country no electricity or telephone. One stretch of road on the Placencia peninsula is now sprinkled with massive McMansions, gated communities, and condo projects, built on filled land next to the lagoon.

Belize's lack of infrastructure is nothing new. As late as the 1980s open sewers were common all over Belize City. Even today, in some rural villages, especially in Toledo District, telephone service is a rare commodity, and drinking water comes from a community well. With the unemployment rate in Belize in the low double digits, and with good, high-paying jobs scarce, many hope that the new housing boom will provide a needed economic boost and sustainable job growth. But environmentalists are taking a darker view.

In the Hopkins area, near Sittee Point, environmentalists worry that some of the tallest mangroves in the Western Hemisphere will fall prey to developers. It is illegal to remove endangered mangroves in Belize without a government permit, but this rule, like many other environmental protections, is often ignored. It isn't unusual for homeowners and developers with waterfront property to simply tear out these precious trees and deal with possible fines later.

Belize effectively has no zoning or comprehensive land-use planning, though there is now a country-wide building code that applies to individual buildings and houses. Environmental regulations, while strict in theory—every development is required to have a formal Environmental Impact Plan approved by the national government—often fail in practice. Protective regulations and permit procedures are circumvented, flouted, or just plain ignored. Government officials, whose resources are stretched thin, often can't provide oversight on development projects. According to environmentalists, some government officials are corrupt; they believe that developers can do what they like, if the price is right.

Economic growth, the environment, and the housing boom in Belize are complex, with parties facing off on a multitude of issues. Who knows if everyone will ever see eye to eye?

—Lan Sluder

6

WHERE TO STAY

For expanded hotel reviews, visit Fodors.com.

In addition to the resorts and hotels listed below, Hopkins has about 20 small guesthouses, mostly run by local villagers but also by some expats who have found that the easygoing Hopkins life suits them. Typically just two or three rooms are built next to the home of the owner, who has an eye to tapping the growing tourism market in Hopkins. Most don't look like much from the outside, but have the necessities including electricity and, usually, private baths. Among the better ones are **Wabien Guest House** (☎ 523/7010), **Yugadah Inn** (☎ 503/7089), **Seagull's Nest Guest House** (☎ 522/0600), **Whistling Seas Vacation Inn** (☎ 608/0016), **Ransoms Seaside Gardens** (☎ No phone), and **Laruni Cabins** (☎ 523/7026). Rates in most cases are less than BZ$100 for a double, with the least expensive ones, usually a block or two back from the water, costing less than BZ$50 for a double. At these guesthouses it's usually not necessary to make reservations. When you arrive in the village, just walk around until you find one that suits you.

$ 🏨 **All Seasons Guest House.** The four small but immaculate rooms in this European-style guesthouse are designed around jungle themes. **Pros:** pleasant, very clean rooms; lovely garden, handy to the excellent Chef Rob's restaurant. **Cons:** rooms in main house not directly on the sea. ⊠ *Opposite Chef Rob's* ⊠ *Box 251, Dangriga* ☎☎ *523/7209* ⊕ *www. allseasonsbelize.com* ↩ *4 rooms, 3 apartments, 1 cabaña* ⚅ *In-room: no a/c, kitchen, no TV, Wi-Fi.*

$$$ 🏨 **Almond Beach Resort & Spa.** Variety is the spice of beach life at this
RESORT   resort with an assortment of rooms, suites, and villas. **Pros:** variety of accommodations; spa. **Cons:** resort has gone through recent changes. ⊠ *Hopkins* ☎ *520/7040, 866/910–7373* ⊕ *www.almondbeachbelize. com* ↩ *20 rooms* ⚅ *In-room: safe, kitchen, Wi-Fi. In-hotel: restaurant, bar, pool, gym, spa, beach, water sports.*

$$ 🏨 **Beaches and Dreams Seafront Inn.** Refugees from Alaska's harsh win-
★   ters purchased this small beachfront inn, turning it into one of our favorite kick-back beach spots. **Pros:** kick-off-your-shoes atmosphere; steps from the sea; good restaurant. **Cons:** in summer, hotel goes bare-bones. ⊠ *Sittee Point* ☎☎ *523/7259* ⊕ *www.beachesanddreams.com* ↩ *5 rooms* ⚅ *In-room: no a/c, no TV. In-hotel: restaurant, bar, beach, water sports* ○ *Breakfast.*

$$$$ 🏨 **Belizean Dreams.** This collection of three-bedroom, three-bath condos
★   is among the most upmarket accommodation choices on the Southern Coast. **Pros:** deluxe condo apartments; units can be combined and configured to meet your needs. **Cons:** don't expect the same kind of hands-on management as at a small inn. ⊠ *Hopkins* ☎ *523/7272, 800/456–7150 in U.S. and Canada* ⊕ *www.belizeandreams.com* ↩ *9 3-bedroom villas (available as 1-, 2-, or 3-bedroom units)* ⚅ *In-room: kitchen, Wi-Fi. In-hotel: restaurant, bar, pool, spa, beach, water sports* ○ *Multiple meal plans.*

$$$$ 🏨 **Hamanasi.** With beautifully landscaped grounds, top-notch accom-
Fodor's Choice   modations, and an excellent dive program, Hamanasi (Garífuna for
★   "almond") is among Belize's superior beach and dive resorts. **Pros:** well-run, deluxe lodging in beautiful beachside setting; excellent dive trips and inland tours. **Cons:** expensive restaurant; pricey accommodations (but worth it); diving requires a long boat trip to the reef or atolls. ⊠ *P.O. Box 265, Dangriga* ☎ *520/7073, 877/552–3483 in U.S.* ⊕ *www. hamanasi.com* ↩ *8 rooms, 13 suites* ⚅ *In-room: no TV, Wi-Fi. In-hotel: restaurant, bar, pool, beach, water sports, business center* ○ *Breakfast.*

$$ 🏨 **Hopkins Inn.** Greg and Rita Duke are helpful hosts at their little beach-front cottage colony in Hopkins, featuring four cozy cabins with tile floors, ceilings paneled in local hardwoods, fridges, fans, and porches

with sea views. **Pros:** on the beach; helpful owners. **Cons:** you may be awakened by the sound of roosters. ✉ *Hopkins* ☎ *523/7283* ⊕ *www. hopkinsinn.com* ⊋ *4 cottages* ♿ *In-room: no a/c, no TV. In-hotel: beach* ▭ *No credit cards* ¶◯¶ *Breakfast.*

$$$ ▦ **Jaguar Reef Lodge.** After operating a while as part of a three-property complex of sister resorts, Jaguar Reef Lodge, in Hopkins for more than 20 years, is now back as an independent beach resort; choose between whitewashed, thatch-roofed cabañas and newer colonial style suites. **Pros:** attractive and well-kept grounds; lovely beachside location. **Cons:** service can be inconsistent; operation has gone through several major changes in recent years. ✉ *P.O. Box 297, Dangriga* ☎ *533/7040, 888/731–1132 in U.S. and Canada* ⊕ *www.jaguarreef.com* ⊋ *20 units* ♿ *In-room: safe, kitchen, Wi-Fi. In-hotel: restaurant, bar, pool, beach, water sports, business center.*

$ ▦ **Jungle by the Sea.** Although not actually in the jungle, this group of
★ seven wood cabañas on stilts, also known as Jungle Jeanie's, is on about 2 acres of beachfront nicely shaded by coconut palms. **Pros:** comfortable cabañas; lovely stretch of beach; quiet location. **Cons:** short hike to other resorts or to in-town restaurants and bars. ☎☎ *523/7047* ⊕ *www. junglebythesea.com* ⊋ *7 cabañas* ♿ *In-room: no a/c, kitchen, no TV. In-hotel: restaurant, bar, beach, water sports.*

$$$$ ▦ **Kanantik Reef & Jungle Resort.** At this all-inclusive luxury resort, you
★ can experience the Barrier Reef without having to make decisions more complicated than whether to have fish or steak for dinner. **Pros:** stunning beachside setting; stress-free all-inclusive. **Cons:** remote location keeps you isolated from local people and culture; expensive. ✉ *Off Southern Hwy., between Hopkins and Placencia peninsula* ✉ *P.O. Box 150, Dangriga* ☎ *520/8048, 877/759–8834 in U.S.* ⊕ *www.kanantik. com* ⊋ *25 cabañas* ♿ *In-room: no TV. In-hotel: restaurant, bar, pool, beach, water sports, business center, some age restrictions* ¶◯¶ *Multiple meal plans.*

$$$ ▦ **Parrot Cove Lodge.** Under new management and separated from its two larger sister hotels next door, of which it was a temporary part, Parrot Cove is again an independent beach resort. **Pros:** comfy, small beachside resort; good restaurant. **Cons:** standard rooms are small. ✉ *False Sittee Point, Hopkins* ☎ *523/7225, 877/207–7139 in U.S.* ⊋ *5 rooms, 1 suite, 1 1-bedroom house, 1 house with 2 2-bedroom suites* ♿ *In-room: Wi-Fi. In-hotel: restaurant, bar, pool, beach, water sports.*

¢ ▦ **Tipple Tree Beya Hotel.** This tiny beachfront guesthouse in the heart of Hopkins village provides a comfortable, no-frills alternative to the coast's upmarket resorts. **Pros:** steps from the water; hammocks on the porch. **Cons:** basic, not overly large rooms; can be hot in summer. ✉ *Hopkins* ☎☎ *520/7006* ⊕ *www.tippletree.com* ⊋ *4 rooms, 1 with shared bath, 1 cabin* ♿ *In-room: no a/c, no TV. In-hotel: beach, water sports.*

THE OUTDOORS
BIRD-WATCHING
Cockscomb Basin Wildlife Sanctuary has excellent birding, with some 300 species identified in the reserve. You can also sometimes see the jabiru stork, the largest flying bird in the Western Hemisphere, in the

marsh areas just to the west of Hopkins Village. Keep an eye out as you drive into the village from the Southern Highway. North of Hopkins is Fresh Water Creek Lagoon, and south of the village is Anderson Lagoon. These lagoons and mangrove swamps are home to many waterbirds, including herons and egrets. A kayak trip on the Sittee River should reward you with kingfishers, toucans, and various flycatchers. About 30 minutes by boat off Hopkins is Man-o-War Caye, a bird sanctuary that has one of the largest colonies of frigate birds in the Caribbean, more than 300 nesting birds. **Hamanasi, Jaguar Reef,** and other hotels arrange bird-watching trips. Costs for guided birding tours run from BZ$50 to BZ$200 per person, depending on where you go and the length of time.

DISTANCES

Hopkins is less than 10 minutes by road (about half paved but pot-holed) from the paved Southern Highway and is ideally situated for a variety of outdoor adventures, both land and sea. Here's the distance from Hopkins to selected points of interest:

■ Belize Barrier Reef: 10 mi (17 km)

■ Cockscomb Basin Wildlife Sanctuary: 10 mi (17 km)

■ Glover's and Turneffe atolls: 25 mi (42 km)

■ Mayflower Bocawina National Park: 15 mi (25 km)

CANOEING AND KAYAKING

When kayaking or canoeing on the Sittee River, you can see many birds and, possibly, manatees and crocodiles. Manatees also are often spotted in the sea just off the Hopkins shore. If you go on a tour with a licensed guide from a local lodge, expect to pay BZ$100–BZ$150 per person. Several hotels in Hopkins, including **Tipple Tree Beya Hotel, Hopkins Inn, Jungle by the Sea,** and **All Seasons Guest House,** rent kayaks, canoes, and other water equipment by the hour or day. Although it's possible to do sea kayaking from Hopkins, often the water is choppy. Long sea-kayaking trips should be tried only by experienced kayakers, preferably with a guide.

CAVING

Caving tours from Hopkins typically go to St. Herman's Cave and the Crystal Cave at Blue Hole National Park on the Hummingbird Highway. Cost is around BZ$120 per person.

DIVING

Diving off Hopkins is very good to terrific. The Barrier Reef is closer here—about 10 mi (17 km) from shore—than it is farther south. Diving also is fairly costly here. Half-day, two-tank dive trips to the South Water Caye Marine Reserve are around BZ$200–BZ$280, not including regulator, BCD, wet suit, and other equipment rental, which can add BZ$50. Dive shops with fast boats can also take you all the way to the atolls—Turneffe, Glover's, and even Lighthouse. These atoll trips generally start early in the morning, at 6 or 7 am, and last all day. Costs for three-tank atoll dives are around BZ$380–BZ$400 for Glover's and Turneffe, and BZ$580 for Lighthouse. In late spring, when whale sharks typically show up, local dive shops offer dives to see the Belizean behemoths at Gladden Spit Marine Reserve for around BZ$400. Marine park fees (sometimes included in dive trip charges) are BZ$10 each for South Water and Glover's marine reserves, and BZ$20 for Gladden Spit.

Hamanasi. One of the best diving operations in Southern Belize is at Hamanasi. Here you'll find the newest equipment and the biggest boats. ☎ 520/7073 ⊕ *www.hamanasi.com.*

HIKING

Most hiking trips go to Cockscomb Basin Wildlife Sanctuary, where there are a dozen short hiking trails near the visitor center. Full-day trips to Cockscomb generally cost about BZ$120–BZ$150 per person from Hopkins and can be booked through your hotel. If you're a glutton for punishment, you can go on a guided hike to Victoria Peak, the second-highest mountain peak in Belize. The 40-mi (67-km) hike from the visitor center at Cockscomb Basin Wildlife Sanctuary to the top entails inclines of 45 to 60 degrees. Most of these trips require three to five days up and back and cost in the range of BZ$500 per person (minimum of two people). One guide who will take you is **Marcos Cucul** (⊕ *www.mayaguide.bz*). He is a jungle survival guide who is a member of the Belize National Cave and Wilderness Rescue Team.

HORSEBACK RIDING

Local lodges arrange horseback-riding trips, working with ranches near Belmopan and Dangriga. A full-day horseback trip, including transportation to the ranch and lunch, is around BZ$150 per person.

MANATEE-WATCHING TOURS

Local lodges offer trips to Gales Point and the Southern Lagoon to try to spot Antillean manatees, a subspecies of West Indian manatees. These large aquatic mammals—adults weigh 800 to 1,200 pounds—are related to elephants. They're found in shallow waters in lagoons, rivers, estuaries, and coastal areas in much of Belize, and are especially common in the lagoons around Gales Point. These gentle herbivores can live 60 years or longer. The cost of manatee-spotting trips varies, but is around BZ$150 per person. Under Belize government guidelines, you're not permitted to feed manatees, to swim with them, or to approach a manatee with a calf.

SNORKELING

Snorkeling off Hopkins is excellent, though expensive compared with the Northern Cayes. Half-day snorkeling trips from Hopkins to the Belize Barrier Reef, usually a pristine section of it in the South Water Caye Marine Reserve, cost from BZ$100 to BZ$150 per person. These snorkel trips are almost twice as pricey as those to Hol Chan from Ambergris Caye or Caye Caulker, partly because the trip out and back to snorkel sites here is longer, and also because there's less competition to hold prices down. Full-day whale-shark snorkeling trips (usually whale sharks are best seen in late spring and early summer, around the time of a full moon) are about BZ$300–$350.

WINDSURFING

Windsurfing is a growing sport in Hopkins, as the wind is a fairly consistent 10 to 15 knots, except in August and September, when it sometimes goes calm. The best winds are in April and May.

Windschief. Windschief rents well-maintained windsurfing equipment for BZ$20 for the first hour, then BZ$10 for additional hours, or BZ$60 a day. Private lessons are BZ$60 an hour. Catamaran rentals are BZ$120 a day. Several hotels also rent windsurfing equipment. Windschief also has beach cabañas and a bar. ☎ 523/7249 ⊕ *www.windsurfing-belize. com.*

SHOPPING

Shopping is limited in Hopkins, where the local "shopping center" is a small clapboard house with a few dozen items for sale. Locals traditionally make much of what they use in daily life, from cassava graters to fishing canoes and paddles, and drums and *shakas* (shakers made from a calabash gourd filled with seeds). Around the village, you'll see individuals selling carvings and other local handicrafts made from shells and coconuts. Also, several small shops or stands, including **Wood Work Shop, Kulcha Gift Shop,** and **Tribal Arts,** few of which have phones, sell locally made crafts. You can bargain for the best price, but remember that there are few jobs around Hopkins and that these craftspeople are trying to earn money to help feed their families.

Hamanasi. Hamanasi has a well-stocked gift shop. ☎ 520/7073.

Jaguar Reef Resort & Spa. This resort has a fine little gift shop filled with pottery and embroidery as well as Garífuna crafts. The store also carries Marie Sharp's superb hot sauces, music CDs, and drugstore items like sunscreen and the crucial no-see-um bug repellent. ☎ 520/7040.

COCKSCOMB BASIN WILDLIFE SANCTUARY

10 mi (17 km) southwest of Hopkins Village.

GETTING HERE AND AROUND

Maya Centre, at the entrance of the road to Cockscomb, is at Mile 15 of the Southern Highway. You can drive here, or any local bus on the Southern Highway will drop you. From Maya Centre it's 6 mi (10) km to the park. You can drive, hike (about two hours), or take a local taxi (about BZ$30 one way). Admission to the sanctuary is BZ$10, and is collected at the crafts shop at Maya Centre.

TIMING

Most visitors come to Cockscomb only on a day visit. However, for the best chance to see wildlife and even a jaguar, a stay of several nights is best.

EXPLORING

🕙 **Cockscomb Basin Wildlife Sanctuary.** The mighty jaguar, once the undisputed king of the Central and South American jungles, is now endangered. But it has a haven in the Cockscomb Basin Wildlife Sanctuary, which covers 128,000 acres of lush rain forest in the Cockscomb Range of the Maya Mountains. With the Bladen Nature Reserve to the south, the jaguars have a continuous corridor of about 250,000 acres. Thanks to these reserves, as well as other protected areas around the country, Belize has the highest concentration of jaguars in the world.

Fodor'sChoice
★

Some visitors to Cockscomb are disappointed that they don't see jaguars and that wildlife doesn't jump out from behind trees to astound them as they hike the trails. The experience at Cockscomb is indeed a low-key one, and seeing wildlife requires patience and luck. You'll have the best chance of seeing wild animals, perhaps even a jaguar or one of the other large cats, if you stay overnight, preferably for several nights, in the sanctuary. You may also have better luck if you go for an extended hike with a guide. Several nearby lodges, such as **Hamanasi,** offer night hikes to Cockscomb, departing around dusk and returning around 9 pm.

Cockscomb Basin also has native wildlife aside from the jaguars. You might see other cats—pumas, margays, and ocelots—plus coatis, kinkajous, deer, peccaries, and, last but not least, tapirs. Also known as the mountain cow, this shy, curious creature appears to be half horse, half hippo, with a bit of cow and elephant thrown in. Nearly 300 species of birds have been identified in the Cockscomb Basin, including the Keel-Billed Toucan, the King Vulture, several hawk species, and the Scarlet Macaw.

Within the reserve is Belize's best-maintained system of jungle and mountain trails, most of which lead to at least one outstanding swimming hole. The sanctuary also has spectacular views of Victoria Peak and the Cockscomb Range. Bring serious bug spray with you—the reserve swarms with mosquitoes and tiny biting flies called no-see-ums—and wear long-sleeve shirts and long pants. The best times to hike anywhere in Belize are early morning, late afternoon, and early evening, when temperatures are lower and more animals are on the prowl.

You have to register in a thatch building at Maya Centre on the Southern Highway before proceeding several miles to the visitor center. In the same building is an excellent gift shop selling baskets, wood and fabric crafts, and slate carvings by local Maya craftspeople, at good prices. Buying crafts at this shop, which is run as a co-op by local residents, generally gets more of the money into local hands than if you buy from a commercial gift shop. At Maya Centre there is also a small butterfly farm.

The road from Maya Centre to the Cockscomb ranger station and visitor center winds 6 mi (10 km) through dense vegetation—splendid cahune palms, purple mimosas, orchids, and big-leaf plantains—and as you go higher the marvelous sound of tropical birds, often resembling strange windup toys, grows stronger and stronger. This is definitely four-wheel-drive terrain. You may have to ford several small creeks as well as negotiate deep, muddy ruts. At the end, in a clearing with hibiscus and bougainvillea bushes, you'll find a little office, where you can buy maps of the nature trails, along with restrooms, several picnic tables, cabins, and a campground. The Belize Audubon Society manages the Cockscomb and can assist in making reservations for the simple accommodations in the sanctuary.

Altogether there are some 20 mi (33 km) of marked trails. Walking along these 12 nature trails is a good way to get to know the region. Most are loops of ½–1½ mi (1–2 km), so you can do several in a day. The most strenuous trail takes you up a steep hill; from the top is a magnificent view of the entire Cockscomb Basin.

Hotels and tour operators and guides in Hopkins, Placencia, and Dangriga offer tours to Cockscomb; Hopkins is closest to the sanctuary. ⊠ *Outside Maya Centre, Maya Centre* ☎ *227/7369, 223/5004 Belize Audubon Society in Belize City* ✆ *base@btl.net* ⊕ *www.belizeaudubon. org/protected_areas/cockscomb-basin-wildlife-sanctuary.html* 🎫 *BZ$10* 🕙 *Daily 8–4:30.*

WHERE TO STAY

For expanded hotel reviews, visit Fodors.com.

Although most visitors come to Cockscomb on day trips and stay in Hopkins, Placencia, or Dangriga, you can camp in the reserve for BZ$10 per night per person, or for a little more money you can stay in pleasant rooms in a dormitory with solar-generated electricity starting at BZ$40 per person. Also, a small house and three cabins, each with private bath, can accommodate up to four or six people (BZ$106–$150 per house/cabin). An old, primitive cabin with 10 bunk beds is BZ$16 per person. There's a communal kitchen for cooking. No fishing or hunting is allowed in the reserve, and pets are prohibited. Book in Belize City through the **Belize Audubon Society** (☎ *223/5004* ⊕ *www. belizeaudubon.org*).

¢ 🏠 **Tutzil Nah Cottages.** Gregorio Chun and his family, including brothers Ouscal and Julian, Mopan Maya people who've lived in this area for generations, provide accommodations in simple thatch cabañas. **Pros:** near Maya Centre; owners highly knowledgeable about Cockscomb; interesting tours available. **Cons:** very basic accommodations. ⊠ *Near Maya Centre, Mile 13½, Southern Hwy., Maya Centre* ☎ *533/7045* ⊕ *www.mayacenter.com* 🛏 *2 cabañas, 1 with share bath* ☖ *In-room: no a/c, no TV.*

PLACENCIA PENINSULA

28 mi (47 km) south of Dangriga by road.

The Placencia peninsula is fast becoming one of the major visitor destinations in Belize, one that may eventually rival Ambergris Caye as the most popular resort area in the country. It's one 16-mi (26-km) long peninsula, with three different but complementary areas: Northern Peninsula/Maya Beach, Seine Bight, and Placencia Village.

The former dirt track that ran 25 mi (41 km) from the Southern Highway to the tiny community of Riversdale and then down the peninsula to Placencia Village has been paved, and the road is now in excellent condition (beware the speed bumps, however). Beginning at Riversdale, at the elbow where the actual peninsula joins the mainland, you'll get a quick glimpse through mangroves of the startlingly blue Caribbean. As you go south, the Placencia Lagoon is on your right, and behind it in the distance rise the low Maya Mountains, the Cockscomb Range ruffling the tropical sky with its jagged peaks. On your left, a few hundred feet away, beyond the remaining mangroves and a narrow band of beach, is the Caribbean Sea. A line of uninhabited cayes grazes the horizon.

The northern end of the peninsula from Riversdale south to Maya Beach once had just a few small seaside houses, and Maya Beach was a sleepy beach community. Now the towering five-story buildings of the Copal Beach condominium development, currently under construction, rise up out of the flat peninsula land. "For Sale" signs dot the roadside, supersize beach- and lagoon-side mansions are going up at The Placencia Residences and elsewhere, and several new condominium communities and resorts are open or planned (though some are struggling to find buyers, and one large one, Bella Maya, has closed.) These new resorts and condo developments join a small group of laid-back seaside hotels and cabins. The

> ## JAGUARS
>
> Jaguars are shy, nocturnal animals that prefer to keep their distance from humans, so the chances of viewing one in the wild are slim. The jaguar, or *el tigre*, as it's known in Spanish, is a supremely independent creature that shuns even its own kind. Except during a brief mating period and the six months the female spends with her cubs before turning them loose, jaguars roam the rain forest alone.

beaches at the upper end of the peninsula are some of the best on mainland Belize, and more restaurants and shops are starting to open here. There's now even a small bowling alley in Maya Beach, Jaguar Lanes.

Roughly midway down the peninsula is the Garífuna village of Seine Bight, struggling to adapt to change. At both the north and south ends of the village upscale resorts and condo developments have sprung up to take advantage of the appealing beaches.

On a sheltered half-moon bay at the southern tip of the peninsula is Placencia Village. Founded by pirates, and long a Creole village, the community is now inhabited by an extraordinary mélange of people, local and expatriate. Most of the hotels in the village are modest, and the shops have tiny selections. Never mind, once you arrive you'll probably just want to lie in a hammock with a good book, perhaps getting up long enough to cool off in the gentle waves or to sip a Belikin at one of the village saloons.

From anywhere on the Placencia peninsula you can dive along the reef, swim in the warm sea water, look for scarlet macaws in Red Bank Village to the southwest (between December and February), explore the Mayan ruins at Mayflower and hike to the waterfalls there, or, on a full day trip, travel to the Mayan sites at Lubaantun and Nim Li Punit near Punta Gorda, or treat yourself to some of the best sportfishing in the country.

GETTING HERE AND AROUND

Both Tropic Air and Maya Island Air fly from Belize City to Placencia, and also from Punta Gorda. Tropic Air also has at least one flight daily between Placencia and Belmopan. The airstrip is about 2 mi (3 km) north of the center of Placencia Village. A so-called international airport is under construction about 2 mi (3 km) northwest of the Placencia peninsula, though in mid-2011 construction on the airport had slowed to a standstill. Details on when and if the airport will open or the flights it will have are, as of this writing, only speculative.

By road, from the Southern Highway at Mile 22.2, it's about 8¼ mi (14 km) to Riversdale, 15¼ mi (26 km) to Maya Beach, 19 mi (31 km) to Seine Bight, and 25 mi (41 km) to Placencia Village. The road is completely paved. Ritchie's Bus Line has buses from Dangriga to Placencia at 11 am and 4:30 pm, and from Placencia to Dangriga at 5:45 am and 12:45 pm. The main bus stop in Placencia is in the village near the Shell station.

Since there's no point-to-point bus service on the peninsula, and taxis are expensive (BZ$50 one-way between Placencia Village and The Placencia hotel area at the northern end of the peninsula), a rental car can be handy. If you haven't rented one in Belize City, you can rent one locally. Currently there are three car-rental agencies on the peninsula, plus a branch of Belize City's Budget agency. Expect to pay BZ$160 and up per day for a rental.

Contacts Barefoot Services ⊠ *Main St., Placencia* ☎ *629/9602* ⊕ *www. barefootservicesbelize.com* ⊘ *Closed Sat..* **Jagz Car Rentals** ☎ *604/7471, 604/7471* ⊕ *www.genietravelbelize.com.*

TIMING
It takes but a couple of days to explore all of the Placencia peninsula. How long you spend here depends on how much beach and water-sports time you want. Many visitors stay a week or longer.

SAFETY AND PRECAUTIONS
The influx of construction workers to the peninsula, some from Guatemala and Honduras, has somewhat changed the security situation here. Petty thefts and break-ins are more common. However, overall the Placencia peninsula is safe.

NORTHERN PENINSULA AND MAYA BEACH

36 mi (61 km) south of Dangriga by road.

Some of the best beaches on the Placencia peninsula—and therefore on mainland Belize—are at the northern end of the peninsula and the Maya Beach areas. The light khaki-color sand is soft, the surf is gentle, and, while the Barrier Reef is miles off the coast here as it is elsewhere in this part of Belize, there is good snorkeling a short kayak ride away, around False Caye just east of Maya Beach.

GETTING HERE AND AROUND
From the Southern Highway you go about 8¼ mi (14 km) east to Riversdale, where the Placencia peninsula formally meets the mainland. From there, head south through the northern end of the peninsula 7 mi (12 km) to Maya Beach.

WHERE TO EAT
$$ ✕**Mango's of Maya Beach.** Frank Da Silva, long-time chef at the award-
SEAFOOD   winning restaurant at Inn at Robert's Grove, has taken over Mango's, raising this casual beachside, thatch-roofed eatery and bar to a new level. The chef brought with him some of his favorites from Robert's Grove, such as conch fritters with chipotle mayonnaise (BZ$1.50 each). Many of the dishes are bar snacks, such as fajitas (chicken BZ$20,

shrimp BZ$28, lobster BZ$32), peel-and-eat shrimp (BZ$20 for ½ pound), or chicken wings. You can also sip a beer, enjoy the sea view, and feast on bigger dishes like filet mignon (BZ$38) or baby back ribs (BZ$32). Open 11 am to midnight daily except Monday. ✉ *Maya Beach* ☎ *523/8102* ✆ *Closed Mon.*

$$$
SEAFOOD
Fodor's Choice
★

✕ **Maya Beach Hotel Bistro.** Before ending up here, owners John and Ellen Lee (he's Australian, she's American) traveled the world and worked in 20 countries. They obviously figured out what travelers love, because their bistro by the beach is one of our favorite restaurants in all of Belize. It won "Restaurant of the Year" honors in 2011 from the Belize Tourism Board. The Bistro has been expanded, to provide more beachside seating. The

menu changes occasionally, but among the standards you'll go gaga over are five-onion cioppino, mixed seafood in a robust tomato and vegetable stew; boathouse pie, fish filet in truffle and bourbon sauce, topped with puff pastry and feta-mashed potatoes; potato-encrusted snapper with shrimp; and cocoa-dusted pork chop on a risotto cake. Dinner entrées are mostly priced from BZ$28 to BZ$56. The Bistro has added a selection of small plates and appetizers including fish cakes, a shrimp corn dog, and honey-coconut ribs, from BZ$12 to BZ$28. Open for breakfast, lunch, and dinner daily, although the owners usually close for a few weeks in summer. At breakfast, don't miss the fresh-baked cinnamon role—it's big enough for Godzilla. ✉ *Maya Beach* ☎ *520/8040* ⊕ *www.mayabeachhotel.com/restaurant.html* ⚓ *Reservations essential.*

WHERE TO STAY
For expanded hotel reviews, visit Fodors.com.

$$
★

⌂ **Barnacle Bill's Beach Bungalows.** "Barnacle Bill" Taylor, known as the wit of Maya Beach, and wife Adriane rent a pair of wooden Mennonite bungalows set among palm trees on a lovely beach about 80 feet from the sea; each cottage is on stilts and has a private bath and a kitchen where you can prepare your own meals. **Pros:** friendly spot; helpful owners; nice place just to relax. **Cons:** don't expect luxury. ✉ *23 Maya Beach Way* ☎☎ *533/8110* ⊕ *www.barnaclebills-belize.com* ⤵ *2 cottages* ⚓ *In-room: no a/c, kitchen, no TV, Wi-Fi. In-hotel: beach, water sports, some age restrictions.*

$$$

⌂ **Green Parrot Beach Houses.** This resort has Mennonite-built cottages, some showing a little age, along a nice stretch of beach, each with a kitchenette and dining area. **Pros:** good option for families; pleasant beach area. **Cons:** no swimming pool. ✉ *No. 1 Maya Beach, 4 mi*

(6½ km) north of Seine Bight ☎ *523/2488, 734/667–2537 in the U.S.* ⊕ *www.greenparrot-belize.com* ⬅ *6 cabins, 2 cabañas* ⚐ *In-room: no a/c, no TV. In-hotel: restaurant, bar, beach, water sports* ❍| *Breakfast.*

$$ 🏨 **Maya Beach Hotel.** This is the kind of small, unpretentious beachfront
★ hotel that many come to Belize to enjoy, but few actually find. **Pros:** like a small beach hotel should be; good value; excellent restaurant. **Cons:** rooms are only a couple of steps up from basic; Wi-Fi is a little spotty. ⊠ *Maya Beach* ☎☎ *520/8040, 800/503–5124 in U.S.* ⊕ *www. mayabeachhotel.com* ⬅ *5 rooms, 3 apartments, 2 houses* ⚐ *In-room: kitchen, no TV, Wi-Fi. In-hotel: restaurant, bar, pool, beach, water sports.*

$$ 🏨 **Maya Breeze Inn.** At this small resort choose from three cabins and two suites on the seaside, or opt for a room in the small lagoon-side lodge. **Pros:** variety of accommodations; attractive pool. **Cons:** lagoon-side rooms don't have the best views. ⊠ *Maya Beach, 2 mi (3 km) north of Seine Bight, 5 Maya Beach Way* ☎☎ *523/8106* ☎ *888/458–8581 in U.S.* ⊕ *www.mayabreezeinnandresort.com* ⬅ *3 cabins, 2 suites, 4 rooms* ⚐ *In-room: safe, kitchen. In-hotel: pool, beach, water sports, business center.*

$$$ 🏨 **The Placencia.** Transplant an upscale Florida or Texas condo community to Belize, and you might end up with something like The Placencia, formerly called Zeboz. **Pros:** beautiful beach; huge pool; attractive condos. **Cons:** sprawling gated complex lacks personality; rarely many guests; a BZ$50 cab ride to Placencia village. ⊠ *6 mi (10 km) north of Seine Bight* ☎ *520/4110* ⊕ *www.theplacencia.com* ⬅ *92 condo apartments* ⚐ *In-room: kitchen, Wi-Fi. In-hotel: restaurant, bar, pool, tennis court, spa, beach, water sports* ❍| *Multiple meal plans.*

$$ 🏨 **Singing Sands.** New owners, who also have purchased the Inn at Robert's Grove, have upgraded this small beachfront resort. **Pros:** small, owner-run beach hotel; pleasant cottages. **Cons:** smallish rooms. ⊠ *714 Maya Beach Rd., 6 mi (10 km) north of airstrip* ☎☎ *520/8022, 888/201–6425* ⊕ *www.singingsands.com* ⬅ *6 cabañas, 4 apartments* ⚐ *In-room: no TV, Wi-Fi. In-hotel: restaurant, bar, pool, beach, water sports.*

SEINE BIGHT

47 mi (77 km) south of Dangriga.

Like Placencia, its Creole neighbor to the south, Seine Bight is a small coastal fishing village. It may not be for long, though, as Placencia's resorts are stretching north to and through this Garífuna community, one of six predominantly Garífuna centers in Belize. The beach, especially south of Seine Bight, is excellent, though near the village garbage sometimes mars the view. Hotels do rake and clean their beachfronts, and several community cleanups have been organized in an effort to solve this problem. All the businesses catering to tourists are along the main road (actually, it's the only road) that leads south to Placencia Village. This road is paved. The name Seine Bight derives from a type of net, called a seine, used by local fishermen. Bight means an indentation or inward bend in the coastline.

Several small resorts and tracts of beachfront near Seine Bight have been sold, and there are plans, when the economy improves, for the development of a large but low-rise resort.

GETTING HERE AND AROUND

By road, Seine Bight is around 19 mi (31 km) from the Southern Highway. By air, you'll fly into the Placencia airstrip.

TIMING

You can explore Seine Bight in a few hours at most. How long you stay depends on how much beach and water time you want. Many visitors stay a week or more.

WHERE TO EAT

$$$ ✕**Danube.** Wiener schnitzel and Fleischfondue in Placencia? If you have
AUSTRIAN a yen for something different, most of the Austrian and Hungarian dishes are very good, if a bit pricey. Danube has a pleasant, relaxed atmosphere with art on the walls by the co-owner, Simone Gareis, and a screened porch for outdoor dining. ⊠ *On main road 2½ mi (4 km) north of the Placencia airstrip, Placencia Rd.* ☎ *610/0132* ⊕ *www. danubebelize.com* ☉ *No lunch. Closed Tues. and late Aug.–late Sept.*

WHERE TO STAY

For expanded hotel reviews, visit Fodors.com.

$$$ ⌂**The Inn at Robert's Grove.** The Inn at Robert's Grove's founders Bob
★ and Risa Frackman sold the hotel in late 2010, and new owners (who also operate the nearby Singing Sands) appear to be gradually reshaping and upgrading the resort while maintaining the elements that made this one of the top spots in Belize. **Pros:** complete resort facilities; gorgeous seaside rooms and suites; lots of on-site activities. **Cons:** nothing particularly exotic here; not inexpensive. ⊠ *½ mi (1 km) south of Seine Bight, Placencia Rd.* ☎ *523/3565, 800/565–9757 in U.S., 888/501–3808 in U.S.* ⊕ *www.robertsgrove.com* ⌂ *20 rooms, 32 suites* ⌂ *In-room: kitchen, Wi-Fi. In-hotel: restaurant, bar, pool, tennis court, gym, spa, beach, water sports, business center* ❙◯❙ *Multiple meal plans.*

$$ ⌂**Laru Beya Villas.** Laru Beya, a condo colony whose name means "on
★ the beach" in the Garífuna language, sits on 7 beachfront acres. **Pros:** well-designed rooms and suites; a good value. **Cons:** minigolf course needs maintenance. ⊠ *½ mi (1 km) south of Seine Bight, south of Robert's Grove* ☎ *523/3476, 800/813–7762 in U.S. and Canada* ⊕ *www. larubeya.com* ⌂ *30 units* ⌂ *In-room: kitchen, Wi-Fi. In-hotel: restaurant, bar, pool, beach, water sports.*

$$$ ⌂**Maine Stay Cabanas.** These well-designed cabañas, available either as two bedrooms with two baths or one bedroom with one bath, on a 400-foot (122-meter) stretch of beautiful beach, are ideal for families and for longer stays. **Pros:** attractive and comfortable suites; ideal for families and for longer stays. **Cons:** no restaurant on-site; no pool. ⊠ *Placencia Rd.* ☎ *523/3507, 877/458–7580* ⊕ *www.traversbelize.com* ⌂ *1 2-bedroom, 2-bath and 1 1-bedroom, 1-bath cabaña* ⌂ *In-room: kitchen, Wi-Fi. In-hotel: beach, water sports, laundry facilities.*

6

CLOSE UP

A Creole Primer

The Creole language is associated with the Creole or black people of Belize, especially those around Belize City. But people all over Belize know the Creole language and speak it daily. You'll hear Creole spoken by Mennonite farmers, Chinese shopkeepers, and Hispanic tour guides. Creole was brought to Belize by African slaves and former slaves from Jamaica and elsewhere in the Caribbean. Creole words are primarily of English origin, with some words from several West African tongues, Spanish, Miskito (an indigenous language of Central America, spoken by some 200,000 people in Honduras and Nicaragua), and other languages.

Spoken in a lilting Caribbean accent and combined with a grammar and syntax with West African roots, the language, despite English word usage, is difficult for foreigners to understand. Plurals aren't used often in Creole. For some, knowing how to speak Creole is a test you have to pass before you can become a "real" Belizean. However, with the increasing number of Hispanic immigrants in Belize, it's heard less and less, while Spanish is heard more and more.

Here are a few Creole words and phrases. If you want to learn more, get the *Kriol-Inglish Dikshineri* (Paul Crosbie, Editor-in-Chief) published by the Belize Kriol Project and available in gift shops and bookstores in Belize.

Ah mi gat wahn gud guf taim: I had a really good time

Bashment: Party

Bwah: Boy

Chaaly prise: A large rat, after Sir Charles Price, an 18th-century Jamaican planter

Chinchi: A little bit

Dis da fi wi chikin: This is our chicken (well-known slogan of a Mennonite chicken company)

Dollah: A Belize dollar

Fowl caca white and tink eh lay egg: A chicken sees its white droppings and thinks it laid an egg (said of a self-important person)

Grind mean: Ground meat

Gyal: Girl

Humoch dis kaas?: How much is this?

Ih noh mata: It doesn't matter

Madda rass: Foolishness (literally, mother's ass)

Tiga maga but eh no sic: Tiger's skinny but he's not sick (that is, don't judge a book by its cover)

Waawa: Foolish

Wangla: Sesame seed or candy made from sesame seeds

Weh di beach deh?: Where's the beach?

Yerrisso: Gossip, from "Ah her so" (so I hear)

SHOPPING

Lola's Art. Painter and writer Lola Delgado moved to Seine Bight from Belize City in the late 1980s. Her workshop, Lola's Art, displays her bold, cheerful acrylic paintings of local women and scenes (BZ$100 and up). She also sells hand-painted cards and some of her husband's wood carvings. Espresso and pastries are available. The workshop is up a flight of steps in a tiny wooden house off the main street, behind the football field. ☎ *601/1913* ⊕ *www.lolasartinbelize.blogspot.com.*

PLACENCIA VILLAGE

5 mi (8 km) south of Seine Bight, 52 mi (85 km) south of Dangriga.

Placencia Village is a mini version of Key West, laid-back, hip, and full of atmospheric watering holes. At the end of the road, the village is the main residential center on the peninsula, with a population of around 800, predominantly Creoles. It is also the peninsula's commercial hub—if you can call a small village a hub—with a half-dozen grocery stores, a couple of hardware stores, and the majority of the region's restaurants and bars. Traffic on the Main Road (also called Placencia Road) through the village is surprisingly heavy, and parking can be problematical. Most of the hotels in the village proper are budget spots, but just north of the village, between it and the airport, are several upscale beach resorts and condo developments.

Sometimes billed as the world's narrowest street, a single concrete path through the village called the Sidewalk is just wide enough for two people. Setting off purposefully from the southern end of the village near the harbor, the path meanders through everyone's backyard. It passes wooden cottages on stilts overrun with bougainvillea and festooned with laundry, along with a few shops and tour offices, and then, as if it had forgotten where it was headed in the first place, peters out abruptly in a little clearing. Paved sidewalks and dirt paths run between the Sidewalk and the Main Road through Placencia Village. Stroll along the Sidewalk, and you've seen the village. If you don't mind its being a little rough around the edges, you'll be utterly enchanted by this rustic village, where the palm trees rustle, the waves lap the shore, and no one is in a hurry.

Along the Sidewalk and the Main Road are most of the village's guesthouses and cafés, which serve rice and beans, burgers, and seafood.

GETTING HERE AND AROUND

By road, Placencia Village is around 25 mi (41 km) from the Southern Highway. By air, you'll fly into the Placencia airstrip. From the airstrip to the village is a BZ$12 taxi ride for up to two people, BZ$6 each for three or more. You can also get here by boat, the Hokey Pokey, from Independence/Mango Creek across the Placencia Lagoon, BZ$10. There are two Ritchie buses a day to Placencia Village from Dangriga.

Contacts Hokey Pokey ✉ *Main road at Texaco dock* ☎ *523/4045 Placencia Tourism Center.*

Placencia Village

KEY
❶ *Restaurants*
① *Hotels*
···· *Path*

CARIBBEAN SEA

NOT TO SCALE

TIMING

Placencia Village is small and can be seen in a day or less. How long you choose to stay depends on how much relaxing and beach and water time you desire. Many visitors stay a week or longer.

SAFETY

Most visitors say they feel safe on the Placencia peninsula. However, petty theft is a perennial problem, especially in Placencia Village. Quite a few budget travelers report thefts from their hotel rooms. A few Placencia hotels, and most of the more upscale resorts up the peninsula, have security guards. Note that at night the village and its beachfront are not well lighted.

WHERE TO EAT

$$
SEAFOOD
✕ **De Tatch Café.** This open-air bar and restaurant with a "tatch" (thatch) roof long has been one of the most popular hangouts in the village. Try the huge shrimp burrito and wash it down with a few cold Belikins. If you go fishing and catch something, the restaurant will prepare it for you. Breakfasts are good here, too. ⊠ *In village near Seaspray Hotel* ☎ *523/3148* ☉ *Closed Mon.*

$$$ ✕ **La Dolce Vita.** In a slightly Fellini-esque setting, upstairs over Wallen's
ITALIAN Store, La Dolce Vita brings authentic antipasti, bruschetta, and pasta
dishes to Placencia. Try the signature penne dolce vita, with a shrimp
and zucchini sauce (BZ$27) or the linguini with calamari, octopus,
and shrimp (BZ$30). The Rome-born chef-owner, Simone DeAngelis,
imports Italian pastas, olive oils, and wines to make sure everything
is top quality. With opera music playing in the background, it's like
being in a small, family-run restaurant in Italy. ✉ *On main road in
Placencia Village, above Wallen's Store, Main Rd.* ☎ *523/3115* ⊕ *www.
ladolcevitaplacencia.com* ☽ *No lunch.*

$$ ✕ **Pickled Parrot Bar & Grill.** This feet-in-the-sand restaurant and bar with
AMERICAN a thatch roof is in the heart of Placencia. Owner Wende Bryan offers
pizza (from BZ$34), chili, and burgers. ✉ *Off main road, behind Wal-
len's Market* ☎ *624/2651* ☽ *Closed Sat.–Sun.*

$$$ ✕ **Rumfish y Vino.** This hip spot run by transplanted New Yorkers, in a
SEAFOOD breezy second-floor location near the Placencia BTIA office, is a good
place to have drinks, tapas, and pasta. Try the "small plates" of Thai
curry shrimp or *pescado relleño* (red snapper stuffed with shrimp).
Bigger dishes include paella. There's a good selection of Italian and
California wines. ✉ *Placencia Village, near BTIA office* ☎ *523/3293.*

$$$ ✕ **Secret Garden Restaurant and Spa.** What was Placencia's first coffee-
INTERNATIONAL house has gone upmarket under a new management team, serving
★ sophisticated international meals at dinner, with dishes like seared tuna,
Korean barbecue, snapper in banana leaf, or vegetable fettuccine with
tomato pesto. At breakfast you can still get good coffee, along with
crepes, French toast and pastries. If you're feeling self-indulgent, a spa is
attached to the tropical-feeling Secret Garden restaurant. Breakfast and
dinner only. ✉ *In village, behind Wallen's store* ☎ *523/3420* ⊕ *www.
secretgardenplacencia.com* ☽ *No lunch; closed Mon.*

$ ✕ **The Shak.** In a shack at the beginning of the Sidewalk, overlooking
CAFÉ Placencia harbor, The Shak is the spot for fruit smoothies. For lunch
there are several curries and stir-fries. Open daily except Tuesday. ✉ *Placencia Harbor, at beginning of Sidewalk* ☎ *622/1686* ▭ *No credit cards.*

$ ✕ **Sweet Dreams Bakery.** This Swiss-owned bakery on the Sidewalk in
BAKERY Placencia Village sells fresh-baked breads and desserts, along with piz-
zas and daily specials such as meatloaf with mashed potatoes, all made
without artificial ingredients. Some bakery items can be quite expensive—ask prices before buying. ✉ *On west side of sidewalk near center
of Placencia Village* ☎ *523/3418* ⊕ *www.belizebakery.tripod.com* ▭ *No
credit cards.*

¢ ✕ **Tutti-Frutti.** Authentic, Italian-style gelato is the thing here, and it's
CAFÉ absolutely delicious, the equal of any you'll find in New York, Buenos
Fodor's Choice Aires, or even Rome. Try the tropical fruit flavors, such as banana, lime,
★ coconut, papaya, and mango, or an unusual flavor such as sugar corn,
all made from natural ingredients. Beware: You may become addicted
and return day after day to sample new flavors. The only negative here
is that the owners can be a little less than friendly. ✉ *In village on main
road, next to BTIA office., Main Rd.* ☎ *No phone* ▭ *No credit cards*
☽ *Closed Sept.–Oct.*

6

$$
LATIN AMERICAN

✗**Wendy's.** No, not that Wendy's. This Wendy's is a local restaurant operated by Wendy Lemus. It moved to a new location in an attractive new building, and unfortunately prices have increased, while the service has decreased. However, the grilled fish is still fresh and delicious, and there are many dishes to choose from, including creole items like cowfoot's soup for lunch on Friday and mestizo dishes like escabeche with fresh flour tortillas. Gibnut is served on Monday only. ⊠ *Main Rd.* ☎ *523/3335* ⊕ *www.wendyscuisine.com.*

$
CAFÉ

✗**Yoli's Bar & Grill.** The best views in the village are from your table at Yoli's. Built on a pier jutting out into the Placencia Harbor, Yoli's attracts a sizeable crowd at night. It's also a pleasant place to sip a Belikin and enjoy the sea breezes at lunch. Meals are simple, highlighting local seafood, hamburgers, and basic Belizean fare. Food is cooked at Merlene's restaurant nearby (owned by members of the same family) and brought out to the pier. ⊠ *Harborfront in Bakader area* ☎ *523/3183.*

WHERE TO STAY

For expanded hotel reviews, visit Fodors.com.

$$$$
★

Chabil Mar Villas. Chabil Mar means "beautiful sea" in Ketchi Mayan, and the sea and almost 400 feet of beach here are indeed gorgeous at this gated condo development. **Pros:** beautiful grounds; luxurious condos, lovely stretch of beach; every comfort and convenience is at hand. **Cons:** expensive. ⊠ *Main road north of Placencia Village* ☎ *523/3606, 866/417–2377 in U.S. and Canada* ⊕ *www.chabilmarvillas.com* ➪ *4 1- and 18 2-bedroom condos* ⌂ *In-room: safe, kitchen, Wi-Fi. In-hotel: restaurant, bar, pool, beach, water sports, laundry facilities.*

¢

Deb & Dave's Last Resort. This simple budget spot in Placencia Village is owned by Deb and Dave Vernon, and while it's nothing fancy, the rooms are spotless, and it's set in pleasant gardens. **Pros:** good value in budget accommodations; clean; well-run. **Cons:** not directly on the beach. ⊠ *Placencia Village, near Tipsy Tuna* ☎ *523/3207* ➪ *4 rooms with shared baths* ⌂ *In-room: no a/c, no TV.*

¢

Lydia's Guest House. For cheap and cheerful, plus friendly and clean, stay at this budget guesthouse in Placencia Village. **Pros:** can't beat the price; you have kitchen privileges. **Cons:** basic, backpacker-style accommodations. ⊠ *North end of Placencia Village* ☎ *523/3117* ⊕ *www. lydiasguesthouse.com* ➪ *8 rooms, all with shared bath, 2 cabañas, 1 house* ⌂ *In-room: no a/c, kitchen, no TV.*

¢

Manatee Inn. The Manatee Inn is good value for your money with clean, simply furnished rooms in a two-story woodframe lodge. **Pros:** comfortable budget accommodations. **Cons:** beach is a couple of hundred feet away. ⊠ *At north end of Placencia Village* ☎ *523/4083* ⊕ *www.manateeinn.com* ➪ *6 rooms, 2 apartments* ⌂ *In-room: no a/c, no TV.*

¢

Seaspray Hotel. There's no whirlpool or room service at this blue-and-white hotel, you just get a clean room (14 of them are on the beach) at a fair price. **Pros:** good value; right in the middle of things. **Cons:** can be noisy at times. ✉ *Near middle of Placencia Village* ☎ *523/3148* 🌐 *www.seasprayhotel.com* *19 rooms, 1 cabin* *In-room: no a/c, kitchen, no TV. In-hotel: restaurant, beach.*

$ **Tradewinds.** If you're yearning for a cottage right on the beach but don't want to spend a lot of money, then this little cottage colony is for you. **Pros:** cute cottages by the sea; near many restaurants and bars. **Cons:** rooms are small; some cottages need refurbishing; beach sand nearby is coarse; no parking nearby. ✉ *South Point* ☎ *523/3122* *9 cabins* *In-room: no a/c, no TV. In-hotel: beach, water sports.*

$$$$ Fodor's Choice ★ **Turtle Inn.** Francis Ford Coppola's second hotel in Belize is if nothing else exotic, with the furnishings, art, and most of the construction materials selected in Bali by the film director and his wife. **Pros:** memorable resort; delightful outdoor showers; superb service. **Cons:** no a/c; food and drinks are surprisingly expensive. ✉ *Placencia Rd., 2 mi (3 km) north of Placencia village* ☎ *824/4912 concierge, 800/746–3743 in U.S. and Canada* 🌐 *www.coppolaresorts.com* *17 cabañas, 7 2-bedroom cabañas, 1 house* *In-room: no a/c, no TV, Wi-Fi. In-hotel: restaurant, bar, pool, spa, beach, water sports* *Breakfast.*

$ **Westwind.** A favorite with anglers and beachcombers, this is a dependable, no-frills spot to rest your head. **Pros:** what a beachcomber looks for; friendly and secure. **Cons:** not for the luxury-minded. ✉ *Beachfront, near middle of Placencia Village* ☎ *523/3255* 🌐 *www.westwindhotel.com* *12 rooms, 1 suite, 1 house* *In-room: no TV. In-hotel: beach, business center.*

> **WORD OF MOUTH**
>
> "It is a wonderful drive down the Hummingbird Highway, absolutely beautiful through the orange groves. They were harvesting and pulping at the pulp plants and the aroma of oranges was heavenly. On to Placencia, which was lovely—stayed down at Placencia Point. Favorite places to eat—of course Tutti Frutti, Rumfish [y Vino], the upstairs Italian restaurant [La Dolce Vita], but [our] all-time favorite was Maya Beach Bistro—ate there twice. Yes, the pumpkin green chili soup is really that good! Went out to snorkel trip to Ranguana, which was gorgeous." —joan95448

SPORTS AND ACTIVITIES

Jaguar Lanes. About the last place you'd expect to find a bowling alley is Maya Beach, but Jaguar Lanes is here, and it's fun! This little four-lane alley, with jaguar murals on the walls and pine ceilings, has everything your lanes back home have, except you have to keep score on paper. Games are BZ$6, and shoe rental BZ$2.50. ✉ *Maya Beach* ☎ *664/2583* ⏲ *Closed Thurs.*

SHOPPING

The highlight of shopping on the Placencia peninsula is going to the grocery store, and the largest (Wallen's Market) is about the size of convenience store, so you get the picture. The larger resorts, including Inn at Robert's Grove and Turtle Inn, do have gift shops. In Placencia Village a few small gift shops and arts-and-craft galleries are on the Sidewalk.

VACATION RENTAL HOUSES

In addition to hotels and beach resorts, Placencia has a growing number of vacation rentals, private homes, and apartments that are available on a weekly, sometimes daily, basis. Among these are:

$$$ **Captain's House.** This is a three-bedroom house on the beach on the north end of Placencia Village, constructed almost entirely of mahogany (BZ$400 a night or BZ$2,500 weekly, plus tax). ☎ 523/4018, 203/975–8480 in the U.S. ⤴ 1 house.

$$$$ **Casa del Sol.** One of the most luxurious houses on the peninsula, Casa del Sol has a swimming pool, beach, and four bedrooms and four baths, renting for BZ$1,350 a night plus 9% tax (one- and two-bedroom sections of it are also available, starting at BZ$500 a night, plus tax). ☎ 523/3481 ⊕ www.casadelsolbelize.com ⤴ 1 house, rented as a whole house or in 1- and 2- bedroom units.

$$ **Easy Living Apartments.** Four modern two-bedroom apartments reside in the center of the village, with fully equipped kitchens. ☎ 523/3481 ⊕ www.easyliving.bz ⤴ 4 2-bedroom apartments.

¢ **Garden Cabanas.** Two small cottages with full kitchens are tucked away in a garden setting in the village, a few minutes from the beach; BZ$480 to BZ$700 weekly, or BZ$80 to BZ$120 nightly, plus tax. ☎ 605/0586 ⊕ www.gardencabanas.com ⤴ 2 cottages.

$ **Las Amigas.** Two cabañas near the water in the village have kitchenette, bedroom, and veranda (BZ$800 for six nights or BZ$150 nightly, in-season, plus 9% tax). ⊠ North end of village, Placencia ☎ 523/4018 for Destinations Belize, Placencia ⊕ www.lasamigasbelize.com ⤴ 2 cottages.

$$$ **The North Beach.** A villa run by the owners of Deb & Dave's Last Resort, The North Beach has suites with sea views, air-conditioning, cable TV, and phone, from BZ$300 plus tax. ☎ 523/3207 ⊕ www.thenorthbeach.com ⤴ 4 suites in 1 house.

$ **One World Rentals.** These eight apartments in three cottages, built in 2005 and 2008, are behind Rumfish y Vino restaurant, from BZ$700 weekly or BZ$110 nightly in-season, plus tax. ☎ 523/3103 ⊕ www.oneworldplacencia.com ⤴ 8 apartments in 3 cottages.

¢ **Toucan Lulu.** Six beachfront, self-catering units reside in a quiet area of Placencia Village, from BZ$90 to BZ$200 nightly in-season, plus tax. ☎ 628/8474 ⊕ www.toucanlulu.com ⤴ 6 cottages.

A Piece of Belize. Leo Hulse's carvings from zericote, rosewood, and other hardwoods are beautiful souvenirs of Belize. ⊠ About midway on the Sidewalk ☎ 205/5511.

Art 'n Soul Gallery. This little gallery on the south end of the Sidewalk has paintings by owner Greta Leslie, along with work by other Belizean artists and some jewelry, too. ⊠ South end of the Sidewalk ☎ 503/3088.

Sunova Beach Gift Shop. This spot sells T-shirts, wood carvings, and local art. ⊠ On sidewalk near Tipsy Tuna ☎ 523/4060.

Wallen's Market. The oldest grocery in Placencia, Wallen's Market has the basics, and it's even air-conditioned. Wallen's also has a pharmacy and hardware store. ⊠ *Main Rd., across from soccer field* ☎ *523/3128* ⊙ *Daily 9–5.*

NIGHTLIFE

Nightlife in Placencia is generally limited to drinking at a handful of local bars, of which Barefoot and Tipsy Tuna are perhaps the most popular. You can hear live music on weekends at Barefoot, Tipsy Tuna, or Eclipse.

Barefoot Beach Bar. This roadside bar is always busy. Expect lots of rum drinks and plenty of cold beer, along with bar food. Live music Thursday to Sunday nights. ⊠ *Main Rd., next to MnM* ☎ *523/3515* ⊙ *Daily 11 am–midnight.*

Eclipse Entertainment Club. Placencia's only real nightclub has live entertainment and a DJ on weekends. There's an outdoor dance floor. Cover charge of BZ$10–$20. ⊠ *Main Rd., north of airstrip* ☎ *523/3288* ⊙ *Thurs.–Sun. 9 pm–2 am.*

J-Byrds Bar. J-Byrds Bar attracts a fairly hard-drinking crowd, and there's a dance party on Friday nights. ⊠ *At docks, Placencia Village* ☎ *523/3412.*

Tipsy Tuna. The popular Tipsy Tuna has an inside sports bar and an open-air beach bar. There's live music some weekend nights, and you can always shoot pool or watch sports on a big-screen TV. Fill up on bar snacks like burgers, fajitas, tacos, and shrimp baskets. There's karaoke some nights and Garífuna drumming occasionally. ⊠ *On the Sidewalk near beach* ☎ *523/3089* ⊕ *www.tipsytunabelize.com* ⊙ *Open daily 11:30 pm–2 am.*

THE OUTDOORS

FISHING

The fly-fishing on the flats off the cayes east of the Placencia peninsula is some of Belize's best. This is one of the top areas in the world for permit. The area from Dangriga south to Gladden Caye is called "Permit Alley," and the mangrove lagoons off Punta Ycacos and other points south of Placencia are also terrific permit fisheries. You'll encounter plentiful tarpon—they flurry 10 deep in the water at times—as well as snook. You can also catch king mackerel, barracuda, wahoo, and cubera snapper. However, a lingering impact of Hurricane Iris in 2001 is that there are no longer as many good bonefish flats close to shore at Placencia. Bonefish are still around, but they're now several miles away, off the cayes.

GUIDES

Most of the better hotels also can arrange guides, many of whom pair with specific hotels. Fishing guides in Placencia are down-to-earth, self-taught guys who have fished these waters for years. They use small skiffs called *pangas*. For more information and help matching a local guide to your specific needs, get in touch with **Mary Toy at Destinations Belize** (☎ 523/4018 ⊕ www.destinationsbelize.com). You may want to talk with Wayne Castellanos (☎ 634/2852), considered one of the best fishing guides in the area. **Wyatt Cabral** (☎ 523/3534 ⊕ www.wyattsfishing. com) is native of Placencia who is considered another one of the best fly-fishing guides. Another well-known fly-fishing guide is **Julian Cabral** (☎ 610/1068).

Expect to pay around BZ$500–BZ$750 for a full day of fly-fishing, spin casting, or trolling. That includes your guide, boat, and lunch. If you're on a budget, you can rent a canoe and try fishing the Placencia lagoon on your own, where you may catch snook, barracuda, and possibly other fish.

GEAR

The guides usually provide trolling gear for free, but they charge about BZ$40 a day for light spin-casting tackle gear, and you may be happier with your own spinning gear. If you're serious about fly-fishing, of course you'll want to bring your own gear. Don't forget to bring polarized sunglasses, a good fishing hat, insect repellent, lots of sunscreen and lip salve, and, if you're wading, thick-soled flats boots.

SAILING

The Moorings and Sunsail offer bareboat and captained sail charters out of Placencia. Bareboat charters have to stay inside the reef.

The Moorings. Based at Laru Beya Marina along with sister charter company Sunsail, The Moorings offers bareboat and captained catamaran charters, with a week's bareboat sailing going for around BZ$7,600–BZ$14,000. ✉ Laru Beya Marina, Laru Beya Resort, Placencia ☎ 523/3206, 888/952–8420 in U.S. ⊕ www.moorings.com.

Sunsail. In 2011, Clearwater, Florida–based international charter company Sunsail began offering a limited number of sail charters from Placencia, operating out of the same marina as TUI Travel sister company The Moorings at Laru Beya Resort. Week-long Sunsail bareboat charters are around BZ$7,500 to $13,000. ✉ Laru Beya Marina, c/o Laru Beya Resort, Placencia ☎ 888/350, 523/4057.

SCUBA DIVING

This far south, the reef is as much as 20 mi (33 km) offshore, necessitating boat rides of 45 minutes to nearly two hours reach dive sites. Because this part of the reef has fewer cuts and channels, it's also more difficult to get out to the seaward side, where you'll find the best diving. As a result, most of the diving in this region is done from offshore cayes, which are surrounded by small reefs, usually with gently sloping drop-offs of about 80–100 feet. This isn't the place for spectacular wall dives—you're better off staying in the north or heading out to the atolls. Near Moho Caye, southeast of Placencia, you'll find brilliant red-and-yellow corals and sponges that rarely appear elsewhere in Belize.

Two marine reserves off Placencia are popular snorkeling and diving spots. Laughing Bird Caye, Belize's smallest marine reserve, about 13 mi (22 km) off Placencia, is a popular spot for snorkeling. Whale sharks, Rhincodon typus, gentle giants of the sea, appear off Placencia in the Gladden Spit area, part of the Gladden Spit and Silk Caves Marine Reserves 26 mi (43 km) east of Placencia, in late spring and early summer. You can snorkel or dive with them on day trips (around BZ$180–BZ$200 for snorkel trips, BZ$330–BZ$370 for dives) from Placencia. The best time to see whale sharks is three or four days before and after a full moon, March through June. Admission fee to each of these marine reserves is BZ$20; the admission typically is included in the dive or snorkel shop fee.

Diving costs a little more in Placencia than elsewhere. Full-day trips to the reef, including two-tank dive, all gear, and lunch, run BZ$190–BZ$260 per person. Two- and three-tank dive trips to Glover's Atoll are around BZ$300–BZ$440. Snorkeling trips start at around BZ$80 to BZ$100, and a snorkeling tour to Glover's Atoll is around BZ$175–BZ$220.

GUIDES

Most of the larger resorts, like the Inn at Robert's Grove and Turtle Inn, have dive shops and also offer snorkel trips. Avadon Divers is considered one of the best dive shops in the region.

Avadon Divers. Avadon Divers, which won the 2011 Belize Tourism Board's award for "Best Tour Operator of the Year," is generally considered the best dive operation in Placencia. ☎ 503/3377, 888/509–5617 in U.S. ⊕ www.avadondiversbelize.com.

Ocean Motion. For snorkeling trips check with Ocean Motion, on the Sidewalk in the heart of Placencia Village. A day snorkeling trip to Laughing Bird Caye is BZ$122 per person and a day trip to Ranguana Caye is BZ$154. ☎ 523/3363 ⊕ www.oceanmotionplacencia.com.

Seahorse Dive Shop. Brian Young runs the respected Seahorse Dive Shop. Local reef dives are BZ$214 including tax and gear. Glovers Atoll diving is BZ$340 including tax, gear, park fees, and lunch. If you don't dive, you can snorkel on any of these trips for BZ$120. ☎ 523/3166 ⊕ www.belizescuba.com.

Splash Dive Center. At the end of the Sidewalk, at the harbor, Splash Dive Center offers dive and snorkel trips. ☎ 523/3058 ⊕ www.splashbelize.com.

The Deep South

WORD OF MOUTH

"I will admit there is something about Toledo that is drawing me in. Maybe because I really value 'off the beaten trail' and it seems like such an untouched area in regards to tourism."

—rlk679

By Lan Sluder   Toledo District in the Deep South has Belize's only extensive, genuine rain forest, and its canopy of trees conceals
a plethora of wildlife, including jaguars, margays, tapirs,
and loads of tropical birds. The area's rich Mayan heritage is just being unearthed, with archaeologists at work at
Pusilha, Nim Li Punit, Uxbenká, and elsewhere. Contemporary Maya—mainly Mopan and Ketchi—still live in villages
around the district, as they have for centuries, along with
the Garífuna, Creoles, East Indians, and others who constitute the Toledo population of about 30,500.

Lush, green, tropical Toledo also calls to chocolate lovers, as it's home
to hundreds of small cacao growers. Cadbury's Green & Black gets
some of its organic chocolate for Maya Gold chocolate bars from
Toledo, and several small Belizean chocolate makers, including Cotton
Tree, Goss, and Kakaw, create gourmet candy from organic Toledo
cacao beans. In 2007 a cacao festival was organized, and it continues
annually in May (dates vary—see ⊕ *www.toledochocolate.com*).

Toledo also has rice plantations, citrus orchards, and stands of mangos,
pineapples, bananas, and coconuts, so you'll never go hungry here.

For many years, ill-maintained roads, spotty communications, and the
country's highest annual rainfall—as much as 180 to 200 inches—kept
Belize's southernmost region off-limits to all but the most adventurous
of travelers. The precipitation hasn't changed, but with improvements
to the Southern Highway—beautifully paved the entire way from Dangriga to Punta Gorda—and the opening of new lodges and hotels, the
riches of Toledo District are finally becoming accessible. The San Antonio Road, from the area called "The Dump" on the Southern Highway
to the Guatemala border, is currently being paved. When and if the road
is completed, perhaps in 2012–2013, it's expected that a new, legal land
border crossing between Belize and Guatemala will further open the
Deep South to tourism and development. Local residents are split on
the wisdom of this. Some say it will mean not only more tourism dollars
but also new Guatemalan markets for Toledo farm products. Others
worry that the new border crossing will create new problems for Toledo.

Other areas of Belize (not to mention Guatemala and Honduras) may
have more spectacular ruins than Toledo, but where the Deep South
shines is in its contemporary Mayan culture. Dozens of Mopan and
Ketchi villages exist much as they have for centuries, as do the Garífuna
villages of Punta Negra and Barranco and the town of Punta Gorda
(PG). You can visit some of the villages and even stay awhile in guesthouses or homestay programs.

TOP REASONS TO GO

Rain Forests. The greenest, lushest jungles in Belize are in Toledo, fed by heavy rains and temperatures that stay mostly above 70°F. Red ginger, bright yellow-and-orange lobster claw, masses of pink on mayflower trees, and orchids of all colors splash the emerald-green landscape. Scarlet-rumped tanagers, black-headed trogans, green kingfishers, and rose-ate spoonbills join hundreds of other birds in the rain-forest cacophony.

Outpost Atmosphere. Punta Gorda has that end-of-the-road feel, as if it's the last outpost on Earth. Yes, the Southern Highway does end

here—but it's more than that. Here you get the feeling that even in today's world of 7 billion people there are still places where you could, if you needed to, hide out for a while and not be found.

Fishing. Among serious anglers, Southern Belize has a reputation for having one of the world's great permit fisheries, and for its large populations of tarpon and bonefish. The flats off Punta Ycacos are prime permit and bonefish grounds, and freshwater lagoons near Punta Negra hold snook, small tarpon, and other fish.

Don't expect to come to Toledo and lounge on the sand. The area doesn't have good beaches except for a few accessible only by boat: the coastal waters of the Gulf of Honduras are often muddy from silt deposited by numerous rivers flowing from the Maya Mountains. What *can* you expect? Exceptional fishing (Toledo has one of the world's best permit fisheries) and cayes off the coast that are well worth exploring. The closest are the Snake Cayes; farther out are the Sapodilla Cayes, the largest of which is Hunting Caye, with a horseshoe-shape bay at the caye's eastern end with beaches of white coral where turtles nest in late summer. The downside is that visits to the cayes and to inland sites usually require expensive tours, as distances are considerable, and public transportation is limited.

ORIENTATION AND PLANNING

GETTING ORIENTED

The main road to the Deep South is the paved Southern Highway, which runs 100 mi (164 km) from the intersection of the Hummingbird Highway/Stann Creek District Highway to Punta Gorda.

As you travel south on the Southern Highway, the Great Southern Pine Ridge is on your right, starting at about Mile 55. Farther in the distance are the Maya Mountains. On your left (though not visible from the highway) is the Caribbean Sea, and farther south, beyond Punta Negra, the Gulf of Honduras.

Branching off the Southern Highway are mostly unpaved roads, some barely more than muddy trails that lead to small villages. The San Antonio Road from the Southern Highway is currently being paved and extended to the Guatemala border, where an official border crossing is expected to be established. Completion date is uncertain, but should be by 2013.

Punta Gorda. Many of the handful of restaurants and shops in PG open and close at the whim of their owners, and therein lies some of the charm of this little town. It's a sleepy, friendly, overgrown village with a beautiful setting on the bay.

The Maya Heartland. Nothing in Belize is quite like the Maya Heartland, where contemporary Mayan villages sit next to ancient ruins. Here also you'll see verdant rain forests, rice plantations, and cacao farms.

PLANNING

WHEN TO GO

June through September is the peak of the rainy season in Toledo. Unless you love a good thunderstorm, come between December and early May, when most of Toledo gets only about an inch of rain a week.

GETTING HERE AND AROUND

AIR TRAVEL

Maya Island Air and Tropic Air fly south to Punta Gorda from both the municipal (BZ$$204–$BZ214 one-way) and international (BZ$214–BZ$245 one-way) airports in Belize City, typically with stops at Dangriga and Placencia. Local security and Belize Airports Authority fees add BZ$6.50 to each ticket. There are four or five flights daily to PG on each airline. The Punta Gorda airstrip is on the town's west side; from the town square, walk four blocks west on Prince Street.

Contacts Maya Island Air ⊠ *Punta Gorda airstrip, Punta Gorda* ☎ *722/2856 in PG, 233/1140 in Belize City* ⊕ *www.mayaregional.com.* **Tropic Air** ⊠ *PG Airstrip, Prince St., Punta Gorda* ☎ *722/2008 in PG, 226/2012 in San Pedro (main office), 800/422–3435 in U.S.* ⊕ *www.tropicair.com.*

BOAT TRAVEL

Requena's, the most reliable operator, provides daily boats departing at 9:30 am from the docks on Front Street, Punta Gorda, to Puerto Barrios, Guatemala. The trip takes about an hour and can be rough. The fare is BZ$40 one-way. Requena's returns to PG at 2 pm. Three other water-taxi services, Pichilingo, Memo's, and Marisol, run water taxis for around BZ$44 one-way. The Pichilingo boat departs from PG at 2 pm, Memo's at 1 pm, and Marisol at 4 pm. From Puerto Barrios, Pichilingo departs at 10 am, Memo's at 3:15 pm, and Marisol at 1 pm. Boats to Livingston, Guatemala, depart on Tuesday and Friday only at 10 am. These boats are small open boats for pedestrians only; there is no auto ferry between Guatemala and Punta Gorda. You must pay a BZ$37.50 exit fee when departing from PG and about a US$10 exit fee when departing from Guatemala for Belize. To make a reservation, you need to provide your full name, date of birth, nationality, and passport number. If you're flying to PG just to catch the water taxi to Puerto Barrios, take the 8 am Maya Island flight from the municipal airstrip in Belize City. Requena's will pick you up at the airstrip.

Contact Requena's Charter Service ⊠ *12 Front St., Punta Gorda* ☎ *722/2070* ⊕ *www.belizenet.com/requena.*

BUS TRAVEL

James Bus Lines dominates the route between PG and points north. Currently there are nine daily local bus departures from PG to Belize City, and one express with limited stops. The first bus is at 3:50 am and the last one at 3:50 pm. An equal number of James Line buses come from the Novelo's bus station in Belize City to Punta Gorda daily, beginning at 5:15 am. It's a six- to seven-hour trip to or from Belize City via Belmopan and Dangriga, depending on whether it's an express or local bus. Between Belize City and PG, fare is around BZ$22 for local and BZ$24 for express. Most buses are old U.S. Bluebird school buses—they're usually crowded, cramped, and have no air-conditioning. If you have the budget, fly.

Off the Southern Highway public transportation is very limited. On market days (generally Monday, Wednesday, Friday, and Saturday) buses leave the main plaza in PG around noon. Buses, mostly old American school buses operated by local entrepreneurs, go to different villages, returning on market days very early in the morning. There's no published schedule—you have to ask locally. Fares are modest, BZ$2–BZ$4. As of this writing, buses served the villages of Barranco, Big Falls, Crique Jute, Crique Sarco, Golden Stream, Indian Creek, Jalacte, Laguna, San Antonio, San Marcos, San Miquel, San Pedro Columbia, Pueblo Viejo, and Silver Creek.

Information James Bus Line ⊠ *7 King St., Punta Gorda* ☎ *702/2049, 664/2185.*

CAR TRAVEL

The paving of the Hummingbird and Southern highways has made the journey to Punta Gorda much shorter and more pleasant. Off the Southern Highway most roads are unpaved. In dry weather they're bumpy yet passable, but after heavy rains the dirt roads can turn into quagmires even for four-wheel-drive vehicles. Most tertiary roads are not well marked, so you may have to stop frequently for directions. Despite this, expensive taxis and infrequent bus service to and from the Mayan villages are arguments for renting a car. There are no major car-rental companies in Punta Gorda, but Sun Creek Lodge has a few rental cars. They start at around BZ$120 per day or BZ$720 per week, plus tax, for a Toyota 4Runner.

Contact Sun Creek Lodge ⊠ *About 14 mi [23 km] northwest of Punta Gorda, off Mile 86, Southern Hwy.* ☎ *604/2124* ⊕ *www.suncreeklodge.de/englisch/home.html.*

TAXI TRAVEL

Taxis in the Deep South are available mostly in PG. Your hotel can call one for you. Any trip within PG should cost around BZ$7, with additional charges for extra stops. You can also hire a taxi to take you to nearby villages, but negotiate the rate in advance; it could be anywhere from BZ$20 to BZ$150, or more, depending on the destination. If you want a car and driver, a taxi likely will charge you around BZ$300 a day.

EMERGENCIES

Hospital **Punta Gorda Hospital** ⊠ *Main St. at south end of town, Punta Gorda* ☎ *722/2026.*

MONEY MATTERS

The only banks in Punta Gorda are Belize Bank and ScotiaBank. Happily, both have ATMs that accept foreign-issued ATM cards (on the PLUS, CIRRUS, and Visa Electron systems).

Banks and ATMs **Belize Bank** ⊠ *30 Main St., at Hospital St., Punta Gorda* ☎ *722/2324.* **ScotiaBank** ⊠ *Prince and Main Sts., Punta Gorda* ☎ *722/0098.*

SAFETY

Punta Gorda is generally a safe, friendly town. Indeed, Toledo District has the lowest murder rate in Belize, and one of the lowest rates of other serious crimes. With normal precautions you should have no problem walking around, even after dark. The nearby Mayan villages are also relatively free of crime. Guatemala's Caribbean coast, just a short boat ride away, has a reputation for lawlessness, which can occasionally spill over into Toledo.

ABOUT THE RESTAURANTS

With relatively few tourists coming to the region, and most local residents unable to afford to eat out regularly, restaurants in Toledo often are here today and gone tomorrow. Even those that stick around often open and close at the whim of the owner or the cook. Those that do make it are usually basic spots serving local fish and staples like stew chicken with beans and rice. Prices are low—you'll rarely pay more than BZ$25 for dinner. Nearly all Toledo restaurants are in PG.

ABOUT THE HOTELS

The entire Toledo District has only about 30 hotels, most of them in and around Punta Gorda. Most are small and owner-run. You can usually show up without reservations and look for a place that suits you. Clean rooms are under BZ$100, and for BZ$150–BZ$200 you can stay at a charming small inn. Several jungle lodges have rates of BZ$300 or more, and a couple of the lodges are among the most expensive in the entire country.

WHAT IT COSTS IN BELIZE DOLLARS					
	¢	$	$$	$$$	$$$$
RESTAURANTS	under BZ$8	BZ$8–BZ$15	BZ$15–BZ$25	BZ$25–BZ$50	over BZ$50
HOTELS	under BZ$100	BZ$100–BZ$200	BZ$200–BZ$300	BZ$300–BZ$500	over BZ$500

Restaurant prices are per person for a main course at dinner. Hotel prices are for two people in a standard double room, including tax and service.

TOURS

TIDE Tours, a subsidiary of the Toledo Institute for Development and Environment, a nonprofit organization promoting ecotourism in Toledo, does not itself run tours but instead acts as a clearinghouse for several good tour operators. It can arrange fishing, kayaking, snorkeling, and cultural tours, as well as trips to Mayan ruins. Bruno Kuppinger at Sun Creek Lodge and IBTM Tours specializes in adventure tours, some definitely not for couch potatoes, including the weeklong Maya Divide hiking trip and trips to Doyle's Delight, the highest peak in Belize. Garbutts Marine on Joe Taylor Creek offers dependable boat trips to the Snake and Sapodilla cayes and to Port Honduras Marine Reserve, along with fishing trips. Romero's Charters and Tours, while not a tour operator, has a driver service that can take you to any of the inland destinations. Blue Belize Tours and Charters, run by PhD marine biologist Rachel Graham and fishing and tour guide Dan Castellanos, can arrange sea and inland tours and trips. Dr. Graham won the 2011 Gold Award from the Whitley Fund for Nature in the U.K. for her work with whale sharks in Belize. For birding, it's hard to beat George Alford, who can be contacted through TIDE. Several of the hotels, including Hickatee Cottages, offer kayaking on the Moho River.

During the Cacao Festival in May, and by advance arrangement at other times, the Toledo Cacao Growers Association (TCGA), which represents over 1,000 small cacao growers in southern Belize, offers tours of working cacao farms. Cacao Trail tours can also be arranged through TIDE, IBTM, and others.

For a tour of the Garífuna village of Barranco, where famed Belize musician Andy Palacio was born and now is buried, check with tour guide Alvin Loredo, reachable by the community telephone in the Barranco. Two-hour tours include Palacio's burial site, a visit to the local Garífuna dabuyaba temple, the tiny House of Culture museum, and a lunch of Garífuna food. Cost is around BZ$14, including admission to the House of Culture but not lunch. You'll have to get to Barranco on your own. By car, drive on the Southern Highway north to Jacintoville, and turn west and go 9 mi (15 km) on the dirt road via San Felipe and Santa Ana to Barranco. Figure a little over an hour from Punta Gorda, depending on road conditions.

"Ranger patrol hikes" are organized by the Ya'axche Conservation Trust, a nongovernmental organization that among other things owns and manages the 15,000-acre Golden Stream corridor preserve north of Punta Gorda. These hikes start at the field station at Golden Stream, with a climb of the fire tower for a bird's-eye view of the area, and then "ranger work" such as wildlife logs, patrols, and biodiversity transects. This is something of an adventure in an area not normally accessible to visitors. Check with Hickatee Cottages for details.

The Toledo Tour Guide Association has about 20 members. All are licensed by the Belize government. Some of these tour guides work for the larger tour operators, and others work independently.

Contacts Barranco Village Tour by Alvin Loredo ✉ *Barranco* ☎ *709/2010 Barranco community telephone.* **Blue Belize Tours and Charters** ✉ *139 Front St., Punta Gorda* ☎ *722/2678* ⊕ *www.bluebelize.com.* **Bruno Kuppinger, Sun Creek Lodge and IBTM Tours** ✉ *Sun Creek Lodge, off Mile 86, Southern Hwy.* ☎ *604/2124* ⊕ *www.suncreeklodge.de/englisch/home.html.* **Garbutt's Marine** ✉ *Joe Taylor Creek, Punta Gorda* ☎ *722/0070* ✎ *garbuttsmarine@yahoo.com.*

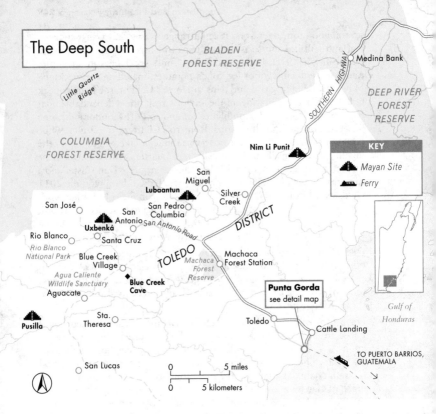

BLADEN
FOREST RESERVE

Medina Bank

Little Quartz Ridge

DEEP RIVER
FOREST
RESERVE

COLUMBIA
FOREST RESERVE

SOUTHERN HIGHWAY

Nim Li Punit

San Miguel

Lubaantun

Silver Creek

San José

San Antonio

San Pedro Columbia

Uxbenká

Santa Cruz

San Antonio Road

DISTRICT

Rio Blanco

Rio Blanco National Park

Blue Creek Village

TOLEDO

Machaca Forest Reserve

Machaca Forest Station

Agua Caliente Wildlife Sanctuary

Blue Creek Cave

Aguacate

Punta Gorda
see detail map

Gulf of Honduras

Pusilla

Sta. Theresa

Toledo

Cattle Landing

San Lucas

TO PUERTO BARRIOS, GUATEMALA

0   5 miles

0   5 kilometers

KEY

▲ Mayan Site

🚢 Ferry

Hickatee Cottages ✉ *Ex-Servicemen Rd., Punta Gorda* ☎ 662/4475 ⊕ *www.hickatee.com.* **Romero's Charter and Tours** ✉ *Forest Home* ☎ 722/2625 ✉ *rcharters@btl.net.* **TIDE Tours** ✉ *14 Front St., Punta Gorda* ☎ 722/2129 ⊕ *www.tidetours.org.* **Toledo Cacao Growers Association** ✉ *Main St., Punta Gorda* ☎ 722/2992 ✉ *tcga@btl.net.*

VISITOR INFORMATION

The office of the Belize Tourism Industry Association (BTIA), on Front Street near the water-taxi dock, is open Tuesday–Saturday 9–noon and 1–4:30, and Sunday 9–noon.

Information Belize Tourism Information Center ✉ *Front St.* ☎ 722/2531 ✉ *btiatoledo@btl.net.*

PUNTA GORDA

102 mi (164 km) south of Placencia.

Most journeys south begin in the region's administrative center, Punta Gorda. PG (as it's affectionately known) isn't your typical tourist destination. Though it has a wonderful setting on the Gulf of Honduras, it has no real beaches. There are few shops of interest to visitors, a few simple restaurants, and little nightlife. Don't expect many tourist services.

So why, you ask, come to PG? First, simply because it isn't on the main tourist track. The accoutrements of mass tourism are still, refreshingly, missing here. Schoolchildren may wave at you, and residents will strike up a conversation. Toledo has stunning natural attractions, too, such as clean rivers for swimming and cave systems with Mayan artifacts that rival those in the Cayo District. Also, with several new hotels to choose from, it's a comfortable base from which to visit surrounding Mayan villages, offshore cayes, and the high bush of the Deep South.

Settled in 1867 by ex-Confederate immigrants from the United States and later a magnet for religious missionaries, Punta Gorda once had 12 sugar estates, each with its own mill, but the sugar industry in Toledo has been replaced by rice farming, citrus groves, and small cacao plantations. After World War II, Great Britain built an important military base here, but when that closed in 1994 the linchpin of the local economy was yanked out. With some increase in tourist dollars and foreigners' growing interest in real estate here, PG is starting to pick up again, but hasn't lost its frontier atmosphere.

GETTING HERE AND AROUND
To best see the sights of Toledo, you'll need a rental car. Otherwise you'll be stuck paying high tour rates or waiting hours for infrequent bus service. If you've flown or bused in to PG, rent a car from Bruno at Sun Creek Lodge (he'll deliver to PG). If you'd like a knowledgeable local guide to ride with you in your rental car, Celiano Pop charges around BZ$80 a day. With a day's notice he can show you the villages and even arrange a traditional Mayan lunch for BZ$6 in one of the villages.

From the intersection of the Hummingbird and Southern highways it's a straight shot 100 mi (164 km) down the Southern, with only a well-marked right turn near Independence to slow you down. On the Southern Highway about 20 mi (33 km) north of Punta Gorda, at about Mile 83, you'll come to an intersection. If you turn left you'll stay on the Southern Highway to PG; if you bear right onto the San Antonio Road, you'll go to Lubaantun, San Antonio Village, and other Mayan villages. Assuming that you continue on the Southern Highway, at about Mile 95 you have two options for reaching downtown PG. You can turn right on the mostly unpaved Saddleback Road and go 5 mi (8 km). To enter from the prettier Bay of Honduras side, as most visitors do, stay straight on the paved Southern Highway and go the same distance.

Contacts Celiano Pop ✉ *Papishaw Rd.* ☎ *624/2518* ✍ *cuxlinha@hotmail.com* ⊕ *www.cuxlinha.com.*

EXPLORING

☼ **Cotton Tree Chocolates.** From cacao beans to final candy bars, you can see how chocolate is made at Cotton Tree Chocolates, a small chocolate factory on Front Street. It is associated with Cotton Tree Lodge. You'll get a short guided tour of the chocolate-making process and you can buy bars of delicious milk or dark chocolate. ✉ *2 Front St.* ☎ *670/0557* ▦ *Free* ☾ *Mon.–Fri. 8–noon and 1:30–5; Sat. 8–noon.*

OUTDOOR ACTIVITIES

Punta Gorda and Toledo offer great opportunities for outdoor activities—fishing, diving, snorkeling, sea and river kayaking, and caving. The problem has been that due to so few visitors to the Deep South and the limited number of tour operators, visitors often arrived to find that few tours were actually available on a given day, or if they were running, tended to cost much more than in other parts of Belize. An attempt to schedule tours to always run on specific days—for example, to Port Honduras Marine Reserve for snorkeling on Monday and to Blue Creek for caving on Tuesday—has fizzled out. Still, with tourism

> **TO MARKET, TO MARKET**
>
> On market days—Monday, Wednesday, Friday, and Saturday, with Wednesday and Saturday usually being the largest—the town comes to life with vendors from nearby Mayan villages and even from Guatemala. They pack the downtown market area with colorful fruit and vegetable stands. Fresh fish also is sold in a building at the market, daily except Sunday, and for a small fee you can have your fish cleaned.

slowly increasing, more tours are being offered, and most prices are reasonable. Try to go with a group of four to six, as many tours have a price based on a group of up to six people, not per person.

Among the most popular tours are those to the Snake Cayes. An all-day trip of snorkeling, fishing, and beach bumming costs around BZ$500 for up to four people, plus the BZ$10 per person Port Honduras Reserve entrance fee. Another popular tour combines Blue Creek caves and Agua Caliente Wildlife Sanctuary; it's around BZ$130 per person, with a minimum of two people. Tours to Lubaantun, often in combination with a visit to Rio Blanco National Park and its waterfall, are around BZ$130 a person (two-person minimum).

☾ **Agua Caliente Wildlife Sanctuary.** Hot springs, freshwater lagoons, caves, and hiking trails dot the Agua Caliente Wildlife Sanctuary, a good-sized nature preserve. You can fish here as well. ⊠ *About 13 mi (21 km) west of Punta Gorda* ✛ *From Punta Gorda, take Southern Hwy. 10 mi (16 km) north. Turn left on Laguna Rd. and go 3 mi (5 km). The trail to the wildlife sanctuary begins in the village. Ask a local resident to show you where it begins.*

☾ **Bladen Forest Reserve.** Ever been freshwater snorkeling? Check out the Bladen River in the Bladen Forest Reserve. The river snakes through the reserve, allowing for excellent kayaking, canoeing, swimming, and, yes, freshwater snorkeling. The 100,000-acre Bladen Forest Reserve is co-managed by the Belize Forestry Department and the Ya'axche Conservation Trust.

Tours of the Bladen Reserve also are given by interns from a 1,153-acre private reserve managed by the Belize Foundation for Research and Environmental Education (BFREE). The BFREE reserve adjoins four protected areas: Bladen Nature Reserve, Cockscomb Basin Sanctuary, Deep River Forest Reserve, and Maya Mountain Forest Reserve. Camping and simple bunkhouse accommodations are available at BFREE for

HISTORY

The Maya, mostly a group called the Manche Chol Maya, established sizable ceremonial centers and midsize cities in Toledo beginning almost 2,000 years ago. Uxbenká is one of the oldest centers, dating to AD 200. In the Classic period, Lubaantun, which flourished in the 8th and 9th centuries, is thought to have been the administrative center of the region, but for reasons still unclear it was abandoned not long after this. In southern Belize as elsewhere in Mesoamerica, the Mayan civilization began a long, slow decline a little more than 1,000 years ago.

Spanish conquistadors, including Hemán Cortés himself in 1525, came through southern Belize in the early 16th century, but the Maya resisted the Spanish and, later, Britain's attempts to control and tax them.

The British, who arrived as loggers, tried to put the Maya in "reservations," and eventually, in the 18th and 19th centuries, moved nearly the entire Manche Chol population to the highlands of Guatemala.

In the late 19th century, groups of Mopan and Ketchi Maya began moving into southern Belize from Guatemala, establishing more than 50 villages around Toledo. Around the same time, Garífuna from Honduras settled in Punta Gorda, Barranco, and Punta Negra.

Southern Belize, with its rain and remoteness from Belize City, has languished economically for most of the 20th century. The paved Southern Highway and planned new road from Guatemala may help boost tourism and development in the region in coming years.

around BZ$80 to BZ$120 per person per day, meals included. Additional charges may apply for transportation, canoe rental, laundry, and other services. ✉ *Off Mile 59, Southern Hwy.* ☎ *614/3896 for BFREE* ☎☎ *722/0108 for Ya'axche Conservation Trust* ● *www.bfreebz.org and www.yaaxche.org/bladen_nature_reserve.html.*

Columbia Forest Reserve. One of the largest undisturbed tropical rain forest areas in Central America is the Columbia Forest Reserve. It's in a remote area north of San José Village, and the karst terrain—an area of irregular limestone in which erosion has produced sinkholes, fissures, and underground streams and caves—is difficult to navigate, so the only way to see this area is with a guide and with advance permission from the Belize Forestry Department. It has extremely diverse ecosystems because the elevation ranges from about 1,000 to over 3,000 feet, with sinkholes as deep as 800 feet. You'll find areas of true "high bush" here: old-growth tropical forest with parts that have never been logged at all. Much of the rich flora and fauna of this area has yet to be documented. For example, one brief 12-day expedition turned up 15 species of ferns never found before in Belize, along with several new species of palms, vines, and orchids. Bruno Kuppinger at SunCreek Lodge is among the guides who offer adventure trips into the Columbia Forest Reserve. ✉ *North of San José Village* ☎ *722/2765.*

Itzama Ethnobotanical Gardens. A medicinal plant garden, Itzama Ethnobotanical Gardens was conceived and created by local Maya traditional healers, members of the Ketchi Maya Healers Association. Initial funding was from the Canadian government. There are about 100 species of medicinal plants transplanted to the garden. If you want to tour this small, informal, but highly educational garden, you should call or email Victor Cal at the Belize Indigenous Training Institute and make an appointment in advance. ⊠ *Southern Hwy., between Golden Stream and Indian Creek* ☎ *702/0134* ✉ *vikcal045@hotmail.com.*

🕙 **Rio Blanco National Park.** This is a tiny national park (105 acres) with a big waterfall. The Rio Blanco waterfall splashes over rough limestone boulders into a deep pool, which you can jump into for a refreshing swim. You reach the waterfall after hiking a well-marked trail. Upstream a short distance from the falls is a nice area for a picnic, shaded by trees and flowering bushes. ⊠ *30 mi (49 km) west of Punta Gorda between Santa Cruz and Santa Elena villages, on road to Jalacte.*

🕙 **Sarstoon-Temash National Park.** One of the wildest and most remote areas of Belize is the Sarstoon-Temash National Park, between the Temash and Sarstoon rivers in the far south of Toledo District on the border of Guatemala. Red mangroves grow along the river banks; animals and birds rarely seen in other parts of Belize, including white-faced capuchin monkeys, can be spotted here, along with jaguars (if you're lucky), ocelots, and tapirs, along with more than 200 species of birds. The only way to see this 42,000-acre area is with a guide by boat. Contact the Sarstoon and Temash Institute for Indigenous Management (SATIIM) for a guide. SATIIM, among other things, is involved in efforts to oppose oil and gas exploration in the Sarstoon-Temash. ⊠ *About 13 mi (21 km) south of Punta Gorda by boat* ☎ *722/0103* ⊕ *www.satiim.org.bz* 💲 *BZ$20.*

🕙 **Toledo Botanical Arboretum.** The Toledo Botanical Arboretum is an organic farm with a growing collection of fruit trees (more than 50 varieties) and hundreds of other local plants and trees. The farm and gardens are part of the Dem Dats Doin' organization run by Yvonne and Alfredo Villoria. For a tour, call in advance. ⊠ *1¼ mi (2 km) from turnoff to Lubaantun* ☎ *772/2470* 💲 *BZ$10.*

FISHING

For bonefish and tarpon, head to the estuary flats in the Port Honduras marine reserve at the end of the Río Grande, or go northward to Punta Ycacos. In the Marine Reserve, anglers pay a one-day park fee of BZ$20, or BZ$60 for three to seven days. There is no fee for the Punta Ycacos, unless you fish in the Port Honduras reserve. For a full day of fly-fishing with a local guide and boat, you'll pay around BZ$550–BZ$650 for two anglers.

Blue Belize Tours and Charters. Blue Belize Tours is operated by Dr. Rachel Graham, a marine biologist specializing in sharks, and Dan Castellanos, an experienced local fisherman and licensed guide. Fishing trips include spincasting, trolling, and catch-and-release fly-fishing, for around BZ$650 a day for up to two to four persons, depending on the type of fishing. ⊠ *139 Front St.* ☎ *722/2678* ⊕ *www.bluebelize.com.*

TIDE Tours. TIDE Tours offers fly-fishing for bonefish or permit, from BZ$900 per day for two persons, not including 12.5% tax or reserve entry fees. ✉ *14 Front St.* ☎ *722/2129* ⊕ *www.tidetours.org.*

SCUBA DIVING

This far south the reef has pretty much broken up, but individual cayes have their own small reef systems. The best of the bunch is at the Sapodilla Cayes, seven cayes with great wall dives. Lime Caye here has camping, and Hunting Caye has a lighthouse. The only drawback is that because they're 40 mi (64 km) off the coast, a day's dive trip costs around BZ$300 per person or more, depending on how many people go. The Snake Cayes, with several notable dive sites, are closer in, about 30 km (18 mi) northeast of Punta Gorda. The four Snakes—East, West, South, and Middle—are so named because of boa constrictors that once lived there.

Reef Conservation International. Reef Conservation International operates marine conservation trips from Franks Caye in the Sapodilla Cayes Marine Reserve. You can stay there in basic accommodations. There's plenty of snorkeling and diving, but you can also assist marine biologists and other Reef CI staff in monitoring and preserving the Barrier Reef. Four night packages including diving, dive equipment, lodging, and meals start at BZ$1,990 per person. ✉ *Franks Caye* ☎ *626/1429, 606/0074* ⊕ *www.reefci.com.*

TIDE Tours. TIDE Tours can arrange diving, snorkeling, and other trips to the Sapodilla and Snake cayes. ✉ *14 Front St.* ☎ *722/2129* ⊕ *www. tidetours.org.*

SNORKELING

The turquoise waters lapping up the shores of the usually deserted white-sand beach on Snake Caye are good for snorkeling, as are the Sapodilla Cayes at the southern end of the Belize Barrier Reef.

Blue Belize Tours and Charters. Blue Belize Tours has full-day snorkeling tours to the Snake (BZ$500) or Sapodillas (BZ$650) cayes, for up to six persons. Keep in mind that travel time by boat to the Sapodilla Cayes is about two hours, and 45 minutes to the Snake Cayes—with gas at near BZ$12 gallon, that's one reason for the high costs. ✉ *139 Front St.* ☎ *722/2678* ⊕ *www.bluebelize.com.*

Garbutt's Marine. Garbutt's Marine offers all-day snorkeling trips to the Snake Cayes for around BZ$450 for up to three persons or BZ$120 per person for four to six people. Full-day trips to the Sapodilla Cayes are BZ$600 for up to three persons, or BZ$160 per person for four to six people. Garbutt's also offers overnight camping and a cabin at Lime Caye. ✉ *Joe Taylor Creek* ☎ *722/0072* ✍ *garbuttsmarine@yahoo.com.*

TIDE Tours. TIDE Tours can arrange full-day snorkeling trips to Snake Caye in the Port Honduras Marine Reserve. For two people, it's BZ$280 per person, and for four persons, BZ$160 per person, all plus 12.5% tax and BZ$10 per person reserve entry fee. The cost includes lunch and snorkel equipment. ✉ *14 Front St.* ☎ *722/2129* ⊕ *www.tidetours.org.*

WHERE TO EAT

$ **Bamboo Chicken.** This casual bar and restaurant, new in 2011, doesn't
AMERICAN actually serve "bamboo chicken" (a local name for iguana), but it does
offer cold beer and light meals and bar snacks in a breezy location
directly on the bayfront on Front St. There's a pier at the restaurant
where you can swim in the bay. ⊠ *Front St., Punta Gorda* ☎ *No phone*
▭ *No credit cards.*

$ **Earth Runnins Café and Bakut Bar.** Many visitors and expats enjoy this
ECLECTIC café's Rastafarian vibe. It's a laid-back (read: service can sometimes
seem to be in slow motion) spot for a beer and a bite to eat. Runnins is
a Rasta word for happenings, and Bakut is a local tree with pink flowers and long seed pods with edible but smelly seeds—the tree is locally
known as Stinking Toe. Local seafood is a specialty here. Try the conch
curry or snapper cooked in a banana leaf, or the curried chicken wrap
on roti bread. For vegetarians the Mediterranean plate with hummus
and babaganoosh is a good choice. Check out the bar, which was made
from a large rosewood tree that was felled by Hurricane Iris in 2001,
and have a lime daiquiri made from Belizean rum and local organic
limes. There's live music some nights. Open for breakfast, lunch, and
dinner Wednesday–Sunday. ⊠ *13 Main Middle St.* ☎ *702/2007* ▭ *No
credit cards* ⊘ *Closed Mon. and Tues.*

$ **Gomier's Restaurant and Soy Centre.** This is one of the best restaurants
VEGETARIAN in PG—when and if it's open. It opens only if the St. Lucia–born owner,
Ingnatius "Gomier" Longville, feels like cooking, and you won't know
that until about the time the restaurant is supposed to open. When it is
open, Gomier's does excellent vegetarian meals, from organic ingredients grown locally by the owner. It pays to go with the vegetarian dish
of the day, which could be stir-fried tofu or vegan spaghetti. A fresh fish
dish sometimes is available. The owner also offers cooking classes, for
around BZ$100 a day. ⊠ *Alejandro Vernon St., near 'Welcome to Punta
Gorda' sign on Front St.* ☎ *722/2929* ▭ *No credit cards* ⊘ *Closed Sun.
and Mon.; unpredictable hrs.*

$ **Grace's.** An established spot, Grace's has genuine value and serves
LATIN AMERICAN a hearty plate of beans and rice and other Belizean staples. Get a seat
near the entrance and eye the town's street life. This is a good place for
a full breakfast of eggs, bacon, fry jacks (a Belizean version of a sopa-
pilla), and, of course, beans. For lunch and dinner you can always get
chicken, but you can usually get fresh fish, too, plus pizza, chow mein,
hamburgers, and several dozen other dishes. ⊠ *21 Main St.* ☎ *702/2414*
▭ *No credit cards.*

$ **Mangrove Inn at Casa Bonita.** You're seated here in a first-floor screened
INTERNATIONAL porch or in the breezeway of this house across the street from the water
★ in Cattle Landing. The chef and co-owner, Iconie Williams, formerly
operated one of PG's best restaurants, also called Mangrove Inn, and
she reopened it here in the B&B in her home. She cooks different dishes
every evening, but you'll usually have a choice of seafood (snapper,
snook, or shrimp, BZ$14–BZ$20) or hearty fare like lasagna (BZ$15).
It's all delicious and inexpensive. Open daily for dinner only, except
Sunday. BYOB—Bring Your Own Belikin—as the restaurant doesn't

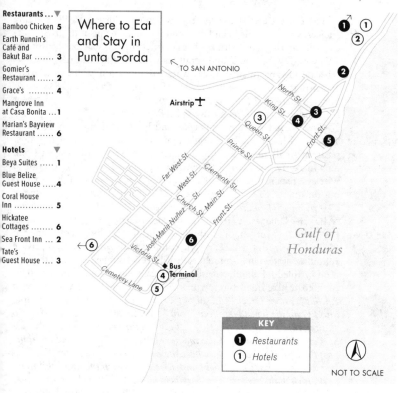

Where to Eat
and Stay in
Punta Gorda

TO SAN ANTONIO

Airstrip

North St.
King St.
Queen St.
Prince St.
Front St.

Far West St.
West St.
Clements St.
Church St.
Main St.
José María Núñez
front St.
Victoria St.
Cemetery Lane

◆ Bus
Terminal

*Gulf of
Honduras*

KEY

❶ *Restaurants*

① *Hotels*

NOT TO SCALE

have a license to serve alcohol. ✉ *Front St. in Cattle Landing area* ☎ *631/1596* ▭ *No credit cards* ☾ *Dinner only; closed Sun.*

$ ✕ **Marian's Bayview Restaurant.** On the third level of a nondescript con-
LATIN AMERICAN crete building, with a thatch roof palapa, Marian's has little atmo-
★ sphere—though there is indeed a view of the bay—but the Indian and
Belizean food is inexpensive and well prepared. Marian usually cooks
only two or three dishes each evening, and you choose among them.
It might be a freshly caught snapper seasoned with a blend of Belizean
and East Indian spices or a plate of Belizean beans and rice, and they're
both delicious. ✉ *76 Front St., south of market* ☎ *722/0129.*

WHERE TO STAY

For expanded hotel reviews, visit Fodors.com.

$ ⊡ **Beya Suites.** From the verandas on the second- or third-floor rooftop
terrace of this bright pink, waterfront hotel (*beya* means beachfront in
the Garífuna language), you have expansive views of the water. **Pros:**
views of the water; Belizean-owned. **Cons:** most units are not really
suites. ✉ *6 Front St., Hopeville* ☎ *722/2188* ⊕ *www.beyasuites.com* ⇌ *8
rooms, 2 suites* ⌂ *In-room: kitchen, Wi-Fi. In-hotel: restaurant, bar.*

7

$ ☆ 🏠 **Blue Belize Guest House.** At this welcome addition to PG lodging choices, you can settle in and do your own thing in one of the five attractive self-catering flats, with kitchens or kitchenettes, spacious bedrooms, TVs with DVD players, and verandas with hammocks. **Pros:** spacious self-catering apartments; breezy waterfront location; well-guided tours and fishing trips. **Cons:** no a/c. ⊠ *139 Front St.* ☎ *722/2678* ⊕ *www. bluebelize.com* ➾ *4 1-bedroom apartments, 1 2-bedroom apartment* ⚴ *In-room: no a/c, kitchen, Wi-Fi* ❑ *Breakfast.*

$ Fodor'sChoice ★ 🏠 **Coral House Inn.** Americans Rick and Darla Mallory renovated this 1938 British colonial–era house and turned it into one of the most pleasant small guesthouses in the country. **Pros:** one of the best small inns in Belize; most comfort amenities provided, from a/c to pool to wireless; reasonable prices. **Cons:** no restaurant, so you'll have to go out for dinner. ⊠ *151 Main St.* ☎ *722/2878* ⊕ *www.coralhouseinn.net* ➾ *4 rooms, 1 1-bedroom house* ⚴ *In-room: Wi-Fi. In-hotel: bar, pool.*

$ Fodor'sChoice ★ 🏠 **Hickatee Cottages.** A charming and enthusiastic young British couple, Ian and Kate Morton, opened this delightful small lodge at the edge of PG in 2005, with Caribbean-style cottages with zinc roofs and private verandas, nestled in lush foliage. **Pros:** lovely cottages; some of the best food in Toledo; helpful, friendly owners; excellent value. **Cons:** a longish hike or bike ride from town; no air-conditioning. ⊠ *Ex-Servicemen Rd. (aka Boom Creek Rd.), about 1 mi (1½ km) from PG* ✛ *Coming into PG on the bayside, follow Front St. through town, past the Texaco station, through the market area, and then turn right immediately past St. Peter Claver church. Take the next left onto Main St. and continue past the hospital; bear right where the road becomes Cemetery La. Follow Cemetery La. for 2 blocks and, when you reach the small children's park, turn 'half-left' onto Ex-Servicemen Rd. Go 1 mi (1½ km) farther to Hickatee Cottages, on left* ☎ *662/4475* ✉ *cottages@hickatee.com* ⊕ *www.hickatee.com* ➾ *6 rooms, 1 suite* ⚴ *In-room: no a/c, no TV. In-hotel: restaurant, bar, pool* ❑ *Breakfast.*

$ 🏠 **Sea Front Inn.** With its pitched roofs and stone-and-wood facade, this four-story hotel may remind you of a Swiss ski lodge. **Pros:** appealing waterfront location; one-of-a-kind rooms. **Cons:** upper-story rooms require climbing a lot of steps. ⊠ *Front St.* ☎ *722/2300* ⊕ *www. seafrontinn.com* ➾ *12 rooms, 2 suites, 5 1-bedroom apartments, 1 2-bedroom apartment* ⚴ *In-room: kitchen, Wi-Fi. In-hotel: restaurant, bar.*

$$ ★ 🏠 **Sirmoor Hill Farm Bed and Breakfast.** This newly opened B&B, in a restored 100-year-old colonial home on a 775-acre farm near Punta Gorda, is among the most appealing small lodgings in Belize. **Pros:** charming guestrooms in restored colonial ranch house; breezy and beautiful hilltop country setting with pool; friendly, gregarious hosts. **Cons:** not a lot of privacy; no restaurants nearby. ⊠ *New Road, near Belize Defence Forces camp, Punta Gorda* ☎ *722/0052* ➾ *2 rooms with shared bath* ⚴ *In-room: no a/c, no TV, Wi-Fi. In-hotel: pool* ❑ *Breakfast.*

¢ 🏠 **Tate's Guest House.** If you don't demand luxury or soft beds, you couldn't find a nicer spot in PG. **Pros:** clean accommodations at near backpacker rates. **Cons:** few frills. ⊠ *34 José Maria Nuñez St.* ☎ *722/0147* ➾ *5 rooms* ⚴ *In-room: no a/c, kitchen* ▭ *No credit cards.*

THE MAYA HEARTLAND

Drive a few miles out of town, and you find yourself in the heartland of the Maya people. Half the population of Toledo is Maya, a far higher proportion than in any other region. The Toledo Maya Cultural Council has created an ambitious network of Maya-run guesthouses, and in 1995 it initiated the Mayan Mapping Project. By collating oral history and evidence of ancient Mayan settlements, the project hopes to secure rights to land that the Maya have occupied for centuries, but that the Belizean government has ceded to multinational logging companies. There's also a separate, privately run Mayan homestay program, where you stay in local homes rather than in guesthouses. *See Where to Stay, below, for information on these two programs.*

The Maya divide into two groups: Mopan Maya– and Ketchi-speaking peoples from the Guatemalan highlands. Most of the latter are recent arrivals, refugees from repression and overpopulation. Each group tends to keep to itself, living in separate villages and preserving unique traditions. Among the Ketchi villages in Toledo are Crique Sarco, San Vincente, San Miquel, Laguna, San Pedro Columbia, Santa Teresa, Sunday Wood, Mabelha, and Corazon. Mopan Maya villages include San Antonio, Pueblo Viejo, and San José.

GETTING HERE AND AROUND
Since bus service to rural villages is limited at best, a car is almost a necessity unless you want to take guided tours.

TIMING
You can see the highlights in a day or two, but to explore the region thoroughly takes longer. Distances are not great, but roads are poor to terrible, and it takes time just to get around the district.

HEALTH AND SAFETY
Malaria is a problem in rural areas of Toledo. If you're going to spend any time in the bush, discuss with your physician whether to use chloroquine or other malaria prophylaxis. In rural areas the water is often from community wells; you should drink bottled water. Otherwise, the Maya Heartland is very safe.

EXPLORING

MAYA VILLAGES
Blue Creek. Don't miss Blue Creek, a beautiful stretch of river dotted with turquoise swimming holes. A path up the riverbank leads to dramatic caves. The entrance to Hokeb Ha Cave is fairly easy to explore on your own (although you should be a strong swimmer), but others require a guide or a tour. International Zoological Expeditions, a Connecticut-based student travel and research organization, has established a jungle lodge at Blue Creek, with seven rustic cabañas and a restaurant. To visit this part of Blue Creek, you need an okay from the **IZE Blue Creek Rainforest Lodge** (☎ *508/655–1461 in the U.S. or ✉ ize2belize@aol. com*). ITMB at SunCreek Lodge, TIDE Tours, and other tour operators offer trips to Blue Creek, providing lights and other necessary equipment. Don't swim in the river at night—a highly poisonous snake called

Belize's Multicultural Gumbo

The celebration of Belize's historic multiculturalism begins on its flag: the two young men—one black and the other white—are woodcutters standing beneath a logwood tree. Under them is a Latin inscription: *sub umbra floreat*—"In the shade of this tree we flourish."

Belize is a rich gumbo of colors and languages. Creoles, once the majority, now make up only about a quarter of the population. Creoles in Belize are descendants of slaves brought from Jamaica to work in the logging industry. By the early 18th century, people of African descent came to outnumber those of British origin in Belize. The two groups united early in the country's history to defeat a common enemy, the Spanish. Most of the Creole population today is concentrated in Belize City and Belize District, although there are predominantly Creole villages elsewhere, including the villages of Gales Point, Crooked Tree, and Placencia. English is the country's official language and taught in school, although an English dialect, Creole, is widely spoken.

Mestizos are the fastest-growing group in Belize and make up about half the population. These are persons of mixed European and Maya heritage, typically speaking Spanish as a first language and English as a second. Some migrated to Belize from Mexico during the Yucatán Caste Wars of the mid-19th century. More recently, many "Spanish" (as they're often called in Belize) have moved from Guatemala, El Salvador, Honduras, or elsewhere in Central America. According to the 2010 Belize Census, more than 33,000 residents of Belize were born in other Central American countries. Mestizos are concentrated in northern and western Belize.

Numbering close to a million at the height of the Mayan kingdoms, the Maya today constitute only about one-tenth of the Belize population of 313,000. There are concentrations of Yucatec Maya in Corozal and Orange Walk districts, Mopan Maya in Toledo and Cayo districts, and also Ketchi Maya in about 30 villages in Toledo. Most speak their Mayan dialect and either English or Spanish, or both.

About one in 20 Belizeans is a Garífuna. The Garinagu (the plural of Garífuna) are of mixed African and Carib Indian heritage. Most originally came to Belize from Honduras in the 1820s and 1830s. Dangriga and Punta Gorda are towns with large Garífuna populations, as are the villages of Seine Bight, Hopkins, and Barranco. Besides their own tongue—an Arawakan-based language with smatterings of West African words—many Garinagu speak English and Creole and sometimes Spanish.

Other groups include more than 11,000 Mennonites, sizable communities of East Indians, and Chinese, mostly from Taiwan and Hong Kong. Belize's original white populations were English, but today's "gringos" are mostly expats from the United States and Canada, with some from the United Kingdom and various Commonwealth countries, numbering some 3,000. All these groups find in this tiny country a tolerant and amiable home.

Whatever the background of its citizens, Belize's population is young. More than two out of five Belizeans are under 15 years of age, and the median age is just 22.

the fer-de-lance likes to take nocturnal dips. ✛ *If going on your own from PG, drive north on the Southern Hwy. to the dump and turn west on the San Antonio Rd. (currently being paved). Drive to the village of Mafredi and turn left toward Blue Creek. Go about 9 mi (15 km) to the entrance to the Blue Creek research station.*

San Antonio. The Mopan Maya village of San Antonio, a market town 35 mi (56 km) west of Punta Gorda, is Toledo's second-largest town, with a population of more than 2,000. It was settled by people from the Guatemalan village of San Luis, who revere their former patron saint. The village church, built of stones carted from surrounding Mayan ruins, has a stained-glass window donated by another city with a connection to the saint: St. Louis, Missouri. The people of San Antonio haven't forgotten their ancient heritage: Each June 13, they take to the streets for a festival that dates back to pre-Columbian times. The road to San Antonio is currently being paved. ✛ *Drive north on the Southern Hwy. to the Dump, and turn left and follow the San Antonio Rd. to San Antonio village.*

San Pedro Columbia. The Ketchi Maya village of San Pedro Columbia is a cheerful cluster of brightly painted buildings and thatch houses off the San Antonio Road. ✛ *From PG, drive north on the Southern Hwy. to the Dump, and turn west on the San Antonio Rd. Just before the village of San Antonio, turn right on a dirt track (watch for a sign) to San Pedro Columbia.*

GARÍFUNA VILLAGE

Barranco. Although the Maya are by far the largest population in rural Toledo, this is also a home to the Garífuna. Barranco, a small village of fewer than 300 people about an hour by road from Punta Gorda, is the best-known Garífuna center in Toledo. The village, the southernmost coastal village in Belize, has electricity and a community phone, one or two shops, a bar, a police station, a health clinic, and a school. It was the birthplace of Andy Palacio, the Punta rock musician with a worldwide following, who died in 2008 at age 46. Palacio is buried in Barranco, and you can visit his grave. A guided village tour takes a couple of hours and includes, in addition to a visit to the Palacio gravesite, stops at the Dabuyaba (Garífuna temple), the House of Culture, and a cassava factory, all providing lots of information on the local culture. Lunch in a local home is also possible. A good guide is Alvin Loredo (reach him on the Barranco community telephone, ☎ *709/2010*), who charges around BZ$8 per person per hour. TIDE, Blue Belize Tours and Charters, and other tour operators also offer tours to Barranco. ✛ *From PG, drive north to Jacinto village (watch for the water tower) and turn west on the dirt road to San Felipe, Santa Ana, and Barranco villages. It's about 9 mi (15 km) on the dirt road to Barranco, but it may take you as long as 45 minutes after you leave the Southern Hwy.* ☎ *709/2010 Barranco community telephone.*

MAYAN RUINS

Ꮳ ★ **Lubaantun.** Lubaantun, which lies beyond the village of San Pedro Columbia, is a Late Classic site discovered in 1924 by German archaeologist Thomas Gann, who gave it a name meaning "place of fallen stones." Lubaantun must have been an awe-inspiring sight: on top of a conical hill, with views to the sea in one direction and the Maya Mountains in the other, its stepped layers of white-plaster stone would have towered above the jungle like a wedding cake. No one knows exactly what function the structures served, but the wealth of miniature masks and whistles found suggests it was a center of ceramic production. The trio of ball courts and the central plaza with tiered seating for 10,000 spectators seems like a Maya Madison Square Garden. There's a small visitor center at the site.

In the last century Lubaantun became the scene of what is allegedly the biggest hoax in modern archaeology. After it was excavated in the 1920s, a British adventurer named F. A. Mitchell-Hedges claimed to have stumbled on what became known as the Crystal Skull. Mitchell-Hedges described the incident in a potboiler, *Danger, My Ally*, in 1951. According to the book, the Crystal Skull was found under an altar at Lubaantun by his daughter Anna. Mitchell-Hedges portrayed himself as a serious archaeologist and explorer: in truth, he was a magazine hack who was later exposed in England as an adventurer. The Crystal Skull made good copy; also known as the Skull of Doom, it was supposedly used by Mayan high priests to zap anyone they didn't care for. Mitchell-Hedges claimed it was 3,600 years old and had taken 150 years to fashion by rubbing a block of pure rock crystal with sand. A similar skull, in the possession of the British Museum, shows signs of having been manufactured with a dentist's drill. However, some archeologists believe the crystal skull may be authentic, possibly of Aztec origin. Anna Mitchell-Hedges, who died in 2007, adamantly refused to allow the Crystal Skull to be tested and denied all requests by the Belizean government to return it. It is now owned by her caregiver, Bill Homann. Most tour operators in PG can arrange trips to Lubaantun. ⊠ *20 mi (33 km) northwest of Punta Gorda, about 1 mi (1½ km) from village of San Pedro Columbia* 🎫 *BZ$20* ⊘ *Daily 8–5.*

☺ ★ **Nim Li Punit.** Nim Li Punit, a Late Classic site discovered in 1976, has 26 unearthed stelae, including one, Stela 14, that is 30 feet tall—the largest ever found in Belize and the second largest found anywhere in the Mayan world. Nim Li Punit, which means "Big Hat" in the Ketchi Mayan language, is named for the elaborate headgear of a ruler pictured on Stela 14. Shady trees cool you off as you walk around the fairly small site (you can see it all in an hour or so). Stop by the informative visitor center on the premises to learn more about the site. Nim Li Punit is near the Ketchi village of Indian Creek, and children (and some adults) from the village usually come over and offer jewelry and crafts for sale. ⊠ *27 mi (44 km) northwest of Punta Gorda off Mile 72½, Western Hwy.* ✛ *From PG, drive north on the Southern Hwy. about 27 mi (44 km) to Indian Creek village. Turn west at the Nim Li Punit sign and go about ½ mi (1 km) on a dirt road to the site. James Line buses (locals, not express) will drop you at the entrance road.* 🎫 *BZ$20* ⊘ *Daily 8–5.*

☺ **Uxbenká.** Uxbenká, or "ancient place," is on the eastern edge of Santa Cruz Village, about 3 mi (5 km) west of San Antonio. This small ceremonial site has a main plaza with six structures, and a series of smaller plazas. More than 20 stelae have been found here, six of them carved. This site is not officially open to visitors, but if you ask a villager in Santa Cruz, you can probably get an informal guided tour, or go with a TIDE or other tour from PG (about BZ$200), which also include a visit to the nearby Yok Balum cave. ⊹ *From PG, drive north on the Southern Hwy. to the Dump and turn west on the San Antonio Rd. Drive past San Antonio village about 3 mi (5 km) to Santa Cruz village.* ▨ *BZ$5 donation.*

WHERE TO EAT

$
LATIN AMERICAN
⨉**Coleman's Café.** This longtime local favorite serves simple but tasty Belizean dishes such as stew chicken with beans and rice. Sit at tables with checkered oilcloth tablecloths under a covered patio, open to the breezes, and enjoy genuine Belizean hospitality. ⊠ *Big Falls Village, near rice mill* ☎ 720/2017 ⊟ *No credit cards.*

WHERE TO STAY

For expanded hotel reviews, visit Fodors.com.

$$$
★
▦ **Cotton Tree Lodge.** Named after the silk cotton tree (also called the kapok or ceiba), a giant specimen of which stands near the main building, this lodge sits beside the Moho River about 15 mi (24 km) from Punta Gorda—most guests arrive by boat to stay at the thatch cabañas among the fig tress. **Pros:** stunning riverside setting, complete with rope swing to play Tarzan in the river; lots of activities. **Cons:** sometimes buggy; no a/c. ⊠ *San Felipe village* ⊠ *P.O. Box 104, Punta Gorda* ☎ 670/0557, 866/480–4534 in U.S. ⊕ *www.cottontreelodge.com* ⇆ *11 cabañas* ♿ *In-room: no a/c, no TV. In-hotel: restaurant, bar, water sports, business center* |⊙| *Multiple meal plans.*

$$$
★
▦ **The Lodge at Big Falls.** Relax beside a meandering jungle river, listen to otters splash, and admire colorful butterflies at this small lodge on 30 placid acres beside the Rio Grande River. **Pros:** it's fun to tube or swim in the river; excellent birding; good food. **Cons:** meals are pricey. ⊠ *Off Mile 79, Southern Hwy.* ⊠ *P.O. Box 103, Punta Gorda* ☎ 732/4444 ⊕ *www.thelodgeatbigfalls.com* ⇆ *8 cabañas* ♿ *In-room: no a/c, no TV. In-hotel: restaurant, bar, pool, water sports, business center.*

$$$$
★
▦ **Belcampo Lodge.** New owners have moved this former fishing lodge far up the scale of luxury, renovating the main lodge, adding a gorgeous spa, and redoing the cottages. **Pros:** great views of sea and jungle from hilltop location; incredible spa; the top lodge option near PG. **Cons:** extremely pricey and, some would say, overpriced. ⊠ *5 mi (8 km) north of Punta Gorda* ⊠ *Box 135, Punta Gorda* ☎ 722/0050 ⊕ *www. machacahill.com* ⇆ *12 cottages* ♿ *In-room: no TV, Wi-Fi. In-hotel: restaurant, bar, pool, spa* |⊙| *Multiple meal plans.*

$
▦ **Sun Creek Lodge.** This little lodge is operated by Bruno Kuppinger, a native of Germany, who maintains the simple, comfortable thatch cabañas that have outdoor showers. **Pros:** inexpensive; landscaped setting; excellent adventure tours available. **Cons:** some accommodations are basic. ⊠ *San Marcos Rd., about 14 mi (23 km) northwest of Punta*

7

HELPING OUT IN BELIZE

Church and mission trips. This typically involves a week to several weeks of volunteer work in a medical or dental clinic, or building churches or homes, or other hands-on assistance. Usually these volunteer groups are based outside of Belize, often at a church or school or as a part of a local medical society. In most cases, volunteers pay for their own transportation to Belize, along with personal expenses in the country, but food and lodging may be provided by the mission. Your best bet is to contact your church, college, or local medical society and ask if they know of upcoming mission trips to Belize.

Independent volunteering. Find a worthwhile organization and volunteer your services. Conservation organizations, churches, libraries, medical clinics, humane societies, and schools are among those that may welcome volunteers. You typically won't receive any lodging or food in return for your volunteer activities. To arrange this kind of independent volunteer work, you usually need to be in Belize and make personal contact with the organization you are seeking to help.

Organized volunteer programs. These volunteer programs often revolve around conservation, such as working with wildlife or reef preservation. A few programs offer volunteer opportunities in education, animal care, or social work. Some programs require volunteers to pay a placement fee, which can be several hundred dollars or more, plus pay for room, board, and transportation to Belize. In other programs, volunteers do not pay a fee and they may receive food and lodging in exchange for their volunteer work, but they usually have to pay transportation and incidental expenses out of pocket. For longer-term volunteering, consider the U.S. Peace Corps, which has a significant presence here.

Some organizations that accept volunteers in Belize:

Belize Audubon Society. The Belize Audubon Society, the oldest and largest conservation group in Belize, which manages nine protected areas and parks in Belize, accepts some qualified volunteers to assist in its park management, conservation, tourism development, and other programs. The BAS requires a minimum three-month commitment for its overseas volunteers working inland, and one-month for volunteers in marine program. Although the BAS prefers to partner with universities to get its interns, it does also accept individual volunteer applications. The BAS does not pay for lodging or living expenses. ⊠ *12 Fort St., Belize City* ⊠ *P.O. Box 1001, Belize City* ☎ *223/5004* ⊕ *www.belizeaudubon. org.*

Belize Zoo and Tropical Education Center. The Belize Zoo, one of the great conservation organizations in Central America, and the adjoining Tropical Education Center have a wide range of education and outreach programs. A few motivated volunteers are accepted to assist Belize Zoo and TEC programs. The Zoo says it's looking for volunteers to help guide and teach Belizean students, to help manage the animals, and in certain professional and skill areas including web design, art, plumbing, electrical work, photography, marketing, and aquarium development. In some cases, volunteer placements at the Belize Zoo involve a placement fee. ✉ Box 1787, Belize City ☎ 220/8003 ⊕ www.belizezoo.org.

Cornerstone Foundation. This nonprofit's programs include cultural, community service, AIDS prevention, and peace-related volunteer programs in Cayo District. Volunteers commit for a minimum of one week and up to three months. For longer programs, individuals pay US$385 to US$485 a month for bunk-style housing and food. Fees for one-week programs start at US$199. Volunteers at Cornerstone must have travel and basic medical insurance. ✉ 43 Church St., San Ignacio ☎ 824/2373 ⊕ www.cornerstonefoundationbelize.org.

Green Reef. Green Reef is a private, nonprofit conservation group based in San Pedro, devoted to protecting the marine and coastal resources. Green Reef operates five- to seven-day study abroad programs where students from middle school and high school to college do volunteer work and learn about the ecology of Baccalar Chico National Park and Marine Reserve on North Ambergris Caye. Fees are charged. ✉ 100 Coconut Dr., San Pedro ☎ 226/2833 ⊕ www.greenreefbelize.org.

Monkey Bay Wildlife Sanctuary. Monkey Bay is a private wildlife sanctuary and environmental education center on 1,070 acres near the Belize Zoo. It has some volunteer intern opportunities in conservation and community service, usually with a minimum one-month commitment. Monkey Bay also offers homestay programs, as well as 12- to 21-day education and adventure programs

for students (middle school to university). Volunteer programs for interns require payments of BZ$300 a week to cover room and board. ✉ Box 187, Belmopan ☎ 820/3032 ⊕ www.monkeybaybelize.org.

Plenty International. Plenty, founded in 1974, places several volunteers annually in Toledo District and elsewhere. Volunteers ideally should have medical, midwifery, marketing, farming, or other skills. The minimum commitment is usually three months, and a nominal (US$30) placement fee is charged. There are no stipends or other payments to volunteers, and travel expenses are not paid, but in some cases volunteers may receive assistance with food and housing. Currently Plenty is working to help Toledo youth develop organic home gardens and is accepting applications for volunteers to help implement the garden program. ✉ Box 394, Summertown, TN 38483 ☎ 913/964–4323 ⊕ www.plenty.org.

WWOOF Belize. WWOOFING in Belize allows you to trade work on an organic farm in return for room and board and in some cases a small stipend. Conditions and terms of work vary considerably from farm to farm, but keep in mind you'll usually be involved in hard physical labor for several hours a day under hot, humid, and buggy conditions. Currently there are more than 15 farms in the WWOOF Belize network. To participate in WWOOF Belize, you have to join WWOOF Latin America Network and pay a fee of US$5 for membership in WWOOF Belize. ⊕ www.wwoofbelize.com.

—Lan Sluder

Gorda, off Mile 86, Southern Hwy. ☎ *604/2124* ⊕ *www.suncreeklodge. com* ➴ *6 cabañas, 3 with shared bath* ⚬ *In-room: no a/c, kitchen, no TV. In-hotel: restaurant* ❏ *Breakfast.*

¢ ⌨ **T.E.A.** The Toledo Ecotourism Association arranges stays in one of nine participating Mayan and Ketchi villages, including Blue Creek, San Antonio, Laguna, Pueblo Viejo, and Medina Bank, and also one Garífuna village, Barranco. **Pros:** true cultural experience; rare opportunity to participate in Mayan village life while having some personal privacy. **Cons:** very basic lodgings and facilities. ✉ *Front St., Punta Gorda* ✉ *Box 157, Punta Gorda* ☎ *722/2531* ✍ *teabelize@yahoo.com* ⚬ *In-room: no a/c, no TV* ▭ *No credit cards* ❏ *All meals.*

$$ ⌨ **Tranquility Lodge.** Owners Sheila and Rusty Nale, who for many years ran a popular condotel on Ambergris Caye, have upgraded the rooms at this small lodge and added two thatched casitas. **Pros:** tranquil rural setting; newly upgraded rooms; good creek swimming. **Cons:** not near restaurants and bars. ✉ *San Felipe Rd., Jacintoville* ⊹ *About 9 mi (15 km) north of Punta Gorda, turn west off the Southern Hwy. onto San Felipe Rd. Go a few hundred feet and turn right at the first side road, a palm-lined road to the lodge* ☎ *677/9921, 800/819–9088 in U.S.* ⊕ *www.tranquility-lodge.com* ➴ *4 rooms, 2 casitas* ⚬ *In-room: no a/c, safe, no TV, Wi-Fi. In-hotel: restaurant, bar.*

$ ⌨ **Village Homestay Network.** The Village Homestay Network arranges for visitors to stay with one of about 15 or 20 Mayan families in one of two Toledo villages: Aguacate, a Ketchi village, and Na Luum Cah, a Mopan village. **Pros:** unique opportunity to get up close and personal with the indigenous community. **Cons:** basic lodging even by backpacker standards; little personal privacy. ✉ *53 Main Middle St., Punta Gorda* ☎ *722/2470 for Aguacate village, 664/9419 for Na Luum Cah village* ✍ *demdatsdoin@btl.net or quichpan_luum@yahoo.ca* ⚬ *In-room: no a/c, no TV* ▭ *No credit cards* ❏ *All meals.*

Side Trip to Guatemala

EL PETÉN WITH TIKAL AND OTHER MAYAN SITES

WORD OF MOUTH

"Climbing to the top of [Tikal's] Temple V was especially spellbinding, gazing through the mist at the great city. No guardrails at the top, so it is not for the faint of heart! We saw lots of coatimundis around the grounds, beautiful wild turkeys, spider and howler monkeys, as well as many exotic birds."

—Cattail

Updated by
Ian Sluder

The jungles of El Petén, Guatemala, were once the heartland of the Mayan civilization. The sprawling empire—including parts of present-day Mexico, Belize, Honduras, and El Salvador—was made up of a network of cities that held hundreds of thousands of people, but a millennium ago this fascinating civilization went into a mysterious decline and soon virtually disappeared. The temples that dominated the horizon were swallowed up by the jungle.

Today ancient ruins seem to just crop up from El Petén's landscape. In comparison with the rest of Guatemala, which has 15 million people in an area the size of Tennessee, El Petén is relatively sparsely populated, although this is changing. Fifty years ago El Petén had fewer than 20,000 residents. Due to massive immigration from other areas of Guatemala, El Petén now has more than half a million people (almost twice the population of the entire country of Belize). Still, nature reigns supreme, with vines and other plants quickly covering everything that stands still a little too long. Whatever your primary interest—archaeology, history, birding, biking—you'll find plenty to do and see in this remote region.

Four-wheel-drive vehicles are required to get to many of the archaeological sites (but not to Tikal), while others, such as those in the Mirador Basin, are reachable only by boat or on foot. The difficulty doesn't just enhance the adventure, it gives you time to take in the exotic scenery and rare tropical flora and fauna that are with you all the way.

If you drive instead of fly from Belize, you'll notice the difference in Guatemala almost the instant you cross the border. Spanish replaces English, and except in some hotels and other tourist businesses very little English is spoken. Prices for everything from beer to meals to lodging are considerably lower. Starting at the border, bribes and petty corruption are a way of life. While poverty is much in evidence in some areas of this part of Guatemala, there are pockets of prosperity, too. Most major roads in the Petén are now beautifully paved, and the towns of Flores and Santa Elena bustle with activity.

The Petén may be vast and remote, but the traveler's focus takes in a far more limited area. Ruins dot the entire region, but excavation has begun on only a few of them. In the center of the region on Lago Petén Itzá sits Flores, its administrative center, and its twin town of Santa Elena, the site of the regional airport. Northeast are the famed ruins of Tikal.

HISTORY

At its peak, the Mayan civilization developed one of the earliest forms of writing, the first mathematical system to use zero, complex astronomical calculations, advanced agricultural systems, and an inscrutable belief system. It was during this zenith that spectacular cities such as Tikal were built. By the time the Europeans arrived, the Mayan civilization had already mysteriously collapsed.

Until the 1960s the Petén region was a desolate place. This all changed when the Guatemalan government began offering small tracts of land in El Petén for US$25 to anyone willing to settle it. The landless moved in droves, and today the population is more than 500,000—a 25-fold increase in around 50 years.

Unemployment in El Petén is high, and tourism—mostly associated with Tikal and other Mayan sites—is the main industry. Many make ends meet through subsistence farming, logging, hunting for *xate* (palm leaves used in the floral industry) in the wild, and marijuana cultivation. Exploration for oil is underway in a few areas as well.

A new and disturbing industry has also come to the region: the running and smuggling of hard drugs, with the violence and brutality that often accompanies it. Drug cartels, including Los Zetas, under continuing pressure from the Mexican government, have moved some of their operations to El Petén. Beginning in late 2010 there was a wave of violence associated with these drug runners: In October 2010 a large group of armed men attacked a Guatemalan army outpost between Flores and Tikal, resulting in four deaths. Then, in May 2011 more than two-dozen farm workers in La Libertad southwest of Flores were murdered and decapitated, allegedly by members of the Zetas cartel. Also in 2011, several Guatemalan government officials were kidnapped or killed in the Petén.

ORIENTATION AND PLANNING

8

GETTING ORIENTED

The Petén is rugged country where major roads are few and far between and highways are all but nonexistent. But because there are only two airports—one in Guatemala City, the other in Flores—you're forced to do most of your travel by land. Many of the roads in El Petén are still unpaved, the exceptions being the road from Santa Elena–Flores to Tikal, the road from Río Dulce in the south to Santa Elena–Flores, most of the road from the Belize border to the crossroad junction to Tikal and Flores, and a few others.

Tikal. Arguably the most impressive of all Mayan sites, and rivaling even Machu Picchu in Peru and Angkor Wat in Cambodia in its ancient splendor, Tikal is a must-see, if only on a day trip from Belize.

Tikal Environs. Set at the end of causeway in Lake Petén, the town of Flores is a charming and walkable small town, with almost a Mediterranean air. The village of El Remate, closer to Tikal and on the lake, is another pleasant base for exploring the region.

Other Mayan Sites in El Petén. El Mirador, about 80 mi (133 km) north of Flores near the Mexican border, is a huge site, but at present getting there requires a multi-day, 45-mi (75-km) trek from the village of Carmelita. The complexes of Yaxhá, El Zotz, Nakúm, and Uaxactún are

TOP REASONS TO GO

TIKAL

Tikal is usually ranked as the most impressive of all Mayan sites. Although Caracol and other Mayan sites in Belize are magnificent, none truly rivals Tikal in visual impact. You'll never forget the jungle setting, rich with wildlife and birds.

OTHER MAYAN RUINS

Tikal is the best known, but hardly the only important Mayan site in El Petén. El Mirador was a giant city-state, likely larger than Tikal, and in the Mirador Basin are the remains of at least four other centers, including Nakbé, El Tintal, Xulnal, and Wakná. The Guatemalan government has grandiose plans to make Mirador a tourist attraction that would rival Tikal, if not outdo it. Other Mayan sites in El Petén include Yaxhá, Nakúm, Uaxactún, Aguateca, Dos Pilas, and El Zotz.

LOW PRICES

In comparison with Belize, the Petén is rife with travel bargains. Overall, price levels in Guatemala for hotels, meals, and tours are a third to half less than in Belize.

FLORES AND PETÉN ITZÁ

The island town of Flores, separated from the grungier Santa Elena by a causeway across part of Lake Petén Itzá, has a charming European feel, with red-roof houses and cobblestone streets.

SHOPPING FOR HANDICRAFTS

The indigenous population creates countless kinds of handicrafts. There's an open-air market in Santa Elena, and Flores has a number of little shops. The village of El Remate is known for its unique wood carvings, and the border town of Melchor also has a few shops catering to tourists.

scattered around Tikal. Poor roads and possible bandit incidents limit the number of visitors. Farther removed, southwest of Flores, off the road to Cobá in Las Verapaces, are the town of Sayaxché and its nearby Ceibal ruins, along with several other Maya sites including Aguateca.

PLANNING

WHEN TO GO

It's warm here year-round. The rainy season is May to November. Occasional showers are a possibility the rest of the year, but shouldn't interfere with your plans. March and April are the hottest months, with December and January a few degrees cooler than the rest of the year. July and August see an influx of visitors during prime North American and European vacation time. Also prime visitor times around Tikal are Easter week and Christmas/New Year.

GETTING HERE AND AROUND

AIR TRAVEL

Aeropuerto Internacional Santa Elena (FRS), or the Mundo Maya International Airport, often referred to as the Flores airport, is less than ½ mi (1 km) outside town. Taxis and shuttles meet every plane and charge about 20 quetzales per person to take you into Flores. The airport has service to and from Belize City, Guatemala City, and, at times, Cancún. United-Continental no longer has nonstop service from the U.S. to Flores.

Tropic Air offers twice-daily flights between the international airport in Belize City and Flores. Fares are US$224 or BZ$448 round trip, not including international air exit taxes from Belize (US$39.25 or BZ$78.50) and US$33 from Guatemala. Tropic Air's Flores flights also have continuing service between Flores and Guatemala City.

TACA and TAG operate flights between Guatemala City and Santa Elena–Flores that take less than an hour and cost from around US$140 each way or US$240 round trip on TACA and usually slightly less on TAG. Check with TAG regarding its luggage weight allowance, as the allowance on TAG's puddle jumpers has been only 20 pounds.

Contacts TACA (☎ 501/7926–1238, 2470–8222 in Guatemala City, or 800/493-8426 in U.S. ⊕ www.taca.com). **TAG** (☎ 502/2360–3038 ⊕ www.tag.com.gt). **Tropic Air** (☎ 501/226–2012 in Belize, 800/422–3435 in U.S. and Canada ⊕ www.tropicair.com).

BUS TRAVEL

Fuente del Norte and San Juan Travel run daily buses from the Marine Terminal in Belize City to Santa Elena–Flores. Fuente del Norte has better buses. Fuente del Norte buses depart from the Marine Terminal at 10 am and return from Santa Elena at 5 am. San Juan minibuses leave the Marine Terminal at 2:30 pm and return at 5 am. (Schedules change frequently so check locally.) Cost is US$27 one-way. The 146-mi (235-km) trip takes around five hours, including border crossing. Agents with desks in the Marine Terminal, including Mundo Maya, can book the buses for you.

When leaving Belize by land, there's a US$18.75 exit fee, and a Q20 entrance fee to Guatemala. Returning to Belize by land there is no exit fee from Guatemala or entrance fee for Belize.

The 42-mi (70-km) paved route between Santa Elena–Flores and Tikal is served by scheduled minibus shuttles, operated by San Juan Travel and other companies. They cost around Q50–Q60 one way. The trip takes a little over an hour.

Contacts Fuente del Norte (✉ Terminal de Buses, Santa Elena ☎ 502/7926–2999 ⊕ www.grupofuentedelnorte.com). **Mundo Maya Deli** (✉ Marine Terminal, Belize City ☎ 501/223–1235). **San Juan Travel** (✉ Calle 2, Santa Elena ☎ 501/7926–0042 or 5847–4738).

CAR TRAVEL

Main roads in El Petén, such as between Flores/Santa Elena and Tikal, are paved and in very good shape. The road from the Belize border toward Tikal and Flores has some short unpaved sections in the first few miles but is otherwise paved and the entire road is usually in good condition. Secondary roads, however, often are in poor repair and not well marked. Some roads are impassable during the rainy season, so check with the tourist office before heading out on seldom traveled roads, such as those to the more remote ruins surrounding Tikal. A four-wheel-drive vehicle, *doble-tracción,* is highly recommended.

From the Belize border it's about 62 mi (100 km) by road to Tikal, and from the Belize border to Flores it's slightly longer (70 mi or 112 km). This road, except for some dusty streets in the scruffy Guatemalan border town of Melchor de Mencos, is in good condition and nearly all paved. At El Cruce, also known as Ixlú, the road splits, turning north to Tikal and southwest to Santa Elena and Flores. Both roads are nicely paved. If, instead of going on to Tikal, you turn northwest near the village of El Remate, the road (mostly unpaved) takes you around the north side of Lake Petén Itzá, passing the villages of San José and San Andrés, and eventually ends up at the town of San Benito, adjoining Santa Elena. Driving, by car or van, the trip to Tikal from the Belize border is roughly 1½ hours, depending on road and weather conditions.

If you're not booked on a tour, you can get around El Petén by renting a four-wheel-drive vehicle. Several major rental agencies, including Hertz, have offices at Aeropuerto Internacional Santa Elena. Tabarini is a local company that usually has a good selection at competitive prices. Rates start at around US$35 a day for a compact car, or US$60–$70 a day for a four-wheel drive SUV. You need a valid driver's license from your own country to drive in Guatemala. Crystal Auto Rental in Belize City permits its vehicles to be taken into Guatemala (the El Petén/Tikal area only). Car rentals in Belize usually are more expensive than in Guatemala.

Local Agencies **Crystal** (⊠ *Mile 5, Northern Hwy., Belize City* ☎ *501/223–1910*). **Hertz** (⊠ *Aeropuerto Internacional Santa Elena* ☎ *501/7950–0204*). **Tabarini** (⊠ *Aeropuerto Internacional Santa Elena* ☎ *501/7926–0253 or 7926–0277*).

TAXI TRAVEL

After you cross the border from Belize into Melchor de Mencos, you can hire a taxi to take you and your party direct to Tikal or, if you prefer, to Flores. You'll usually pay Q350–Q550 (US$45–US$70) for the taxi, not per person, depending on your bargaining ability. A taxi to El Remate from the border will be less, as little as Q200 (US$25). Taxis from the Santa Elena–Flores airport to Tikal are around Q350–400 (US$45–$50). A taxi from the Santa Elena airport into Flores is Q20 (about US$2.50) per person.

EMERGENCIES

El Petén's only hospital is in San Benito, a suburb of Santa Elena. Medical facilities in El Petén are not as modern as in the rest of the country. If you're really sick, consider getting on the next plane to Guatemala City. Centro Médico Maya in Santa Elena has physicians on staff, though little or no English is spoken. Asistur, a tourist assistance service overseen by INGUAT, can help you locate English-speaking physicians and arrange an ambulance—dial 1500 anywhere in Guatemala, 24 hours a day.

Contact Emergency Services **Asistur** (☎ *502/2421–2810 or 1500 or 502/5414–3594*). **Police** (☎ *502/7926–1365 or 110 or 120*). **Centro Médico Maya** (⊠ *Av. 4, Santa Elena* ☎ *502/7926–0180*). **Hospital Nacional** (⊠ *San Benito* ☎ *502/7926–1333*).

BORDER FORMALITIES

The Belize border is about 9 mi (15 km) from San Ignacio, just west of the town of Benque Viejo del Carmen. Belize has built a new customs-and-immigration building at the border. Border crossings here are usually quick and easy.

Upon arrival at the border, you'll be approached on the Belize side by money changers asking if you want to exchange U.S. or Belize dollars for Guatemalan quetzales. Another group will approach you on the Guatemala side. The rate given by money changers may be a little less than you'll get at an ATM or bank, but you may want to exchange enough at least for your first day in Guatemala. You'll usually get better rates on the Guatemala side.

Belize formalities include paying your US$18.75 (BZ$37.50) exit fee. Guatemala border officials will ask for a Q20 (US$2.50) entrance fee at this border. Most visitors to Guatemala, including citizens of the United States, Canada, and European Union, do not need visas, and passports are normally stamped with a permit to enter for 90 days.

Melchor de Mencos is a scruffy border town with unpaved streets. Shops on the main drag sell Guatemalan crafts. Some of the basic hotels in town are actually brothels.

There's no safe long-term parking at the Belize border, so if you are driving a rental car you should arrange to park it elsewhere. Only a handful of Belize rental companies allow their vehicles to be taken into Guatemala (try Crystal in Belize City). Note, however, that Belize insurance isn't valid in Guatemala, and Guatemalan insurance currently isn't sold at the border.

8

Pharmacy Farmacia Nueva (✉ Av. Santa Ana, Flores ☎ 502/7926–1387).

MONEY MATTERS

The exchange rate between the U.S. dollar and the Guatemalan quetzal floats—that is, it changes depending on market conditions. As of this writing, the Guatemalan quetzal is roughly Q7.8 to US$1, but at most hotels and shops in El Petén you'll get a little less.

Although U.S. dollars are seldom refused in Guatemala, using quetzales will make transactions easier and less confusing. You can exchange U.S. dollars at any bank and in high-end hotels. If you need to exchange money, do so before heading off on your jungle adventure. Note that since 2009 Guatemala has a new Q200 note; previously, the largest denomination was Q100.

There are several banks in Santa Elena, but few anywhere else in the region, and none at Tikal park. Those on Calle 4, Santa Elena's main street, have ATMs that work with foreign ATM cards with MasterCard or Visa logos on the PLUS or CIRRUS systems. In Guatemala Visa debit cards are more widely used in ATMs than are MasterCard debit cards. Several gas stations between Santa Elena and Ixlú also have bank ATMs. In Flores there is an ATM next to Hotel Petén on Calle 30 de Junio. Banrural has an office in Flores but no ATM there. There is a bank office, Banquetzal, at the Flores airport that will exchange money.

Banks **Banrural** (✉ *Calle 4 at Av. 3, Santa Elena* ☎ *502/7926–1002*). **Banco Industrial** (✉ *Calle 4, Santa Elena* ☎ *502/7926–0281*). **Banquetzal** (✉ *Aeropuerto Internacional Santa Elena, Santa Elena* ☎ *502/7926–0711*).

HEALTH

If you've been traveling in Belize, where you can generally drink the water and usually eat even street food with no problem, Guatemala's health and hygiene standards come as an unpleasant surprise. Tap water is rarely potable, and even better restaurants may not pass a health inspection. To prevent traveler's diarrhea, drink only bottled water and avoid raw vegetables—on their own or in salads—unless you know they've been thoroughly washed and disinfected. Be wary of strawberries and other unpeeled fruits. Heat stroke is another risk, but one that can easily be avoided. The best way to avoid it is to do as the locals do (wake early and retire at midday for a siesta) and drink lots of water.

SAFETY

Most crimes directed at tourists in El Petén have been pickpocketings, muggings, and thefts from cars. However, there have been a number of incidents over the years involving armed groups stopping buses, vans, and private cars, both at Tikal park and on the road from Tikal to the Belize border.

In mid-2011 murderous attacks on Guatemalan farm workers and Guatemalan government officials in the Petén (including the decapitation of 25 campensinos on a farm southwest of Flores), allegedly by members of Mexico's Los Zetas drug cartel, prompted the U.S. Embassy in Belize to "strongly recommend against" travel to Flores and Tikal. For several months some tour operators in San Ignacio and elsewhere in Cayo District suspended doing tours to Tikal, but as of this writing most have resumed tours. ⚠ **Tourists have not been specifically targeted, but due to the growing threat of drug cartel–related violence in El Petén you should check the current U.S. State Department travel advisories and ask locally before traveling to Tikal, Flores, and environs.**

In town, keep your camera in a secure bag, don't wear flashy jewelry or watches, and don't handle money in public. Hire taxis only from official stands at the airport, outside hotels, and at major intersections. If you can avoid it, don't drive after sunset. One common ploy used by highway robbers is to construct a roadblock, such as logs strewn across the road, and then hide nearby. When unsuspecting motorists get out of their cars to remove the obstruction, they are waylaid. ⚠ **If you come upon a deserted roadblock, don't stop; turn around.**

The increase in adoption of Guatemalan children has caused some people—particularly rural villagers—to fear that children will be abducted by foreigners. Limit your interaction with children you do not know, and be discreet when taking photographs.

ABOUT THE RESTAURANTS

In El Petén you have a couple of choices for dining: *comedores*, which are small eateries along the lines of a U.S. café or diner, with simple and inexpensive local food; and restaurants that, in general, are a little nicer and serve a wider selection of food, often with an international or American flavor. Restaurants are mostly in Flores and other towns. Elsewhere you'll probably eat in hotel or lodge dining rooms.

Some restaurants serve wild game, or *comida silvestre*. Although often delicious, the game has usually been taken illegally. You might see *venado* (venison), *coche del monte* (mountain cow or peccary), and *tepezcuintle* (paca, a large rodent) on the menu.

ABOUT THE HOTELS

El Petén now has a wide range of lodging options, from suites at luxurious lakeside resorts to stark rooms in budget hotels. The island town of Flores has many lodging choices, though most are mediocre at best, and the number of hotels there keeps prices competitive. The hotels in the much larger Santa Elena, the gateway to Flores, are generally larger and more upscale than the places in Flores, but with less atmosphere. El Remate, about 22 mi (35 km) from Flores on the road to Tikal, is a pleasant alternative, with several excellent small, mostly inexpensive hotels. At Tikal itself are three lodges that have the great advantage of being right at the park. On the north side of Lago de Petén Itzá are several hotels, including a couple of the most upscale in the region: Francis Ford Coppola's La Lancha and the largest resort hotel in the area, Hotel Camino Real Tikal.

WHAT IT COSTS IN GUATEMALAN QUETZALES					
	¢	$	$$	$$$	$$$$
RESTAURANTS	under Q40	Q40–Q70	Q70–Q100	Q100–Q130	over Q130
HOTELS	under Q160	Q160–Q360	Q360–Q560	Q560–Q760	over Q760

Restaurant prices are per person for a main course at dinner. Hotel prices are for two people in a standard double room, including tax (up to 22%, almost always included in the quoted room price) and service.

Many hotels in El Petén have high and low seasons. They charge higher rates during the dry season, December through April, especially at the peak times of Christmas and Easter, and sometimes also during the July to August vacation season. Advance reservations are a good idea during these periods, especially at Tikal park lodges.

TOURS

Flores-based Martsam Travel, run by Lileana and Benedicto Grijalva, offers many different types of tours in the area. Tikal Connection specializes in trips to hard-to-get-to Mayan sites such as El Mirador—its prices may be a little higher than some. The long-established La Casa de Don David in El Remate arranges well-run trips to Tikal, Yaxhá, and El Zotz, along with horse-riding and birding tours. Tip tour guides about 10% of the tour price.

Contacts La Casa de Don David (✉ El Remate ☎ 502/7928–8469 ⊕ www. lacasadedondavid.com.com). **Martsam Tour & Travel** (✉ Calle Centroamérica and Av. 30 de Junio, Flores ☎ 502/7867–5093 ⊕ www.martsam.com). **Tikal Connection** (✉ Aeropuerto Internacional Santa Elena, Santa Elena ☎ 502/5871–1169 ⊕ www.tikalcnx.com).

FROM BELIZE

Many tour operators in the San Ignacio, Belize, area operate day and overnight or multinight Tikal tours. You'll pay more in Belize than in Guatemala, but you reduce the hassle factor—you'll probably be picked up at your Cayo hotel, whisked across the border, provided with a guide to Tikal, and fed lunch (hotel accommodations are arranged if you're staying overnight). You'll typically pay US$125 to US$150 (BZ$250 to BZ$300) for a day tour to Tikal from San Ignacio, and US$250 to US$350 (BZ$500 to BZ$700) for an overnight trip. When comparing tour costs, check to see if border fees and Tikal admission are included. ⇨ *See the Cayo and Adventure Vacations chapters for more information.*

VISITOR INFORMATION

Arcas, which returns illegally captured animals to the wild, is a great resource on the flora and fauna of El Petén. The staff at INGUAT, Guatemala's tourism promotion agency, is courteous, professional, and knowledgeable. INGUAT has two offices in El Petén, one in Flores just on the Flores side of the causeway to the island and one at Aeropuerto Internacional Santa Elena. CINCAP (Centro de Información sobre de Naturaleza, Cultura y Artesanías), on the central plaza in Flores, has tourism information and historical exhibits on the Petén. The owner of Café Arqueológico Yaxhá in Flores also is very knowledgeable about the area.

Contacts Arcas (✉ *Barrio La Ermita, 6 mi [10 km] east of Santa Elena in San Benito* ☎ *502/5208–0968* ⊕ *www.arcasguatemala.com*). **CINCAP** (✉ *Parque Central, Flores* ☎ *502/7926–0718*). **INGUAT** (✉ *Playa Sur, Flores* ☎ *502/5116–3182* ✉ *Aeropuerto Internacional Santa Elena* ☎ *502/7926–0533 at airport*).

TIKAL

22 mi (35 km) north of El Remate, 42 mi (68 km) northeast of Flores.

GETTING HERE AND AROUND

If you're in Belize City, take the Fuente del Norte or San Juan Travel bus from the Marine Terminal to Flores, or from the San Ignacio area cross the border (take a taxi to the border and walk across) and then go by taxi to Tikal. You can also take an escorted tour from San Ignacio, or fly Tropic Air from the international airport in Belize City.

TIMING

You can visit Tikal on a day trip from the San Ignacio area and get a good sense of its grandeur. Depending on your schedule, you may choose to spend the night either at Tikal park so you can see the ruins in the morning (a must for birders), or in Flores, El Remate, or elsewhere along the shores of Lake Petén Itzá. You can easily spend two days, or longer, exploring the ruins. You may want to hire a guide for your first day, then wander about on your own on the second. If you have additional time, consider an extension in El Petén. The town of Flores, with its lakeside bistros and cobblestone streets, merits at least a half-day stroll.

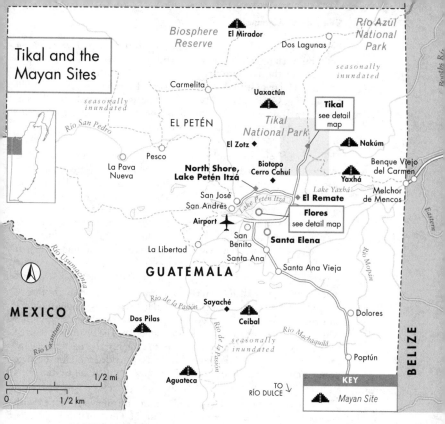

Tikal and the Mayan Sites

Biosphere Reserve

El Mirador

Dos Lagunas

Río Azúl National Park

seasonally inundated

Carmelita

Uaxactún

Tikal see detail map

seasonally inundated

EL PETÉN

Río San Pedro

Pesco

La Pava Nueva

Tikal National Park

El Zotz ◆

Nakúm

North Shore, Lake Petén Itzá

Biotopo Cerro Cahuí ◆

Benque Viejo del Carmen

Yaxhá

San José

San Andrés

Lake Petén Itzá

Lake Yaxhá

◆ **El Remate**

Melchor de Mencos

Airport

San Benito

Flores see detail map

Santa Elena

La Libertad

Santa Ana

Santa Ana Vieja

Río Mopán

GUATEMALA

Río Usumacinta

MEXICO

Río Lacantún

Río de la Pasión

Sayaché ◆

Ceibal

Dos Pilas

Río de la Pasión

Río Machaquilá

Dolores

seasonally inundated

Poptún

BELIZE

0 ⎯⎯⎯ 1/2 mi
0 ⎯⎯⎯ 1/2 km

Aguateca

TO RÍO DULCE ↓

KEY

▲ *Mayan Site*

SAFETY AND PRECAUTIONS

Taxis and tourist buses are sometimes magnets to bandits in El Petén. Taxi drivers taking passengers from the Belize border to Flores or Tikal remove taxi insignia from their vehicles before leaving the border. The bandits take passengers' valuables; occasionally passengers have been assaulted. Keep in mind, however, that some 300,000 international visitors come to Tikal every year, and the vast majority of them have no problems with crime.

Fodor's Choice ★

Tikal is one of the most popular tourist attractions in Central America—and with good reason. Smack in the middle of the 222-square-mi (575-square-km) Parque Nacional Tikal, the towering temples are ringed on all sides by miles of verdant forest. The area around the ruins is great for checking out creatures, such as howler and spider monkeys that spend their lives high above the forest floor in the dense canopy of trees. Colorful birds like yellow toucans and scarlet macaws are common sights. The latest jaguar census found that there are at least seven of these magnificent cats resident in the park boundaries.

Although the region was home to Mayan communities as early as 600 BC, Tikal itself wasn't established until sometime around 200 BC. One of the first structures to be built here was a version of the North Acropolis. Others were added at a dizzying pace for the next three centuries.

By AD 100 impressive structures like the Great Plaza had already been built. But even though it was a powerful city in its own right, Tikal was still ruled by the northern city of El Mirador. It wasn't until the arrival of a powerful dynasty around AD 300 that Tikal arrogated itself to full power. King Great Jaguar Paw sired a lineage that would build Tikal into a city rivaling any of its time. It's estimated that by AD 500 the city covered more than 18 square mi (47 square km) and had a population of close to 100,000.

The great temples that still tower above the jungle were at that time covered with stucco and painted with bright reds and greens, and the priests used them for elaborate ceremonies meant to please the gods and assure prosperity for the city. What makes these structures even more impressive is that the Maya had no metal tools to aid in construction, had no beasts of burden to carry heavy loads, and never used wheels for anything except children's toys. As a hierarchical culture, they had a slave class, and the land was rich in obsidian, a volcanic glass that could be fashioned into razor-sharp tools.

By the 6th century Tikal governed a large part of the Mayan world, thanks to a leader called Caan Chac (Stormy Sky), who took the throne around AD 426. Under Caan Chac Tikal became an aggressive military and commercial center that dominated the surrounding communities with a power never before seen in Mesoamerica. The swamps protected the city from attack and allowed troops to spot any approaching enemy. Intensive agriculture in the *bajos* (lowlands) provided food for the huge population. A valuable obsidian trade sprang up, aided by the city's strategic position near two rivers.

Tikal thrived for more than a millennium, forming strong ties with two powerful centers: Kaminal Juyu, in the Guatemalan highlands, and Teotihuacán, in Mexico City. The city entered a golden age when Ah-Cacao (Lord Chocolate) ascended the throne in AD 682. It was Ah-Cacao and his successors who commissioned the construction of the majority of the city's most important temples. Continuing the tradition of great structures, Ah-Cacao's son commissioned Temple I, which he dedicated to his father, who is buried beneath it. He also ordered the construction of Temple IV, the tallest temple at Tikal. By the time of his death in 768, Tikal was at the peak of its power. It would remain so until its mysterious abandonment around AD 900.

For almost 1,000 years Tikal remained engulfed by the jungle. The conquistadors who came here searching for gold and silver must have passed right by the overgrown ruins, mistaking them for rocky hills. The native Peténeros certainly knew of the ancient city's existence, but no one else ventured near until 1848, when the Guatemalan government dispatched archaeologists to the region. Tikal started to receive international attention in 1877, when Dr. Gustav Bernoulli commissioned locals to remove the carved wooden lintels from across the doorways of Temples I and IV. These items were sent to a museum in Basel, Switzerland.

In 1881 and 1882 English archaeologist Alfred Percival Maudslay made the first map showing the architectural features of this vast city. As he

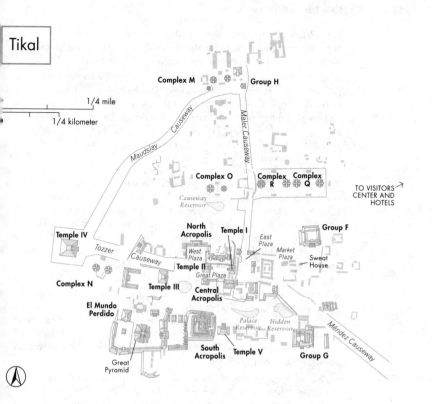

1/4 mile

1/4 kilometer

Complex M   Group H

Maudslay Causeway

Maler Causeway

Complex O   Complex R   Complex Q

Causeway Reservoir

TO VISITORS
CENTER AND
HOTELS

Temple IV

Tozzer

North Acropolis   Temple I   East Plaza   Group F

West Plaza   Market Plaza   Sweat House

Causeway

Temple II   Great Plaza

Complex N   Temple III   Central Acropolis

El Mundo Perdido   Palace Reservoir   Hidden Reservoir

Méndez Causeway

Great Pyramid   South Acropolis   Temple V   Group G

began to unearth the major temples, he recorded his work in dramatic photographs—you can see copies in the museum at Tikal. His work was continued by Teobert Maler, who came in 1895 and 1904. Both Maler and Maudslay have causeways named in their honor. In 1951 the Guatemalan air force cleared an airstrip near the ruins to improve access for large-scale archaeological work. Today, after more than 150 years of digging, researchers say that Tikal includes some 3,000 buildings. Countless more are still covered by the jungle. ⌧ *Parque Nacional Tikal* ☎ *No phone* ⊕ *www.tikalpark.com* 🎫 *Q150* ⊙ *Daily 6–6.*

EXPLORING

WITH A GUIDE   Guides make the visit more interesting, though don't believe everything they tell you, as some guides have their own pet theories on the decline of the Maya or other subjects that they love to expound to tourists. Near the parking lot at Tikal is an information kiosk where you can hire guides. Rates are somewhat negotiable, but expect to pay about Q400 (a little over US$50) for a tour for up to four or five people. In a large group you may pay as little as Q60 (US$8) per person. Groups are not supposed to exceed 20 people. If you're staying more than one day, consider hiring a guide for the first day, and then wandering on your own after that. You can buy a map of the park near the visitor's center for Q20. Note that many but not all guides speak English. Roxy Ortiz is perhaps the most recommended guide at the park. An archaeologist, she is highly knowledgeable. She works out of the nearby Tikal Inn.

ON YOUR OWN   Wear comfortable shoes and bring water—you'll be walking about 6 mi (10 km) if you intend to see the whole site. As you enter Tikal, keep to the middle trail. You'll soon arrive at the ancient city's center, filled with awe-inspiring temples and intricate acropolises. The pyramid that you approach from behind is **Temple I,** known as the Temple of the Great Jaguar because of the feline represented on one of its carved lintels. It's in what is referred to as the **Great Plaza, or Gran Plaza,** one of the most beautiful and dramatic in Tikal. The Great Plaza was built around AD 700 by Ah-Cacao, one of the wealthiest rulers of his time. His tomb, comparable in magnitude to that of Pa Cal at the ruins of Palenque in southern Mexico, was discovered beneath the Temple of the Great Jaguar in the 1960s. The theory is that his queen is buried beneath **Temple II,** called the Temple of the Masks for the decorations on its facade. It's a twin of the Temple of the Great Jaguar. In fact, construction of matching pyramids distinguishes Tikal from other Mayan sites.

The **North Acropolis,** to the west of Ah-Cacao's temple, is a mind-boggling conglomeration of temples built over layers and layers of previous construction. Excavations have revealed that the base of this structure is more than 2,000 years old. Be sure to see the stone mask of the rain god at Temple 33. The **Central Acropolis,** south of the Great Plaza, is an immense series of structures assumed to have served as administrative centers.

If you climb to the top of one of the pyramids, you'll see the gray roof combs of others rising above the rain forest's canopy but still trapped within it. **Temple V,** to the south, underwent a US$3 million restoration project and is now open to the public. **Temple IV,** to the west, is the tallest known structure built by the Maya. Although the climb to the top is difficult, the view is unforgettable.

To the southwest of the plaza lies the **South Acropolis,** which hasn't been reconstructed, and a 105-foot-high pyramid, similar in construction to those at Teotihuacán. A few jungle trails offer a chance to see spider monkeys and other wildlife. Outside the park, a somewhat overgrown trail halfway down the old airplane runway on the left leads to the remnants of old rubber-tappers' camps and is a good spot for bird-watching.

At park headquarters are two small archaeological museums that display Mayan artifacts. They are a good resource for information on the enigmatic rise and fall of the Maya people, though little information is in English.

Museo Lítico or Stelae Museum has stelae found at Tikal and interesting photos from early archaeological excavations. ⊠ *Near visitor center* ⌨ *Q10* ☼ *Daily 8–5.*

Museo Tikal, also known as the Tikal Sylvannus G. Morley Museum, has a replica of Ha Sawa Chaan K'awil's burial chamber and some ceramics and bones from the actual tomb (the jade, however, is replica). ⊠ *Near visitor center* ⌨ *Free with ticket from Museo Lítico* ☼ *Daily 8–5.*

EXPLORING TIPS

Visitors generally are not allowed inside the ruins outside of opening hours (6 am to 6 pm). The exception is that visitors staying at one of the three park lodges (or camping at the park) may visit the park at sunrise and sunset, but only with a guide. The cost is Q275 (or around US$35) including Q100 special admission fee and a three-hour tour of the major temples. This admission fee is only for the duration of the tour and doesn't allow you to stay in the park after the tour, so if you want to see more you have to also purchase a regular admission for Q150. The rules about these sunrise and sunset tours change from time to time—ask park rangers or official guides about the current policy. If you are able to see sunrise in the park, perhaps the best place to see it is at the top of Temple IV.

Even if you don't take one of the extra-cost sunrise or sunset tours, if you stay at one of the three lodges on the grounds you get a jump-start

on the day-tour visitors and have the advantage of being here late in the afternoon, after most everyone else has left.

We do hear tales of visitors sneaking in at night or slipping guards bribes to pass, but we advise against that. The trails are not lit, and climbing the pyramids is risky in the dark. There's also a slight chance of robbery.

Formerly, if you purchased your entrance ticket after 3:30 pm you could use the same ticket for your next day's entry. However, in 2011 park officials stopped permitting that, so you have to buy another admission the following day. Of course, this could change, so if you're arriving late, ask.

If you have only one day or less at the park, try to see the highlights: Temples IV and V, both of which can be climbed, the Great Plaza, Mundo Perdido, and the Plaza of the Seven Temples.

8

WHERE TO STAY

There are three hotels on the park grounds: Tikal Inn, Jungle Lodge, and Jaguar Inn. At all of these you pay for the park location rather than amenities and great service. Electric power is from generators, which usually run from around 5 or 6 am to 10 or 11 pm, and power may be off at times during the day, although batteries may provide limited lighting throughout the night. Bring a flashlight! None of the hotels at the park has air-conditioning. Since the hotels here have a captive audience, service is not always as friendly or helpful as it could be, and at busy times reservations are sometimes "lost," even if you have confirming email. Camping is also available, at the park campsite (US$7 for a tent, US$3.50 for a hammock) or at the Jaguar Inn. Several *comedores* are at the entrance to the park, Imperio Maya and Comedore Tikal currently being the best, and you can also get snacks and drinks in the parking lot (but not in the park itself) and at the hotels. All the hotels have room-only rates, but if you are booking through a travel agent you may be required to take a package that includes meals and a Tikal tour. The restaurant at Jaguar Inn currently is the best of the lodge eateries.

For expanded hotel reviews, visit Fodors.com.

$$ 🏨 **Jaguar Inn.** Although this small hotel won't win any travel awards and has the feel of a backpacker's place, it's considerably less expensive than the other two hotels in the park (around US$65 double), attracts well-traveled guests, and has a good restaurant. **Pros:** cheapest lodging at the park; camping available; good restaurant. **Cons:** basic rooms somewhat jammed together; no pool. ⊠ *Parque Nacional Tikal* ☎ *502/7783–3647 front desk, 7926–0002* reservations ⊕ *www.jaguartikal.com* ⇦ *13 rooms, camping area* ⚂ *In-room: no a/c, no TV. In-hotel: restaurant, Wi-Fi hotspot.*

$$$$ 🏨 **Jungle Lodge.** Built more than 50 years ago to house archaeologists working at Tikal, this hotel, the largest and arguably the best in the park, has cute duplexes with porches but not much privacy. **Pros:** arguably the best of the three lodges in the park; swimming pool; clean and adequate accommodations. **Cons:** you are paying for location; food is mediocre. ⊠ *Parque Nacional Tikal* ☎ *502/2477–0570* ⊕ *www.junglelodgetikal.com* ⇦ *12 rooms with shared baths, 36 bungalows, 2 suites* ⚂ *In-room: no a/c, no TV. In-hotel: restaurant, bar, pool, business center* ⦿ *Breakfast.*

$$$–$$$$ 🏨 **Tikal Inn.** This cluster of comfortable bungalows, set farthest from the park entrance, wraps around a well-manicured garden and a pool. **Pros:** good location in the park; swimming pool. **Cons:** poor service at times; rooms are hot; limited hot water and electricity. ⊠ *Parque Nacional Tikal* ☎ *502/7926–1917* ⦿ *7926–0065* ⊕ *www.tikalinn.com* ⇦ *18 rooms, 18 bungalows* ⚂ *In-room: no a/c, no TV. In-hotel: restaurant, bar, pool, business center* ⦿ *Breakfast (with bungalow rooms).*

> **WATCH FOR THE ANIMALS!**
>
> Obey Tikal's 45 kph (27 mph) speed limit; it's designed to give you time to stop for animals that cross the road within the confines of the park. Be particularly careful of the raccoon-like coatimundi that locals call a *pizote,* which scurries with abandon across the road. At the park entrance a guard gives you a time-stamped ticket to be collected by another guard when you arrive at the visitor center. If you cover the 9-mi (15-km) distance in less than 20 minutes, you'll be deemed to have been speeding and possibly fined.

TIKAL ENVIRONS

Flores, a charming small town in Lake Petén Itzá connected to the mainland by a causeway, is the main point of interest beyond Tikal. Stay in a small inn or hotel, eat at lakeside bistros, and explore the cobblestone streets on foot. Santa Elena, at the entrance to Flores, is a bustling commercial center but is far less frequented by tourists. El Remate, a village on the shore of the lake, has a number of small, mostly budget, hotels and is a handy, low-key jumping-off point for Tikal if you don't stay in the park.

FLORES

★ *133 mi (206 km) north of Río Dulce, 38 mi (61 km) northeast of Sayaxché.*

The red-roof town of Flores, on an island surrounded by the waters of Lago Petén Itzá, is on the site of the ancient city of Tatyasal. This was the region's last unconquered outpost of Mayan civilization, until finally falling to the Spanish in 1697. The conquerors destroyed the city's huge pyramids.

Today the capital of the department of Petén is a pleasant place to explore, with its narrow streets lined with thick-walled buildings painted pink, blue, and purple. Flowering plants droop over balconies, and there's a central square presided over by a colonial church.

Sadly, many of the hotels in Flores are also pedestrian, rarely rising above mediocrity. Flores is crying out for a truly special small inn, one that's as charming as the town itself.

Connected to the mainland by a bridge and causeway—don't be put off by the Burger King at the entrance to the causeway, or the new Mundo Maya International Mall shopping center there—Flores serves as a base for travelers to El Petén. It's also the center of many nongovernmental organizations working for the preservation of the Mayan Biosphere, an endangered area covering nearly all of northern Petén. Flores is also one of the last remaining vestiges of the Itzá, the people who built Mexico's monumental Chichén Itzá.

In the 1800s, before it was a departure point for travelers headed for the ruins, Flores was called Devil's Island because of the prison on top of the hill (a large white church stands there now). Since 1994 the building has been home to the **Centro de Información sobre la Naturaleza, Cultura, y Artesanía de Petén** (⊠ *North side of Parque Central* ☎ *502/7926–0718* ⊗ *Weekdays 8–5*). This center has a small museum with photographs of the region and information about local resources, such as allspice, chicle (a chewing-gum base made from tree sap), and *xate* (a shade palm used in floral decorations). A gift shop sells wood carvings, woven baskets, cornhusk dolls, and even locally made peanut butter.

GETTING HERE AND AROUND

From the airport in Santa Elena, Flores is a short Q20 per-person taxi ride. Minibuses (Q50 per person) will bring you from Tikal park. A taxi from the Belize border takes about 1½ hours and costs US$45 to US$70 for up to four persons. Minibuses from Melchor de Mencos near the Belize border are only Q30, but are packed and drop you in Santa Elena. Flores itself is best seen on foot or in tuk-tuks (small motorcycle rickshaw taxis). The street resurfacing project in 2009–2010 resulted in many nicely cobblestoned streets in town, especially on Flores's malecón along the water.

TIMING

You can easily experience the highlights of Flores in a day or less, but it's a pleasant place to relax for longer. If visiting Tikal park from Flores, you'll require an additional one to two days.

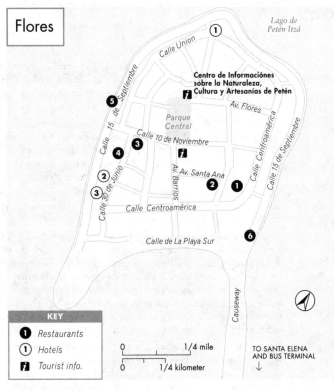

Flores

*Lago de
Petén Itzá*

Calle Union

Calle 15 de Septiembre

Centro de Informaciónes
sobre la Naturaleza,
Cultura y Artesanías de Petén

Av. Flores

Parque
Central

Calle 10 de Noviembre

Av. Santa Ana

Calle Barrios

Av. Centroamérica

Calle 15 de Septiembre

Calle 30 de Junio

Calle Centroamérica

Calle de La Playa Sur

Causeway

KEY

❶ *Restaurants*

① *Hotels*

ℹ *Tourist info.*

0   1/4 mile

0   1/4 kilometer

TO SANTA ELENA
AND BUS TERMINAL
↓

SAFETY AND PRECAUTIONS

Flores generally is a safe small town, but avoid flashing wads of money
or jewelry, and don't wander alone on isolated streets after dark.

WHERE TO EAT

¢–$

CENTRAL
AMERICAN

★

✕ **Café Arqueológico Yaxhá**. This restaurant combines a cultural and educational experience with good food. German architect Dieter Richter,
who has worked on projects at Yaxhá and Naranjo, started this café.
You can browse a collection of books, photos, maps, and other information about the Mayan world while you enjoy a *hamburguesa* (Q35)
or one of the "pre-Columbian" dishes such as *Pollo Xni Pec* (chicken
in a chili sauce served with rice, squash, and yucca, Q48). You can also
book tours to Yaxha and elsewhere. There's a small jade shop at the restaurant. ✉ *Calle. 15 de Septiembre* ☎ *502/5830–2060 or 7926–0367.*

¢–$$$

STEAK HOUSE/
CENTRAL
AMERICAN

✕ **Capitán Tortuga**. The large, cartoonlike Capitán Tortuga sign may fool
you into thinking this restaurant is just for kids, but the excellent grilled
steak and seafood options make this one of Flores's best restaurants.
The *pinchos* (grilled kebabs) are cooked on an open barbecue, sending
enticing aromas throughout the restaurant. There's a nice patio out
back, which offers tremendous sunset views of the lake. You can swim
off the dock. There's a decent selection of wines from Chile. ✉ *Calle 30
de Junio and Callejón San Pedrito* ☎ *502/7926–0247.*

¢–$ ✕**Cools Beans/El Café Chilero.** Sit in a leafy garden and sip a latte or lem-
CAFÉ onade at this cool coffeehouse. Breakfast, served all day, is Q15–Q20, and light meals, beer, and snacks are also available. Free Wi-Fi. ✉ *Calle 15 de Septiembre near causeway* ☎ *502/5571–9240* ▭ *No credit cards* ⊘ *Closed Tues.*

$–$$$ ✕**La Luna.** With its homemade paper lampshades illuminating lovely
CONTINENTAL blue walls, La Luna inspires romance on any moonlit night. But you
★ can just as easily fall in love with what we think is the most creative restaurant in town when you stop in for a delicious lunch. Choose from inventive dishes, including wonderful vegetarian options like the stuffed squash in white sauce. Many people drop by for a drink at the bar. ✉ *Calle 30 de Junio* ☎ *502/7926–3346* ⊘ *Closed Sun.*

¢–$ ✕**Las Puertas.** On a quiet side street, Las Puertas was named for its six
LATIN AMERICAN screened doors. It's a favorite hangout for locals and travelers alike. The friendly couple who run the place take great pride in serving only the freshest foods. Notable are the delicious sandwiches made with home-made bread and mozzarella cheese and the giant goblets of incredible iced coffee. In the afternoon you can relax with a fruit drink as you play one of the many board games. Films are shown in the afternoon and evening. Don't forget to stop back at night for a hearty dinner and live music. ✉ *Calle Central at Av. Santa Ana* ☎ *502/7926–1061* ⊘ *Closed Sun.*

¢–$ ✕**Pizzeria Picasso.** If you find yourself returning to Pizzeria Picasso, it's
PIZZA because the brick-oven pizza (around Q80 for a large one) is hot and delicious. The decor, featuring a print of Picasso's *Guernica*, is another draw. If you're not in the mood for pizza, there is a variety of pastas as well. Save room for cheesecake or tiramisu and a cup of steaming cap-puccino. ✉ *Calle 15 de Septiembre* ☎ *502/7926–0673* ⊘ *Closed Mon.*

WHERE TO STAY

If you are looking for a great hostel, check out Los Amigos in Flores (✉ *Calle Central* ☎ *502/7867–5075* ⊕ *www.amigoshostel.com*) as one of the coolest and most popular hostels around, with a tropical court-yard and a good, cheap restaurant with a lot of vegetarian choices. Besides dorm beds and hammocks, there are rooms with private baths (Q150, around US$19).

For expanded hotel reviews, visit Fodors.com.

$$ 🏨 **Hotel Petén.** An arabesque plunge pool graces the central courtyard of this lovely lodging, said to be the oldest hotel in Flores. **Pros:** modern hotel with great sunset views of the lake. **Cons:** four flights of stairs to get to top-floor rooms. ✉ *Calle Centroamerica, off Calle 30 de Junio* 🏨 *502/7926–0692* ⟿ *21 rooms* ⌂ *In-hotel: restaurant, bar, pool, business center* ⦿ *Breakfast.*

$–$$ 🏨 **Hotel Sabana.** This small hotel, with four floors in one section and five in another, offers simple rooms that open onto a terrace overlooking the pool. **Pros:** dependable choice with some amenities. **Cons:** a lot of stairs to climb. ✉ *Calle Union and Av. Libertad* 🏨 *502/7926–1248* ⊕ *www.hotelsabana.com* ⟿ *28 rooms* ⌂ *In-hotel: restaurant, bar, pool.*

$–$$ 🏨 **Hotel Santana.** Since it sits right on the water, many of the rooms open up onto wide balconies with wicker chairs where you can enjoy

8

the view. **Pros:** lovely views of the lake; good ice cream. **Cons:** mish-mash of building styles and materials, but it seems to work; rates are higher than you'd expect for what you get. ⊠ *Calle 30 de Junio, Playa Poniente* ☎ *502/7867–5123* ⊕ *www.santanapeten.com* ↘ *35 rooms* ⌂ *In-room: safe. In-hotel: restaurant, pool, business center.*

NIGHTLIFE

Raices (⊠ *Calle Sur* ☎ *502/5521–1843*) is the island's disco, but it is also a restaurant. **Las Puertas** (⊠ *Calle Central at Av. Santa Ana* ☎ *502/7867–5242*) has live music some nights. The artsy **La Luna** (⊠ *Calle 30 de Junio* ☎ *502/7926–3346*) has a pleasant atmosphere for enjoying a nightcap, and it usually stays open until 11 pm.

SPORTS AND THE OUTDOORS
BOATING
Boat trips on Lake Petén Itzá can be arranged through most hotels in Flores or by haggling with boat owners who congregate behind the Hotel Santana. Tours (Q80–Q160) often include a stop at Paraíso Escondido, a small mainland park northwest of Flores.

SANTA ELENA

¼ mi (½ km) south of Flores.

Although it lacks the charms of neighboring Flores, gritty Santa Elena is pretty much unavoidable. Most services that you'll need for your trip to El Petén, from currency exchange to gas stations, are offered here. Mundo Maya International Mall, a new shopping center near the causeway to Flores, has a large grocery store and other shops. There are also more upscale hotels here than in Flores.

GETTING HERE AND AROUND
Tuk-tuks—the motorized three-wheeled taxi rickshaws manufactured in Asia—ply the streets of Flores and, to a lesser degree, Santa Elena. Most trips are Q10 or less.

TIMING
Santa Elena is a place to sleep in a decent hotel, get money from an ATM, and buy picnic supplies. There's little to see in Santa Elena itself. At most, you'll use it as a base for exploring other parts of El Petén, so how long you stay here depends on your exploration plans.

SAFETY AND PRECAUTIONS
Some gas stations in Santa Elena have armed guards 24 hours a day, so that should tell you something. The better hotels are quite safe, however, and most visitors never experience any crime.

WHERE TO STAY
For expanded hotel reviews, visit Fodors.com.

$$$ 🏨 **Hotel La Casona del Lago.** Santa Elena's newest, spiffiest hotel sits on the lakeshore of Santa Elena near the causeway to Flores and has splendid views. **Pros:** Newest of Santa Elena hotels; fine views of Flores; bright, large rooms. **Cons:** In increasingly congested area near causeway; not a lot of character; 15-minute walk to main part of Flores. ⊠ *Calle 1*

☎ *7952–8700* ⤴ *33 rooms* ♿ *In-hotel: restaurant, bar, poolbusiness center, Wi-Fi.*

$$$$ ⬚ **Petén Espléndido**. You're not in Flores, but the views of that pretty island from your private balcony are the next best thing. **Pros:** full-service hotel in Santa Elena; only elevator in the Petén; nice views of Flores. **Cons:** a bit like a U.S. chain motel; smallish rooms. ✉ *At foot of causeway leading to Flores* ☎ *502/2360–8140 (reservations) or 7774–0700 (front desk)* ⊕ *www.petenesplendido.com* ⤴ *62 rooms* ♿ *In-room: safe. In-hotel: restaurant, room service, bar, pool, business center, Wi-Fi.*

$$$–$$$$ ⬚ **Villa Maya**. You could lie in bed and count the birds flying by your
★ window at these modern villas on a lagoon east of Santa Elena. **Pros:** beautiful lake views; quiet and peaceful setting. **Cons:** not near restaurants and shopping. ✉ *Laguna Petenchel, 5 mi (8 km) east of Santa Elena* ☎ *5415–1592, or 866/599–6674 in U.S. and Canada* ⊕ *www.villasdeguatemala.com* ⤴ *56 rooms* ♿ *In-room: no TV (some). In-hotel: restaurant, room service, bar, pools, business center.*

SPORTS AND THE OUTDOORS

There are several caves in the hills behind Santa Elena with interesting stalactite and stalagmite formations and subterranean rivers. The easiest to visit is Actun Kan, just south of town.

☼ **Ixpanpajul Parque Natural** (✉ *Ruta a Santa Elena, Km 468* ☎ *502/2336–0576* ⊕ *www.ixpanpajul.com* ☉ *Open daily 6–6*) is a private nature reserve sitting on a large stand of primary rain forest. Hiking the suspended bridges of the skyway will give you a bird's-eye view of the indigenous flora and fauna that make the rain forest the most biodiverse ecosystem on the planet. The park also offers myriad adventure opportunities from nighttime ATV tours to horseback rides to mountain-bike excursions. The Tarzán Canopy Tour (zip line) costs around Q125. There is camping (from Q30 per person), and rental cabañas are available. The entrance to the reserve is 6 mi (10 km) south of Santa Elena.

EL REMATE

18½ mi (30 km) northeast of Flores.

A mellow little town on the eastern shore of Lago Petén Itzá, El Remate is known for its wood carvings, made by families that have dedicated themselves to this craft for generations. Just west of El Remate is the Biotopo Cerro Cahuí, and you can rent a canoe or kayak (around Q10 or US$1.20 an hour) at El Remate to explore the lake. Because it's less than one hour from both Tikal and Yaxhá, El Remate makes a good base for exploring the area.

With more than 1,600 acres of rain forest, **Biotopo Cerro Cahuí** (✉ *1.2 mi [2 km] west of El Remate on the lakeshore road* ☎ *No phone* ⊠ *Q40, daily 8–4*) is one of the most accessible wildlife reserves in El Petén. It protects a portion of a mountain that extends to the eastern edge of Lago Petén Itzá, so there are plenty of opportunities for hiking. Two well-maintained trails put you in proximity of birds like ocellated turkeys, toucans, and parrots. As for mammals, look up to spot the long-armed spider monkeys or down to see squat rodents called *tepezcuintles*. Tzu'unte, a 4-mi (6-km) trail, leads to two lookouts with views of nearby lakes. The upper lookout, Mirador Moreletii, is known by locals as Crocodile Hill, because from the other side of the lake, it looks like the eye of a half-submerged crocodile. Los Ujuxtes, a 3-mi (5-km) trail, offers a panoramic view of three lakes. Both hikes begin at a ranger station, where English-speaking guides are sporadically available. Some robberies and attacks on tourists have taken place in the reserve, so ask locally about safety conditions before you explore on your own.

GETTING HERE AND AROUND

El Remate, near the El Cruce or Ixlú crossroads, is about an hour by car from the Belize border and about a half hour from Flores.

TIMING

Most visitors use El Remate as a base for visits to Tikal and other nearby Mayan sites, so the length of stay depends on how much time you want to spend seeing ruins.

WHERE TO EAT AND STAY

For expanded hotel reviews, visit Fodors.com.

$$–$$$
CENTRAL
AMERICAN

✕ **El Muelle.** True to its name, this long-established restaurant has a pier into the lake, where you can swim. It's popular with Guatemalan families. You have to try the local whitefish from the lake, served whole and usually fried. El Muelle also has hotel rooms in a wooden building. ⊠ *Calle Principal, El Remate* ☎ *502/5514–9785.*

$$
★

⌂ **La Casa de Don David.** Owners Don David Kuhn (originally from Florida) and his Guatemalan wife, Doña Rosa, have lived in the area for 30 years and are a great source of travel tips; rooms are simple and clean with private baths, and most have air-conditioning. **Pros:** knowledgeable host; attractive grounds; good restaurant. **Cons:** not a lot of frills. ⊠ *On road to Biotopo Cerro Cahuí near junction with road to Tikal* ☎ *501/5306–2190 or 7928–8469* ⊕ *www.lacasadedondavid.com* ⮐ *13 rooms* ⚲ *In-room: a/c (some), no TV. In-hotel: restaurant, business center* ❑ *Breakfast.*

$$

⌂ **La Mansión del Pájaro Serpiente.** Perched high on the hillside, La Mansión del Pájaro Serpiente has some of the prettiest accommodations in El Petén. **Pros:** pretty little cabins set on a hillside; lake views (though it's not directly on the lake); lovely grounds; swimming pool. **Cons:** not for those who can't walk up and down steep hills; furnishings in rooms a little dated. ⊠ *On main hwy. south of El Remate* ☎ *502/7926–849 or 570294348* ⮐ *11 rooms* ⚲ *In-room: a/c (some), no TV (some). In-hotel: restaurant, bar, pool* ❑ *No credit cards.*

$$

⌂ **Posada del Cerro.** A new choice in El Remate, Posada del Cerro is near the entrance to Biotopo Cerro Cahuí, offering great views. **Pros:** rustic but charming rooms and modern apartments; great views. **Cons:** a little more expensive than most lodging in El Remate. ⊠ *Near entrance to Biotopo Cerro Cahuí* ☎ *502/5376–8722* ⊕ *www.posadadelcerro.com* ⮐ *4 rooms in cabañas, 2 apartments, 1 dorm that can be used as a family cottage* ⚲ *In-room: no a/c, kitchen (some), no TV. In-hotel: restaurant, bar* ❑ *No credit cards.*

SPORTS AND THE OUTDOORS

The fun folks at **Tikal Canopy Tour** (⊠ *Near entrance gate to Tikal park, about 40 minutes by car from Flores* ☎ 5819–7766 ⊕ *www.canopytikal.com*) have expeditions that take you to the true heart of the rain forest—not on ground level, but more than 100 feet up in the air. In the canopy you'll see monkeys and maybe even a sloth. The tour, which costs US$30 per person, ends with an exhilarating 300-foot-long ride down a zip line.

SHOPPING

Although most souvenirs here are similar to those found elsewhere in Guatemala, the beautiful wood carvings are unique to El Petén. More than 70 families in this small town dedicate themselves to this craft. Their wares are on display on the side of the highway right before the turnoff for the Camino Real and La Lancha hotels on the road to Tikal, and also in small shops in El Remate.

WORD OF MOUTH

"La Lancha is gorgeous! If you are staying overnight near Tikal, stay here! It is in a beautiful and serene setting on Lake Petén Itza. . . . There are only 10 rooms, and they weren't at capacity so once again we felt like we had the place almost to ourselves. The service was impeccable without being too in-your-face. The staff were so friendly and they work so hard. Speaking of breakfast, lunch, and dinner, the food was amazing. There are a lot of stairs at La Lancha so if you are injured, handicapped, or just plain lazy this wouldn't be the place for you."

—sessa

8

NORTH SHORE, LAKE PETÉN ITZÁ

8 mi (13 km) west of El Remate.

The small villages of San Pedro, San José, and San Andrés, on the northwest shore of Lake Petén Itzá, have beautiful views of the sparkling lake. Several upscale lodges and hotels have opened here, and the area is accessible via bus or car on an improved (but bumpy) dirt road from El Remate or Santa Elena, or in the clockwise direction from San Benito.

WHERE TO STAY

For expanded hotel reviews, visit Fodors.com.

$$$$ **Camino Real Tikal.** To experience the natural beauty of the jungles surrounding Lago Petén Itzá without sacrificing creature comforts, many head to Camino Real Tikal. **Pros:** most upscale large hotel in El Petén; beautiful setting on the lake. **Cons:** somewhat remote; as a larger hotel it gets some tour groups. ⊠ *Lote 77, Parcelamiento Tayasal, 3 mi (5 km) west of El Remate, San José* ☎ 7926–0204 ⊕ *www.caminoreal.com.gt* ⤢ 72 rooms ⌂ *In-room: safe, Wi-Fi. In-hotel: 2 restaurants, room service, bars, pool, gym, water sports, business center* ⦿ *Breakfast.*

$$$$ **La Lancha.** Francis Ford Coppola's lodge in Guatemala isn't quite as Fodor's Choice luxe as his two properties in Belize, though it is the only one with air-conditioning, but everything is done in exquisite taste. **Pros:** lovely lake views; good restaurant. **Cons:** expensive (for Guatemala); somewhat

remote; lots of steep steps; in the duplex units you can hear your neighbors. ⊠ *8 mi (13 km) west of El Remate, San José* ☎ *502/7928–8331, 800/746–3743 in U.S.* ⊕ *www.blancaneauxlodge.com* ⤶ *10 casitas* ⌂ *In-room: a/c, no TV. In-hotel: restaurant, room service, bar, pool, Wi-Fi hotspot* ⭐ *Some meals.*

$$$$
Fodor's Choice
★

🔲 **Ni'tun Ecolodge.** After hiking through the jungle, you'll love returning to this charming cluster of cabins owned by a former coffee farmer. **Pros:** small, very personal lodge experience; excellent food; engaging owners. **Cons:** somewhat off the beaten path; steep steps. ⊠ *1 mi (2 km) west of San Andrés, northwest of Flores* ☎ *502/5201–0759* ⊕ *www. nitun.com* ⤶ *4 cabins* ⌂ *In-room: no a/c, no TV. In-hotel: restaurant, bar, business center* ⭐ *Breakfast.*

OTHER MAYAN SITES IN EL PETÉN

Although Tikal is the most famous, El Petén has hundreds of archaeological sites, ranging from modest burial chambers to sprawling cities. The vast majority have not been explored, let alone restored. Within a few miles of Tikal are several easy-to-reach sites. Because they're in isolated areas, it's a good idea to go with a guide.

EXPLORING

Nakúm lies deep within the forest, connected to Tikal via jungle trails that are sometimes used for horseback expeditions. You cannot visit during the rainy season, as you'll sink into mud up to your ankles. Two building complexes and some stelae are visible. ⊠ *16 mi (26 km) east of Tikal.*

The 4,000-year-old city of **Uaxactún** (pronounced Wah-shank-TOON) was once a rival to Tikal's supremacy in the region. It was conquered by Tikal in the 4th century and lived in the shadow of that great city for centuries. Inscriptions show that Uaxactún existed longer than any other Mayan city, which may account for the wide variety of structures. Here you'll find a Mayan observatory.

Uaxactún is surrounded by thick rain forest, so the trip can be arduous, but as it's difficult to get here, you most likely won't have to fight the crowds as you do at neighboring Tikal, leaving you free to enjoy the quiet and mystic air of the ruins. The rock-and-dirt road is passable during the drier seasons and nearly impossible at other times without a four-wheel-drive vehicle. You'll need to secure a permit to visit Uaxactún. The administration building in Tikal is on the road between the Jaguar Inn and the Jungle Lodge. Obtaining a permit is sometimes easier said than done, but with a little persistence and perhaps a small *mordida* (bribe), you should be able to get past the guards into the administration area where they grant the free permits. Sometimes police will ask to accompany you on the trip, which is helpful for two reasons: it prevents potential robberies, and, most important, will give you an extra person to push if your vehicle gets stuck. ⊠ *16 mi (24 km) north of Tikal.*

Overlooking a beautiful lake of the same name, the ruins of **Yaxhá**, about halfway between the Belize border and Flores, are divided into two sections of rectangular structures that form plazas and streets. The city was probably inhabited between the Pre-Classic and Classic periods. The ruins are being restored by a German organization in coordination with the Guatemalan government. Yaxhá was featured on the 2005 reality TV show *Survivor*, and that has helped make

it the second-most visited site in the Petén after Tikal. Lake Yaxhá, surrounded by virgin rain forest, is a good bird-watching spot. During the rainy season only a four-wheel-drive vehicle—or setting out on horseback, motorcycle, or on foot—will get you to Yaxhá; the rest of the year the road is passable. Day trips to Yaxhá from Flores or El Remate cost about US$25 to $30 per person, sometimes including lunch. **El Sombrero ecolodge** (✉ *Yaxhá* ☎ *502/7861–1688*) is near the entrance to Yaxhá if you want to stay overnight and explore the ruins more thoroughly. ✉ *30 mi (48 km) south of Flores, 19 mi (30 km) east of Tikal* ▱ *Q80.*

A popular ecotourism destination, **El Zotz** is where you'll find the remnants of a Mayan city. On a clear day you can see the tallest of the ruins at Tikal from these unexcavated ruins. The odd name, which means "the bat" in Q'eqchí, refers to a cave from which thousands of bats make a nightly exodus. Troops of hyperactive spider monkeys seem to have claimed this place for themselves, swinging through the treetops and scrambling after each other like children playing a game of tag. Unlike those in Tikal, however, these long-limbed creatures are not used to people and will shake branches and throw twigs and fruit to try to scare you away. Mosquitoes are fierce, especially in rainy season; bring your strongest repellent. ✉ *15 mi (24 km) west of Tikal* ▱ *Q50.*

El Mirador, once equal in size and splendor to Tikal, may eventually equal Tikal as a must-see Mayan ruin. It's just now being explored, but elaborate plans are being laid to establish a huge park four times the size of Tikal. The Mirador Basin contains the El Mirador site itself, four other known Mayan cities that probably were as large as Tikal (Nakbé, El Tintal, Xulnal, and Wakná), and many smaller but important sites—perhaps as many as 80 to 100 cities. The Mirador Basin is home to an incredible diversity of plant and animal life, including 200 species of birds, 40 kinds of animals (including several endangered ones, such as jaguars), 300 kinds of trees, and 2,000 different species of flora. It has been nominated as a UNESCO World Heritage Site. Currently, fewer than 2,500 visitors get to El Mirador annually, as it's a difficult trek requiring five or six days of hiking (round trip). The jumping-off point for the trek is Carmelita Village, about 50 mi (84 km) north of Flores.

8

There are no hotels in the Mirador Basin, and no roads except for dirt paths. Local tour companies can arrange treks, but guides likely will speak only Spanish. Hiking tours start at around US$300 per person. It's also possible to visit El Mirador by helicopter—one option is with a Guatemala City–based company called Ecotourism & Adventure Specialists. One-day trips from Flores start at around US$600–$700 per person, with a minimum of four persons. ⊠ *Ecotourism & Adventure Specialists, 4 Av. 7-95 Zona 14, 2nd level, Guatemala City 01014 Guatemala* ☎ *502/5115–6634 or 800/297–1880 in the U.S.* ✛ *40 mi (66 km) northwest of Tikal* ⊡ *Q60.*

Mayan Sites

WORD OF MOUTH

"Caracol is probably the grandest of the Mayan sites in Belize—there's plenty to study/gawk at. It's done almost exclusively as a day trip out of the Cayo or Mountain Pine Ridge regions over a very rough road through dense jungle—the vehicles travel in a caravan led by the Belize military, which is actually kind of cool. Lamanai is also an impressive site, with magnificent pyramids and fascinating carved masks in the sides of the temples. The setting is also spectacular, right on the New River lagoon. Most people do it as a day trip. The ride down the New River to reach it is pretty fascinating (the first boat in and first to leave probably see the best wildlife on the river)."

—RAC

By Lan Sluder

Visiting Belize without touring any Mayan sites is like going to Greece and not seeing the Acropolis and the Parthenon. For at least five millennia, the Maya left their imprint on what is now Belize, and today some of the Mayan world's most awe-inspiring ruins are yours to explore. Archaeologists have identified more than 600 significant Mayan sites in Belize, and doubtless many more are yet to be discovered.

You can choose from among more than a dozen major excavated sites that are open to visitors, in all parts of the country, from Corozal and Orange Walk districts in the north to Cayo in the west and Toledo in the south. Some, such as Cahal Pech or Xunantunich, are by the roadside and easily reached; others, such as La Milpa or Cerros, will have you tramping the bush like Indiana Jones. Even the most accessible sites aren't overrun with hordes of travelers—at some you may be the only visitor, other than perhaps a troop of howler monkeys or a flock of parrots. This chapter fills you in on the fascinating history of the Maya in Belize, exposes some of the secrets of their great architecture, suggests itineraries for visiting the most interesting sites, and provides tips for touring the realm of the Maya.

NOTABLE MAYAN SITES IN BELIZE

The following are our picks for the most notable Mayan sites in Belize. See the destination chapters for detailed information on the sites, including hours and admission fees. Fees at most sites for non-Belizeans are usually around BZ$20, while Caracol is BZ$30, and Actun Tunichil Muknal is BZ$50. This is in addition to any fees for guides or tours.

NORTHERN BELIZE

Altun Ha. The most visited Mayan site in Belize, though not the most impressive, is popular with cruise-ship passengers and for those staying on Ambergris Caye or Caye Caulker. It's a little more than an hour's drive north of Belize City. One of the temples at Altun Ha is prominently pictured on Belikin beer bottles.

Cerros. Although the few remaining original structures here are weathered, and there's no museum or visitor center, Cerros—like Tulum in the Yucatán—enjoys a glorious location right beside the water.

Chan Chich. The lodge of the same name was built literally on top of this minor ceremonial site. It can be reached by car or charter flight and is best visited in connection with a stay at the lodge.

Cuello. It's one of the oldest Mayan sites in the region, settled more than 2,500 years ago. It's on the property of a rum distillery near Orange Walk Town, and you have to get permission in advance to visit it.

La Milpa. The third-largest Mayan site in Belize (only Caracol and Lamanai are larger), La Milpa is in the early stages of exploration and excavation. It can be visited through advance arrangement with Programme for Belize, on whose land it sits.

★ **Lamanai.** Boat your way up the New River to the shores of the New River Lagoon to see this ruin, which has the most beautiful setting of any Mayan site in Belize. You can also reach it by road from Orange Walk Town. Lamanai has a small museum and a resident troop of howler monkeys.

Noh Mul. This ruin, settled around 350 BC, is about 10 mi north of Orange Walk Town on private land.

Santa Rita. Corozal Town is built on what was the large Mayan trading center known as Chactemal (or Chetumal, as the capital of Quintana Roo, Mexico, is known today). A part of the ruins, now called Santa Rita, is on a hill on the outskirts of town. At this writing Santa Rita is not officially open to the public, although you can walk around the small site.

THE CAYO

Fodor's Choice ★ **Actun Tunichil Muknal.** "ATM," near Belmopan, provides the most rewarding Mayan cave experience in Belize, and indeed in the entire region. Many visitors say it is the highlight of all their travels in Central America. To see the cave, you have to take a 45-minute hike and a brief swim, and be a part of a guided tour. Only about 30 guides are certified to lead trips to ATM.

Barton Creek Cave. You can canoe through part of this 7-mi (11-km) wet-cave system once used by the Maya for human sacrifices. It's about a half hour off the Chiquilbul Road on the way to the Mountain Pine Ridge.

Cahal Pech. This small Late Classic site, with a lovely location on a hill overlooking San Ignacio, is easily accessible from town. It has a little museum.

Fodor's Choice ★ **Caracol.** The largest and most significant site in Belize is a must if you're in the Cayo. It's an all-day trip from San Ignacio through the Mountain Pine Ridge, but it's well worth the time. There's a museum and visitor center, and extensive excavations have been underway for more than 20 years.

Che Chem Ha. This cave on private land south of Benque Viejo has artifacts dating back 2,000 years.

El Pilar. Set on low hills above the Mopan River at the Guatemalan border is one of the largest sites in Belize, but little of it has been excavated.

Pacbitun. Near San Antonio village on the road to the Mountain Pine Ridge, Pacbitun dates back to at least 1000 BC. It's on private land.

★ **Xunantunich.** Though it's not one of the largest sites in Belize, Xunantunich is one of the easiest and most pleasant to visit. To reach it, you cross the Mopan River on a quaint, hand-pulled ferry. There's a well-done museum and visitor center. It's off the Western Highway, west of San

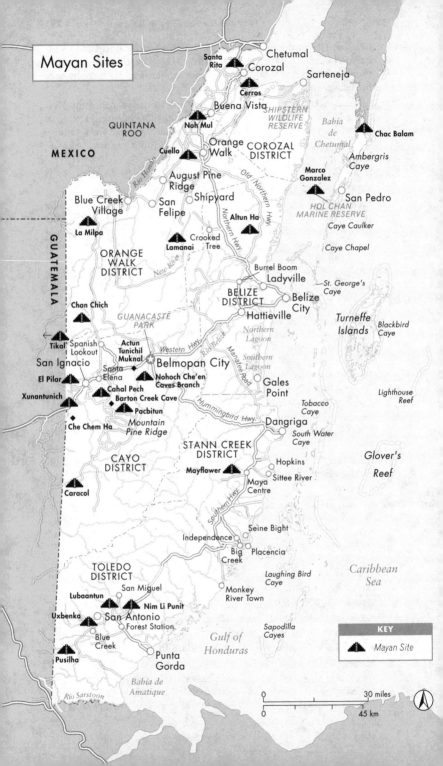

Mayan Sites

Santa Rita
Chetumal
Corozal
Sarteneja
Cerros
Buena Vista
Bahía de Chetumal
Chac Balam
QUINTANA ROO
Noh Mul
MEXICO
Cuello
Orange Walk
COROZAL DISTRICT
Ambergris Caye
HIPSTERN WILDLIFE RESERVE
August Pine Ridge
Shipyard
Marco Gonzalez
San Pedro
Blue Creek Village
San Felipe
Altun Ha
HOL CHAN MARINE RESERVE
La Milpa
Caye Caulker
ORANGE WALK DISTRICT
Lamanai
Crooked Tree
Caye Chapel
New River
GUATEMALA
Burrel Boom
Ladyville
St. George's Caye
Chan Chich
BELIZE DISTRICT
Belize City
Turneffe Islands
Blackbird Caye
GUANACASTE PARK
Hattieville
Northern Lagoon
Tikal
Spanish Lookout
Actun Tunichil Muknal
Western Hwy
Belmopan City
San Ignacio
Santa Elena
Nohoch Che'en Caves Branch
Gales Point
Lighthouse Reef
El Pilar
Cahal Pech
Southern Lagoon
Xunantunich
Barton Creek Cave
Pacbitun
Tobacco Caye
Che Chem Ha
Mountain Pine Ridge
Hummingbird Hwy
Dangriga
South Water Caye
Glover's Reef
CAYO DISTRICT
STANN CREEK DISTRICT
Caracol
Mayflower
Hopkins
Sittee River
Maya Centre
Southern Hwy
Independence
Seine Bight
Caribbean Sea
Big Creek
Placencia
Laughing Bird Caye
TOLEDO DISTRICT
San Miguel
Lubaantun
Nim Li Punit
Monkey River Town
Sapodilla Cayes
Uxbenka
San Antonio
Forest Station
Blue Creek
Gulf of Honduras
Punta Gorda
Pusilha
Bahía de Amatique
Rio Sarstoon

0 30 miles
0 45 km

Ignacio. In May 2009 parts of the tallest structure at Xunantunich, El Castillo, were damaged by an earthquake. As of this writing, climbing to the top of this structure is no longer permitted, so you can't enjoy the panoramic views of the Cayo and Guatemala.

SOUTHERN BELIZE

★ **Lubaantun.** Occupied for less than 200 years in the Late Classic period, Lubaantun is unusual in that no stelae were ever found here, and the precisely fitted building stones, laid without mortar, have rounded corners. The controversial "Crystal Skull" supposedly was found here. Lubaantun is near San Pedro Columbia village, about 20 mi (32 km) from Punta Gorda.

Mayflower. This Classic-period site, off the Southern Highway just south of Dangriga, is in the early stages of excavation. Waterfalls nearby make the setting appealing.

★ **Nim Li Punit.** Off the Southern Highway north of Punta Gorda is Nim Li Punit ("Big Hat" in Ketchi), a small but pretty site. There's a visitor center.

Pusilha. At a site near Aguacate Village on the Moho River is this collection of extensive but low-lying structures on a small hill. Also visible are the remains of a stone bridge. It is officially closed to the public, though you can ask locally to see it. Because of its remote location off the main highway, there aren't many visitors who make the trip out here.

AMBERGRIS CAYE

Although there are no large Mayan sites on the cayes, Ambergris Caye has several small ruins. **Chac Balam** can be visited on a boat tour to Bacalar, at the far north end of the island. **Marco Gonzalez,** at the south end of the island, is difficult to find without a local guide.

9

EL PETÉN, GUATEMALA

Fodor'sChoice **Tikal.** Along with Copán in Honduras and Palenque in Mexico, Tikal is
★ considered by many to be the most impressive of all Mayan sites. The Petén area is home to several other ruins, including **Nakúm, El Ceibal, Uaxactún, Yaxhá, Yaxchilán, El Zotz,** and **El Mirador.** Some, like El Mirador, are extremely remote, requiring a multiday jungle trek.

SEEING THE RUINS

Most visitors to Belize are not serious "Maya buffs" who spend all their time touring ruins. Instead, they opt to visit Mayan sites as just one aspect of their beach or mainland vacation. If this is your first trip to Belize, we recommend you do the same. Following are the sites that are easily visited from the most popular areas.

Ambergris Caye and Caye Caulker. Tour operators on these islands run trips to **Lamanai** (usually a full-day trip by boat and road) and to **Altun Ha**

(normally a half-day trip, although it may be longer if it includes lunch and a spa visit at Maruba Spa). You can also visit **Tikal** on an overnight trip by air to Flores, Guatemala, with a change of planes in Belize City. It's also possible to arrange boat tours of small ruins on Ambergris Caye, including **Chac Balam** at Bacalar.

Belize City. Tour operators based in Belize City, most of which cater to cruise ships, offer day trips by road, boat, or air to **Lamanai** and by road to **Altun Ha,** and also by road to **Xunantunich** and other ruins, including **Cahal Pech** near San Ignacio. The tours to San Ignacio may be combined with a stop at the Belize Zoo. You can also visit **Tikal** on a day or overnight trip by air from the international airport in Belize City to Flores.

TIPS

Tour operators in each area offer day or part-day trips (and in a few cases, overnight trips) to the sites. Tours may not operate every day, especially off-season, and there may be a minimum number of participants required for the tour to run. Tour operators may be able to provide tours to less-visited sites with an advance arrangement. Except for certain caves such as Actun Tunichil Muknal, which can be visited only with a guide, most Mayan sites can be visited independently—you just need a rental car, or, in a few cases, bus fare.

San Ignacio makes a good jumping-off spot to see Tikal, either on a day trip or overnight. It's also a good base for visiting Caracol, Xunantunich, Cahal Pech, and El Pilar.

Corozal Town. Tour operators in Corozal Town can arrange a full-day trip by road and boat to **Lamanai.** They also offer boat trips to **Cerros** or a visit to nearby **Santa Rita** by car, if you don't have your own. By advance arrangement, tour operators may be able to offer road tours of **Cuello, La Milpa, Noh Mul,** or other less-visited sites.

San Ignacio, Belmopan, and Mountain Pine Ridge. Tour operators in the San Ignacio, Belmopan, and Mountain Pine Ridge areas focus on the many Mayan sites in the Cayo, including **Caracol, Xunantunich, Cahal Pech,** and **El Pilar.** Tours to Caracol typically require a full day, while the other sites can each be done in a half day or less. There are also guided tours of notable caves, including **Actun Tunichil Muknal** (full day) and **Che Hem Ha** (half day). Day and overnight tours by road to **Tikal** are also offered.

Hopkins and Placencia. Tour operators in Hopkins and Placencia offer half-day tours to the **Mayflower** ruins (sometimes combined, on a full-day trip, with a visit to the Cockscomb Basin Wildlife Sanctuary). They also offer full-day trips by road to the ruins near Punta Gorda, mainly **Lubaantun** and **Nim Li Punit.** You can also fly from Dangriga or Placencia, via Belize City, to Flores to see **Tikal.**

Punta Gorda. Tour operators in Punta Gorda and nearby focus on trips by road to the ruins of **Lubaantun, Nim Li Punit,** and, less commonly, **Pusilha.** These tours usually include visits to modern Maya villages near Punta Gorda. You can also fly from Punta Gorda, with a change of planes in Belize City, to Flores to see **Tikal.**

GREAT ITINERARY: MAYAN SITES BLITZ

If you want to see the top Mayan sites in one trip, base yourself in the Cayo for a few days. Information on tour operators and guides, and on admissions to specific sites, is in destination chapters.

If after a few days in western Belize and Guatemala you still haven't had your fill of things Mayan, you can add extensions to northern Belize and to Punta Gorda in southern Belize.

DAY 1: SAN IGNACIO

San Ignacio is an easy jumping-off spot for seeing several small but fascinating nearby ruins. If you get an early start, you can take in **Xunantunich, Cahal Pech,** and **El Pilar.** Both Cahal Pech and Xunantunich can be reached by bus (albeit with a short hike after the bus ride in both cases), but a taxi or rental car is needed to get to El Pilar. Guided tours of all these sites can be arranged in San Ignacio or at lodges and hotels in the area. (⇨ *See The Cayo, Chapter 5*)

DAY 2: CARACOL

Caracol, the most important Mayan site in Belize, deserves a full day. You can drive yourself—or go on a tour. There is no bus transportation in the Mountain Pine Ridge. Even if you arrive independently, you can hire a guide to show you around once you're at the site, or you can tour it on your own. There's an informative museum and visitor center. Due to a series of bandit incidents in 2008–2010, trips to Caracol are being done in convoys, protected by Belize Defence Forces soldiers. Check locally for updates. (⇨ *See The Cayo, Chapter 5*)

DAYS 3 AND 4: TIKAL

Tikal is by far the most impressive Mayan site in the region and shouldn't be missed (though you should check in advance about travel warnings to the area). Many operators offer day tours of Tikal from the San Ignacio area. (⇨ *See El Petén, Chapter 8*)

TIPS

Altun Ha, the ruin closest to Belize City, gets crowds of cruise-ship day-trippers; so if you go, try to avoid days when there are several cruise ships in port.

Be aware of your surroundings, and before heading anywhere remote by yourself, check with the locals to find out if there have been any recent safety issues.

On your visit to Tikal, stay at one of the three lodges at the park if possible—you'll be able to visit the ruins early in the morning or late in the afternoon, when howler monkeys and other animals are active and most day visitors have left.

Pack plenty of bug juice with DEET. Mosquitoes are especially bad around Cerros and at the ruins near Punta Gorda.

9

A MAYAN PRIMER

CHRONOLOGY

Traditionally, archaeologists have divided Mayan history into three main periods: Pre-Classic, Classic, and Post-Classic. Although some academics question the validity of such a uniform chronology, the traditional labels are still in use.

The **Pre-Classic** (circa 3,000 BC–AD 250) period is characterized by the influence of the Olmec, a civilization centered on the Gulf Coast of present-day Mexico. During this period cities began to grow, especially in the southern highlands of Guatemala and in Belize, and it's at this time that Belize's Cuello, Lamanai, Santa Rita, Cahal Pech, Pacbitun, and Altun Ha sites were first settled.

By the **Late Pre-Classic** (circa 300 BC–AD 250) period the Maya had developed an advanced mathematical system, an impressively precise calendar, and one of the world's five original writing systems. In Belize, Cerros was established during the Late Pre-Classic period.

During the **Classic** (circa 250 BC–AD 900) period, Maya artistic, intellectual, and architectural achievements literally reached for the stars. Vast city-states were crisscrossed by a large number of paved roadways, some of which still exist today. The great cities of Caracol (Belize), Palenque (Mexico), Tikal (Guatemala), and Quirigu (Guatemala) were just a few of the powerful centers that controlled the Classic Maya world. In AD 562 Caracol—which at its height was the largest city-state in Belize, with a population of about 150,000—conquered Tikal. Other notable Classic period sites in Belize include Xunantunich, El Pilar, and Lubaantun.

The single largest unsolved mystery about the Maya is their rapid decline during the **Terminal Classic** (AD 800–900) period and the centuries following. Scholars have postulated that climate change, pandemic disease, drought, stresses in the social structure, overpopulation, deforestation, and changes in the trade routes could have been responsible. Rather than a single factor, several events taking place over time could well have been the cause.

The Maya of the **Post-Classic** (AD 900–early 1500s) period were heavily affected by growing powers in central Mexico. Architecture, ceramics, and carvings from this period show considerable outside influence. Although still dramatic, Post-Classic cities such as Chichén Itzá and Uxmal pale in comparison to their Classic predecessors. By the time the Spanish conquest reached the Yucatán, the Maya were scattered, feuding, and easy to conquer. Several sites in Belize, including Lamanai, were continuously occupied during this time, and even later.

KEY DATES

Here are some key dates in the history of the Maya in Belize and in the El Petén area of Guatemala. Most of the dates are approximate, and some dates are disputed.

BC

3114	Date of the creation of the world, or 0.0.0.0.0 according to the Long Count calendar
3000	Early Olmec and Mayan civilizations thought to have begun
2500	Cuello established
2000	Santa Rita established
1500	Lamanai established
1000	Cahal Pech established
900	Olmec writing system developed; Caracol established
800	Tikal established
500	First Mayan calendars carved in stone
400–300	First written Mayan language
250	Altun Ha established
200	First monumental buildings erected at Tikal and El Mirador

AD

400–600	Tikal becomes leading city-state, with population of perhaps 200,000
553	Accession of Lord Water as Caracol ruler
562	Caracol conquers Tikal
599	Accession of Lord Smoke Ahau as Caracol ruler
618	Accession of Kan II as Caracol ruler
631	Caracol defeats Naranjo; Caracol's population is 150,000
700	Lubaantun established
800	Cahal Pech abandoned
895	Xunantunich abandoned
899	Tikal abandoned
900	Classic period of Mayan history ends
900–1500	Maya civilization in decline, many cities abandoned
1000	Southern Belize Mayan centers mostly abandoned
1050	Caracol abandoned
1517	Spanish arrive in Yucatán and begin conquest of Maya
1517–1625	Diseases introduced from Europe cause death of majority of Maya
1524–25	Hernán Cortés passes through Belize en route to Honduras, after leading expeditions to conquer the Aztecs in Mexico
1546–1600s	Maya in Belize rebel against Spanish
1695	Tikal ruins rediscovered by Spanish
1700s	Lamanai continuously occupied over 3,000 years

9

1724	Spanish abolish *encomienda* system of forced Maya labor
1839	John Lloyd Stephens and Frederick Catherwood visit Belize
1847	Caste Wars in Yucatán begin
1881	Early archaeological work begins at Tikal, by Alfred Maudslay
1894	Thomas Gann begins exploring Xunantunich and other Belize ruins
1936	Caracol ruins rediscovered by a lumberman
1956	William Coe and others begin excavations at Tikal
1992	Rigoberta Menchu, a Maya from Guatemala, wins Nobel Peace Prize
2006	Mel Gibson's *Apocalypto,* set in a crumbling Mayan civilization, and with actors speaking Yucatec Maya, filmed in Veracruz
2012	The predicted end of the world, 13.0.0.0.0 in the Long Count calendar; or, by other interpretations, just the transition of one age to another.

HISTORY IN BRIEF

Anthropologists believe that humans from Asia crossed a land bridge, in what is now the Bering Strait in Alaska, into North America about 25,000 years ago. Gradually these Paleoindians, or "Old Indians," whose ancestors probably were Mongoloid peoples, made their way down the continent, establishing Native American or First Nation settlements in what is now the United States and Canada. Groups of them are thought to have reached Mesoamerica, which includes, besides Belize, much of central Mexico, Guatemala, Honduras, and Nicaragua, around 20,000 to 22,000 years ago.

These early peoples were hunter-gatherers. The Olmec civilization, considered the mother culture of later Mesoamerican civilizations including that of the Maya, arose in central and southern Mexico 3,000 to 4,000 years ago. The Olmecs developed the first writing system in the New World, dating from at least 900 BC. They also had sophisticated mathematics and created complex calendars. The Olmecs built irrigation systems to water their crops.

As long ago as around 3000 BC—the exact date is in question and has changed as archaeologists have made new discoveries—the Maya began to settle in small villages in Belize and elsewhere in the region. They developed an agriculture based on the cultivation of maize (corn), squash, and other fruits and vegetables. Some archeologists believe that the Maya—like other Indians in the region as well as in the South American Amazon—augmented soils with charcoal, pottery fragments, and organic matter to create *terra preta* (Portuguese for dark soil), very fertile earth that stood up to hard tropical rains. In Belize, small settlements were established as early as 2500 BC at Cuello in what is now Orange Walk District in northern Belize. Then, over the next 1,000 years or so, settlements arose at Santa Rita in Corozal and Lamanai in Orange Walk, and at Cahal Pech, Caracol, and elsewhere in Cayo District in western Belize. What would become the great city-states of the region, including Tikal in today's Petén region of Guatemala and Caracol in the Cayo, was first settled around 900 to 700 BC.

Two or three centuries before the time of Christ, several Mayan villages grew into sizable cities. The Maya began to construct large-scale stone buildings at Tikal and elsewhere. Eventually, Tikal, Caracol, and other urban centers each would have thousands of structures—palaces, temples, residences, monuments, ball courts, even prisons. Although the Maya never had the wheel, and thus no carts or wagons, they built paved streets and causeways, and they developed sophisticated crop irrigation systems.

At its height, in what is known as the Classic period (250 BC to AD 900), the Maya civilization consisted of about 50 cities, much like ancient Greek city-states. Each had a population of 5,000 to 100,000 or more. Tikal, the premier city in the region, may have had 200,000 residents in and around the city during its heyday, and Caracol in Belize probably had nearly as many. The peak population of the Maya civilization possibly reached 2 million or more, and as many as a million may have lived in Belize alone—more than three times the current population.

The Mayan culture put a heavy emphasis on religion, which was based on a pantheon of nature gods, including those of the sun, moon, and rain. The Mayan view of life was cyclical, and Mayan religion was based on accommodating human life to the cycles of the universe.

Contrary to what scholars long believed, however, Mayan society had many aspects beyond religion. Politics, the arts, business, and trade were all important and dynamic aspects of Mayan life. Dynastic leaders waged brutal wars on rival city-states. Under its ruler Lord Smoke Ahau, Caracol, the largest city-state in Belize, conquered Tikal in AD 562, and less than a hundred years later conquered another large city, Naranjo (also in Guatemala).

The Maya developed sophisticated mathematics. They understood the concept of zero and used a base-20 numbering system. Astronomy was the basis of a complex Mayan calendar system involving an accurately determined solar year (18 months of 20 days, plus a five-day period), a sacred year of 260 days (13 cycles of 20 days), and a variety of longer cycles culminating in the Long Count, based on a zero date in 3114 BC, or 0.0.0.0.0—the date that the Maya believed was the beginning of the current cycle of the world.

The Mayan writing system is considered the most advanced of any developed in Mesoamerica. The Maya used more than 800 "glyphs," small pictures or signs, paired in columns that read from left to right and top to bottom. The glyphs represent syllables and, in some cases, entire words, that can be combined to form any word or concept. There is no Mayan alphabet. Mayan glyphs can represent either sounds or ideas, or both, making them difficult to accurately interpret. The unit of the writing system is the cartouche, a series of three to 50 glyphs, the equivalent of a word or sentence in a modern language.

As in most societies, it's likely that the large majority of the Maya spent much of their time simply trying to eke out a living. In each urban area the common people lived in simple thatch dwellings, similar to those seen in the region today. They practiced a slash-and-burn agriculture. Farmers cleared their small plots by burning the bush, then planting maize, squash, sunflowers, and other crops in the rich ash. After two or three years, when the soil was depleted, the plot was left fallow for several years before it could be planted again.

Beginning around AD 800, parts of the Mayan civilization in Belize and elsewhere in Mesoamerica began to decline. In most areas the decline didn't happen suddenly, but over decades and even centuries, and it took place at different times. For example, the cities in the Northern Lowlands of the Yucatán, such as Chichén Itzá, flourished for several more centuries after Tikal and Caracol were abandoned.

Scholars are still debating the reasons for the decline. Climatic change, lengthy droughts, overpopulation, depletion of arable land, social revolutions by the common people against the elites, epidemics, and the impact of extended periods of warfare all have been put forth as reasons. Earthquakes, hurricanes, and other natural disasters may have played a role at certain sites. It may well have been a combination of factors, or there may have been different causes in different regions.

Whatever the reasons, the Mayan civilization in Belize and elsewhere in Mesoamerica never regained its Classic period glory. By the time the Spanish arrived in the early 1500s only a few of the Mayan cities, mainly in the Highlands of Guatemala, were still thriving. Most of the great cities and trading centers of Belize and Guatemala, including Caracol and Tikal, had long been abandoned. Lamanai and a few other urban settlements were still inhabited.

Seeking gold and other plunder, the Spanish began their conquest of the Maya in the 1520s. Some Mayan states offered fierce resistance, and the last Mayan kingdom, in Mexico, was not vanquished until almost 1700. The Maya in Belize rebelled against the Spanish several times, but there was one enemy against which the Maya were defenseless: European disease. Smallpox, chicken pox, measles, flu, and other infectious diseases swept through the Mayan settlements. Scientists believe that within a century nearly 90% of the Maya had been wiped out by "imported" diseases.

Mayan resistance to European control continued from time to time. In 1847 Mayan Indians in the Yucatán rose up against Europeans in the bloody Caste Wars, which lasted until 1904. This had a major impact on Belize, as many Mexican Mestizos (persons of mixed Indian and European heritage) and Maya moved to northern Belize to escape the violence. Sarteneja, Orange Walk Town, and Ambergris Caye were among the areas at least partly settled by refugees from the Yucatán.

Much of the Mayan civilization was buried under the tropical jungles for centuries, and Westerners knew little about it. In the process of trying to convert the Maya to Christianity in the 16th century, the Spanish burned most of the codices, Mayan "books" made of deer hide or bleached fig-tree paper. Only in the last few decades have scholars made progress in deciphering Mayan glyphic writing.

In 1839 two British adventurers, John Lloyd Stephens and Frederick Catherwood, visited Central America, including Belize, and explored a number of the Mayan sites. Their books, especially *Incidents of Travel in Central America, Chiapas, and Yucatán,* with text by Stephens and illustrations by Catherwood, brought the attention of the world to the Mayan past.

In the late 1800s the first systematic archaeological excavations of Tikal and Mayan sites in Belize were begun. Alfred Maudslay, an Englishman, conducted excavations at Tikal in 1881–82, and Harvard's Peabody Museum did fieldwork there between 1895 and 1904. Sylvanus Morley, a well-known Maya expert, conducted work at Tikal at times between 1914 and 1928. In 1956 the University of Pennsylvania began the first large-scale excavation project at Tikal. In Belize, Thomas Gann, a British medical officer stationed in what was then British Honduras, carried out the first excavations of several major Belize Mayan sites, including Santa Rita, Xunantunich, Lubaantun, sites on Ambergris Caye, and others, starting in 1894. Since then, many university and museum teams, including ones from the University of Pennsylvania, the Royal Ontario Museum, Tulane University, the University of Texas, the University of California, and the University of Central Florida, have conducted extensive fieldwork in Belize. Drs. Diane and Arlen Chase, of the University of Central Florida, have been at work at the largest site in Belize, Caracol, since 1983.

About 30,000 Maya live in Belize today, according to the 2010 Belize Census, of which about 17,000 are Ketchi, 11,000 are Mopan, and 2,000 are Yucatec. In southern Belize they're predominantly Ketchi and Mopan Maya; in western Belize, Mopan Maya; and in northern Belize, Yucatec Maya. The largest concentration of Maya in Belize is in the small villages in Toledo District near Punta Gorda.

The end of the world, or at least its current cycle, will take place on December 21, 2012, according to the Long Count calendar of the ancient Maya. However, others say that the Maya did not see this as the end of the world but rather as a transition from one age to another.

DOS AND DON'TS FOR VISITING RUINS

■ **If it's allowed, do climb the temples and enjoy the views from the top.** At most sites you're free to climb the ruins. (However, at some, including Tikal, visitors are now prevented from climbing some structures.) The views from El Castillo at Xunantunich, from structures at Cerros of Chetumal Bay, and from Lubaantun to the sea, are among the most memorable. Be warned, though: most of the steps are very steep.

■ **Do descend into Xilbalda.** The Maya called the underworld Xilbalda. You can experience it by visiting one of the caves once used by the Maya. Actun Tunichil Muknal, "The Cave of the Stone Sepulchre," near Belmopan, is our favorite. Che Chem Ha near San Ignacio is another cave with many Mayan artifacts. Ho Keb Ha, also known as Blue Creek Cave, is a cave system near Blue Creek village in Toledo. Barton Creek Cave, en route to the Mountain Pine Ridge and more than 7 mi (11½ km) long, was once used by the Maya for human sacrifices; today you can float it in a canoe. All of these caves are best visited with a guide. Actun Tunichil Muknal and Che Chem Ha, at the very least, absolutely require one. Private land, especially in the Cayo and Toledo, often contains caves with Mayan artifacts.

■ **Do look for wildlife at the ruins and en route.** One of the best things about the ruins and their surroundings is that they're home to many birds and wild creatures. On the long drive to Caracol, for example, you'll pass through pine ridge and broadleaf jungle, and you may see brocket deer, oscellated turkey, and coatimundi. En route to Caracol, we once saw a small crocodile sunning at the bridge over the Macal River and, on another occasion, a fer-de-lance at DiSilva village. You're sure to see many beautiful butterflies. The trip up the New River to Lamanai is another good opportunity to see birds and wildlife on the riverbanks, and once you get to Lamanai chances are good that you'll spot howler monkeys. Tikal is a great place to see howler and spider monkeys, coatis, and other wild creatures.

■ **Don't ever take any artifact from a Mayan site, not even a tiny pottery fragment.** The theft of Mayan antiquities is a serious crime. Luggage is sometimes searched at the international airport, and if any Mayan artifacts are found, you could be in hot water.

■ **Don't be surprised to find Mayan ruins in unexpected places.** There are at least 600 known Mayan sites in Belize, and the number of ruins out there probably runs into the thousands. Nearly every jungle lodge in Belize has some kind of Mayan site on the grounds, and some lodges, such as Pook's Hill, Nabitunich, Chan Chich, and Maya Mountain, have hosted archaeological digs. Mayan artifacts still remain in many caves, and pottery fragments can be as common as weeds in the backyards of many private homes. After all, at the height of the Mayan kingdoms, there were perhaps a million Maya living in Belize, and their traces are everywhere.

ARCHITECTURE

One look at the monumental architecture of the Maya, and you might feel transported to another world (perhaps that's why Tikal was used as the rebel base in the original 1977 *Star Wars*). The breathtaking structures are even more impressive when you consider that they were built 1,000 to 2,000 years ago or more, without iron tools, wheels, or pulleys. The following is a brief explanation of the architecture you see at a Mayan ruin.

INFLUENCES

Mayan architecture, even the great temples, may echo the design of the typical thatch hut ordinary Maya used for thousands of years. The rectangular huts had short walls made of a limestone mud and were topped by a steeply tilted two-sided thatch roof. Caves—ever-important Mayan ceremonial sites—were also influential. Many aboveground Mayan temples and other monumental structures have cavelike chambers, and the layout of Mayan cities probably reflected the Mayan cosmology, in which caves played a critical role.

BUILDING MATERIALS

With few exceptions, the large buildings in Mayan cities were constructed mostly from limestone, which was widely available in Belize and the Mexican Yucatán. Quarries were often established close to a building site so that workers didn't have to haul stone long distances. The Maya used limestone for mortar, stucco, and plaster. Limestone was crushed and burned in wood-fired kilns to make lime. A cement-like mortar was made by combining one part lime with one part of a white soil called *sahcab,* and then adding water.

The Maya also used wood, which was plentiful in Mesoamerica. In fact, some of the early temples were probably constructed of wood poles and thatch, much like the small houses of the Maya; unfortunately, these buildings are now lost.

TOOLS

The Maya were behind the curve with their tool technology. They didn't have iron tools, pulleys to move heavy weights, or wheels to build carts. They didn't have horses or other large animals to help them move materials. Instead, they used large numbers of laborers to tote and haul stones, mortar, and other building materials.

Obsidian, jade, flint, and other hard rocks were used to make axes, knives, and saws. The Maya had mason's kits to cut and finish limestone, and they had the equivalent of a plumb bob and other tools to align and level stones. The Maya were skilled stoneworkers, although the degree of finish varied from city to city.

CITY LAYOUT

In most Mayan cities large plazas were surrounded by temples and large pyramids, probably used for religious ceremonies and other important public events. Paved causeways connected the plazas. Away from the city center were sprawls of "suburbs"—smaller stone buildings and traditional thatch huts.

Most cities had ball courts, and although the exact rules are unclear, players used a ball of natural rubber (rubber was discovered by the Olmecs) and scored points by getting the ball through a hoop or goalpost. "Sudden death" had a special meaning—the leader of the losing team was sometimes killed by decapitation.

Adventure Vacations

By Lan Sluder

These days more travelers than ever are seeking trips with an active or adventure component, and tour operators are responding with an ever-increasing selection of exciting itineraries. Belize, with its opportunities for many different kinds of activities, is at the leading edge of the adventure-travel trend.

In Belize you can select something easy, like cave tubing, snorkeling, fishing, horseback riding, hiking, birding, wildlife-spotting, and canoeing. Or you can go for jungle trekking, caving, windsurfing, sea kayaking, or mountain-biking expeditions that require higher degrees of physical endurance and, in some cases, considerable technical skill. You can rough it or opt for comfortable, sometimes even luxurious, accommodations; put adventure at the center of your trip or make it only a sideline; go for a multiweek package or only a day trip. Study multiple itineraries and packages to find the trip that's right for you.

PLANNING YOUR ADVENTURE

Choosing a tour package carefully is always important, but it becomes even more critical when the focus is adventure or sports. When wisely chosen, special-interest vacations lead to distinctive, memorable experiences—just pack your curiosity along with the bug spray.

Belize Tourism Board. For additional information about a specific activity or destination within Belize, contact the Belize Tourism Board, or one of the tour operators listed in each section and in the chart at the end of the chapter. ⊠ *64 Regent St., Belize City* ⊠ *P.O. Box 325, Belize City* ☎ *227/2420* ⊕ *www.travelbelize.org.*

CHOOSING A TRIP

With dozens of options for special-interest and adventure tours in Belize, including do-it-yourself or fully guided package trips, it's helpful to think about certain factors when deciding which company or package will be right for you.

■ **Are you interested in adventure travel on the sea or the mainland or both?** Belize offers two very different adventure environments: the sea and the mainland. The Caribbean, various bays and lagoons, the Barrier Reef that runs 185 mi (303 km) along the eastern coast of the country, and three South Pacific–style atolls are perfect for activities such as fishing, sailing, diving, snorkeling, and windsurfing. Inland, you can rappel hundreds of feet into a limestone sinkhole, explore an underworld labyrinth of caves full of Mayan artifacts, hike the rain forest, ride horses or bikes to remote waterfalls, or tube down underground rivers. Some travelers prefer to concentrate on either water or land activities, but you can combine the two. Just be sure to give yourself enough time.

■**How strenuous a trip do you want?** Adventure vacations commonly are split into "soft" and "hard" adventures. Hard adventures, such as strenuous jungle treks and extended caving trips, usually require excellent physical conditioning and previous experience. Most hiking, biking, canoeing-kayaking, cave tubing, snorkeling, brief cave tours, and similar soft adventures can be enjoyed by persons of all ages who are in good health and are accustomed to a reasonable amount of exercise. A little honesty goes a long way—recognize your own level of physical fitness and discuss it with the tour operator before signing on. Keep in mind that for most of the year in Belize you'll face hot weather and high humidity, conditions that can take a lot out of you, even if you're in good shape.

■**Would you like to pick up new skills?** Belize is a great place to pick up new skills, whether it's how to paddle a kayak, how to rappel down a cliff face, or how to dive. For example, you can take a quick resort diving course to see if you like scuba, or you can do a complete open-water certification course, usually in three to four days. Before committing to any program, do some research to confirm that the people running it are qualified. Check to see if the dive shop or resort is certified by one of the well-known international dive organizations, such as the Professional Association of Diving Instructors (PADI), the largest certification agency in the world, or National Association of Underwater Instructors (NAUI), the second largest. Among the other how-to programs or lessons offered in Belize are kayaking, kayak surfing (riding the sea swells driven through the Barrier Reef by prevailing trade winds), horseback riding, snorkeling, and windsurfing. The sky's the limit, literally: you can go parasailing and, at times, you can even score skydiving lessons.

■**Do you want an "off-the-shelf" tour package or do you prefer to build your own trip?** You can opt to buy a prepackaged adventure or special-interest trip, complete with full-time guides who will do everything from meeting your international flight to cooking your meals, or you can go the more independent route, arranging local guides or tour operators on a daily, or even hourly, basis. Because English is the official language in Belize and most tour operators have email and Web sites, it's easy to put together an adventure package à la carte. Many package tour operators also offer you the ability to combine two or more trips or to create a custom itinerary. It all comes down to whether you're happier doing it yourself or having someone else take care of all the logistics and details.

■**How far off the beaten path do you want to go?** As one of the least densely populated countries in the hemisphere—more than two-fifths of the country is devoted to nature reserves and national parks—Belize offers many off-the-beaten-path experiences. Although many trips described in this chapter might seem to be headed into uncharted territory, tour operators carefully check each detail before an itinerary goes into a brochure. You won't usually be vying with busloads of tourists for photo ops, but you'll probably run into occasional small groups of like-minded travelers. Journeys into truly remote regions, such as Victoria Peak in the Maya Mountains, typically involve camping or the simplest of accommodations, but they reward with more abundant wildlife and locals who are less accustomed to the clicking of cameras.

10

■ **What sort of group is best for you?** At its best, group travel offers curious, like-minded people companions with which to share the day's experiences. Do you enjoy mixing with people from other backgrounds, or would you prefer to travel with people of different ages and backgrounds? Inquire about group size; many companies have a maximum of 10 to 16 members, but 30 or more is not unknown. The larger the group, the more time spent (or wasted) at rest stops, meals, and hotel arrivals and departures.

If groups aren't your thing, most companies will customize a trip for you. In fact, this has become a major part of many tour operators' business. Your itinerary can be as flexible or as rigid as you choose. Such travel offers all the conveniences of a package tour, but the "group" is composed of only you and those you've chosen as travel companions. Responding to a renewed interest in multigenerational travel, many tour operators also offer family trips, with itineraries carefully crafted to appeal both to children and adults.

MONEY MATTERS

■ **How much are you willing to spend?** Tours in Central America can be found at all price points, and Belize has an adventure for every budget. Local operators are usually the best deal. Tours that are run by as many local people and resources as possible are generally cheaper, and also give the greatest monetary benefit to the local economy. These types of tours are not always listed in guidebooks or on the Internet, so often they have to be found in person or by word of mouth. Safety and date specificity can fluctuate. Amenities such as lodging and transportation may be very basic in this category. Some agencies pay attention to the environment, whereas others do not. You really have to do your research on every operator, no matter the cost, to be sure you get what you need. When you find the right match, the payoff in terms of price and quality of experience will be worth it.

On the other end of the spectrum, the large (often international) tour agencies are generally the most expensive; however, they provide the greatest range of itinerary choices and highest quality of services. They use the best transportation, like private tour buses and boats, which rarely break down. First-rate equipment and safe, reliable guides are the norm. Dates and times are set in stone, so you can plan your trip down to the time you step in and out of the airport. Guides are certified, and well paid. When food and lodging is provided it is generally of high quality. If you are a traveler who likes to have every creature comfort provided for, look for tour operators more toward this end of the spectrum.

■ **Are there hidden costs?** Make sure you know what is and is not included in basic trip costs when comparing companies. International airfare is usually extra. Sometimes domestic flights in-country are too. Is trip insurance required, and if so, is it included? Are airport transfers included? Visa fees? Departure taxes? Gratuities? Although some travelers prefer the option of an excursion or free time, many, especially those visiting a destination for the first time, want to see as much as possible.

Paying extra for a number of excursions can significantly increase the total cost of the trip. Many factors affect the price, and the trip that looks cheapest in the brochure could well turn out to be the most expensive. Don't assume that roughing it will save you money, as prices rise when limited access and a lack of essential supplies on-site require costly special arrangements. ■ TIP➜ **Tour prices operated by companies in Belize incur a 12.5% Goods and Services Tax. In some cases, the GST is not included in the tour prices shown.**

CRUISES

CRUISES AROUND THE CAYES AND ATOLLS

Few things in life compare with the experience of being on a sailboat in the Caribbean—the caress of the wind and the salt spray on your face, the sun on your back, and all around the mint green, turquoise, and vodka-clear sea. Companies listed below provide day sails as well as longer, multiple-night trips.

Season: Year-round

Locations: Most day sails and longer crewed trips start in San Pedro, Caye Caulker, or Placencia. The boats visit nearby islands, snorkel spots, and dive destinations. Generally, they stay inside the Barrier Reef.

Cost: Day sails on a crewed boat start at under BZ$100 per person and may include lunch and drinks. Overnight and longer trips can run BZ$300–BZ$2,000 or more per day, depending on the size of the boat, the number in your party, and what's included.

Tour Operators: Belize Sailing Charters; El Gato; Raggamuffin Tours; Winnie Estelle

Raggamuffin Tours does day sails around the northern cayes, as well as a BZ$700-per-person, two-night/three-day island-hopping trip from Caye Caulker to Placencia. The nights are spent camping on Tobacco and Rendezvous cayes (camping equipment provided), with stops at Goff and Southwater cayes. Belize Sailing Charters has day sails on catamarans from Placencia. Several boats, including *El Gato* and *Winnie Estelle,* do day trips out of San Pedro. Sailboat owners tend to be free spirits who may pick up and sail to another port at the drop of a yachting cap, so check locally to see what boats are still sailing.

10

YACHT CHARTERS

A crewed or bareboat sailing charter lets you explore the Belize Barrier Reef and little-visited cayes at your own pace. Most charters are for a week, though shorter charters may be available off-season. Placencia and San Pedro are the two main sailboat charter bases in Belize. You sail inside the reef, protected from ocean swells. A typical day? Wake to a private sunrise over the Caribbean. Have breakfast and a quick swim. Dive or snorkel all morning, snag some lobsters or conchs (if in season), and then drop anchor at a remote island for a barbecue on

CLOSE UP

Ecotourism in Belize

Central America is the original eco-tourism destination; as a result, you'll see the term used liberally everywhere. For lodging it can be used to describe a deluxe private cabaña on a well-tended beach or a hut in the middle of nowhere with pit toilets. It may also point to environmental conservation efforts by parks or tour companies that are conscious of natural resources and their role in not depleting them. Or it may mean just the opposite. Wildlife parks, butterfly farms, rain forests, and Mayan ruins are some of the incredible ecodestinations in this area. And mountain biking, bird-watching, jungle hiking, scuba diving, cave tubing, fishing, and white-water rafting are just some of the eco-activities.

You can do your part to protect the natural heritage of Belize and the Tikal area of Guatemala by being an ecologically sensitive traveler. Where possible, choose green hotels, those that have taken care to protect the environment and that have energy-efficient cooking, lighting, and cooling systems, and that recycle and dispose of waste responsibly. Be culturally sensitive, as both countries have highly diverse populations, each with different cultural attitudes and perspectives. Also, try to do business with companies that hire local people for positions at all levels, and where

possible choose local restaurants and hotels over chain properties. When diving or snorkeling, avoid touching or breaking coral, and don't take part in swim-with-dolphins or swim-with-manatees tours, as most naturalists say these programs disturb the animals. Also, use ecofriendly sunscreen. On caving or hiking trips, take nothing but photographs and leave nothing of yours behind. When visiting Mayan sites, never remove anything, not even a tiny shard of pottery.

For the most part, Belize has reaped the benefits of the growing tourism industry, drawing in much-needed capital to bolster national coffers. The costs of tourism are less obvious, however. Among other effects, indigenous communities are undermined by increasingly tourist-oriented economies—cultivating a plot of land may no longer support a family, but selling knickknacks in the streets just might. Where tourists come, expats often follow, and land, especially beachfront land, is quickly priced out of the reach of locals. There's no easy solution to this dilemma, and balancing the advantages of tourism against its drawbacks is, and will remain, a constant struggle for Belize. The long-term effects are as much dependent on the attitudes and behavior of visitors as they are on prudent national policies.

the beach. In the afternoon, relax with a rum and tonic and enjoy the warm trade winds. Go ashore to a beachside restaurant for a seafood dinner. Then relax on your boat before drifting off to sleep under Central American stars.

Season: Year-round

Locations: Inside the Barrier Reef—either the northern cayes from San Pedro, Ambergris Caye, or the southern cayes from Placencia.

Cost: Bareboat sailing charters range from about BZ$1,000 to BZ$2,500 per night for two to eight people (not all operators offer daily charters), and BZ$7,000–BZ$16,000 or more for weeklong charters for two to eight people, plus provisions. For crews, add about BZ$300 a day for a skipper and BZ$220 a day for a cook, in both cases plus food and gratuity. Marine reserve use fees add about BZ$20 per day per person.

Tour Operators: Belize Sailing Charters; Legacy Adventures; The Moorings; Raggamuffin Tours; Sunsail; TMM Belize

TMM Belize, with a base in San Pedro, has catamarans for weekly bareboat or crewed charter. The Moorings, with a base in Placencia, has a selection of 31- to 54-foot catamarans and monohulls. Sunsail, new to Placencia in 2011, offers cats for charter. About once a month, Belize Sailing Charters offers a nine-night private catamaran sail from Placencia to the Rio Dulce in Guatemala, with a visit by land to Tikal, for around BZ$20,000 for two persons. Legacy Adventures has seven-night/eight-day trips from Cucumber Marina near Belize City on its 65-foot catamaran with a crew of five for BZ$35,200 for up to six persons. Rates include all meals, drinks, fishing, diving, and tours. Raggamuffin Tours runs multiday crewed trips, with camping stops at two islands, from Caye Caulker to Placencia.

LEARNING VACATIONS

ART AND ARCHAEOLOGY

Some travelers want a quick look at a country's major sights, while others prefer to immerse themselves in the culture. In Belize this means participating in a "dig" at a Mayan archaeological site, usually under the direction of a university archaeological team. Other tours don't get involved with archeological digs but focus on the history of the Mayan civilization.

Season: Sessions run only a few weeks of the year, usually in spring or summer.

Locations: Archaeological digs that accept volunteer workers are mostly in Orange Walk District.

Cost: Archaeological programs start at around BZ$1,440 per person for a one-week volunteer session, and BZ$2,240 to BZ$3,500 for a two-week session. Some programs offer academic college credit. Prices don't include transportation to Belize or incidental personal expenses.

Tour Operators: Elderhostel; Maya Research Program; University of Texas Mesoamerican Archaeological Research Laboratory

Elderhostel offers a 14-day program in Belize, Guatemala, and Honduras on the history of the Maya, with insight into modern-day issues affecting their community, starting at around BZ$6,000 per person. It also offers seven-night coral reef and rain-forest programs in Belize. The Maya Research Program, established in 1992, has two-week volunteer programs in the Blue Creek area of Orange Walk District, at BZ$3,500

10

(BZ$3,000 for students). Digs at Nojol Nah and Chum Balam-Nal near Blue Creek began in 2008. The University of Texas Mesoamerican Archaeological Research Laboratory (MARL) accepts volunteers at its field station in the Rio Bravo Conservation area of Orange Walk District, located on Programme for Belize lands. Volunteers (who pay a fee to participate) must commit for at least one week and may stay as long as three weeks. The program usually runs from February to April, with other options in summer, some for academic credit. Volunteers live in a rustic dorm setting and learn the basics of field archaeology through lectures and hands-on experience.

CULTURAL TOURS

A few programs offer the chance to live with the modern-day Maya or Garífuna at a homestay or village guesthouse program. You can also spend a week learning how to process cacao or spend four days learning to cook Belizean—including Mayan—recipes.

Season: Year-round

Locations: Homestay and village guesthouse programs are in Toledo District near Punta Gorda. There's also a homestay tour at Indian Church Village in Orange Walk District.

Cost: Village guesthouse programs start at BZ$45 per person per night, including lodging, activities, and meals. Homestays start at around BZ$35 per person per night. The Chocolate Week near Punta Gorda costs BZ$2,730 per person including lodging and meals. Belizean cooking classes cost BZ$150 per person per day.

Tour Operators: Banana Bank Lodge; Beyond Touring; Cotton Tree Lodge; Dems Dats Doin'; Maya Centre Women's Group; Maya Village Homestay Program; Maya Mountain Lodge & Tours; Toledo Ecotourism Association

The Toledo Ecotourism Association (T.E.A.) program allows visitors to participate in the village life of the Maya while maintaining some personal privacy. You stay in small guesthouses in one of nine Mopan and Kek'chi Mayan villages in Toledo District, including San Antonio, San Miguel, and Blue Creek. Barranco, a predominantly Garífuna village, also has a guesthouse. The guesthouses are very simple, with traditional thatch roofs and outdoor latrines. There is no running water or electricity in the guesthouses. You take meals in the homes of villagers and participate in the routines of village life. The program, endorsed by the Belize Tourism Board, is a collective owned by more than 200 members and is designed to promote cultural exchange. The cost is around BZ$84 a day for two, including meals. A separate, somewhat different program, the Maya Village Homestay Program, run privately by Dem Dats Doin' (which also operates an eco-farm and a private tourist information office in Punta Gorda) arranges stays for visitors in homes in Aguacate and San Jose villages in Toledo. A related homestay program in Nah Luum Cah Mopan village is run by German Sho. Again, the accommodations are extremely simple—you may share a room with the family in a small thatch building with dirt floor. Two people pay a total of BZ$82 a day, including lodging and meals, plus a one-time BZ$20 registration fee. Homestays at Maya Center at the entrance to the Cockscomb Wildlife Sanctuary can be arranged through the Maya Center Women's Group, a group of about 50 Mopan women who have banded together to sell handicrafts. Beyond Touring offers some homestay and other cultural programs at Indian Church Village near Lamanai. In Toledo, Cotton Tree Lodge's Chocolate Week program, held on two different weeks in the spring, lets you "work your way through the entire practical process from scratch, starting with the cacao fruit on the tree and ending with the chocolate in your mouth." Banana Bank Lodge, set on a 4,000-acre ranch near Belmopan, has occasional "agricultural tours" that introduce visiting farmers or others interested in agriculture to Mennonite and other farm operations in Belize. Maya Mountain Lodge & Tours has a two-day BZ$150 cooking class that teaches you to prepare Mayan and Belizean recipes, and Thai dishes, too.

ECO-ORIENTED VOLUNTEER PROGRAMS

If you have more time than money, and want to help Belizeans and Belize, you may want to look into eco-oriented volunteer programs.

Season: Year-round

Locations: Throughout Belize

Cost: From BZ$770 a month, including lodging and some meals, but not including transportation to Belize, mandatory health insurance, some food, and incidental personal expenses.

Tour Operators: Belize Audubon Society; Cornerstone Foundation; Green Reef Belize Coral Caye Conservation NGO; Monkey Bay Wildlife Sanctuary

With the Belize Audubon Society (BAS), you can apply for volunteer jobs at its marine or mainland parks or at its office in Belize City. People with education, community development, and conservation experience and skills make especially good candidates. The BAS is Belize's premier conservation organization and manages or co-manages nine national parks and monuments. Volunteers usually must commit for a minimum of three months (one month at marine areas) and must pay for their own accommodations and food. BAS also has internships, typically arranged through partnerships with foreign universities. The nonprofit Cornerstone Foundation, based in San Ignacio, Cayo, provides volunteer opportunities in community development, ecology, health care, and other areas. Volunteers, who live in communal lodging, can work for periods of from one week to three months. Cornerstone charges BZ$2,310 per person for a three-month program, and that fee includes lodging but not food (except for lunches five days a week), transportation, or personal expenses. Cornerstone's one-week visitor programs, with volunteers paying BZ$398 a week, involve volunteers in community work such as painting a school or beautifying a park. Green Reef on Ambergris Caye is a nonprofit dedicated to the sustainable use of Belize's marine resources. It occasionally accepts volunteers, who must provide their own lodging, food, and transportation expenses. The NGO also has week-long study abroad programs for middle and high school students at Bacalar Chico reserve. Monkey Bay, a private environmental education center, accepts volunteers for a minimum of one week (a month's advance notice is required); a BZ$300 per week charge covers meals and accommodations. Volunteers work about 30 hours a week on outdoor projects such as maintaining organic gardens. Monkey Bay also has internship and homestay programs. ⇨ *See also the sidebar on volunteering in Belize on page 264.*

THE OUTDOORS

BIRD-WATCHING TOURS

When selecting a bird-watching tour, ask questions. What species might be seen? What are the guide's qualifications? Does the operator work to protect natural habitats? How large are the birding groups? What equipment is used? (In addition to binoculars and a birding guidebook, this should include a high-powered telescope, a recorder to record and play back bird calls, and a spotlight for night viewing.)

Season: Year-round, though more common from December to March, when birds from the north winter in Belize and there's less rain.

Locations: Cayo, Orange Walk, Stann Creek, and Toledo Districts

Cost: From BZ$1,600 per person for a six-day/five-night birding trip, including guides, lodging, and some meals. On an à la carte basis, short birding hikes with a local guide cost from BZ$30 per person, though at some jungle lodges such as Chaa Creek local birding hikes are free.

Tour Operators: Belize Birding Tours; Chan Chich Lodge; Hidden Valley Inn; The Lodge at Chaa Creek; Nature Treks; Paradise Expeditions; Victor Emanuel Nature Tours; Wildside Nature Tours

Nearly 600 species of birds have been spotted in Belize, and every year five or more additional species are found in the country. Birders flock to Belize to see exciting species such as the jabiru stork, the largest flying bird in the Western Hemisphere; the harpy eagle with its 7-foot wingspan; the beautiful but endangered scarlet macaw; the keel-billed toucan, the national bird of Belize; 21 species of hummingbirds; and endangered or rare species such as the yellow-headed parrot, oscellated turkey, orange-breasted falcon, and chestnut-breasted heron. Birding hot spots in Belize include Crooked Tree Wildlife Sanctuary, the Mountain Pine Ridge, the area around Chan Chich Lodge at Gallon Jug, and the Cockscomb Basin. *Birds of Belize,* by H. Lee Jones and Dana Gardner, is the bible of Belize birding, although some complain that the 484-page, 2.2-pound birding guide is heavy and cumbersome in the field. The operators listed above offer trips to the best birding areas in Belize. Victor Emanuel Nature Tours (VENT) has 2012–2013 tours to Chan Chich, Crooked Tree, Hidden Valley Inn, and Machaca Hill Lodge. Wildside Nature Tours has 11- to 14-day birding trips that visit Crooked Tree, Cockscomb, Cayo, and Tikal, from BZ$5,600 per person, not including airfare. Paradise Expeditions, based in Cayo and connected with Crystal Paradise Lodge, has five- to 11-night birding trips to various parts of Belize, starting at BZ$2,500 per person.

ECOTRIPS

With about two-fifths of Belize dedicated to national parks and reserves, the country is a natural for ecotripping.

Season: Year-round

Locations: Throughout Belize

Cost: From BZ$100 for day trips and BZ$2,000 for backpacker trips

Tour Operators: Belize Audubon Society; Belize Trips; Beyond Touring; Chaa Creek Expeditions; Chan Chich Lodge; Chocolate's Tours; G.A.P. Adventures; Hamansi Eco Tours; Hidden Valley Inn; International Zoological Expeditions; Journeys International; Red Mangrove Eco Adventures; Terra Incognita Ecotour; TIDE Tours; Victor Emanuel Nature Tours

Park rangers and local guides at Cockscomb Basin Wildlife Sanctuary, managed by the Belize Audubon Society, provide guided nature tours of Cockscomb and can also arrange multiday treks to Victoria Peak, one of the highest mountains in the country. Hamanasi and other resorts in Hopkins and Placencia run day tours to Cockscomb. On Caye Caulker, Lionel "Chocolate" Heredia who with his wife helped make the Swallow Caye Wildlife Sanctuary a reality, runs ecologically conscious manatee-watching tours. Red Mangrove Eco Adventures also offers manatee and other tours from Caye Caulker. International Zoological Expeditions has bases at Blue Creek in Toledo District and on South Water Caye off Dangriga; from both areas it runs educational and nature programs for students, teachers, and others. Victor Emanuel Nature Tours runs tours, oriented to birding but including wildlife spotting, at Chan Chich Lodge, Hidden Valley Inn, and at Crooked Tree. TIDE organizes nature tours in beautiful Toledo. G.A.P. Adventures' 16- to 59-day trips through Mexico and Central America, starting at around US$1,000 per person offer a mix of Mayan ruins, cultural tours, birding, and beaching, and include time in Belize. Transportation and simple hotels are included, but not meals. The 59-day Mexico & Central America Journey from Mexico City to Panama City includes five days in Belize. Restricted to those between 18 and 39, it costs US$4,299. Journeys International offers eight- and nine-day trips in Belize, and Terra Incognita Ecotours has eight-night tours. At many jungle lodges, including, notably, Chan Chich, Chaa Creek, duPlooy's, Blancaneaux, Lamanai Outpost, Lodge at Big Falls, Caves Branch, and Pook's Hill (⇨ *see individual chapters for details on these lodges)*, you can hire a local guide to take you on a guided nature walk or a longer wildlife-spotting trip.

10

LE CAMPING AND LODGES

Belize has a few developed campgrounds, and it does offer primitive camping on some cayes and at some national parks on the mainland. Several hotels and lodges also offer a camping option. Because there are dozens of jungle lodges in Belize, most are not covered in this section. ⇨ *See individual chapters for information on lodges.*

Season: Year-round

Locations: Throughout Belize

Cost: Camping from BZ$10 per person per night

Tour Operators: Belize Audubon Society; Caves Branch Adventure Co. & Jungle Lodge; Glovers Atoll Resort; IBTM (Bruno Kuppinger); Inglewood Camping Grounds; Island Expeditions; Macal River Jungle Camp at Chaa Creek; Seakunga Adventures; Slickrock Adventures; Toadal Adventure

Caves Branch Adventure Co. & Jungle Lodge offers bunkhouse camping at its lodge off the Hummingbird Highway and as a part of its many overnight jungle treks. For a more upscale camping experience, Chaa Creek has small casitas on raised platforms at its Macal River Jungle Camp, near its main lodge in the Cayo. Rates are BZ$110 per person including tent casita and breakfast and dinner, plus 19% hotel tax and service, and provides access to Chaa Creek's facilities. Several small hotels and lodges, including the Trek Stop and Clarissa Falls in Cayo and Jungle by the Sea and Tipple Tree Beya Inn, both in Hopkins, allow camping on their property for a small fee. Another camping option in the Cayo is Inglewood Camping RV Park, which offers tent camping for BZ$20 for two and even has RV hookups with water and Wi-Fi for BZ$30 a night plus 9% tax plus electricity. Seakunga Adventures specializes in kayaking and camping trips, with base camps in the Sapodilla Cayes, Glover's Atoll, and elsewhere. Both Slickrock Adventures and Island Expeditions offer camping on the cayes and inland as part of their kayaking and other adventure trips. Slickrock has a one-week adventure package at its base at Glover's Reef, with sea kayaking, kayak surfing, windsurfing, diving, fishing, and more for BZ$4,150 per person. David Vernon's Toadal Adventure in Placencia offers excellent sea and river kayak trips. The budget-level Glover's Atoll Resort provides primitive camping facilities at its beautiful island, Northeast Caye, on Glover's Atoll for BZ$198 a week per person. Basic tent-camping facilities are available at several national parks and reserves, including Cockscomb and Half Moon Caye, both of which are managed by the Belize Audubon Society. Most of the remote islands off the Belize coast are now privately owned, and camping is allowed only with permission of the owner or caretaker. Bruno Kuppinger at IBTM/Sun Creek Lodge near Punta Gorda runs extreme camping and trekking trips, including the weeklong Maya Divide trip and expeditions to Doyle's Delight, the highest peak in Belize. Note that in most areas of Belize budget hotels are available for only a little more than the cost of camping—you may find that the extra comfort and security of a hotel, plus not having to lug camping gear around the country, outweigh the small savings of roughing it.

PHOTO SAFARIS

A photo safari can sharpen your photography skills while letting you visit some of the most scenic spots in Belize.

Season: Year-round

Locations: Cayo District, Guatemala

Cost: From around BZ$6,000 per person

Tour Operators: Nature Photography Adventure

Nature Photography Adventure runs a "Secrets of the Maya" weeklong photo safari to Belize and Tikal. The company also has a "Wild Bunch" photo-safari trip to Belize and Guatemala, with an emphasis on remote caves. You have to be physically fit to join this trip.

SPORTS

BICYCLING

Despite heat, humidity, bad drivers, and rough roads, cycling is a big sport in Belize, and you often see local cyclists risking life and limb to train on the Western or Northern highways. Mountain biking, however, is only beginning to take hold in Belize, mostly in the Mountain Pine Ridge. Some jungle lodges offer guests mountain bikes.

Season: Year-round

Locations: Mountain Pine Ridge for mountain biking

Cost: From BZ$150 per person for a full-day mountain-biking expedition; some hotels and lodges rent bikes from BZ$10 to BZ$20 a day, or provide them free for guests.

Tour Operators: Ceiba International; Green Dragon Adventure Travel; Hidden Valley Inn; The Lodge at Chaa Creek; Tropical Expeditions Belize

Ceiba International offers six-day mountain-biking trips in the Mountain Pine Ridge and elsewhere in Cayo District, with stays at upscale lodges for around BZ$4,000 per person. Mountain biking is especially good on the 90 mi (150 km) of private hiking and mountain biking trails at Hidden Valley Inn in the Mountain Pine Ridge. The Lodge at Chaa Creek also offers mountain biking. Tropical Expeditions has a nine-day/eight-night "Ride & Explore" trip that begins in Placencia at Lobster Fest in June and ends in Caye Caulker. Green Dragon Adventure Travel has several short bike tours in the Cayo District.

CANOEING AND KAYAKING

Belize has some of the best sea kayaking in Central America. Thanks to the Barrier Reef, a literal barrier to big waves and swells, the sea inside the reef is usually much calmer than the open ocean. Belize also has good kayaking and canoeing on inland rivers and lagoons.

Season: Year-round

10

Locations: Sea kayaking around Ambergris Caye, Caye Caulker, and elsewhere along the coast inside the Barrier Reef; canoeing and kayaking on the Macal, Mopan, Sibun, Swasey, Hondo, New, Belize, and other rivers, and on the Progresso, Placencia, Northern, Southern, New, and other lagoons.

Cost: Day kayaking and canoe trips from BZ$150 a person; kayaking tours from BZ$1,600 per person for four days, BZ$2,800 per person for seven days. Many beach resorts provide kayaks to guests at no charge.

Tour Operators: Belize Trips; Caves Branch Adventure Co.; G.A.P. Adventures; International Zoological Expeditions; Island Expeditions; Saddle Caye South; Seakunga; Slick Rock Adventures; Toadal Adventure

There are two types of kayaking trips: base kayaking and expedition kayaking. On a base kayaking trip you have a home base—usually a caye—from which you take day trips (or longer). On an expedition-style trip you travel from island to island or up mainland rivers. Typically, base kayaking is easier, but expedition kayaking is more adventurous.

Toadal Adventures, based in Placencia, provides top-notch sea and river expedition kayak trips that usually last for four to six days in southern Belize; it can customize trips to your specific schedule and interests. Island Expeditions and Slick Rock Adventures both do complete expedition packages, several of which combine sea and river kayaking and base and expedition aspects. They both focus on Glover's Atoll and land activities in central and southern Belize. Seakunga also runs both base camp and expedition-style kayaking trips at Glover's Atoll as well as the Sapodilla Cayes in southern Belize, and other locales. International Zoological Expeditions has eight- to 10-day trips, usually with an educational component such as ethnobotanical walks or mapping an island. IZE's trips combine time inland at Blue Creek in Toledo and at South Water Caye. Saddle Caye South in Placencia offers self-guided kayak trips—in effect, kayak and camping gear rentals—and five-day island-hopping expeditions with guide, kayaks, camping gear, meals, and support boat. G.A.P. Adventures has a weeklong island-hopping kayak trip, starting and ending in Placencia, for around BZ$2,800 per person. You paddle for two to four hours a day, with stops at Pumpkin Caye, the Silk Cayes, and the Sapodilla Cayes. Most of the trips by all operators provide opportunities for snorkeling, fishing, hiking, and caving as well as kayaking. Several Belize-based operators, including Caves Branch Adventure Co., and a number of the other jungle lodges, run day and overnight kayaking trips in the Cayo District. In addition, rental kayaks are available in Placencia, Hopkins, San Pedro, and Caye Caulker for do-it-yourselfers. Some hotels also provide kayaks for their guests.

CAVE TUBING

An activity you'll find in few places outside Belize is cave tubing. You drift down a river, usually the Caves Branch River in the Cayo District, in a large rubber inner tube. At certain points the river goes underground, and you float through eerie underground cave systems, some with Mayan artifacts still in place. The only light is from headlamps.

Season: Year-round, though seasonal rains June through November can sometimes raise water levels too high for tubing, and during dry season (February–May) some river levels may occasionally become too low.

Locations: Rivers in Cayo District, primarily the Caves Branch River and Barton Creek

Cost: From BZ$100 per person for a half-day trip

Tour Operators: Action Belize; Belize Trips; Caves Branch Adventure Co. & Jungle Lodge; Cave-Tubing in Belize; Cayo Adventure Tours; Chaa Creek Expeditions; Discovery Expeditions; Ecological Tours and Services; Green Dragon Adventure Travel; Jaguar Paw/Chukka Caribbean; Windy Hill Resort & Tour Co.

In the last decade since Jaguar Paw Lodge (now no longer operating as a lodge) and Caves Branch Adventure Co. & Jungle Lodge first introduced it, cave tubing has become one of the most popular soft-adventure activities in Belize. It's the number one mainland shore excursion of cruise-ship passengers, and on days when several large ships are docked in Belize City you should expect inner-tube traffic jams. Several Belize City–based tour operators, including Action Belize, Ecological Tours, and Discovery Expeditions, cater to the cruise-ship day-trippers with cave tubing trips for around BZ$120 per person. Cave tubing and zip-line combo tours are around BZ$200 per person. In addition, Cayo-based tour operators, including Chaa Creek Expeditions, Caves Branch Adventure Co., Jaguar Paw/Chukka Caribbean, Cayo Adventure Tours, Green Dragon Adventure Travel (aka Belize Jungle Dome Tours), and Windy Hill Resort & Tour Co., run cave-tubing day trips. Belize Trips can arrange custom cave-tubing trips for individuals or groups. The drill with most of these operations is the same. You pile into a van or bus for a short drive to a parking area near the Caves Branch River off the Western Highway, next door to Jaguar Paw, hike a short distance, and then pop into the Caves Branch with your inner tube for a float on the river and through several caves. Depending on where you're launched into the river, you float through anywhere from three to seven caves, some of which have ancient pottery shards and other artifacts of the Maya. Most of the caverns are very dark, and guides normally provide headlamps. The activity level is usually light, and even some people who can't swim or who are in their 70s and 80s go cave tubing. Caves Branch Adventure Co. & Jungle Lodge offers longer and more active (and more expensive) cave-tubing trips. In the "River of Caves" cave-tubing trip, you float underground for a total of nearly 7 mi (11 km). San Ignacio–based tour operators, including Cayo Adventure Tours, also offer tubing at Barton Creek Cave.

10

CAVING

Belize has some of the most extensive cave systems in Central America. One cave system in the Chiquibul Wilderness is 35 mi (56 km) long. Only serious, highly trained cavers need consider the remote, difficult caves of Belize, but more casual adventurers can find fairly easy day trips to caves like Actun Tunichil Muknal, frequently described by visitors as a highlight of their Belize vacation.

Season: Year-round

Locations: Cayo and Toledo districts

Cost: Day trips to caves from BZ$70 per person.

Tour Operators: Caves Branch Adventure Co. & Jungle Lodge; PACZ Tours

A small number of tour companies, including PACZ, are permitted to take visitors into Actun Tunichil Muknal (ATM) cave. From a basing area off the Western Highway in the Cayo District, you walk about 45 minutes to the "Cave of the Stone Sepulchre" in Roaring Creek Valley. Entering the cave requires a short swim. Once you make your way inside the cave formation, your headlamp reveals hundreds of Mayan artifacts—thought to have been used in rituals to *Chac,* the Rain God of the Maya—as well as human remains. Guests at Pook's Hill Lodge, the lodge closest to ATM, can hike with a guide from the lodge to the cave. Most visitors find visiting ATM an amazing experience. There are several other easy-to-moderate caves in the Cayo that can be visited on day tours, including Che Chem Ha, Rio Frio, and Barton Creek. Caves Branch Adventure Co. & Jungle Lodge, widely considered the premier caving guide operation in the country, conducts day and overnight caving trips. Some of the trips are rated moderate and others difficult.

FISHING

Drop your hook in Belize and you're almost guaranteed to catch something. Lagoons and shallow flats are ideal for bonefish. The Barrier Reef supports grouper, snapper, and jacks. In the blue water beyond the reef, anglers will find tuna, sailfish, and pompano. Some of the world's best permit fisheries are off the coast of southern Belize. The estuaries and river mouths are home to tarpon and snook. It's even possible to achieve a "grand slam" in Belize—that is, catch tarpon, permit, and bonefish all in one day on a catch-and-release basis. Fishing licenses are now required for saltwater fishing in Belize (except for shore and pier fishing)—your hotel or fishing guide will arrange for the license, or you can get it online from the Coastal Zone Management Authority and Institute (⊕ *www.coastalzonebelize.org*). Marine reserves, those that permit fishing, also charge a small daily use fee.

Season: Year-round, with best fishing for tarpon May–September; permit, February–November; snook, November–March; bonefish, April–November; sailfish, January–June.

Locations: All coastal areas and the cayes

Cost: Local fishing guides with boats charge from BZ$400 to BZ$600 per day for reef and flats fishing, more for deep-sea angling; complete fishing packages including meals, accommodations, and guides for seven days, from BZ$3,500-$4,000 per person (not including airfare).

Tour Operators: Belize River Lodge; Destinations Belize; El Pescador; Fishing International; Glover's Atoll Resort; International Zoological Expeditions; Isla Marisol Resort; Machaca Hill Rainforest Canopy Lodge; Rod & Reel Adventures; Turneffe Flats Lodge; Turneffe Island Lodge; Whipray Caye Lodge

The best-known fishing lodges in Belize aren't skunky fishing camps but high-end resorts catering to affluent anglers who, after a hard day on the water, expect ice-cold cocktails, equally icy air-conditioning, and Sealy Posturepedic mattresses. El Pescador on North Ambergris Caye, Machaca Hill Canopy Lodge (formerly El Pescador PG) in Punta Gorda, two lodges on Turneffe Atoll (Turneffe Flats and Turneffe Island Lodge), and several beach resorts in Placencia and Hopkins offer fishing with a touch of luxury—everything from guides to cold drinks included. Fishing travel companies like Fishing International and Rod & Reel Adventures typically book with fishing lodges.

Belize River Lodge, the oldest fishing lodge in Belize (it's been in continuous operation since 1960) operates live-aboard boats including a 58-foot Hatteras yacht. It also runs fishing skiffs from its lodge on the Belize River.

If you want a less expensive fishing vacation, you can make your own arrangements for lodging and meals and hire your own local fishing guides in San Pedro, Placencia, Hopkins, Punta Gorda, and elsewhere. Mary Toy's Destinations Belize in Placencia is a compromise between a total package and doing it all yourself. She can help you arrange moderate accommodations, some meals, and guides for light-tackle or fly-fishing day trips (or for longer periods). She also puts together moderately priced packages for fishing in Placencia and elsewhere in southern Belize.

LIVE-ABOARDS

If you're serious about diving and want to hit the best dive spots in Belize, morning, noon, and night, with as many as six dives a day, live-aboard dive boats are your best bet.

Season: Year-round

Locations: Live-aboards concentrate on dives around Belize's three atolls—Lighthouse, Turneffe, and Glover's—with most dives at Lighthouse and Turneffe. The boats depart from Belize City.

Cost: Expect to pay about BZ$3,000–BZ$5,600 for six days of diving. That price includes all dives, meals, airport transfers, and stateroom accommodations on the dive boat. It does not include airfare to Belize, tips, alcoholic beverages, equipment rentals, Nitrox, marine park fees, and incidentals.

Tour Operators: Belize Aggressor; Dancer Fleet

The Dancer Fleet's 138-foot *Sun Dancer II,* which can hold up to 20 passengers in 10 staterooms, departs from Belize City on Saturday afternoon and moors at either Turneffe or Lighthouse Atoll. For the next six days divers explore these two atolls, getting as many as five dives a day. The ship moves two or three times a day. The itinerary of the 18-passenger *Belize Aggressor* is similar to that of the *Sun Dancer II,* with passengers embarking in Belize City on a Saturday and spending time until the next Friday at Turneffe and Lighthouse atolls, with as many as five or six dives each day.

Adventures to Get Your Heart Rate Up

Most adventure tours and trips in Belize can be handled by anyone used to a reasonable amount of activity. Even couch potatoes can hack it. But a few are more physically challenging and require a higher level of fitness or skill. Here are three adventures that will send your heart rate soaring:

Climb Victoria Peak. This may be the toughest trek in Belize. You need a guide, and the trip takes a total of four to five days up and back. Though Victoria Peak is only 3,675 feet high, and the top of the mountain is just 17 mi (28 km) from the visitor center at Cockscomb Basin Wildlife Sanctuary, the going—through tropical jungle—is rough, hot, and humid, with slopes of up to 60 degrees. Another peak experience is to climb to the top of Doyle's Delight, a few feet higher than Victoria Peak and now considered the highest mountaintop in Belize.

Dive the Blue Hole. The bottom of Blue Hole, a large underwater sinkhole at Lighthouse Atoll, is more than 400 feet down. Although not an inherently difficult dive, it's deep, and it's best done only by experienced divers. Hammerhead, tiger, and other sharks prowl the hole. Be forewarned: over the years, at least three divers have died making the dive. If you don't dive, you can snorkel the Blue Hole; most dive boats also welcome snorkelers.

Rappel the Black Hole. Caves Branch Adventure Co. runs a two-day jungle expedition that starts with a rappel more than 200 feet into the Actun Loch Tunich sinkhole, followed by a trip through more than 10 mi (6 km) of underground river. For a longer and even more intense jungle trek, consider Caves Branch's seven-day "Lost World Expedition."

SCUBA DIVING AND SNORKELING

Belize has the largest living coral reef system in the Western and Northern hemispheres, and three of the only four coral atolls outside the South Pacific. Here you can see more than 300 species of tropical fish, 100 types of coral, and many large sea creatures, including hammerheads, whale sharks, manatees, and manta rays. It's no wonder that the scuba diving and snorkeling in Belize are considered among the best in the world. Belize has more than 50 dive shops and snorkel tour operators, so only a representative sample of the top operators is included here. (⇨ *See individual chapters for more information on dive and snorkel shops and on specific dive destinations.*)

Season: Year-round

Locations: Serious divers focus on the three atolls—Lighthouse, Turneffe, and Glover's—which have dedicated dive lodges and are the destinations of most live-aboard dive boats. Good recreational diving options abound all around the northern cayes and off the southern coast. For snorkeling, Hol Chan Marine Reserve near Ambergris Caye is the most popular spot, and at Shark-Ray Alley, now a part of Hol Chan, you can swim with stingrays and nurse sharks. There's also excellent snorkeling along most of the Barrier Reef, patch reefs, and at the atolls.

Cost: Snorkel trips from BZ$50 per person; two-tank dives from BZ$100; one-week dive packages, including hotel, meals, and dives, from BZ$2,500 per person.

Tour Operators: Amigos del Mar; Avadon Divers; Belize Aggressor; Belize Dive Connection; Belize Diving Services; Belize Trips; Carlos Tours; Chocolate's Tours; Destinations Belize; Ecologic Divers, Glover's Atoll Resort; Frenchie's Dive Shop; Hamanasi Eco Tours; Isla Marisol; Lil' Alphonse Tours; Patojo's Scuba Center; Dancer Fleet; Raggamuffin Tours; Red Mangrove Eco Adventures; Reef Conservation International; SEAduced; Sea Horse Dive Shop; SEArious Adventures; Sea Sports Belize; Tsunami Adventures; Turneffe Flats; Turneffe Island Lodge

The largest concentration of dive shops and dive-trip operators (and also snorkel-boat operators) is on Ambergris Caye. It's a short boat ride to the spur-and-groove formations along the Barrier Reef and to Hol Chan Marine Reserve. Several San Pedro operators with speedboats, including Amigos del Mar, Ecologic Divers, and Patojo's, can take you to the Blue Hole, the largest ocean sinkhole in the world, with depths of more than 400 feet. Lil' Alphonse Tours specializes only in snorkeling and does a terrific job at it. The cleverly named SEAduced and SEArious Adventures both do snorkel trips around Ambergris Caye and to Caye Caulker. Frenchie's and Belize Diving Services on Caye Caulker take divers to the same sites as the dive shops on Ambergris Caye, and operators such as Carlos Tours, Chocolate's Tours, Tsunami Adventures, and Raggamuffin offer local trips. Almost a dozen dive lodges and hotels are on Belize's atolls, including Turneffe Flats, Turneffe Island Lodge, Thatch Caye, Isla Marisol, Glover's Atoll Resort, and others. Live-aboard dive boats also dive the atolls—the *Belize Aggressor* and Dancer Fleet's *Sun Dancer II* live-aboards leave from and return to Belize City.

Almost a dozen dive lodges and hotels are on Belize's atolls, and live-aboard dive boats also cluster here. Off the southern coast—served by Hamanasi Eco Tours, Sea Horse Dive Shop, Avadon Divers, Reef Conservation International, and other operators—you can dive less-visited sites such as the Silk Cayes, home to large numbers of whale sharks in spring, and Belize's largest marine park, South Water Caye Marine Reserve.

Belize City–based dive operations generally concentrate on the cruise market. These include Belize Dive Connection and Sea Sports Belize.

10

HORSEBACK RIDING

Time to tack up and hit the trail! You can ride to waterfalls in the Mountain Pine Ridge or to Mayan ruins and caves in the Cayo.

Season: Year-round

Locations: Cayo District

Cost: From BZ$1,330 per person for horseback-riding packages for four days/three nights, including lodging; from BZ$60 for a half-day ride.

Tour Operators: Banana Bank Lodge; Equitours; Mountain Equestrian Trails

Two well-established Belize outfits offer horseback-riding tours. At Banana Bank Lodge you can ride one of about 100 horses (predominantly quarter horses) on a 4,000-acre ranch that hugs the banks of the Belize River. At Mountain Equestrian Trails you can take day rides or multi-night horseback trips into the Mountain Pine Ridge and the high bush of the Cayo District. U.S.-based Equitours offers riding tour packages in the Cayo, with extensions to Tikal. The Lodge at Chaa Creek, Cahal Pech Village, Caves Branch Adventure Co. & Jungle Lodge, Pook's Hill Lodge, and duPlooy's Lodge, all in the Cayo, and Maruba Spa off the Old Northern Highway and Cotton Tree Lodge in Toledo also arrange horseback-riding trips.

MULTISPORT

Multisport simply means that you can take part in a series of different activities—hiking, kayaking, cave tubing, birding, swimming, snorkeling. With so many land and water activities packed into one small country, Belize is ideal for multisporting, and many Belize-based and international tour operators provide trips that exercise nearly every muscle in your body.

Season: Year-round

Locations: Throughout Belize

Cost: Day tours from BZ$100 per person; package tours from BZ$900 per person for four days.

Tour Operators: Adventure Center; Adventure Life; Beyond Touring; Caves Branch Adventure Co.; Cayo Adventure Tours; Chaa Creek Expeditions; Destinations Belize; G.A.P. Adventures; Hamanasi Eco Tours; International Zoological Expeditions; Island Expeditions; Nature Treks; PACZ Tours; Seakunga Adventures; Slick Rock Adventures; TIDE; Toadal Adventure Belize; Wilderness Travel; Windy Hill Tour Co.

Many Belize adventure trips include a bunch of different activities. For example, the eight-day Land of Belize trip offered by Adventure Center (US$1,100 per person not including meals) starts with a day in Belize City, then moves on to caving, biking, and hiking in the Cayo, followed by a visit to Tikal, and ending with snorkeling or diving off Caye Caulker. Adventure Life offers a similar trip, at US$1,400 per person, with hiking, paddling, snorkeling, and visits to Mayan sites. Island Expeditions' 10-night Ultimate Adventure trip (US$2,469 per person) begins with sea kayaking, diving, snorkeling, and boardsailing at Glover's Atoll and on the southern part of the Belize Barrier Reef, then switches to caving, hiking, and canoeing/rafting on the mainland. Seakunga's 11- or 12-night multisport tour, Caves to Cayes (from US$1,979), combines sea kayaking, mountain biking, and inflatable-river-rafting activities. The other tour companies listed above offer a similar variety of activities in many areas of Belize.

ZIP-LINING

Zip lines allow you to experience the jungle at canopy level, suspended in a harness 50 to 80 feet in the air, zooming from one platform in the trees to another.

Season: Year-round

Locations: Cayo District

Cost: From BZ$120 per person (from BZ$190 including transportation from Belize City)

Tour Operators: Calico Jack; Jaguar Paw/Chukka Caribbean

Jaguar Paw, which opened the first zip line in Belize, is now operated as part of the Chukka Caribbean tour company. The Chukka Canopy Tour of the Lost World Cave zip line has five traverses above a cave opening. Calico Jack's Ultimo Explorer two-hour zip-line tour involves nine runs, 15 platforms, and 2,700 feet of cable. Many tour operators in Belize offer visits to one of these zip lines. There is also a zip line near the entrance of Tikal park.

10

Tour Operators

Below is contact information for all tour operators mentioned in this chapter, including Belize-based operators or those based in the United States or elsewhere. The list is selective—we've chosen established firms that offer a good selection of itineraries.

Action Belize ⊠ *Mile 2, Northern Hwy., Action Belize Marina, Belize City* ☎ *223/2987, 888/383–6319* ⊕ *www.actionbelize.com.*

Adventure Center ⊠ *1311 63rd St., #200, Emeryville, California, USA* ☎ *510/654–1879, 800/228–8747* ⊕ *www.adventurecenter.com.*

Adventure Life ⊠ *1655 S. 3rd. St. W, Suite 1, Missoula, Montana, USA* ☎ *406/541–2677, 800/344–6118* ⊕ *www.adventure-life.com.*

Amigos del Mar ⊠ *San Pedro* ☎ *226/2706, 800/345–9786* ⊕ *www.amigosdive.com.*

Avadon Divers ⊠ *Placencia Rd., Placencia* ☎ *503/3377, 888/509–5617 in U.S.* ⊕ *www.avadondiversbelize.com.*

Banana Bank Lodge ⊠ *P.O. Box 48, Belmopan City* ☎ *832/2020* ⊕ *www.bananabank.com.*

Belize Aggressor ⊠ *209 Hudson Trace, Augusta, Georgia, USA* ☎ *706/993–2531, 800/348–2628 in U.S. or Canada* ⊕ *www.aggressor.com.*

Belize Audubon Society ⊠ *12 Fort St., Belize City* ☎ *223/5004* ⊕ *www.belizeaudubon.org.*

Belize Birding Tours ☎ *877/571–0653 in U.S.* ⊕ *www.belizebirdingtours.com.*

Belize Diving Services ⊠ *Chapoose St., near soccer field, Caye Caulker* ☎ *226/0143* ⊕ *www.belizedivingservices.net.*

Belize Dive Connection ⊠ *P.O. Box 1818, Belize City* ☎ *223/5086, 888/223–5403* ⊕ *www.belizediving.com.*

Belize River Lodge ⊠ *Riverview, Ladyville* ☎ *225/2002, 888/275–4843* ⊕ *www.belizeriverlodge.com.*

Belize Sailing Charters ⊠ *Main St., Point Peninsula, Placencia* ☎ *523/3138, 505/717–7301 U.S. number* ⊕ *www.belizesailingcharters.com.*

Belize Trips (Katie Valk) ⊠ *P.O. Box 1108, Belize City* ☎ *610/1923, 561/210–7015 in U.S.* ⊕ *www.belize-trips.com.*

Beyond Touring ⊠ *3036 Lake Shore Dr., Deerfield Beach, Florida, USA* ☎ *954/415–2897* ⊕ *www.beyondtouring.com.*

Calico Jack's ⊠ *7 Mile, Off Mountain Pine Ridge Rd., El Progresso, Cayo* ☎ *820/4078* ⊕ *www.calicojacksvillage.com.*

Carlos Tours ⊠ *Front St. at Calle del Sol, Caye Caulker* ☎ *226/0058.*

Cave-Tubing in Belize ⊠ *Belize City* ☎ *605/1575* ⊕ *www.cave-tubing.com.*

Caves Branch Adventure Co. & Jungle Lodge ⊠ *Mile 41½ Hummingbird Hwy., Belmopan* ☎ *673/3454, 866/357–2698* ⊕ *www.cavesbranch.com.*

Cayo Adventure Tours ⊠ *29 Burns Ave.* ☎ *824/3246* ⊕ *www.cayoadventure.com.*

Ceiba International ⊠ *P.O. Box 2274, Flagstaff, Arizona, USA* ☎ *800/217–1060.*

Chaa Creek Expeditions ⊠ *P.O. Box 53, San Ignacio* ☎ *824/2037, 877/709–8708 in U.S* ⊕ *www.chaacreek.com.*

CLOSE UP

Chocolate's Tours ⊠ *Front St., Caye Caulker* ☏ *226/0151.*

Chan Chich Lodge ⊠ *Gallon Jug* ⊠ *P.O. Box 37, Belize City* ☏ *223/4419, 800/343–8009 in U.S.* ⊕ *www.chanchich.com.*

Cornerstone Foundation ⊠ *43 Church St., San Ignacio* ☏ *824/2373* ⊕ *www.cornerstonefoundationbelize. org.*

Cotton Tree Lodge ⊠ *Moho River, San Felipe* ☏ *670/0557, 866/480– 4534 in U.S.* ⊕ *www.cottontreelodge. com.*

Dancer Fleet ⊠ *15291 NW 60 Ave., Suite 201, Miami, Florida, USA* ☏ *305/669–9391, 800/932–6237* ⊕ *www.dancerfleet.com.*

Dems Dats Doin' ⊠ *P.O. Box 73, Punta Gorda* ☏ *722/2470* ⊕ *www.mayavillagehomestay.com.*

Destinations Belize ⊠ *General Delivery, Placencia* ☏ *523/4018* ⊕ *www. destinationsbelize.com.*

Discovery Expeditions ⊠ *5916 Manatee Dr., Buttonwood Bay, Belize City* ☏ *223/0748* ⊕ *www. discoverybelize.com.*

Ecologic Divers ⊠ *Beachfront, San Pedro* ☏ *226/4118, 800/244– 7704 in U.S. and Canada* ⊕ *www. ecologicdivers.com.*

Ecological Tours & Services ⊠ *Tourism Village, Fort St., Belize City* ☏ *223/4874* ⊕ *www.ecotoursbelize. com.*

Elderhostel ⊠ *11 Avenue de Lafayette, Boston, Massachusetts, USA* ☏ *800/454–5768* ⊕ *www.roadscholar. org.*

El Gato ⊠ *San Pedro* ☏ *226/2264* ⊕ *www.ambergriscaye.com/elgato.*

El Pescador ⊠ *P.O. Box 17, San Pedro* ☏ *226/2398, 800/242–2017* ⊕ *www. elpescador.com.*

Equitours ⊠ *P.O. Box 807, Dubois, Wyoming, USA* ☏ *307/455–3363, 800/545–0019* ⊕ *www.ridingtours. com.*

Fishing International ⊠ *5510 Skylane Blvd., Suite 200, Santa Rosa, California, USA* ☏ *707/542– 4242, 800/950–4242* ⊕ *www. fishinginternational.com.*

Frenchie's Dive Shop ⊠ *Beachfront, Front St., Caye Caulker* ☏ *226/0234* ⊕ *www.frenchiesdivingbelize.com.*

G.A.P. Adventures ⊠ *19 Charlotte St., Toronto, Ontario, Canada* ☏ *416/260– 0999, 888/800–4100* ⊕ *www. gapadventures.com.*

German Sho. Maya Village Homestay Program in Nah Luum Cah ⊠ *Nah Luum Cah* ☏ *664/9419* ✉ *quichpan_ luum@yahoo.ca.*

Glovers Atoll Resort ⊠ *P.O. Box 2215, Belize City* ☏ *520/5016* ⊕ *www. glovers.com.bz.*

Green Dragon Adventure Travel ⊠ *Mile 47, Western Hwy., Banana Bank, Belmopan City* ☏ *822/2124* ⊕ *www.greendragonbelize.com.*

Green Reef Belize Coral Reef Conservation NGO ⊠ *100 Coconut Dr., San Pedro* ☏ *226/2833* ⊕ *www. greenreefbelize.org.*

Hamanasi Eco Tours ⊠ *Hamanasi, Sittee River Rd., Hopkins* ☏ *533/7073* ⊕ *www.hamanasi.com.*

10

Tour Operators (continued)

Hidden Valley Inn ✉ *P.O. Box 170, Belmopan City* ☎ *822/3320, 866/443–3364* ⊕ *www.hiddenvalleyinn.com.*

IBTM Tours (Bruno Kuppinger) ✉ *Sun Creek Lodge, Mile 14, Southern Hwy., Toledo* ☎ *604/2124* ⊕ *www.suncreeklodge.de/englisch/home.html.*

Inglewood Camping RV Park ✉ *Mile 68¼, Western Hwy., San Ignacio* ☎ *824/3555* ⊕ *www.inglewoodcampingrvpark.com.*

International Zoological Expeditions (IZE) ✉ *210 Washington St., Sherborn, Massachusetts, USA* ☎ *508/655–1461* ⊕ *www.ize2belize.com.*

Isla Marisol Resort ✉ *P.O. Box 10, Dangriga* ☎ *520/2056, 866/990–9904* ⊕ *www.islamarisolresort.com.*

Island Expeditions ✉ *P.O. Box 69, D'Arcy, British Columbia, Canada* ☎ *604/452–3212, 800/667–1630* ⊕ *www.islandexpeditions.com.*

Jaguar Paw/Chukka Caribbean at Jaguar Paw ✉ *P.O. Box 698, Belize City* ☎ *223/4438, 877/424–8552 in U.S.* ⊕ *www.chukkacaribbean.com.*

Journeys International ✉ *907 Aprill Dr., Suite 3, Ann Arbor, Michigan, USA* ☎ *800/255–8735 in U.S., 734/665–4407* ⊕ *www.journeys.travel.*

Legacy Adventures ✉ *Cucumber Marina, Western Hwy., Belize City* ☎ *670/4354* ⊕ *www.legacycharter.com.*

Lil' Alphonse Tours ✉ *Coconut Dr., San Pedro* ☎ *226/3136.*

The Lodge at Chaa Creek ✉ *Chial Rd., on Macal River, San Ignacio* ☎ *877/709–8708 in U.S., 824/2037* ⊕ *www.chaacreek.com.*

Macal River Jungle Camp at Chaa Creek ✉ *P.O. Box 53* ☎ *824/2037, 877/709–8708 in the U.S.* ⊕ *www.chaacreek.com.*

Machaca Hill Rainforest Canopy Lodge ✉ *P.O. Box 135, Punta Gorda* ☎ *722/0050* ⊕ *www.machacahill.com.*

Maya Center Women's Group ✉ *Southern Hwy., Maya Center* ✉ *P. O. Box 108, Dangriga* ☎ *603/9256.*

Maya Mountain Lodge & Tours ✉ *Cristo Rey Rd., San Ignacio* ☎ *824/2164* ⊕ *www.mayamountain.com.*

Maya Research Program ✉ *1910 E. Southeast Loop 323, Tyler, Texas, USA* ☎ *817/831–9011* ⊕ *www.mayaresearchprogram.org.*

Monkey Bay Wildlife Sanctuary ✉ *Western Hwy., Belmopan* ☎ *820/3032* ⊕ *www.monkeybaybelize.org.*

The Moorings ✉ *Laru Beya Marina, Placencia* ☎ *523/3206, 888/952–8420 in U.S.* ⊕ *www.moorings.com.*

Mountain Equestrian Trails (M.E.T.) ✉ *Mile 8, Mountain Pine Ridge Rd., Cayo* ☎ *669/1124, 800/838–3918* ⊕ *www.metbelize.com.*

Nature Photography Adventure ✉ *P.O. Box 1900, Missouri, USA* ☎ *417/683–6881* ⊕ *www.naturephotography.us.*

Nature Treks ✉ *P.O. Box 542, Massachusetts, USA* ☎ *781/789–8127* ⊕ *www.naturetreks.net.*

PACZ Tours ✉ *30 Burns Ave., San Ignacio* ☎ *824/0536* ⊕ *www.pacztours.net.*

CLOSE UP

Paradise Expeditions ⊠ *P.O. Box 106, San Ignacio* ☎ *670/2473* ⊕ *www.birdinginbelize.com.*

Patojo's Scuba Center ⊠ *Beachfront, North end of town, San Pedro* ☎ *226/2283* ⊕ *www.ambergriscaye.com/tides.*

Raggamuffin Tours ⊠ *Front St., Caye Caulker* ☎ *226/0348* ⊕ *www.raggamuffintours.com.*

Red Mangrove Eco Adventures ⊠ *Caye Caulker* ☎ *607/1440* ⊕ *www.mangrovebelize.com.*

Reef Conservation International ⊠ *Punta Gorda* ☎ *606/0074* ⊕ *www.reefci.com.*

Rod & Reel Adventures ⊠ *32617 Skyhawk Way, Eugene, Oregon, USA* ☎ *541/349–0777, 800/356–6982* ⊕ *www.rodreeladventures.com.*

Saddle Caye South/Kayak Belize ⊠ *Placencia* ☎ *517/626–6680* ✎ *sherry@kayakbelize.com* ⊕ *www.kayakbelize.com.*

SEAduced ⊠ *Tarpon St., Vilma Linda Plaza, San Pedro* ☎ *226/4118.*

SeaHorse Dive Shop ⊠ *Point Placencia, Placencia* ☎ *523/3166, 800/991–1969 Tropic Horizon, U.S. representative* ⊕ *www.belizescuba.com.*

Seakunga Adventures ⊠ *Placencia Rd., 1 mi (2 km) north of airstrip, Placencia* ☎ *523/3644, 800/781–2269* ⊕ *www.seakunga.com.*

SEArious Adventures ⊠ *Beachfront between Tarpon and Black Coral sts., San Pedro* ☎ *226/4202* ⊕ *www.seariousadventures.com.*

Sea Sports Belize ⊠ *83 N. Front St., Belize City* ☎ *223/5505* ⊕ *www.seasportsbelize.com.*

Slickrock Adventures ⊠ *P.O. Box 1400, Moab, Utah, USA* ☎ *435/259–4225, 800/390–5715* ⊕ *www.slickrock.com.*

Sunsail ⊠ *Laru Beya Marina, Placencia* ☎ *523/4057, 888/350–3568 in the U.S..*

Terra Incognita Ecotours ⊠ *4016 West Inman Ave., USA* ☎ *855/326–8687* ⊕ *www.ecotours.com.*

Thatch Caye ⊠ *P.O. Box 146, Dangriga* ☎ *603/2414, 800/435–3145* ⊕ *www.thatchcayebelize.com..*

TIDE ⊠ *14 Front St., Punta Gorda* ☎ *722/2129* ⊕ *www.tidetours.org.*

TMM (Belize) Ltd. ⊠ *Coconut Dr., San Pedro* ☎ *226/3026, 800/633–0155* ⊕ *www.sailtmm.com.*

Toadal Adventure Belize (David Vernon) ⊠ *Pt. Placencia, Placencia* ☎ *523/3207* ⊕ *www.toadaladventure.com.*

Toledo Ecotourism Association (T.E.A.) ⊠ *San Antonio, Toledo* ☎ *722/2531* ✎ *teabelize@yahoo.com.*

10

Tropical Expeditions Belize ⊠ *1149 Coney Dr., Belize City* ☎ *223/6939* ⊕ *www.tropicalexpeditionsbelize.com.*

Tsunami Adventures ⊠ *Front St., Caye Caulker* ☎ *226/0462* ⊕ *www.tsunamiadventures.com.*

Turneffe Flats Lodge ⊠ *P.O. Box 10670, Bozeman, Montana, USA* ☎ *220/4046, 888/512–8812* ⊕ *www.tflats.com.*

Tour Operators (continued)

Turneffe Island Resort ✉ 440 *Louisiana, Suite 900, Houston, Texas, USA* ☎ 713/236–7739 ⊕ *www. turneffelodge.com.*

University of Texas Mesoamerican Archaeological Research Laboratory ✉ *MARL, 1 University Station R7500, Austin, Texas, USA* ☎ 512/232–7049 ⊕ *uts.cc.utexas.edu/~marl.*

Victor Emanuel Nature Tours ✉ *2525 Wallingwood Rd., Suite 1003, Austin, Texas, USA* ☎ 512/328–5221, 800/328–8368 ⊕ *www.ventbird.com.*

Whipray Caye Lodge ✉ *General Delivery, Placencia* ☎ 610/1068.

Wilderness Travel ✉ *1102 9th St., Berkeley, California, USA* ☎ 510/558–2488, 800/368–2794 ⊕ *www. wildernesstravel.com.*

Wildside Nature Tours ✉ *539 Prince Frederick St., King of Prussia, Pennsylvania, USA* ☎ 888/875–9453 *in U.S.,* 610/564–0941 ⊕ *www. wildsidetoursinc.com.*

Windy Hill Resort & Tour Co. ✉ *Graceland Ranch, San Ignacio* ☎ 824/2017, 800/946–3995 ⊕ *www. windyhillresort.com.*

Winnie Estelle ✉ *San Pedro* ☎ 226/2427 ⊕ *www.ambergriscaye. com/winnieestelle.*

Travel Smart
Belize

WORD OF MOUTH

"My family and friends just returned from a Belize/
Guatemala trip. We are pretty frugal and willing
to skip some amenities. We also went in the rainy
season and skipped making reservations. Upon
arriving in Belize City, we took a cab to the bus
station and a bus (not express) to San Ignacio. It
was a long hot trip with many stops along the way
but it was a good experience (and cheap). We
stayed at Parrot Nest for less than $50 a night per
cabin. ATM was great and Hode's is a must-eat
stop! We took a *colectivo* to Flores, Guatemala,
and stayed there for a couple of days. Tikal was
great and we were able to take a private tour
(of sorts) into a pyramid to see hieroglyphs and
bones—Way cool!"   —Buddy_C

GETTING HERE AND AROUND

▮ AIR TRAVEL

TO BELIZE

All international flights to Belize fly into the international airport (BZE) in Ladyville near Belize City. The major U.S. departure gateways are Atlanta, with daily flights on Delta to Belize City (most flights are regional jets with one-class service, with service significantly reduced in summer and fall); Charlotte, with daily nonstops on US Airways to Belize City (with fewer flights, usually weekends only, in the summer and fall); Houston, with service two or three times daily, depending on the time of year, on United/Continental; and Miami and Dallas-Fort Worth with daily nonstop service from each city on American. United/Continental has a weekly nonstop from Newark. TACA flies to Belize City from several U.S. cities with a change of planes in San Salvador, El Salvador.

To Belize City it's roughly 2 hours from Miami and Atlanta; 2½ hours from Dallas, Houston, and Charlotte; and 4½ hours from Newark.

Tropic Air, one of two Belizean airlines, offers twice-daily service between Belize City's international airport and Flores, Guatemala, with continuing service to and from Guatemala City. Maya Island Air, another Belizean airline, in 2009 introduced international service connecting Cancún, Mexico, Guatemala City, and San Pedro Sula, Honduras, with Belize City, but by mid-2011 this international service had been suspended, and it's unclear when or whether the service will resume.

Airfares to Belize are often twice or more the cost of a ticket to Cancún or Cozumel, Mexico, so, if you have the time, it may pay to fly into the Yucatán and take a bus. From Cancún or Playa del Carmen a first-class or deluxe ADO bus costs US$25 or less, and takes five to six hours, to Chetumal, Mexico, a border town where you can transfer to a Belize bus to Belize City (US$6–$7) or take a water taxi to San Pedro, Ambergris Caye, or to Caye Caulker (US$30–$40).

WITHIN BELIZE

Domestic planes are single- or twin-engine island-hoppers. The carriers are Tropic Air and Maya Island Air, both of which fly to San Pedro on Ambergris Caye and Caye Caulker as well as Corozal Town, Dangriga, Placencia, and Punta Gorda. Tropic Air also has service between Placencia and Belmopan City, between Belize City and Belmopan City, and between San Pedro and Sarteneja in Corozal District. For those going to certain remote inland resorts, Tropic Air has flights on demand to Kanantik, Hidden Valley Inn, and Lamanai Outpost. Maya Island Air also has service on demand to Savannah near Placencia. In addition, as noted above, Tropic Air has service to and from Flores, Guatemala, with continuing service to and from Guatemala City.

Belize domestic flights on Maya Island and Tropic Air from and to the international airport are between BZ$250 and BZ$500 round-trip and about BZ$144 to BZ$400 round-trip between the municipal airstrip in Belize City and domestic destinations. A Belize Airports Authority Rider Fee of BZ$5 is added to the cost of tickets, and BZ$1.50 security fee if using the international airport. Currently, Maya Island includes this fee in its fares, while Tropic adds it to the quoted fare.

Charter services such as Javier Flying Service and Cari Bee Air Service will take you almost anywhere for around BZ$400 per hour and up; Javier has flights to Chan Chich Lodge. Both Maya Island and Tropic also have charter services. Astrum Helicopters, based near Belize City, offers transfers, aerial property tours, and custom sightseeing and photography tours anywhere in Belize. Costs for up to six people in the Bell 206 helicopters are around BZ$2,000 an hour. Fixed rates apply for transfers to specific resorts, starting at BZ$2,500 for four persons.

You'll save 10% to 40% on flights within Belize by flying to and from the municipal airport near downtown Belize City, rather than to or from the international airport north of the city in Ladyville. If you're arriving at the international airport, a transfer by taxi to the municipal airport is BZ$50 (for up to four persons, not per person); transferring to the municipal airport makes more sense for families or groups traveling together. If you need to fly between the Belize City area and another part of the country, it's always at least a little cheaper to fly to or from municipal.

Air Contacts American Airlines ☎ *800/433–7300 in U.S. and Canada, 223/2522 in Belize City* ⊕ *www.aa.com.* **Astrum Helicopters** ☎ *501/222–5100* ⊕ *www.astrumhelicopters.com.* **Cari Bee Air Service** ☎ *224/4253.* **United/Continental** ☎ *800/864–8331 in U.S., 223/2613 in Belize, 800/538–2929 in Canada* ⊕ *www.united.com.* **Delta Airlines** ☎ *800/221–1212 in U.S., 800/241–4141 for international reservations, 223/3504 in Belize* ⊕ *www.delta.com.* **Javier Flying Service** ☎ *824/0460* ⊕ *www.javiersflyingservice.com.* **Maya Island Air** ☎ *223/1140* ⊕ *www.mayaregional.com.* **TACA** ☎ *800/400–8222 in U.S., 501/227–7363 in Belize, 502/2470–8222 in Guatemala* ⊕ *www.taca.com.* **Tropic Air** ☎ *226/2012, 800/422–3435 in U.S. and Canada* ⊕ *www.tropicair.com.* **US Airways** ☎ *800/428–4322 in U.S. and Canada, 800/622–1015 for international reservations and in Belize* ⊕ *www.usairways.com.*

Airlines and Airports Airline and Airport Links. Airline and Airport Links has links to many airlines and airports. ⊕ *www.airlineandairportlinks.com.*

Airline Security Issues Transportation Security Administration ☎ *866/289–9673 in U.S.* ⊕ *www.tsa.gov.*

AIRPORTS

International flights arrive at the Philip Goldson International Airport (BZE) in Ladyville, 9 mi (15 km) north of Belize City, probably the world's only airport with a mahogany ceiling. Small domestic airports (which include landing strips with a one-room check-in) in Belize are in Belize City municipal (TZA), Belmopan (BCV), Corozal (CZH), Dangriga (DGA), Savannah (SVH) Placencia (PLJ), Punta Gorda (PND), San Pedro (SPR), Caye Caulker (CUK), and Sarteneja (SJX).

The future of a new, privately funded international airport under construction near the north end of the Placencia peninsula is unclear. As of this writing, construction work has essentially stopped, and the airport remains unfinished.

Philip Goldson International Airport has security precautions similar to those in the United States; the domestic airstrips have limited security systems, but there has never been an airline hijacking in Belize. For international flights, arrive at the airport at least two hours before departure; for domestic flights, about half an hour. For connections from international flights to domestic flights, allow 45 minutes. In Belize, domestic airlines with more passengers than seats sometimes simply add another flight.

Belize Belize Municipal Airstrip (TZE) ✉ *On seafront off Princess Margaret Dr., Belize City.* **Philip Goldson International Airport** ✉ *9 mi (15 km) north of Belize City center, off Northern Hwy., Ladyville* ☎ *225/2045* ⊕ *www.pgiabelize.com.*

❚ BOAT TRAVEL

Since Belize has about 200 mi (325 km) of mainland coast and some 400 islands in the Caribbean, water taxis, passenger ferries, and private boats are key.

BELIZE VIA CANCÚN

Due to the high cost of flights into Belize City, an increasing number of visitors to Belize are opting to fly into Cancún, which has inexpensive charter and scheduled flights from many points in the U.S., Canada, and even Europe. Visitors can save as much as one-half on the cost of airfare to Belize, even after paying for the cost of first-class buses from Cancún to the Belize border at Chetumal. The downside? Getting from Cancún to most destinations in Belize takes a full day of travel, so you have to add an extra day coming and going to your trip.

On arrival at Cancún International Airport (CUN), you have two choices to get to Belize. You can take an ADO shuttle bus to the Cancún City bus terminal, with service hourly or more frequently depending on the time of day, 48 Mexican pesos (about US$4 at current exchange rates), and then take an ADO bus from Cancún City to Chetumal, with buses approximately hourly, 284 Mexican pesos (about US$24) for first-class or 340 Mexican pesos (about US$29) for deluxe. Most buses on this route are first-class. Or, you can take an ADO shuttle from the airport to Playa del Carmen, with shuttle service approximately every half-hour from 10 am to 10 pm (116 Mexican pesos or US$10, about an hour). Then, from Playa take an ADO bus to Chetumal; fares are 238 Mexican pesos (about US$20) for first-class, or 284 Mexican pesos (about US$24) for deluxe. Most service on this route is first-class. Note that most ADO buses from Playa to Chetumal leave from the newer bus terminal, Terminal Alterna at Avenida 20 and Calle 12, rather than the older terminal near the water at Avenida 5 and Juarez. It's a little over 5 hours from Cancún to Chetumal, and a little over 4 hours from Playa del Carmen.

ADO first-class and deluxe buses are modern and comfortable, with reserved seats, ice-cold air-conditioning, videos, and bathrooms. Use the ADO Web site w*www.ado.com.mx* to make reservations in advance.

Buses arrive in Chetumal at the ADO terminal. There are no buses to Belize from the main bus station, the ADO terminal, in Chetumal, but you can take a taxi (15 Mexican pesos or about US$1.25) to the nearby Nuevo Mercado (New Market) terminal and connect there with a bus bound for Belize. Depending on the state of bus service in Belize, which changes frequently, BBOC buses leave Nuevo Mercado for Corozal Town and Belize City three or four times daily (BZ$16 from Chetumal to Belize City, about 3½ hours). Other buses from several bus lines including Gilharry, Tillett, Venus, and others, leave from the border and also from Corozal Town. You also can take a water taxi from Chetumal to San Pedro or Caye Caulker, Belize, or use a transfer service to cross the border. (xSee Bus Travel and Boat and Water-Taxi Travel.)

FERRIES AND PRIVATE BOATS

A local ferry company, Coastal Xpress, provides scheduled boat transportation up and down the east side of Ambergris Caye.

Several private boats make the run from Dangriga to Tobacco Caye for BZ$35 per person one-way. They leave Dangriga around 9:30 am and return from Tobacco Caye later in the day. Check at the Riverside Café in Dangriga or ask your hotel on Tobacco Caye.

Information Coastal Xpress ⊠ *Amigos del Mar Pier Beachfront, San Pedro* ☎ *226/2007* ⊕ *www.coastalxpress.com.* **Requena's** ⊠ *12 Front St., Punta Gorda* ☎ *722/2070* ⊕ *www. belizenet.com/requena.* **Riverside Café** ⊠ *5 Riverside Dr., south bank of North Stann Creek, Dangriga* ☎ *523/3499.* **Water Jets International.** Also confusingly known as San Pedro Water Jets International, Water Jets Express, and San Pedro-Jet Express. ⊠ *Black Coral St., on back side of island near soccer field, San Pedro* ☎ *226/2194* ⊕ *www.sanpedrowatertaxi. com.*

WATER TAXIS

There are three main water-taxi companies, with fast boats that hold up to 50 to 100 passengers, connecting Belize City with San Pedro (Ambergris Caye) and Caye Caulker. They also connect San Pedro with Caye Caulker and these islands with Chetumal, Mexico.

Most scheduled water taxis allow two pieces of luggage per person, along with miscellaneous personal items. Bicycles and other larger items may be permitted, if there's space, but you may be charged extra. Life jackets are carried on board the boats but aren't handed out to passengers. Seas, especially in the south between Dangriga and Placencia and Puerto Cortes, and also between Punta Gorda and Puerto Barrios, can be rough. Postpone your trip if the weather looks bad, or, in the case of private charters, if the boat offered looks unseaworthy or crowded.

The Belize water-taxi business is still in a state of flux, and schedules and rates are subject to change.

DEPATURE POINTS

Caye Caulker Water Taxi boats depart from the Marine Terminal at 10 North Front Street near the Swing Bridge; San Pedro Belize Express boats leave from the Brown Sugar dock at 111 North Front Street near the Tourism Village; Water Jets International boats, also known as San Pedro Water Jets Express leave from the Marine Terminal at 10 North Front Street.

ARRIVAL POINTS

Caye Caulker Water Taxi boats arrive at the Main Public Pier on Front Street on Caye Caulker, and on San Pedro they arrive at the Texaco Marina; on Caye Caulker, San Pedro Belize Express boats arrive at the pier near the basketball court on Front Street, and in San Pedro they arrive at the pier at on Black Coral Street on the east (sea) side of the island, next to Wahoo's Bar & Grill; on both Caye Caulker and Ambergris Caye the Water Jets International terminals are on the back (lagoon) side of the islands.

RIDE TIMES AND FARES

From Belize City it's a 45-minute ride to Caulker and 75 minutes to San Pedro. Going between Caulker and San Pedro takes about 30 minutes. Fares vary a little among companies. At press time, one-way fares between Belize City and Caye Caulker were BZ$24 on Water Jets International, BZ$20 on Caye Caulker Water Taxi Association, and BZ$20 on San Pedro Belize Express; one-way fares between Belize City and San Pedro were BZ$35 on Water Jets International, BZ$30 on Caye Caulker Water Taxi Association, and BZ$30 on San Pedro Belize Express.

Two of these water-taxi companies, Water Jets International and San Pedro Belize Express, also have daily service between the Muelle Fiscal or municipal pier in

Chetumal, Mexico, and San Pedro and Caye Caulker, a trip of about 90 minutes to San Pedro, for US$30–US$35 to San Pedro and US$35–US$40 to Caulker, or the equivalent in Mexican pesos, though sometimes in Chetumal you can negotiate a lower rate.

Another company, Thunderbolt, has daily service between Corozal Town and San Pedro for BZ$45 one-way. The trip takes 90 minutes to two hours, depending on weather conditions and whether there is a stop in Sarteneja. In Corozal, the Thunderbolt leaves from the Reunion Pier in the center of town; it arrives in San Pedro at the dock on Black Coral Street on the back side of the island near the soccer field.

Information Caye Caulker Water Taxis Association ☎ 223/5752 ⊕ www.cayecaulkerwatertaxi.com. **San Pedro Belize Express Water Taxi** ☎ 223/2225 ⊕ www.belizewatertaxi.com.

REACHING REMOTE CAYES AND ATOLLS

To reach the more remote cayes and the atolls, you're basically left to your own devices, unless you're staying at a hotel where such transfers are arranged for you. The resorts on the atolls run their own boats, but these usually aren't available to the general public.

There are no water taxis along the coast of mainland Belize—none from Belize City to Corozal Town, Hopkins, Placencia, or Punta Gorda. However, weekly ferries run from Dangriga and Placencia to Puerto Cortes, Honduras. D-Express leaves from Placencia on Friday morning and the Nesymein Neydy from Dangriga also on Friday morning. D-Express returns from Puerto Cortes Monday morning and Nesymein Neydy also on Monday morning. Cost is BZ$110 one-way.

Four water-taxi companies—Requena's, Pichillingo, Meno's, and Marisol—currently go from Punta Gorda (PG) to

Puerto Barrios, Guatemala. Rates are BZ$40–BZ$45 one-way. Requena's provides daily boats departing at 9:30 am from the docks on Front Street, Punta Gorda, to Puerto Barrios, Guatemala. The fare is BZ$40 one-way. Requena's returns to PG at 2 pm. Three other water-taxi services, Pichilingo, Memo's, and Marisol, run water taxis for around BZ$44 one-way. The Pichilingo boat departs from PG at 2 pm, Memo's at 1 pm, and Marisol at 4 pm. From Puerto Barrios, Pichilingo departs at 10 am, Memo's at 3:15 pm, and Marisol at 1 pm. Boats to Livingston, Guatemala, depart from Punta Gorda on Tuesday and Friday only at 10 am.

The trip between PG and Puerto Barrios takes about an hour and can be rough. These water taxis are small open boats for pedestrians only; there is no auto ferry between Guatemala and Punta Gorda.

Information D-Express ☎ 202/4506 Placencia BTIA office. **Nesymein Neydy** ☎ 604/4738.

TRAVEL TIMES FROM BELIZE CITY		
To	By Air	By Car or Bus
San Pedro	20 minutes	n/a
Caye Caulker	15 minutes	n/a
Corozal Town	1–2 hours (via San Pedro)	2–3 hours
San Ignacio	n/a	2–3 hours
Placencia	50 minutes	3½–4 hours
Punta Gorda	1 hour	4–6 hours
Cancún, Mexico	1 hour	8–11 hours

▍BUS TRAVEL

There's frequent bus service on the Northern and Western highways and to southern Belize via the Hummingbird and Southern highways. Elsewhere service is spotty. There's only limited municipal bus service in Belize City, on Lopez, Arrow

Line, Haylock, and other independent lines. Fares are BZ$1 to $2 depending on the route and the bus line.

Buses can get you just about anywhere cheaply (about BZ$2–BZ$30 for inter-town trips) and quickly. Expect to ride on old U.S. school buses or retired North American Greyhound buses. On some routes there are a few express buses with air-conditioning and other comforts. These cost a few dollars more.

■TIP→ Be prepared for tight squeezes—this can mean three people in a two-person seat—and watch for pickpockets. Drivers and their assistants (in Guatemala, *cobradors* or *ayudantes*, fare collectors, who call out the stops) are knowledgeable and helpful. They can direct you to the right bus, and tell you when and where to get off. To be sure you're not forgotten, try to sit near the driver.

Most buses on main routes run according to more-or-less reliable schedules; on less-traveled routes the schedules may not mean much. Buses operate mostly during daylight hours, but they run until around 9 pm on the western route between Belize City and San Ignacio. The Belize Tourism Board sometimes has schedules for popular routes. Also check online for the Belize Bus Blog (⊕ *www.belizebus.wordpress.com*), which has generally up-to-date information on Belize bus rates and schedules and also on other types of transportation in Belize. Buses in Belize accept only cash in U.S. or Belize dollars.

In August 2011 Mexican bus line ADO (⊕ *www.ado.com.mx*) began offering daily express service between Belize City and Cancún, using executive-class 44-seat Mercedes buses with reserved reclining seats, air-conditioning, bathrooms, and videos. These buses leave late in the evening in both directions, allowing passengers to sleep en route and arrive early in the morning. Buses make brief stops at Playa del Carmen, Tulum, Corozal Town,

and Orange Walk Town. Fare is around US$39 (BZ$78) one-way.

Inexpensive public buses, also of the converted school bus variety, crisscross Guatemala, but they can be slow and extremely crowded, with a three-per-seat rule enforced. Popular destinations, such as Tikal or Santa Elena, use Pullman buses, which are as well equipped as North American bus lines. Your hotel or INGUAT office can help you make arrangements. Fares on public buses in Guatemala are a bargain.

■TIP→ In Guatemalan cities you pay the bus driver as you board. On intercity buses, fare collectors pass through the bus periodically. Buses follow loose schedules, sometimes waiting to leave until the bus fills up. On some routes the day's very last bus isn't always a sure thing. Schedules for Pullman buses are usually observed.

Reservations are usually not needed or expected in Belize or Guatemala, even for Pullman or express departures. The terminals in Belize City and some towns have ticket windows where you can pay in advance and get a reserved seat. If you board at other points, you pay the driver's assistant and take any available seat. Arrive at terminals about a half hour before departure.

Belize Companies James Bus Line ⊠ *7 King St., Punta Gorda* ☎ *702/2049.*

Guatemala Companies Autobuses del Norte ⊠ *Guatemala City, Guatemala* ☎ *502/2251–0079 in Guatemala City, 502/7924-8131 in Santa Elena, Guatemala* ⊕ *www.adnautobusesdelnorte.com.* **Fuente del Norte** ⊠ *7 Calle 8a Y 9a 8-46, Zona 1, Guatemala City, Guatemala* ☎ *502/7947–7070 in Guatemala, 223/0457 in Belize* ⊕ *www.grupofuentedelnorte.com.*

CAR TRAVEL

GASOLINE

Modern gas stations—Texaco, Esso, and Shell brands, some of them with convenience stores and 24-hour service—are in Belize City and most major towns. In more remote areas, especially in the south, fill up the tank whenever you see a station. Unleaded gas costs around BZ$11–$12 a gallon. Diesel fuel is slightly less. Attendants who pump gas for you don't expect a tip, though they are happy to accept it.

Prices at Guatemala's service stations aren't quite as high as in Belize. At most stations an attendant will pump the gas and make change. Plan to use cash, as credit cards sometimes aren't accepted.

PARKING

In Belize City, with its warren of narrow and one-way streets, downtown parking is often at a premium. For security, try to find a guarded, fenced parking lot, and don't leave your car on the street overnight. Elsewhere, except in some areas of San Ignacio and Orange Walk Town, there's plenty of free parking.

There are no parking meters in Belize. In most cities and towns parking rules are laxly enforced, although cars with license plates from elsewhere may attract a ticket.

ROAD CONDITIONS

All four main roads in Belize—the Western Highway, Northern Highway, Southern Highway, and Hummingbird Highway—are completely paved. These two-lane roads are generally in good condition. The once-horrendous Placencia Road is now completely paved. Signage is good along the main highways; large green signs direct you to major sights.

Elsewhere in Belize, expect fair to stupendously rough dirt, gravel, and limestone roads; a few unpaved roads may be impassable at times in the rainy season.

FROM/TO	ROUTE	DISTANCE
Belize City–Corozal Town	Northern Highway	99 mi (160 km)
Belize City–San Ignacio	Western Highway	72 mi (116 km)
Belize City–Placencia	Western, Hummingbird, and Southern highways	147 mi (237 km)
Belize City–Punta Gorda	Western, Hummingbird, and Southern highways	200 mi (323 km)
San Ignacio–Placencia	Western, Hummingbird, and Southern highways	113 mi (182 km)

Immense improvements have been made to Guatemala's ravaged roads. A highway from Río Dulce to Tikal has cut travel time along this popular route significantly. In the Petén, the road from Belize toward Tikal has a few short stretches near the border without pavement, but after that, both to Tikal and to Flores, it's paved and in excellent condition. Roads in remote areas are frequently unpaved, rife with potholes, and treacherously muddy in the rainy season. Four-wheel-drive vehicles are recommended for travel off the beaten path. In cities, expect narrow brick streets. Road signs are generally used to indicate large towns; smaller towns may not be so clearly marked. Look for intersections where people seem to be waiting for a bus—that's a good sign that there's an important turnoff nearby.

ROADSIDE EMERGENCIES

When renting a car, ask the agency what it does if your car breaks down in a remote area. Most agencies in Belize send a driver with a replacement vehicle or a mechanic to fix the car. For help in Guatemala, your best bet is to call the National or Tourist Police. In either country, consider renting a cell phone (⇨ *Phones, under Communication in Essentials.*).

Emergency Services **Belize Police** ☎ *911 for emergencies.* **Guatemalan National Police.** The local equivalent of 911 in Guatemala is 120, 122, and 123. ☎ *120 for emergencies, 122 for emergencies, 123 for emergencies.* **Guatemalan Tourist Police.** POLITUR (Tourist Police) is a joint National Police and INGUAT tourism information service. ☎ *502/2421–2810 for 24-hour security information provided by INGUAT, 120 for emergencies.*

RULES OF THE ROAD

Driving in Belize and Guatemala is on the right. Seat belts are required, although the law is seldom enforced. There are few speed-limit signs, and speed limits are rarely enforced. However, as you approach villages and towns watch out for "sleeping policemen," a local name for speed bumps. Belize has about a dozen traffic lights, and only Belize City and downtown San Ignacio have anything approaching congestion. One unusual aspect of driving in Belize, likely a hold-over from British Honduras days when driving was on the left, is that vehicles turning left against traffic are not supposed to hold up cars behind them; instead, they are supposed to pull over to the right and wait for a break in traffic to turn.

Despite the relatively small number of private cars in Belize, traffic accidents are the nation's number one cause of death. Belizean drivers aren't always as skilled as they think they are, and drunk drivers can be a problem. Guatemala's narrow roads and highways mean you can be stuck motionless on the road for an hour while a construction crew stands around a hole in the ground. Always allow extra travel time for such unpredictable events, and bring along snacks and water. In both Belize and Guatemala, be prepared to stop for police traffic checks. Usually tourists in rental cars are checked only cursorily. Otherwise, if you observe the rules you follow at home, you'll likely do just fine. Just don't expect everyone else to follow them.

RENTAL CARS

Belize City and the international airport in Ladyville have most major car-rental agencies as well as several local operators. There also are car-rental agencies in Corozal Town, San Ignacio, Placencia, and Punta Gorda. Prices vary, but all are high by U.S. standards (BZ$120–BZ$275 per day), and vehicles are often a few years old with quite a few miles. Off-season, rates are a little lower. A few resorts have rental cars for about BZ$150–BZ$180 per day.

For serious safaris, a four-wheel-drive vehicle is invaluable. But since unpaved roads, mudslides in rainy season, and a general off-the-beaten-path landscape are status quo here, all drivers will be comforted with a four-wheel-drive vehicle.

Car rental has never really caught on in Guatemala, which, given the narrowness of the roads, is just as well. If you do rent a car, opt for four-wheel drive, which will run around US$65 a day. Several international and local car-rental companies are based at the Flores airport.

In Belize and Guatemala, rental-car companies routinely accept driver's licenses from most other countries without question. Most car-rental agencies require a major credit card for a deposit, and some require you be over 25.

Most Belize agencies don't permit their vehicles to be taken into Guatemala or Mexico. Crystal in Belize City does permit its vehicles to be taken into Guatemala, as do a couple of the car-rental companies in San Ignacio, although without any insurance coverage while in Guatemala. There is no place to buy Guatemalan liability insurance at the Belize-Guatemala border.

On Belize's cayes you can't rent a car, but you can rent a golf cart, at prices not much less than renting a car. You'll need a driver's license and a credit card.

CAR-RENTAL INSURANCE

If you own a car, your personal auto insurance may cover a rental to some degree, though not all policies protect you abroad; always read your policy's fine print. If you don't have auto insurance, then seriously consider buying the collision- or loss-damage waiver (CDW or LDW) from the car-rental company, which eliminates your liability for damage to the car. Some credit cards offer CDW coverage, but it's usually supplemental to your own insurance and rarely covers SUVs, minivans, luxury models, and the like. If your coverage is secondary, you may still be liable for loss-of-use costs from the car-rental company. But no credit-card insurance is valid unless you use that card for *all* transactions, from reserving to paying the final bill. All companies exclude car rental in some countries, so be sure to find out about the destination to which you are traveling.

In Belize CDW insurance costs BZ$25–BZ$40 a day, and you may still be liable for the first BZ$1,000–BZ$4,000 in damages.

Major Agencies **Budget**. Offices at the international airport, in Belize City, and in Placencia. ✉ *Mile 2½ Northern Hwy., Belize City* ☎ *223/2435 in Belize* ✎ *reservations@budget-belize.com* ⊕ *www.budget-belize.com.* **Cayo Auto Rentals** ✉ *81 Benque Rd., San Ignacio* ☎ *824/2222* ⊕ *www.cayoautorentals.com.* **Crystal**. Offices at the international airport and in Belize City. ✉ *Mile 5, Northern Hwy., Belize City* ☎ *223/1600 in Belize, 800/777-7777 toll-free in Belize* ⊕ *www.crystal-belize.com.* **Hertz**. Offices at international airport and near Tourism Village in Belize City. ☎ *800/654-3001 in U.S. for international reservations, 225/3300 in Belize* ⊕ *www.hertzbelize.com.*

∎ CRUISE SHIPS

Over two-thirds of a million cruise passengers visit Belize annually, all arriving on big ships that call on Belize City. Because of shallow water near shore, passengers are brought ashore in small boats called tenders. Although Carnival Cruise Lines agreed to build a new US$50 million cruise terminal in Belize City, construction has been indefinitely delayed. Studies have been done for a new cruise terminal in Placencia village; its future is uncertain, as many local residents strongly oppose it.

On arrival in Belize City, most passengers take snorkel, cave tubing, or Mayan ruin tours, or just wander around the historic Fort George area, visiting the Tourist Village.

Cruise Lines **Carnival Cruise Line** ☎ *305/599-2600, 800/227-6482* ⊕ *www.carnival.com.* **Costa Cruises** ☎ *954/266-5600, 800/462-6782* ⊕ *www.costacruise.com.* **Holland America Line** ☎ *206/281-3535, 877/932-4259* ⊕ *www.hollandamerica.com.* **Norwegian Cruise Line** ☎ *866/234-7350* ⊕ *www.ncl.com.* **Princess Cruises** ☎ *661/753-0000, 800/774-6237* ⊕ *www.princess.com.* **Regent Seven Seas Cruises** ☎ *877/505-5370* ⊕ *www.rssc.com.* **Royal Caribbean International** ☎ *305/539-6000, 866/562-7625* ⊕ *www.royalcaribbean.com.* **Seabourn Cruise Line** ☎ *305/463-3000, 877/301-2174* ⊕ *www.seabourn.com.*

▌ SHUTTLES

Belize has some shuttle service, primarily between Belize City and San Ignacio, though shuttles also are available to Placencia, Chetumal, Mexico, and elsewhere. Most hotels and lodges will arrange van transfers for guests to and from the international airport in Belize City for BZ$250–BZ$400 for up to four passengers. William's Shuttle in the Cayo offers van transfers to and from Belize City (rates depend on the number of passengers). Belize Shuttles in Belize City has both scheduled and on-demand shuttles between the international airport and San Ignacio, at BZ$70 per person for the scheduled shuttles and BZ$180 for a private shuttle for up to three persons and BZ$30 for additional persons. In the north, Belize VIP Transfers will whisk you across the border to Chetumal for BZ$70 per person (not including the BZ$37.50 Belize exit fee).

San Juan Travel and Fuente del Norte (which has the nicer equipment) run daily vans or minibuses between Belize City and Flores, Guatemala, for BZ$50–$60. These fares don't include exit fees of BZ$37.50 when leaving Belize by land. Linea Dorada no longer operates on this route.

Shuttles in Guatemala are private minivans that hold up to eight passengers. They're faster and more comfortable than public buses. Public minivans from the Belize border to Santa Elena near Flores cost around US$5; they're often packed. Taxi shuttles from the border to Tikal or Flores are around US$45–US$70 for up to four passengers, depending on your bargaining ability. Shuttles between Flores and Tikal charge a flat US$5 per person round-trip and run frequently, starting at 5 am from Flores.

Reservations are generally required for shuttle service in both Belize and Guatemala. Some may ask for payment up front; before obliging, be sure you're dealing with a reputable company.

Belize Company **Belize Shuttles**
☎ *631/1749 in Belize, 757/383–8024 in U.S.* ✉ *reserve@belizeshuttlesandtransfers. com* ⊕ *www.belizeshuttlesandtransfers.com.* **Belize VIP Transfers** ☎ *422/2725* ⊕ *www. belizetransfers.com.* **William's Shuttle** ✉ *belizeshuttle@yahoo.com* ⊕ *www.parrot-nest.com/belize-shuttle.html.*

Guatemala Companies **Fuente del Norte** ☎ *502/7947–7070* ⊕ *www. grupofuentedelnorte.com.* **San Juan Travel** ☎ *502/7926–0042.*

ESSENTIALS

■ ACCOMMODATIONS

Regardless of the kind of lodging, you'll usually stay at a small place of two to 50 rooms; the owners often actively manage the property. Thus, Belize accommodations usually reflect the personalities of their owners, for better or worse.

APARTMENT AND HOUSE RENTALS

You can most easily find vacation rentals on Ambergris Caye. Marty Casado's Ambergris Caye Web site has a good selection of rental houses and condos. Vacation Rentals By Owner (VRBO) has scores of rentals on Ambergris Caye and elsewhere in Belize. There also are some vacation rental houses in Placencia and Hopkins and on Caye Caulker. *Individual chapters in this guide direct you to vacation rental sources.*

Information Ambergis Caye Web Site ⊕ *www.ambergriscaye.com.* **Vacation Rentals By Owner (VRBO)** ⊕ *www.vrbo.com.*

BEACH HOTELS

Beach hotels range from a basic seaside cabin on Caye Caulker to a small, deluxe resort such as Turtle Inn on the Placencia peninsula or Hamanasi near Hopkins. On Ambergris Caye many resorts are "condotels"—low-rise condo complexes with individually owned units that are managed like a hotel.

HOSTELS

Information Hostelling International—USA ☎ *301/495–1240* ⊕ *www.hihostels.com.*

JUNGLE LODGES

Jungle lodges are concentrated in the Cayo, Toledo, and Orange Walk districts, but they can be found most anywhere except the cayes. Jungle lodges need not be spartan; nearly all have electricity (though the generator may shut down at 10 pm), a number have swimming pools, and a few have air-conditioning. The typical lodge has a roof of bay-palm thatch and may remind you of a Mayan house gone upscale.

STAYING ON THE CAYES

Lodging choices on remote cayes appeal to the diving and fishing crowd. Amenity levels vary greatly, from cabins with outdoor bathrooms to simple cottages with composting toilets to comfortable villas with air-conditioning.

TRADITIONAL HOTELS

Traditional hotels, usually found in larger towns, can be basic budget places or international-style hotels such as the Radisson Fort George in Belize City.

CANCELLATIONS

As most hotels have only a few rooms, a last-minute cancellation can have a big impact on the bottom line. Most properties have a sliding scale for cancellations, with full refunds (minus a small administrative fee) if you cancel 60 or 90 days or more in advance, with reduced refund rates for later cancellations, and often no refunds at all for cancellation 30 to 45 days out. Practices vary greatly, so check on them.

RATES

In the off-season—generally May–November, though dates vary by hotel—most properties discount rates by 20% to 40%. Although hotels have published rates, in the off-season at least you may also be able to negotiate a better rate, especially if you're staying more than one or two nights. ■TIP➔ **Walk-in rates are usually lower than pre-booked rates, and rooms booked direct on the Internet may be lower than those booked through agents.**

Most hotels allow children under a certain age to stay in their parents' room at no extra charge, but others charge for them as extra adults; find out the cutoff age for discounts.

All prices for Belize are in Belize dollars for a standard double room in high season with no meals included, including service charges and 9% hotel tax.

■ COMMUNICATIONS

INTERNET

Belize is wired. DSL high-speed (though not always the "high speed" you may be accustomed to) Internet is available in most populated areas, and cable Internet is offered in Belize City, Placencia, and elsewhere. In more remote areas, there's the option of satellite Internet. There are Internet cafés in San Pedro, Caye Caulker, Belize City, San Ignacio, Placencia, Hopkins, Corozal Town, Punta Gorda, and other areas. Rates are usually BZ$10–BZ$20 an hour. Most offices of the main phone company, Belize Telemedia, Ltd., have computers with DSL Internet connections (BZ$10 per half hour). BTL also has Wi-Fi hot spots at the international airport (free) and elsewhere.

CYBERCAFÉS AND INTENET CAFES

Cybercafés are now common in Belize City and in most towns and resort areas all over Belize. The problem is that these lightly capitalized businesses frequently are here today and gone tomorrow. Your best bet is just to scout the area where you're staying for an open Internet café. If you're visiting on a cruise ship, Click & Sip is inside the Tourism Village in Belize City. Rates vary, but typically you'll pay around BZ$5–$10 for a half hour, BZ$8–BZ$15 for an hour. There is free Belize Telemedia Ltd. Wi-Fi at the international airport.

Cybercafes Cybercafes lists more than 4,000 Internet cafés worldwide. ⊕ www.cybercafes. com.

Internet Cafés Click & Sip Internet Café
✉ Fort St., in Tourism Village, Belize City
☎ 223/1305.

INTERNET AT ACCOMMODATIONS

Most mid-level and upscale hotels, and some budget ones, now provide Internet access, typically Wi-Fi for your laptop, tablet computer, or Internet-enabled cell phone, and also a few computers in the office or lobby, at no charge. A few hotel operators still charge a fee, up to BZ$30 a day. In towns and resort areas this is usually DSL, but with speeds of only 1 Mbps down or less. At jungle lodges and other remote properties, the access is usually via a satellite system, with very limited bandwidth. At these lodges you're usually asked to use the Internet for email only and not to upload or download large files.

■TIP→ If you're traveling with a laptop in Belize, be aware that the power supply may be uneven, and most hotels don't have built-in current stabilizers. At remote lodges power is often from fluctuating generators. Bring a surge protector and your own disks or memory sticks to save your work.

PHONES

CALLING WITHIN BELIZE

All Belizean numbers are seven digits. (In Guatemala there are eight digits.) The first digit in Belize is the district area code (2 for Belize District, 3 Orange Walk, 4 Corozal, 5 Stann Creek, 6 for mobile phones, 7 Toledo, and 8 Cayo). The second indicates the type of service (0 for prepaid services, 1 for mobile, 2 for regular landline). The final five digits are the phone number. Thus, a number such as 22x/xxxx means that it's a landline phone in Belize District.

To dial any number in Belize, local or long distance, you must dial all seven digits. When dialing from outside Belize, dial the international access code, the country code for Belize (501), and all seven digits. When calling from the United States, dial 011/501–xxx–xxxx.

Belize has a good nationwide phone system. There are pay phones on the street in the main towns. All take prepaid phone cards rather than coins. Local calls cost BZ25¢; calls to other districts, BZ$1. Dial 113 for directory assistance and 115 for operator assistance. For the correct local time, dial 121. You can get phone numbers in Belize on the Web site of Belize Telemedia Ltd.

CALLING OUTSIDE BELIZE

To call the United States, dial 001 or 10–10–199 plus the area code and number. You'll pay around BZ$1.50 a minute. Pay phones accept only prepaid BTL phone cards, available in shops at BTL offices in denominations from BZ$5 to BZ$75. BTL blocks many foreign calling cards and also attempts to block even computer-to-computer calls on Skype and similar services.

The country code is 1 for the United States and Canada, 502 for Guatemala, 52 for Mexico, 61 for Australia, 64 for New Zealand, and 44 for the United Kingdom.

Resources **Belize Telemedia Ltd.**
☎ *800/225–5285 toll-free in Belize* ⊕ *www.belizetelemedia.net.*

MOBILE PHONES

If you have a multiband phone and your service provider uses the GSM 850/1900 digital system (like AT&T) you can use your phone in Belize on BTL's DigiCell system. You'll need a new SIM card (your provider may have to unlock your phone for you to use a different SIM card). The SIM card will cost about BZ$50, and you'll also need a prepaid phone card. Both items and also rental cell phones (starting at BZ$10 a day or BZ$70 a week) are available at the BTL office at the international airport (near the rental car kiosks), at some BTL offices, and at a number of private shops and stores around Belize that are DigiCell distributors.

Another option is a small BTL competitor, Smart!, which operates a nationwide cell-phone system that uses CDMA technology (like Verizon in the United States). At one of its offices—in Belize City, Corozal Town, Orange Walk Town, Belmopan City, San Ignacio, San Pedro, or Benque Viejo—you can reprogram your unlocked 800 MHz or 850 MHz CDMA phone for use in Belize. There's an activation fee of BZ$40, and you'll need to purchase a prepaid plan with per-minute rates for outgoing calls of BZ55¢ to BZ70¢ (incoming calls, text messages, and voice mail are free).

You may also be able to activate your own cell phone for use in Belize. Check with your service provider, but be aware that international roaming charges are high. Typically, you'll pay US$3 or more per minute to use your cell in Belize.

Contacts **BTL International Airport Office**
☎ *225/4162, 800/225–5285 toll-free in Belize*
⊕ *www.telemedia.com.* **Smart!** ⊠ *Mile 2½ Northern Hwy., Belize City* ☎ *1090 (number works on Smart! phones only), 280/1000 in Belize City* ⊕ *www.smart-bz.com.*

▌ CUSTOMS AND DUTIES

At the international airport in Belize City it rarely takes more than 30 minutes to clear immigration and customs.

Duty-free allowances for visitors entering Belize include 1 liter of liquor and one carton of cigarettes per person. Customs officials may confiscate beer, including beer from Guatemala or Mexico, as Belize protects its domestic brewing industry. The exception is beer from countries in CARICOM, of which Belize is a member.
■ **TIP➔** When arriving by international air at Philip Goldson International Airport you can buy up to four bottles of spirits or wine at the duty-free shop in the arrival terminal near the baggage claim area. These won't be counted toward your regular import allowance.

In theory, electronic and electrical appliances, cameras, jewelry, or other items of value must be declared at the point of entry, but unless these are new items you plan to leave in Belize, you probably will not be required to declare them. You should have no trouble bringing in a laptop for personal use.

Firearms of any type are prohibited, as are fresh fruits and vegetables. Although a couple of dozen food items, including meats, rice, beans, sugar, and peanuts, require an import license, grocery items in small amounts for personal use, in their original packages, are usually allowed.

To take home fresh seafood of any kind from Belize, you must first obtain a permit from the Fisheries Department. There's a 20-pound limit. It is illegal to export any Mayan artifact from Belize.

You may enter Guatemala duty-free with a camera, up to six rolls of film, any clothes and articles needed while traveling, 500 mg of tobacco, 3 liters of alcoholic beverages, two bottles of perfume, and 2 kg of candy. Unless you bring in a lot of merchandise, customs officers probably won't even check your luggage, although a laptop may be somewhat scrutinized.

It's illegal to export most Mayan artifacts. If you buy any such goods, do so only at a well-established store, and keep the receipt. You may not take fruits or vegetables out of Guatemala.

Information in Belize Belize Fisheries
☎ 501/224–4552.

U.S. Information U.S. Customs and Border Protection ☎ 877/227–5511 in U.S., 703/526–4200 for international callers ⊕ www.cbp.gov. **U.S. State Department** ☎ 202/647–4000 State Dept. main switchboard, 888/407–4747 hotline for U.S. travelers, 877/487–2778 passport information ⊕ www.travel.state.gov.

LOCAL DO'S AND TABOOS

CUSTOMS OF THE COUNTRY
Patience and friendliness go a long way in Belize. Don't criticize local ways of doing things—there's usually a reason that may not be obvious to visitors—and, especially with officials, adopt a respectful attitude.

GREETINGS
Belizeans are incredibly kind and friendly. Greet folks with a "Good morning" before asking for directions, for a table in a restaurant, or when entering a store or museum, for example. It will set a positive tone and you'll be received much more warmly for having done so.

SIGHTSEEING
Don't take pictures inside churches. Do not take pictures of indigenous people without first asking their permission. Offering them a small sum as thanks is customary.

LANGUAGE
English is Belize's official language. Spanish is widely spoken especially in northern and western Belize. Several Maya dialects and the Garífuna language are also spoken. Some Mennonite communities speak German. Creole, which uses versions of English words and a West African–influenced grammar and syntax, is spoken as a first language by many Belizeans, especially around Belize City.

Around Tikal, wherever tourist traffic is heavy, you'll find a few English speakers; you'll have considerably less luck in places off the beaten path. In general, very little English is spoken in El Petén, and in some small villages in the region absolutely none. In addition, many Guatemalans will answer "yes" even if they don't understand your question, so as not to appear unkind or unhelpful. To minimize such confusion, try posing questions as "Where is so-and-so?" rather than asking "Is so-and-so this way?"

EATING OUT

For information on food-related health issues, see ⇨ Health.

MEALS AND MEALTIMES

You can eat well in Belize thanks to a gastronomic gumbo of Mexican, Caribbean, Mayan, Garífuna, English, and American dishes (on the American side, think fried chicken, pork chops, burgers, and T-bone steaks). On the coast and cayes, seafood—especially lobster, conch, snapper, and grouper—is fresh, relatively inexpensive, and delicious.

Try Creole specialties such as cow-foot soup (yes, made with real cows' feet), "boil up" (a stew of fish, potatoes, plantains, cassava and other vegetables, and eggs), and the ubiquitous "stew chicken" with rice and beans. Many Creole dishes are seasoned with red or black *recado,* a paste made from annatto seeds and other spices.

In border areas, enjoy Mestizo favorites such as *escabeche* (onion soup), *salbutes* (fried corn tortillas with chicken and a topping of tomatoes, onions, and peppers), or *garnaches* (fried tortillas with refried beans, cabbage, and cheese).

In Dangriga and Punta Gorda or other Garífuna areas, try dishes such as *sere lasus* (fish soup with plantain balls) or cassava dumplings.

Breakfast is usually served from 7 to 9, lunch from 11 to 2, and dinner from 6 to 9. Few restaurants are open late. Remember, though, that small restaurants may open or close at the whim of the owner. Off-season, restaurants may close early if it looks as if there are no more guests coming, and some restaurants close completely for a month or two, usually in September and October. Unless otherwise noted, the restaurants listed in this guide are open daily for lunch and dinner.

■ TIP➔ Other than at hotels, Belize restaurants are often closed on Sunday.

RESERVATIONS AND DRESS

Reservations are rarely needed in Belize or the Tikal area. The exceptions are for dinner at jungle lodges and at small restaurants where the owner or chef needs to know in advance how many people are dining that night. We mention reservations only when they're essential.

A few restaurants in Belize City have a dress code, which basically means that you can't wear shorts at dinner. We mention dress only when men are required to wear a jacket or a jacket and tie, which is nearly unheard of in Belize.

ELECTRICITY

There's no need to bring a converter or adapter, as electrical current is 110 volts, the same as in the United States, and outlets take U.S.-style plugs. In a few remote areas lodges and hotels may generate their own electricity, and after the generators are turned off at night, power, if there's any, comes only from kerosene lanterns or your flashlight.

EMERGENCIES

In an emergency, call 911 nationwide. There are police stations in Belize City and in Belmopan City, in the towns of Benque Viejo, Corozal, Dangriga, Orange Walk, Punta Gorda, San Ignacio, and San Pedro, and in Placencia Village and a few other villages. Police try to respond quickly to emergencies, although lack of equipment, supplies, and training may sometimes reduce their effectiveness.

Police are generally polite, professional, and will do what they can to help. In Belize City and in most tourist areas, including Placencia and San Pedro, there are special tourist police whose job is to patrol areas where visitors are likely to go and to render any assistance they can, including providing directions.

Most Belizeans are extremely solicitous of the welfare of visitors to the country. In an emergency, it's likely that bystanders or people in the area will gladly offer to help, usually going out of their way to render any assistance they can.

Your hotel can provide the names of nearby physicians and clinics. You can also go to the emergency room of public hospitals in Belize City and major towns. Don't worry about payment—in an emergency, you'll be treated regardless of your ability to pay, though after being treated you may be asked to pay what you can. Private hospitals (there are two in Belize City and one in San Ignacio) may ask for some guarantee of payment. ⇨ *For more information, see Health, below.*

Guatemala police, overwhelmed at times by the amount of crime—in 2010 there were 55 murders a day in Guatemala City alone—may not be able to respond effectively to emergencies. For tourist assistance in Guatemala, dial 1500 from any phone, or dial the equivalent of 911— either 120, 122, or 123.

American Embassy **Embassy of the United States in Belize** ⊠ *Floral Park Rd., Belmopan City* ☎ *822/4011 office hours, 610/5030 emergency number after office hours* ✍ *emb-belize@state.gov* ⊕ *belize.usembassy.gov.*

▌ HEALTH

Many medicines requiring a doctor's prescription at home don't require one in Belize; drugstores often sell prescription antibiotics, sleeping aids, and painkillers. However, pharmacies generally have a very small inventory, and only the most commonly prescribed drugs are available. In Belize private physicians often own an associated pharmacy, so they sell you the medicine they prescribe. A few pharmacies are open 24 hours and deliver directly to hotel rooms. Most hotel proprietors will direct you to such services.

CRITTERS

Sand flies (also sometimes referred to as no-see-ums, or as sand fleas, which are a different insect) are common on many beaches, cayes, and in swampy areas. They can infect you with leishmaniasis, a disease that can cause the skin to develop sores that can leave scars. In rare cases, the visceral form of leishmaniasis, if untreated, can be fatal.

Use repellent containing a high concentration of DEET insect repellent to help deter sand flies. Some say lathering on Avon's Skin So Soft or any oily lotion such as baby oil helps, too, as it drowns the little bugs.

The botfly or beefworm is one of the most unpleasant of Central American pests. Botfly eggs are deposited under your skin with the help of a mosquito, where one can grow into larva, a large living worm. To rid yourself of your unwanted pal, cover the larva's airhole in your skin with Vaseline, and after it suffocates you can remove it with a sterile knife. Or see your doctor. The good news is that unless you spend a lot of time in the bush in Belize, you are unlikely to encounter botflies.

Virtually all honeybees in Belize and Guatemala are Africanized. The sting of these killer bees is no worse than that of regular bees, but the hives are much more aggressive. If attacked by Africanized bees, try to get into a building, vehicle, or under water.

Scorpions are common in Belize and around Tikal. Their stings are painful, but not fatal. There are many poisonous snakes in Belize and lowland Guatemala, including the notorious fer-de-lance and small but deadly coral snakes. Most visitors never even see a snake, but if bitten can go to medical centers for antivenom.

Crocodiles (called alligators by Belizeans) are present in many lagoons and rivers, but very rarely are they known to attack humans.

Divers and snorkelers may experience "itchy itchy" or *pica pica*, a skin rash, in spring and early summer, when the tiny larvae of thimble jellyfish may get on the skin. Putting Vaseline or other greasy lotion on the skin before entering the water may help prevent the itch, and applying Benadryl, vinegar, or even Windex to the affected area may help stop the itch.

If you're a light sleeper, you might want to pack earplugs. Monkeys howling through the night and birds chirping at the crack of dawn are only charming on the first night of your nature excursion.

FOOD AND DRINK

Belize has a high standard of health and hygiene, so the major health risk is sunburn, not digestive distress. You can drink the water in Belize City, the Cayo, Placencia, on Ambergris Caye, and in most other areas you're likely to visit, though you may prefer the taste of bottled water. In remote villages, however, water may come from shallow wells or cisterns and may not be safe to drink.

On trips to Tikal or other areas in Guatemala, assume that the water isn't safe to drink. Bottled water—*agua mineral* or *agua pura* in Spanish—is available even at the smallest *tiendas* (stores) and is cheaper than in North America. Eating contaminated fruit or vegetables or drinking contaminated water (even ice) could result in a case of Montezuma's revenge, or traveler's diarrhea. Also skip uncooked food and unpasteurized milk and milk products.

INFECTIOUS DISEASES

HIV/AIDS is an increasing concern in Central America. This is especially true in Belize, where the incidence on a per capita basis is the highest in the region.

According to the U.S. Centers for Disease Control and Prevention, there's a limited risk of malaria, hepatitis A and B, dengue fever, typhoid fever, and rabies in Central America. In most urban or easily accessible areas you need not worry. However, if you plan to spend a lot of time in the jungles, rain forests, or other remote regions, or if you want to stay for more than six weeks, check the CDC Web site.

In areas where malaria and dengue are prevalent, sleep under mosquito nets. If you're a real worrier, pack your own—it's the only way to be sure there are no tears. Although most hotels in Belize have screened or glassed windows, your room probably won't be completely mosquito-proof. Wear clothing that covers your arms and legs, apply repellent containing at least 30% DEET, and spray for flying insects in living and sleeping areas.

There's no vaccine for dengue, but you can take antimalarial pills; chloroquine (the commonly recommended antimalarial for Belize and Guatemala) is sold as Aralen in Central America. It must be started a week before entering an area with malaria risk. Malarone is prescribed as an alternative, and it can be started only two days before arrival in a risk area. Don't overstress about this: in Belize there are fewer than 1,000 reported cases of malaria a year, mostly in the far south, actually fewer cases than are reported in the United States. In Guatemala, El Petén is a risk area.

You should be up-to-date on shots for tetanus and hepatitis A and B. Children traveling to Central America should have current inoculations against measles, mumps, rubella, hepatitis, and polio.

Health Warnings National Centers for Disease Control & Prevention (CDC) ☎ 800/232-4636 ⊕ www.cdc.gov/travel. **World Health Organization (WHO)** ⊕ www. who.int.

MEDICAL INSURANCE AND ASSISTANCE

Consider buying trip insurance with medical-only coverage. Neither Medicare nor some private insurers cover medical expenses anywhere outside of the United States. Medical-only policies typically reimburse you for medical care (excluding that related to preexisting conditions) and hospitalization abroad, and provide for evacuation. You still have to pay the bills and await reimbursement from the insurer, though.

Another option is to sign up with a medical-evacuation assistance company. A membership in one of these companies gets you doctor referrals, emergency evacuation or repatriation, 24-hour hotlines for medical consultation, and other assistance. A few credit cards, such as American Express Platinum, include medical evacuation among their perks. International SOS Assistance Emergency and AirMed International provide evacuation services and medical referrals. Medjet-Assist offers medical evacuation.

Medical Assistance Companies AirMed International ☎ *205/443–4840, 800/356–2161* ⊕ *www.airmed.com.* **International SOS Assistance Emergency** ☎ *215/942–8226 international alarm center in U.S.* ⊕ *www.internationalsos.com.* **MedjetAssist** ☎ *800/527–7478* ⊕ *www.medjetassist.com.*

Medical-Only Insurers International Medical Group ☎ *800/628–4664, 317/655–4500* ⊕ *www.imglobal.com.* **Wallach & Company** ☎ *800/237–6615, 540/687–3172* ⊕ *www. wallach.com.*

▌ HOURS OF OPERATION

Belize has three local banks, Heritage Bank (formerly Alliance Bank), Atlantic Bank, and Belize Bank, and two international ones, First Caribbean International (formerly Barclays) and ScotiaBank. Hours vary, but are typically Monday–Thursday 8–2 and Friday 8–4. There are branches of Belize Bank and Atlantic Bank at the international airport, with longer hours.

Belize is a laid-back place that requires a certain amount of flexibility when shopping or sightseeing. Stores tend to open according to the whim of the owner, but generally operate 8–noon and 2–8. Larger stores and supermarkets in Belize City and in towns such as San Ignacio and San Pedro don't close for lunch.

On Friday some shops close early, and many are only open a half day on Saturday. On Sunday, Belize takes it easy: few shops are open, and many restaurants outside of hotels are closed. Most Mayan sites in Belize are open 8–5. Guatemala's Tikal ruins are open daily 6–6.

HOLIDAYS

New Year's Day (January 1); Baron Bliss Day (officially March 9, but date may vary); Good Friday; Holy Saturday; Easter Monday; Labour Day (May 2); Sovereign's Day (May 24); National Day (September 10); Independence Day (September 21); Columbus Day (October 12); Garífuna Settlement Day (November 19); Christmas Day; Boxing Day (December 26).

▌ MAIL AND SHIPPING

When sending mail to Central America, be sure to include the city or town and district, country name, and the words "Central America" in the address. Don't use the abbreviation "CA" or your mail may end up in California, USA. Belizean mail service is very good, except to and from remote villages, and the stamps, mostly of wildlife, are beautiful. An airmail letter from Belize City takes about a week to reach the United States, longer—sometimes several weeks—from other areas.

An airmail letter to the United States is BZ60¢, a postcard, BZ30¢; to Europe, BZ75¢ for a letter, BZ40¢ for a postcard. The post office in Belize City is open Monday–Thursday 8–5 and Friday 8–4:30.

EXPRESS SERVICES

If you have to send something fast, use FedEx or DHL Worldwide Express, which are expensive but do the job right. Both have offices in Belize City and agents elsewhere. In San Pedro, Mail Boxes Etc. can wrap and ship your packages.

Express Services DHL Worldwide Express
⊠ *38 Hydes Ln., Belize City* ☎ *223/4350.*
FedEx ⊠ *6 Fort St., Belize City* ☎ *223/1577.*
Mail Boxes Etc. ⊠ *Coconut Dr., San Pedro*
☎ *227/4770* ⊕ *www.mbe-belize.com.*

POST OFFICES

There are two post offices in Belize City (N. Front Street and Queen's Square) as well as in Belmopan, Benque Viejo, Caye Caulker, Corozal Town, Dangriga, Independence, Ladyville, Orange Walk Town, Placencia, Punta Gorda, San Pedro, and San Ignacio. Mail service from Belize City to and from the United States and other countries is generally fast and reliable (airmail to and from the United States usually takes about five to seven days). To and from outlying towns and villages service is slower, and for remote villages may take weeks. For faster, though expensive, service use DHL and FedEx.

Post Office Main Post Office ⊠ *N. Front St., Belize City* ☎ *227/2201.*

▌ MONEY

There are two ways of looking at the prices in Belize: Either it's one of the cheapest countries in the Caribbean or one of the most expensive countries in Central America. A good hotel room for two will cost you upward of BZ$250; a budget one, as little as BZ$40. A meal in one of the more expensive restaurants will cost BZ$50–BZ$75 for one, but you can eat the classic Creole dish of stew chicken and rice and beans for BZ$8. Prices are highest in Belize City and on Ambergris Caye.

ITEM	AVERAGE COST IN BELIZE
Cup of Coffee	BZ$2
Glass of Wine	BZ$10–BZ$18
Glass of Beer	BZ$3–BZ$10
Sandwich	BZ$6–BZ$14
One-Mile Taxi Ride in Belize City	BZ$7
Museum Admission	BZ$10–BZ$20

Prices throughout this guide are given for adults. Substantially reduced fees are usually available for children, students, and senior citizens.

ATMS AND BANKS

Your own bank will probably charge a fee for using ATMs abroad; the foreign bank you use will also charge a fee. However, extracting funds as you need them is a safer option than carrying around a large amount of cash. That said, do *not* go to Belize expecting to get all your cash from ATMs, as machines sometimes are down or out of money. As a backup, carry some U.S. currency, a credit card, and perhaps a few traveler's checks.

ATMs in Belize give cash in Belize dollars. There are ATMs in Belize City (including two at the international airport), Corozal Town, Orange Walk Town, San Pedro, Caye Caulker, Belmopan, San Ignacio, Spanish Lookout, Dangriga, Placencia, and Punta Gorda. Most ATMs in Belize have a BZ$500 daily limit. Belize Bank's 25 ATMs around the country take ATM cards issued outside Belize on the CIRRUS, MasterCard, PLUS, and Visa networks. Atlantic Bank's 12 ATMs also accept foreign cards on the CIRRUS, MasterCard, PLUS and Visa networks. First Caribbean International Bank's six ATMs and ScotiaBank's 11 ATMs around the country also accept foreign-issued ATM cards. Heritage Bank has ATMs, but as of this writing they only accept ATM cards issued in Belize. Other bank offices you see in Belize City or San Pedro are likely international banks; they are set up to do business with individuals and companies outside of Belize and do not provide retail banking services in Belize.

In the Petén you can get cash in quetzales from ATMs in Flores and Santa Elena.

The biggest employer in Belize—the Belize government—pays most employees on the 14th or 15th of the month, and on those days in particular banks in Belize are jammed, with customer lines often snaking around the outside of the building. Banks are also usually busy on Friday. You should have a four-digit PIN. ATM scams—where the ATM "eats" your card or your PIN is stolen—are rare in Belize but increasingly common in Guatemala. Most banks offer cash advances on credit cards issued by Visa and MasterCard for a fee ranging from BZ$10 to BZ$30.

CREDIT CARDS

It's a good idea to inform your credit-card company before you travel, especially if you're going abroad and don't travel internationally very often. Otherwise, the credit-card company might put a hold on your card owing to unusual activity—not a good thing halfway through your trip.

Record all your credit-card numbers—as well as the phone numbers to call if your cards are lost or stolen—in a safe place, so you're prepared should something go wrong. Both MasterCard and Visa have general numbers you can call (collect if you're abroad) if your card is lost, but you're better off calling the number of your issuing bank, since Master-Card and Visa usually just transfer you to your bank; your bank's number is usually printed on your card.

In Belize, MasterCard and Visa are widely accepted, American Express less so, and Discover and Diner's hardly at all.

▪ TIP→ **Hotels, restaurants, shops, and tour operators in Belize sometimes levy a surcharge for credit-card use, usually 5%** but ranging from 2% to 10%. This practice happily has become less common, but it still happens. If you use a credit card, ask if there's a surcharge. Most credit-card issuers now also charge an international exchange fee, usually 2% to 3%, even if the foreign purchase is denominated in U.S. dollars.

Reporting Lost Cards American Express ☎ *800/528–4800 in U.S., 954/473–2123 collect from abroad* ⊕ *www.americanexpress. com.* **Diners Club** ☎ *800/234–6377 in U.S., 702/797–5532 collect from abroad* ⊕ *www. dinersclub.com.* **Discover** ☎ *800/347–2683 in U.S., 801/902–3100 from abroad* ⊕ *www. discovercard.com.* **MasterCard** ☎ *800/307– 7309 in U.S., 636/722–7111 collect from abroad* ⊕ *www.mastercard.com.* **Visa** ☎ *800/847–2911 in U.S., 303/967–1096 from abroad* ⊕ *www.visa.com.*

CURRENCY AND EXCHANGE

Because the U.S. dollar is gladly accepted everywhere in Belize, there's little need to exchange it. When paying in U.S. dollars, you may get change in Belize or U.S. currency, or in both.

The Belize dollar (BZ$) is pegged to the U.S. dollar at a rate of BZ$2 per US$1, and nearly all shops, stores, hotels, restaurants, and other businesses honor that exchange rate. Note, however, that moneychangers at Belize's Mexico and Guatemala borders operate on a free-market system and pay a rate depending on the demand for U.S. dollars, sometimes as high as BZ$2.15 to US$1. Banks (and ATMs) generally exchange at BZ$1.98 or less.

The best place to exchange Belize dollars for Mexican pesos is in Corozal, or at the Mexico-Belize border where the exchange rate is quite good. At the Guatemala border near Benque Viejo del Carmen, you can exchange Belize or U.S. dollars for quetzales—money changers will approach you on the Belize side and also on the Guatemala side. Usually the money changers on the Guatemala side offer better rates.

When leaving Belize, you can exchange Belizean currency back to U.S. dollars (up to US$100) at Belize Bank at the international airport. The Belize dollar is difficult if not impossible to exchange outside of Belize.

In Belize most hotel, tour, and car-rental prices are quoted in U.S. dollars, while most restaurant prices are in Belize dollars. In this guide, all Belize prices are quoted in Belize dollars. Because misunderstandings can happen, if it's not clear, always ask which currency is being used.

TRAVELER'S CHECKS

Traveler's checks should be in U.S. dollars, and the American Express brand is preferred. Most hotels and travel operators accept traveler's checks, and some restaurants and gift shops do. However, even in Belize City and popular tourist areas such as San Pedro, clerks at groceries and other shops may be reluctant to accept traveler's checks or will have to get a supervisor's approval to accept them. Some places charge a small fee, around 1% or 2%, if you pay with a traveler's check. Most banks will cash them for a fee of 1% to 2%, but it may require a long wait in line. In all cases, you will need your passport in order to use or cash a traveler's check.

▌PACKING

Pack light. Baggage carts are scarce at Central American airports, and international luggage limits are increasingly tight. Tropic Air and Maya Island Air officially have 70-pound (32-kilogram) weight limits for checked baggage. However, in practice the airlines rarely weigh luggage, and if you're a little over it's usually no problem. Occasionally, if the flight on the small Cessna or other airplane is full and there's a lot of luggage, some bags may be sent on the next flight, usually no more than an hour or two later.

Bring casual, comfortable, hand-washable clothing. T-shirts and shorts are acceptable near the beach and in tourist areas. More modest attire is appropriate in smaller towns, and the same long sleeves and pants will protect your skin from the ferocious sun and mosquitoes. Bring a hat to block the sun from your face and neck. If you're on a boat, you'll want a tight-fitting cap or hat with chinstrap to keep it from being blown away.

If you're heading into the mountains or highlands, especially during the winter months, bring a light sweater, a jacket, and something warm to sleep in, as nights and early mornings can be chilly. Sturdy sneakers or hiking shoes or lightweight boots with rubber soles for wet or rocky surfaces are essential. A pair of sandals (preferably ones that can be worn in the water) are good, too.

Be sure to bring insect repellent, sunscreen, sunglasses, and an umbrella. Other handy items include tissues, a plastic water bottle, and a flashlight (for occasional power outages or use in areas without streetlights). A mosquito net for those roughing it is essential, but people staying in hotels or lodges—even budget-level ones—rarely need one. Snorkelers should consider bringing their own equipment, especially mask and snorkel, if there's room in the suitcase. Divers will save money—typically BZ$50 a day in rentals—by bringing their own equipment. Sand and high humidity are enemies of your camera equipment. To protect it, consider packing your gear in plastic ziplock bags. Also bring your own condoms and tampons. You won't find either easily or in familiar brands.

▌PASSPORTS AND VISAS

To enter Belize, only a valid passport is necessary for citizens of the United States, Australia, Canada, CARICOM member states, Great Britain, Hong Kong, European Union countries, Mexico, New Zealand, Norway, and Venezuela; no visa is required. Nationals of other countries require a visa and/or clearance by the immigration office. Check the Belize Tourist Board Web site for updates on visas. You can also check with the Belize Immigration and Nationality Department.

If upon arrival the customs official asks how long you expect to stay in Belize, give the longest period you might stay—you may legally stay for up to 30 days on the tourist card you'll receive on entry—otherwise, the official may endorse your passport with a shorter period.

You can renew your entry permit at immigration offices for a fee of BZ$50 per month for the first six months; after six months, it costs BZ$100 a month for up to six more months, at which time you may have to leave the country for 72 hours to start the process over (sometimes this rule isn't enforced). Note that renewals aren't guaranteed, but normally are routinely granted.

If you're young with a backpack and entering Belize by land from Mexico or Guatemala, there's a slight chance you'll be asked to prove you have enough money to cover your stay. You're supposed to have US$60 a day, though this requirement is rarely enforced. A credit card also may work.

Citizens of the United States, Canada, and most other Western countries do not need a visa when entering Guatemala from Belize.

Info in Belize Belize Immigration and Nationality Department ☏ 802/0284 ⊕ www.governmentofbelize.gov.bz. Belize Tourism Board ✉ 64 Regent St., Belize City ☏ 227/2427 ⊕ www.travelbelize.org. Belize Tourism Industry Association (BTIA) ✉ 10 N. Park St., Belize City ☏ 227/1144 ⊕ www.btia.org.

U.S. Passport Information U.S. Department of State ☏ 877/487–2778 ⊕ travel.state.gov.

GENERAL REQUIREMENTS FOR BELIZE	
Passport	Must be valid for 6 months after date of arrival.
Visa	Not required for Americans, Canadians, and European Union citizens, among others; a tourist card good for up to 30 days is issued free upon arrival
Vaccinations	Yellow fever only if coming from an infected area such as parts of Africa
Driving	Valid driver's license from your home country
Departure Tax	By international air: US$39.25, usually included in the cost of your airline ticket; if not, it must be paid in U.S. dollars or by credit card. By land border into Mexico or Guatemala: US$18.75, payable in U.S. or Belize dollars. By water taxi or boat: usually US$18.75, payable in U.S. or Belize dollars

▌ RESTROOMS

You won't find many public restrooms in Belize, but hotels and restaurants usually have clean, modern facilities with American-style—indeed American-made—toilets. Hot-water showers in Belize often are the on-demand type, powered by butane gas.

Restrooms in Guatemala use Western-style toilets, although bathroom tissue generally shouldn't be flushed but discarded in a basket beside the toilet.

Find a Loo The Bathroom Diaries. The Bathroom Diaries is flush with unsanitized info on restrooms the world over—each one located, reviewed, and rated. ⊕ www.thebathroomdiaries.com.

▌ SAFETY

CRIME

There's considerable crime in Belize City, but it rarely involves visitors. When it does, Belize has a rapid justice system:

the offender often gets a trial within hours or days and, if convicted, can be sent to prison ("the Hattieville Ramada") the same day. Tourist police patrol Fort George and other areas of Belize City where visitors convene. Police are particularly in evidence when cruise ships are in port. If you avoid walking around at night (except in well-lighted parts of the Fort George area), you should have no problems in Belize City.

Outside of Belize City, and possibly the rougher parts of Dangriga and Orange Walk Town, you'll find Belize to be safe and friendly. Petty theft, however, is common all over, so don't leave cameras, cell phones, and other valuables unguarded.

Thefts from hotel rooms, especially in Placencia Village, occur occasionally. Given the hundreds of thousands of visitors to Belize, however, these incidents are isolated, and the vast majority of travelers never experience any crime in Belize.

In 2005–2006 and again in 2009–2011 there were sporadic incidents at Belize–Guatemala border areas. In several cases, masked men believed to be from Guatemala held up tourist vehicles in the Mountain Pine Ridge and elsewhere in western Belize. In other cases, Guatemalans seeking land or trying to harvest xate (a plant used by florists) have moved across the Belize border, creating incidents with Belize authorities.

The road from the Belize border toward Tikal has long been an area where armed robbers stopped buses and cars, and there also have been incidents at Tikal Park itself. In mid-2011 murderous attacks on Guatemalan farm workers and Guatemalan government officials in the Petén (including the decapitation of more than two dozen workers on a farm southwest of Flores) allegedly by members of Mexico's Los Zetas drug cartel prompted the U.S. Embassy in Belize to "strongly recommend against" travel to Flores and Tikal. Ask locally about crime conditions before traveling to Tikal.

If you are an American citizen, consider enrolling in the U.S. Statement Department's Smart Traveler Enrollment Program (⊕ *travelregistration.state.gov/ibrs/ui*), which makes it easier to locate you and your family in case of an emergency. Many other countries have similar programs.

CONCERNS FOR WOMEN

Many women travel alone or in small groups in Belize without any problems. Machismo is not as much a factor in the former British Honduras as it is in Latin countries in the region. Unfortunately, in the past Guatemala has been the site of some disturbing assaults on women. These have occurred on buses, usually late at night in remote areas. Women should avoid making such trips alone. A more common complaint is catcalling, which is typically more of an annoyance than a legitimate threat. Most women, locals and foreigners alike, try to brush it off. That said, however, women make up a large percentage of the travelers in Guatemala, and the vast majority have positive experiences.

SCAMS

Most Belizeans and Guatemalans are extremely honest and trustworthy. It's not uncommon for a vendor to chase you down if you accidentally leave without your change. That said, most organized scams arise with tours and packages, in which you're sold a ticket that turns out to be bogus. Arrange all travel through a legitimate agency, and always get a receipt. If a problem does arise, the Belize Tourism Board or INGUAT may be able to help mediate the conflict.

Advisories and Other Information Transportation Security Administration (TSA) ☎ *866/289-9673* ⊕ *www.tsa.gov*. **U.S. Department of State** ⊕ *www.travel.state.gov*.

▌ TAXES

The hotel tax in Belize is 9%, and a 12.5% Goods and Services Tax (GST) is charged on meals, tours, and other purchases at the hotel, along with most other purchases in Belize including car rentals and tours. The GST is supposed to be included in the cost of meals, goods, and services, but some businesses add the tax on instead.

When departing the country by international air, even on a short hop to Flores, Guatemala, you'll pay US$39.25 departure tax and fees. This must be paid in U.S. dollars or by credit card. However, many airlines include the departure tax in the airline ticket price. Don't pay twice—check your airline to see if the tax is included.

When leaving Belize by land to either Guatemala or Mexico, there's a border exit fee of BZ$30, plus a conservation fee of BZ$7.50. This may be paid in either U.S. dollars or Belize dollars, but not by credit card. For departures by boat to Guatemala or Honduras, you'll also pay the BZ$7.50 conservation fee and the BZ$30 exit fee, in U.S. or Belize dollars. Those in transit through Belize, staying less than 24 hours, can avoid paying the BZ$7.50 conservation fee but have to fork out the other taxes and fees.

Most Guatemalan hotels and some tourist restaurants charge an additional 10% to 20% tourist tax. The airport-departure tax is US$30. Guatemalan border officials charge a Q20 fee (about US$2.50) when entering Guatemala at Melchor de Mencos.

▌ TIME

Belize and Guatemala time is the same as U.S. Central Standard Time. Daylight saving time is not observed. (Note that Mexico does observe daylight saving time.)

Time Zones **Timeanddate.com** ⊕ *www.timeanddate.com/worldclock.*

▌ TIPPING

Belize restaurants rarely add a service charge, so in better restaurants tip 10%–15% of the total bill. At inexpensive places,

leave small change or tip 10%. Many hotels and resorts add a service charge, usually 10%, to bills, so at these places additional tipping isn't necessary. In general, Belizeans tend not to look for tips, though with increasing tourism this is changing. It's not customary to tip taxi drivers.

In Guatemala, restaurant bills do not typically include gratuities; 10% is customary. Bellhops and maids expect tips only in the expensive hotels. Guards who show you around ruins and locals who help you find hotels or give you little tours should also be tipped. Children will often charge a quetzal to let you take their photo.

TIPPING GUIDELINES FOR BELIZE	
Bartender	BZ$1–BZ$5 per round of drinks, or 10% of the cost of the drinks
Bellhop	BZ$1–BZ$4 per bag, depending on the level of the hotel
Hotel Doorman	BZ$2–BZ$4 if he helps you get a cab
Hotel Maid	BZ$4–BZ$8 a day (either daily or at the end of your stay, in cash); nothing additional is required if a service charge is added to your bill, though some guests tip extra directly to the maid
Hotel Room-Service Waiter	BZ$2–BZ$4 per delivery, even if a service charge has been added
Porter at Airport	BZ$2 per bag
Taxi Driver	Not usually tipped, unless he or she carries your luggage or performs other extra services
Tour Guide	10% of the cost of the tour
Waiter	10%–15%, with 15% being the norm at high-end restaurants; nothing additional if a service charge is added to the bill
Fishing Guides	BZ$40–BZ$80 a day

▌VISITOR INFORMATION

ONLINE RESOURCES

For information on Belize, visit the official site of the Belize Tourism Board at ⊕ www.travelbelize.org. Unfortunately, changes at the BTB have made the Web site less useful than it used to be, but things may have improved by the time you read this. Belize Explorer (⊕ *www.belizeexplorer.com*), formerly the ToucanTrail.com site operated by the BTB, now is a private site that provides information on budget hotels—those priced under US$70 double. The **Belize Tourism Industry Association** (⊕ *www.btia.org*) also provides visitor information, mainly through information offices and monthly publications for visitors in Placencia and Punta Gorda.

The Belize Forums (⊕ *www.belizeforum.com/belize*) is an active online community of Belize visitors and residents; many regulars are happy to answer questions, though occasionally discussions become heated. Also, Lan Sluder, the author of this guide and other books on Belize, has his own site called ⊕ *www.belizefirst.com*.

Belize Bus Blog (⊕ *belizebus.wordpress.com*) has detailed and comprehensive information on bus, water taxi, shuttle, and other transportation in Belize.

For destination-specific information, check out *Ambergriscaye.com* for San Pedro; *GoCayeCaulker.com*, *CayeCaulkerBelize.net*, and *CayeCaulker.org* for Caye Caulker; *BelmopanCityOnline.com* for Belmopan; *Belizex.com* for the Cayo district and elsewhere; *Placencia.com* and *DestinationsBelize.com* for Placencia; *SouthernBelize.com* or for Punta Gorda and southern Belize; *HopkinsBelize.com* and *CometoHopkins.com* for the Hopkins area; and *NorthernBelize.com*, *Corozal.com*, and *BelizeNorth.com* for northern Belize. There also are hundreds of personal blogs on living in and visiting Belize.

For information on Guatemala, contact that country's tourist board, INGUAT.

Contacts Belize Tourism Board (BTB) ⊠ 64 *Regent St., Belize City* ☎ 227/2420 ⊕ www.travelbelize.org ⊗ *Open Mon.–Thurs. 8–5; Fri. 8–4.* **Belize Tourism Industry Association (BTIA)** ☎ 227/1144 ✑ info@btia.org ⊕ www.btia.org. **INGUAT** ☎ *502/2421–2800 general information, 502/2421–2810 tourist assistance* ✑ info@inguat.gob.gt ⊕ www.visitguatemala.com.

INDEX

A

Accommodations, 346–347
Actun Chechem Ha, 188
Actun Tunichil Muknal, 21, 166, 173–174, 177, 295, 298
Adventure vacations, 310–334
Agua Caliente Wildlife Sanctuary, 252
Air travel. ⇨ See Plane travel
Aji Tapa Bar and Restaurant ✕, 89
Almond Tree Hotel Resort 🏨, 150–151
Altun Ha, 128, 137–139, 294, 297–298
Ambergris Caye, 20, 78–90, 92–104, 297
Apartment and house rentals, 346
Archeological sites, 19, 294–307
Ambergris Caye, 297
architecture, 306–307
Cayo region, 159, 166, 173–174, 175, 177, 178, 188, 189, 191, 192, 198–199, 295, 297
Deep South, 259, 261–263
Guatemala, 269–270, 276–280, 290–292, 297–298
itinerary recommendations, 299
Northern Belize, 127, 128, 137–139, 142–144, 150, 153, 294–295
sightseeing, 199, 297–298
Southern Belize, 208, 214, 227, 297
tours, 315–316
Architecture, 37, 306–307
Art and archaeology vacations, 315–316
Art galleries, 44, 188–189, 197, 216, 229, 233, 238–239
ATMs, 354–355
Atolls, The, 68, 120–123
Azul Resort 🏨, 95

B

Bacalar Chica Marine & Nature Reserve, 81–82
Banana Bank Lodge 🏨, 170
Banana Beach Resort 🏨, 97
Barnacle Bill's Beach Bungalows 🏨, 229
Barracuda Bar & Grill ✕, 217
Barranco, 261
Bars and clubs, 56–57, 100–102, 239
Barton Creek Cave, 21, 191, 295
Beach hotels, 346
Beaches
Cayes and atolls, 67
Southern Coast, 203, 204, 214, 228
Beaches and Dreams Seafront Inn 🏨, 220
Belcampo Lodge 🏨, 263
Belikin Beer, 29, 51
Belize Barrier Reef, 26, 81
Belize Botanical Gardens, 177
Belize City, 14, 36–63, 298
children, activities for, 49–50, 61, 62
emergencies, 43
history, 47
lodging, 53–55, 63
money matters, 44–45
nightlife and the arts, 56–57
orientation and planning, 37–39
outdoor activities and sports, 57–59
price categories, 50, 54
reasons to go, 37
restaurants, 50, 52–53
safety concerns, 46
shopping, 59–60
side trips, 60–63
tours, 45, 59
transportation, 38–39, 42–43
visitor information, 45
Belize Jungle Dome 🏨, 170
Belize Supreme Court, 48
Belize Zoo, 61, 166
Belizean Dreams 🏨, 220
Belmopan City, 159, 165–175, 298
Benque House of Culture, 188
Benque Viejo, 159, 188–190
Bicycling, 197, 321
Billy Barquedier National Park, 213
Biotopo Cerro Cahuí, 287–288
Bird watching, 19, 318–319
Cayo region, 160, 167–168, 171–172, 178, 185, 192, 195
Guatemala, 287–288
Northern Belize, 135, 143, 147, 154–155
Southern Coast, 221–222, 225
Black Hole, 326
Black Orchid Resort 🏨, 63
Bladen Forest Reserve, 252–253
Blancaneaux Lodge 🏨, 20, 195
Bliss Center for the Performing Arts, 48, 57
Blue Belize Guest House 🏨, 258
Blue Creek, 259, 261
Blue Hole, 21, 122, 166, 326
Blue Water Grill ✕, 87
Boat and ferry and water-taxi travel, 337, 339–340
Cayes and atolls, 69–71
Deep South, 246
Northern Belize, 129–130
Southern Coast, 205, 240
Boating, 80–81, 107–108, 286
Border formalities, 273
Bowling, 237
Bus travel, 340–341
Belize City, 39, 42
Cayo region, 161
Deep South, 247
Guatemala, 271
Northern Belize, 130
Southern Coast, 205–206
Business hours, 353
Butterfly migrations, 167

C

Cacao Festival, 135
Café Arqueológico Yaxhá ✕, 284
Cahal Pech, 177, 295, 298
Cahal Pech Village Resort 🏨, 181
Camino Real Tikal 🏨, 289
Camping, 320
Cayo region, 186
Deep South, 252–253
Guatemala, 281
Canoeing, 321–322
Cayo region, 172, 185–186
Deep South, 252
Southern Coast, 222
Canopy tours, 172–173, 289, 329
Capricorn ✕, 89
Car rentals, 343–344
Car travel, 342–343
Belize City, 42
Cayo region, 161

PHOTO CREDITS

ABOUT OUR WRITER

Belize First magazine founder Lan Sluder has been banging around Belize since 1991. In addition to authoring *Living Abroad in Belize, San Pedro Cool,* and other books on the country, he's written about it for *Caribbean Travel & Life,* the *Bangkok Post,* and Canada's *Globe & Mail,* among other publications. His favorite parts of Belize? Sarteneja and Punta Gorda. His children, though, prefer San Pedro and Caye Caulker.